MYSTICAL DIMENSIONS OF ISLAM

by ANNEMARIE SCHIMMEL

MYSTICAL DIMENSIONS OF ISLAM

The University of North Carolina Press
Chapel Hill

Manufactured in the United States of America
Cloth, published 1975, ISBN 0-8078-1223-4
Paper, published 1978, ISBN 0-8078-1271-4
First printing, October 1975
Second printing, August 1976
Third printing, April 1978
Fourth printing, March 1981
Fifth printing, November 1983

Library of Congress Cataloging in Publication Data

Schimmel, Annemarie.
Mystical dimensions of Islam.

Includes bibliographical references.
1. Sufism. I. Title.
BP189.2.S34 297'.4 73-16112
ISBN 0-8078-1223-4
ISBN 0-8078-1271-4 (pbk.)

TO THE SAINTS OF SHIRAZ

CONTENTS

ILLUSTRATIONS

ABBREVIATIONS

Since this book is intended primarily for the general reader, we have—though reluctantly—refrained from having too many footnotes or too large a bibliography. The reader will find much additional information about personalities, terminology, and historical facts in the *Encyclopedia of Islam* (1913–36; 2d ed., 1960–); the relevant articles have not been mentioned in the footnotes.

The following frequently cited works are abbreviated in the text:

A Abū Nuᶜaym al-Iṣfahānī. *Ḥilyat ul-auliyā͗*. 10 vols. Cairo, 1932.

AD Farīduddīn ᶜAṭṭār. *Dīwān-i qaṣā͗id wa ghazaliyāt*. Edited by Saᶜīd Nafīsī. Tehran, 1339 sh./1960. Number of poem cited.

AP *Armaghān-i Pāk*. Edited by Sheikh Muḥammad Ikrām. Karachi, 1953.

B Rūzbihān Baqlī. *"Sharḥ-i shaṭḥiyāt," Les paradoxes des soufis*. Edited by Henri Corbin. Tehran and Paris, 1966. Paragraphs cited.

BA Rūzbihān Baqlī. *"ᶜAbhar al-ᶜāshiqīn," Le jasmine des fidèles d'amour*. Edited by Henri Corbin. Tehran and Paris, 1958. Paragraphs cited.

BO John K. Birge. *The Bektashi Order of Dervishes*. 1937. Reprint. London, 1965.

CL Henri Corbin. *L'Homme de lumière dans le soufisme iranien*. Paris, 1971.

D Jalāluddīn Rūmī. *Dīwān-i kabīr yā Kulliyāt-i Shams*. Edited by Badīᶜuz-Zamān Furūzānfar. Vols. 1–7. Tehran, 1336 sh./1957. Number of poem cited.

G Abū Ḥāmid al-Ghazzālī. *Iḥyā͗ ᶜulūm ad-dīn*. 4 vols. Bulaq, 1289 h./1872–73.

H ᶜAlī ibn ᶜUthmān al-Hujwīrī. *The "Kashf al-Maḥjūb," the Oldest Persian Treatise on Sufism by al-Hujwiri.*

Translated by Reynold A. Nicholson. Gibb Memorial Series, no. 17. 1911. Reprint. London, 1959.

IK Khwāja Mīr Dard. *ᶜIlm ul-kitāb*. Bhopal, 1309 h./1891–92.

K Abū Bakr Muḥammad al-Kalābādhī. *The Doctrine of the Sufis*. Translated by A. J. Arberry. Cambridge, 1935.

L Abū Naṣr as-Sarrāj. *Kitāb al-lumaᶜ fīʾt-taṣawwuf*. Edited by Reynold A. Nicholson. Leiden and London, 1914.

M Jalāluddīn Rūmī. *Mathnawī-i maᶜnawī*. Edited and translated by Reynold A. Nicholson. 6 vols. London, 1925–40. Volume and line cited.

MC Jalāluddīn Rūmī. *Mathnawī-i maᶜnawī*. Commentary by Reynold A. Nicholson. 2 vols. London, 1925–40.

MM Marijan Molé. *Les mystiques musulmans*. Paris, 1965.

MT Farīduddīn ᶜAṭṭār. *Manṭiq aṭ-ṭayr*. Edited by M. Jawād Shakūr. Tehran, 1962.

N Maulānā ᶜAbdurraḥmān Jāmī. *Nafaḥāt al-uns*. Edited by M. Tauḥīdīpūr. Tehran, 1336 sh./1957.

NS Reynold A. Nicholson. *Studies in Islamic Mysticism*. 1921. Reprint. Cambridge, 1967.

P Louis Massignon. *La passion d'al-Ḥosayn ibn Mansour Al-Hallāj, martyr mystique de l'Islam exécuté à Bagdad le 26 Mars 922*. 2 vols. Paris, 1922.

Q Abūʾl-Qāsim al-Qushayrī. *Ar-risāla fī ᶜilm at-taṣawwuf*. Cairo, 1330 h./1912.

QR Abūʾl-Qāsim al-Qushayrī. *Ar-rasāʾil al-qushayriyya*. Edited and translated by F. M. Hasan. Karachi, 1964.

R Hellmut Ritter. *Das Meer der Seele. Gott, Welt und Mensch in den Geschichten Farīduddin ᶜAṭṭārs*. Leiden, 1955.

S Abūʾl-Majd Majdūd Sanāʾī. *Ḥadīqat al-ḥaqīqat wa sharīᶜat aṭ-ṭarīqat*. Edited by Mudarris Rażawī. Tehran, 1329 sh./1950.

SD Abūʾl-Majd Majdūd Sanāʾī. *Dīwān*. Edited by Mudarris Rażawī. Tehran, 1341 sh./1962.

T Farīduddīn ᶜAṭṭār. *Tadhkirat al-auliyāʾ*. Edited by Reynold A. Nicholson. 2 vols. 1905–7. Reprint. London and Leiden, 1959.

U Farīduddīn ᶜAṭṭār. *Muṣībatnāme*. Edited by N. Fiṣāl. Tehran, 1338 sh./1959.

V Farīduddīn ʿAṭṭār. *Ushturnāme*. Edited by Mahdi Muḥaqqiq. Tehran, 1339 sh./1960.

W Paul Nwyia, S.J. *Exegèse coranique et langage mystique*. Beirut, 1970.

X ʿAlī ibn Aḥmad ad-Daylamī. *Sīrat-i Ibn al-Hafīf ash-Shīrāzī*. Translated by Junayd-i Shīrāzī. Edited by Annemarie Schimmel. Ankara, 1955.

Y Yūnus Emre. *Divan*. Edited by Abdülbâki Gölpınarlı. Istanbul, 1943.

FOREWORD

To write about Sufism, or Islamic mysticism, is an almost impossible task. At the first step, a wide mountain range appears before the eye—and the longer the seeker pursues the path, the more difficult it seems to reach any goal at all. He may dwell in the rose gardens of Persian mystical poetry or try to reach the icy peaks of theosophic speculations; he may dwell in the lowlands of popular saint worship or drive his camel through the endless deserts of theoretical discourses about the nature of Sufism, of God, and of the world; or he may be content to have an all-around glimpse of the landscape, enjoying the beauty of some of the highest peaks bathed in the sunlight of early morning, or colored by the violet haze of a cool evening. In any case, only the elect few will reach the farthest mountain on which the mythical bird, Sīmurgh, lives—to understand that they have reached only what was already in themselves.

Thus, to set out and delineate some main features of Sufism, both historically and phenomenologically, will yield no result that satisfies everybody: it is easy to overlook certain aspects and give too much weight to others. The amount of oriental and occidental literature existent in print and in manuscript is beyond counting, so that even from this viewpoint a full account is not to be achieved.

Yet, my students at Harvard have urged me to put together the notes that formed the basis of several courses on Sufism—notes that consist both of literary evidence and of personal experiences with numerous friends in the Islamic East, mainly in Turkey and in Pakistan. My thanks are due to all of those who have helped me—be it only by casual remarks—to formulate my ideas about Sufism and to those who took part in the growth of this book.

I wish to thank especially Dr. Charles Forman of Wheaton College, Norton, Massachusetts, who was kind enough to go through the manuscript to polish it from the linguistic standpoint and to suggest some simplifications.

With special gratitude I acknowledge a generous subsidy from the Ozai-Durrani Funds, Harvard University, which was given in support of the exploration of Indo-Muslim culture contained in this book.

My mother has, during many years, and especially during the period of final typing, shown the virtues of patience and love, which are so typical of the true Sufi; she never failed to encourage me in my work.

ANNEMARIE SCHIMMEL

THE ARABIC ALPHABET AND NOTE ON TRANSCRIPTION

There is no single, commonly accepted system of transliterating languages written in Arabic characters. Furthermore, the transcription system changes according to the languages concerned; thus, an Arabic *ḍ* would be a *ż* in Persian, a *z* in Modern Turkish. European scholars have used a wide variety of transcription systems, and one of the main problems is posed by the transliteration of oriental names into a Western alphabet. Throughout this book the generally accepted American transcription system has been used. In the following list the other possible transcriptions of each letter have been indicated after the semicolon. *T* means "modern Turkish alphabet."

Letter in basic form	*Numerical value*	*Name and transcription*
ا	1	*alif*: ā, ʾ, carrier of the initial vowel.
ب	2	*bāʾ*: b
ت	400	*tāʾ*: t
ث	500	*thāʾ*: th; ṯ; T: s
ج	3	*jīm*: j; ǧ, dj, dsch; T: c
ح	8	*ḥā*: ḥ; T: h
خ	600	*khāʾ*: kh; ḫ, x; T: h
د	4	*dāl*: d
ذ	700	*dhāl*: dh; ḏ; T: z
ر	200	*rāʾ*: r
ز	7	*zāy*: z
س	60	*sīn*: s
ش	300	*shīn*: sh; š, sch; T: ş
ص	90	*ṣād*: ṣ; s, ç; T: s
ض	800	*ḍād*: ḍ; non-Arabic, ż; T: z

ط	9	*ṭāʾ*: ṭ; T: t
ظ	900	*ẓāʾ*: ẓ; z
ع	70	*ʿayn*: ʿ, or unnoticed
غ	1000	*ghayn*: gh; ġ, g; T: ğ
ف	80	*fāʾ*: f
ق	100	*qāf*: q; ḳ, k, gh; T: k
ک	20	*kāf*: k
ل	30	*lām*: l
م	40	*mīm*: m
ن	50	*nūn*: n
ه	5	*hāʾ*: h
و	6	*wāw*: w; v, ū, ō, ou
ی	10	*yāʾ*: y; j, ī, ē.

The additional Persian letters:

ژ	*zhāʾ*: zh; j
چ	*chāʾ*: ch; č, tsch; T: ç
پ	*pāʾ*: p
گ	*gāf*: g

Urdu, Sindhi, Panjabi, and Pashto, as well as other Islamic languages of non-Arabic origin, have added a number of letters and diacritical marks to secure the correct pronounciation.

The diphthongs, او, *a+u*, and *a+y*, ای, are transcribed as *aw, au, o, ow*, and *ay, aj, ei, ej*, respectively.

The three short vowels, which are not expressed in writing, are transcribed as *a, e; i, e;* and *u, o* respectively.

THE MUSLIM YEAR

The Muslim year is a lunar year of 354 days, 12 months of 29 and 30 days. The calendar begins with Muhammad's emigration from Mecca to Medina in 622; thus the year 300 h.=912–13 A.D., 600 h.=1203–4 A.D., 1000 h.=1591–92 A.D., and 1300 h.=1822–23 A.D.

Muḥarram: *10,* ʿAshūra, *the memorial of Ḥusayn ibn ʿAlī's death at Kerbela on 10 Muḥarram 680* A.D.

Ṣafar

Rabīʿ ul-awwal: *12, birthday of the Prophet.*

Rabīʿ ath-thānī: *11, anniversary of ʿAbduʾl-Qādir Gīlānī.*

Jumādā al-ūlā

Jumādā al-ākhira

Rajab: *at the beginning,* raǵāʾib-*nights (conception of the Prophet). 27,* miʿrāj, *the Prophet's ascension to Heaven.*

Shaʿbān: *14–15,* shab-i barāt, *when the destinies are fixed for the coming year.*

Ramaḍān: *the month of fasting. In one of the last three odd nights—generally thought to be the twenty-seventh—the* laylat ul-qadr, *during which the Koran was revealed for the first time.*

Shawwāl: *begins with the* ʿīd ul-fiṭr, *the feast of breaking the fasting.*

Dhūʾl-Qaʿda

Dhūʾl-Ḥijja: *the month of Pilgrimage to Mecca* (ḥajj). *From the tenth to the twelfth, the* ʿīd ul-aḍḥā, *Feast of Sacrifices.*

MYSTICAL DIMENSIONS OF ISLAM

Glory to God Who has not vouchsafed to His creatures any means of attaining unto knowledge of Him except through impotence to attain unto knowledge of Him.

Somebody asked Abū Ḥafṣ: "Who is a Sufi?"
He answered:
"A Sufi does not ask who a Sufi is."

1. WHAT IS SUFISM?

In recent years many books have been published on Sufism and the spiritual life in Islam. Each of them has touched upon a different facet, for the phenomenon usually called Sufism is so broad and its appearance so protean that nobody can venture to describe it fully. Like the blind men in Rūmī's famous story, when they were made to touch an elephant, each described it according to the part of the body his hands had touched: to one the elephant appeared like a throne, to another like a fan, or like a water pipe, or like a pillar. But none was able to imagine what the whole animal would look like (M 3:1259–68).[1]

Such is the case with Sufism, the generally accepted name for Islamic mysticism. To approach its partial meaning we have to ask ourselves first, what *mysticism* means. That *mysticism* contains something mysterious, not to be reached by ordinary means or by intellectual effort, is understood from the root common to the words *mystic* and *mystery*, the Greek *myein*, "to close the eyes."

1. See Fritz Meier, "Zur Geschichte der Legende von den Blinden und dem Elefanten," in "Das Problem der Natur im esoterischen Monismus des Islams," *Eranos-Jahrbuch* 14 (1946): 174. "The Blind Men and the Elephant," a Hindu fable by John Godfrey Saxe. Shāh Walīullāh of Dehli speaks of the blind who tried to describe a tree according to the part their hands touched; see Shāh Walīullāh, *Lamaḥāt*, ed. Ghulām Muṣṭafā Qāsimī (Hyderabad, Sind, n.d.), p. 4.

Mysticism has been called "the great spiritual current which goes through all religions." In its widest sense it may be defined as the consciousness of the One Reality—be it called Wisdom, Light, Love, or Nothing.[2]

Such definitions, however, merely point our way. For the reality that is the goal of the mystic, and is ineffable, cannot be understood or explained by any normal mode of perception; neither philosophy nor reason can reveal it. Only the wisdom of the heart, *gnosis,* may give insight into some of its aspects. A spiritual experience that depends upon neither sensual nor rational methods is needed. Once the seeker has set forth upon the way to this Last Reality, he will be led by an inner light. This light becomes stronger as he frees himself from the attachments of this world or—as the Sufis would say—polishes the mirror of his heart. Only after a long period of purification—the *via purgativa* of Christian mysticism—will he be able to reach the *via illuminativa,* where he becomes endowed with love and gnosis. From there he may reach the last goal of all mystical quest, the *unio mystica.* This may be experienced and expressed as loving union, or as the *visio beatifica,* in which the spirit sees what is beyond all vision, surrounded by the primordial light of God; it may also be described as the "lifting of the veil of ignorance," the veil that covers the essential identity of God and His creatures.

Mysticism can be defined as love of the Absolute—for the power that separates true mysticism from mere asceticism is love. Divine love makes the seeker capable of bearing, even of enjoying, all the pains and afflictions that God showers upon him in order to test him and to purify his soul. This love can carry the mystic's heart to the Divine Presence "like the falcon which carries away the prey," separating him, thus, from all that is created in time.

One can find these essentially simple ideas in every type of mysticism. The mystics of all religions have tried to symbolize their experiences in three different groups of images: The never-ending quest for God is symbolized in the "Path" on which the "wayfarer" has to proceed, as in the numerous allegories dealing with Pilgrim's Progress or the Heavenly Journey. The transformation

2. The best introduction to mysticism is still Evelyn Underhill, *Mysticism: A Study in the Nature and Development of Man's Spiritual Consciousness* (1911; paperback ed., New York, 1956).

of the soul through tribulation and painful purification is often expressed in the imagery of alchemy or similar processes from nature and prescientific science: the age-old dream of producing gold from base material is realized on the spiritual level. Eventually, the nostalgia of the lover and the longing for union was expressed by symbols taken from human love; often a strange and fascinating combination of human and divine love permeates the verses of the mystics.

Notwithstanding similarities of description of mystical experiences, it is advisable to distinguish between two main types, which have been classified as Mysticism of Infinity and Mysticism of Personality. The former type has found its highest and purest expression in the system of Plotinus and in the Upanishads, particularly as elaborated in Shankara's *advaita* philosophy. Sufism comes close to it in some of the forms developed by the Ibn ᶜArabī school. Here, the Numen is conceived as the Being beyond all being, or even as the Not-Being, because it cannot be described by any of the categories of finite thought; it is infinite, timeless, spaceless, the Absolute Existence, and the Only Reality. By contrast the world possesses only a "limited reality," which derives its conditioned existence from the Absolute Existence of the Divine. It may be symbolized as the boundless ocean in which the individual self vanishes like a drop, or as the desert, which shows itself in ever new sand dunes that hide its depths, or as the water out of which the world is crystallized like ice. This type of mysticism was often attacked by prophets and reformers, because it seemed to deny the value of the human personality and to result in pantheism or monism, thus constituting the greatest threat to personal responsibility. The idea of continuous emanation in contrast to the unique divine act of creation was considered, by both Muslim and Christian mystics, to be incompatible with the Biblico-Koranic idea of a *creatio ex nihilo*. In the so-called Mysticism of Personality, the relation between man and God is perceived as that of creature and Creator, of a slave in the presence of his Lord, or of a lover yearning for his Beloved. This type is more commonly found in earlier Sufism.

These two types of mystical experience, however, are rarely met with in their purest forms. Especially in mystical poetry, an author may describe God in terminology taken from a pure love relation and a few lines later use language that lends itself to an exclusively "pantheistic" interpretation.

A differentiation between the "voluntaristic" and the "gnostic" approaches to mystical experience is somewhat easier. The mystic of the voluntaristic type wants to "qualify himself with the qualities of God," as the Prophetic tradition says, and to unite his own will completely with God's will, thus eventually overcoming the theoretical difficulties posed by the dilemma of predestination and free will. This mysticism can be seen as a practical life process. The mystic of the gnostic type strives for a deeper knowledge of God: he attempts to know the structure of His universe or to interpret the degree of His revelations—although no mystic could ever dare to "know" His Essence. Did not Dhū᾿n-Nūn (d. 859), usually regarded as one of the founders of speculations about *maᶜrifa,* or gnosis, warn his fellow mystics: "To ponder about the Essence of God is ignorance, and to point to Him is associationism (*shirk*), and real gnosis is bewilderment" (N 34)? Despite this bewilderment, the gnostic approach often led to the building of theosophical systems with its adherents tending to interpret every aspect of mysticism in the light of their own particular theories, sometimes even denying the simple experience of loving submission. In Islamic mysticism, both aspects are equally strong, and in later periods they are intermingled.

In their formative period, the Sufis admitted of a twofold approach to God. As Hujwīrī (d. circa 1071) says in his discussion of the states of "intimacy" and "respect":

> There is a difference between one who is burned by His Majesty in the fire of love and one who is illuminated by His Beauty in the light of contemplation. (H 367)

> There is a difference between one who meditates upon the Divine acts and one who is amazed at the Divine Majesty; the one is a follower of friendship, the other is a companion of love. (H 373)

One might also recall the distinction made by Jāmī in speaking of the two types of advanced Sufis: some are those

> to whom the Primordial Grace and Lovingkindness has granted salvation after their being submerged in complete union and in the wave of *tauḥīd* [unification], [taking them out] of the belly of the fish "Annihilation" on the shore of separation and in the arena of permanent subsistence, so that they might lead the people towards salvation.
>
> The others are those who are completely submerged in the ocean of

Unity and have been so completely naughted in the belly of the fish "Annihilation" that never a news or trace comes to the shore of separation and the direction of subsistence . . . and the sanctity of perfecting others is not entrusted to them. (N 8–9)

The distinction that modern history of religions makes between the so-called "prophetic" and the "mystic" spirit is clearly visible in Jāmī's description of the two types of mystics—those who practice complete reclusion (*Weltabkehr*) and are solely concerned with their own salvation in the first "flight of the one toward the One," and those who return from their mystical experience in a higher, sanctified state of mind and are able to lead other people on the right path.

Approaches to the phenomenon "Sufism" are manifold. To analyze the mystical experience itself is next to impossible since words can never plumb the depths of this experience. Even the finest psychological analysis is limited; words remain on the shore, as the Sufis would say. It would be easier to understand Sufism through an analysis of given structures: the French scholar Henri Corbin, in his books on Ibn ʿArabī, has shown to what depths such a study of structure underlying a specific mystical-philosophical system can lead. Analyses of the language of mysticism and the development of the "mystical lexicon" (Louis Massignon and, more recently, Paul Nwyia) can help illuminate the formative period of Sufi thought. The study of symbols and images used by the mystics and of the degree of their interdependence belongs to this field; it opens the way to an examination of the contribution of Sufism to the development of Islamic languages, literatures, and arts.

Since Sufism is to a very large extent built upon the principle of the disciple's initiation, the different methods of spiritual education, the exercises practiced in the Sufi orders, the psychological phases of the progress, the formation of orders, and their sociological and cultural role are rewarding fields of research. Of prime importance here are the penetrating studies of the Swiss scholar Fritz Meier.

European scholars have responded to the phenomenon of Islamic mysticism in different ways, as can be understood from these remarks. Europe's first contact with Sufi ideas can be traced back to the Middle Ages: the works of the Catalanian mystic and scholar Ramon Lull (d. 1316) show a remarkable influence of Sufi literature.[3] The first figure from the history of Sufism to be introduced into European literature was Rābiʿa al-ʿAdawiyya, the great woman saint of the eighth century; her legend was brought to Europe by Joinville, the chancellor of Louis IX, in the late thirteenth century. Rābiʿa's figure was used in a seventeenth-century French treatise on pure love as a model of Divine love,[4] and her story has been retold more than once in the West, the latest echo being a contemporary German short story (Max Mell, "Die schönen Hände").

Travelers who visited the Near and Middle East in the sixteenth and seventeenth centuries brought back information about rites of the dervishes, with both the ritual dance of the Whirling Dervishes (Mevlevis) and the strange performances of the Howling Dervishes (Rifāʿī's) attracting casual visitors. In 1638 the learned Fabricius of Rostock University edited and translated, for the first time, a poem by the great Egyptian mystic Ibn al-Fāriḍ (d. 1235).

Most of the information about oriental spirituality, however, was derived from the translations of Persian classical poetry—Saʿdī's *Gulistān* has been one of the favorite books of European intellectuals since Adam Olearius produced its first complete translation into German in 1651. A century later, Sir William Jones at Fort William, Calcutta, fostered the study of Persian poetry, among other subjects, and as a result the first translations of Ḥāfiẓ became available in the West. His ideas about Sufi poetry have influenced many English-speaking orientalists, although one may find, in some works on Sufism written during the nineteenth century, rather absurd views in wild confusion. Ḥāfiẓ's poetical imagery—unfortunately mostly taken at face value—has largely colored the Western image of Sufism.

In the nineteenth century, historical sources and important Sufi texts were made available in print both in the Middle East and in Europe, so that scholars could begin to form their own ideas about the origin and early development of Sufism. Yet most of the sources available were of rather late origin and rarely contained reliable information about the earliest stages of the mystical movement in Islam. That is why the interpreters usually agreed that Sufism must be a foreign plant in the sandy desert of Islam, the

3. Annemarie Schimmel, "Raymundus Lullus und seine Auseinandersetzung mit dem Islam," *Eine Heilige Kirche*, fasc. 1 (1953–54).

4. Henri Bremond, *Histoire du sentiment religieux en France*, vol. 9 (Paris, 1928).

religion that was so little known and even less appreciated and that could not possibly be related to any finer and higher spiritual movement.[5]

A German professor of Divinity, F. A. D. Tholuck, produced the first comprehensive book on Sufism in 1821, called *Ssufismus sive theosophia persarum pantheistica,* and four years later an anthology called *Blüthensammlung aus der Morgenländischen Mystik.* Amazingly enough, Tholuck—himself a good Protestant and therefore not at all prone to mystical ideas—understood that "the Sufi doctrine was both generated and must be illustrated out of Muhammad's own mysticism." This statement is all the more surprising in view of the miscellaneous character of the manuscripts and printed books at his disposal.[6]

During the following decades, several theories about the origin of Sufism were brought forth, as A. J. Arberry has shown in his useful book *An Introduction to the History of Sufism.*[7] It will suffice to mention a few of those theories.

E. H. Palmer, in his *Oriental Mysticism* (1867), held that Sufism is "the development of the Primaeval religion of the Aryan race"[8] —a theory not unknown to some German writers during the Nazi

5. Basic sources are: A. J. Arberry, *Sufism: An Account of the Mystics of Islam* (London, 1950), which deals with the history of the classical period of Sufism; Marijan Molé, *Les mystiques musulmans* (Paris, 1965), the best short introduction to Sufism, its history and meaning; G.-C. Anawati and Louis Gardet, *Mystique musulmane* (Paris, 1961), a fine study of the early period of Sufism and of Sufi practices, mainly *dhikr,* "recollection," as seen by Catholic theologians. See also Louis Gardet, *Expériences mystiques en terres nonchrétiennes* (Paris, 1953). Cyprian Rice, O. P., *The Persian Sufis,* 2d ed. (London, 1969), is a lovable and understanding booklet about mystical experience. Fritz Meier, *Vom Wesen der islamischen Mystik* (Basel, 1943), is a small but weighty book that stresses the importance of initiation in Sufism; it contains rich source material. Seyyed H. Nasr, *Ideals and Realities of Islam* (London, 1966; New York, 1967), contains a number of important remarks about the Iranian aspect of Sufism, which is dealt with more fully in the same author's *Sufi Essais* (London, 1972). Inayat Khan, *The Sufi Message,* which has been reprinted many times, is a modern and subjective, yet impressive interpretation. Idries Shah, *The Sufis,* as well as his other books, should be avoided by serious students.

6. Friedrich August Deofidus Tholuck, *Ssufismus sive theosophia persarum pantheistica* (Berlin, 1821), and the same author's *Blüthensammlung aus der Morgenländischen Mystik* (Berlin, 1825), are still quite revealing.

7. The history of Sufi studies in Europe has been discussed by A. J. Arberry in *An Introduction to the History of Sufism* (London, 1942).

8. E. H. Palmer, *Oriental Mysticism: A Treatise on Sufistic and Unitarian Theosophy of the Persians* (1867; reprint ed., London, 1969), is immature but has some good points; John P. Brown, *The Dervishes* (1868; reprint ed., London, 1968), gives much important material, though it is not scholarly.

period. In any case, Sufism has often been considered a typically Iranian development inside Islam. There is no doubt that certain important Iranian elements have survived through the ages beneath its surface, as both Henri Corbin and Seyyed H. Nasr have recently emphasized.[9]

Many eminent scholars, mainly in Great Britain, have stressed the importance of Neoplatonic influences upon the development of Sufism. Nobody would deny that Neoplatonism had deeply permeated the Near East—the so-called "Theology of Aristotle" (which is, in fact, Porphyry's commentary on Plotinus's *Enneads*) was translated into Arabic as early as 840. Neoplatonism was "in the air," as Reynold A. Nicholson pointed out in the famous introduction to his selection from Jalāluddīn Rūmī's lyrical poetry in 1898—the first book in the long list of his still unrivaled publications in the field of Sufism.[10] Nicholson, however, understood that the early ascetic movement can be explained without difficulties from its Islamic roots and that, therefore, the original form of Sufism is "a native product of Islam itself." Since Islam grew out of a soil in which ancient oriental, Neoplatonic, and Christian influences were strong, a number of secondary influences may have worked upon Islam even in its earliest phase.

It is only natural that the Christian influences should have interested many European scholars (Adalbert Merx, Arend Jan Wensinck, Margaret Smith),[11] who mainly tried to explore the relations of Muslims with the Syrian monks. The best studies in this field have been written by the Swedish Bishop Tor Andrae, to whom we also owe the classical discussion of the veneration of the Prophet Muhammad in mystical Islam.[12]

The problem of influences becomes more difficult when one thinks of the relations with religious traditions outside the Near

9. See also Emil Brögelmann, *Die religiösen Erlebnisse der persischen Mystiker* (Hannover, 1932); a short survey is given by A. H. Zarrinkoob, "Persian Sufism in Its Historical Perspective," *Iranian Studies* 3 (1970): 3–4.

10. Reynold A. Nicholson, *The Mystics of Islam* (1914; reprint ed., Chester Springs, Pa., 1962), is still a classic, though it is outdated at certain places. His *Studies in Islamic Mysticism* (1921; reprint ed., Cambridge, 1967), contains three excellent studies on outstanding personalities (Abū Saʿīd, Ibn al-Fāriḍ. Jīlī); and his *The Idea of Personality in Sufism* (Cambridge, 1923) is a collection of lectures.

11. Adalbert Merx, *Ideen und Grundlinien einer allgemeinen Geschichte der Mystik* (Heidelberg, 1893). Arend Jan Wensinck, *Abūʾl-farağ Bar hebreaus, The Book of the Dove* (Leiden, 1919).

12. Tor Andrae, *I Myrtenträdgården* (Uppsala, 1947). For his other works see the Bibliography.

Eastern world.[13] Many scholars were, and some still are, inclined to accept Indian influences on the formative period of Sufism, beginning with Alfred von Kremer (1868) and Reinhart P. Dozy (1869). But even Max Horten's numerous articles in this field could not bring any stringent proof of such influences[14] in the early period; for later times, the situation is slightly different.[15]

For the earliest period, influences from Turkestan are much more important, as Richard Hartmann has shown; Ignaz Goldziher had already pointed out parallel traditions in Islamic mystical tales and Buddhist stories, but this kind of parallelism can be easily traced back to the common sources, e.g., the Indian fables of the Hitopadeśa and Panchatantra, which were translated into the Near Eastern languages before and shortly after the advent of Islam. And the miracles of saints are the same all over the world. The Turkestani contribution is, however, highlighted in our day by some Turkish mystics who show a tendency of speaking of a typically "Turkish" type of mysticism that comprises a strict Mysticism of Infinity, which describes God as "positive Not-Being." But such generalizations are dangerous.

Even the rather far-fetched possibility of early Chinese—i.e., Taoist—influences on Sufism has been discussed (first by Omar Farrukh). For the later period, the Japanese scholar Toshihiko Izutsu has drawn some interesting parallels between Taoist structures of thought and Ibn ᶜArabī's mystical system.[16]

The study of a single mystic's life and work can occupy a scholar throughout his life: Louis Massignon's research into the personality of al-Ḥallāj, the "martyr of divine love," is the best example for this approach; Hellmut Ritter's masterly book on ᶜAṭṭār, *Das*

13. See Ignaz Goldziher, "Materialien zur Entwicklungsgeschichte des Sufismus," *Wiener Zeitschrift für die Kunde des Morgenlandes* 13 (1899). Reynold A. Nicholson, "A Historical Enquiry concerning the Origin and Development of Sufism," *Journal of the Royal Asiatic Society*, 1906, p. 303; Richard Hartmann, "Zur Frage nach der Herkunft und den Anfängen des Sufitums," *Der Islam* 6 (1915); Annemarie Schimmel, "The Origin and Early Development of Sufism," *Journal of the Pakistan Historical Society*, 1958.

14. Max Horten, *Indische Strömungen in der islamischen Mystik* (Heidelberg, 1927–28); like his article "Der Sinn der islamischen Mystik," *Scientia*, July 1927, this book should be used with caution.

15. Robert C. Zaehner, *Hindu and Muslim Mysticism* (London, 1960), is well documented and thought-provoking, though it overstresses the Indian elements.

16. Omar Farrukh, *At-taṣawwuf fiʾl-Islām* (Beirut, 1957). For parallels see Toshihiko Izutsu, *A Comparative Study of the Key Philosophical Concepts of Sufism and Taoism*, 2 vols. (Tokyo, 1966–67).

Meer der Seele (The Ocean of the Soul), is the result of an ideal combination of strict philology combined with aesthetic and religious understanding. On the other hand, an investigation of a particular mystical attitude, like Benedikt Reinert's study of *tawakkul*, "trust in God," reveals the various facets of one single stage of the Path and sheds light on many kindred problems.

Whether we concentrate upon the history of Sufism, by using a vertical cut, or upon its methods, expressions, and experiences, by taking a cross section, the main problem is the fact that previously unknown manuscripts frequently come to light.[17] The libraries of the Islamic countries, and those in the West, still contain many works that may shed new light upon any of the problems at stake. Even now there is so much material available in the different languages of Islam that any generalization seems impossible.[18] That is why this book can give only a glimpse of a few aspects of Sufism; even this will, probably, be tinged by a personal predilection for mystical poetry derived from the large area of Iranian cultural influence.

How did the Sufis themselves interpret the meaning of the word Sufism?

In interpreting Islamic mystical texts, one must not forget that many sayings to which we give a deep theological or philosophical meaning may have been intended to be suggestive wordplay; some of the definitions found in the classical texts may have been uttered

17. For this problem see Fritz Meier, "Ein wichtiger Handschriftenfund zur Sufik," *Oriens* 20 (1967).

18. As an antidote to the large amount of Arabic and Persian sources, one should consult Ibn al-Jauzī, *Talbīs Iblīs* (Cairo, 1340 h./1921–22), translated by David Samuel Margoliouth as "The Devil's Delusion," *Islamic Culture* 12 (1938), a poisonous book attacking the degeneration of Sufism in the twelfth century. Oriental scholars have published a number of general studies on the history of Sufism in the last twenty years, during which there has been a growing interest in the spiritual life of Islam. Abūʾl-ʿAlāʾ ʿAffīfī, *At-taṣawwuf: ath-thaurat ar-rūḥiyya fīʾl-Islām* [Sufism, the Spiritual Revolution in Islam] (Cairo, 1963); Muḥammad Muṣṭafā Ḥilmī, *Al-ḥayāt ar-rūḥiyya fīʾl-Islam* [Spiritual Life in Islam] (Cairo, 1954); M. Qāsim Ghanī, *Taʾrīkh-i taṣawwuf dar Islām* [History of Sufism in Islam] (Tehran, 1330 sh./1951). Among the anthologies of Sufi texts produced in the West, the following useful collections should be mentioned: Johannes Pedersen, *Muhammedansk mystik* (Copenhagen, 1923); Margaret Smith, *Readings from the Mystics of Islam* (London, 1950); Margaret Smith, *The Sufi Path of Love* (London, 1954); Martino Mario Moreno, *Antologia della Mistica Arabo-Persiana* (Bari, Italy, 1951); Émile Dermenghem, *Vies des saints musulmans* (Algiers, 1942); Virginia Vacca, *Vite e detti di Santi Musulmani* (Torino, n.d.). Specialized studies and anthologies will be mentioned in relevant places.

by the Sufi masters as a sort of *koʾan*, a paradox meant to shock the hearer, to kindle discussion, to perplex the logical faculties, and thus to engender a nonlogical understanding of the real meaning of the word concerned, or of the mystical "state" or "stage" in question. The resolution of apparent contradictions in some of these sayings might be found, then, in an act of illumination. This is at least one possible explanation of the fact that the masters give many different answers to the same question. This "willful paradox" and "pious highfalutin" was perhaps "intended to make their flesh creep a little for their health's sake," as W. H. Temple Gairdner puts it, who with full right asks: "Do we not take their language too seriously? It parades as scientific; it is really poetico-rhetorical."[19] Indeed, one aspect of mystical language in Sufism that should never be overlooked is the tendency of the Arabs to play with words. The structure of the Arabic language—built upon triliteral roots—lends itself to the developing of innumerable word forms following almost mathematical rules. It might be likened to the structure of an arabesque that grows out of a simple geometric pattern into complicated multiangled stars, or out of a flower motif into intricate lacework. A tendency to enjoy these infinite possibilities of the language has greatly influenced the style of Arabic poets and prose writers, and in many sayings of the Sufis one can detect a similar joy in linguistic play; the author indulges in deriving different meanings from one root, he loves rhymes and strong rhythmical patterns—features inherited by the mystics of the Persian, Turkish, and Indo-Muslim tongues. But this almost magical interplay of sound and meaning, which contributes so much to the impressiveness of a sentence in the Islamic languages, is lost in translation. So also are the numerous hidden allusions inherent in every root of the Arabic tongue, which point to the whole range of historical, theological, and poetical experiences that may have been present in the mind of the author of an apparently simple statement or an easy-flowing verse.

Another problem is posed by the fondness of many Sufi authors for inventing classifications, usually tripartite, to define certain mystical states; they often press the meaning of a word rather than explain it. The titles of the books composed by Sufis, particularly

19. W. H. Temple Gairdner, *Al-Ghazzālī's "Mishkāt al-anwār": The Niche for Lights* (London, 1915), p. 71.

in the postclassical centuries, show the same peculiarities; they allude to mystical states, to technical expressions, and often contain in themselves a whole spiritual program; other authors may give, by the numerical value of the title, the date of its composition.

What, then, did the Sufis say about the origin of the name *taṣawwuf*, which we translate as Sufism (or, the older form, Sufiism)?

Their definitions go back to the earliest period and thus defy the tendency of some modern Western writers to apply this name only to the later "theosophical" aspect of Islamic mysticism. Some of the pious would even ask the Prophet when he blessed them with his appearance in their dreams: "What is Sufism?" (N 255) Hujwīrī, in the mid-eleventh century, summed up the discussion:

Some assert that the Sufi is so called because he wears a woollen garment (*jāma-i ṣūf*), others that he is so called because he is in the first rank (*ṣaff-i awwal*), others say it is because the Sufis claim to belong to the *aṣḥāb-i Ṣuffa* (the people of the Bench who gathered around the Prophet's mosque). Others, again, declare that the name is derived from *ṣafā* (purity). (H 30)

Another—Western—definition, namely the derivation from Greek *sophos*, "wise," is philologically impossible. The derivation from *ṣūf*, "wool," is now generally accepted—the coarse woolen garment of the first generation of Muslim ascetics was their distinguishing mark. Kalābādhī, one of the early theoretical writers on Sufism (d. ca. 990), says in this respect:

Those who relate them to the Bench and to wool express the outward aspect of their conditions: for they were people who had left this world, departed from their homes, fled from their companions. They wandered about the land, mortifying the carnal desires, and making naked the body; they took of this world's good only so much as is indispensable for covering the nakedness and allaying hunger. (K 5)

But Sufism is more. Junayd, the undisputed leader of the Iraqian school of mysticism (d. 910), wrote: "Sufism is not [achieved] by much praying and fasting, but it is the security of the heart and the generosity of the soul" (QR 60). Junayd is also credited with a definition in which he sees the prototypes of the Sufis in the prophets as mentioned in the Koran (in later times the ascent through the different stages of the prophets, or the identification with the spirit of one of them, is one aspect of certain Sufi schools):

Sufism is founded on eight qualities exemplified in eight apostles: the generosity of Abraham, who sacrificed his son; the acquiescence of Ishmael, who submitted to the command of God and gave up his dear life;

the patience of Job, who patiently endured the afflictions of worms and the jealousy of the Merciful; the symbolism of Zacharias, to whom God said "Thou shalt not speak unto men for three days save by signs" (Sūra 3:36) and again to the same effect "When he called upon his Lord with a secret invocation" (Sūra 19:2); the strangerhood of John, who was a stranger in his own country and an alien to his own kind amongst whom he lived; the pilgrimhood of Jesus, who was so detached therein from worldly things that he kept only a cup and a comb—the cup he threw away when he saw a man drinking in the palms of his hand, and the comb likewise when he saw another man using his fingers instead of a comb; the wearing of wool by Moses, whose garment was woollen; and the poverty of Muhammed, to whom God Almighty sent the key of all treasures that are upon the face of the earth, saying, "Lay no trouble on thyself, but procure every luxury by means of these treasures," and he answered, "O Lord, I desire them not; keep me one day full fed and one day hungry." (H 39–40)

Some of Junayd's contemporaries emphasized the ascetic side of Sufism, a complete break with what is called "the world" and egotism: "Sufism is to possess nothing and to be possessed by nothing" (L 25).

"Sufism is freedom and generosity and absence of self-constraint" (L 57). Ruwaym's (d. 915) advice to young Ibn Khafīf, "Sufism is to sacrifice one's soul—but do not occupy yourself with the small-talk of the Sufis!" (X 90) shows that the danger of talking too much in a sort of technical and quasi-esoteric language was felt quite early. The Sufi should rather insist upon "faithfulness with the contract" (N 226) and should be free, "neither tired by searching nor disappointed by deprivation" (L 25). "The Sufis are people who prefer God to everything and God prefers them to everything else" (L 25). Some decades after Dhū'n-Nūn (d. 859), who is credited with the last sayings, Sahl at-Tustarī defined the Sufi: "It is he whose blood is licit and whose property is allowed [i.e., he who can be killed and whose property can be legally given to the faithful] and whatever he sees, he sees it from God, and knows that God's loving-kindness embraces all creation" (B 370).

The social and practical aspect of Sufism is understood from definitions like those of Junayd and Nūrī, according to whom "Sufism is not composed of practices and sciences, but it is morals" (H 42), and "who surpasses you in good moral qualities surpasses you in Sufism" (N 311). It means to act according to God's orders and laws, which are understood in their deepest spiritual sense without denying their outward forms. This way of life is possible only through loving devotion: "Sufism is the heart's being pure from the pollution of discord"—a sentence which Hujwīrī (H 38) explains as follows: "Love is concord, and the lover has but one duty in the world, namely to keep the commandment of the beloved, and if the object of desire is one, how can discord arise?"

The Sufis have spoken of the threefold meaning of *taṣawwuf* according to the *sharīʿa*, the Muslim law, the *ṭarīqa*, the mystical path, and the *ḥaqīqa*, the Truth. It is a purification on different levels, first from the lower qualities and the turpitude of the soul, then from the bondage of human qualities, and eventually a purification and election on the level of attributes (L 27–28).

But there are also warnings against "Sufism." Shiblī (d. 945), as was so often the case, wanted to shock his audience when he asserted: "Sufism is polytheism, because it is the guarding of the heart from the vision of the 'other,' and 'other' does not exist" (H 38). He thus attacks the ascetic who closes his eyes to the created world and wants to concentrate exclusively upon God—but since God is the only Reality, how can one think of "otherness" and so try to avoid it? Therefore, "a true Sufi is he who is not," as Kharaqānī says, with a paradox that has been repeated by other mystics (N 298, 225).

The Islamic mystics enjoyed the play with the root *ṣafā*, "purity," when they discussed Sufism and the qualities of the ideal Sufi: "He that is purified by love is pure (*ṣāfī*), and he who is purified by the Beloved is a Sufi" (H 34), i.e., he who is completely absorbed in the Divine Beloved and does not think of anything but Him has attained the true rank of a Sufi. It is not surprising that the Sufis made attempts to designate Adam as the first Sufi; for he was forty days "in seclusion" (like the novice at the beginning of the Path) before God endowed him with spirit; then God put the lamp of reason in his heart and the light of wisdom on his tongue, and he emerged like an illuminated mystic from the retirement during which he was kneaded by the hands of God. After his fall he performed acts of penitence in India for 300 years until God "elected" him (*iṣṭafā*; see Sūra 3:25) so that he became pure (*ṣāfī*) and thus a true Sufi.[20]

Even a poet who cannot be called exactly a mystic, namely Khāqānī, the greatest panegyrist of Iran (d. 1199), claims: "I am pure since I am a servant of the purity of the Sufi"; and in one of the long chains of oaths that he likes to insert in his *qaṣīdas* he swears "by the Sufis who love afflictions and are enemies of wellbeing." He is thus close to Rūmī, who a century later defined Sufism in this way:

20. Quṭbaddīn al-ʿIbādī, *At-taṣfiya fī aḥwāl aṣ-ṣūfiyya, or Ṣūfīnāme*, ed. Ghulām Muḥammad Yūsufī (Tehran, 1347 sh./1968), p. 27.

"What is Sufism? He said: To find joy in the heart when grief comes" (M 3:3261). Khāqānī alluded to the Sufis

> who carry in their waterbowl the water of life, like Khiḍr,
> and whose rods are as miraculous as the rod of Moses.[21]

Later Persian, Turkish, and Urdu literature abounds in poems that praise the wonderful qualities of this or that Sufi saint or describe the miracles worked by a mystical leader.

Sufism meant, in the formative period, mainly an interiorization of Islam, a personal experience of the central mystery of Islam, that of *tauḥīd,* "to declare that God is One." The Sufis always remained inside the fold of Islam, and their mystical attitude was not limited by their adherence to any of the legal or theological schools. They could reach their goal from any starting point—neither the differences between the legal *madhhabs* nor theological hairsplitting was, basically, of interest to them. Hujwīrī sums up the early Sufi attitude toward science and theology when he poignantly observes: "Knowledge is immense and life is short: therefore it is not obligatory to learn all the science . . . but only so much as bears upon the religious law" (H 11). That means: enough astronomy to find the direction of Mecca as required for the correct performance of prayer, enough mathematics to figure out the legal amount of alms one has to pay—that is what the Sufi, like every good Muslim, should know. For God has condemned useless knowledge (Sūra 2:96), and did not the Prophet say: "I take refuge with Thee from knowledge that profiteth naught" (H 11)?[22] *ʿIlm,* "knowledge," the pursuit of which is incumbent upon every male and female Muslim, is the knowledge of a Muslim's practical duties: "Do not read *ʿilm* except for the true life. . . . Religious science is jurisprudence and exegesis and tradition—whoever reads anything else, becomes abominable" (U 54). True gnosis, namely the gnosis of the One, is not attained through books, and many a legend tells how a Sufi who had reached, or thought he had reached, his goal threw away his books, for: "Books, ye are excellent guides, but it is absurd to trouble about a guide after the goal has been reached" (NS 21).

"To break the ink-pots and to tear the books" was considered by some mystics the first step in Sufism. The great saint ʿUmar Suhrawardī, who studied scholastic theology in his youth, was blessed by

21. Khāqānī, *Diwan,* ed. Sajjādī (Tehran, 1338 sh./1959), qaṣīda p. 250, 51, 369.
22. N 32 attributed to Abū Hāshim aṣ-Ṣūfī.

a saint who put his hands on his chest and made him forget all he had studied, "but he filled my breast with the *ᶜilm ladunnī*" (Sūra 18:65), the "knowledge immediately derived from God" (N 515). ᶜAbdu'l-Qādir Gīlānī performed a miracle by suddenly washing away the text of a philosophy book he considered dangerous to his disciple (N 517); other Sufis were urged by dreams to cast their precious collections of books into a river (N 432).

This predilection for immediate knowledge as contrasted with legalistic scholarship was expressed in later times by many poets and mystics who ridiculed the founders of the great law schools, especially Abū Ḥanīfa (d. 767) and Shāfiᶜī (d. 820). Sanā'ī's verse (attributed to both ᶜAṭṭār [AD 100] and Rūmī [D 498]) is a case in point:

> Abū Ḥanīfa has not taught love,
> Shāfiᶜī has no traditions about it.
>
> (SD 605)

Sanā'ī (d. 1131) has often contrasted the *Sufi* with the *Kūfī*, the learned lawyer Abū Ḥanīfa from Kufa, and still in eighteenth-century Sindhi mystical poetry the Sufi is called *lā-kūfī*, "non-Kūfī," i.e., not bound to a particular religious rite.[23]

The Sufis claimed that the whole wisdom was included in the letter *alif*, the first letter in the alphabet and symbol of God (see Appendix 1). Are not many scholars who rely upon books "like the donkey which carries books" (Sūra 62:5)? Did not Noah live for nine hundred years, with only the recollection of God? And, as Rūmī adds with a slightly ironical bent, "he had not read the *risāla* nor the *Qūt al-qulūb*" (M 6:2652–53), the two handbooks of moderate Sufism. For although the Sufis often condemned the bookishness of scholars and admonished their disciples to "strive to lift the veils, not to collect books,"[24] it is a fact that they themselves were among the most productive writers in Islamic history. And many of their theoretical works are no more readable or enjoyable than the dogmatic treatises that they attacked in their poems.

The main target of Sufi criticism was philosophy, influenced by Greek thought: "There is nobody more distant from the law of the

23. For the whole complex see Annemarie Schimmel, "Shah ᶜAbdul Laṭīf's Beschreibung des wahren Sufi," in *Festschrift für Fritz Meier*, comp. Richard Gramlich (Wiesbaden, 1974).

24. Maulānā ᶜAbdurraḥmān Jāmī, *Lawā'iḥ* (Tehran, 1342 sh./1963), no. 24, p. 40.

Hashimite prophet than a philosopher" (U 54; see also MT 291), says ᶜAṭṭār, echoing Sanāʾī's sentiments when he wrote:

> From words like "primary matter" and "primary cause"
> you will not find the way into the Presence of the Lord.[25]

The whole "Universal Reason" is nothing in the presence of a single divine order, "Say!" (U 45)—a fine pun on *kull*, "universal," and *qul*, "say," the divine address to the Prophet. The "little philosopher" is both the laughing stock and the scapegoat for the mystics. Strangely enough, Ibn Sīnā (Avicenna, d. 1037) has become the representative of dry rationalism, although he was as much of a mystical thinker as some of those classified as Sufis.[26] Perhaps the Sufi aversion to him, though already visible in Sanāʾī's poetry (SD 57), was fostered by a story about Majduddīn Baghdādī (d. 1219): "He saw the prophet in his dream and was informed by him that 'Ibn Sīnā wanted to reach God without my mediation, and I veiled him with my hand, and he fell into the fire' " (N 427).

Such an anti-intellectualism, as it was sensed by the orthodox, could lead to dangers for the communal life. One might mention the type of the "wise idiot,"[27] represented in Islamic lore first by Buhlūl, a strange character who lived during the caliphate of Hārūn ar-Rashīd (d. 809). To him, as later to many unknown and unnamed mentally deranged persons, are ascribed sayings in which they give frank expression of their criticism of contemporary life. But since they were insane they escaped punishment: "God has freed them from order and prohibition" (N 296). They are set free by God from their normal state as "slaves" and live in perfect loving union with Him, as ᶜAṭṭār points out (MT 245). The type of the *majdhūb*, the "enraptured one" who, under the shock of a mystical vision or any psychological experience, is bereft of his senses and walks around in a fashion prohibited by the religious law (i.e., stark naked) belongs to the darker side of the Sufi world. Many a mystical leader has complained about simpletons who attracted, by their strange behavior and their alleged miracle mongering, the interest of the crowd, who took them for representatives of true spirituality.

25. Abūʾl-Majd Majdūd Sanāʾī, "Sanāʾīʾābād," in *Mathnawīhā*, ed. Mudarris Rażawī (Tehran, 1348 sh./1969), line 42.

26. Henri Corbin, *Avicenna and the Visionary Recital* (New York and London, 1960).

27. Paul Loosen, "Die weisen Narren des Naisaburi," *Zeitschrift für Assyriologie* 27 (1912), deals with this type of mentally deranged "wise" man or "saint."

In the introduction to his *Nafaḥāt al-uns*, Jāmī poignantly criticizes the imitators of the different Sufi types and their vain and dangerous attitudes. The innumerable verses of Persian poets who juxtapose *mollā* and lover, pulpit and gallows, and claim that true love is the greatest enemy of reason and that the lover should be comparable to *Majnūn*, the demented lover who was the laughing stock of children, may have enhanced the importance of this class of illiterate, crude, and sometimes even very nasty "saints."

Comparatively harmless types, living on the charity of the pious, did not really endanger the Sufi movement; but the degeneration of the wandering dervishes or *faqīrs*, the "poor," who performed miracles and were beyond the law (*bī sharᶜ*), has done much to bring Sufism into discredit. It was such people whom European travelers in the East met first, so that one of the honorific names given to the genuine mystic, *faqīr*, "poor," has become, in German, the designation of a mere trickster.

From the very beginning, the mystics strictly distinguished between the true Sufi, the *mutaṣawwif* who aspires at reaching a higher spiritual level, and the *musṭawif*, the man who pretends to be a mystic but is a useless, even dangerous, intruder. They knew well that the spiritual path is "hard to travel except for those who were created for that purpose" (H 4), and that it is impossible to become a true Sufi if one is not born that way: "This patched frock must have been sewn in pre-eternity," for, as much as a person may strive to reach the rank of a Sufi, "no ass can turn into a horse by energy and zeal" (U 70–71). Therefore, the complaint about the decline of Sufism almost coincides with its beginning; a saying of the ninth-century mystic, the Persian Yaḥyā ibn Muᶜādh, warns his fellow mystics: "Avoid the society of three classes of men—heedless savants, hypocritical Koran-readers, and ignorant pretenders to Sufism" (H 17; cf. B 411). Poets have satirized the self-styled Sufi (S 666), and in the eleventh century it was repeatedly said: "Today Sufism is a name without reality, but formerly it was a reality without name. . . . The pretence is known and the practice unknown" (H 44). People were content with empty confession, and "blind conformity has taken the place of spiritual enthusiasm" (H 7). The mystical concerts in which the Sufis might become enraptured and begin to spin around their axis were taken, by many, for the essence of Sufism. And to pretend mystical knowledge and experience was—and still is—quite easy. The stock of delightful stories and the legends of ancient saints could always attract people; well-recited verses might move the listeners to tears; and it was certainly easier to beg food at the doors of the rich and give a blessing in exchange than to pursue a normal profession. Thus a saint of the eleventh century angrily declared: "I looked into Hell, and I saw that most of its inhabitants were those donning a patched frock and carrying a food-bowl" (B 309). These accursed people are, as Baqlī explains the saying, the traitors to mysticism, those who claim gnosis but have only the external color of truth, because they lack knowledge of the Muhammadan religious law. "Their prayer-direction is the charming beloved [*shāhid*], the candle [*shamᶜ* at joyous meetings] and the belly [*shikam*]" (SD 82). As time passed the complaints about the degeneration of Sufism became more eloquent. ᶜUrfī, one of Akbar's court-poets (d. 1591), says in a quatrain:

> The Sufi is busy with deceiving men and women,
> The ignorant one is busy with building up his body,
> The wise man is busy with the coquetry of words,
> The lover is busy with annihilating himself.[28]

He thus attributes to the lover the quality that should be that of the Sufi: namely, to annihilate himself in the Beloved.

The word *Sufi* became a pejorative expression; the great mystic of Delhi in the eighteenth century, Mīr Dard, insistently repeated that he did not want to be called a Sufi, but rather "a true Muhammadan." He did not hesitate to call the representatives of mystical doctrines opposed to his stern, law-bound mysticism "pig-natured," and he often expressed his contempt for the "shopkeeper sheikh," the "seller of patched frocks" who was found everywhere in the country. He would have agreed completely with his Arabian contemporary al-Badr al-Ḥijāzī, whose satire on the decline of Sufism Arberry has translated:[29]

> Would that we had not lived to see every demented madman held up by his fellows as a *Pole*!
> Their *ulema* take refuge in him, indeed, they have even adopted him as a Lord, instead of the Lord of the Throne.
> For they have forgotten God, saying "So-and-so provides deliverance from suffering for all mankind."

28. Muhammad ᶜUrfī Shīrazī, *Kulliyāt*, ed. Ali Jawāhirī (Tehran, 1336 sh./1957), p. 448.

29. Arberry, *Sufism*, p. 128.

When he dies, they make him the object of pilgrimage, and hasten to his shrine, Arabs and foreigners alike;
Some kiss his grave, and some the threshold of his door, and the dust . . . .

Ḥijāzī has put his finger on the danger of the exaggerated veneration of the spiritual master, the sheikh or *pīr* (see chapter 5), what Muhammad Iqbal has called "pirism," which means the absolute sway of the leader over his followers and the attendant exploitation of ignorant peasants and villagers.

In their criticism of saint worship and pirism—a facet of popular Islam the danger of which one can scarcely realize without having lived in the East—Muslim modernists and moderate Sufis are united. But to reach this point, we have first to travel the long road through the outward history of Sufism. We shall see how this movement has assumed various shapes appropriate to the times and the personalities of its leaders, though its substance has remained the same.

2. HISTORICAL OUTLINES *of* CLASSICAL SUFISM

THE FORMATIVE PERIOD

"Islamic mysticism is the attempt to reach individual salvation through attaining the true *tauḥīd,*" says one of the leading Western orientalists.[1] In fact, the quintessence of the long history of Sufism is to express anew, in different formulations, the overwhelming truth that "there is no deity but Allah" and to realize that He alone can be the object of worship.

The history of Sufism is a chart showing some of the stations on this path of interpretation, some of the forms in which this one reality was expressed, some of the different ways in which the mystics

1. Hans Heinrich Schaeder, "Zur Deutung des islamischen Mystik," *Orientalistische Literaturzeitung* 30 (1935): 845.

tried to reach their goal, whether individually or collectively, through gnosis or through love, by means of asceticism or through practices leading to ecstatic rapture. Its external history is a history of the spiritual, theological, and literary movements inside Islam. At the same time, because of its deep roots in the ritual practices taught by the Koran, Sufism reflects the different attitudes of Muslims toward "the world"; thus we find among the mystics antiworldly ascetics and active fighters for the glory of their faith, austere preachers of repentance and enthusiastic hymnodists praising God's eternal loving-kindness, builders of highly sophisticated theosophical systems and enraptured lovers of Eternal Beauty.

The aims of all the mystics are essentially the same. For, as Henri Corbin has stated, "the religious conscience of Islam is centered upon a fact of meta-history" (W 46), namely, upon the transhistorical fact of the primordial covenant as understood from the Koranic word in Sūra 7:171. Before creation, God called the future humanity out of the loins of the not-yet-created Adam and addressed them with the words: "Am I not your Lord?" (*alastu bi-rabbikum*), and they answered: "Yes, we witness it" (*balā shahidnā*). The idea of this primordial covenant (*mīthāq*) between God and humanity has impressed the religious conscience of the Muslims, and especially the Muslim mystics, more than any other idea. Here is the starting point for their understanding of free will and predestination, of election and acceptance, of God's eternal power and man's loving response and promise. The goal of the mystic is to return to the experience of the "Day of *Alastu*," when only God existed, before He led future creatures out of the abyss of not-being and endowed them with life, love, and understanding so that they might face Him again at the end of time.

Sufism traces its origins back to the Prophet of Islam and takes inspiration from the divine word as revealed through him in the Koran.[2] God has manifested His will, or rather Himself, in the words of the holy book, which is, basically, the only means by which man can know Him. The Koran was accepted relatively early by the faithful as uncreated and coeternal with God. It has been for every Muslim, and particularly for the mystics, the "unique lexicon," the

2. On Koranic exegesis see Ignaz Goldziher, *Die Richtungen der islamischen Koranauslegung* (Leiden, 1920); Paul Nwyia, *Exegèse coranique et langage mystique* (Beirut, 1970), an excellent analysis of early Sufi language, adds to Louis Massignon's classical study, *Essai sur les origines du lexique technique de la mystique musulmane*, 3d ed. (Paris, 1968).

"essential textbook of his sciences, the key for his *Weltanschauung*," as Louis Massignon has put it (P 465). For everything concerning worldly and spiritual affairs can be found in this book, and its interpretation in different ages shows how the self-understanding of the Muslim community grew and changed. The mystics have played a decisive role in the development of the Koranic sciences; their hermeneutical methods range from a simple verbal interpretation to symbolical and allegorical exegesis, without, however, denying the value of the exterior meaning of the Koranic words. For the devout—some of whom could find up to seven thousand meanings in a single Koranic verse—the holy book was "the resurrection," for, as Ḥallāj had claimed, "in it there are the signs of Divine Lordship [*rubūbiyya*], information of the resurrection, and news about the future till the eternity of eternities. Whosoever knows the Koran is, so to speak, in the Resurrection" (B 265). The words of the Koran have formed the cornerstone for all mystical doctrines: the early Sufis lived under the threat of the Last Judgment as described in the terrifying words of many *sūras*, until they discovered the promise of mutual love between God and man (Sūra 5:59); they found in it the different stages of the human soul, which rises from the "soul that commands evil" (*an-nafs al-ammāra*) to the "soul which is at peace with God" (*an-nafs al-muṭmaʾinna*). They read that God is closer to man than his jugular vein (Sūra 50:16) and is, at the same time, the Lord and Creator of the universe, immanent and transcendent. "The sights do not reach Him" (Sūra 6:103), but "whithersoever ye turn there is the Face of God" (Sūra 2:109). God has "put signs into nature and into the human soul" (Sūra 51:21), and it is necessary to see and to understand them.

God, as revealed in the Koran, is both the stern Judge and the Merciful and Compassionate; He is All-knowing and Wise, but He is also the Most Cunning. The numerous and often contradictory attributes given to Allah in the Koran form the chain of the ninety-nine most beautiful names—names that were to play an important role in later mystical theories and in the life of prayer and were sometimes used in almost magical connections. The hope of discovering the Greatest Name of God has inspired many a Sufi who dreamed of reaching the highest bliss in this world and the next by means of this blessed name. God appears, through the Koranic words, as the only real Agent who creates and predestines human actions. He is the Absolute Personality—as the Sufis defined it: "He alone has the right to say 'I' " (W 249)—and the Reality, *al-ḥaqq*, a word that was used by most of the later mystics to designate God.

Just as the scholastic theologians defined God by forty-one attributes—twenty attributes of necessity, twenty of impossibility, and one of possibility—many of the later Sufis invented complicated systems to draw closer to the mystery of the divine, the Absolute Being, the Pure Existence, or whatever names they might find. Pious mystics have often objected to these pseudophilosophical definitions containing names and words not found in the Koran and therefore ill becoming Him who revealed Himself in the holy book.

But the Koran contains more than the description of God and of the otherworld; it also regulates the practical and moral life of the community, and the Sufis meticulously followed its injuctions. Further, the recitation of the Koran was an important means of leading the spirit into a meditative state, or even of producing a mystical rapture. Recited in beautiful tones, the rhythmic and musical wording of the holy book carried the minds of the devout into higher spheres and might open a higher level of understanding to them. The language of the Koran was common to Muslims all over the world; it has helped to shape the expressions not only of theologians or lawyer divines but of poets and men of letters; it permeated the Islamic community as a living force. Even though millions of men and women did not and do not understand its Arabic wording, they still sense the numinous quality of the book and live with it. One can certainly speak of a "koranization" of the memory[3]; and everyone who has read Persian, Turkish, or any other Islamic idiom knows how strongly the language of the Koran has penetrated the literature and everyday language, and how beautifully the "letters of the Koran" have been elaborated according to the artistic taste of Persians, Turks, Indians, and Africans, creating the most exquisite calligraphy—the typical art of the mystics.

Sufism traces its origin back to the Prophet himself. He is described in the Koran as *ummī*, "illiterate" (Sūra 7:157–58), a quality that is central to the understanding of Islamic religiosity: just as in Christianity, where God reveals Himself through Christ—the word made flesh—the virginity of Mary is required in order to produce an immaculate vessel for the divine word, so in Islam, where God reveals Himself through the word of the Koran, the Prophet had to be

3. Paul Nwyia, *Ibn ᶜAṭāʾ Allāh et la naissance de la confrèrie šāḏilite* (Beirut, 1972), p. 46.

a vessel that was unpolluted by "intellectual" knowledge of word and script so that he could carry the trust in perfect purity.

Muhammad is the first link in the spiritual chain of Sufism, and his ascension through the heavens into the divine presence, to which the first lines of Sūra 17 allude, became the prototype of the mystic's spiritual ascension into the intimate presence of God. According to the tradition, esoteric wisdom was transmitted from Muhammad to his cousin and son-in-law ᶜAlī ibn Abī Ṭālib, the fourth of the righteous caliphs (d. 661). Other members of his family and his friends, according to legend, were endowed with mystical insight or pursued mystical practices. The traditions (*ḥadīth*) that go back to the Prophet, or at least are attributed to him, served the Sufis when they elaborated their own definitions of the various stages and states. Every tendency within Islam, and so within Sufism, found material to support its claims from Prophetic traditions. In later times a considerable number of *ḥadīth* that are not found in the official collections as they were compiled in the second half of the ninth century were used by the Sufis. In a comparatively short time, Muhammad's personality gained great importance for the spiritual life of his community: He was the ideal leader, and the duty of every Muslim was to imitate him. His veneration soon reached mythical heights, until he was conceived by the medieval mystics as the Perfect Man par excellence, the cause and goal of creation, the friend of God and the intercessor on behalf of his community (see chapter 4).

The Western student of Islam, used to the traditional picture of Muhammad as it emerged during hundreds of years of hatred and enmity in the Christian world, will be surprised to see the strong "mystical" qualities attributed to this man who was, according to the usual Western understanding, a mere politician, shrewd and sensual, or, at the best, the founder of a heresy derived from Christianity. Even most recent studies of the Prophet, which have shown his sincerity and his deep religious concern, do not convey that quality of mystical love that his followers feel for him.

We do not know how many of the later tales of Muhammad's ascetic piety are true and how many simply reflect the ideals of later mystical devotion. A number of his sayings about the importance of prayer, and mainly of the night vigils, seem to be authentic, and "when his eyes slept his heart did not sleep," as his beloved young wife Āᶜisha relates. The classical manuals of Sufism contain large collections of sayings in which the Prophet exhorts the faithful to constant prayer and to the recollection of God during every moment of life (L 64; G 1:265–66). Indeed, a prophet who was so certain of being God's instrument must have relied upon prayer; for through prayer he could experience, over and over again, the presence of Him who had sent him.

Mystical tradition includes some of Muhammad's companions among the spiritual ancestors of Sufism—we have already mentioned the so-called *ahl aṣ-ṣuffa*, "the People of the Bench," poor and pious members of the community who lived in the mosque of Medina. Among the Prophet's companions, Abū Dharr al-Ghifārī (d. 653) is often mentioned as "un socialiste avant la lettre," as Louis Massignon puts it; it is to him that the tradition ascribes many sentences about poverty, and he appears as the prototype of the true *faqīr*, the poor person who possesses nothing but is totally possessed by God, partaking of His everlasting riches.

Even more important is Salmān al-Fārisī, a Persian-born barber who was taken into Muhammad's household and became the model of spiritual adoption and mystical initiation—he is, thus, the symbol of the Persians, who were adopted into Islam, and links the Arabian world with the Iranian tradition. His spirituality was later considered a decisive element in the history of Persian Sufism and in Shia thought.[4] Salmān the Barber was later regarded as the patron saint of small artisans, just as some of the ninth- and tenth-century Sufis were to become patrons of the artisan groups whose professions they shared; Salmān came to stand for the impact of Sufism on the large masses (see MM 5).

Another name mystically connected with the Prophet is that of Uways al-Qaranī, who is supposed to have lived in Yemen and who never met the Prophet.[5] It is said that Muhammad knew of his piety and uttered these famous words: "The breath of the Merciful (*nafas ar-Raḥmān*) comes to me from Yemen." Uways, about whom the tradition relates that he spent all his nights in prayer (T 1:21), became, for the later Sufis, the prototype of the inspired Sufi who has been guided solely by divine grace, knowing of the Prophet without outward connection. Thus *uwaysī*, or, as the Turks say, *veysi meshreb*, is the mystic who has attained illumination outside the regular mystical path and without the mediation and guidance of a

4. Louis Massignon, "Salmān Pāk et les prémices spirituelles de l'Islam iranien," *Société des études iraniennes* 7 (1934).

5. A. S. Husaini, "Uways al-Qaranī and the Uwaysi Sufis," *Moslem World* 57, no. 2 (April 1967).

living sheikh. And the "breath of the Merciful" has become, in poetical language, the symbol for the act of divine guidance, which, like the morning breeze, opens the contracted bud of the human heart.

Out of this nucleus of pious people around Muhammad has emerged a definition that was adopted by the Sufis: that is, the threefold attitude of *islām, īmān,* and *iḥsān.*[6] The Koran speaks of *islām* and *īmān; islām* is the complete and exclusive surrender of the faithful to God's will and his perfect acceptance of the injunctions as preached in the Koran, whereas *īmān,* "faith," constitutes the interior aspect of Islam. Thus a *muslim* need not be a *muʾmin* "one who has faith," but the *muʾmin* is definitely a *muslim.* As to *iḥsān,* it was added—according to most traditions by the Prophet himself—with the meaning "that you worship God as if you see Him," for even though man does not see God, God always sees man, and the Koran asserts that "mercy is with those who practice *iḥsān* [*al-muḥsinūn,* 'those who do well']" (Sūra 7:54). With the addition of this third element the complete interiorization of Islam begins; for the believer has to feel that he stands every moment in the presence of God, that he has to behave with awe and respect, and must never fall back into the "sleep of heedlessness," never forget the all-embracing divine presence.

We know little about the earliest appearance of ascetic tendencies in Islam. But when, in 661, ʿAlī, the fourth caliph, was assassinated and the dynasty of the Omayyads came to power, the different trends within the community became more conspicuous. The continuous expansion of the Muslim Empire made the pious ponder the discrepancy between the eschatological threat in the early Koranic revelations and the necessity to expand the realms of Muslim rule by conquering more and more of the lands of the infidels. These conquests were led by a dynasty whose members were anything but representative of Muslim ideals: the Omayyads were always accused of utter worldliness and impious behavior (with the exception of ʿUmar II, 717–20). The resistance of the pious circles to the government grew stronger and was expressed in theological debates about the right ruler of the faithful and the conditions for the leadership of the community. The negative attitude toward the government engendered during these decades has significantly shaped the

6. Arend Jan Wensinck, *Concordance et indices de la tradition musulmane* (Leiden, 1936–71), 1: 467b.

feeling of the pious throughout the history of Islam; the Sufis would often equate "government" with "evil." Medina, the city of the Prophet, was one center of pious conservatives; other groups lived in the new Muslim settlements in Iraq, a province where the love for Muhammad's family was particularly strong and which was antagonistic to Syria, the country where the Omayyad rulers had set up their capital.

The name that stands for the early ascetic, antigovernmental attitude is that of the patriarch of Muslim mysticism, Ḥasan al-Baṣrī (d. 728).[7] He saw the glorious conquests of the Arabs in 711, the memorable year when they crossed the straits of Gibraltar (which still bears the name of the Muslim conqueror Ṭāriq, *jabal Ṭāriq*, "Ṭāriq's mountain"), and when they also reached Sind, the lower Indus valley, and laid the foundation of a Muslim rule that still continues in present Pakistan; in the same year, 711, the Muslims reached the borders of Transoxania, which was destined to become an important center of Muslim learning and piety. Ḥasan al-Baṣrī, however, sober and clearsighted as he was, sensed the dangers inherent in a society that had become interested in conquest alone, in collecting wealth and worldly goods, while tending to forget the Koranic word (Sūra 55:26): "Whatever is on earth is perishing save His Face." He used to admonish his listeners to live strictly according to the rules laid down by the Koran so that they would not be ashamed at Doomsday: "O son of Adam, you will die alone and enter the tomb alone and be resurrected alone, and it is with you alone that the reckoning will be made!" Why care so much for this perishable world? "Be with this world as if you had never been there, and with the Otherworld as if you would never leave it." Many centuries later his words still echo in Persian, Turkish, and Pashto mystical verses.

Ḥasan al-Baṣrī was deeply steeped in the sadness and fear so typical of ascetics of all religions. "It was as if Hellfire had been created exclusively for him and for ʿUmar II," says one historian. His preaching and his exhortations, produced in beautiful sonorous Arabic, influenced many a pious soul in Iraq and elsewhere. His scrupulosity and his fear of the Day of Judgment are reflected in many sayings of his contemporaries or of later Muslims, who might

7. Hans Heinrich Schaeder, in "Hasan al-Basri," *Der Islam* 13 (1923), dealt for the first time with Ḥasan but never completed his study. Hellmut Ritter, "Ḥasan al-Baṣrī, Studien zur Geschichte der islamischen Frömmigkeit," *Der Islam* 21 (1933), gave an excellent analysis. Quotations are taken from Ritter's article.

exclaim, when thinking of God's terrible wrath and of their own sinful lives: "O that I were dust and ashes!"—a saying that was projected back even into the mouth of Muhammad's most trustworthy companions (cf. Sūra 78:41).

Louis Massignon has seen in Ḥasan and in the ascetics who followed him a "realistic critical tendency" as opposed to the more "idealistic tradition" that prevailed in Kufa, the seat of the first Shia groups and the home town of Abū Hāshim, the first to be called *aṣ-Ṣūfī*. It is true that the first ascetic tendencies in Basra and its environment were almost exclusively devotional and lacked any interest in speculative thought. In contrast with the growing luxury of life, the men and women of these groups advocated strict renunciation of the world and what was in it and relied upon the Prophet's word: "If ye knew what I know ye would laugh little and weep much." Therefore they were known as "those who constantly weep" (*al-bakkāʾūn*), for both the miserable state of the world and the meditation of their own shortcomings made them cry in hope of divine help and forgiveness. Ibn ar-Rūmī, the Iraqi poet of the ninth century, has dramatically described them in one of his poems, and Kharaqānī, in the eleventh century, attests that "God is fond of His servant's crying" (N 299). It is, therefore, not surprising that one of Ḥasan al-Baṣrī's disciples founded a settlement of ascetically inclined people in Abbadan on the Persian Gulf: that disciple was ʿAbduʾl Wāḥid ibn Zayd (d. 794), described as a typical representative of the virtue of *waraʿ*, "abstinence," and of permanent sadness. Through him, Ḥasan's ideals reached Syria, where Abū Sulaymān ad-Dārānī (d. 830) and his disciple Aḥmad ibn Abīʾl-Ḥawārī (d. 851) are the best-known members of the Basrian ascetic movement.

A new chapter in the history of Islam was opened when the Abbasids—related to Muhammad's uncle ʿAbbās—came to power in 750. According to the traditional interpretation, the long rule of this dynasty (their last member was killed by the Mongols in 1258) marks the high tide of Muslim culture and civilization. Arts and sciences, law and philology, theology and philosophy were developing; every branch of human knowledge was cultivated. The legal injunctions of the Koran were brought into a more systematic form by the scholars who are considered the founders of the four orthodox law schools: Abū Ḥanīfa (d. 767), Mālik ibn Anās (d. 795), ash-Shāfiʿī (d. 820), and Aḥmad ibn Ḥanbal (d. 855). They took into account legal points ranging from obscure matters pertaining to laws of inheritance to the smallest details for the correct performance of the ritual prayer or the pilgrimage. The four schools differed from each other only on minor points; they were all founded upon the Koran and the *sunna*, i.e., the Prophetic tradition, and made the *ijmāʿ*, the consensus of the "doctors of law" on a certain point, an instrument for introducing innovative legal decisions. They differed on the degree of personal judgment that was granted to the jurist in making his decisions. As early as the late tenth century, the possibility of free investigation into the sources of law (*ijtihād*) in matters that previously had been decided was no longer permitted; this led to a fossilization of jurisprudence, and the *ijmāʿ*, once a force for creative change in Islam, became the cause of its stagnation. Although Islamic law was never codified, the classical handbooks, along with their commentaries and scholia, were handed down verbatim through the generations—and the Sufis have often raised their voices against the spiritless legalism that stifled free development of the personal spiritual life.

Theological issues were widely discussed, mainly in connection with the problem of the legitimacy of the leader of the community, which embraces the question of predestination as well as the problem of whether or not a grave sinner can remain within the pale of Islam. The first attempts at defining the central theme of Islam, the unity of God, were made at approximately the same time, with theologians gradually learning the skills of dialectical disputation and logic. They fought relentlessly against any trace of Manichaean dualism, of Christian trinitarianism, or of whatever seemed to constitute *shirk*, "associating anything with God," i.e., worship of anything besides the sovereign ruler Allah. Defense of God's absolute unity led to discussions concerning the attributes of God, from which ensued the problem of whether the Koran, as God's own word, was created (according to the Muʿtazila) or uncreated (according to the followers of Aḥmad ibn Ḥanbal and the majority of the faithful). But here, too, the zeal for accuracy of definition led the scholars into hairsplitting discussions—as had been the case with the legalists—and Maʿrūf al-Karkhī, a leading Sufi of the early ninth century in Baghdad, sighed: "When God loves His servant, He opens for him the door of actions [i.e., religious and pious acts] and closes the door of theological disputations."[8] The theological

8. ʿAbdur Raḥmān as-Sulamī, *Kitāb ṭabaqāt aṣ-Ṣūfiyya*, ed. Nūraddīn Sharība (Cairo, 1953), p. 87.

discussions had repercussions upon religious thought in general, as, indeed, was the case with the new interest in Greek science and philosophy. The reign of the caliph Maʾmūn (813–33) marks the beginning of that remarkable activity of Arab translators (many of whom were non-Muslims) who made Greek science and philosophy available to Muslim scholars; these, in turn, elaborated the given data, adding many new practical insights. The noteworthy results of their scholarship deeply influenced Western thought and science in the later Middle Ages.

All these currents helped develop the language; the jurists, the theologians, and the translators gave Arabic a greater pliability, adding new dimensions to an already rich and beautiful language. The mystics, too, made considerable contributions in this regard—Paul Nwyia, noting the "adventures of the mystics" in language, has highlighted the fact that, "thanks to the mystics, in the Arabic language, an authentic language, that of experience, was born" (W 4). The writings of the early Sufis show not only variety of expression but an increasing profundity of thought as the mystical experience is refined. In the prayers of some of the Sufis in the tenth century, or in certain poems by Ḥallāj, the ineffable experience has been abstracted in words of unforgettable beauty.

A similar development is visible, in later times, in the non-Arab countries: the literary language of Iran owes much to writers who gave voice to mystical yearnings in Persian; Turkish was transformed by the mystical poet Yūnus Emre (d. circa 1321) into a delightful literary idiom. Likewise the Indo-Muslim languages (Sindhi, Panjabi, and to a great extent Urdu and Pashto) are in large part the result of the speech and song of mystical leaders who could not address their simple disciples in high-flown theological Arabic or poetical Persian; in order to express the mysteries of divine love and devotion, they were obliged to use the vernaculars, making them vehicles of the most lofty thought. Then they emerged as languages well able to serve as a literary medium for nonmystical writers.

The expansion of the Islamic Empire during the late Omayyad and early Abbasid periods had brought the Muslims into contact with large groups of non-Muslims representing different cultural levels and varied traditions. The presence of Zoroastrian influences must certainly be accepted from the beginning of the Abbasid period, when the capital was shifted from Damascus to Baghdad. Persian noblemen served at the court; Persian traditions from the "Book of Kings" were incorporated into the Arabic narrative literature, helping to shape the image of the ideal ruler; and Persian mythology was to become a substitute for the weak pre-Islamic Arabic tradition. In Eastern Iran and Transoxania, the Muslims met Buddhists whose ascetic practices were of some interest to them. Their contacts with Hinduism as a religion were negligible in this period, although India contributed extensively to the development of Islamic mathematics and astronomy. But India in general was considered the country of the sage, and the home of magical practices performed by blackish, ugly people. Manichaeism, so widespread in the Near and Middle East, and in Central Asia, attracted the interest of the theologians, and more than one mystic was accused of Manichaean inclinations. Mandaeans and Jews constituted a small, but active, minority.

The most significant contacts of the early Abbasid Muslims were with Christians, split into numerous groups ranging from the Nestorians to the many Monophysite sects and churches.[9] Christian ascetics and hermits who inhabited places in Iraq and the mountains of Lebanon are mentioned frequently in Sufi stories—and in pre-Islamic poetry there were already allusions to the light shining forth from the Christian hermit's cell. A meeting with a Christian ascetic or with a wise monk is a fictional element in Sufi legends of early times: such a person usually explains some mystical truths to the seeker; or the disciple admires his austerity but is informed by a heavenly voice that all his asceticism will not gain him salvation since he has no faith in Muhammad. Jesus, the last prophet before Muhammad according to Koranic revelation, appears to the Sufis as the ideal ascetic and also as the pure lover of God. A homeless pilgrim, wandering without knowing where to put his head, he instructs the devout about the importance of modesty, peace, and charity, for "just as the seed does not grow but from dust, so the

9. There are several studies devoted to the mystics of the first three centuries: Henry Frederick Amedroz, "Notes on Some Sufi Lives," *Journal of the Royal Asiatic Society*, 1912; Margaret Smith, *Studies in Early Mysticism in the Near and Middle East* (London, 1931), deals with the relationships between Christian and Islamic mysticism. The same problem has been discussed by Tor Andrae, "Zuhd und Mönchtum," *Le monde oriental* 25 (1931), and in several other studies by this Swedish theologian. His posthumously published book *I Myrtenträdgården* (Uppsala, 1947), translated into German by Hans Helmhart Kanus as *Islamische Mystiker* (Stuttgart, 1960), is an excellent introduction to the pre-Ḥallājian development of Sufism and deserves an English translation.

seed of wisdom does not grow but from a heart like dust."[10] It is the Jesus of the Sermon on the Mount whose image is reflected in sayings of the first generations of Sufis, and he continued to be a favorite figure in later Sufi poetry as well: he and his virgin mother become exalted symbolic figures—the woman unspoiled by worldly concern, the pure receptacle of the divine spirit, and the prophet born out of the divine command, surnamed "Spirit of God," became models of the pure spiritual life.

It is even possible that the first Sufis adopted from the Christian ascetics the woolen garment from which their name derives. These Sufis were people who meticulously fulfilled the words of the law, prayed and fasted, constantly recollecting God, and were absolutely bound by Koran and tradition. Thus says one of them: "Sometimes Truth knocks at my heart for forty days, but I do not permit it to enter my heart unless it brings two witnesses, the Koran and the Prophetic tradition" (L 104). The country of incomparable ascetic achievement was Khurasan in the northeastern part of the Abbasid Empire. A saying ascribed to one of the ninth-century Khurasanian ascetics serves well as an introduction to the mentality typical of this remarkable group: "Who wants to attain to the highest honor should prefer seven to seven: poverty to wealth, hunger to satiety, the low to the elevated, humiliation to honor, modesty to pride, sadness to joy, death to life" (N 45). As late as the thirteenth century Jalāluddīn Rūmī alludes in one of his verses to the ascetics of Herat and Merw-i Taliqan, declaring that even they would be intoxicated if the scent of the wine of love were to reach them from the Maghreb, the far west (D 1966). But this scent very rarely reached them, though perhaps more true mystical love is hidden beneath their outward austerity than a modern reader can realize.[11]

One of the most famous conversion stories in early Sufism is that of Fuḍayl ibn ᶜIyāḍ. He was a highwayman, albeit a magnanimous one, between the cities of Abiward and Sarakhs. One day, on the way to his beloved, he happened to hear a verse from the Koran and immediately gave up banditry, thereafter devoting himself to the study of the Prophetic tradition in Kufa. He died in Mecca in 803.

10. Abū Ṭālib al-Makkī. *Qūt al-qulūb fī muᶜāmalāt al-maḥbūb*, 2 vols. (Cairo, 1310 h./1892–93), 2:74.

11. Early ascetic Sufism has beeen treated by Paul Klappstein, *Vier turkestanische Heilige, ein Beitrag zum Verständnis der islamischen Mystik* (Berlin, 1919), and Jakob Hallauer, *Die Vita des Ibrahim ibn Edhem in der Tedhkiret al-Ewlija des Ferid ed-Din Attar* (Leipzig, 1925)—both rather superficial.

Fuḍayl is a typical representative of early orthodox asceticism, "and when he died, sadness was taken away from the world" (Q 9). This sadness is reflected in many of his sayings. He disliked the company of people, and in words reminiscent of his contemporary Rābiʿa, the woman saint, he said: "When night comes I am happy that I am alone, without separation, with God, and when morning comes I get distressed because I detest the view of those people who enter and disturb my solitude" (T 1:31). Although Fuḍayl was married, he considered family life one of the greatest obstacles on the way to God; he was seen smiling only once in thirty years—when his son died. This event was, for him, a sign of divine grace: "When God loves His servant, He afflicts him, and when He loves him very much He takes hold of him and leaves for him neither family nor wealth" (G 4:282). (The feeling of happiness at the death of family members was not unknown among medieval Christian mystics either, as the story of Angela di Foligno shows).[12] Even Jalāluddīn Rūmī wrote, quite without feeling, in a verse of his *Mathnawī*: "The death of his children was for him like sweetmeat" (M 3:1927); and the indifference of some Indo-Muslim Chishtī saints of the thirteenth and fourteenth centuries to the death of family members is well known. On the other hand, many of the great Sufis and founders of mystical fraternities were married and had large families—Aḥmad-i Jām had forty-two children (N 357), and ʿAbdu'l-Qādir Gīlānī had forty-nine sons. Yet so rare is it to find any approval of happy family life in Sufi sayings that one is quite unprepared for the exception one meets in Mīr Dard, the saint of Delhi in the eighteenth century, who exclaimed in one of his books: "I love my wife and my children dearly."[13]

Among the early ascetics, a preference for celibacy was common in spite of the Prophet's example of married life and his advice to raise a family. But, as Dārānī says, "the sweetness of adoration and undisturbed surrender of the heart which the single man can feel the married man can never experience" (G 2:22). The restlessness caused by marriage, the distraction from God, has often been described by the Sufis (N 217), and the sorrows of family life might be regarded as "punishment for the execution of legally permitted lusts" (N 185). Fuḍayl's elder contemporary, Ibrāhīm ibn Adham

12. Evelyn Underhill, *Mysticism: A Study in the Nature and Development of Man's Spiritual Consciousness* (1911; paperback ed., New York, 1956), p. 216.

13. Khwāja Mīr Dard, "Nāla-yi Dard," no. 70, in *Chahār risāla* (Bhopal, 1310 h./1892–93).

(d. circa 790), whom he met at Mecca, expressed such a notion in a striking sentence often quoted in Sufi poetry and prose: "When a man marries he embarks on a ship, and when a child is born he suffers shipwreck" (L 199). Ibrāhīm ibn Adham—"the key of mystical sciences," as Junayd called him (H 103)—has become, in Islamic tradition, one of the proverbial examples of true poverty, abstinence, and trust in God. According to the legend, he renounced the princely life in Balkh, the old Buddhist capital where he was born (a story embellished with echoes of the Buddha legend). He later became the subject of many pious tales in Eastern Islamic lands. A romance was even composed about his adventures and was known particularly in the Malayan archipelago.

> Although his residence was Balkh,
> Balkh became corrected, namely *talkh* ["bitter"],

says ʿAṭṭār (U 264), with a pun: by changing the diacritical dots of the first letter of Balkh, he implies that the former seat of power and wealth became bitter for the young, highborn ascetic.

Ibrāhīm is credited with making the first classification of the stages of *zuhd*, "asceticism." Because of its tripartition, which was common after the ninth century, it looks like a word from some later source, for it discerns: (a) renunciation of the world, (b) renunciation of the happy feeling of having achieved renunciation, and (c) the stage in which the ascetic regards the world as so unimportant that he no longer looks at it.

The stories of the degree of asceticism achieved by these early Sufis sound somewhat incredible to a modern mind; yet they counted it happiness to live completely free of worldly things, even though they might use only a brick for a pillow (N 49) and a worn-out mat of straw for a bed (if they did not prefer to sleep in a seated position or refrain from sleep at all). They cared neither for their outward appearance nor for their attire, and although they strictly observed the ritual purity required for prayer, Ibn Adham was proud of the huge number of lice living in his coat, and as late as 900, a maidservant of a Sufi from Baghdad exclaimed: "O God, how dirty are Thy friends—not a single one among them is clean!" (N 621).

One of Fuḍayl's disciples was Bishr, called *al-Ḥāfī*, "the barefooted one," who considered even shoes to be a "veil" on the path to God. Bishr, like his master, came from Merw and, also like Fuḍayl, was converted by a miracle: on the road he found a piece of paper, which he took with him because the name of God was written on it —this pious act of the otherwise worldly man was soon recompensed when, by divine grace, he was transformed into a Sufi. He settled in Baghdad, where he died, after a perfectly scrupulous life, in 841. Bishr is said to have dwelt upon the concept of *ikhlāṣ*, "absolute sincerity," in every thought and action, an attitude that was elaborated to perfection by his younger contemporary in Baghdad, al-Ḥārith al-Muḥāsibī.

Among the early Khurasanian Sufis, the former merchant Shaqīq al-Balkhī (d. 809) is worthy of mention. Recent research has shown that he was not only an expert on *tawakkul,* "absolute trust in God" —a path taken up by his disciples Ḥātim al-Aṣamm (d. 851) and Ḥātim's pupil Abū Turāb an-Nakhshabī (d. 859)—but that he was also the first to discuss the "mystical states" and was deeply concerned with what he calls "the light of pure love of God" (W 228). With this idea he comes close to the saint of Basra, Rābiᶜa al-ᶜAdawiyya, who died only a few years before him (801).[14]

Rābiᶜa was "that one set apart in the seclusion of holiness, that woman veiled with the veil of sincerity, that one enflamed by love and longing . . . , lost in union with God, that one accepted by men as a second spotless Mary . . . " (T 159). Rābiᶜa is generally regarded as the person who introduced the element of selfless love into the austere teachings of the early ascetics and gave Sufism the hue of true mysticism. Jāmī has beautifully explained the difference between these ascetics and the genuine Sufis: "The ascetics regard the Beauty of the Otherworld with the light of faith and certitude and despise the world, but are still veiled by a sensual pleasure, namely the thought of Paradise, whereas the true Sufi is veiled from both worlds by the vision of the Primordial Beauty and Essential Love" (N 10).

Rābiᶜa was a slave girl, set free by her master. The most famous story illustrative of the singlemindedness of her devotion is this: Once, in the streets of Basra, she was asked why she was carrying a torch in one hand and a ewer in the other, and she answered: "I want to throw fire into Paradise and pour water into Hell so that these

14. Margaret Smith, *Rābiᶜa the Mystic and Her Fellow-Saints in Islam* (Cambridge, 1928), is a fundamental study that also deals with the role of women in Sufism in general. ᶜAbdur Raḥmān Badawī, *Shāhidat al-ᶜishq al-ilāhī, Rābiᶜa al-ᶜAdawiyya* (Cairo, 1946).

two veils disappear, and it becomes clear who worships God out of love, not out of fear of Hell or hope for Paradise."[15]

This love for love's sake has become the central topic of Sufism; almost every mystical poet in Islam has expressed the idea that "the lover must be in the way of love so that he does not remember Hell or Paradise" (N 597). For "a few houris and castles" that are promised to the pious in Paradise are mere veils hiding the eternal divine beauty—"when He fills your mind with Paradise and houris know by certain that He keeps you far from Himself" (MT 204). It would certainly be better if God took away Paradise or cast the ascetic who feared hellfire into that very fire, for both Paradise and Hell are created, and thus distinct from God (T 1:73).

Rābiᶜa's love of God was absolute; there was no room left for any other thought or love. She did not marry, nor did she give the Prophet a special place in her piety. The world meant nothing to her. She would shut the windows in spring without looking at the flowers and become lost in the contemplation of Him who created flowers and springtime. This story has often been retold by the mystical poets of Iran. Every true mystic should know that "the gardens and the fruits are inside, in the heart," as Rūmī says in his version of Rābiᶜa's story (M 4: 1357; see also U 198). Rābiᶜa seems to have been the first Sufi to speak about the jealous God—a concept not unknown to prophetic piety; but whereas the jealous God of the orthodox does not allow anybody to *worship* anything besides Him, Rābiᶜa's God "will suffer none to share with Him that love which is due to Him alone."[16] And so she addresses Him in small poetical effusions:

O Beloved of hearts, I have none like unto Thee,
therefore have pity this day on the sinner
  who comes to Thee.
O my Hope and my Rest and my Delight,
the heart can love none other but Thee.[17]

In such perfect love, the mystic has "ceased to exist and passed out of self. I am one with Him and altogether His."[18] Rābiᶜa had meditated upon the Koranic statement that God's love precedes man's

15. Smith, *Rābiᶜa*, p. 98.
16. Ibid., p. 108.
17. Ibid., p. 55.
18. Ibid., p. 110.

love: "He loves them and they love Him" (Sūra 5:59): "Love has come from Eternity and passes into Eternity and none has been found in seventy thousand worlds who drinks one drop of it until at last he is absorbed in God, and from that comes the saying: He loves them and they love Him" (T 1:67). It was this Koranic passage that provided the Sufis of the following generations with proof for their theories of the mutual love between the Creator and the creature.

There is nothing left to distract the lover from God—the spiritual eye sees nothing but Him when the eye of the body is closed. He is enough for the loving soul: "O my Lord, whatever share of this world Thou dost bestow on me, bestow it on Thine enemies, and whatever share of the next world Thou doest give me, give it to Thy friends—Thou art enough for me" (T 1:73). Rābiʿa's prayer has been repeated, with variations, by Sufis of all ages, probably in the most shocking form by Shiblī (d. 945), the mystic of Baghdad whose paradoxes are famous in Sufi history: "O God, hand this world and the Otherworld over to me so that I may make a morsel from this world and throw it into a dog's mouth, and make a morsel of the Otherworld and put it into a Jew's mouth, for both are veils before the true goal" (T 2:165). For Rābiʿa the only thing that mattered was the hope of God and the word of His praise, which was sweeter than any other word. The nightly prayer, one of the pivots of early ascetic life, becomes, with her, a sweet and loving conversation between lover and beloved:

> O God, the night has passed and the day has dawned. How I long to know if Thou hast accepted my prayers or if Thou hast rejected them. Therefore console me for it is Thine to console this state of mine. Thou hast given me life and cared for me, and Thine is the glory. If Thou want to drive me from Thy door, yet would I not forsake it, for the love that I bear in my heart towards Thee.[19]

It was a daring prayer, often repeated by the early Sufis, that the true lover would not leave the door of the beloved even if driven away.

Rābiʿa was not the only woman saint in the eighth century; several women chose the mystical path, sighing for the heavenly beloved who, though absent from their sight, is never absent from their hearts. Because of her intense feelings Rābiʿa was accepted as the model of selfless love even by those who otherwise despised

19. Ibid., p. 27.

women—but since in the unity of God the lovers no longer have a separate existence, no distinction can be made between man and woman (T 1:59).

During the ninth century different trends in the mystical teachings and the approach to God emerged, and religious experiences were expressed in various styles and forms. But the roots of these developments went back to an earlier period. That has been shown very clearly in Père Nwyia's research. He has emphasized that Jaʿfar aṣ-Ṣādiq, the sixth imām of the Shia (d. 765), was certainly one of the greatest teachers of early Sufism. His commentary on the Koran, part of which is preserved in Sulamī's *tafsīr*, shows an exceptional insight into mystical phenomena (W 161). Jaʿfar discerned the four different aspects of the Koran: expression, for the common people; allusion, for the privileged or elite; touches of grace (*laṭāʾif*), for the saints; and finally the "realities," for the prophets (W 167). This pluralistic structure of the holy book led Jaʿfar to sketch a hierarchical structure of the faithful according to the degree of their interior knowledge—a principle developed by later Sufis when they identified the "stages" and "stations" and then divided them into those for the common people, for the elect, and for the elite of the elite. The hierarchical principle is also found in later theories of saintship, and it is a typical facet of Shia thought as well. Imām Jaʿfar alluded to a structure of mystical experience that leads in twelve stages from source to source, which looks like a preparation for the stations through which the Sufi initiate has to pass on the Path. Some of Jaʿfar's hermeneutic principles seem to contain thoughts that were, until recently, ascribed to later mystics; he even analyzed the "theopathic locutions," the so-called *shaṭḥiyāt*, in which the mystic utters words that he should not say. Jaʿfar's model case for such an experience is the conversation between Moses and God on Mount Sinai (Sūra 20:11–21).

Moses was the prophet who heard God—heard His voice speaking in him and through him; but Muhammad was blessed with the vision of God during his ascension—he entered the intimate proximity of the beloved, and here, as Jaʿfar's modern interpreter states, "the language of experience becomes the language of love" (W 187). That means that before the time of Rābiʿa the first steps were taken in the direction of an authentic love mysticism. The definition of divine love as given by Jaʿfar, and often repeated by later mystics, is this: "a divine fire that devours man completely" (W 187).

SOME MYSTICAL LEADERS OF THE LATE NINTH CENTURY

The discoveries about the earliest Sufis show that some of the definitions attributed to mystics of the ninth century can probably be dated much earlier. They also show how Shia and Sufi ideas were, at that early stage, interdependent. But many problems still await solution. The thoughts of Jaʿfar and, perhaps, other early mystical thinkers must have been at work beneath the surface, permeating the mystical life until they appeared in the sayings of a number of Sufis, all near contemporaries, who reveal the potential variety within the mystical life. I refer to Dhūʾn-Nūn the Egyptian (d. 859), Bāyezīd Bisṭāmī the Iranian (d. 874), Yaḥyā ibn Muʿādh from Rayy (d. 871), and al-Ḥārith al-Muḥāsibī the Iraqi (d. 857).

Dhūʾn-Nūn is one of the most attractive and intriguing figures in the history of early Sufism, aptly called "one of the most eminent of their hidden spiritualists" (H 100). Thaubān ibn Ibrāhīm, surnamed Dhūʾn-Nūn, "he with the fish," was born of Nubian parents in Ikhmim in Upper Egypt; he studied religious sciences and is reported to have transmitted traditions from Mālik ibn Anās, the founder of the Maliki law school. Dhūʾn-Nūn was "the unique [authority] of his time in scholarship and piety and mystical state and culture" (Q 8). During the Muʿtazilite persecution of the orthodox he, too, was imprisoned, because of his belief in the doctrine that the Koran was uncreated; the caliph Mutawakkil, however, deeply impressed by one of his sermons, set him free. He was accused of being a philosopher and an alchemist, and the genuineness of his mystical state was sometimes doubted; Ibn an-Nadīmʾs *Fihrist* (2: 862) in the tenth century mentions two of his works among alchemistic scriptures. We know little about his life, and his teachings are still scattered in the hagiographic books. Ibrāhīm al-Qaṣṣār, who saw him in his childhood, remembers that he was disappointed by the great mystical leader who was outwardly so humble and meek, but Dhūʾn-Nūn reproached the boy, whose thoughts he had read by means of his inner power (N 166). Many miracles are ascribed to him, and in strange legends he figures as a kind of magician whom men and jinn obeyed. It is said that "he traveled the road of blame." But when he died, legend asserts, "it was written on his forehead: 'This is the friend of God, he died in love of God, slain by God' " (H 100). This love of God has been expressed in one of his sayings (which has also been attributed to other mystics because it shows very well the inclination of the early Sufis to speak in allusions without divulging the secret of their loving intimacy with God): "O God! Publicly I call Thee 'My Lord,' but in solitude I call Thee 'O my Beloved'!" (A 9:332). According to the tradition, Dhūʾn-Nūn formulated for the first time a theory of *maʿrifa,* intuitive knowledge of God, or gnosis, as opposed to *ʿilm,* discursive learning and knowledge; many sayings about "love" and "intimacy" are also attributed to him. However, we would scarcely agree with Edward G. Browne, who considers him "the first to give to the earlier asceticism the definitely pantheistic bent and quasi-erotic expression which we recognize as the chief characteristics of Sufism."[20] Nicholson was inclined to accept Neoplatonic influences upon Dhūʾn-Nūn. Since this mystic lived in Egypt, where Neoplatonic and hermetic traditions were in the air, and was regarded by some of his contemporaries as a "philosopher," he may well have been acquainted with some Neoplatonic ideas. In a famous passage, he has described the gnostic (*ʿārif*), the true mystic with spiritual insight; but we do not find a "philosophical" approach in these words of his:

> The gnostic becomes more humble every hour, for every hour is drawing him nearer to God. The gnostics see without knowledge, without sight, without information received, and without observation, without description, without veiling and without veil. They are not themselves, but in so far as they exist at all they exist in God. Their movements are caused by God, and their words are the words of God which are uttered by their tongues, and their sight is the sight of God, which has entered into their eyes. So God Most High has said: "When I love a servant, I, the Lord, am his ear so that he hears by Me, I am his eye, so that he sees by Me, and I am his tongue so that he speaks by Me, and I am his hand, so that he takes by Me."[21]

This last-quoted *ḥadīth qudsī,*[22] an extra-Koranic word attributed to God, forms one of the cornerstones of mystical teaching in Sufism: man is, through acts of supererogatory piety, slowly lifted above his own base qualities and instead distinguished by the good qualities seen in God, until he completely lives in Him and through Him.

Dhūʾn-Nūn's alleged "philosophical-gnostic" character is not re-

20. Edward G. Browne, *A Literary History of Persia,* 4 vols. (1902; reprint ed., Cambridge, 1957), 2:505.

21. Margaret Smith, *Readings from the Mystics of Islam* (London, 1950), no. 20; see A 9:385 ff.

22. *Ṣaḥīḥ al-Bukhārī,* ed. L. Krehl and W. Juynboll (Leiden, 1862–1908), 4:231.

flected in another of his sayings either: "I knew God by God, and I knew what is besides God by the Messenger of God" (L 104). "The sign of the lover of God is to follow the Friend of God, i.e., the Prophet, in his morals, and his deeds and his orders and his customs" (T 1:125).

Stories connected with the Greatest Name of God are told about this mystic; but his reply in the following anecdote reveals the pious Muslim rather than a man who relies upon magical practice: "One said to Dhūʾn-Nūn: 'Show me the Greatest Name of God.' He said: 'Show me the smallest one!'—and scolded him"[23] Dhūʾn-Nūn emphasized God's incredible majesty and power and, inspired by two of the Koranic names of God, *al-muḥyī*, "He who bestows life," and *al-mumīt*, "He who kills," he appropriately described the state of the mystic: "Nothing sees God and dies, even as nothing sees God and lives, because His life is everlasting, and who ever sees Him, remains in Him and is made everlasting" (A 9:373). The theories of *fanā* and *baqā*, "annihilation, extinction," and "everlasting life, duration" in God, central topics of Sufism, are developed here out of the Koranic context.

Dhūʾn-Nūn, like most of the mystics, often juxtaposed the divine qualities and names. *Jamāl*, "eternal beauty," and *jalāl*, "eternal majesty," coinciding in *kamāl*, "eternal perfection," are the qualities of Him who must be addressed as "Thou art who Thou art, eternally, in eternity."[24] God, the eternal perfection to which no created being has access, reveals Himself to man under the aspects of beauty and fascination, kindness and mercy, or under the aspects of majesty and wrath, power and revenge. More than a thousand years after Dhūʾn-Nūn, the German theologian Rudolf Otto has built up a theological system based upon the contrast between the *mysterium tremendum* and the *mysterium fascinans*, which constitute the two main qualities of the Numen; he has, thus, expressed in scientific language a truth that had been known to every Sufi in the world of Islam for centuries. Dhūʾn-Nūn frequently dwelt upon the quality of majesty, *jalāl*, the *tremendum*, in God—an approach typical of early Islamic thought. That is why he believed affliction to be indispensable to man's spiritual development; it is the "salt

23. ʿAbdul Wahhāb ash-Shaʿrānī, *Lawāqiḥ al-anwār al-qudsiyya* (Cairo, 1311 h./1893–94), p. 144.

24. Reynold A. Nicholson, *The Mystics of Islam* (1914; reprint ed., Chester Springs, Pa., 1962), p. 183.

of the faithful, and when the salt lacks, the faithful becomes rotten" (A 9:373). The faithful lover enjoys the tribulations sent by his beloved, as Dhūʾn-Nūn has said; but the great mystic disliked those who turned this attitude into a mere show: "When one of his brethren, a so-called lover, was boasting during his illness: 'Who suffers from the pain which God sends him, does not love God,' he replied: 'I would rather say: "He who boasts of his love of God, does not love Him"'" (T 1:123).

One of the most attractive aspects of Dhūʾn-Nūn is his poetic talent and his wonderful command of the Arabic language. He composed small, charming poems—a new development in Sufism, although Rābiʿa is credited with a few poetical exclamations. He praised the Lord in long, hymnlike poems and popularized a kind of romantic mystical story, a literary type often found in later hagiographic works. He told how he wandered along the Nile, or strolled alone in the desert, when suddenly he would meet a stranger who revealed to him mysteries of the Path: "He met a woman at the sea shore and asked her: 'What is the end of love?' And she answered: 'O simpleton, love has no end.' And he asked: 'Why?' She said: 'Because the Beloved has no end'" (T 1:123). This story is typical of Dhūʾn-Nūn's tendency to introduce a dramatic element into the discussion of complicated problems that cannot be resolved through intellectual efforts. The answer of the unknown woman (in other cases it may be a slave girl, a negro, or an old anchorite) points immediately to the heart of the matter: since love is the essence of the divine, it is, like God Himself, without beginning and without end.

The romantic and poetic aspect of Dhūʾn-Nūn can be understood best from his prayers. The Koran asserts that everything created worships God; everything utters praise and thanks to its creator in its own tongue, which may be the human voice, the humming of the bee, the growing of the leaves, the scent of the flower, or just the *lisān ul-ḥāl*, the "state of speaking by itself," someone's whole attitude. The created world gains, thus, a religious meaning—a meaning that the early ascetics had lost sight of because they considered it to be a detestable veil that distracted them from God. But for Dhūʾn-Nūn and the generations of Sufis following him, the worth or worthlessness of the world is determined not by itself, but by man's relation to it. It is again regarded as God's creation and thus as something dependent upon Him and belonging to Him. That is how Dhūʾn-Nūn felt:

O God, I never hearken to the voices of the beasts or the rustle of the trees, the splashing of the waters or the song of the birds, the whistling of the wind or the rumble of the thunder, but I sense in them a testimony to Thy Unity, and a proof of Thy incomparability, that Thou art the All-Prevailing, the All-Knowing, the All-True. (A 9:342)

Such psalmlike prayers of praise, in beautiful, rhythmic rhyme-prose are unforgettable, and they deeply impressed the mystical writers of later centuries. The great poets of Iran understood the language of the flowers and birds as clearly as Dhūʾn-Nūn; the proems of ʿAṭṭār's epics translate this praise of the creatures into human poetical language, and he was able to express the silent yearning of all creatures in the forty chapters of his *Muṣībatnāma*. Dhūʾn-Nūn's compatriot Shaʿrānī, the last great mystic of Egypt in the sixteenth century, tells a story that reminds the reader immediately of Dhūʾn-Nūn's hymnic praise:

Whoever recollects God in reality, forgets all else besides Him, because all the creatures recollect Him, as is witnessed by those who experience a revelation (*kashf*). I experienced this state from evening prayer until one third of the night was over, and I heard the voices of the creatures in the praise of God, with elevated voices so that I feared for my mind. I heard the fishes who said: Praised be the King, the Most Holy, the Lord.[25]

The late thirteenth-century mystical poet Yūnus Emre, who declared that he would praise the Lord together with the stones and the fountains, with the gazelles and with the prophets, was just as faithful an interpreter of the Koranic words that everything was created in order to worship and praise the Creator as was his seventeenth-century compatriot Merkez Efendi, about whom a charming story was told to me by Turkish friends:

The *sheikh* of the Khalvati order in Istanbul, Sünbül Efendi, in looking for a successor, sent his disciples forth to get flowers to adorn the convent. All of them returned with large bunches of lovely flowers; only one of them—Merkez Efendi—came back with a small, withered plant. When asked why he did not bring anything worthy of his master, he answered: "I found all the flowers busy recollecting the Lord—how could I interrupt this constant prayer of theirs? I looked, and lo, one flower had finished its recollection. That one I brought." It was he who became the successor of Sünbül Efendi, and one of the cemeteries along the Byzantine wall of Istanbul still bears his name.

The poetic aspect of Dhūʾn-Nūn has been highlighted because

25. Ash-Shaʿrānī, *Lawāqiḥ*, p. 156. See also the description of Kāzarūnī in T 2:295.

that is most conspicuous in his sayings. A detailed study of his life and work would, in all probability, reveal many previously unknown aspects of his teachings and show whether he was, indeed, the first "theosophist" among the Sufis or rather the hymnodist who rediscovered the divine glory as praised by the creatures. In later times Dhūʾn-Nūn became a subject of tales and legends.

Another early saint has been almost completely transformed into a kind of Sufi symbol—Abū Yazīd (Bāyezīd) Bisṭāmī (d. 874).[26] His personality looms large on the horizon of early Persian Sufism. Few mystics have impressed and perplexed their contemporaries and successive generations as much as this ascetic from the little place known as Bistam (Basṭām) in northwestern Iran. Strange experiences and great faith are ascribed to him. His theopathic locutions and paradoxes attracted another, though very different, mystic, Junayd (d. 910), the leader of the Baghdad school, who, however, held that Bāyezīd had not reached the final goal of the seeker.

Numerous attempts at explaining Bāyezīd's personality and his enigmatic utterances have been made in Europe. The finest one is the short and penetrating study by Hellmut Ritter. R. C. Zaehner has stressed the possibility of Indian influences upon Bāyezīd. The import of the story that Bāyezīd's mystical master was a certain Abū ʿAlī as-Sindī, i.e., from Sind, is still doubtful; even if this man had been from the lower Indus valley and not from a village called Sind close to Bistam, it seems scarcely possible to draw far-reaching consequences from this geographical fact: not every man from Sind could be expected to know all the intricacies of Hindu monistic philosophy. It is, of course, tempting to imagine such an acquaintance with Vedantic speculations on the part of Bāyezīd, and some of the equations brought forth by Zaehner seem very plausible; yet it seems more likely that the mystic of Bistam should have reached his goal by means of the Islamic experience of *fanā*, annihilation, as he formulated it for the first time, rather than by an experience

26. Hellmut Ritter, "Die Aussprüche des Bāyezīd Bisṭāmī," in *Westöstliche Abhandlungen, Festschrift für Rudolf Tschudi,* ed. Fritz Meier (Wiesbaden, 1954). Reynold A. Nicholson, "An Early Arabic Version of the Miʿrāj of Abū Yazīd al-Bisṭāmī," *Islamica* 2 (1925). On possible Indian influences see Robert C. Zaehner, *Hindu and Muslim Mysticism* (London, 1960), and the critical article by M. ʿAbdur Rabb, "The Problem of Possible Indian Influence on Abū Yazīd al-Bisṭāmī," *Journal of the Pakistan Historical Society,* January 1972. ʿAbdur Raḥmān Badawī, *Shaṭaḥāt aṣ-ṣūfiyya, I: Abū Yazīd al-Bisṭāmī* (Cairo, 1949).

that, in the Vedantic sense, would have led him to an extension of the *atman*, "the innermost self," until it realizes its unity with the essence of everything as expressed in the words *tat twam asi*, "that is you." Bāyezīd hoped for a complete extinction of the traces of self, not for an extension of anything created (cf. MM 56). The negative way is his; but he was also the first to describe the mystical experience in terms of the image of the *miʿrāj*, the heavenly journey of the Prophet. His sayings burn with hopeless longing and possess a weird beauty, and they are often frightening in their powerful imagery. His yearning is absolute, and so is his disappointment.

Bāyezīd's nephew, to whom we owe the transmission of many of his sayings, once asked him about his renunciation, and he answered:

> Renunciation (*zuhd*) has no value. I was three days in renunciation, on the fourth day I had finished it. The first day I renounced this world, the second day I renounced the Otherworld, the third day I renounced everything save God; when the fourth day came, nothing was left to me but God. I reached a desperate longing. Then I heard a voice addressing me: "O Bāyezīd, you are not strong enough to endure with Me alone." I said: "That is exactly what I want." Then the voice said: "You have found, you have found!" (T 1:167)

God is so overwhelming that man becomes nothing even when thinking of His name or pronouncing the word *Allāh* with proper awe: "Bāyezīd once uttered the call to prayer and fainted. When he came to his senses he said: 'It is amazing that a man does not die when uttering the call to prayer.' "[27] But then, how are we to understand his description of his flight beyond space three times thirty thousand years—until eventually he found nothing but Bāyezīd in the divine throne and behind the veil that hides God? And again there is his reply to someone who asked him: When does man reach God? "O you miserable one—does he reach Him at all?"[28] One of his mystical friends—the traditions about the name differ—sent him a prayer rug on which to pray; but he answered: "I have put together the worship of the inhabitants of the heavens and the seven earths and put it into a pillow and put that pillow under my cheek" (T 1:144). And at other times, when somebody came to see him, he replied: "I myself am in search of Bāyezīd."[29]

His sentences are paradoxes, wrapped in wonderful imagery: for

27. Ritter, "Bayezid," in *Westöstliche Abhandlungen*, ed. Meier, p. 234.
28. Ibid., p. 240.
29. Ibid.

twelve years he was the blacksmith of his self until he made of himself a pure mirror (T 1:139); he saw "longing" as a palace in which the sword "horror of separation" is placed and a narcissus stem "union" given in the hand of hope—but even after seven thousand years the narcissus is fresh and green, for no one has ever attained it (T 1:166).

Bāyezīd might acknowledge at one moment that he eventually found that God had remembered him before he remembered God, knew him before he had known Him, and that God's love of man precedes man's love of God (A 10:34); but at another moment the same Bāyezīd sighs:

> As soon as I attained to His Unity I became a bird with a body of Oneness and wings of Everlastingness, and I continued flying in the air of Quality for ten years, until I reached an atmosphere a million times as large, and I flew on, until I found myself in the field of Eternity and I saw there the Tree of Oneness. . . . And I looked, and I knew that all this was a cheat.

Then again, he exclaimed, with the pride of one who had found his goal:

> He got up once and put me before Himself and addressed me: "O Bāyezīd, my creatures desire to behold thee." So I said: "Adorn me with Thy Unity and dress me with Thy I-ness and raise me to Thy Oneness so that, when Thy creatures see me, they may say: We have seen Thee, and it is Thou and I am no longer there." (L 382)

It must have been in such a state of rapture that Bāyezīd said: "*Subḥānī*—Praise be to Me, how great is My Majesty!" This typical *shaṭḥ* has puzzled many later mystics and has often been repeated by the poets of Iran and Turkey and Muslim India as proof of the unitive state reached by the perfected mystic. Sarrāj, to give one example of moderate Sufi interpretation, understands Bāyezīd to be talking "as if he were reciting the Koranic word: 'I am God, there is no God besides Me' " (Sūra 20:14) (L 390)—which is certainly a mild explanation. Bāyezīd came to attain this state by an austere *via negationis* and constant mortification, by emptying himself of himself, until he had reached, at least for a moment, the world of absolute unity where, as he said, lover, beloved, and love are one (T 1:160), and where he himself is the wine, the wine-drinker, and the cupbearer (T 1:159)—a formulation used by later Persian poets in their hymns praising the purifying and transforming power of divine love.

A strange figure of dark fire, Bāyezīd stands lonely in early Iranian Sufism. His paradoxes constantly yield new meaning, yet they continue to be elusive—unless the reader were to share the mystic's experience. Or would one, then, return and claim with Bāyezīd that "everything was a cheat"?

Whatever the experiences of the mystic from Bistam were, his personality inspired many later writers. His name occurs, in poetry, more frequently than that of any other mystic, with the exception of "Manṣūr" Ḥallāj, with whom he was sometimes associated, although Ḥallāj believed that "poor Abū Yazīd" had arrived only at the threshold of the divine (P 250). The poets could easily contrast his unflinching faith and deep religious engagement with the "infidelity of Yazīd" (playing on the similarity of their names); the second Omayyad caliph Yazīd was responsible for the tragedy of Kerbela, in which the Prophet's grandson was killed, together with his family, in 680, and his name has become anathema to every pious Muslim. Thus Sanāʾī asks:

> Who ever agreed with the Yazīd "base soul,"
> how could he know the state of Bāyezīd?
>
> (S 632)

For the "soul that inspires evil" is similar to the cruel enemy of the Prophet's family and thus stands in contrast to the great mystical leader. "Bāyezīd of his time" has become an honorary epithet for a man of outstanding mystical piety, and Sufi pretenders have been warned "not to make themselves Bāyezīds" (M 6:2548). In his *Mathnawī*, Rūmī tells the legend that Bāyezīd's disciples rebelled against him when he exclaimed: "Under my garment there is nothing but God!" But when they tried to kill him, the strokes of their knives wounded themselves (M 4:2102–40), for the perfect saint is a pure mirror who reflects the attributes of others to them. In another passage he relates the story of a Zoroastrian who refused to accept Islam because he felt too weak to embrace a religion that had produced spiritual heroes like Bāyezīd (T 1:149; M 5:3358)—a story that has been taken over, in our day, by Muhammad Iqbal in his *Jāwīdnāme* (1932), where it serves to assert the spiritual strength of the Islamic religion and the true Muslims.

There are still sacred places dedicated to the memory of the lonely mystic of Bistam in the remotest corners of the Islamic world: in Zousfana in the Maghreb and in Chittagong in Bangla Desh, where huge, whitish turtles inhabit a tank to which people come to obtain blessings for themselves and for their children.

Sufi hagiography often mentions a letter sent to Bāyezīd by Yaḥyā ibn Muᶜādh, who wrote: "'I am intoxicated from having drunk so deeply of the cup of His love.'—Abū Yazīd wrote to him in reply: 'Someone else has drunk up the seas of Heaven and earth, but his thirst is not yet slaked: his tongue is hanging out and he is crying "Is there any more?" ' " (A 10:40). Bāyezīd's metaphysical thirst has never been quenched; he belongs to those who,

> even if they would drink every day seven seas of union from this goblet, they would say from thirst to thirst:
>
> Standing in the water, athirst
> and not being granted a drink . . . .
>
> (B 442)

His correspondent Yaḥyā ibn Muᶜādh ar-Rāzī was a completely different type, personifying another major trend in early Sufism.

Yaḥyā came from Rayy (near present Tehran), lived for a while in Balkh, and died, in 871, in Nishapur, "and he spoke constantly about hope" (Q 16). According to Hujwīrī, he was the author of many books—which seem to be lost—and his sayings "are delicately moulded and pleasant to the ear and subtle in substance and profitable in devotion" (H 122). Indeed, the scattered words and short poems that have come down to us from the "preacher Yaḥyā" are pleasantly different in style from the utterances of the Khurasanian and the Baghdadian Sufis. He was mainly a preacher who called people to God, and, although a number of Sufis are related to have preached in public, he is the only one to be distinguished by the title *al-wāᶜiẓ*, "the preacher." He also talked about divine love, and to him is ascribed the famous saying: "Real love does not diminish by the cruelty of the beloved, nor does it grow by His grace, but is always the same" (A 10:58)—an idea that has been worked out by the Persian poets to its final consequences.

Yaḥyā held that "one mustard seed of love is better than seventy years of worship without love" (T 1:306). Religion is, for him, hope in God, whose mercy is infinite and who listens to the prayer of the human heart.

The preacher from Rayy once spoke about the difference between the person who comes to attend a banquet for the sake of the banquet and the one who attends in the hope of meeting his friend; such is the difference between the ascetic who longs for Paradise for the sake of joy and bliss and the lover who hopes for the beatific vision of his eternal beloved (P 516). Yaḥyā spoke the oft-repeated word: "Death is beautiful, for it joins the friend with the Friend!" (T 1:308). The most characteristic expression of Yaḥyā's piety is the reflection, in a number of his prayers, of an almost "evangelical" trust in the compassionate God. In dialectical form, they show the contrast between the helpless sinner and the Almighty Lord who can forgive His miserable creatures out of His inexhaustible treasure of mercy:

O God, Thou hast sent Moses and Aaron to Pharaoh the rebel and said, "Talk mildly with him"—O God, this is Thy kindness towards one who claimed to be God; how, then, is Thy kindness towards one who is Thy servant out of his innermost soul? . . . O God, I fear Thee because I am a slave, and I hope in Thee because Thou art the Lord! . . . O God, how should I not hope in Thee, while Thou art merciful, and how should I not fear Thee because Thou art powerful? O God, how can I call upon Thee, being a rebellious slave, and how could I not call upon Thee who art a merciful Lord? (T 1:309–10)

Yaḥyā deeply trusted in God's forgiveness, which can cover every sin, for no matter how near perfect a man may be, sinning is part of human nature: "O God, though I can not refrain from sin, Thou canst forgive sins" (T 1:310). And this God will lead him eventually to the place that He chooses out of His loving-kindness: "O God, I have done nothing for Paradise, and I have no strength to endure Hell—everything is left to Thy mercy!" (T 1:310). The preacher from Rayy stands amazed and overwhelmed before the mystery of divine love—is it not the greatest miracle of grace that God, the ever rich who needs nothing, should love men? How, then, should man, who is so much in need of God, not love Him? He sums up his whole feeling in one short prayer: "Forgive me, for I belong to Thee" (T 1:310).

Among Yaḥyā's successors—though not exclusively his disciples—there are two main ones in central and western Iran who are mentioned by later authors. His disciple in Nishapur was Abū ʿUthmān al-Ḥīrī (d. 910), who had been educated in part by Shāh Kirmānī in the spiritual tradition of Khurasan. Al-Ḥīrī is regarded as one of the great leaders of his time, who established Sufism in Nishapur; but he was criticized by some contemporaries for thinking too much of the purification of the soul without turning his views exclusively to God. He is regarded as one of the first to introduce a strict system of education for his disciples, a trend that developed finally into the *perinde ac cadaver* obedience that distinguishes later Sufi education.[30] The second master of Rayy is Yūsuf ibn Ḥusayn ar-Rāzī (d. 916), who belongs to the line of the ascetic Abū Turāb and who seems to have met Dhūʾn-Nūn in his early years. He is credited with sayings about *ikhlāṣ,* "perfect sincerity," as well as with sentences about the constant recollection of God.

Rābiʿa ushered in a new and productive period in the development of the mystical life in Iraq. Among the many Sufis who lived and worked in the capital, Baghdad, as well as in other Iraqian cities, mention must be made of Rābiʿa's younger contemporary Maʿrūf al-Karkhī (d. 815). Legends speak of his strong mystical power; his prayers were heard, and after his death people from Baghdad would cross the Tigris to the section of Karkh and pray for rain at his tomb. He was among the first to speak about divine love, and his teaching that one cannot learn love, for it is a divine gift and not an acquisition (T 1:272), has had a great impact on mystical thought. Qushayrī attributes to Maʿrūf special strength in *riḍā,* perfect contentment with God's decrees (Q 9).

Maʿrūf's disciple Sarī as-Saqaṭī, "the huckster" (d. circa 867), gratefully acknowledged that his teacher's blessings had enabled him to achieve high spiritual rank. The biographers claim that Sarī was the first to discuss the various mystical states (*aḥwāl*), a central topic of mystical writers. His piety and scrupulosity are reflected in the remark that he was afraid that his nose might turn black because of his sins. In his meetings he used to discuss topics of mystical love, which he was apparently the first to define as "real mutual love between man and God"—a scandal to the orthodox, who accepted "love of God" only in the sense of obedience. Also attributed to Sarī are sayings about the problem of *tauḥīd,* "to declare that God is one," which was later elaborated by his disciple and nephew Junayd. A delightful episode preserved in the *Nafaḥāt al-uns* reveals the great Sufi leader in a very human light: "During his illness people used to visit him and would ask him for his blessings and prayers, and he, eventually exhausted, taught them to

30. For the whole problem see Fritz Meier, "Ḫurāsān und das Ende der klassischen Sufik," in *La Persia nel medioevo* (Rome, 1971).

pray: 'O God, teach us how to behave when visiting the sick' " (N 54; A 10:122).

During those years when Sarī was discussing the mystical stages, his compatriot al-Ḥārith al-Muḥāsibī (d. 857) was writing his fundamental books on mystical psychology.[31] Born in Basra in 781, he was probably influenced by the teachings of Ḥasan al-Baṣrī's followers. Muḥāsibī belonged to the Shāfiᶜī school of law, as did Junayd, Rūdhbārī, and many other Sufis; but he also acquired the theological and philosophical vocabulary of the Muᶜtazila—which brought criticism from the Hanbalites. Yet the study of Muᶜtazilite theological methods gave him greater eloquence, and it is he who gave Sufism a highly developed technical language.

Muḥāsibī—whose surname is derived from *muḥāsaba,* the constant analysis of even the most secret motions of the soul and the heart—taught the relentless fight against man's lower nature, not just the outward struggle of the ascetic against the "flesh," but a subtle psychological analysis of every thought as well as uninterrupted spiritual training. Such training, of course, goes along with utmost scrupulosity. Muḥāsibī claimed to have a nerve in his finger that would warn him whenever food was not perfectly clean legally (N 572). He has described very eloquently the state of the seeker of the path to God:

> God has appointed self-mortification for the seeker, for the training of his soul. Men are ignorant of the high station of that one who is preoccupied with his Lord, who is seen to be thinking little of this world, who is humble, fearful, sorrowful, weeping, showing a meek spirit, keeping far from the children of this world, suffering oppression and not seeking revenge, despoiled, yet not desiring requital. He is dishevelled, dusty, shabby, thinks little of what he wears, wounded, alone, a stranger—but if the ignorant man were to look upon the heart of that seeker, and see how God has fulfilled in him what He promised of His favor and what He gives Him for exchange for that which he renounces of the vain glory of the world and its pleasure, he would desire to be in that one's place, and would realise that it is he, the seeker after God, who is truly rich, and fair to look upon, who tastes delight, who is joyous and happy, for he has attained his desire and has secured that which he sought from his Lord.[32]

Muḥāsibī's subtle analysis of *riyā,* "hypocrisy," and his whole meth-

31. Margaret Smith, *An Early Mystic of Baghdad* (London, 1935). Joseph van Ess, *Die Gedankenwelt des Ḥāriṯ al-Muḥāsibī, anhand von Übersetzungen aus seinen Schriften dargestellt und erläutert* (Bonn, 1961), is an excellent analysis of Muḥāsibī's teachings. Some of Muḥāsibī's works have been edited; these are listed under his name in the Bibliography.

32. Smith, *Readings,* no. 12.

odological approach became fundamental and indispensable to the early Sufis; Ghazzālī, the master of moderate medieval mysticism, depends largely upon him.

Among the disciples of Sarī as-Saqaṭī, Abū Bakr al-Kharrāz (d. 899) is known in the West through Arberry's translation of his *Kitāb aṣ-ṣidq*, "The Book of Truthfulness."[33] His mystical hints, *ishārāt*, seem to have influenced Junayd. Tradition credits him with having been the first to discuss the theory of *fanā*, "annihilation," and *baqā*, "permanent life in God." Recently discovered documents reveal that he can be regarded as one of Junayd's masters and that he contributed to mystical psychology in his *Kitāb al-farāgh*, which has been analyzed by Père Nwyia (W 240 ff.).

Nwyia has also brought to light Kharrāz's importance for the definition of *tauḥīd*, in which he anticipates some of Junayd's and even Ḥallāj's ideas: "Only God has the right to say 'I,' for whoever says 'I' will not reach the level of gnosis." That is why Satan was punished, for he said, "*I* am better than Adam," and that is why the angels had to prostrate themselves before Adam, for they had claimed, "*We* are higher than he." The only true subject is, in fact, God. Kharrāz goes even further by showing that this divine "I" is ontologically connected with the divine name *al-Ḥaqq*, "the Reality"—this seems to be the nucleus of Ḥallāj's famous phrase *anāʾl-Ḥaqq* (W 249). From these theories we can understand how ʿAbdullāh-i Anṣārī, the leading mystic and hagiographer of Herat in the eleventh century, could make the remark: "Abū Saʿīd [sic] Kharrāz would have needed a trifle lameness, for nobody could walk along with him" (N 74).

Kharrāz was writing a treatise on saintship at almost the same time that Sahl at-Tustarī (d. 896) was discussing the problem of saintship and Tirmidhī was working on his book *Khatm al-auliyāʾ*, "The Seal of Saints." This coincidence indicates that during the last two or three decades of the ninth century the necessity for a systematization of mystical thought was being felt, and that the problem of sanctity and saintship was one of the central ones at the time.

Sahl's name stands for a certain tendency that was rejected in part by subsequent generations. It is, however, difficult to find heterodox trends in the teachings of this apparently introverted

33. Abū Bakr al-Kharrāz, *Kitāb aṣ-ṣidq, The Book of Truthfulness*, ed. and trans. A. J. Arberry (Oxford, 1937).

ascetic, who was praised by Junayd as "the proof of the Sufis" (QR 59). He had spent a couple of years in the ascetic settlement at Abbadan and was eventually exiled to Basra. His most frequently cited theory is that of the obligatory character of repentance, which should be a permanent state in the faithful. This austere outlook fits the ascetic life in which Sahl tried to combine *tawakkul* and work; for, as he thought, it would be an offense to the Prophetic tradition to avoid or condemn work as a means of gaining one's livelihood, but an offense against the faith to neglect "trust in God."[34]

Sahl tried to remain aloof from the theological discussions that had shaken the Muslim community in the preceding decades; he advocated the duty of obeying the political ruler. Instead, he retired into the sweetness of his inner life and found there the peace that the disturbed outward world could not give him. He wrote an extensive commentary on the Koran in which he discussed the fourfold meaning of each verse. His theories of saintliness are highly interesting: he spoke of a pillar of light formed from the souls of those who are predestined to become saints—it was the time in both Sufi and Shia circles that theories about the preexistent light of Muhammad were being developed, and other mystics had put forth the theory that the souls of the true lovers belong to a divine light. According to Sahl, only the saints are predestined to attain the mystery of lordliness, *sirr ar-rubūbīya*—here lies, probably, one source of Ḥallāj's similar theories, for Ḥallāj had lived with Sahl for a while.

Sahl's teaching was continued by his disciple Ibn Sālim (d. 909); hence their school was known as the Sālimiyya. The author of the first comprehensive manual of Sufism, Abū Ṭālib al-Makkī, belonged to this group.

Sahl's younger contemporary at-Tirmidhī developed peculiar ideas about sainthood.[35] Tirmidhī is surnamed *al-Ḥakīm*, "the philosopher," which points to the fact that through him Hellenistic philosophical ideas were penetrating Sufism. Tirmidhī died early in the tenth century in Mecca, where he lived after the study of

34. Cihad Tunc, "Sahl ibn ʿAbdullah at-Tustarī und die Sālimīya" (Ph. D. diss., University of Bonn, 1970). Tunc is a Turkish theologian; his discussion of Sahl is not fully satisfactory.

35. Osman Yaḥyā, "L'oeuvre de Tirmiḏī, essai bibliographique," *Mélanges Louis Massignon*, 3 vols. (Damascus, 1956–57), 3:411ff.; Nicholas Heer, "Some Biographical and Bibliographical Notes on al-Ḥakīm at-Tirmidhī," in *The World of Islam: Studies in Honour of Philip K. Hitti*, ed. R. Bailey Winder and James C. Kritzeck (London, 1960).

Shafiite law in Balkh and a prolonged stay in Iraq. He, too, wrote a commentary on the Koran "in the light of the questions which his own experience posed to him and which he interpreted in a vocabulary enriched by the philosophical rapport and the experiences of the earlier mystics" (W 156). He thus gave the words a more profound meaning, and it is significant that the founder of the Naqshbandī order in the fourteenth century attributed to him a particular power when the disciple undergoes the process of directing his concentration toward the spirit of one of the great masters (N 119).

Tirmidhī's main contribution to the theory of Sufism is probably his "Seal of the Saints," in which he developed the terminology of sainthood that has been used since that time. The leader of the Sufi hierarchy is the *quṭb*, "pole" or "pivot," or *ghauth*, "help." The saints govern the universe, certain groups of three, seven, forty, or three hundred saints being entrusted with various duties in maintaining the world order (see Chapter 4). Like the prophets, whose seal is Muhammad, the saints have their seal, the last and culminating figure in the hierarchy.

The degrees of sainthood as sketched by Tirmidhī are related to the degree of illumination and gnosis reached by the person in question—it is not a "hierarchy of love." With him, the emphasis upon gnosis, *maᶜrifa*, becomes more explicit; he thus prepares the way for later theosophic speculation.

But while Sahl and Tirmidhī wrote about saintship and gnosis, ᶜAmr al-Makkī (d. 909) was probably the first to compose a systematic treatise on the degrees of love, intimacy, and proximity.

The undisputed master of the Sufis of Baghdad was Abūʾl-Qāsim al-Junayd, who is considered the pivot in the history of early Sufism.[36] The representatives of divergent mystical schools and modes of thought could refer to him as their master, so that the initiation chains of later Sufi orders almost invariably go back to him.

Like many other mystics, Junayd came from Iran; born in Nihawand, he settled in Baghdad and studied law according to the Shafiite rite. In Sufism he was educated by his uncle Sarī as-Saqaṭī;

36. A. J. Arberry, "Junaid," *Journal of the Royal Asiatic Society*, 1935, p. 499; A. H. Abdel Kader, *The Life, Personality and Writings of al-Junayd*, Gibb Memorial Series, n.s. 22 (London, 1962). See the review of Abdel Kader's book by Joseph van Ess, *Oriens* 20 (1967). A fine analysis is given in Zaehner, *Hindu and Muslim Mysticism*, pp. 135 ff.

Muḥāsibī's psychological insight seems to have impressed him, and the influence of Kharrāz on his formation is apparently greater than has been proved at the moment. One of his fellow Sufis, al-Ḥaddād, is reported to have said: "If intellect (*ʿaql*) were a man, it would have the form of Junayd" (N 80), a saying that alludes to the seriousness, sobriety, and penetrating mind of the master.

Junayd—faithful to the Muḥāsibī tradition—sees in Sufism a way of constant purification and mental struggle: "We did not take Sufism from talk and words, but from hunger and renunciation of the world and cutting off the things to which we were accustomed and which we found agreeable" (Q 19). The mystical life meant, for him, the permanent striving to return to one's origin, that origin that was in God and from which everything proceeds, so that eventually the mystic should reach the state "in which he was before he was." That is the state of the primordial covenant (Sūra 7:171), when God was alone and what is created in time was not yet existent. Only then can man realize perfect *tauḥīd*; only then can he witness that God is one from eternity to eternity.

The tremendous majesty of God in His aloneness and unity permeates every thought of Junayd; he feels that majesty whose will must be accepted in every moment of life, and before whom the servant becomes nothing through constant obedience, worship, and permanent recollection of His name, until he reaches the "annihilation in the object mentioned," when the recollecting human is no longer separated from the object of his recollection, God. Unification means, for Junayd, "the separation of the Eternal from that which has been originated in time by the Covenant" (H 281); and it also means "to go out of the narrowness of temporal signs into the wide fields of eternities" (L 29). Like other mystical leaders, Junayd spoke about the different stations and stages on the Path; he praised poverty, *faqr*, which is "an ocean of affliction, yet its affliction is completely glory" (L 174). Mystical love means, to him, "that the qualities of the Beloved replace the qualities of the lover" (L 59); it is a transformation of the lover on the level of attributes.

A major aspect of Junayd's teaching is his emphasis on the state of sobriety (*ṣaḥw*) as contrasted to intoxication (*sukr*). Bāyezīd Bisṭāmī preferred mystical intoxication because it obliterates the human attributes and annihilates man completely in the object of adoration, taking him out of himself. Junayd and his followers, however, considered the "second sobriety" the highest and preferable state: after the ecstatic intoxication man becomes once more aware of himself in the "life in God," when all his attributes, transformed and spiritualized, are restored to him. *Fanā*, "annihilation," is not the ultimate goal, but *baqā*, "remaining," a new life in God.

Junayd's claim, like that of Bāyezīd, is absolute; he concentrated every thought, every love, every inclination, every admiration, every fear, and every hope on God and asked Him to annihilate everything that might exist outside this perfect concentration (A 10:282).

Junayd knew very well that mystical experience and thought cannot be rationalized and that it is dangerous to speak openly about the deepest mysteries of faith in the presence of the uninitiated (particularly since orthodox circles viewed the activities of the Sufis with growing suspicion). It was for this reason that he had rejected Ḥallāj, who was to become the model for all who are punished because they speak openly about the mysteries of love and unity. Junayd, therefore, refined the art of speaking in *ishārāt*, subtle allusion to the truth—a trend, attributed first to Kharrāz, that became characteristic of later Sufi writings. His letters and short treatises are written in a cryptic style; their language is so dense that they are difficult to understand for one not acquainted with his peculiar way of thinking and teaching. This language of exquisite beauty rather veils than unveils the true meaning.

One of Junayd's friends in Baghdad was Ruwaym (d. 915); in fact, the Baghdad Sufis were divided in their preferences between these two masters. Anṣārī admitted 150 years later that he "would prefer one hair of Ruwaym to a hundred of Junayd" (N 95).

Ruwaym is remembered by later hagiographers mainly because he did not practice the same extraordinary austerities as many of his contemporaries and did not overemphasize *tawakkul*, absolute trust in God. "He disguised himself in the attitude of a rich man" (N 95). Ibn Khafīf, the Shirazi Sufi leader, relates how Ruwaym's little daughter, prettily dressed in red, ran into her father's arms, and he caressed her and explained to his surprised visitor that he liked to care for his family and would not leave everything to *tawakkul* (X 85). For him, *tawakkul* meant trust in God's eternal promise to look after His creatures (L 52), but it did not mean to turn completely away from worldly concerns.

Two more figures of the Baghdad circle should be mentioned, both of them famous for their love. They are Abū'l-Ḥusayn an-

Nūrī (d. 907) and Sumnūn, whose sobriquet was *al-Muḥibb*, "the lover" (d. after 900).

Nūrī had been a disciple of Sarī as-Saqaṭī and was, thus, a confrère of Junayd; after having spent some years in Raqqa in northern Iraq, he had returned to the capital. He is the greatest representative of that pure love that had been introduced by Rābiʿa, a disinterested love for which God has not asked and for which He will not recompense the lover. That his love—a love that rejoices in suffering—was not only theoretical was proved when Ghulām Khalīl brought charges against the Sufis of Baghdad in 885. Accused of heresy, and likely to be sentenced to capital punishment, Nūrī offered his life to save his companions; the caliph, touched by such magnanimity, investigated the case, found the Sufis to be good Muslims, and set them free. Brotherly love was, for Nūrī, the perfect expression of truthfulness as well as of genuine spiritual poverty, which meant preferring others to himself.

Nūrī was considered a heretic (*zindīq*) by the orthodox because he spoke of being a lover (*ʿāshiq*) of God, a strong term that was misinterpreted by the theologians (see B 389). His love was overwhelming, and in his enthusiasm he tended to "tear the veils" (L 59) and therefore expose himself to blame and danger. He was, however, not only the representative of a love that overflows all borders and tempts man to seemingly blameworthy acts; he also composed a number of theoretical works that have only recently come to light. Like Shaqīq, he speaks of the light of God, which is the first thing to appear when God wants to guide a person on the mystical path (W 348). His *Maqāmāt al-qulūb* "The Stations of the Hearts," contains a fine analysis of the psychological stages and their "seats" in the human heart. Nwyia (W 326) has drawn the attention of scholars to Nūrī's colorful imagery, which until recently was known only from his short musical poems and some fragments of prose. But to truly appraise his power of expression, one should read Nūrī's elaborate comparison of the heart to a house in which a king, Certitude, resides, assisted by two viziers, Fear and Hope, and surrounded by ten chiefs, which are the main duties of a pious Muslim. Another description of the cleaning of this house reminds us immediately, in its consequences, of Jalāluddīn Rūmī's famous verses about the lover who is admitted to the abode of the beloved only after he has become annihilated, for "there is no room for two I's in this narrow house" (M 1:3056–63)—an echo of a basic mystical experience through the centuries. Nūrī's description of the seven citadels, surrounded by seven ramparts and a wall, as God has built them in the heart, is somewhat reminiscent of St. Theresa's *Interior Castle*, though the Baghdad Sufi does not reach the psychological depth of the great Carmelite nun.

Nūrī's definition of the heart as a garden prefigures later Persian garden poems: the garden of the heart is either blessed or destroyed by rain—rain being, in the East, a symbol of divine activity and, generally, of divine mercy. Nūrī speaks of the two-fold rain, one of grace and mercy and one of divine wrath and revenge; the first one is revealed by thunders of majesty in the hearts of those who repent, by the lightning of desire in the hearts of the ascetics, by the showers of generosity in the hearts of the lovers, and by the breeze of appeasement in the hearts of the gnostics. But the thunderstorm of revenge sends the thunder of rupture into the hearts of the idolaters, the lightning of hatred into the hearts of the hypocrites, the rains of enmity into the hearts of the oppressors, and the wind of the veiling screen into the hearts of those who transgress the law. Nūrī was, as can be understood from these few details, indeed a forerunner of the later poets, who never tired of expressing their mystical experiences in the imagery of gardens, flowers, rains, and fruits—those poets who would symbolize the word coming to them from the beloved by the life-bestowing morning breeze, or the advent of the Prophet by a merciful rain that quickens the parched hearts of mankind.

Nūrī seems not to have been a conforming member of the Baghdad Sufi circles. There are stories that recount Junayd's criticizing him for exuberant words and startling miracles. Indeed, his way of educating his lower soul was quite peculiar: he was afraid of lions and therefore stayed in the lion-infested forests along the Tigris to conquer his fear.[37] Does he not remind us of the age-old mythological tales in which the hero goes into the forest, the symbol of his unconscious, in order to overcome the animals, which represent his lower instincts? Nūrī's death, too, occurred in a strange way: enraptured by the recitation of a verse, he ran into a nearby reedbed where the reeds had just been cut; the razor-sharp edges of the stumps hurt his feet without his being aware of the pain; soon afterward he died from the wounds.

37. Ibn al-Jauzi, *Talbīs iblīs* (Cairo, 1921–22), p. 381, dwells intensely upon this frequently told story.

Among the friends who had been tried and imprisoned with Nūrī was Sumnūn the Lover, who called himself "the Liar": "He, without fear, and completely love, he without reason and completely heart, that moth of the candle of Beauty, that man confused by the dawn of union"—that is how ʿAṭṭār introduced him in lovely rhyming sentences (T 2:82). He told touching stories about the Lover: the lamps in the mosque shattered when Sumnūn began preaching about disinterested and selfless love, and birds killed themselves while listening to his heart-rending sermons. Before ʿAṭṭār, Hujwīrī had said that Sumnūn "held a special *madhhab* in love and considered love the root and the foundation of the way towards God" (H 398). Later, Jāmī related that men and women gave up their spirits during his preaching.

Sumnūn considered love superior to gnosis (P 39)—a problem much discussed at that time among the Sufis. The solution finally depends upon the personal attitude of each traveler on the mystical path. Sumnūn knew, like Dhū'n-Nūn and all those who had experienced divine love, that it is always connected with affliction. When he was asked why, he replied: "In order that not every ordinary person may claim love, for he will run away when he sees affliction" (T 2:85). Love is the true religion of the spiritual elite, and its subtlety and depth cannot be conveyed by words. The metaphors that Sumnūn the Lover used to express the ineffable experience of this love, of which he was only a fragile vessel, are not taken from the vocabulary of worldly love. Rather, they are perfectly chaste, lucid, almost immaterial:

> I have separated my heart from this world—
> My heart and Thou are not separate.
> And when slumber closes my eyes,
> I find Thee between the eye and the lid.
>
> (A 10:310)

There is a direct line from the verses of Sumnūn to the sublime poems being written at the same time by the most famous mystic of Baghdad and of the whole early period of Sufism, al-Ḥallāj.

AL-ḤALLĀJ, MARTYR OF MYSTICAL LOVE

When Ḥallāj was in prison, he was asked: "What is love?" He answered: "You will see it today and tomorrow and the day after tomorrow." And that day they cut off his hands and feet, and the next day they

The Martyrdom of al-Ḥallāj, from a manuscript of Amīr Khosrau's Dīwān, *seventeenth-century India.*

The Walters Art Gallery, Baltimore

put him on the gallows, and the third day they gave his ashes to the wind . . . .

This story, told by ʿAṭṭār (T 2:142), conveys in a nutshell the secret of Ḥallāj's life, love, and death. With the intuition of a great psychologist, ʿAṭṭār has condensed into these words the tragedy of a man who deeply influenced the development of Islamic mysticism and whose name became, in the course of time, a symbol for both suffering love and unitive experience, but also for a lover's greatest sin: to divulge the secret of his love.

European scholars have been attracted by Ḥallāj's fate since his name was first discovered in Arabic sources. After the British scholar Edward Pocock (d. 1691), it was the German protestant theologian F. A. D. Tholuck who drew attention to him whom he calls "the Sufi most famous (*inclytissimus*) by fame and fate"[38] who "removed the veil of pantheism publicly with incredible audacity." The quotation that Tholuck then gives is both wrongly spelled and wrongly interpreted so that Ḥallāj's image was seriously distorted in subsequent times.

Tholuck regarded Ḥallāj as a pantheist; that became the opinion of the nineteenth-century scholars, and it was, and to some degree still is, accepted by a number of theologians. Some have accused Ḥallāj of blasphemy, while others considered him a secret Christian. This latter view was taken up in the late nineteenth century by August Müller and lingers on in the minds of some scholars. Other orientalists, in the light of the sources at hand, tended to regard him as a neuropath or as a pure monist. Alfred von Kremer tried to locate the source of Ḥallāj's famous word *anāʾl-Ḥaqq*, "I am the Absolute Truth," in Indian sources, and Max Horten drew the comparison between this mystical statement and the *aham brahmasmi* of the Upanishads, in which a number of oriental scholars have also concurred. Max Schreiner and Duncan Black Macdonald regarded Ḥallāj as a full-fledged pantheist; contrary to them, Reynold A. Nicholson stressed the strict monotheism and the very personal relation between man and God in Ḥallāj's thought. Finally, Adam Mez dwelt upon possible connections between the great Sufi and Christian theology.

Now, thanks to the lifelong work of Louis Massignon, the environment and influences on Ḥallāj have been explored so that his

38. Friedrich August Deofidus Tholuck, *Ssufismus sive theosophia persarum pantheistica* (Berlin, 1821), p. 68.

life and teachings have become better known and better understood in the West.[39] Massignon has edited the difficult rhyming prose of the *Kitāb aṭ-ṭawāsīn* and has collected Ḥallāj's scattered poems, which, in marvelous density, give utterance to the transcendence of God and His immanence in the human heart. The mystery of loving union is celebrated in verses free of any trace of the symbolism of profane love. Massignon devoted his whole life to the exploration of the spiritual world of Ḥallāj, adding more and more details, which he set forth in a monumental biography of the martyr-mystic that first appeared in 1922—just one thousand years after Ḥallāj's execution. In fact, Ḥallāj is, as Hans Heinrich Schaeder says in his review of Massignon's book, the martyr of Islam par excellence because he exemplified the deepest possibilities of personal piety to be found in Islam; he demonstrated the consequences of perfect love and the meaning of submission to the unity of the divine beloved—not with the aim of gaining any sort of private sanctity but in order to preach this mystery, to live in it and to die for it.

Who was this man who has been the object of both hatred and love, the model of suffering, the arch-heretic of orthodox writings, the ideal of enraptured Sufis?

Ibn an-Nadīm, relying upon certain inimical sources, said of him in the tenth century:

> Al-Ḥusayn ibn Manṣūr al-Ḥallāj was a crafty man and a conjurer who ventured into the Sufi school of thought, affecting their ways of speech. He laid claim to every science, but nevertheless [his claims] were futile. He even knew something about the science of alchemy. He was ignorant, bold, obsequious, but courageous in the presence of sultans, attempting great things and ardently desiring a change of government. Among his adherents he claimed divinity, speaking of divine union . . . .[40]

This—together with the paragraphs that follow in Ibn an-Nadīm's book—articulates the conventional reading of Ḥallāj's personality. Sober historical facts, however, though sometimes not too clear, reveal something close to the following picture of his life:

39. Louis Massignon, *La passion d'Al-Ḥosayn ibn Mansour Al-Ḥallaj, martyr mystique de l'Islam exécuté à Bagdad le 26 Mars 922*, 2 vols. (Paris, 1922); see Hans Heinrich Schaeder's review, *Der Islam* 15 (1926). Massignon, "Le *diwan* d'al-Ḥallāj, essai de reconstitution," *Journal asiatique*, 1931; new edition as separate book (Paris, 1955). Massignon and Paul Kraus, *Akhbār al-Ḥallāj, texte ancien relatif à la prédication et au supplice du mystique musulman al-Ḥosayn b. Mansour al-Ḥallaj*, 3d ed. (Paris, 1957). See the Bibliography for other works by Massignon. Roger Arnaldez, *Hallaj ou la religion de la croix* (Paris, 1964).

40. *The Fihrist of al-Nadīm*, ed. and trans. Bayard Dodge, 2 vols. (New York, 1970), 1:474.

Ḥusayn ibn Manṣūr al-Ḥallāj, born in the province of Fars in 858, grew up in Wasit and Tustar, where cotton was cultivated and where cotton carders (that is the meaning of *ḥallāj*) like his father could pursue their occupation. The young man attached himself to Sahl at-Tustarī and accompanied him to Basra. Later he became a disciple of ʿAmr al-Makkī in Baghdad and also of Junayd. He became estranged from ʿAmr when he married another mystic's daughter. She remained his only wife, and much information about Ḥallāj's later life is given on the authority of their son Ḥamd. After a short while, Ḥallāj's father-in-law began to regard him as a "cunning sorcerer and miserable infidel." In connection with his first pilgrimage, Ḥusayn stayed in Mecca for a year, undergoing terrible hardships in asceticism. After his return to Baghdad, Junayd foretold—according to the legends—an evil end for his former disciple. At this point the tradition contains the following anecdote:

When he knocked at Junayd's door, the master asked: "Who is there?" and he answered: "*anāʾl-Ḥaqq*, I am the Absolute [or Creative] Truth [or the True Reality]."

This sentence has become the most famous of all Sufi claims. In fact, it appears in a chapter of Ḥallāj's *Kitāb aṭ-ṭawāsīn* and was probably taken from this source very early. In this chapter Ḥallāj discusses his own claim together with that of Pharaoh and Satan, Pharaoh having asserted, according to the Koran, "I am your highest Lord" (Sūra 79:24) and Satan, "I am better than Adam" (Sūra 7:12). Ḥallāj, then, asserts his own claim, "I am the Absolute Truth." This passage led later mystics into deep speculations about the two different "I's," that of Pharaoh and that of the loving mystic; the solution is given in the divine revelation that "Pharaoh saw only himself and lost Me, and Ḥusayn saw only Me and lost himself" (N 444), so that the "I" of the Egyptian ruler was an expression of infidelity but that of Ḥallāj expressed divine grace (M 2:2522).

Whatever the reason for the statement *anāʾl-Ḥaqq* may have been, Junayd uttered his verdict against his former disciple, accusing him of propagating an unsound religious claim. The antagonism of the other mystics of the Baghdad school, especially of ʿAmr al-Makkī and his group, mounted. Ḥallāj left the capital. For five years he traveled, ultimately reaching Khurasan, where he discussed religious problems with the people; it was there, his son thinks, that he was surnamed *ḥallāj al-asrār*, "the cotton carder of the innermost hearts," since he knew all things hidden in the human heart and soul.

During a second pilgrimage to Mecca, 400 disciples accompanied him, and eventually, in 905, Ḥallāj took a boat to India. His enemies ascribed this journey to his desire to learn magic, specifically, the rope trick. But he told his family that his aim was to call the heathen to God. From Gujerat he wandered through Sind, the lower Indus valley, which had been a part of the Muslim Empire since 711. The seeds he sowed there grew in later centuries in the mystical poetry of this province. From Sind, Ḥallāj traveled to the northern borders of India, then to Khurasan, to Turkestan, and eventually to Turfan—Massignon has suggested that he may have gone with the caravans that brought brocade from his home town of Tustar to the East and returned with Chinese paper to the Islamic countries. Some sources say that his words were written down on precious paper decorated in the style of the Manichaean manuscripts from Central Asia. In the eyes of the Baghdad government these externals drew suspicion upon him. An even greater cause for suspicion was his supposed relations with the Carmathians, who ruled not only Bahrain but also northern Sind and Multan—places that the mystic had just visited. Did he not, after all, receive letters from distant Eastern lands in which he was addressed by strange names?

The *Akhbār al-Ḥallāj*, a collection of anecdotes about Ḥallāj, gives a vivid impression of his life in Baghdad before and especially after his return from this last long journey. He is described preaching and calling people to God, in intense love and excessive asceticism. But in spite of his constant preoccupation with prayer and ascetic practices, Ḥallāj was sure that he had not completely fulfilled his duties toward God. In his ascetic mood he would prefer to feed the black dog at his side, the image of his lower nature, instead of taking food himself. At the same time he claimed miraculous powers; in Mecca he produced sweetmeat from Yemen, and he sent down heavenly food in the middle of the desert.

One can understand how his behavior encouraged opposition on the part of both political and religious circles. Because of that Ḥallāj performed the pilgrimage once more, this time staying for two years in the holy city of Mecca. Then he bought a house in Baghdad, but soon Muḥammad ibn Dāʾūd, the son of the founder of the Zahirite school of law, denounced him, inciting other scholars to join in attacking the man who claimed to have reached real union with his divine beloved, an idea that the representatives of platonic love could not accept.

Aside from the subtle problems of mystical love, political and social problems were at stake. Ḥallāj was a friend of the chamberlain Naṣr al-Qushūrī, who favored better administration and juster taxation, dangerous ideas in a time when the caliph was almost powerless and the viziers, though all-powerful for a short period, changed frequently. The Shia groups who supported the vizier Ibn al-Furāt considered Ḥallāj as dangerous as did the Sunni orthodox wing surrounding the "pious vizier" ʿAlī ibn ʿIsā. All of them were afraid that the effect on the people of spiritual revival might have repercussions on the social organization and even on the political structure. The idea of converting the hearts of all Muslims and teaching them the secret of personal sanctification and not just of blind acceptance would certainly have been dangerous for a society whose religious and political leaders lived in a state of stagnation with neither the strength nor the intention to revitalize the Muslim community.

At the end of 912 Ḥallāj was apprehended while traveling near Sus; for three days he was set in a pillory, then imprisoned. Both the caliph's mother and the chamberlain Naṣr—who called him "a righteous man"—tried to make his imprisonment as comfortable as possible; but his situation grew worse during the financial crisis of 919, when the vizier Ḥāmid tried by every means to have him executed. Searching the houses of his disciples, the police found fragments of correspondence in cryptic letters, partly decorated with picturesque forms, probably calligraphic signs representing the name of ʿAlī and some of the divine names. But years passed before the vizier could force the highest judge of Iraq to sign Ḥallāj's death sentence. On 26 March 922 he was put to death.

The story goes that Ḥallāj went dancing in his fetters to the place of execution, reciting a quatrain about mystical intoxication; then he asked his friend Shiblī to lend him his prayer mat and performed a prayer during which he once more touched the mystery of the ineffable unity and separation of man and God. When people began to throw stones at him, Shiblī—so the legend has it—threw a rose, and Ḥallāj sighed. Asked the reason for his sigh, he answered: "They do not know what they do, but he should have known it."

And the saying that "the rose, thrown by the friend, hurts more than any stone" has become a Turkish proverb.

Ḥallāj's last words were: "*ḥasb al-wājid ifrād al-wāḥid lahu*—it is enough for the lover ['who has found in ecstasy'] that he should make the One single"—i.e., that his existence should be cleared away from the path of love (H 311). That is genuine *tauḥīd,* fully interiorized, and paid for with the lover's blood.

Ḥallāj's hands and feet were cut off, and he was put on the cross or, more probably, on the gallows, then decapitated; his body was burned and the ashes thrown in the Tigris. This was the death for which his whole life had been a preparation. He had often urged the people of Baghdad to kill him so that he might be united with God and they might be recompensed for defending their simple and sincere faith. One of his most touching hymns begins with the words:

> *Uqtulūnī yā thiqātī—inna fī qatlī ḥayātī.*
> Kill me, o my trustworthy friends, for in my being killed is my life—

words that have been repeated by mystics throughout the ages as a basis for their meditations.

Ḥallāj's comprehensive work—of which the *Fihrist* gives a list—is preserved only in fragments. Mention has already been made of his *Kitāb aṭ-ṭawāsīn,* probably written during his imprisonment.[41] It contains eight chapters, each of them called *ṭāsīn,* after the mysterious letters at the beginning of Sūra 27, which are said to indicate divine majesty and power. This little book deals with problems of divine unity and with prophetology. It contains a discussion between God and Satan, in which the latter refuses to obey the divine order to prostrate himself before Adam and, true *muwaḥḥid* (confessor of divine unity) that he is, is caught in the dilemma between God's eternal will that nobody should worship any being save Him and His explicit order to fall down before a created being. This situation has sometimes served to explain Ḥallāj's own hopeless dilemma. Ḥallāj's satanology inspired a number of later mystics to develop these ideas (see Chapter 4).

Portions of the *Kitāb aṭ-ṭawāsīn* are beautiful hymns in honor of the Prophet. Among the traditions that he personally affirmed, Ḥal-

41. Ḥusayn ibn Manṣūr al-Ḥallāj, *Kitāb aṭ-ṭawāsīn, texte arabe . . . avec la version persane d'al-Baqlī,* ed. and trans. Louis Massignon (Paris, 1913).

lāj included the saying that "God has not created anything he loves more than he loves Muhammad and his family" (B 639). If there is any doubt as to whether Ḥallāj was a faithful Muslim, one need only read his description of Muhammad in the "Ṭāsīn as-sirāj" of the *Kitāb aṭ-ṭawāsīn.* These short, rhyming sentences achieve new heights in the veneration of the Prophet:

> All the lights of the Prophets proceeded from his light; he was before all, his name the first in the book of Fate; he was known before all things, all being, and will endure after the end of all. By his guidance have all eyes attained to sight . . . . All knowledge is merely a drop, all wisdom merely a handful from his stream, all time merely an hour from his life . . . .

In another chapter, Ḥallāj describes the fate of the moth that approaches the flame and eventually gets burned in it, thus realizing the Reality of Realities. He does not want the light or the heat but casts himself into the flame, never to return and never to give any information about the Reality, for he has reached perfection. Whoever has read Persian poetry knows that the poets choose this story of the moth and the candle as one of their favorite allegories to express the fate of the true lover (SD 311; an almost word-for-word Persian poetical paraphrase is found in ʿAṭṭār's *Manṭiq aṭ-ṭayr,* when the poet speaks of the seventh and last valley of the mystical journey [MT 258]). Through the medium of Persian poetry the same symbol reached Europe. Goethe's famous poem "Selige Sehnsucht," in his *West-Östlicher Divan,* reflects this very mystery of dying in love and reaching a new, higher life in union. The Goethean *Stirb und werde,* "die and become," translates very well the Prophetic tradition "die before ye die" (in order to gain new life), which formed one of the cornerstones of Sufism and, of course, of Ḥallāj's theories.[42]

Ḥallāj's poetry is a very tender and intense expression of mystical yearning. Its language is chaste; the favorite symbols are the wine cup, the crescent, the goblet of intoxicating mystical joy, the virgin, the soul bird, and similar images. He sometimes uses cabalistic word plays and relies on the secret meaning of the letters of the alphabet; alchemistic expressions are also found at times. All of his verses are weighted with deep theological and mystical meaning and filled with enigmas, but so great is their beauty that they can be enjoyed even by those who do not care for deep religious interpretation but

42. Al-Ḥallāj, "Ṭāsīn al-fahm," *Kitāb aṭ-ṭawāsīn,* pp. 16ff. Hans Heinrich Schaeder has studied the symbolism of the moth and the candle in his essay "Die persische Vorlage von Goethes Seliger Sehnsucht," in *Festschrift E. Spranger* (Berlin, 1942).

do enjoy Arabic poetry at its best—an extremely refined art with many overtones that evoke strange and fascinating echoes in the reader (see P 904). One can understand from his poems what Ḥallāj meant when he declared that God is visible in every trace of His creation, and although the common folk, the blind and dumb, animal-like creatures, do not recognize Him, the mystic drinks not a single drop of water without discovering His vision in the cup. God is He "who flows between the pericardium and the heart, just as the tears flow from the eyelids." Some of Ḥallāj's great hymns reveal abysses of loneliness, like his threnody for all things on earth that are left blind and hopeless because the witness has gone and left them alone.

A small part of Ḥallāj's theology can be reconstructed from the scattered fragments of his commentary on the Koran preserved in the *Tafsīr* of Sulamī (d. 1021), one of the leading authorities on the mystical theology of his time. The *Riwāyāt*—collected by Rūzbihān Baqlī in the late twelfth century—allow some insight into the working of Ḥallāj's mind. They consist of traditions that are not very different from, and are often verbally congruent with, the generally accepted *ḥadīth*; yet they are introduced not by a chain of human transmitters, as is the rule in *ḥadīth* transmission, but by a chain going back to cosmic and supernatural powers, to stars and sun, to angels and spirits. That is the way Ḥallāj authenticated these traditions for himself. This personal acceptance and realization of the religious truth was, perhaps, one of his most original contributions to Muslim spiritual life; it even led him to the doctrine of the *isqāṭ al-farāʾiḍ*, i.e., that certain religious duties can be exchanged for other acts that are more useful at the moment. Instead of performing the pilgrimage, he advised people to invite orphans and to feed and dress them and make them happy for the day of the Great Feast. Such ideas, of course, were not acceptable to the legalists.

Some of Ḥallāj's letters have been preserved, as have a few of his prayers and a small number of isolated sayings, which often have a dialectical form that seems to be typical of the mystical mind: "Do not let yourself be deceived by God, nor cut off your hope from Him; do not wish His love, and do not resign from loving Him." By such paradoxes the ineffable mystery of the love relation between man and God is disclosed. And this love relation is, in fact, the central theme of Ḥallāj's prayers and sermons. Love, for Ḥallāj, was certainly not sheer obedience: "Love is that you remain standing in front of your beloved, when you are deprived of your qualities and when the qualification comes from His qualification." This love is realized through suffering—man can be united with the divine will by accepting suffering and even longing for it: "Suffering is He Himself, whereas happiness comes from Him." That is one of the decisive sayings of Ḥallāj. But this suffering is not a means of dehumanizing man and bringing him back into his first state, "as he was before he was," as was held by the followers of Junayd. Ḥallāj did not advocate destruction for the sake of destruction; he saw in suffering a positive value by means of which man might understand that *ʿishq*, "love," is the essence of the essence of God and the mystery of creation. The word *ʿishq*, with its connotation of "passionate, overflowing love," came to mean, for him, dynamic divine love; but this term was considered dangerous, if not illicit, even by moderate Sufis. In Ḥallāj's theory, the compensation for having offered God unconditional love was the beatific vision, without an intervening "I."

The sentence *anāʾl-Ḥaqq*, "I am the Absolute Truth," or, as it was translated later, "I am God," led many mystics to believe that Ḥallāj was a pantheist, conscious of the unity of being. Ḥallāj's theory, however, maintains the absolute transcendence of God beyond the dimensions of created things, his *qidam*, the preeternity that separates Him forever from the *ḥadath*, "what is created in time." However, in rare moments of ecstasy the uncreated spirit may be united with the created human spirit, and the mystic then becomes the living personal witness of God and may declare *anāʾl-Ḥaqq*. We must remember that, according to Ḥallāj, God's nature contains human nature within it. This human nature was reflected in the creation of Adam, and Adam became *huwa huwa*, "exactly He." This theory has led many critics to the assumption that the Christian dogma of the incarnation influenced Ḥallāj, an assumption seemingly supported by his use of the Christian terms *lāhūt*, "divine nature," and *nāsūt*, "human nature." But his theories are too complicated to be reducible to this or that influence. Indeed, they so intimately reflect the uniqueness of Ḥallāj's thought that it is useless to trace each one back to its source.

Ḥallāj was willing to suffer for himself and for others. The mystery of his death is aptly described in Émile Dermenghem's words about the true Muslim saint:

The saint is he who takes upon him the sins and the pain of the world; the unjust death is, for him, one of his means of accomplishments. He is the "great Help" and the consolation of the people. He is a living accusation for the world: his existence insults the tyrants, his death makes tremble his executioners, his canonisation is a victory of faith, of love, and of hope.[43]

This is the spirit in which Ḥusayn ibn Manṣūr al-Ḥallāj went to the gallows. Since he was put to death by the government—or the establishment—his influence became even stronger after his execution than it had been during his lifetime.[44] About the year 1000 the Syrian poet Maᶜarrī wrote that in his day people still stood on the banks of the Tigris awaiting Ḥallāj's return.

Persian poetical tradition has praised Ḥallāj; the founders of the mystical fraternities as well as the theoreticians of Sufism frequently referred to him—sometimes in terms of pity, sometimes in admiration, and sometimes rejecting him or declaring him to be merely a beginner on the mystical Path. The fact that he proclaimed the secret of love openly made him appear to more sober mystics as one who had not reached his goal: for them he resembled the kettle that sings as long as the water is not yet boiling; when the water boils and evaporates, the kettle becomes silent. Other mystics have accused him of believing that the human and divine natures can be united, resulting in the heretical doctrine of *ḥulūl*, "incarnation." Even Hujwīrī, in a book written in the mid-eleventh century—unfortunately no longer extant—in spite of all his admiration for Ḥallāj, felt obliged to declare him "not firmly settled."

A great number of Sufi poets, however, have shown their predilec-

43. Émile Dermenghem, *Le culte des saints dans l'Islam maghrebin* (Paris, 1954), p. 94.

44. Louis Massignon, "La survie d'al-Ḥallāj," *Bulletin d'études arabes Damas* 11 (1945–46); Massignon, "La legende de Hallacé Mansur en pays turcs," *Revue des études islamiques*, 1941–46; Massignon, "L'oeuvre Hallagienne d'Attār," *Revue des études islamiques*, 1941–46; Massignon, "Qiṣṣat Ḥusayn al-Ḥallāj," *Donum Natalicum H. S. Nyberg*, ed. E. Gren et al. (Uppsala, 1954). Annemarie Schimmel, ed. and trans., *Al-Halladsch, Märtyrer der Gottesliebe* (Cologne, 1969), an anthology compiled from Ḥallāj's writings and from poetry and prose by Muslim authors from different countries; Schimmel, "The Martyr-Mystic Ḥallāj in Sindhi Folk-Poetry," *Numen* 9 (1962): 3; Abdulghafur Rawan Farhadi, "Le majlis de al-Ḥallāj, de Shams-i Tabrezi et du Molla de Roum," *Revue des études islamiques*, 1954, a Persian passion play, *taᶜziya*; Salih Zeki Aktay, *Hallac-ī Mansur* (Istanbul, 1942), a Turkish tragedy; M. Salih Bhatti, *Manṣūr Ḥallāj* (Hyderabad, Sind, 1952); Ṣalāḥ ᶜAbduʾṣ-Ṣabūr, *Maʾsāt al-Ḥallāj* (Beirut, 1964), trans. K. J. Semaan as *Murder in Baghdad* (Leiden, 1972). Almost every collection of modern Arabic poetry contains some poems in honor of al-Ḥallāj, for example, the works of Adonis and al-Bayātī.

tion for Ḥallāj, and the Persian tradition largely follows the example set by Ibn Khafīf of Shiraz, who had visited him in prison and defended him, even to the extent of calling him an *ᶜālim rabbānī*, "a divinely inspired master." Some of Ḥallāj's disciples sought shelter in Iran during the critical years of Ḥallāj's persecution, and there they secretly transmitted his ideas. We owe the preservation of the most important Ḥallājian texts to Rūzbihān Baqlī, the mystic of Shiraz who stands in the Ibn Khafīf tradition; Rūzbihān's commentaries on the *Kitāb aṭ-ṭawāsīn* and on many other sayings of the master are the most valuable source for our understanding of large parts of Ḥallāj's theology. Another leading representative of the Ḥallājian tradition in Iran—though from a different point of view—is Farīduddīn ᶜAṭṭār, the poet (d. 1220 in Nishapur). He had accepted Ḥallāj as his spiritual guide in a vision, and Ḥallāj's name recurs often in ᶜAṭṭār's lyrical and epic poetry. ᶜAṭṭār's description of Ḥallāj's suffering, found in his hagiographical work *Tadhkirat al-auliyāʾ*, has deeply influenced almost all later mystics who wrote about the martyr-mystic in the Persian-speaking lands—Turkey, Iran, Central Asia, and India. The details of his account of Ḥallāj's execution are repeated in nearly every subsequent book; they have been poetically elaborated in many languages—Persian, Turkish, Urdu, Sindhi, Panjabi, and Pashto—but in substance they remained unchanged.

The work of the greatest of the mystical poets to write in Persian, Jalāluddīn Rūmī, contains numerous allusions to the fate of Manṣūr, "the victorious," as Ḥallāj is often called after his father; some of his utterances and verses have been embellished by Rūmī in an entirely ingenious way. Turkish Sufi tradition also shows a strong penchant for Manṣūr. In the Bektashi order, his name is connected with the central place of initiation, which is called *dār-e Manṣūr*, "the gallows of Manṣūr"; Bektashi poets from the fourteenth century onward have often imitated the "unitive cry," *anāʾl-Ḥaqq*, and have heard echoes of these words everywhere. And one ought not fail to mention Nesīmī, the Ḥurūfī poet (executed in 1417) who considered himself "a new Manṣūr" and reenacted in his own life the passion and death of Ḥallāj.

Most recently Turkish literature has borne witness to the abiding inspiration of Ḥallāj with the appearance of a play called *Manṣūr-e Ḥallāj*; its author tries to establish his hero as an heir to Zoroastrian ideas. The date of the play is especially significant: it was written in 1940, at a time when Islamic religious instruction was banned from Turkish schools and laicism had reached its apex.

In Iran, the name of the martyr-mystic has become a commonplace in the verses of almost all poets; they allude to the gallows and the sad fate of the lover, sometimes even likening the tresses of their beloved to the rope of Manṣūr's gallows. They see the red rose on its bough as a symbol of Ḥallāj on the gallows tree, and they find the word *anāʾl-Ḥaqq* manifest in the heart of every atom and every drop of water. Even among the *taʿziyas,* the plays written in commemoration of Ḥusayn ibn ʿAlī's martyrdom at Kerbela on the tenth of Muharram 680, Enrico Cerulli has discovered one piece that deals with the fate of Ḥallāj, who is here in strange juxtaposition with Maulānā Rūmī and his mystical preceptor and beloved Shams-i Tabrīz (the combination of Ḥallāj and Shams is also known from Indo-Muslim folk poetry). The tragic figure of Manṣūr occurs in modern Persian drama, too.

The poets in Iran and Afghanistan were outdone in their devotion to the Ḥallājian tradition by the Indian poets writing in Persian who made use of the figure of Ḥallāj from the eleventh century on. The images and forms they used are almost identical with those found in classical Persian poetry. An even stronger predilection for Manṣūr is to be found in the mystical folk songs composed in the vernaculars of Muslim India and adjacent areas. The Pathans knew the name of the martyr of love (who is even mentioned in their proverbs), as did the Panjabis. His name occurs in most of the mystical Panjabi songs as the representative of love, contrasted with the dry asceticism of the theologians and the bookishness of the mollahs. Ḥallāj is mentioned just as frequently in Sindhi poetry: one can scarcely find any book of mystical verses in Sindhi or its northern dialect, Siraiki, that does not contain allusions to him or his fate. He is the great lover; he plays "the drum of unity" (a modern Turkish poet, Asaf Halet Çelebi, has also written a fine poem on the "drum of Manṣūr"); his goblet is filled with the primordial wine of unity; and he is one of those who must suffer because of their overflowing passion and because God loves them too much. He is the model for every loving soul who will gladly suffer and die for the sake of his love; but he is also in constant danger because it is not permitted to proclaim the word of love openly—

> The secret that is hidden in the breast is not a sermon;
> you cannot utter it in the pulpit, but on the gallows.

That is—since the days of Sanāʾī—one of the central ideas in Persian and Indo-Muslim poetry, which has found its finest expression in the verse just quoted by Ghālib (d. 1869). Or is the poet, perhaps, declaring that death is the only legitimate way to express the secret of loving union? And does he aver that the ultimate experience is communicable through the silent language of martyrdom, for in the martyr (*shahīd*) God has His true witness (*shāhid*)?

There is nothing more touching than to hear the plaintive Sindhi folk songs in a remote corner of the Indus valley through which the great mystic had wandered in order to call the people to God a thousand years ago:

> When you want to know the way of love,
> ask those who are like Manṣūr.

In our day, there is renewed interest throughout the Islamic world in the figure of Ḥallāj, thanks, in large part, to Massignon's comprehensive work. Muhammad Iqbal (d. 1938), who in his youth described the great mystic as a pantheist—as he had seen him through hundreds of Persian, Urdu, and Panjabi poems—later recognized Ḥallāj's strong personal religious commitment and saw in him one of the few who had attained to an experience of the divine higher than that of ordinary people. He recognized that Ḥallāj had called the slumbering Muslims to a personal realization of the truth, thus coming into conflict with the religious authorities who were afraid of any ardent witness for the living God. In the scene in Jupiter-Heaven in the *Jāwīdnāme* that depicts his spiritual journey through the spheres, Iqbal has even treated Ḥallāj as a sort of medieval forerunner of himself and has emphasized his dynamic concept of love and faith as an ideal for every free Muslim.

Even in the Arab lands, in which Ḥallāj was less renowned than in those areas influenced by the Persian mystical tradition, he has gained fame recently: the philosopher ʿAbduʾr-Raḥmān Badawī has likened Manṣūr's experience to that of Kierkegaard, seeing in him a true existentialist. Poets like Adonis in Lebanon and ʿAbduʾl Wahhāb al-Bayātī in Iraq have written sensitively of the secret of his personality; and a young socialist writer from Egypt, Ṣalāḥ ʿAbduʾṣ-Ṣabūr, has composed a *Tragedy of Ḥallāj*. Its form shows influences of Eliot's dramatic technique. The interesting aspect of the work is the intensity with which the author highlights the social side of Ḥallāj's message.

Ḥallāj's name has found its way into the remotest corners of the Islamic world. It can be discovered in the folklore of East Bengal and the Malayan archipelago; it has been used by some Sufi fraternities in their celebrations, and a Tunisian order has an entire litany in honor of the martyr-mystic. Manṣūr's suffering through "gallows and rope" has become a symbol for the modern progressive writers in India and Pakistan who underwent imprisonment and torture for their ideals like "the victorious" of old.

In Ṣalāh ʿAbdu'ṣ-Ṣabūr's tragedy the members of the chorus sing about the words of Ḥallāj:

—And we will go, to scatter in the plough furrows of the peasants what we have stored up from his words . . . .
—And we will preserve them among the merchants' goods.
—And we will give them to the wind that wanders o'er the waves.
—And we will hide them in the mouths of singing camel-drivers who traverse the desert.
—And we will note them down on papers, to be kept in the folds of the frock.
—And we will make them into verses and poems.

All of them:
Tell me—what would become of his words,
if he were not martyred?

THE PERIOD OF CONSOLIDATION: FROM SHIBLĪ TO GHAZZĀLĪ

Ḥallāj represents the culminating point of early Sufism; but the mystical impetus of the early Baghdad school continued in a number of Sufis who lived shortly after him and represented, again, different aspects of Sufism. Ḥallāj's most faithful friend, Ibn ʿAṭā'—with whom he had exchanged some beautiful poetical letters—was killed in connection with Ḥallāj's execution and, thus, paid for his friendship with his life. Another friend, Abū Bakr ash-Shiblī, survived Ḥallāj by twenty-three years.

Shiblī had been a high governmental official before his conversion to the mystical life. When he died in 945 at the age of eighty-six, he left behind a considerable number of sayings and paradoxes upon which following generations often pondered. His strange behavior resulted from time to time in his confinement in an asylum; thus he was spared, according to his own statement, the fate of Ḥallāj, for he tried to express some of Ḥallāj's lofty ideas in more comprehensible language. In one poem he compares himself to a frog:

> Now praised be God, that like a frog am I
> Whose sustenance the watery deeps supply.
> It opens its mouth, and straightway it is filled.
> It holds its peace, and must in sorrow die.

Shiblī's contemporaries and later Sufis are divided in their feelings about him—Junayd called him "the crown of these people" (N 180), whereas others, acknowledging his strong mystical "state," yet held that he was not a proper interpreter of *tauḥīd* (N 145). The sayings and short, delicately expressed verses attributed to him[45] show his overwhelming feeling of God's unity and of the love that removes from the heart all but the beloved or consumes all but the will of the beloved (Q 190). "To love Him for His acts of grace means to be a polytheist" (A 10:369), for, in the tradition of Rābiᶜa, God has to be the only goal for the lover who not only loves Him with his heart but all of whose limbs "are hearts pointing to Thee" (L 91). Similarly, "the best recollection is to forget recollection in vision" (L 220). God, the ever living and everlasting, should be the only object of love: "Shiblī saw somebody weeping because his beloved had died and blamed him: 'O fool, why do you love someone who can die?' " (T 2:172). God's face, i.e., His essence, is the proof for the lover on the day "when proofs are required" (L 209).

Like Nūrī, Shiblī sometimes used the kind of imagery that became commonplace in later Persian poetry. Thus he describes the "gnostics," those who know God by intuitive knowledge and are, therefore, the nearest perfect of men:

> They are comparable to springtime: thunder clashes and the clouds pour rain, the lightning flashes and the wind blows, the buds open and the birds sing—such is the state of the gnostic: his eye weeps, his mouth smiles, his heart burns, he gives away his head, he mentions the name of the Beloved and walks around His door. (T 2:177)

Such a description could have come from any of the later Persian

45. Abū Bakr Shiblī, *Dīwān*, ed. Kāmil M. ash-Shaybī (Cairo, 1967).

mystics, who so often compared their condition to clouds and lightning; they knew that the weeping of the cloud is indispensable for the growth of a flower out of a heart that should be like soil.

When mentioning Muhammad's name in the call to prayer, Shiblī is reported to have said: "If Thou hadst not ordered it, I would not mention another name besides Thee" (Q 17). He therefore regarded as infidel and polytheist anyone who might think of the angels Michael and Gabriel—for, according to the Prophetic tradition, in the moment of closest proximity there is no room even for Gabriel, who is pure spirit; lover and beloved are alone, without separation (B 413).

Rūzbihān Baqlī preserved many of Shiblī's paradoxes, which foreshadow trends that became explicit in later mysticism. When he told his disciples to go away and to know that wherever they were they were under his protection and he would be with them, he points to the power of *himma,* that "high spiritual ambition," or "power," that is strong enough to keep safe those who believe in the master. Being united in perfect *tauḥīd* with God, he can protect his disciples wherever they may wander about (B 322), since he himself works and walks through God. The claim of the sheikh to possess this strong *himma* is reflected in many legends about saints of later times.

Another story told about Shiblī is typical of the so-called *munāqara,* "quarrel," of saints: He threw one of his fellow mystics into the Tigris, saying, "If he is sincere, he will be saved, like Moses; if not, he will be drowned, like Pharaoh." A few days later he was challenged by that very person to take live charcoals from an oven without being hurt (B 494). It seems that this kind of contest was not uncommon among the early Sufis; later sheikhs used to settle questions of priority in a similar way.

Baqlī explains Shiblī's exclamation that "fire of Hell will not touch me, and I can easily extinguish it," when he says, faithfully interpreting the genuine mystical experience, that "in the world those who have been drawn close to God are burnt by the fire of pre-eternal love so that it is for them that God ordered the fire to be 'cool and pleasant' [Sūra 21:69], as He did for Abraham" (B 460). In another saying, Shiblī claimed that hellfire could not burn even a single hair on his body. Baqlī sees here a manifestation of what he calls *iltibās,* the envelopment of the human being in the light of preeternity: the divine uncreated light is incomparably stronger than the created fire of Hell. For, according to a *ḥadīth* of which the Sufis were particularly fond, Hell addresses the true believer with the words: "Thy light has extinguished my flames" (B 452). The mystic who has been surrounded by the primordial and everlasting divine light is no longer subject to the change of mystical states, to death, Paradise, and Hell. Such a person may leave the early station of renunciation and abstinence and become a perfect lover; by love he becomes "like a lion in the forest of affliction" (B 154).

Shiblī's daring paradoxes find a counterpart in the less often quoted but extremely interesting sayings of his contemporary Abū Bakr al-Wāsiṭī, who came from Farghana, settled for a while in Baghdad, and then returned to Khurasan. He too belonged to the group of Junayd and Nūrī, but his sayings bear the stamp of a very independent personality. "He would have needed a trifle of mercy" (N 74), says Anṣārī, who praises him as the "leader of *tauḥīd*" and "the master of the East in the science of subtle allusions" (N 175). Complete isolation and absolute concentration upon Him who is recollected are expressed in his sentences. According to him, the utterance of the formula *Allāhu Akbar*, "God is greater" (than everything), during the act of ritual prayer is "as if one said 'Thou art too mighty to be joined by prayer, or to be separated from by omitting to pray': for separation and union are not personal notions, they follow a course preordained in eternity" (K 144).

The overwhelming greatness of God, who teaches man how to pray and who addresses him before man dares to address Him, is visible through every word written by Niffarī.[46] This Iraqian mystic, who died in 965, left writings, called *Mawāqif* and *Mukhāṭabāt*, that seem to have been studied carefully by later Sufis. Even Ibn ᶜArabī may have been inspired by the daring ideas of this mystical thinker. Niffarī spoke of the state of *waqfa*, "standing," during which he was addressed by God, who inspired him to write down His words either during or after this experience. Niffarī's whole work, thus, is presented as a replica of Muhammad's experience, a dialogue in which man becomes the confidant of God (W 358),

46. Muḥammad ibn ᶜAbdiᵓl-Jabbār an-Niffarī, *The "Mawāqif" and "Mukhāṭabāt" of Muḥammad ibn ᶜAbdiᵓl-Jabbār al-Niffarī with Other Fragments*, ed. A. J. Arberry, Gibb Memorial Series, n.s. 9 (London, 1935). Of special importance are the texts recently discovered and edited by Père Nwyia: Paul Nwyia, *Trois oeuvres inédites de mystiques musulmans: Šaqīq al-Balḫi, Ibn ᶜAṭā, Niffarī* (Beirut, 1973).

as it is described by Père Nwyia (whose study on Niffarī opens previously undiscovered perspectives in the experiences of the mystic). Such a dialogue between God and the mystic is not alien to later Sufis, who not infrequently claimed that God spoke to them, and a comparison between Niffarī's experiences as set forth in his books with those of the eighteenth-century Indo-Muslim mystic Mīr Dard (contained in his *ʿIlm ul-kitāb*) would yield significant similarities.

Niffarī's sayings are full of paradoxes. They show the perfect passing away of the mystic, who has passed beyond all the veils between the human and the divine; at the same time they make clear the impossiblity of expressing mystical experience at all. The center of Niffarī's experience is that of prayer; over and over he is taught by God to recollect Him, and then again the impossibility of this task is put before him: "Thoughts are contained in letters, and fancies in thoughts; the sincere recollection of Me is beyond letter and thoughts, and My name is beyond recollection."[47] God wants His servant to rest in His recollection, but: "Do not speak, for he that reaches unto Me does not speak."[48] How, then, is recollection to be performed? And what meaning does it have? "My recollection is the electest thing I have manifested, and My recollection is a veil."[49] For this recollection is contained in letters, and Niffarī "unmasked the idolatry of the letter" (W 370) at a time when Muslim orthodoxy was going more and more by the letter and becoming increasingly intellectualized. It was he who spoke of the *ḥijāb al-maʿrifa*, "the veil of gnosis" (W 380), which, tender and subtle as it may be, can constitute the greatest barrier between man and God.

Niffarī clearly formulated the theory—probably known to mystics before him—that prayer is a divine gift: "To Me belongs the giving: if I had not answered thy prayer I should not have made thee seeking it."[50] It is an idea well known in Christian tradition, where it found its most famous expression in the words of Pascal: "You would not seek Me if you had not found Me." Much earlier, it became a cornerstone of the Muslim theology of prayer and was most poetically expressed by Jalāluddīn Rūmī (see Chapter 3).

47. *Maw.*, no. 55/20.
48. *Mukh.*, no. 22/5.
49. *Maw.*, no. 49/2.
50. *Mukh.*, no. 42/10.

Niffarī also expressed the feeling of the persistent love with which God follows man in a divine address that can be compared, as his modern commentator has in fact done, to Francis Thompson's *Hound of Heaven*.[51]

In certain aspects the late tenth century was the period of organization and consolidation for Sufism. It was the time during which, on the political level, the influence of different Shia groups grew in every part of the Muslim Empire. Since 945—the year of Shiblī's death—Baghdad had been under the control of the Iranian Buwaihids, a Shia dynasty; Northern Syria was ruled by the Ḥamdanite dynasty, which was also Shia—Aleppo for a short time rivaling Baghdad as a gathering place for poets, philosophers, and musicians. Central Arabia had been conquered, in 930, by the Carmathians, an extreme Shia group whose capital was located in Bahrain and whose branches extended to the Indus valley; there, at Multan, Ḥallāj had been in touch with them, according to the tradition. In North Africa, the Shiite Fatimid dynasty was gaining in power; in 969 they conquered Egypt, there to establish a splendid rule that was to last for two centuries.

It is a well-known fact that many of the Sufis—and many of the pious Sunnites in general—felt a kind of sentimental allegiance to the family of the Prophet without believing in Shia doctrines. The veneration of ʿAlī was widespread among the Muslims, and he was often regarded as an important link in the spiritual chain leading the Sufi masters back to the Prophet. Widespread, too, was the veneration of the *sayyid*s, Muhammad's descendants through ʿAlī and Fāṭima. Even in our day some of the *sayyid* families in countries like Muslim India or Pakistan consider themselves exalted above the common Muslim, surrounded by a sanctity or transmitting a *baraka* (spiritual power, blessing) that gives them a peculiar status. This veneration shown to the *ahl al-bayt,* the Prophet's family, constitutes in later times a very important aspect of popular Sufism.

The relationship between Shia thought as it crystallized in the ninth and tenth centuries and the theories of Sufism that emerged at about the same time has not yet been completely elucidated;[52]

51. *Maw.*, no. 11/16.

52. Kāmil M. ash-Shaybī, *As-ṣila bayn at-taṣawwuf waʾt-tashayyuʿ* (Cairo, ca. 1967). See Seyyed H. Nasr, "Shiʿism and Sufism," in *Sufi Essais* (London, 1972).

but some of the Sufi teachings about the primordial light of Muhammad and the theories of saintship seem to correspond very closely in their hierarchical structure to Shiite theories about the imamate and the gradual initiation of adepts into the deeper realms of faith, into new levels of spiritual interpretation. The role played by Jaʿfar aṣ-Ṣādiq's commentary on the Koran in the formation of some Sufi ideas has already been mentioned. In later times, the connections between these two forms of Muslim spirituality became visible once more in the development of the Sufi fraternity located in Ardebil in Northwestern Iran—from a regular Sufi order it turned into the cell of Shia propaganda in Iran. The activities of this group resulted eventually in the victory of Shah Ismail the Safawid in 1501, and at that time Shiism became the official creed of Iran. It seems symptomatic that both in Arabic and in early European sources the Safawid ruler is often called "Sufi" or the "Grand Sophi." Yet from that time onward Sufism and the Shia creed were rarely combined, and only a few Shia orders exist today. In spite of the relatively close relationship between the two movements in the period of formation, the Sufi congregations usually supported the Sunni case and often became defenders of the official Sunnite creed under the later Abbasid caliphs (MM 86).

During the Abbasid period the need was felt to formulate some of the main lines, a *Leitbild,* of moderate Sufism. The case of Ḥallāj had confronted the Sufis with the danger of persecution, and even without his tragic death one might well have felt that the Path had to be made accessible to people who could never reach the abysses of mystical experience Ḥallāj had reached, or who could not be compared in sobriety to Junayd, in burning love to Nūrī, or in paradoxical speech to Shiblī. It was left to men like Ibn Khafīf of Shiraz (d. 982, at about 100 years of age)[53] and similar mystics to teach the Path, to make it understandable—at least in part—to the intellectuals, and to set an example to larger groups of the faithful.

It would, however, be wrong to speak of a real "reconciliation" between Sufism and orthodoxy. For the Sufis were, on the whole,

53. ʿAlī ibn Aḥmad ad-Dailamī, *Sīrat-i Ibn al-Ḫafīf ash-Shīrāzī,* ed. Annemarie Schimmel (Ankara, 1955). See Annemarie Schimmel, "Zur Biographie des Abu ʿAbdallah ibn Chafīf aš-Šīrāzī," *Die Welt des Orients,* 1955; and Schimmel, "Ibn Khafīf, an Early Representative of Sufism," *Journal of the Pakistan Historical Society,* 1959. N 600 mentions that the famous poet Saʿdī (d. 1292) lived close to Ibn Khafīf's tomb (which is now in a rather dark quarter of Shiraz, close to the charcoal sellers).

as good Muslims as the rest of the community in Baghdad, Nishapur, or Egypt. They did not reject the religious law but rather added to it—additions that made more exacting demands on their personal lives. The genuine mystical practices, like the performance of the *dhikr*, the constant recollection of God, occupied only part of their time. Many Sufis followed normal professions to earn their livelihoods. The surnames of some of them point to these professions: *saqaṭī*, "huckster"; *ḥallāj*, "cotton carder"; *nassāj*, "weaver"; *warrāq*, "bookseller" or "copyist"; *qawārīrī*, "glassmaker"; *ḥaddād*, "blacksmith"; *bannāʾ*, "mason" were among them. Some would work regularly and use a trifle of their gain for themselves, distributing the main part to the Sufis, so that it could be said, for example, that a person "veiled his saintliness under the modest shape of a cupper" (N 572). Some left their original professions after they had gained fame as mystical leaders and attracted a few disciples. Others were trained as theologians, traditionalists, or jurists in one of the four schools of law. Still, it was considered important to prove to the world the perfect orthodoxy of Sufi tenets, and therefore a number of books were composed almost simultaneously in the last quarter of the tenth century.

The oldest authority is Abū Naṣr as-Sarrāj, from Tus in eastern Iran (d. 988), whose *Kitāb al-lumaʿ fīʾt-taṣawwuf* is an excellent exposition of the doctrines of the Sufis, with numerous quotations from the sources. The matters at stake are lucidly laid before the reader.[54] Sarrāj, who was for a while a disciple of Ibn Khafīf, is close enough to the great masters of the Path to understand and interpret their sayings and their way of life. His definitions of the different states and stations, his long quotations from Sufi prayers and letters, his words about the behavior of the Sufis at home and on their journeys, and his explanations of difficult expressions are of great value to the student of Sufism, though his book apparently has not been as widely read as other handbooks. Sarrāj himself had reached a high rank in practical Sufism; according to one story, he was discussing some mystical problems with his friends on a cold winter day, "and the sheikh got into a 'state' and put his face on the fireplace and prostrated himself before God in the midst of the fire without being hurt" (N 283).

54. *Kitāb al-lumaʿ fīʾt-taṣawwuf*, ed. Reynold A. Nicholson, Gibb Memorial Series, no. 22 (Leiden and London, 1914); A. J. Arberry, ed., *Pages from the "Kitāb al-lumaʿ"* (London, 1947).

A near contemporary of Sarrāj, al-Kalābādhī, who died in Bukhara about 990, wrote his *Kitāb at-taᶜarruf* in an effort to find a middle ground between orthodoxy and Sufism.[55] His book is, on the whole, the somewhat dry exposition of a Hanafi jurist and not as enjoyable as Sarrāj's study. Yet the work contains valuable material for the study of early Sufism; it was widely read, along with a commentary, in medieval Muslim India. A commentary of 222 Prophetic traditions is also ascribed to Kalābādhī. The study of Muhammad's sayings was regarded as essential by the Sufis, who tried to follow their beloved Prophet's example as closely as possible.

The third book written during this period was Abū Ṭālib al-Makkī's comprehensive *Qūt al-qulūb*, "The Food of the Hearts."[56] Though Makkī (d. 996 in Baghdad) was considered a follower of the Sālimiyya school, his book had a pronounced influence on later Sufi writings. Ghazzālī relied heavily upon this work, and quotations in later sources—in Rūmī's *Mathnawī* and in medieval Indian books—show how widely it was used.

Shortly after the composition of these three theoretical books on the tenets and doctrines of Sufism, two attempts were made to deal with the Sufis in the same way as Arab historians had dealt with scholars, heroes, philologists, and other groups: by dividing them into "classes" belonging to succeeding periods. Sulamī (d. 1021) called his work simply *Ṭabaqāt aṣ-ṣūfiyya*, "The Classes of the Sufis." Abū Nuᶜaym al-Iṣfahānī (d. 1037) chose for his ten-volume work the more romantic title *Ḥilyat al-auliyā*ᵓ, "The Ornament of the Saints."[57] Beginning with the Prophet and his companions, Abū Nuᶜaym brought together every available bit of information about the pious and their deeds; his book is a storehouse of information, which, however, must be used with caution. Yet even in its present edition, which is not free from mistakes, the book is indispensable for the study of the biographies of early Sufis.

Sulamī's *Ṭabaqāt* has constituted a source for later hagiographers.[58] Half a century after his death, the book was expanded and

55. Abū Bakr Muḥammad al-Kalābādhī, *At-taᶜarruf li-madhhab ahl at-taṣawwuf*, ed. A. J. Arberry (Cairo, 1934), trans. A. J. Arberry as *The Doctrine of the Sufis* (Cambridge, 1935).

56. Abū Ṭālib al-Makkī, *Qūt al-qulūb fī muᶜāmalāt al-maḥbūb*, 2 vols. (Cairo, 1310 h./1892–93).

57. Abū Nuᶜaym al-Iṣfahānī, *Ḥilyat al-auliyā*ᵓ, 10 vols. (Cairo, 1932–38).

58. ᶜAbdur-Rahmān as-Sulamī, *Kitāb ṭabaqāt as-Ṣūfiyya*, ed. Johannes Pedersen (Leiden, 1960), has an extensive introduction; Sulamī's *Kitāb* has also been edited by Nūraddīn Sharība (Cairo, 1953). For other editions see the Bibliography under

translated into Persian by ʿAbdullāh-i Anṣārī, the patron saint of Herat; his translation, in turn, was revised and brought up to date in the late fifteenth century by Jāmī, also in Herat, in his *Nafaḥāt al-uns.*

Sulamī dealt not only with the biographies of the mystics, but also with the different strands of Sufism as they had developed by his time. He thus concerned himself with the group of the Malāmatiyya, to whom he devoted a special treatise.[59] He distinguishes between the orthodox people, the *ahlal-maʿrifa,* "gnostics," i.e., the true Sufis, and the *malāmatiyya,* "those who draw blame (*malāma*) upon themselves."

The ideal of the Malāmatiyya developed out of a stress on *ikhlāṣ,* "perfect sincerity"; Anṣārī sometimes praises a person for his "perfect *malāma* and sincerity" (N 340). Muḥāsibī had taught that even the slightest tendency to show one's piety or one's religious behavior was ostentation. Thus the Malāmatīs deliberately tried to draw the contempt of the world upon themselves by committing unseemly, even unlawful, actions, but they preserved perfect purity of heart and loved God without second thought. Typical is the story told by Jāmī: "One of them was hailed by a large crowd when he entered a town; they tried to accompany the great saint; but on the road he publicly started urinating in an unlawful way so that all of them left him and no longer believed in his high spiritual rank" (N 264). These pious relied upon the Koranic words, "and they do not fear the blame of a blaming person" (Sūra 5:59), and probably also thought of the *nafs lawwāma,* "the blaming soul," the conscience that warned them at every step in the religious life (Sūra 75:2). But the attitude itself is not novel—Marijan Molé (MM 72–74) has shown that, particularly among the early Syrian Christians, there was a similar trend to hide one's virtuous actions; stories about some of these Christian saints, who would rather live as actors or rope-dancers than show their deep religious concern, at once call to mind anecdotes about the Malāmatiyya.

Sulamī. Süleyman Ateş, *Sülemi ve tasavvufi tefsiri* (Istanbul, 1969), is a Turkish study of the famous commentary on the Koran by Sulamī, a work that still awaits a critical edition.

59. Richard Hartmann, "As-Sulamī's 'Risālat al-Malāmatīya,' " *Der Islam* 8 (1918), is a fine analysis of Sulamī's treatise. For the whole problem see Abdülbâki Gölpınarlı, *Melâmilik ve Melâmiler* (Istanbul, 1931); Abūʾl-ʿAlāʾ Affifi, *Al-malāmātiyya waʾṣ-ṣūfiyya wa ahl al-futuwwa* (Cairo, 1945); Morris S. Seale, "The Ethics of Malāmātīya Sufism and the Sermon of the Mount," *Moslem World* 58 (1968): 1; and the discussion in Nwyia, *Ibn ʿAṭāʾ Allāh,* p. 244.

Al-malāma tark as-salāma, "blame is to give up well-being," says Ḥamdūn al-Qaṣṣār, one of the first among the Khurasanian Sufis to adopt this way of life (H 67). Sulamī sees them as veiled from the vulgar by God's jealousy: He has granted them all kinds of spiritual graces, but does not expose them to the view of the common people; their outward behavior is that of people who live in separation from God, but inwardly they dwell in the sweetness of divine union. They thus prefigure the lover in Persian poetry, who was to describe himself in terms of a detestable creature, calling the hatred of the "others" upon himself, but never revealing the secret of his intense love.

Hujwīrī, half a century after Sulamī, is more critical of the *malāmatī* attitude, for even in the actions of those who want to attract blame upon themselves he sees a trace of subtle hypocrisy: "The ostentatious men purposely act in such a way as to win popularity, while the *malāmatī* purposely acts in such a way that people reject him. Both have their thought fixed on mankind and do not pass beyond that sphere" (H 6). That may sound hard, but from the viewpoint of a perfect mystic every interest in people's reaction—be it positive or negative—is a sign of selfishness, and therefore of imperfection.

Jāmī regarded the *malāmatī* as sincere, *mukhliṣ,* whereas the true Sufi is *mukhlaṣ,* made sincere by God (N 10), not by an act that can be attributed to himself. But Jāmī, writing in the mid-fifteenth century, saw the problem that was involved in the whole *malāmatī* attitude more clearly than his predecesssors had. The problem had arisen when people affiliated themselves with the Malāmatiyya or claimed to be one of them without accepting the difficult burden of genuine *malāmatī* practices: "Now a group has brought forth licentiousness and treating lightly of the Divine law and heresy and lack of etiquette and respectlessness—but *malāmat* was not, that somebody would act by showing no respect to the law: it was, that they did not care for the people in their service of God." Thus complains Anṣārī as early as the eleventh century, not long after Sulamī, in a discussion of the life of Ḥamdūn al-Qaṣṣār (N 61). Jāmī accepted Anṣārī's assessment and went on to contrast the *malāmatī,* who adheres to the duties and performs many supererogatory acts of piety in secret, and the *qalandar,* the wandering dervish who performs only the absolute minimum in religious duties. The *qalandar,* in his description, is the less rigorous mystic, who enjoys his unfettered life. The *qalandar* is chiefly known in the West as a kind of free thinker—even a charlatan—without deeper religious concern; but this, Jāmī asserts, is not true of the genuine *qalandar* (N 15).

Sulamī influenced successive generations mainly as teacher and biographer. Through his disciple, Naṣrābādī, the mystical chain reaches Abū Saᶜīd ibn Abīʾl-Khair, to whom the first Persian mystical quatrains are, erroneously, ascribed and who was the first to draw up a simple monastic rule for his Sufi community (see Chapter 5). The spiritual chain from Sulamī also leads to al-Qushayrī (d. 1074) through his father-in-law Abū ᶜAlī ad-Daqqāq. Qushayrī took up once more the task of writing a treatise on Sufism.[60] His *Risāla* describes Sufi teachings and practices from the viewpoint of a full-fledged Ashᶜarite theologian; this school—to which Ibn Khafīf had belonged as well—flourished in Iran and elsewhere under the Seljukids. Qushayrī's *Risāla*—written in 1046—is probably the most widely read summary of early Sufism; it was analyzed in the West prior to most other books on Sufism. It is comparable, in some ways, to Sarrāj's *Kitāb al-lumaᶜ*, beginning with short biographies of the Sufis and containing detailed chapters on Sufi terminology and expressions. Some of the author's shorter treatises give a good insight into his own spiritual experiences, especially into his prayer life.[61]

One of Qushayrī's colleagues, who had attended his meetings and had visited almost every leading Sufi of his time, was Hujwīrī from Ghazna. He later came to Lahore, the capital of the Ghaznawids in India, and he died there in 1071. His shrine, called that of Data Ganj Bakhsh, is still a popular place of pilgrimage in Lahore.[62] Hujwīrī's important innovation is that he wrote his *Kashf al-maḥjūb*, "Unveiling of the Hidden," in Persian and thus ushered in a new period in mystical literature. A monument of early Persian and noteworthy for its expressiveness, the *Kashf*, "which belongs to the valid and famous books" (N 316), contains much interesting information rarely found in other sources. Although the author's

60. Abūʾl-Qāsim al-Qushayrī, *Ar-risāla fī ᶜilm at-taṣawwuf* (Cairo, 1330 h./1911–12). Richard Hartmann, *Al-Kuschairis Darstellung des Sufitums* (Berlin, 1914), is a very useful analysis of the *Risāla*.

61. Abūʾl-Qāsim al-Qushayrī, *Ar-rasāʾil al-qushayriyya*, ed. and trans. F. M. Hasan (Karachi, 1964). The most important treatise was edited and analyzed by Fritz Meier, "Qušayris Tartīb as-sulūk," *Oriens* 16 (1963).

62. ᶜAlī ibn ᶜUthmān al-Hujwīrī, *Kashf al-maḥjūb*, ed. V. A. Žukovskij (Leningrad, 1926; reprint ed., Tehran, 1336 sh./1957); al-Hujwīrī, *The "Kashf al-Maḥjūb," The Oldest Persian Treatise on Sufism by al-Hujwīrī*, trans. Reynold A. Nicholson, Gibb Memorial Series, no. 17 (1911; reprint ed., London, 1959).

inclination toward systematization sometimes goes too far, it is singularly valuable in its approach and its balanced discussion.

The eastern provinces of Iran have always been proud to be a fertile soil for mystically inclined souls. A contemporary of Qushayrī and Hujwīrī was ᶜAbdullāh-i Anṣārī (1006–89), whose work, like that of Hujwīrī, was written in part in his Persian mother tongue.[63] It proves the breadth of spirit of Sufism that two masters so totally different in their outlook as Qushayrī and Anṣārī could live at close proximity during the same politically restless period. While Qushayrī followed the Ashᶜarite creed of the ruling Seljukids, Anṣārī belonged to the stern Hanbalite school of law. The traditional idea that Hanbalite rigorism and mystical emotion are mutually exclusive can no longer be maintained—not only was Anṣārī an energetic representative of this school, but ᶜAbduʾl-Qādir Gīlānī, the founder of the most widespread mystical fraternity, also belonged to this *madhhab*. Perhaps it was precisely the strict adherence to the outward letter of the God-given law and the deep respect for the divine word that enabled Anṣārī and his fellow Hanbalites to reach a deeper understanding of the secrets of the revelation.

Anṣārī's father had been a mystic, too; when the boy was still small, his father had left his family to join friends in Balkh. The young scholar pursued his studies in Herat and Nishapur. He tried several times to perform the pilgrimage to Mecca but was detained because of confused political circumstances in the eastern provinces occasioned by the untimely death in 1030 of Maḥmūd of Ghazna, the conqueror of northwestern India and supporter of the caliph and of Muslim orthodoxy.

Although young Anṣārī did not reach Mecca, his life was changed by his meeting with the distinguished mystic Kharaqānī in 1034, shortly before the master died at the age of eighty. Kharaqānī's sayings, preserved in the *Tadhkirat al-auliyā* and elsewhere, show tremendous force, but are devoid alike of any learnedness or theological systematization. This illiterate peasant, who could not pronounce Arabic correctly (N 336, 353), was a typical *uwaysī*, initiated not by a living master but by the powerful spirit of Bāyezīd Bisṭāmi. Legends dwell on the spiritual relation between these two men: it is said that the scent of Kharaqānī reached Bāyezīd long before his

63. Serge de Laugier de Beaureceuil, *Khwadja Abdullah Ansari, mystique hanbalite* (Beirut,1965), is a fine study of Anṣārī and his work. Père Beaureceuil has also edited some of Anṣārī's works with their commentaries.

spiritual disciple was born (M 4:1802–50) and that Kharaqānī used to pray every evening in Kharaqān, then mysteriously be transported to Bistam—a distance of about 1500 kilometers—pray there, and then perform the morning prayer back in his own village (T 2:201).

Kharaqānī's prayers burn with intense love and yearning, as when he swore that he would not give his soul to the angel of death, for he had received it from God, and only to Him would he return it (T 2:212). Longing for God made him melt away, but the Lord told him, in one of his rare dreams after long periods of sleeplessness, that the longing he had endured for sixty years was nothing, "for We have loved thee already in the pre-eternity of eternities" (T 2:253). And he was sure that he would be resurrected among the martyrs, "for I have been killed by the sword of longing for Thee" (T 2:229), as he asserts.

This enthusiastic and demanding master caused a spiritual change in ʿAbdullāh-i Anṣārī, with the result that Anṣārī began to write his commentary on the Koran, which was, unhappily, never finished. The advent of the Seljuks in eastern Iran in 1041 brought affliction on Anṣārī; he was persecuted, spent years in destitution, and endured much suffering at the hands of the authorities in their defense of Ashʿarite theology. The grand vizier Niẓāmulmulk even exiled him from Herat in 1066, but he was soon called back. Shortly afterward the caliph himself honored the famous orator and mighty preacher whose fame had spread around Herat. Eventually Anṣārī lost his sight and spent the last eight years of his life in darkness and under the threat of another expulsion. He died in Herat on 8 March 1089.

Anṣārī's productivity is amazing in light of the difficulties he had to face during his career. Among the great number of books written in both Arabic and Persian, the *Manāzil as-sāʾirīn,* "The Stations on the Way," has had several commentators.[64] The mystic of Herat also translated Sulamī's *Ṭabaqāt* into the Persian vernacular of his region. But in spite of his many works in theoretical Sufism, his smallest book has won him the greatest admiration: the *Munājāt,* "Orisons," a prayer book in rhyming Persian prose, interspersed with some verses, in which he pours out his love, his longing, and his

64. Hellmut Ritter, "Philologika VIII: Anṣārī Herewi.—Senāʾī Ġaznewī," *Der Islam* 22 (1934); Vladimir Ivanow, "Ṭabaqāt of Anṣārī in the Old Language of Herat," *Journal of the Royal Asiatic Society,* January–July 1923.

advice.[65] Its simple and melodious Persian prose makes this small book a true vade mecum for anyone who needs a devotional aid for meditation in lonely hours.

Nothing shows better the change in emphasis and style, in Sufi outlook and expression, than a comparison of Anṣārī's *Munājāt* with another small book written in the same mixture of poetry and prose in the same city of Herat 400 years later, by the author who reworked Anṣārī's hagiographical book and relied heavily upon him, namely the *Lawāʾiḥ*, by Maulānā Jāmī. This book has become one of the most widely used manuals of later Sufi teachings—but how far is its intellectual and rational approach to the divine truth, its high-flown technical expression about absolute existence and relative being, from the intense earnestness and simplicity of Anṣārī's orisons!

At the same time that Anṣārī was being persecuted by the Seljuk government, another mystic was cooperating with that regime and lending it support through his writings. That was Abū Ḥāmid al-Ghazzālī, Ashʿarite theologian and, later, mystic, who has often been called the greatest Muslim after Muhammad. An anecdote told by Jāmī illustrates how highly esteemed he was in most moderate Sufi circles: "The North African Sufi leader Abūʾl-Ḥasan ash-Shādhilī (d. 1258) saw in a dream vision that the Prophet of Islam was extolling himself with Ghazzālī before Moses and Jesus . . . and he had ordered the punishment of some who had denied him, and the marks of the whip remained visible on their bodies until they died" (N 373).

Ghazzālī was born in Tus, near present-day Meshed, in 1058, three years after the Seljuks had taken over the rule in Baghdad. His life was closely connected with the fate of this dynasty, whose power grew in the ensuing years to extend over all of Iran and parts of eastern Anatolia. Abū Ḥāmid, along with his younger brother Aḥmad, followed the usual course of theological studies; the teacher to whom he owed most and with whom he worked closely was al-Juwainī, surnamed the *imām al-ḥaramayn* (d. 1083). Niẓāmulmulk, the vizier, appointed Ghazzālī professor at the Niẓāmiyya *madrasa* in Baghdad. With the zeal of an ardent adherent of Ashʿarite theology, the vizier had founded colleges (*madrasa*) all over the Seljuk

65. ʿAbdullāh-i Anṣārī, *Munājāt ū naṣāʾiḥ* (Berlin, 1924); this little book has been reprinted many times. Anṣārī, *The Invocations of Shaikh Abdullah Ansari*, trans. Sir Jogendra Singh, 3d ed. (London, 1959); Singh's translation lacks the rhyming patterns, which are essential, and the poetic flavor.

territories. They served as training institutions for theologians and proved to be models for later colleges in the Muslim world.

The school at Baghdad, the seat of the caliphate, was without doubt the most important among the institutions founded by Niẓāmulmulk. It therefore caused great amazement when the successful professor Ghazzālī, after a breakdown in 1095, left his teaching position to enter the spiritual life. After long journeys that led him to Syria, Jerusalem, and perhaps Egypt, Abū Ḥāmid returned to his home and family and once more taught in his hometown of Tus. There he died in December 1111.[66]

Ghazzālī's literary activity was as great as that of any of his colleagues; his books cover different branches of learning, but mainly theology and its confrontation with philosophy. We are fortunate enough to possess his spiritual autobiography, written after his "conversion." It is called *Al-munqidh min aḍ-ḍalāl,* "The Deliverer from Error," and has often been translated;[67] it has even been compared to Augustine's *Confessions*, though it conveys nothing of the author's earlier external life. Rather it shows his attempts at coping with the various elements of Islamic intellectual life that confronted him in the course of his studies and his teaching. He had studied the works of the philosophers who, inspired by Greek thought, had developed the logical tools required for scholarly discussion, but who had nevertheless remained, in the opinion of the faithful, outside the pale of orthodox Islam. Ghazzālī's works refuting the philosophical doctrines were in turn refuted by Averroes (d. 1198), the

66. The literature about Ghazzālī is almost inexhaustible; some major works and translations are: Duncan Black Macdonald, "The Life of al-Ghazzālī," *Journal of the American Oriental Society* 20 (1899); Arend Jan Wensinck, *La pensée de Ghazzālī* (Paris, 1940); W. Montgomery Watt, *Muslim Intellectual: A Study of Al-Ghazali* (Edinburg, 1963). The first independent study on Ghazzālī appeared in Berlin in 1858: Reinhard Gosche, *Über Ghazzalis Leben und Werke*; later, the Spanish scholar Asín Palacios devoted a number of books and articles to him. Philosophical investigations of problems of Ghazzālī's thought and faith were introduced by Julius Obermann, *Der religiöse und philosophische Subjektivismus Ġazzālīs* (Leipzig, 1921), a book the main thesis of which can no longer be accepted. Père Farid Jabre has devoted several important books to Ghazzālī's theology. A good introduction into particular problems of Ghazzālī's theological approach is Fadlou Shehadi, *Ghazālī's Unique Unknowable God* (Leiden, 1964); *The Ethical Philosophy of al-Ghazzālī* has been studied by Muhammad Umaruddin (Aligarh, 1951). The Dutch scholar Arend Theodor van Leeuwen sees Ghazzālī, correctly, as apologist: *Ghazālī as apologeet van den Islam* (Leiden, 1947).

67. Abū Ḥāmid al-Ghazzālī, *Al-munqidh min aḍ-ḍalāl,* ed. A. Maḥmūd (Cairo, 1952); translated by W. Montgomery Watt as *The Faith and Practice of Al-Ghazali* (London, 1953); other translations have been done by Claud H. Field (London, 1910); J. H. Kramers (Amsterdam, 1951); and Barbier de Meynard, in *Journal asiatique,* 1877.

greatest Arabic commentator on Aristotle; some of them served medieval Christian theologians in their fight against the Averroist school.

The main source of danger for the Seljuks was, in Niẓāmulmulk's and in Ghazzālī's view, the Ismaili movement, a branch of Shia thought that had gained a firm footing in various parts of the Middle East. Egypt was still ruled by the Fatimid caliphs. During Ghazzālī's lifetime, in 1094, the Persian Ismaili leader Ḥasan-i Ṣabbāḥ took the side of the younger son of the Fatimid caliph during the struggle for succession, with the result that an Ismaili spiritual estate was built up around this Nizar on the mountain castle Alamūt near Kazvin. From there the Ismailis threatened orthodox Muslims and, later, the Crusaders; Niẓāmulmulk fell victim to one of Ḥasan-i Ṣabbāḥ's disciples, known as the Assassins. Ghazzālī wrote several treatises against these *bāṭiniyya,* "the people of esoteric meaning," and in his autobiography tried once more to explain the dangers inherent in the Ismaili system, especially in the doctrine of the necessity of the guidance of an infallible imām, which seemed to him particularly dangerous to the Sunnite community.

Another group with which the medieval scholar concerned himself was his own colleagues, the theologians and lawyer divines—that class of learned men who practically ruled the life of the Muslims by their interpretation of the divine law. Their concern with the outward details of the law had always been a point of criticism for the pious, and particularly for the Sufis. Their worldliness and their many connections with the government aroused those who, acutely conscious of the danger of fossilization of the revealed word under the crust of legal formalism, strove after the interiorization of religion. Ghazzālī wrote: "Those who are so learned about rare forms of divorce can tell you nothing about the simpler things of the spiritual life, such as the meaning of sincerity towards God or trust in Him."[68] Acquainted with all aspects of Muslim intellectual life, and having proved his philosophical and logical adroitness in many defenses of orthodox Islam, Ghazzālī eventually turned to mysticism. Perhaps this was a response to his long-standing skepticism; perhaps a sudden conversion led him to the mystical quest. Whatever the reason, it was typical of Ghazzālī that he approached the mystical Path first from the intellectual side. As he says: "Knowledge was easier for me than activity. I began by reading their books

68. Watt, *Muslim Intellectual,* p. 113.

. . . and obtained a thorough intellectual understanding of their principles. Then I realized that what is most distinctive of them can be attained only by personal experience, ecstasy, and a change of character."[69] We may understand this change to "gnosis because of agnosticism" and agree with W. H. Temple Gairdner's fine remark: "What saved *God* for him from his obliterating agnosticism was the experience of the mystic leap, his own personal *miʿrāj.*"[70] And there it does not matter very much that we do not know who his mystical guide was nor to whom his chain of initiation goes back. We only know that out of his experience came his greatest work, the *Iḥyāʾ ʿulūm ad-dīn,* "Revival of the Religious Sciences," a comprehensive work of forty chapters—forty being the number of patience and trial, the number of days of seclusion that the adept undergoes at the beginning of the Path. The number forty is often identical with "multitude" and is thought to comprise an almost infinite number of items; therefore collections of forty *ḥadīth* (*arbaʿīn*) or of forty pious sentences are very common in the Muslim world. It seems to me typical of Ghazzālī's way of thought that the center of the book, the twentieth chapter, is devoted to the central figure in Islam, the Prophet Muhammad.[71]

The first quarter of the *Iḥyāʾ* is entitled *ʿIbādāt,* "Matters of Worship and Service"; it begins with a chapter on knowledge but deals, in general, with ritual questions like purity, prayers, and devotional acts. Each prescription is preceded by Koranic verses and Prophetic traditions and is explained by the practice of the early faithful and Sufis. The second part of the book deals with the "Customs," and corresponds, to an extent, to the teachings as laid down in the *adab*-books: how to eat and drink, how to lead a married life, and the like

69. Ibid., p. 135.

70. W. H. Temple Gairdner, *The Niche for Lights* (London, 1915), p. 51.

71. Abū Ḥāmid al-Ghazzālī, *Iḥyāʾ ʿulūm ad-dīn,* 4 vols. (Bulaq, Egypt, 1289 h./1872); commentary by the Indian-born scholar Sayyid Murtaḍā az-Zabīdī, *Itḥāf as-sādat al-muttaqīn,* 10 vols. (Cairo, 1311 h./1893–94). The *Iḥyāʾ* has been analyzed in G. H. Bousquet's useful book *"Ihʾyā ʿouloum ad-dīn" ou vivification des sciences de la foi* (Paris, 1955), which contains summaries of all forty chapters. Part translations are: Hans Bauer, *Islamische Ethik,* 4 vols. (Halle, 1916); Hans Wehr, *Al-Ghazālī's Buch vom Gottvertrauen* (Halle, 1940); Herman Henry Dingemans, *Al-Ghazālī's boek der liefde* (Leiden, 1938), not fully satisfactory; Leon Bercher and G. H. Bousquet, *Le livre des bon usages en matière de mariage* (Paris, 1953); Susanna Wilzer, "Untersuchungen zu Ġazzālī's *'kitāb at-tauba,'*" *Der Islam* 32–33 (1955–57); William McKane, *Al-Ghazālī's Book of Fear and Hope* (Leiden, 1962); Nabih A. Faris, *The Book of Knowledge* (Lahore, 1962); Leon Zolondek, *Book XX of al-Gazālī's "Iḥyāʾ ʿulūm ad-Dīn"* (Leiden, 1963); Heinz Kindermann, *Über die guten Sitten beim Essen und Trinken* (Leiden, 1964); Nabih A. Faris, *The Mysteries of Almsgiving* (Beirut, 1966).

—problems that the modern Western reader does not readily relate to religion but that are, in the Islamic (as in the Jewish) view, as much subject to religious rules as is the act of worship. For man should feel every moment that he is in the presence of God, even when occupied by the most worldly activities, and he should be prepared to meet his Lord at any moment of his life.

After the central chapter on the Prophet and his exalted qualities, the third section of the book deals with "Things Leading to Destruction" and the last one with "Things Leading to Salvation." This final part is closest to what we would expect from a mystical writer: it discusses the different stations and states of the wayfarer, like poverty and renunciation, patience and gratitude, love and longing. Here we find some of the finest passages of the whole book, all of which is written in a lucid style with simple, logical arguments. In the chapter on "Love and Longing," Ghazzālī has expressed some of his personal experiences of the Path to God, which never ends but leads to ever new depths.

The whole *Iḥyā*ᵓ may be called a preparation for death: its last chapter is devoted to death in its terrible and its lovable aspects: terrible, because it brings man into the presence of the stern judge at Doomsday, which may be the beginning of everlasting punishment; lovable, since it brings the lover into the presence of his eternal beloved and thus fulfills the longing of the soul, which has finally found eternal peace. All that Ghazzālī teaches in the preceding thirty-nine chapters is only to help man to live a life in accordance with the sacred law, not by clinging exclusively to its letter but by an understanding of its deeper meaning, by a sanctification of the whole life, so that he is ready for the meeting with his Lord at any moment.

This teaching—a marriage between mysticism and law—has made Ghazzālī the most influential theologian of medieval Islam.[72] To fully appreciate his achievement one must remember that during

72. Of Ghazzālī's other works the following translations have been published: Margaret Smith, "Al-Ghazzālī, ar-risāla al-ladunnīya," *Journal of the Royal Asiatic Society*, 1938; Hellmut Ritter, *Das Elixir der Glückseligkeit, aus den persischen und arabischen Quellen in Auswahl übertragen* (Jena, 1923); Mohammed Brugsch, *Die kostbare Perle im Wissen des Jenseits* (Hannover, 1924), an eschatological treatise; Ernst Bannerth, *Der Pfad der Gottesdiener* (Salzburg, 1964), the spurious *Minhāj al-ᶜābidīn*; R. R. C. Bagley, *Ghazālī's Book of Counsel for Kings* (*naṣīḥat al-mulūk*) (Oxford, 1964), a politico-ethical treatise; Franz-Elmar Wilms, *Al-Ghazālīs Schrift wider die Gottheit Jesu* (Leiden, 1966), a translation of *Ar-radd al-jamīl*, a polemic work against Christian theology. Others who have edited or translated some of Ghazzālī's

his lifetime the first signs of Sufi theosophy became visible; certain mystics were more interested in gnostic knowledge than in the practical way of life as taught by the early Sufis. Since Ghazzālī was apprehensive of the dangers of esoteric and gnostic currents inside Islam (as he had shown in his struggle against Ismaili theories) and at the same time scorned the rigidity and pedantry of the scholars and jurists, he undertook in his book to "live through the verities of faith and test those verities through the Sufi experimental method."[73]

It is the life of the heart that matters, and Ghazzālī's method of combining the life of the heart in strict accord with the law and with a theologically sound attitude made even orthodox theologians take the Sufi movement seriously. The moderate Sufi outlook began to color the life of most average Muslims. On the other hand, Ghazzālī's struggle against Hellenistic influences and a more or less Neoplatonic philosophy was probably instrumental in repudiating these currents for a while. During that time, however, they crystallized anew and came back as Sufi theosophy, a new development destined to take shape in the century after Ghazzālī's death.

One of the most puzzling questions among the many unsolved problems for the scholar is where to place Ghazzālī's *Mishkāt al-anwār*, "The Niche for Lights," in the whole body of his writings. It may be regarded as an expression of that set of opinions that the perfected mystic "believes in secret between himself and Allah, and never mentions except to an inner circle of his students."[74] In this book he reaches heights of mystical speculation that are almost "gnostic" when he interprets the Light verse of the Koran (Sūra 24:35) and the tradition about the seventy thousand veils of light and darkness that separate man from God: in his fourfold classification he does not hesitate to put most of the pious orthodox behind the "veils mixed of darkness and light," whereas even certain philosophers are "veiled by pure light." The *Mishkāt al-anwār* shows a highly developed light metaphysics—God is the Light—and many later mystics have relied upon this book rather than upon his *Iḥyāʾ ʿulūm ad-dīn*.

---

works are Ignaz Goldziher, Otto Pretzl, Samuel van den Berghe, Heinrich Frick, and Duncan Black Macdonald. There is a good bibliography in Peter Antes, *Das Prophetenwunder in der frühen Ašʿarīya bis al-Ġazālī* (Freiburg, 1970).

73. Fazlur Rahman, *Islam* (London, 1966), p. 144.

74. Gairdner, *Niche for Lights*, p. 19; see Arend Jan Wensinck, "Ghazālī's *Mishkāt al-anwār*," *Semietische Studien*, 1941.

No thinker of medieval Islam has attracted the interest of Western scholars more than Ghazzālī. Numerous translations of his works are available in Western languages. Discussions about Ghazzālī's true character have been going on for decades. Was he a subjectivist, or a faithful member of the Muslim community who accepted the given religious fact? How can the divergent viewpoints on the several issues of philosophy and theology be explained? To what extent was he sincere in his conversion? Many aspects of his thought have been studied in recent years, but much remains to be done.

Will the admiration reflected in Shādhilī's dream continue? Many a Western scholar, though in milder words, would subscribe to it. Or will Père Anawati's criticism prove right: "Though so brilliant, his contribution did not succeed in preventing the anchylosis that two or three centuries later was to congeal Muslim religious thought"?[75] Or was his greatness itself the reason for the congealing of moderate Islam?

75. G.-C. Anawati and Louis Gardet, *Mystique musulmane* (Paris, 1961), p. 51.

3. THE PATH

THE FOUNDATIONS OF THE PATH

Mystics in every religious tradition have tended to describe the different steps on the way that leads toward God by the image of the Path. The Christian tripartite division of the *via purgativa,* the *via contemplativa,* and the *via illuminativa* is, to some extent, the same as the Islamic definition of *sharīʿa, ṭarīqa,* and *ḥaqīqa.*

The *ṭarīqa,* the "path" on which the mystics walk, has been defined as "the *path* which comes out of the *sharīʿa,* for the main road is called *sharʿ*, the path, *ṭarīq*." This derivation shows that the Sufis considered the path of mystical education a branch of that highway that consists of the God-given law, on which every Muslim is supposed to walk. No path can exist without a main road from which it branches out; no mystical experience can be realized if the binding injunctions of the *sharīʿa* are not followed faithfully first.[1] The path, *ṭarīqa,* however, is narrower and more difficult to walk and leads the adept—called *sālik,* "wayfarer"—in his *sulūk,* "wandering," through different stations (*maqām*) until he perhaps

1. Quṭbaddīn al-ʿIbādī, *At-taṣfiya fī aḥwāl aṣ-ṣūfiya, or Ṣūfīnāme,* ed. Ghūlam Muḥammad Yūsufī (Tehran, 1347 sh./1968), p. 15.

reaches, more or less slowly, his goal, the perfect *tauḥīd,* the existential confession that God is One.

The tripartite way to God is explained by a tradition attributed to the Prophet: "The *sharīʿa* are my words [*aqwālī*], the *ṭarīqa* are my actions [*aʿmālī*], and the *ḥaqīqa* is my interior states [*aḥwālī*]." *Sharīʿa, ṭarīqa,* and *ḥaqīqa* are mutually interdependent:

> The law without truth is ostentation, and the truth without the law is hypocrisy. Their mutual relation may be compared to that of body and spirit: when the spirit departs from the body, the living body becomes a corpse, and the spirit vanishes like wind. The Muslim's profession of faith includes both: the words "There is no god but Allah" are the Truth, and the words "Muhammad is the apostle of God" are the Law. Any one who denies the Truth is an infidel, and any one who rejects the Law is a heretic. (H 383)

"To kiss the threshold of the *sharīʿa*"[2] was the first duty of anyone who wanted to enter the mystical path. The poets have often spoken in verses, and the mystics in poignant sentences, of the different aspects of these three levels (sometimes *maʿrifa,* "gnosis," would be substituted for *ḥaqīqa,* "truth"). Thus it is said in Turkey:

> *Sharīʿa*: yours is yours, mine is mine.
> *Ṭarīqa*: yours is yours, mine is yours too.
> *Maʿrifa*: there is neither mine nor thine.

The meaning is this: in the *ṭarīqa,* the mystic should practice *īthār,* i.e., preferring others to himself, but in the unitive stage the difference between mine and thine has been subsumed in the divine unity.

Once the mystics had identified these three main parts of religious life, they began to analyze the different stages and stations that the wayfarer has to pass on his way. They distinguished between *maqām,* "station," and *ḥāl,* "state": "State is something that descends from God into a man's heart, without his being able to repel it when it comes, or to attract it when it goes, by his own effort" (H 181). Or, as Rūmī puts it more poetically:

> The *ḥāl* is like the unveiling of the beauteous bride,
> while the *maqām* is the [king's] being alone with the bride.
>
> (M 1:1435)

The *maqām* is a lasting stage, which man reaches, to a certain extent, by his own striving. It belongs to the category of acts, whereas

2. Abūʾl-Majd Majdūd Sanāʾī, *Sanāʾīʾābād,* line 39.

the states are gifts of grace. The *maqāmāt*, "stations," define the different stages the wayfarer has attained in his ascetic and moral discipline. He is expected to fulfill completely the obligations pertaining to the respective stations, e.g., he must not act in the station of respect as if he were still in the station of repentance; he also must not leave the station in which he dwells before having completed all its requirements. The states that come over him will vary according to the station in which he is presently living; thus the *qabḍ*, "contraction," of someone in the station of poverty is different from the *qabḍ* of someone in the station of longing.

The mystical theoreticians were not certain whether a state could be appropriated and kept for a while or whether it was a passing experience; they also differ in their classification of the stations and in their description of certain experiences that are seen sometimes as stations, sometimes as states. Even the sequence of the stations is not always clear; it varies according to the capacity of the adept, and God's activity can change stations or grant the wayfarer a state without apparent reason.

Three of the early classifications show the variability of the sequence.

Dhūʾn-Nūn speaks of faith, fear, reverence, obedience, hope, love, suffering, and intimacy; he classifies the last three stations as confusion, poverty, and union (A 9:374).

His younger contemporary in Iran, Yaḥyā ibn Muʿādh, gives a spiritual chain closer to the generally accepted form—repentance, asceticism, peace in God's will, fear, longing, love, and gnosis (A 10:64).

And the Iraqian Sahl at-Tustarī, again a few years younger, defines the sequence as follows: response to God's call, turning toward Him, repentance, forgiveness of sins, loneliness, steadfastness, meditation, gnosis, discourse, election, and friendship (G 4:43).

The manuals of Sufism enumerate still other stations; but the main steps are always repentance, trust in God, and poverty, which may lead to contentment, to the different degrees of love, or to gnosis, according to the mental predilection of the wayfarer. In order to enter the spiritual path, the adept—called *murīd*, "he who has made up his will" (to enter the Path)—is in need of a guide to lead him through the different stations and to point the way toward the goal. *Ad-dīn naṣīḥa*, "religion consists of giving good advice," was a Prophetic tradition dear to the mystics, who saw in the constant supervision of the disciple's way by the mystical guide a *conditio sine qua non* for true progress, though the image of the *sheikh at-tarbīya,* who acutely supervised every breath of the *murīd,* has developed only in the course of time. A later mystic has compared the master—sheikh in Arabic, *pīr* in Persian—to the prophet (for a tradition says that "the sheikh in his group is like the prophet in his people"): "All the prophets have come in order to open people's eyes to see their own faults and God's perfection, their own weakness and God's power, their own injustice and God's justice . . . . And the *shaikh* is also there for the purpose of opening the eyes of his disciples" (N 441). The master who had to teach the method and the exercises had first to test the adept to determine whether he was willing and able to undergo the hardships that awaited him on the Path. The newcomer was sometimes made to wait for days at the sheikh's door, and sometimes as a first test was treated very rudely. Usually three years of service were required before the adept could be formally accepted in a master's group—one year in the service of the people, one in the service of God, and one year in watching over his own heart.

The methods of humiliating future Sufis were numerous. If they were ordered to beg so that they would be rebuked by the people, the intent was not the material profit derived from begging, but the discipline. Shiblī, once a high government official, eventually reached the point of saying: "I deem myself the meanest of God's creatures" (H 359), and only then was he accepted by Junayd. A story that illustrates this attitude very well is told about Majduddīn Baghdādī in the twelfth century:

> When he entered the service of a sheikh, he was made to serve "at the place of ablution," i.e., to clean the latrines. His mother, a well-to-do lady physician, asked the master to exempt the tender boy from this work, and sent him twelve Turkish slaves to do the cleaning. But he replied: "You are a physician—if your son had an inflammation of the gall bladder, should I give the medicine to a Turkish slave instead of giving it to him?" (N 424)

The disciple would probably not have undergone these trials had he not had absolute trust in his master. It was, and still is, a rule that a preformed affinity has to exist between master and disciple. Many Sufis wandered for years throughout the Islamic world in search of a *pīr* to whom they could surrender completely; and a number of sheikhs would not accept a new disciple unless they had seen his name written on the Well-preserved Tablet among their followers (N 536, 538). Did not the Prophet say that the spirits are like armies—those who know each other become friendly with each other?

After the adept had performed the three years of service he might be considered worthy of receiving the *khirqa,* the patched frock, "the badge of the aspirants of Sufism" (H 45). The relation of the novice to the master is threefold: by the *khirqa,* by being instructed in the formula of *dhikr* (recollection), and by company (*ṣuḥbat*), service, and education (N 560). In investing the *murīd* with the patched frock, Sufism has preserved the old symbolism of garments: by donning a garment that has been worn, or even touched, by the blessed hands of a master, the disciple acquires some of the *baraka,* the mystico-magical power of the sheikh. Later Sufism knows two kinds of *khirqa*: the *khirqa-yi irāda,* which the aspirant gets from the master to whom he has sworn allegiance, and the *khirqa-yi tabarruk,* the "frock of blessing," which he may obtain from different masters with whom he has lived or whom he has visited during his journeys—if a master considered him worthy of receiving some of his *baraka.* The *khirqa-yi irāda* is bestowed upon him only by his true mystical leader, who is responsible for his progress.

The *khirqa* was usually dark blue. It was practical for travel, since dirt was not easily visible on it, and at the same time it was the color of mourning and distress; its intention was to show that the Sufi had separated himself from the world and what is in it. In Persian poetry the violet has often been compared to a Sufi who sits, his head on his knees, in the attitude of meditation, modestly wrapped in his dark blue frock among the radiant flowers of the garden. In later times in certain circles mystics would choose for their frocks a color that corresponded to their mystical station (CL 166), and *sabzpūsh,* "he who wears green," has always been an epithet for those who live on the highest possible spiritual level —be they angels, the Prophet, or Khiḍr, the guide of the mystics (cf. V 52).

The patched frock was, of course, often interpreted in a spiritual sense; warnings against attributing too much importance to this woolen dress were not infrequent: "Purity (*ṣafā*) is a gift from God, whereas wool (*ṣūf*) is the clothing of animals" (H 48). Some of the Sufis invented complicated rules for the sewing and stitching of their patched frocks, disputing whether to use thin or coarse thread in putting the patches together, and for some of them these externals were so important that others might accuse them of worshiping the *khirqa* like an idol. The mystical interpretation of the dervish garb is given in a fine passage by Hujwīrī:

Its collar is annihilation of intercourse [with men], its two sleeves are observance and continence, its two gussets are poverty and purity, its belt is persistence in contemplation, its hem is tranquillity in [God's] presence, and its fringe is settlement in the abode of union. (H 56)

The novice who has entered the master's group becomes "like the son of the sheikh"; he is considered part of him according to the tradition, "the son is part of the father." The sheikh helps him to give birth to a true "heart" and nourishes him with spiritual milk like a mother, as it is often repeated.

The Sufis have always been well aware of the dangers of the spiritual path and therefore attributed to the sheikh almost unlimited authority: "When someone has no sheikh, Satan becomes his sheikh," says a tradition, for the satanic insinuations are manifold; the *murīd* may even feel uplifted and consoled by certain experiences that are, in reality, insinuations of his lower self or of a misguiding power. Here the sheikh has to control him and lead him back on the correct path, for

> whoever travels without a guide
> needs two hundred years for a two days journey.
> (M 3:588)

One might read all the books of instruction for a thousand years, but without a guide nothing would be achieved (Y 514).

The master watches every moment of the disciple's spiritual growth; he watches him particularly during the forty-day period of meditation (*arbaʿīn, chilla*) that became, very early, a regular institution in the Sufi path (derived, as Hujwīrī says, from the forty-day fast of Moses, when he hoped for a vision from God, as related in Sūra 7:138). The sheikh interprets the *murīd*'s dreams and visions, reads his thoughts, and thus follows every movement of his conscious and subconscious life. In the first centuries of the Sufi movement the idea was already being expressed that in the hands of the master the *murīd* should be as passive as a corpse in the hands of an undertaker. Ghazzālī, the main representative of moderate Sufism in the late eleventh century, also maintained that complete and absolute obedience is necessary, even if the sheikh should be wrong: "Let him know that the advantage he gains from the error of his sheikh, if he should err, is greater than the advantage he gains from his own rightness, if he should be right."[3] This attitude in later times lent itself to dangerous consequences; indeed, it is one of the reasons for modernist Muslims' aversion to Sufism. But the original intent was genuine: the master should act like a physician, diagnosing and healing the illnesses and defects of the human soul. The image of the master (who is often identified with the true mystical beloved) as the physician who cures the lover's heart occurs frequently in Persian poetry throughout the centuries.

Visiting his master is a religious duty of the disciple (N 115), for he will find from him what he will not find elsewhere. And to serve a master is the highest honor of which a disciple can boast—even if it were only that he "cleaned Junayd's latrines for thirty years" (N 222). Even to have met a leading sheikh at once endows a man with a higher rank (N 115).

Under the guidance of such a trusted master, the *murīd* could hope to proceed in the stations on the Path. The sheikh would teach him how to behave in each mental state and prescribe periods of seclusion, if he deemed it necessary. It was well known that the methods could not be alike for everybody, and the genuine mystical leader had to have a great deal of psychological understanding in order to recognize the different talents and characters of his *murīd*s and train them accordingly.[4] He might exempt a disciple for a time from the forty-day seclusion, for instance, because he was spiritually too weak, or because his spiritual ecstasy might overwhelm him. The isolation of the *murīd* for a period of forty days necessitates a deep change in consciousness, and some of the Sufi theoreticians were aware—as every good sheikh in fact was—that the seclusion might constitute, for weaker adepts, a source of danger rather than of elevation. If he were to concentrate too much upon himself rather than upon God, or if passions might overcome him and make him nervous and angry, it might be better to have him live in the company of other people for his spiritual training[5] because of the mutual influence and good example (L 207).

Generally, the disciple should consider the dark room in which

3. Hamilton A. R. Gibb, *Mohammedanism: An Historical Survey* (London, 1949), p. 150.

4. See Shihābuddīn ᶜUmar as-Suhrawardī, *ᶜAwārif al-maᶜārif* (Printed at the margin of Ghazzālī's *Iḥyā*ᵓ, Bulaq, 1289 h./1872–73), chaps. 26–28.

5. *Ṣūfīnāme*, p. 108.

he observes his seclusion as a tomb, and his frock as a shroud (N 418). Mystics would often retire into seclusion for periods of meditation and were praised if, at the time of their death, they had completed thirty or forty *chilla*. Sometimes they would construct a special *chillakhāna*, a room for seclusion, which might even be subterranean (N 325), close to the center of the fraternity or in a blessed place nearby.

The mystical path has sometimes been described as a ladder, a staircase that leads to heaven, on which the *sālik* slowly and patiently climbs toward higher levels of experience. But the Muslim mystics knew that there is another way of reaching higher experiences: it is the *jadhba*, "attraction," by which a person can be exalted, in one single spiritual experience, into a state of ecstasy and of perfect union. However, it seems typical that the name of *majdhūb*, "the attracted one," was usually given to people who were mentally deranged and who were, in a sense, thrown out of the way of normal behavior by the overwhelming shock of an "unveiling." The sources often described such "attracted" people, who are completely lost and submerged in the divine unity, their eyes "like two cups filled with blood" (N 479), inspiring awe, and at times shocking people by their behavior.

One should not forget, too, that certain Sufis claimed to be traveling the Path without formal initiation. They were called *uwaysī*, recalling the Prophet's contemporary Uways al-Qaranī in Yemen. But even in his case, some legally inclined mystics would hold that he was "spiritually" initiated by the Prophet despite the distance, for initiation by a nonvisible master or by a saint who had died long ago was considered possible in Sufi circles. Thus, Kharaqānī was introduced into the Path through the spirit of Bāyezīd Bisṭāmī, while ʿAṭṭār was inspired by Ḥallāj's spirit. The spirit of the saint is thought to be alive, able to participate actively in the affairs of this world, often appearing in dreams and guiding the wayfarer on his Path, for "the friends of God do not die." Later Sufis—particularly the Naqshbandiyya—practiced a concentration upon the "spiritual reality" of the great masters in order to be strengthened in their mystical pursuits.

A final possibility of initiation from a source other than a human master was through Khiḍr. Khiḍr, identified with the mysterious companion of Moses mentioned in Sūra 18, is the patron saint of travelers, the immortal who drank from the water of life. Sometimes the mystics would meet him on their journeys; he would inspire them, answer their questions, rescue them from danger, and, in special cases, invest them with the *khirqa,* which was accepted as valid in the tradition of Sufi initiation. Thus they were connected immediately with the highest source of mystical inspiration. Ibn ᶜArabī, the theosophist (d. 1240), is one of those who claimed to have received the *khirqa* from Khiḍr.

The mystical Path is long and hard for the *murīd* and requires constant obedience and struggle. The correct initial orientation of the adept is decisive for the success of the journey: who begins in God will also end in Him (L 241). Under the spell of some poetical utterances of later Persian poets, or impressed by dervishes, who were anything but observant of Muslim law, westerners have often regarded the Sufis as representatives of a movement that has freed itself from the legal prescriptions of Islam, no longer caring for religion and infidelity. *Sufi* became almost an equivalent for "free thinker" with many Europeans.

That is, however, not correct. One should not forget that the *sharīᶜa,* as proclaimed in the Koran and exemplified by the Prophet (L 27), together with a firm belief in the Day of Judgment, was the soil out of which their piety grew. They did not abolish the rites but rather interiorized them, as it was said: "The people who know God best are those who struggle most for His commands and follow closest the tradition of His Prophet" (N 117). The performance of ritual prayer, fasting, and pilgrimage to Mecca constituted, for the majority of the early Sufis, the minimal religious obligation without which all possible mystical training would be useless and meaningless. Many of them performed the pilgrimage to Mecca frequently—up to seventy times, if we can believe the hagiographers. They knew that the true seat of the divine spirit was not the Kaaba made of stone but the Kaaba of the faithful worshiper's heart (U 43), in which God might reveal Himself to those who completed the Path.

> When you seek God, seek Him in your heart—
> He is not in Jerusalem, nor in Mecca nor in the *ḥajj,*

says Yūnus Emre (Y 520), voicing the conviction of many of his contemporaries and followers. Yet the pilgrimage remained a central point in the Sufi life, and Mecca was not only a place where the Sufis would meet and join in discussion, but where many of them were blessed with revelations and illuminations.

The recitation of the Koran was another important duty of the mystic: "A disciple who does not know the Koran by heart is like a lemon without scent" (N 131). The divine word is the infallible source of spiritual uplifting; it inspires joy and awe and leads to secret conversations with God, for "God reveals Himself to His servants in the Koran," as ᶜAlī reportedly said (B 584).

Even though Paradise and Hell did not matter to the devotees of mystical love, they were well aware that their deeds would bear fruit, and one of the favorite sayings attributed to the Prophet was constantly repeated by the moderate mystics: "This world is the seedbed for the Otherworld." Every act bears fruit by helping or hindering the adept in his progress toward his goal, and "if you plant colocynth, no sugarcane will grow out of it" (D 1337).

An interesting variation of the *ḥadīth* just quoted is found in the Persian mystical tradition. Rūmī, following Sanāʾī's example, held that every thought that becomes embedded in the heart will turn into a form visible to everybody at the Day of Judgment, just as the thought of the architect becomes visible in the plan of the house, or as the plant grows out of the seed hidden in the soil (M 5:1791–1803), and death will meet man like a mirror, which shows either a beautiful or an ugly face according to his good or evil deeds. The Zoroastrian idea of the witness in Heaven who meets the deceased soul has clearly inspired these ideas. Sanāʾī went even further—he thought that evil thoughts might completely transform man at the end of time so that some people might even appear as animals because they followed bestial instincts and animal lusts in their lifetime (SD 618).

> One has to work day and night,
> to plough and to clean the field of the soul.
>
> (U 264)

And what has been sown during the winter—in the darkness of this material world—will be apparent in the springtime of eternity (M 5:1801).

In this constant watching over one's actions and thoughts, the greatest danger is that the adept may neglect, for a moment, his spiritual duties (*ghaflat*), that he may become entranced by the "sleep of heedlessness," as later poets liked to call this state. The story of Sassuī, the loving wife who found that her husband had been carried away from her while she was asleep, is (in later Sindhi poetry) a perfect illustration of the sleep of heedlessness and negligence that deprives the soul of the company of its Lord and beloved. And while the ordinary believer repents his sins, the elite repents heedlessness (L 44).

The adept should turn with his whole being toward God—*ikhlāṣ,* "absolute sincerity," and giving up selfish thoughts in the service of God are the basic duties of every mystic. A prayer without *ikhlāṣ* is of no avail; a religious thought that is not born out of this sincerity is meaningless, even dangerous. Praise and blame of the crowd do not mean anything to one who has turned wholly and without any qualification to the Lord; and though he will constantly be acting virtuously, he will forget his good and pious actions in his attempt to act solely for God. He forgets, of necessity, the thought of recompense for his works in this world and the world to come.

It is told that Warrāq, one of the early Sufis, was seen wearing a long coat on which he had written the letter *kh* on one side, the letter *m* on the other side, so that he could always remember the *kh* of *ikhlāṣ* and the *m* of *muruwwa,* "virtue." (N 125)

An act of perfect sincerity, done for God's sake, might result in spiritual progress even though it might appear outwardly foolish.

Typical is the story of a not very bright *murīd* whom some mischievous people teased, telling him that he would gain spiritual enlightenment by hanging himself by his feet from the roof and repeating some meaningless words they taught him. He followed their advice in sincerity and found himself illuminated the next morning. (N 320)

An overstressing of the ideal of *ikhlāṣ* has led to the attitude of the *malāmatiyya,* "those who are blamed," those who conceal their virtuous deeds in order to perform their religious duties without ostentation (see chapter 2). For the greatest sin is *riyā,* "hypocrisy" or "ostentation," and the master of psychological analysis in early Sufism, Muḥāsibī, dealt extensively with this danger. Sufi texts tell many stories about people whose hypocrisy was revealed, and they were put to shame. A famous example is this:

A man ostentatiously prayed the whole night through in a mosque he had entered at dusk and where he had heard a sound that seemed to indicate the presence of a human being. But when the call for morning prayer was heard, he discovered that his companion in the mosque was a dog, thus rendering all his prayers invalid and himself impure.

STATIONS AND STAGES

The first station on the Path, or rather its very beginning, is *tauba*, "repentance"; *tauba* means to turn away from sins, to abjure every worldly concern.[6] As the poet says:

Repentance is a strange mount—
it jumps towards heaven in a single moment from the
lowest place.

(M 6:464)

Tauba can be awakened in the soul by any outward event, be it a profane word, which is suddenly understood in a religious sense, a piece of paper on which a relevant sentence is written, the recitation of the Koran, a dream, or a meeting with a saintly person. One of the several stories about Ibrāhīm ibn Adham's conversion is particularly well known:

One night, he heard a strange sound on the roof of his palace in Balkh. The servants found a man who claimed, in Ibrāhīm's presence, to be looking for his lost camel on the palace roof. Blamed by the prince for having undertaken such an impossible task, the man answered that his, Ibrāhīm's, attempt at attaining heavenly peace and true religious life in the midst of luxury was as absurd as the search for a camel on top of a roof. Ibrāhīm repented and repudiated all his possessions. (Cf. M 6:829ff.)

The "world" was considered a dangerous snare on the way to God, and particularly in the time of the old ascetics harsh, crude words were uttered to describe the character of this miserable place, which was compared to a latrine—a place to be visited only in case of need[7]—to a rotting carcass, or to a dunghill: "The world is a dunghill and a gathering place of dogs; and meaner than a dog is that person who does not stay away from it. For the dog takes his own need from it and goes away, but he who loves it is in no way separated from it" (N 65). Most of the Sufis, however, would speak of the transitoriness of the world rather than of its perfect evil; for it was created by God, but it is perishable since nothing but God is everlasting. Why should the ascetic bother about it at

6. See Ignaz Goldziher, "Arabische Synonymik der Askese," *Der Islam* 8 (1918), a study of the technical terms of early Sufism.

7. Abū Ṭālib al-Makkī, *Qūt al-qulūb fī muʿāmalāt al-maḥbūb*, 2 vols. (Cairo, 1310 h./1892–93), 1:244; see Tor Andrae, *Islamische Mystiker* (Stuttgart, 1960), pp. 84ff.

all, since compared to the glory of God, the world is nothing more than a gnat's wing (A 10:84)?

When the disciple leaves this world in his act of repentance, the problem arises as to whether or not he should remember his former sins. Sahl at-Tustarī demands that even after repentance sins should never be forgotten (L 43), for remembrance constitutes a remedy against possible spiritual pride. However Junayd, his contemporary, defined true repentance as "the forgetting of one's sins" (L 43), and Junayd's colleague Ruwaym defined *tauba* as "repenting from repentance," i.e., complete obliteration of the thought of sin and penitence. Junayd's idea is taken up by Hujwīrī: "The penitent is a lover of God, and the lover of God is in contemplation of God: in contemplation it is wrong to remember sin, for recollection of sin is a veil between God and the contemplator" (H 296).

In keeping with his inclination to systematization, Hujwīrī speaks of *tauba* as return from great sins to obedience; *ināba* is the return from minor sins to love, and *auba* the return from one's self to God (H 295). This tripartition is not found elsewhere.

The Sufis knew how often "repentance was broken"—an expression connected, in later Persian poetry, with the breaking of the wine bottle, which induced people to sin again and required renewed repentance. But the mystical leaders were sure that the door of repentance remains open; it is

> a door from the West until the day
> when the sun rises in the West
>
> (M 4:2504)

i.e., until Doomsday, says Rūmī, on whose mausoleum in Konya the famous lines are written:

> Come back, come back, even if you have broken
> your repentance a thousand times.

In the primary stages of the Path, the adept has to increase in abstinence (*wara*ᶜ), caused by fear of the Lord, and in renunciation (*zuhd*). The latter word means, again in the traditional tripartite arrangement of concepts, to give up whatever is ritually and religiously allowed, to give up this world, and eventually to give up everything that distracts the heart from God, even to renounce the thought of renunciation. That includes, of course, giving up the hope for heavenly reward or the fear of Hell.

It was easy for the ascetic to renounce things declared doubtful by Muslim law; but the tendency to renounce even things considered lawful by the community of the faithful sometimes reached absurd degrees. Pious women would not spin in the light of a neighbor's candle; a mystic whose only sheep had grazed on someone else's lawn by mistake would no longer drink its milk, declaring it to be illicit for him after such a transgression. Food or anything belonging to or coming from the ruling classes was regarded as suspect. It is well known that in the old days the most pious scholars refused to accept government offices; even in later periods relations between the Sufis and the rulers were often cold, if not strained, since the mystics were not interested in any contact that might pollute their pure intentions. That is why in anecdotes and in poetry, and so often in ᶜAṭṭār's epics, the dervish is made the mouthpiece of social criticism: he puts his finger on the wound of society and points to the corrupt state of affairs.

For the early considerations of renunciation and "eating the licit," a seemingly characteristic story is told by Hujwīrī in connection with the problem of whether or not a mystic should be a celibate (which he advocates); but the anecdote shows even better the exaggerated *zuhd* and the punishment that follows a single moment of heedlessness:

> One day, when Aḥmad ibn Ḥarb was sitting with the chiefs and nobles of Nishapur who had come to offer their respects to him, his son entered the room, drunk, playing a guitar, and singing, and passed insolently without heeding them. Aḥmad, perceiving that they were put out of countenance, said "What is the matter?" They replied: "We are ashamed that this lad should pass by you in such a state." Aḥmad said: "He is excusable. One night my wife and I partook of some food that was brought to us from a neighbour's house. That same night this son was begotten and we fell asleep and let our devotions go. Next morning we inquired of our neighbour as to the source of the food that he had sent to us, and we found that it came from a wedding-feast in the house of a government official. (H 365)

In later Sufi texts stress is laid not so much on *zuhd* as on its negative counterpart, *ḥirṣ*, "greed," a quality opposed to both renunciation and true poverty. The Persian poets have never ceased warning their readers of greed, which is "a dragon and not any small thing" (M 5:120). This quality was found, as history shows, not only in the worldly leaders but also in many of those who claimed to have attained the highest spiritual rank and who used outward *zuhd* to cover their inner greed. The *zāhid-i ẓāhirparast*, the ascetic who still worships outward things, i.e., who has not reached sincere selflessness and loving surrender, has been ridiculed in many Persian poems.

The forward movement on the Path, as initiated by repentance and renunciation, consists of a constant struggle against the *nafs*, the "soul"—the lower self, the base instincts, what we might render in the biblical sense as "the flesh." The faithful had been admonished in the Koran (Sūra 79:40) to "fear the place of his Lord and hinder the *nafs* from lust." For the *nafs* is the cause of blameworthy actions, sins, and base qualities; and the struggle with it has been called by the Sufis "the greater Holy War," for "the worst enemy you have is [the *nafs*] between your sides," as the *ḥadīth* says (L 12). The Koranic expression *an-nafs al-ammāra biʾs-sūʾ*, "the soul commanding to evil" (Sūra 12:53) forms the starting point for the Sufi way of purification. The holy book contains also the expression *an-nafs al-lawwāma*, "the blaming soul" (Sūra 75:2), which corresponds approximately to the conscience that watches over man's actions and controls him. Eventually, once purification is achieved, the *nafs* may become *muṭmaʾinna* (Sūra 89:27), "at peace"; in this state, according to the Koran, it is called home to its Lord.[8]

The main duty of the adept is to act exactly contrary to the *nafs*'s appetites and wishes. There is nothing more dangerous for the disciple than to treat the *nafs* lightly by allowing indulgences and accepting (facilitating) interpretations, says Ibn Khafīf.[9] It is incumbent upon every traveler on the Path to purge the *nafs* of its evil attributes in order to replace these by the opposite, praiseworthy qualities. Sufi hagiography is full of stories about the ways in which the masters of the past tamed their appetites and, if they failed, the manner of their punishment.

The *nafs* is something very real, and many stories tell of its having been seen outside the body. Sometimes it took the form of a black dog that wanted food but had to be trained and sent away; other mystics saw their *nafs* coming out of their throats in the form of a young fox or a mouse (H 206). The *nafs* can also be compared to a disobedient woman who tries to seduce and cheat the poor wayfarer (the noun *nafs* is feminine in Arabic!). A recurrent image is that of the restive horse or mule that has to be kept hungry and

8. A. Ṭāhir al-Khānqāhī, *Guzīda dar akhlāq ū taṣawwuf*, ed. Iraj Afshar (Tehran, 1347 sh./1968), p. 224.

9. ʿAbdur-Raḥman as-Sulamī, *Kitāb ṭabaqāt aṣ-Ṣūfiyya*, ed. Nūraddīn Sharība (Cairo, 1953), p. 465.

has to undergo constant mortification and training so that, eventually, it serves the purpose of bringing the rider to his goal (H 202–204).[10] Sometimes it is likened to a disobedient camel—Rūmī compares the struggle of the intellect with the *nafs* to the attempts of Majnūn to turn his camel in the right direction, toward the tent of his beloved (M 4:1532)—and it is only natural that poets all over the desert areas, like Shāh ᶜAbduʾl-Laṭīf in Sind, are particularly fond of this comparison. Even the comparison of the *nafs* to a pig is not rare. It is found mainly in ᶜAṭṭār's poetry; like Sanāʾī before him, he felt that those who obeyed their piglike nature would themselves be changed into pigs (U 236–37; R 102–3).

Sometimes the *nafs* has been likened to Pharaoh, the self-centered ruler (U 16; M 4:3621) who did not listen to the call to faith uttered by Moses but claimed a divine rank for himself and consequently was drowned in the Red Sea; or to Abraha, who intruded in the holy city of Mecca and should be scared away with stones (SD 313; cf. Sūra 105).

Old, popular beliefs were revived when the *nafs* was said to take the form of a snake; but this serpent can be turned into a useful rod, just as Moses transformed serpents into rods. More frequent, however, is the idea that the power of the spiritual master can blind the snake; according to folk belief, the snake is blinded by the sight of an emerald (the connection of the *pir*'s spiritual power with the green color of the emerald is significant). Thus, his influence renders the *nafs*-snake harmless (M 3:2548).

The image of training the horse or the dog conveys the most nearly accurate impression of the activity of the Sufi: the lower faculties are not to be killed, but trained so that even they may serve on the way to God. A story told about the Prophet Muhammad well expresses this faith in the training of the base soul; the expression used here for the "lower qualities, instincts," is *shayṭān*, "Satan": "When asked how his *shayṭān* behaved, he answered: '*Aslama shayṭānī*; my *shayṭān* has become a Muslim and does whatever I order him,' " i.e., all his lower faculties and instincts had been turned into useful tools in the service of God. Provided that man obeys God in every respect, the lower soul will obey its master, as everything in the world will obey the one who has completely surrendered his will to the will of God.

10. Annemarie Schimmel, "Nur ein störrisches Pferd," in *Ex Orbe Religionum Festschrift Geo Widengren* (Leiden, 1972).

The struggle against the *nafs* has always been a favorite topic of the Sufis, and they have never tired of warning their disciples of its ruses, not only in the crude forms of sensual appetites but in the guises of hypocrisy and false piety, which must be carefully observed and obliterated.

> The *nafs* has a rosary and a Koran in its right hand,
> and a scimitar and a dagger in the sleeve,
>
> (M 3:2554)

says Rūmī, taking up a warning formulated four hundred years earlier by Dhū'n-Nūn. Even to indulge in constant acts of worship or prayer can become a pleasure for the *nafs*; the mystic, therefore, has to break every kind of habit, for otherwise his *nafs* will overcome him in a subtler way (N 98). The "pleasure derived from works of obedience" should be avoided (N 83), for that is fatal poison.

One of the great dangers for the wayfarer is laziness or leisure; as long as he has not yet reached his goal, it would be better for him to occupy himself with seemingly useless things, like digging one pit after the other (N 156, 90), than to spend a moment in leisure, for "leisure (*farāgh*) is an affliction" (N 90).

The chief means for taming and training the *nafs* were, and still are, fasting and sleeplessness. The first ascetics have often been described as *qā'im al-lail wa ṣā'im ad-dahr*, "spending their nights upright in prayer and maintaining a perpetual fast by day." The old saying that the three elements of Sufi conduct are *qillat aṭ-ṭaʿām, qillat al-manām wa qillat al-kalām*, "little food, little sleep, little talk" (to which often "loneliness, keeping away from men," was added) is still as valid as it was a thousand years ago.

Lack of sleep was considered one of the most effective means on the mystical Path—"the eye is weeping instead of sleeping"[11]—and the caliph ʿUmar (634–44), who was certainly not a Sufi, reportedly said: "What have I to do with sleep? If I slept by day, I would lose the Muslims, and if I slept by night I would lose my soul" (G 1:318). The ascetic spent his nights at prayers recommended in the Koran, which gave him time to enjoy blessed conversation with his Lord through prayer. Many of the mystics would avoid stretching out their legs or lying down when slumber overcame them, for all of

11. Muhammad Gīsūdarāz, *Dīwān anīs al-ʿushshāq* (n.p., n.d.), p. 18.

them hoped for some revelation after the long nights of sleeplessness, which extended over years, if we can believe the sources. The most beautiful story pertaining to this attitude has been told and retold for centuries: Shāh Kirmānī did not sleep for forty years, but eventually he was overwhelmed by sleep—and he saw God. Then he exclaimed: " 'O Lord, I was seeking Thee in nightly vigils, but I have found Thee in sleep.' God answered: 'O Shāh, you have found Me by means of those nightly vigils: if you had not sought Me there, you would not have found Me here' " (H 138). These ascetics and Sufis were hoping—as later poets have expressed it so excellently—to have the vision of a sun that is neither from east nor from west but rises at midnight, and thus to enjoy a spiritual enlightenment not comparable to any worldly light (cf. U 160).

For practical purposes, however, the *qillat aṭ-ṭaʿām*, "to eat little," is even more important than to avoid sleep. The Sufis would fast frequently, if not constantly. Many of them extended the fasting in Ramadan observed by every Muslim; but in order to make fasting more difficult, they invented the so-called *ṣaum dāʾūdī*, which meant that they would eat one day and fast one day, so that their bodies would not become accustomed to either of the two states. "Fasting is really abstinence, and this includes the whole method of Sufism" (H 321).

The first mystic to speak of the "alchemy of hunger" was, as far as we can see, Shaqīq al-Balkhī from the Khurasanian ascetic school. He claimed that forty days of constant hunger could transform the darkness of the heart into light (W 216), and many sayings of the early Sufis praise this hunger, which "is stored up in treasure-houses with Him, and He gives it to none but whom He particularly loves" (L 202). "Hunger is God's food by which He quickens the bodies of the upright" (M 5:1756), says Rūmī, who also argues that, just as the host brings better food when the guest eats little, God brings better, i.e., spiritual, food to those who fast. But "hunger is the food of the ascetics, recollection that of the gnostics" (N 157).

The accounts of the extended periods of fasting of Muslim mystics are astounding, and we have little reason to doubt their authenticity. The wish to die in the state of fasting may induce the Sufi even to throw away the wet piece of cotton that his friends put in his mouth to relieve him in his state of agony (N

245). It would be worth investigating to what extent this restriction to extremely small quantities of food contributed to the longevity of the Sufis. It is astonishing how many of them lived to be very old.

Like the early Christian monks who lived exclusively on the host, the Muslim saints considered hunger the best way to reach spirituality. To be empty of worldly food is the precondition for enlightenment. "Could the reedflute sing if its stomach were filled?" Rūmī asks repeatedly. Man can receive the divine breath of inspiration only when he keeps himself hungry and empty.

Rūzbihān Baqlī tells about a saint who totally fasted for seventy days, during which he remained in the contemplation of *ṣamadiyyat,* "eternity": "In this state food comes to him from the word 'I stay with my Lord who feeds me and gives me to drink' " (Sūra 26:79). "This is no longer the station of struggle, but that of contemplation" (B 364). In cases of this kind, hunger is no longer a means for subduing the *nafs* but a divine grace: adoration is the food for the spiritual man (H 303), and the Sufi is nourished by the divine light (M 4:1640–44). Some mystics, like Ibn Khafīf, have confessed that their goal in permanent fasting and diminishing their food was to be like the angels, who also live on perpetual adoration (X 107).

> Gabriel's food was not from the kitchen,
> it was from the vision of the Creator of Existence.
> Likewise this food of the men of God
> is from God, not from food and dish.
>
> (M 3:6–7)

And why care for the body, which is, as the Sufis liked to say, only "a morsel for the tomb" and should therefore be bony and lean (D 777)?

Some of the ascetics exaggerated fasting and hunger in the preparatory stages to such an extent that one can almost speak of an "idolatry of the empty stomach" (W 216). There are known cases of Sufis who starved to death (L 417). Others not only fasted and restricted their diet to the absolute minimum but, in addition to that, took a purgative on every third day.[12]

Yet the great masters have always acknowledged that hunger is only a means to spiritual progress, not a goal in itself. Just as Abū Saʿīd ibn Abīʾl-Khair, after years of incredible ascetic hardships, eventually enjoyed food—and good food!—many of the later mystics

12. Umar Muhammad Daudpota, *Kalām-i Girhōṛī* (Hyderabad, Sind, 1956), p. 23.

would agree that "the soul-dog is better when its mouth is shut by throwing a morsel into it."[13]

Strangely enough, as early as the tenth century, the fondness of the Sufis for halvah, sweetmeat, is mentioned; and in the eleventh and later centuries poets often speak in derogatory terms of the Sufi with milk-white hair who has made the recollection (*dhikr*) of sugar, rice, and milk his special litany (SD 149). This derogatory attitude is echoed in the poetry of Bedil (d. 1721), who criticized the Sufis whose only *dhikr*, recollection, is to constantly mention food. And Muhammad Iqbal (d. 1938) made the fake *murīd* explain that God, though "closer than the jugular vein" (Sūra 50:16), is not closer to man than his stomach.

Many later orders taught that the middle way, between excessive hunger and excessive eating, was safest for the disciple's progress (N 395). According to the later Naqshbandiyya and other moderate orders, the people who truly fast are those who keep their minds free from the food of satanic suggestions and so do not allow any impure thoughts to enter their hearts: "Such people's sleep is worship. Their walking and going and resting are glorification of God, and their breathing praise of God."

One of the most important stations on the Path is *tawakkul*, complete trust in God and self-surrender to Him. The Swiss scholar Benedikt Reinert has devoted to this subject a book that must be regarded as a model for future research into the concepts of early Sufism.[14] The definition of *tawakkul* is of central importance for an understanding of classical Sufi thought. Dārānī, the spiritual descendant of Ḥasan al-Baṣrī, defined it as the apex of *zuhd*, "renunciation." The problem was soon posed as to whether *tawakkul* was an attribute of the faithful or a consequence of perfect faith. Thus Muḥāsibī, representative of orthodox views, holds that the degree of *tawakkul* can vary in accordance with the degree of faith a person has. Throughout the ninth century—probably beginning with Shaqīq al-Balkhī—the pious discussed the different aspects of this attitude, which Dhū'n-Nūn defined as "complete certitude." According to these definitions, real *tauḥīd* demands *tawakkul*: God, in His absoluteness, is the only actor, and therefore man has to rely completely upon Him. Or, to define it different-

13. Dārā Shikōh, *Sakīnat al-auliyā'*, ed. M. Jalālī Nā'inī (Tehran, 1334 sh./1965), p. 238.

14. Benedikt Reinert, *Die Lehre vom tawakkul in der älteren Sufik* (Berlin, 1968), an excellent study of the development of "trust in God" and its ramifications.

ly: since the divine power is all-embracing, man must have complete trust in this power.

The same end is reached if the problem is approached from the angle of predestination. *Rizq*, "our daily bread," has been guaranteed from preeternity. Why worry, then? Is not one of God's names, *ar-Razzāq*, "He who bestows sustenance"? And He has shown His kindness to every being from his birth, even from the moment of conception, by nourishing him first with blood, then with milk. Since everything is created by and belongs to God, man possesses absolutely nothing of his own; therefore it would be vain to strive to attract or refuse anything. The Muslim creed expressly states that "what has been destined for man cannot possibly miss him," be it food, happiness, or death.

The overwhelming feeling of God's all-encompassing wisdom, power, and loving-kindness is reflected in the Muslim tradition as fully as in some of the Psalms and in the Christian tradition. The word ascribed to the Prophet, "if ye had trust in God as ye ought He would feed you even as He feeds the birds," sounds almost evangelical. This deep trust in God's promise to feed man and bring him up, as it developed out of the Koranic teaching, has permeated Muslim life. Sanāʾī said about 1120:

> If your daily bread is in China,
> the horse of acquisition is already saddled,
> and either brings you hurriedly to it,
> or brings it to you, while you are asleep.
>
> (S 106)

And even today Muslim intellectuals may say: "Wherever your *rizq* is, there you will find it, and it will find you."

The Muslim mystics often use the expression *ḥusn aẓ-ẓann*, "to think well of God," which may sound strange to modern ears, but which means once more the absolute, hopeful trust in God's kindness. God definitely knows what is good for man and gives bread and death, punishment and forgiveness according to His eternal wisdom. This attitude has been a source of strength for millions of Muslims, but it is not to be confused with the stoic acceptance of a blind fate, as it is usually understood in terms of predestinarian ideas. The faith in the *rizq* that will reach man was certainly carried too far by an early mystic who forbade his disciple to stretch out his hand to grasp a dried-up melon skin.

Tawakkul in its interiorized sense means to realize *tauḥīd;* for it would be *shirk khafī,* "hidden associationism," to rely upon or be afraid of any created being. This aspect of *tawakkul* is one of the basic truths in Sufi psychology: as soon as every feeling and thought is directed in perfect sincerity toward God, without any secondary causes, neither humans nor animals can any longer harm the mystic. Thus *tawakkul* results in perfect inner peace. The numerous stories about Sufis who wandered "in *tawakkul*" through the desert without fear of lions or highway robbers, without any provisions, reflect this attitude in a somewhat romantic fashion. Ironically, one of the leading masters of *tawakkul,* Abū Turāb an-Nakhshabī, was devoured by lions in the desert (Q 17).

But exaggerated *tawakkul* might induce man into perfect passivity. Then it might produce strange figures like the dervish who fell into the Tigris; asked whether he wanted to be saved, he said "no," and asked whether he would rather die, he again said "no"—"for what have I to do with willing?" God had decreed at the time of creation whether he was to be drowned or saved. Another story that deals with the unhealthy exaggeration of *tawakkul* is told about Ibrāhīm ibn al-Khawāṣṣ, an Iraqian Sufi who used to wander in the deserts without any provisions (*ʿalāʾt-tawakkul*). But a colleague of his thought even this too lax, since "his Sufi dress begged for him"; he made him wear luxurious attire and then sent him to the desert to practice real trust in God (X 105). This same wayfarer would refuse the company of Khiḍr, the patron of pious travelers, because his graceful company seemed to negate his perfect trust in God alone—had not Abraham, after all, refused help even from Gabriel when Nimrod cast him onto the blazing pyre? And he was rewarded for this act of *tawakkul* by God's changing the fire into a cool rose garden. How, then, could the Sufi ascetic even think of danger if everything was in the hands of God? And why should he get involved in a profession to gain his livelihood if God would send him his food in any case, if there was food predestined for him?

The ascetic regarded everything worldly as contaminated; nothing was ritually clean enough for him to occupy himself with. He would rather spend his days and nights in worship than pollute himself by "practical" work. And even if he did work, why should he try to gain more than was needed just for one day? To store money or goods was regarded as a major sin—did the pious know whether he would still be alive within an hour, or by the next morning? "Extension of hope," *ṭūl al-amal,* is one of the most disliked attitudes in Sufism; Ghazzālī's chapter on "Fear and Hope," in his *Iḥyā᾽ ᶜulūm ad-dīn,* echoes these feelings and gives a lucid picture of the austere outlook of early Sufism. Even mystics who cannot be regarded as typical representatives of strict *tawakkul* often distributed all their money in the evening or gave away everything they had on Friday. They also refused any medical treatment.

The importance of the problem of *tawakkul* for early Sufi thought and practice can be understood from the fact that the earliest standard work on mysticism, Abū Ṭālib al-Makkī's *Qūt al-qulūb,* contains sixty pages (big folio with very small print) about this topic, more than about any other aspect of Sufism. Through Ghazzālī, who drew heavily upon Makkī's book, these ideas became widely known in medieval Islam. However, neither strict Hanbalite orthodoxy nor the moderate Sufis accepted the notion of *tawakkul* in an overstressed form; exaggerations like those just mentioned were criticized by many of the leading pious. They considered this exaggerated attitude a violation of the Prophetic tradition—did not Muhammad himself advise a bedouin: "First tie your camel's knee, and then trust in God"? Sahl at-Tustarī is the perfect example of a mystic who tried to combine a life in the "world" with complete *tawakkul,* and his contemporary Junayd taught his disciples how to regard earning: "The proper method of earning . . . is to engage in works which bring one nearer to God, and to occupy oneself with them in the same spirit as with works of supererogation commended to one, not with the idea that they are a means of sustenance or advantage" (K 73).

In the course of time, *tawakkul* came to be regarded more as a spiritual attitude than as an external practice. If everybody had lived according to the ideals promoted by some of the early ascetics, the whole economic and social fabric of the Muslim Empire would have collapsed. However, as a basic station on the mystical Path and as a spiritual force, an unshakable trust in divine wisdom and power, *tawakkul* is still an important element of Muslim piety.

The central attitude in Sufi life is that of *faqr,* "poverty." The Koran (Sūra 35:16) has contrasted man in need of God with God, the ever Rich, the Self-sufficient, and here lies one of the roots of the Sufi concept of poverty. In fact, the main names under which the mystics have been known in the West—though often in distorted images—are *faqīr,* "poor," and dervish, "poor, mendicant." Poverty was an attribute of the Prophet, who claimed, according to the tradition, *faqrī fakhrī,* "poverty is my pride." There are numerous legends about the destitute state and the poverty of his household and the members of his family.

The Sufis considered outward poverty a necessary station at the beginning of the Path, and they tried to preserve it as long as possible, often throughout their lives. There is no reason to doubt the validity of the stories in which the utter destitution of some of the great mystics is dramatically described. The reed mat on which the mystic slept, and which often constituted his only worldly possession, became in later Persian poetry a symbol of spiritual wealth, since it gives its owner a rank higher than that of Solomon on his air-borne throne:

> Everyone who has to write the manuscript of the etiquette of Poverty
> puts a ruler from the strips of the reed-mat on the pages of his body.[15]

Poverty interpreted in a spiritual sense means the absence of desire for wealth, which includes the absence of desire for the blessings of the otherworld. One of the aspects of true *faqr* is that the mystic must not ask anything of anyone—Anṣārī, though utterly poor, never asked his wealthy friends even for a blanket, though he knew that they would have wanted to give him one, but "since they did not perceive my misery, why ask them?" (N 347). For to ask would mean to rely upon a created being, and to receive would burden the soul with gratitude toward the giver, a burden that was considered most embarrassing and heavy; both in poetry and in everyday speech this feeling of *minnat,* "gratitude," has a negative value for the faithful.

If man has no wish for himself in this world and the next, then he may be called a genuine *faqīr* (N 111). To possess anything means to be possessed by it—the world enthralls those who possess some of its goods, whereas "the true faqīr should not possess anything and thus not be possessed by anything" (L 108). He needs God, nothing else.

15. Abū Ṭālib Kalīm, *Dīwān,* ed. Partaw Baiḍāʾī (Tehran, 1336 sh./1957), ghazal no. 316.

Later Sufis have stretched this concept of absolute poverty so far that even Jesus, the ideal of poverty for the early ascetics, was regarded as imperfect in his poverty; he used to carry a needle with him, which proved that his relation with the world was not yet completely severed, and that is why he was assigned a place only in the fourth heaven, not in the proximity of the Lord. This story belongs among the favorites of Persian poets in their praise of poverty (cf. SD 85).

Hujwīrī spoke, correctly, about the form and the essence of poverty: "Its form is destitution and indigence, but its essence is fortune and free choice" (H 19). The dervish, the Sufi, may be rich if he has the right attitude, which means that his outward wealth and power are of no interest to him and that he would be willing to give them up at any moment. The final consequence—after quitting this world and the next—is to "quit quitting" (*tark at-tark*), to completely surrender and forget poverty, surrender, and quitting. About the year 900, there was discussion in Baghdad and elsewhere about the superiority of the poor or the rich. Most of the Sufis agreed that *faqr* was superior and preferable to wealth, provided that it was combined with contentment (N 417)—and this is the general solution found in later medieval Sufism, as in Abū Najīb as-Suhrawardī's *Ādāb al-murīdīn.*

Many of the early sources are filled with praise for the true *faqīr* and sometimes equate him with the genuine Sufi. Yet Jāmī, following Abū Ḥafṣ ʿUmar as-Suhrawardī's distinction among "ascetic," "poor," and "Sufi," as explained in the *ʿAwārif al-maʿārif,* regarded the *faqīr,* in the technical sense, as inferior to the real Sufi, for whom *faqr* is nothing but a station on the Path. If he makes poverty a goal in itself, the *faqīr* is veiled from God by his very "will to be poor" (N 11). That is basically an elaboration of a saying by Ibn Khafīf: "The Sufi is he whom God has chosen (*iṣṭafā*) for Himself, out of love, and the *faqīr* is he who purifies himself in his poverty in the hope of drawing near [to God]" (N 12).

Others have praised *faqr* as the central quality of the mystic, as Rūmī says in an interesting comparison:

> It is like the highest sheikh, and all the hearts are *murīds,*
> the hearts of the lovers turn around it.
>
> (D 890)

Hujwīrī has described this kind of poverty very beautifully:

Dervishhood in all its meanings is a metaphorical poverty, and amidst all its subordinate aspects there is a transcendent principle. The Divine mysteries come and go over the dervish, so that his affairs are acquired by himself, his actions attributed to himself, and his ideas attached to himself. But when his affairs are freed from the bonds of acquisition, his actions are no more attributed to himself. Then he is the Way, not the wayfarer, i.e., the dervish is a place over which something is passing, not a wayfarer following his own will. (H29)

Faqr, here, is almost equated with *fanā*, "annihilation in God," which is the goal of the mystic, as Rūmī said once in the *Mathnawī* (M 5:672). For ʿAṭṭār poverty and annihiliation constitute the seventh and last vale on the Path leading to God, after the traveler has traversed the valleys of search, love, gnosis, independence, *tauḥīd*, and bewilderment (MT).

Along this line of interpretation a phrase was invented that belongs among the standard sayings of later Sufism: *al-faqr idhā tamma huwa Allāh*, "when *faqr* becomes perfect (complete), it is God." The heart, annihilated in absolute poverty, lives in the eternal richness of God, or, rather, absolute poverty becomes absolute richness. That may be what the author of this sentence felt. Its origin is not known. Sometimes it is called a *ḥadīth*. It has been attributed to Uways al-Qaranī, but that is impossible; Jāmī (N 267) ascribes it to a disciple of Kharaqānī, which would be historically possible. Whatever its source may be, the sentence was used frequently among the mystics after the eleventh century; Rūmī (D 1948) was fond of it, as was Jāmī; and the Sufi orders—Qādiriyya and Naqshbandiyya—made it known as far as Malaysia.[16]

The equation of *faqr* with annihilation, and the emphasis on the negative, nonexistent aspect of things is expressed, in Islamic art, by the large empty hall of the mosque, which inspires the visitor with numinous grandeur. It is also reflected in the negative space in the arabesques or in calligraphy. Only by absolute *faqr* can the created world become a vessel for the manifestations of God, the eternally rich.

There is another Prophetic tradition, however, in which Muhammad claims that "poverty is the 'blackness of face' [i.e., shame]

16. See Hasan Lutfi Şuşut, *Islam tasavvufunda Hacegân Hanedanı* (Istanbul, 1958), p. 156; Maulana ʿAbdurraḥmān Jāmī, *Lawāʾiḥ* (Tehran, 1342 sh./1963), no. 8. See al-Attas, *The Mysticism of Ḥamza al-Fanṣūrī* (Kuala Lumpur, 1970), pp. 46, 226, 462. An inscription from a Qādiriyya *tekke* in Konya, dated 1819, in my possession, contains a Persian quatrain ending with these words. They are also quoted by the Indo-Persian poet Mirza Bedil (d. 1721), *Kulliyāt*, 4 vols. (Kabul, 1962–65), 1:1009.

in both worlds."[17] How is one to interpret this statement after so much praise of *faqr*? Baqlī saw in it a condemnation of the claim to be a *faqīr* (B 605); but Sanāʾī had invented an ingenious interpretation nearly a century before him: just as the Negro—proverbially cheerful in classical Arabic literature—is happy and smiling in spite of his black face, so the true poor person is filled with spiritual happiness and permanent joy in his state of poverty (S 88). This sounds farfetched but is a typical example of the art of interpretation as practiced by the Sufis. It shows, at the same time, the central place attributed to the happiness of poverty among the Sufis, who are the *nihil habentes omnia possedentes.* There is still another interpretation of the "blackness of face": perfect poverty is the state of reaching the pure divine essence, which is the Black Light by which one sees and which itself remains invisible (CL 168, 176)—another interpretation that emphasizes the close relation between *faqr* and *fanā.*

Another station on the Path, which has often been described, is *ṣabr,* "patience," taught by the Koran as the attitude of Job and of Jacob—"and God is with those who show patience" (Sūra 2:103). "*Ṣabr* is to remain unmoved before the arrows of the divine decrees," says Muḥāsibī (W 283). Others would change the words "divine decrees" into "affliction," but the meaning remains the same: perfect patience is to accept whatever comes from God, even the hardest blow of fate. With their tendency to classify the stations and stages, the Sufis divided patient people into three classes: the *mutaṣabbir,* who attempts to be patient; the *ṣābir,* who is patient in afflictions; and the *ṣabūr,* who is perfectly patient under any condition. "To be patient before God's orders is more excellent than fasting and prayer" (N 164).

The old Arabic saying, "patience is the key to happiness," has been repeated thousands of times by mystics and poets, who never tired of inventing new parables to show the necessity of patience: only through patience does the fruit become sweet; only through patience can the seed survive the long winter and develop into grain, which, in turn, brings strength to the people, who patiently wait for it to be turned into flour and bread. Patience is required to cross the endless deserts that stretch before the traveler on the Path and to cross the mountains that stand, with stone-hearted breasts, between him and his divine beloved.

17. Al-Khānqāhī, *Guzīda,* p. 17.

> Patience, O father, is an iron shield,
> on which God has written "victory has come."
>
> (M 5:2479)

Yet patience, indispensable as it is, is only "a messenger from the divine beloved"—

> Patience always says: "I give glad tidings from union with Him."
> Gratitude always says: "I am the possessor of a whole store from Him!"
>
> (D 2142)

Patience is an important milestone on the Path, but a person who has reached the station of gratitude (*shukr*) is already blessed by divine grace. There is no doubt that gratitude is superior to patience; the problem posed by the Sufis of the old school is only whether a patient, poor or a grateful, rich man is closer to God. One might say that patience is more praiseworthy than gratitude, for patience goes against one's body, whereas gratitude conforms to the body, or that the dichotomy of the two states is resolved in the state of *riḍā*, "contentment," which makes man whole.

Gratitude is divided into different ranks: gratitude for the gift, gratitude for not giving, and gratitude for the capacity to be grateful. For though the common man deserves to be applauded when he expresses his gratitude at receiving a gift, the Sufi should give thanks even if his wish is not fulfilled or a hope is withheld.

A famous story about patience and gratitude, repeated in almost every book about early Sufis, appears in Sanāʾī's *Ḥadīqa* in the following form:

> An Iraqian Sufi visited a sheikh from Khurasan and asked him about real Sufism as taught in his country. He replied that, when God sent them something they would eat it and be grateful, if not, they would endure patience and take the wish out of the heart. Whereupon the Iraqian Sufi replied: "That kind of Sufism is what our dogs do in Iraq—when they find a bone they eat it, otherwise they are patient and leave it." Being asked by his companion how he, then, would define Sufism, he answered: "When we have anything we prefer others to ourselves [i.e., give it away], if not, we occupy ourselves with thanks and pray for forgiveness." (S 495)

This story, which has been attributed to various people, clearly shows the higher rank of those who offer thanks even when deprived of everything. It is reminiscent of the prayer of Job, the great model of patience in Christian and Islamic lore: "The Lord gave, and the Lord took away; blessed be the name of the Lord."

On the highest level the Sufis understood that even the capacity for thanking is a divine gift, not a human act (cf. Q 80 ff.), and therefore "it behooves to be grateful for the gratitude" (B 515). The Sufi who acts in this way has before him the example of the Prophet, "who in the highest bliss of being drowned in the ocean of the bounty of gratitude wanted to express his thanks in the tongue without tongues and found himself incapable and said *lā uḥṣī thanāʾan ʿalaika*, 'I cannot count the praise due to Thee' " (B 514). This saying is one of the cornerstones of mystical gratitude. Gratitude, in its deepest sense, is an insight into the wise working of God. As ʿAṭṭār expressed it in his poetical description of the mystical states:

> What is gratitude? To imagine the rose from the thorn,
> and to imagine the nonvisible part to be the whole.
>
> (U 41)

Gratitude toward God teaches man to see with the heart's eye the blessings veiled in affliction. Yet "gratitude is a wild bird the which to catch and to fetter is difficult."[18] Patience, however, is a mount that never fails on the difficult road.

Shukr, gratitude, is related to *riḍā*, which is not a patient bearing and suffering of all the vicissitudes of life, but happiness in poverty and affliction. "*Riḍā* is the joy of the heart in the bitterness of the divine decree" (L 53), says Dhū'n-Nūn. Hujwīrī is probably right in his statement that *riḍā* is a result of love, inasmuch as the lover is content with what is done by the beloved (H 180). It is definitely the attitude of a loving heart, but the Sufis disagree about whether to define it as a station or a state. A verse by Sanāʾī defines the *mufarriḥ*, a medicine to make the heart more cheerful and to calm down nervous tension, a kind of tranquilizer:

> The *mufarriḥ* that the saints make
> is prepared in the hospital of contentment.
>
> (S 341)

The story of Ḥuṣrī, an early tenth-century mystic, points to the essence of contentment: "Ḥuṣrī once said in prayer: 'O God, art Thou content with me that I am content with Thee?' And the answer came: 'O liar—if you were content with Me, you would not

18. *Sanāʾīʾābād*, line 317.

ask whether I am content with you' " (T 2:290). In perfect *riḍā* the mystic should not think about whether or not God has accepted his act of resignation and contentment; he should accept every divine decree, be it wrath or grace, with equanimity and joy. This interior joy, this perfect agreement with God's decrees, transforms the beggar into a king and opens the way toward a participation in the divine will, toward love and "higher predestinarianism."

The mystics differ in their opinions as to whether "fear" and "hope" (*khauf* and *rajāʾ*) are stations or states (Sarrāj feels that they are states). Psychologically, one would prefer that they be classified among the stations, for they belong to the essential and long-standing aspects of mystical life in its primary stages, and even at later levels. To feel fear is essential for every pious Muslim. Did not the Koran speak often of the fear of God, or fear of the Judgment, and does it not contain enough warnings to make the heart of even the most pious tremble with fear? But hope is just as essential, for life would be impossible without hope, and "fear and hope are the two wings of action without which flying is impossible" (L 62). Or, as Sahl saw it: fear is a masculine element, hope a feminine one, and the two together engender the deepest realities of faith (K 89).

The early ascetics emphasized the aspect of fear more than that of hope. They even went so far as to attest that a man who lives in fear inspires his neighbors' trust, for they know that they are secure from his machinations and need not suspect him of meanness (W 223). But even a representative of pure love mysticism, like Rūzbihān Baqlī, praises fear of God as the "whip of divine power [*jabarūtī*], which hits the soul that commands to evil with the lash of 'decent behavior' [*adab*]" (BA 223). The chapter on "Fear and Hope" in Ghazzālī's *Iḥyāʾ ʿulūm ad-dīn* reflects very well the different attitudes of the faithful in regard to these states and demonstrates the strength of the feeling that an equilibrium between both forces is absolutely necessary for a sound religious life (G 4:288).[19]

In the course of time, hope proved stronger than fear, though the advanced mystics knew fear as well and even rejoiced in it. But in their case it is no longer the fear of God's judgment or the terrors of Hell that keeps them on the watch, but rather the fear of God's

19. Al-Makkī, *Qūt*, 2:58ff. See the definition in al-Khānqāhī, *Guzīda*, p. 22: "Who worships God only by fear, is a *ḥarūrī* (i.e., Kharijite), who worships him only by hope is a *murjiʾite,* and who worships him by love, is a *zindīq*, heretic"; only a balanced combination of the three elements constitutes a true Muslim.

makr, His "ruses." In the moment of perfect happiness the mystic can never be sure that God will not use this exalted state as a snare to capture him, to tempt him once more to worldly thought, pride, hypocrisy, to distract him from his highest goal. Miracles, for instance, could be interpreted as divine ruses, for they are still connected with the world; even the small joys of daily life might hide ruses of God that should be feared. And who can be sure that he will be saved or accepted by God? One can hope for it, but never without fear.

However, the notion of "thinking well" of God, i.e., of trusting in His promise to forgive the sinner, proved stronger in mystical life. Did not the tradition attest that God's grace precedes His wrath? Out of this faith grew the whole prayer life of the Sufis. Just as the firm belief in God's unending mercy and the hope for His loving-kindness permeate the prayers of an early Sufi like Yaḥyā ibn Muʿādh, later mystics always relied upon the principle of hope, as Rūmī put it in a lovely comparison:

> [Is there anyone] who has sown the corn of hope in this soil
> to whom the spring of His grace did not grant hundredfold [fruit]?
>
> (D 1253)

But neither fear nor hope is required any longer once the wayfarer has reached his goal:

> The seaman is always on the planks of hope and fear—
> when the plank and the man become annihilated, there remains only submersion.
>
> (D 395)

The stations of fear and hope correspond, in the states, to what is called *basṭ* and *qabḍ*. *Basṭ,* from the root "to get wider and enlarge," means an extension of enthusiastic feeling, a perfect joy and ease that may develop, in some cases, into true "cosmic consciousness," into the feeling of partaking of the life of everything created, into that rapture of which the intoxicated poets of Iran and Turkey have sung so often. It is this state that inspired them to invent long lines of anaphora circling around the beauty of the divine beloved —verses that tried to describe His ineffable, sparkling glory or convey to others the state of happiness in which the whole world is seen in a changed light, transparent and filled with opaline colors of exquisite beauty.

> What is *basṭ*? To leave off the two worlds in one rapture,
> to cast oneself on a hundred new worlds!
>
> (U 42)

But whereas *basṭ* is the experience of extension and perhaps intensification of the self, *qabḍ*, "constraint," means the compression of the soul—"to make one's home in a needle's eye" (U 42)—darkness, the oppressing desert of loneliness in which the mystic spends days and sometimes months of his life. Nevertheless, *qabḍ* has been regarded as superior to *basṭ* by some leading mystics, for, as Junayd says, "when He presses me through fear he makes me disappear from myself, but when He expands me through hope He gives me back to myself" (G 33). In *qabḍ*, the "I" disappears, which is preferable to the extended self-consciousness produced by *basṭ*. In the state of *qabḍ*, the "dark night of the soul," man is left completely to God, without any trace of himself, without strength to want anything; and it is out of this darkness that the light of unitive experience, or of vision, may suddenly appear—like the "sun at midnight."

It is clear, from the previous definitions, that the mystics were fond of the juxtaposition of corresponding states. The manuals enumerate long lists of such mystical states, the true implications of which are difficult for the uninitiated to understand. They speak of *ḥuḍūr wa ghaiba*, "presence and absence," which can be defined as "presence near God and absence from oneself," or vice versa. *Jamᶜ*, "collectedness" and "perfect unification," goes together with *tafriqa*, "separation after union." *Sukr*, "intoxication," is combined with *ṣaḥw*, "sobriety." Eventually the complementary stages of *fanā*, "annihilation," and *baqā*, "duration, remaining in God," are reached. The pair *sukr* and *ṣaḥw* is of special importance to mystical terminology and has been mentioned in connection with Junayd's criticism of Bāyezīd. True sobriety is defined by Hujwīrī as "reaching the goal" (H 230), and the same author says that one of his mystical masters said: "Intoxication is the playground of children, but sobriety is the death-field of men" (H 186).

Before a discussion of the last stations and states on the Path and its goal, a definition that enables a better understanding of some Sufi formulations should be mentioned. It is the word *waqt*, literally, "time," which came to designate the "present moment," the moment in which a certain mystical state is granted to the Sufi. "Time is a cutting sword"; it cuts whatever is before and after it and leaves man in absolute nakedness in the presence of God. The Sufi has therefore been called *ibn al-waqt*, "the son of the present moment," i.e., he gives himself completely to the moment and receives what God sends down to him without reflecting about present, past, and future (cf. N 285). But on the highest level of experience, when the Sufi turns into a *ṣāfī*, "pure," it may be said:

> The Sufi is "son of the Moment" . . .
> The *Ṣāfī* is submerged in the Light of the Majestic,
> not the son of anything, and free from "times" and "states."
>
> (M 3:1426, 1433–34)

LOVE AND ANNIHILATION

The last stations on the mystical path are love and gnosis, *maḥabba* and *maʿrifa*. Sometimes they were considered complementary to each other, sometimes love was regarded as superior, and at other times gnosis was considered higher. Ghazzālī holds: "Love without gnosis is impossible—one can only love what one knows" (G 4:254). The Sufis have tried to define the different aspects of *maʿrifa*, knowledge that is not reached by discursive reason but is a higher understanding of the divine mystery. In later times the term *ʿārif*, "gnostic," has often been used for the advanced mystic in general, for "the faithful sees through God's light, the gnostic sees through God" (L 41). Most of the mystics would agree with the mystical interpretation of Sūra 27:34, "Kings destroy a town when they enter it"; the "king" is interpreted as *maʿrifa*, for this divinely inspired knowledge empties the heart completely of everything so that nothing but God is contained in it (W 170). The scholars and theoreticians of Sufism, like Hujwīrī (H 267), have written many definitions of *maʿrifa*, but the most poignant formulation is that of Junayd: "Gnosis . . . is the hovering of the heart between declaring God too great to be comprehended, and declaring Him too mighty to be perceived. It consists in knowing that, whatever may be imagined in thy heart God is the opposite of it" (K 133).

We shall dwell here mainly upon those mystical currents in which love was praised as the highest possible state, following St. Augustine's dictum, *res tantum cognoscitur quantum diligitur,* "one can know something only insofar as one loves it."[20] The prayer ascribed to the Prophet is a good starting point: "'O God, give me love of Thee, and love of those who love Thee, and love of what makes me approach Thy love, and make Thy love dearer to me than cool water" (G 4:253). In early Sufism the problem of love was the central point of divergence. Orthodoxy accepted *maḥabba* only as "obedience," and even some of the moderate mystics would say that "to love God means to love God's obedience" (T 1:287) or, "true love is to act in the obedience of the beloved" (N 55). Abū Ṭālib al-Makkī sums up the ideas of moderate Sufism: "The Prophet of God made love of God a condition of faith by saying that God and His messenger should be more beloved to the faithful than anything else."[21] And the Sufis were certain that "nothing is dearer to God than that man loves Him" (T 1:321).

When Dhū'n-Nūn expressed the thought that "fear of Hellfire, in comparison with fear of being parted from the beloved, is like a drop of water cast into the mightiest ocean,"[22] he stated very well the main object of this early love mysticism. His younger contemporary, Sarī as-Saqaṭī in Baghdad, who had first formulated the idea of mutual love between man and God, uttered the same feeling in a prayer that has been preserved by Hujwīrī:

> It is the custom of God to let the hearts of those who love Him have vision of Him always, in order that the delight thereof may enable them to endure every tribulation; and they say in their orisons: We deem all torments more desirable than to be veiled from Thee. When Thy beauty is revealed to our heart, we take no thought of affliction. (H 111; cf. A 10:120)

It was apparently Sarī's nephew Junayd who discovered the truth: "Love between two is not right until the one addresses the other, 'O Thou I' " (T 2:29).

The whole complex of love was so inexhaustible that the mystics

20. See "Love, Muhammadan," in *Encyclopedia of Religion and Ethics*, ed. James Hastings, 13 vols. (1908-27), 8:176; Ignaz Goldziher, "Die Gottesliebe in der islamischen Theologie," *Der Islam* 9 (1919), a fundamental study of the early development of mystical love in Islam. Annemarie Schimmel, *Studien zum Begriff der mystischen Liebe im Islam* (Marburg, 1954); Schimmel, "Zur Geschichte der mystischen Liebe im Islam," *Die Welt des Orients*, 1952. A number of scholars have maintained that "love" constitutes the essence of Sufism; see, for example, Mir Valiuddin, *Love of God* (Hyderabad, Deccan, 1968), or the anthology by René Khawam, *Propos d'amour des mystiques muslumanes* (Paris, 1960), and many popular writings.

21. Al-Makkī, *Qūt*, 2:50.

22. Reynold A. Nicholson, *The Mystics of Islam* (1914; reprint ed., Chester Springs, Pa., 1962), p. 116.

invented different stages and used different terms to classify it; yet the definitions given for *ḥubb, maḥabba, wudd,* and *mawadda* are by no means clear. The usual classification of the stages in love dates back to early times. Bāyezīd spoke of the fourfold nature of love: "It has four branches: one from Him, that is His grace, one from you, that is to obey Him, one for Him, and that is your recollecting Him, and one between both of you, and that is love" (A 10:242). Abū Ṭālib al-Makkī knew nine aspects of love, and Hujwīrī gives a classification of the lovers, which Ghazzālī adopted as well, in slightly elaborated form: "Those who regard the favor and beneficence of God toward them and are led by that regard to love the Benefactor, and those who are so enraptured by love that they reckon all favors as a veil and by regarding the Benefactor are led to [consciousness of] His favors" (H 308). As in most of the mystical states, some reach love by more or less rational arguments, ascending from the created to the creator, whereas others are completely lost in the vision of the creator and are brought to contemplate created things only because they are witnesses of His greatness.

Among the different stages of love, the Sufis have mentioned *uns,* "intimacy"; *qurb,* "proximity"; *shauq,* "longing"; and others. The sequence differs according to their personal experiences. The ascending steps are charmingly described in the saying: "The hearts of the gnostics are the nests of love, and the hearts of the lovers are the nests of longing, and the hearts of the longing are the nests of intimacy" (A 10:362). Complete submersion in intimacy is illustrated in the story of a Sufi whose master placed him in a lonely corner. The master then completely forgot him for a week, but when he came and asked his guest to forgive him, the Sufi answered: "Do not worry, God has taken away the fear of loneliness from His friend" (N 94)—the intimacy with God leaves no room for *waḥshat,* "feeling frightened by loneliness." The term *waḥshat* is usually meant as a complementary term to *uns*—it includes the feeling of loneliness in the wilderness, far away from the intimacy and tranquility of home, but also the estrangement from everything created that the Sufi feels in his intimacy with God (G 4:291). *Uns,* on the other hand, is connected with the aspects of divine *jamāl,* the manifestation of God's loving and consoling qualities, and, as such, it is contrasted with *hayba,* "reverence, awe," which awakens in the Sufi's heart at the manifestation of God's grandeur and power (cf. A 9:377).

As to *qurb*, "proximity," the Sufis have always been eager to define it other than spatially; it is an ethical proximity, brought forth by the fulfillment of God's orders, the opposite of separation from God, caused by man's disobedience (H 148). Later mystics invented a complicated system of different grades of *qurb*, like "proximity of the attributes" and "proximity of the names," which refer to the degree to which one is invested with higher, loftier divine attributes. The term *qurb an-nawāfil*, "proximity caused by supererogative works of worship," goes back to a *ḥadīth qudsī* that must have been in circulation in very early times. God says:

> My servant ceases not to draw nigh unto Me by works of devotion, until I love him, and when I love him I am the eye by which he sees and the ear by which he hears. And when he approaches a span I approach a cubit, and when he comes walking I come running. (L 59)

The Naqshbandiyya school in India, however, prefers the *qurb al-farā'iḍ*, caused by the punctual performance of the prescribed ritual duties and as such the "state of the prophets," to the *qurb an-nawāfil*, which is, for them, the station of the saints. It should be added that some mystics would not accept the term *qurb* at all, since it presupposes a duality between lover and beloved, while true Sufism consists of realizing unity (N 222).

This same feeling has led some mystics to deny the station of "longing," for one longs for someone absent, and God is never absent (N 222). Contrary to those who considered longing unnecessary, if not illicit, for a true lover lives constantly with Him who is "closer to you than your jugular vein" (Sūra 50:16), others would boast of their longing, like Bāyezīd: "If the eight Paradises were opened in my hut, and the rule of both worlds were given in my hands, I would not give for them that single sigh which rises at morning-time from the depth of my soul in remembering my longing for Him . . . " (T 1:159).

Others, again, would claim that genuine longing has no end, since the beloved has no end. The more the mystic approaches the divine beloved, the more he apprehends the fathomless depth of His qualities, the abyss of His essence: therefore his longing to plumb deeper and more wonderful mysteries can never end. Ghazzālī has described this state perfectly in the relevant chapter in the *Iḥyā' 'ulūm ad-dīn* (G 4:277). It is this dynamic force of love and longing that has inspired so many Persian poets.

Every moment this love is more endless,
in every time people are more bewildered in it,
(U 9)

says ᶜAṭṭār, and Ḥāfiẓ continues:

The adventure between me and my beloved has no end—
That which has no beginning cannot have an end.

How could this love, inspired by God, be adequately described?

It is greater than a hundred resurrections,
for the resurrection is a limit, whereas love is unlimited.
Love has got five hundred wings, each of them reaching from the Divine Throne to the lowest earth.
(M 5:2189–90)

That is how Rūmī tries to explain the grandeur of love, and ᶜUrfī, in the late sixteenth century, admonishes the lover not to be heedless, "for in that sacred station of love there are a hundred places, the first of which is resurrection!"[23]

The only means of drawing near to the divine beloved is by constant purification and, in exchange, qualification with God's attributes. Junayd has defined this change brought forth by love: "Love is the annihilation of the lover in His attributes and the confirmation of the Beloved in His essence" (H 40). "It is that the qualities of the Beloved enter in the place of the qualities of the lover" (L 59). Many centuries later, Shāh Walīullāh of Delhi (d. 1762) invented an apt symbol for this spiritual purification, using the traditional image of the fire of love: man, like a piece of ice, will be put in a kettle on the flames; thus he will melt, become warm, boil, and eventually, evaporating as steam, be as close as possible to the quality of heat inherent in divine love.[24]

Ghazzālī has compared this purifying love to the "good tree whose root is firm and whose branches are in the sky," as described in the Koran (Sūra 14:24); the fruits show themselves in the heart, on the tongue, and on the limbs (G 4:282). These fruits are obedience to the orders of God and constant recollection of the beloved, which fills the heart and runs on the tongue—the importance of

23. ᶜUrfī-yi Shīrazī, *Kulliyāt*, ed. Ali Jawāhiri (Tehran, 1336 sh./1957), p. 305.

24. Shah Walīullāh, *Saṭaᶜāt*, ed. Ghulām Muṣṭafā Qāsimī (Hyderabad, Sind, 1964), no. 40.

recollection for the development of love has often been emphasized by the mystics (see pp. 167–78). This love is a flame that burns everything except the beloved (M 5:588), just as longing is God's fire, which He kindles in the hearts of His friends to burn down everything that may occupy their hearts (L 64).

Obedience, as the Sufis understood it, is complete surrender—acceptance of the will of the beloved whether it manifests itself in kindness or in wrath. Love neither diminishes by cruelty nor increases by kindness (H 404); and the lover has to remain at the door of the beloved even if driven away—he has "to make his soul a broom at His door" (T 2:193). But even that degree of surrender was not enough for later generations, since it implies a shade of self-will:

> I want union with him, and he wants separation;
> thus I leave what I want so that his wish comes true
> (G 4:117)

—that is how the true lover should act. Pain and death are welcome if the beloved decrees it.

> If you would say "Die!" I would die in full obedience,
> and would say "Welcome to him who calls me to death."
> (N 96; A 10:301)

For death means the annihilation of the individual qualities, the lifting of the veil that separates the primordial beloved from the lover created in time.

"There is nothing good in love without death" (G 4:300); death may be understood as dying to one's own qualities or even as corporeal death, since this leads the lover toward the beloved (A 10:9). The tradition "die before ye die" gave the Sufis the possibility of pondering the implications of the slaying of the lower qualities and the ensuing spiritual resurrection in this life (cf. U 10). But "outward" death was also an aim in itself, as the case of Ḥallāj shows—to lift the disturbing "I" that stands between lover and beloved. Ghazzālī relates a touching story about Abraham, who was called by the angel of death and refused to follow him, since he could not believe that God would kill someone who had loved him so much. But he was addressed: "Have you ever seen a lover who refuses to go to his beloved?" Upon hearing this, he gladly submitted his soul to the angel (G 4:253). The lover who has learned to accept death as a bridge to the beloved should "give his soul with a smile like a rose" (M 5:1255); that is why Ḥallāj danced in fetters when he was led to execution. The idea that the martyr is granted special heavenly privileges, as the Koran attests, has, perhaps, helped in shaping the idea of the "martyr of love," who enjoys a special position with God when he is killed by the sword of longing or has died on the thorny path that leads toward the beloved, where thousands of hearts and livers adorn the thornbushes like red flowers, as Ghālib depicts the way of love. The mystics would rely on the Koranic word: "Do not call them dead who have been slain for God's sake—nay, they are alive" (Sūra 3:163; B 281). It is the sword of *lā*, the first half of the profession of faith, that slays the lover (M 3:4098), and then there remains nothing "but God" (M 5:589). The recompense of those slain by love is more precious than anything else. The Sufis know a wonderful *ḥadīth qudsī*, which was revealed to Shiblī when he asked God about the meaning of Ḥallāj's martyrdom: "Whom My love kills, for him shall I be blood money." The martyr of love will be rewarded by God Himself, no longer separated from Him for whose love he has shed his blood.

Ideas such as these have led the mystics to accept willingly all kinds of tribulations, which were even regarded as signs of special kindness from God. "He is not sincere in his love who does not enjoy the stroke of the friend" (L 50). But even that was not enough—the sincere person is the one who forgets the stroke when looking at the friend.[25] Out of these ideas about suffering, later Sufi poetry developed the motif of the physician who wounds the patient and heals him, the wound being healed only by the one who caused it (A 10:273). Tribulations and afflictions are a sign that God is near, for, to quote Ḥallāj's daring sentence again, "Suffering is He Himself." The more He loves a person, the more He will test him, taking away from him every trace of earthly consolation so that the lover has only Him to rely upon (A 9:345). It is small wonder that a *ḥadīth* about this suffering was very common among the Sufis: "The most afflicted people are the prophets, then the saints, and then so forth." The prophets, being nearest to God, have to suffer most, as is attested to by many Koranic stories, which were embellished in the course of time; and the list of suffering lovers becomes longer from century to century. Affliction, *balā*ʾ, is ingeniously combined with the word *balā*, "Yes," that the souls spoke at the

25. Al-Makkī, *Qūt*, 2:67.

Day of the Covenant, thus accepting in advance every tribulation that might be showered upon them until Doomsday (SD 41; U 133). Just as grape juice is purified by the constant "tribulation" of fermenting until it becomes pure wine, and just as wheat is ground and kneaded and apparently mistreated until it becomes bread, thus the human soul can mature only through suffering. And when the ascetic seeks God's loving-kindness and forgiveness (*raḥma*), the lover seeks his pain (*zaḥma*)—a meaningful pun of Persian poets.

This indulgence in suffering, the feeling that affliction is the fastest steed to bring man to perfection (as Meister Eckhart said just at the time that the greatest Sufis expressed these views)—this attitude has contributed to the development of a certain imagery in later Sufi poetry that is difficult for uninitiated Western readers to appreciate and that has even caused misunderstanding among modern Islamic thinkers. It is an imagery that compares, for example, the lover to the polo ball, rolling without head and feet wherever the friend's polo stick drives him.

Before the tenth century, however, discussions about mystical love and longing were conducted mainly on the theoretical level. The question was one of semantics. The word *maḥabba* had been objected to by the orthodox, but when the first attempts were made to introduce the word *ʿishq*, "passionate love," into the relation between man and God, even most of the Sufis objected, for this root implies the concept of overflowing and passionate longing, a quality that God, the self-sufficient, could not possibly possess; nor was it permissible that man should approach the Lord with such feelings. Nūrī, who probably introduced the use of the word *ʿishq*, defended himself by declaring that "the *ʿāshiq* 'lover' is kept at a distance, whereas the *muḥibb* 'lover' enjoys his love" (B 289).

It was left to Ḥallāj openly to express by this term the inner dynamics of the divine life—"le désir essentiel," as Louis Massignon calls it—an idea that was to influence later Sufi thought decisively until Fakhruddīn ʿIrāqī poetically changed the words of the profession of faith into *lā ilāha illāʾl-ʿishq*, "there is no deity save Love," a formulation that I often heard from Turkish Sufis.

The discussions on mystical love became more complicated in the Baghdad circles about 900, with the introduction of the notion of *ḥubb ʿudhrī*, "platonic love." Jamīl, a noted poet from the tribe of ʿUdhrā in the late seventh century, had sung of his chaste love for Buthayna in delicate verses that almost foreshadow the love lyrics of Spanish and French troubadours; and soon a *ḥadīth* was coined, according to which the Prophet had said: "Whoever loves and remains chaste, and dies, dies as a martyr."

It was Muḥammad ibn Dāʾūd, the son of the founder of the Zahirite law school who composed, in Ḥallāj's day, a book on the ideal chaste love, containing one hundred chapters of poetry about *ḥubb ʿudhrī* and stressing the necessity of the "martyrdom of chastity." He and his followers denied the possibility of mutual love between man and God and excluded every human object from mystical love. Yet two centuries later the two currents merged in the verses of some of the greatest Persian mystical poets.

Another accusation brought against the love theories of the Sufis was that they represented Manichaean ideas. Worship of God by love is the sin of the Manichaeans, the heretics par excellence who imagine that their souls are particles of the eternal divine light, imprisoned in the body, and that a magnetic attraction from the origin of this love will attract them to become united with their origin again. This interpretation is incorrect for the early stages of mystical love, but it points to a development that was inherent in Sufi love theories: love became, with many of the later Sufis, the "growing power" that causes the possibilities of perfection in everything to unfold.[26] The "essential desire" of Ḥallāj's God often turns into a more or less magnetic force that has caused emanation and draws everything back to its source.[27]

But love as experienced by the early Sufis is a strong personal and existential commitment. Ḥallāj did not even hesitate to place it higher than faith (*īmān*): "It is a primordial divine grace without which you would not have learned what the Book is nor what Faith is" (P 610). The mystics felt that the love they experienced was not their own work but was called into existence by God's activity. Did not the Koran attest: "He loves them, and they love Him" (Sūra 5:59)—a word that shows that God's love precedes human love? Only when God loves His servant can he love Him, and, on the other hand, he cannot refuse to love God, since the initiative comes from God (A 10:7). Love cannot be learned; it is the result of divine grace—"If a world would draw love into it, it could not do it, and if they would strive to reject it, they could not do it, for it is a

26. Ibn Sīnā, *"Risāla fiʾl-ʿishq": Traitée sur l'amour,* ed. August Ferdinand Mehren (Leiden, 1894).

27. Fritz Meier, "Das Problem der Natur im esoterischen Monismus des Islams," *Eranos-Jahrbuch* 14 (1946), p. 218, on Nasafī's theories.

gift, not an acquisition. It is divine" (H 398). The Sufis, deepening the general Muslim knowledge that the divine greatness overpowers everything, have always felt that man is far too weak to seek God.

> Not a single lover would seek union
> if the beloved were not seeking it,
>
> (M 3:4394)

sings Rūmī, three hundred years after these ideas had been formulated for the first time. The idea that God was "a hidden treasure that longed to be known" has grown out of this feeling of God's desire to love and to be loved. He is, as Muhammad Iqbal has said in our day, "like us, a prisoner of Desire."[28]

The Sufis have often tried to describe the state of the true lover in poetical images. Bāyezīd saw the springlike quality of love: "I walked in the steppe, it had rained love, and the soil was moist—just as the foot of man walks in a rose garden, thus my feet walked in love" (T 1:155). And Shiblī takes up this spring imagery, which was to become a central theme of Persian poetry: "The 'time' of the gnostic is like a spring day, the thunder roars and the cloud weeps and the lightning burns and the wind blows and the buds open and the birds sing—this is his state: he weeps with his eyes, smiles with his lips, burns with his heart, plays with his head, says the friend's name and roams around his door" (T 2:177). In descriptions like this, technical treatises on Sufism suddenly turn into sheer poetry. Many of these descriptions are couched in the form of a *ḥadīth,* which declares, "verily God has servants who . . .," or take the form of a *ḥadith qudsī,* like the one quoted by Ghazzālī:

> Verily, I have servants among my servants who love Me, and I love them, and they long for Me, and I long for them and they look at Me, and I look at them . . . And their signs are that they preserve the shade at daytime as compassionately as a herdsman preserves his sheep, and they long for sunset as the bird longs for his nest at dusk, and when the night comes and the shadows become mixed and the beds are spread out and the bedsteads are put up and every lover is alone with his beloved, then they will stand on their feet and put their faces on the ground and will call Me with My word and will flatter Me with My graces, half crying and half weeping, half bewildered and half complaining, sometimes standing, sometimes sitting, sometimes kneeling, sometimes prostrating, and I see what they bear for My sake and I hear what they complain from My love. (G 4:278)

28. Muhammad Iqbal, *Zabūr-i ʿajam* (Lahore, 1927), part 2, no. 29; trans. A. J. Arberry as *Persian Psalms* (Lahore, 1948), part 2, no. 29.

These lovers will be granted a special place at Doomsday, beyond the communities of the various prophets, and those who love each other in God will be on a pillar of red garnet and will look down on the inhabitants of Paradise.[29] But a description of mystical love is altogether impossible—no one could put this truth better than Sumnūn, surnamed "the Lover": "A thing can be explained only by something that is subtler than itself. There is nothing subtler than love—by what, then, shall love be explained?" (H 173).

Science would be of no avail on this Path—only the light of gnosis, the light of certainty gained through intuitive knowledge, could help in approaching the mystery of love. The sciences are like eyeglasses, which cannot see by themselves but stand between the eye and the objects, as a seventeenth-century mystic from Sind said, using a modern image but remaining, in substance, faithful to the traditional view. He explains by this image an alleged *ḥadīth* that calls *ʿilm*, "knowledge," the "greatest veil" separating man from God. On the way of love, intellect is like the donkey that carries books (Sūra 62:5); it is a lame ass, whereas love is like the winged *burāq* that brought Muhammad into the presence of God (D 1997).

The contrast between love and discursive reason provided an inexhaustible topic for later poets; they would like

> to hang intellect like a thief
> when love becomes the ruler of the country.
>
> (D 420)

Thus the figure of Majnūn, the demented lover, lost in his contemplation of Laila, might serve as a model for the mystical lover. Love is the most genuine quality of the human race. God created Adam out of love; Adam bears in himself the divine image, and no other created being can follow him in the way of love.

> When the angel falls in love,
> he is the perfect human.
>
> (U 96)

The mystics did not hesitate to give people who do not know love names such as "cow," "jackass," "hard stone," or "animal," based on the Koranic sentence, "they are like beasts, nay, even more

29. Abuʾl-Ḥasan ad-Daylamī, *Kitāb ʿaṭf al-alif al-maʾlūf ilāʾl-lām al-maʿṭūf*, ed. Jean-Claude Vadet (Cairo, 1962), § 101, § 363.

astray" (Sūra 7:178). The expression "lower than a dog" occurs (M 5:2008), for even animals know at least one aspect of love.

The most charming story in this respect, probably told first by ʿAṭṭār (U 129) and retold by ʿIrāqī, deals with a preacher in Shiraz who spoke so poignantly about love that everybody dissolved in tears. A man had inquired of him before the sermon whether by chance he knew where his lost donkey had gone. After the sermon, the preacher asked the community if there was anybody who had never experienced love.

> A certain fool ill-favored as an ass
> in sheer stupidity sprang to his feet.
> "Art thou the man, the elder asked, whose heart
> was never bound by love?" Yea, he replied.
> Then said the sage: "Ho, thou that hadst an ass,
> lo, I have found thine ass. The cropper, quick!"[30]

The genuine lover is the most honored person in both worlds, for the Prophet said: "Man is with him whom he loves." Thus the lover is constantly with God, whom he loves to the exclusion of everything else (T 2:85).

Love is, for the Sufis, the only legitimate way to educate the base faculties. The rules of asceticism in themselves are purely negative; as indispensable as they are, they have to be performed out of love. Only by this method can the *shayṭān*, the lower soul, be transformed —he becomes like Gabriel, and his demonic qualities die (M 6:3648). Having reached this stage, which may be called "loving *tauḥīd*," man sees with the eye of intuitive knowledge and understands the ways of God. Loving acceptance of God's will can resolve the enigma of free will and predestination in a higher unity.

Whether the final station be seen as love or as gnosis, the disciple has to continue in his preparatory activities, like *dhikr* and concentration, which may eventually lead him to the goal, *fanā* and *baqā*.[31] He should concentrate on perfect collectedness in contemplation (*murāqaba*), and from this point he may attain vision (*mushāhada*). But it is a vision that can be described only approximately as presence or proximity, combined with *ʿilm al-yaqīn*,

30. Fakhruddīn ʿIrāqī, *The Song of the Lovers (ʿushshāqnāme)*, ed. and trans. A. J. Arberry (Oxford, 1939), pp. 30 ff.

31. Reynold A. Nicholson, "The Goal of Muhammadan Mysticism," *Journal of the Royal Asiatic Society*, 1913.

"knowledge of certitude" (L 69). The station of sincere *ʿilm al-yaqīn* leads further to *ʿayn al-yaqīn,* "vision of certitude" or "essence of certainty"—the station of the gnostics—until it is consummated in *ḥaqq al-yaqīn,* the "real certitude" or "reality of certainty," which is the place of God's friends.[32] These terms are taken from Sūra 102 and Sūra 56:95, where they have, however, no mystical connotations at all. *Ḥaqq al-yaqīn* is attained in *fanā*; it has been symbolized, in Ḥallāj's *Kitāb aṭ-ṭawāsīn,* as the way of the moth, which experiences *ʿilm al-yaqīn* when it sees the light of the candle, *ʿayn al-yaqīn* when it draws near and feels its heat, and *ḥaqq al-yaqīn* when it is, finally, burned and consumed by the flame.

The true meaning of *fanā* has been one of the controversial topics in the study of Sufism. The German term *Entwerden,* as used by the medieval mystics, is closer to its meaning than words like "annihilation," "being naughted," or "passing away," since it is the opposite of "becoming," *werden.*

Some scholars have tried to equate *fanā* with the Hindu or Buddhist concept of nirvana, but this is incorrect. It is not the experience of being freed from a painful circle of existence, since Islam lacks the idea of karma and accepts the reality of the individual soul. *Fanā* is, in the beginning, an ethical concept: man becomes annihilated and takes on God's attributes—it is the place of the alleged *ḥadīth takhallaqū bi-akhlāq Allāh,* "qualify yourself with the qualities of God," i.e., through constant mental struggle exchange your own base qualities for the praiseworthy qualities by which God has described Himself in the Koranic revelation. The next stage is annihilation in vision, when the soul is surrounded by the primordial light of God. The third and final stage, then, is "annihilation from one's vision of annihilation," in which one is immersed in the *wujūd,* the "existence" of God or, rather, the "finding" of God. For the word *wujūd,* which is usually translated as "existence," means, originally, the "being found"—and that is what the mystic experiences. There is a well-known verse that points to existence as created in time:

> When I said: What have I sinned? she answered:
> Your existence is a sin with which no sin can be
> compared.
>
> (L 59)

32. Al-Khānqāhī, *Guzīda,* p. 208.

Man should recover the state he had on the Day of the Primordial Covenant, when he became existentialized, endowed with individual existence by God, which, however, involved a separation from God by the veil of createdness (cf. MM 65). This veil cannot be lifted completely during one's lifetime. The mystic cannot completely and substantially be annihilated in God, but he may be lost for a while in the fathomless ocean of bewilderment, as it has been defined by Kalābādhī: "*Fanā* . . . may consist of being absent from his own attributes, so that he appears to be really mad and to have lost his reason . . . . For all that he is preserved to perform his duties to God . . . . On the other hand he may be a leader to be followed, governing those who attach themselves to him" (K 131). The problem is whether or not the mystic can return to his own qualities after this experience: "The great Sufis . . . do not hold that the mystic returns to his own attributes after a passing away. They argue that passing-away is a divine bounty and fit for the mystic, a special mark of favour, not an acquired condition: it is a thing which God vouchsafes to those whom He has chosen and elected for Himself" (K 127).

The best interpretation of *fanā* and the following stage, *baqā*, has been given by the Japanese scholar Toshihiko Izutsu,[33] who explains *fanā* as "the total nullification of the ego-consciousness, when there remains only the absolute Unity of Reality in its purity as an absolute Awareness prior to its bifurcation into subject and object"—the state the Sufis would call *jam*ᶜ, "unification, collectedness." The Sufi experiences the return to the moment when God was, and there was nothing else. *Fanā* is "certainly a human experience . . . but man is not the subject of this experience. The subject is rather the metaphysical Reality itself"—we may think of Rūmī's attempt at clarifying the same state with an example taken from grammar: *māta Zayd*, "Zayd died," a sentence in which Zayd is the subject, but not the acting subject (M 3:3683).

Then man may reach the state of *baqā*, "persistence" or "subsistence" in God, and experience the "second separation" or "gathering of the gathering," *jam*ᶜ *al-jam*ᶜ: "Man is resuscitated out of the nothingness, completely transformed into an absolute Self. The multiplicity becomes visible again—but in a changed form, namely

33. Toshihiko Izutsu, "The Basic Structure of Metaphysical Thinking in Islam," in *Collected Papers on Islamic Philosophy and Mysticism*, ed. Mehdi Mohaghegh and Hermann Landolt (Tehran, 1971), p. 39f., an illuminating article.

as determinations of the one Reality." In this state, the mystic acts completely through God.

> When you seek *baqā*, request it from the dervishes—
> the dervishes are the warp and woof of the garment
> (*qabā*) of *baqā*,
>
> (SD 186)

says Sanāʾī, with a fine pun; but for most of the mystics *baqā* is connected particularly with the prophetic activity. God, who has promised the loving soul that he will "become his eye by which he sees," has shown this aspect of religious life, which is turned toward the world in the acts of the prophets. For after the Battle of Badr (624), Muhammad was addressed: "*Mā ramayta idh ramayta,* 'you did not cast when you cast, but God did it' " (Sūra 8:17). And although many Sufis claimed to have attained *baqā*, the distinction between the "saintly" and "prophetic" aspects of *fanā* and *baqā* gained new importance in later Sufi theories, mainly with the Naqshbandīs.

Fanā is not to be confused with *ittiḥād*, "union," a term that presupposes the existence of two independent beings and has, therefore, been regarded as heretic, as has *ḥulūl*, "indwelling," which means the incarnation of the divine in man. Orthodox Muslims accused not only the Christians, but also Ḥallāj and the representatives of love mysticism, of accepting the concept of *ḥulūl*. *Fanā*, however, is the nullification of the mystic in the divine presence.

Later mystics tried to explain the state of *fanā* and *baqā* in wonderful images. The metaphors of Islamic mysticism and philosophy are not merely poetic ornaments but are indicative of a peculiar way of thinking. The Sufis have, for instance, spoken of the experience of the Black Light—the light of bewilderment: when the divine light fully appears in the mystic's consciousness, all things disappear instead of remaining visible (medieval and Renaissance mystics in Germany would speak of the *überhelle Nacht*). Such is the experience of *fanā*—a blackout of everything until the mystic perceives that this blackness is "in reality the very light of the Absolute-as-such," for existence in its purity is invisible and appears as nothing. To discover the clarity of this black light is to find the green water of life, which, according to the legends, is hidden in the deepest darkness—*baqā*, persistence in God, is concealed in the very center of *fanā*.

Ḥallāj had used the allegory of the moth and the candle to allude to the state of extinction. Rūmī, in order to explain Ḥallāj's unitive expression *anāʾl-Ḥaqq*, compares the mystic in this state to a piece of iron that is thrown into the furnace and becomes so hot that it regards itself as fire (M 2:1445), though a substantial union cannot be achieved. This imagery, known from Christian mysticism as well, is also found in the terminology of the Nūrbakhshī mystics in Iran (MM 129).

The same Rūmī has also interpreted Kharaqānī's saying—"there is no dervish in the world, and if there be a dervish, that is non-existent"—in a line that perhaps comes closest to elucidating the mystery of *fanā*:

> Like the flame of the candle in the presence of the sun,
> he is (really) non-existent, (though he is) existent in
> formal calculation.
>
> (M 3:3669–73)

One of the strangest symbols for the experience of *fanā* and *baqā* has been used by mystics from ʿAṭṭār to the eighteenth-century Indian Mīr Dard: The divine essence is compared to a salt mine, into which a dog, or a donkey, falls; thus, losing its low qualities, the animal is transformed into this element and preserved in it. The comparison is all the more fitting since *bā-namak*, "saltish," also means "cute, charming," and can thus be used to describe the charming beloved in whom the lover becomes completely absorbed.[34]

It is in this state of absorption that the mystics have sometimes uttered expressions that do not fit into the orthodox views, or even into moderate Sufism. The so-called *shaṭḥiyāt* (plural of *shaṭḥ*), like Ḥallāj's *anāʾl-Ḥaqq* or Bāyezīd's "Glory be to Me! How great is My Majesty!" are among the most famous of these "theopathic locutions" or paradoxes, to which Rūzbihān Baqlī has devoted a whole book. Their study is one of the most interesting, but also most difficult, topics in the history of Sufism, and the daring, partly jubilant, partly bewildered words that Rūzbihān has put together and interpreted in an existential, authentic way allow a glimpse into the depths of mystical experience, which, however, can never be appropriately expressed in human words.

34. The same expression has also been used for the tomb. For the imagery see Farīduddīn ʿAṭṭār, *Dīwān-i qaṣāʾid wa ghazaliyāt*, ed. Saʿīd Nafīsī (Tehran, 1339 sh./1960), no. 515; Jalāluddīn Rūmī, D 3041, M 2:1344, and M 6:1856; Khwāja Mīr Dard, "Dard-i Dil," no. 161, in *Chahār risāla* (Bhopal, 1310 h./1892–93).

Just as the mystics have constantly invented new symbols to describe the state of *fanā* and *baqā*, they have also attempted to show what *tauḥīd* is. *Tauḥīd*, "to declare that God is One," is the goal of religious life for the Muslim in general and for the Sufi in particular. Hujwīrī speaks of three kinds of *tauḥīd*: "God's unification of God, i.e. His knowledge of His Unity; God's unification of His creatures, i.e. His decree that a man shall pronounce Him to be one, and the creation of unification in his heart; man's unification of God, i.e. their knowledge of the Unity of God" (H 278). For the orthodox mystics, *tauḥīd* meant, first of all, the recognition that there is no agent but God and that everything and everybody are dependent upon Him. This idea could easily lead to the acknowledgment that only He had real existence and that only He had the right to say "I"—that God is the only true subject.

In the chapter on love in the *Iḥyā᾽ ᶜulūm ad-dīn*, Ghazzālī defines the orthodox way of reaching *tauḥīd* very clearly:

> Whoever looks at the world because it is God's work, and knows it because it is God's work, and loves it because it is God's work, does not look save to God and does not know save God, and does not love save God, and he is the true unifier (*muwaḥḥid*) who does not see anything but God, nay who does not even look at himself for his own sake but because he is God's servant—and of such a person it is said that he is annihilated in unification and that he is annihilated from himself. (G 4:276)

This is an elaborated formulation of what an earlier Sufi, quoted by Hujwīrī, had said: "Unification is this: that nothing should occur to your mind except God" (H 158). Junayd, in turn, has taken the idea of *tauḥīd* back to the Day of the Primordial Covenant:

> Unification is this, that one should be a figure in the hands of God, a figure over which His decrees pass according as He in His omnipotence determines, and that one should be sunk in the sea of His unity, self-annihilated and dead alike to the call of mankind to him and his answer to them, absorbed by the reality of the divine unity in true proximity, and lost to sense and action, because God fulfils in him what He hath willed of him, namely that his last state become his first state, and that he should be as he was before he existed. (H 282–83)

True *tauḥīd*, then, means to forget *tauḥīd* (B 383). It is a state in which the sharp-sighted are blinded and men of reason are confused (L 33). The poets have often repeated the verse:

> And in everything there is a witness for Him
> that points to the fact that He is One.
>
> (L 33)

The all-pervading presence of God as witnessed by the *muwaḥḥid* has often been expressed by the Sufis in the saying, "I did not see anything without seeing God before it and after it and with it and in it." Some parts of this sentence can be traced back to early Sufism and have been attributed by some later writers to the first four caliphs of Islam as representing the four different approaches of one who confesses *tauḥīd*.[35] But Hujwīrī has given the more correct version—Muhammad ibn Wāsiᶜ said: "I never saw anything without seeing God therein," which indicates an advanced stage of contemplation in which the mystic sees only the agent. This insight can be developed through perfect faith and is *istidlālī*, "gained through inference." Shiblī, however, exclaimed: "I never saw anything except God." Enraptured (*jadhbī*), he sees only God, nothing else (H 91, 330).

It was easy to move from Shiblī's statement to the feeling expressed in so many Persian and Turkish verses: "In mosques and taverns, in pagan and Muslim only God I saw!" The mystics could support such expressions from the Koran: "Whithersoever ye turn, there is the Face of God" (Sūra 2:109), a sentence that forms one of the cornerstones of later mystical theories, supplying the Sufis with the proof that God, the only agent, the only true existent, is visible, to the enlightened mystic, in every shape and behind every disguise. As Sanāʾī's famous lines attest:

> The word that you speak about faith may be Hebrew or Syrian,
> The place that you seek for God's sake, may be Jablaqa or Jablasa.
>
> (SD 52)

From here it is only one step to the feeling of God's all-embracing presence that Persian poets since ᶜAṭṭār (U 223) have condensed in the sentence *hama ūst*, "Everything is He"—an interpretation of *tauḥīd* that has always been attacked by the more orthodox Sufis because it apparently denies the transcendence of God. It is from these enthusiastic expressions of unity, found in most of the Persian mystics in more or less outspoken form, that Western scholars have gained the impression that Sufism is nothing but measureless pantheism.

Sarrāj, though rather close to the beginnings of Sufi speculation,

35. Al-Attas, *The Mysticism of Ḥamza al-Fanṣūrī*, p. 265.

is certainly right when he says that the manifold definitions of *tauḥīd* defy explanation and convey only a weak shade of the reality—"and if one enters into explanation and expression, then its splendour becomes hidden and disappears" (L 31).

FORMS OF WORSHIP[36]

Ritual Prayer

One of the five pillars of Islam is the ritual prayer (*ṣalāt*; in Persian and in Turkish, *namāz*) to be performed five times a day at prescribed hours between the moment before sunrise and the beginning of complete darkness. In the Koran, night prayer was recommended but not made obligatory for believers. Early Muslim ascetics and mystics regarded ritual prayer, in accordance with the Prophet's saying, as a kind of ascension to Heaven, as a *miʿrāj* that brought them into the immediate presence of God. "Ritual prayer is the key to Paradise," says a tradition; but for the mystics, it was even more. Some of them connected the word *ṣalāt* with the root *waṣala,* "to arrive, be united"; thus, prayer became the time of connection, the moment of proximity to God (L 150). Did not the Koran repeatedly state that all of creation was brought into being for the purpose of worshiping God? Thus, those who wanted to gain special proximity to the Lord, and prove their obedience and love, were, without doubt, those who attributed the most importance to ritual prayer. They might even be able to make the angel of death wait until their prayer was finished (T 2:113).

One of the prerequisites of ritual prayer is that ritual purity (*ṭahāra*) be performed according to the strict rules laid down in the Prophetic tradition. The mystics laid great stress on the meticulous performance of the ablutions, which became, for them, symbols of the purification of the soul (H 293). A good translator of the feelings of his fellow mystics, Shiblī said: "Whenever I have neglected any rule of purification, some vain conceit will rise in my heart" (H 293). Hagiographical literature is filled with stories about

36. Friedrich Heiler, *Das Gebet*, 5th ed. (Munich, 1923); translated by Samuel McComb as *Prayer* (1932; paperback ed., New York, 1958), condensed and without the extensive critical apparatus of the original. Heiler's book is the best introduction to the problem as seen by a historian of religion. Edwin Elliot Calverley, *Worship in Islam, Being a Translation, with Commentary and Introduction, of al-Ghazzālī's Book of the "Iḥyāʾ" on the Worship* (Madras, 1925).

Sufis who indulged in ritual purification to the extent that they would perform the great ablution (*ghusl*) before every prayer or before visiting their spiritual director (N 292), which was, for them, a religious duty comparable to prayer. Some would purify themselves in a river even in the middle of the Central Asian winter; others would become enraptured at the very moment the water for ablution was poured over their hands.[37] And a number of Sufis boasted of being able to perform the morning prayer while still in ritual purity from evening prayer, meaning that they had neither slept nor been polluted by any bodily function. Some of them even reached a state of remaining in ritual purity for several days.

As for the details of ritual prayer, the early Sufis followed the prescriptions of the law exactly. They tried to imitate the model of the Prophet even in the smallest details. Since one tradition holds that Muhammad once performed the *ṣalāt* of tiptoe, some Sufis wanted to follow him in this peculiar way; but a dream vision informed one of them that this was reserved exclusively for the Prophet and that the normal believer need not imitate it (X 24). If confined to bed, they would repeat each prostration and movement twice, since, according to the tradition, "the prayer of the sitting man is worth only half that of the standing person" (X 39; cf. S 144). Stories are told about mystics who, though unable to walk or move at all, regained their strength the very moment the call to prayer was heard, but returned to their state of weakness as soon as they had performed their religious duty.

At the moment the mystic utters the *niya* (the intention to perform his prayer) with the correct number of *rakᶜa*s (units of prostration, genuflection, etc.), he expresses the intention to turn away from everything created. During prayer he feels as if he were waiting before God at Doomsday. Muḥāsibī has described well this feeling of overwhelming awe:

> What predominates in the heart of the mystic while he is at prayer is his sense of the mystery of Him in Whose Presence he stands and the might of Him Whom he seeks and the love of Him Who favours him with familiar intercourse with Himself, and he is conscious of that until he has finished praying, and he departs with a face so changed that his friends would not recognise him, because of the awe that he feels at the Majesty of God. It is so that one who comes into the presence of some king, or someone for whom he yearns and whom he fears, stands in his

37. Mīr ᶜAlī Shīr Qāniᶜ, *Tuḥfat ul-kirām* (Hyderabad, Sind, 1957), p. 386.

presence, with a different attitude from what was his before he entered and goes out with an altered countenance. And how should it not be so with the Lord of the world, Who has not ceased to be nor will cease to be, He Who hath no equal?[38]

Muḥāsibī's younger contemporary Kharrāz, "in a book in which he describes the etiquette of ritual prayer" (L 152 f.), makes us sense even more intensely the mystic's attitude as required in his *ṣalāt:*

When entering on prayer you should come into the Presence of God as you would on the Day of Resurrection, when you will stand before Him with no mediator between, for He welcomes you and you are in confidential talk with Him and you know in whose Presence you are standing, for He is the King of kings. When you have lifted your hands and said "God is most great" then let nothing remain in your heart save glorification, and let nothing be in your mind in the time of glorification, than the glory of God Most High, so that you forget this world and the next, while glorifying Him.

When a man bows in prayer, then it is fitting that he should afterwards raise himself, then bow again to make intercession, until every joint of his body is directed towards the throne of God, and this means that he glorifies God Most High until there is nothing in his heart greater than God Most Glorious and he thinks so little of himself that he feels himself to be less than a mote of dust.[39]

The most touching description of this state of awe, in which every limb joins in the worship until body and mind alike are directed toward God, is Rūmī's story of Daqūqī and his congregational prayer (M 3:2140–44, 2147–48):

Daqūqī advanced to perform the prayer: the company
were the satin robe and he the embroidered border.
Those [spiritual] kings followed his leadership,
[standing] in a row behind that renowned exemplar.
When they pronounced the *takbīrs,* they went forth from
this world, like a sacrifice.
O Imam, the [real] meaning of the *takbīr* is this: "We
have become a sacrifice, O God, before Thee."
At the moment of slaughtering you say *Allāh akbar*: even
so [do] in slaughtering the fleshly soul which ought to
be killed . . . .
Whilst performing the prayer [they were] drawn up in

38. Margaret Smith, *Readings from the Mystics of Islam* (London, 1950), no. 16. Al-Ḥārith al-Muḥāsibī, *Kitāb ar-riᶜāya li-ḥuqūq Allāh,* ed. Margaret Smith (London, 1940), p. 28.

39. Smith, *Readings,* no. 26.

Woman in trance at a saint's tomb in Pakistan.

Photograph by Dr. Jan Marek, Prague

ranks before God as at Resurrection, and engaged in self-examination and orisons.
Standing in God's presence and shedding tears, like one who rises erect on [the day of] rising from the dead.

Notwithstanding their eagerness to perform the *ṣalāt* punctually, some Sufis reached such a state of absolute absorption or rapture that ritual prayer seemed to constitute for them an interruption of their mystical state. Hujwīrī has defined the various types of mystics by their attitudes toward the *ṣalāt*: some hold that it is a means of obtaining the presence of God; others regard it as a means of obtaining absence (H 301). Some would pray hundreds of *rakʿa*s a day in order to remain in constant communion with God; others had to ask somebody else to count their *rakʿa*s during the act of prayer because they themselves were not capable of doing it, since, in their enraptured state, time could expand into thousands of years in one hour (N 455), so that the correct timing would escape them. Some mystics regarded *ṣalāt* as an ascetic discipline that was absolutely necessary to preserve and that the disciples had to follow carefully; others saw and experienced it as an act of divine grace. The Sufi who experienced mystical union through prayer would certainly prolong his *ṣalāt* by adding long litanies of supererogative *rakʿa*s to the basic, prescribed form, whereas the mystic whose rapture or contemplation was more or less interrupted by the prescribed ritual would certainly not perform more than the minimal requirements. When a Sufi was completely lost in ecstasy for a period of days, or even weeks, he was exempt from praying. There were mystics who were transported into an ecstatic state as soon as they pronounced the word "Allah" in the beginning of the call to prayer, without even reaching the next word, *akbar*, "most great" (N 281). And the mystical poets—beginning with Ḥallāj—often spoke of the state in which intoxication and perfect love would make them forget morning and evening and the times of ritual prayer.[40]

The Sufis have interpreted the meaning of the *ṣalāt* differently. Most of them would probably agree with Najmuddīn Kubrā's definition that prayer according to the *sharīʿa* is service, according to

40. Ḥusayn ibn Manṣūr al-Ḥallāj, "*Dīwān*, Essai de reconstitution by Louis Massignon," *Journal asiatique*, January–July 1931, Muqaṭṭaʿa no. 20; see Shiblī in N 181.

the *ṭarīqa,* proximity, and according to the *ḥaqīqa,* union with God.[41]

An esoteric interpretation might see in the different movements of the praying Muslim a representation of the movement of worship found throughout creation: the prostration reminds him of the vegetable state, the *rukūʿ*, "genuflection," of the animal state, and the upright position is the prerogative of human beings. Everything worships God in its own way. The angels spend eternities worshiping the Lord in a single attitude, according to their rank; only man can represent, in his different prayer movements, the fullness of adoration that is the duty of everything created.[42] This idea underlies a Bektashi poem in which the forms of prayer are connected with the name of Adam, the model of humanity:

> When you stand up, an *alif* is formed, ا
> In bending behold: a *dāl* is made; د
> When you have prostrated, a *mīm* takes shape: م
> That is, I tell you, to perceive man—Adam. ا د م
>
> (BO 207)

Other interpreters have seen in the Arabic letters of the name of Muhammad (محمد) the figure of man, prostrate before God. And Bedil, in the late seventeenth century, compares the human life to the movements of ritual prayer:

> Youth is standing upright, old age genuflection, and annihilation prostration.
> In existence and nonexistence one can do nothing but perform the ritual prayer.
>
> (Divan 1:386)

"The prostration of the body is the proximity of the soul" (M 4:11), for God Himself said in the Koran: "Prostrate and draw near" (*usjud waʾqtarib*; Sūra 96:19).

The formulae used during the ritual prayer were also interpreted according to their esoteric meaning—especially the *fātiḥa,* the first Sūra of the Koran, which is recited in Islam as often as, or perhaps even more than, the Lord's Prayer in Christianity:

41. Najmuddīn Kubrā, *Risāla fī faḍīlat aṣ-ṣalāt* (Istanbul Universitesi Kütüphanesi, Arab. 4530), 2b.

42. Henri Corbin, "Imagination créatrice et prière créatrice dans le soufisme d'Ibn Arabi," *Eranos-Jahrbuch* 25 (1956), p. 195.

Praise be to God, Lord of the worlds!
The Compassionate, the Merciful!
King on the day of reckoning!
Thee only do we worship, and to Thee do we cry for help.
Guide Thou us on the straight path,
The path of those to whom Thou hast been gracious; with whom Thou art not angry, and who go not astray.

A *ḥadīth qudsī* makes God declare that He has divided this prayer between Himself and His servant. Relying on this sentence, Ibn ʿArabī found in the seven lines of the *fātiḥa* the perfect expression of the relation between man and God: the first three lines are the action of the faithful directed toward the Lord, the fourth line is a reciprocal action, and the last three lines express the divine activity acting upon man.[43]

The different interpretations the Sufis give of the ritual prayer and its details would fill a large volume. They range from the simple act of obedience to the feeling that God himself performs the prayer, as Ibn al-Fāriḍ says in the *Tāʾiyya:*

Both of us are a single worshipper who, in respect to the united state, bows himself to his own essence in every act of bowing.
None prayed to me but myself, nor did I pray to any one but myself in the performance of every genuflexion.[44]

Even the mystical interpretations of ritual prayer were not sufficient to satisfy the mystic's thirst for more and more intimate discourse with his beloved. The problem of how such prayer might reach God has been posed more than once—perhaps most impressively by Niffarī, who was graced by God's address:

Thou desirest to pray all night, and thou desirest to recite all the sections of the Quran therein; but thou prayest not. He only prays all night who prays for Me, not for any known rosary or comprehended portion of scripture. Him I meet with my face, and he stays through My Self-subsistence, desiring neither for Me nor of Me. If I wish, I converse with him: and if I wish to instruct him, I instruct him.

The people of the rosary depart when they have achieved it, and the people of the portion of the Quran depart when they have read it; but my people depart not, for how should they depart?[45]

43. Ibid., p. 187.

44. Reynold A. Nicholson, *The Idea of Personality in Sufism* (1921; reprint ed., Cambridge, 1967), p. 19; verse 153–54 of the *Tāʾiyya*.

45. Niffarī, *Mukh.*, no. 50.1–2.

True prayer is constant. It cannot be limited to a number of *rakᶜa*s and portions of the Koran, but permeates man's whole being—an idea that in our day has been expressed once more by Muhammad Iqbal, who follows Rūmī's example.[46]

Free Prayer[47]

In part, the longing for more and more intense conversation with God was satisfied by the possibility of uttering free prayers. Adoration, as well as supplication, is an important part of the mystical prayer life, and if the classical rule *lex orandi lex credendi* can be applied anywhere, it certainly applies to the mystical circles in Islam.

"To be deprived of prayer (*duᶜā*) would be a greater loss for me than to be deprived of being heard and granted" (T 1:56). These words of one of the very early Sufis form a keynote for our understanding of the moderate Sufi viewpoint concerning prayer. Prayer can be classified as an intimate conversation, *munājāt*, between man and God, as an exchange of words of love that console the afflicted heart even if they are not immediately answered. It is "the language of yearning for the beloved" (Q 121). From this viewpoint, the importance of night prayer in mystical circles can be properly understood. According to the tradition, Ḥasan ibn ᶜAlī, the Prophet's grandson, was once asked:

> How is it that those people are most beautiful who pray at night?
>
> He said: Because they are alone with the All-Merciful who covers them with light from His light.
>
> (G 1:323)

And another mystic who neglected nightly prayer was accused by God: "He lies who claims to love Me, and when the night comes sleeps away from Me" (H 458). Night prayer, though perhaps worthless in the eyes of the common people, is "like a radiant candle" in God's eyes (M 3:2375).

Only the stern, quietistic mystics—in Islam as well as in other religions—doubted whether it was lawful to utter a prayer at all: God,

46. Annemarie Schimmel, "The Idea of Prayer in the Thought of Iqbal," *Moslem World* 48 (1958): 3.

47. Annemarie Schimmel, "Some Aspects of Mystical Prayer in Islam," *Die Welt des Islam*, n.s. 2 (1952): 2.

they thought, is "too mighty to be joined by prayer, or to be separated from by omitting to pray" (K 144). They thought that silent patience in affliction was more suitable than prayer. One of the leading Khurasanian ascetics and author of a book on renunciation (*Kitāb az-zuhd*), ʿAbdallāh ibn Mubārak, said: "It is about fifty years since I have prayed or wished anyone to pray for me" (Q 144).

Since everything is preordained, why pray? It would be better to leave oneself to complete *tawakkul* and practice perfect contentment with whatever has been sent by God. Even Dhūʾn-Nūn is reported to have told a man who asked him for a prayer: "If something has been preordained by God for you, then many unspoken prayers have already been heard; otherwise: what use has the drowning person for shouting? Only that he is the sooner drowned, and more water comes into his throat" (N 126). However, this attitude of perfect resignation cannot be regarded as typical for the Sufis in general. Most of them firmly believed in the necessity and importance of prayer, since God Himself had ordered in the Koran: "Pray, and I will answer!" (Sūra 40:62).

Ghazzālī, whose *Iḥyāʾ ʿulūm ad-dīn* contains a long chapter about free prayer, formulated an answer to the objection that prayer is incompatible with predestination: predestination includes the possibility of averting evil by prayer "in the same way as a shield averts the arrows: they work against each other" (G 1:298). He repeats here an idea that Yaḥyā ibn Muʿādh had expressed three centuries before him: "When fate meets me with a ruse of affliction, I meet it with a ruse of prayer" (A 10:53). It was Yaḥyā whose prayers echo the problem of sin and grace and always end in hopeful trust in God's forgiveness and help. In fact, the necessity of *istighfār*, "to ask forgiveness," is, as a rule, mentioned among the preparatory stages of true prayer. The early Sufis liked to ponder over the paradoxical relation between human weakness and divine power, and when ʿAṭṭār says in one of his poems:

> I am not, but all evil is from me,
> There is nothing but Thou, but all beneficence is from
> Thee,
>
> (AD 633)

he has given a sophisticated form to the bewilderment that is one of the characteristics of Sufi prayer life. Most of the great authorities on Sufism did, in fact, urge their disciples to continue prayer and to pray trustfully. The sixteenth-century Egyptian mystic Shaᶜrānī has described, in touching words, the dark night of the soul through which he had to pass for a month without being able to pray.[48]

Many mystical masters gave concrete prescriptions even for the so-called "free" prayer—suffice it to mention Ghazzālī's classification of *duᶜā* in the *Iḥyāʾ* (G 1:274), where the rules for each and every possible prayer are so detailed that they amount almost to a new branch of strictly organized worship and seem to lack any free movement of the heart. The correct timing of prayer and the correct attitude during the prayer were regarded as highly important, as was the outward form: rhymed prose, for example, should not be used in free prayer. Yet the great Sufis often composed their finest prayers in rhymed prose. Special importance is attributed to repetitions of prayer formulae and Koranic verses. Three, seven, fifteen, fifty, seventy, and one thousand are the most common numbers for the repetitions. These particular numbers are in accordance with the belief in magical numbers all over the world, but in Islam these rules are regarded as inherited from the Prophet and his companions.[49] The concept of the *duᶜā maʾthūr*, the prayer that is effective because it was first uttered by some pious person or inspired by the Prophet through a dream,[50] has greatly influenced Muslim popular piety, as Constance Padwick has shown in her fine book, *Muslim Devotions*.[51] Through this channel of "approved prayers" and "effective prayers," mystical piety was infused into the large masses and did more to form their religious consciousness than the formulae used in the prescribed ritual.

This popular devoutness of the heart is reflected in one of Rūmī's finest stories, that of the shepherd's prayer, in which Moses, representing established religion, is taught that the heart's stammering and helpless sighing, and even childish imagery in prayer, is more acceptable to God than learned and correct forms—provided the one praying utters his words in perfect sincerity and surrender:

48. ᶜAbdul Wahhāb ash-Shaᶜrānī, *Lawāqiḥ al-anwār al-qudsiyya* (Cairo, 1311 h./1893–94), p. 113.

49. Ignaz Goldziher, "Zauberelemente im islamischen Gebet," *Orientalische Studien Theodor Nöldeke zum siebzigsten Geburtstag gewidmet*, comp. Carl Bezold, 2 vols. (Giessen, 1906), 103 f., on "magical" elements in Muslim prayer.

50. See Abd al-Hamid Farid, *Prayers of Muhammad* (Karachi, 1960).

51. Constance E. Padwick, *Muslim Devotions* (London, 1960), one of the finest books on Muslim piety and religious life.

> Moses saw a shepherd on the way who was saying:
> "O God who choosest (whom Thou wilt):
> Where art Thou, that I may become Thy servant and sew Thy shoes and comb Thy head?
> That I may wash Thy clothes and kill Thy lice and bring milk to Thee, o worshipful One;
> That I may kiss Thy little hand and rub Thy little foot (and when) bedtime comes I may sweep Thy little room,
> O Thou to whom all my goats be a sacrifice, O Thou in remembrance of whom are my cries of ay and ah!"

Moses was horrified at these words: "What babble is this? What blasphemy and raving? Stuff some cotton into your mouth!" (M 2:1720–24, 1728). But he had to learn that the simple-minded shepherd had attained a higher spiritual rank than he, the haughty prophet.

The Sufis knew that prayer, in the sense of petition, is a prerogative of man—though everything created praises God in its own tongue, man alone can address God and speak of his sorrows and hopes, putting them before the wise Lord. Though He has preordained the course of the world, He wishes—as Kāzarūnī has pointed out (T 2:301)—to honor man by answering his prayers. Even more: God longs for human prayer and "He afflicts man out of yearning for his prayer" (L 136). A *ḥadīth* quoted by Qushayrī tells that God orders Gabriel not to answer the prayers of His beloved servant for the pleasure He takes in his voice, and Rūmī has illustrated this rather anthropomorphic view in a story in which he compares humans at prayer to nightingales and parrots, which are put into cages so that their owners may enjoy the sound of their sweet melodies. God loves these prayers, and so he grants them immediate fulfilment only when he dislikes the person who prays—just as one gives a piece of bread to an ugly, old beggar whom one wants to leave the door as soon as possible (M 6:4217–30). This is not a very lofty theological thought, but it is not unusual in Sufi poetry. Rūmī has also spoken of the scent of his burnt liver ascending through his burning prayers into the divine presence (M 5:2259)—strongly reminding us of the Old Testament imagery of the heart and liver as a burnt offering.

Another problem is the matter of how far one can press God in one's prayers. The true lover is allowed to use a language that does not befit common people; the rules of etiquette may be suspended in the relation between lover and beloved (T 2:29). In their lonely prayers, some mystics would utter words that would normally be considered irreverent, even crude, by the average believer (G 4:292). "Muslim Mystics' Strife with God" in their prayers forms a special chapter in the history of Sufism.[52] The numerous stories told by ʿAṭṭār in his epics show how deeply he was concerned with this problem. He depicts enraptured and demented people who leave aside every rule of orthodox prayer and even threaten God in order to obtain this or that favor. "One has to show Him the teeth!" says one of ʿAṭṭār's heroes (U 218) when he asks God to send him some food immediately for an unexpected guest—which food, of course, arrives from the unseen, to the great surprise of the visitors. Such prayers, unbridled by any formalities, are found in the Turkish popular tradition as well, mainly in Bektashi poetry. How often these poets followed Yūnus Emre's example of accusing God of having created a perfectly nonsensical arrangement for the Day of Judgment! Similar words can be heard even today when some village "saint" feels advanced enough to threaten God in order to gain his desired end—an act often approximating magic.

Frequently repeated in this kind of "strife with God," and especially in prayer-poems all over the Islamic world, is the complaint that God afflicts most those whom He loves most and who love Him most. Long lists of suffering prophets and mystics have been drawn up to show God His seeming injustice and, eventually, to bring about a glad acceptance of suffering if He sends it down on the praying mystic himself.

On the whole, the moderate Sufis agree that God's not answering every prayer eventually proves to be as useful for the petitioner as the granting of his wish would be. ʿAbduʾl-Qādir Gīlānī feels that such a divine reluctance keeps man constantly between fear and hope, the ideal state of the pious[53]—but, practically enough, he adds that every prayer that has not been answered will at least be written in the heavenly book on the credit side. "Many a prayer, if heard, would involve destruction, and it is divine wisdom not to answer it" (M 2:140), says Rūmī in the *Mathnawī*, where he frequently discusses those prayers that are not answered out of divine kindness,

52. Hellmut Ritter, "Muslim Mystics' Strife with God," *Oriens* 5 (1952).
53. See Walter Braune, *Die "Futūḥ al-ġaib" des ʿAbdul Qādir* (Berlin and Leipzig, 1933), pp. 100, 143.

because God knows that they would lead, eventually, to destructive results. The real value of prayer is to find consolation in the act of praying, by which human will is made to conform to the divine will. These ideas, so central to prayer theology, and thus to the whole religious life, were taken up once more by Muhammad Iqbal, who often speaks of the miraculous power of true prayer, which ends in a complete conformity of the human to the divine will, in a change and sublimation of man's hopes and anguish.

> He turns the dried-up seed of prayer into a marvelous date-palm,
> Just as in Mary's birth pangs her pain was rewarded by a shower of dates,
>
> (M 5:1188)

Rūmī says, with poetical imagery derived from the Koran (Sūra 19:25). Extreme mystics like the *malāmatiyya* seem to have been unhappy and disappointed when their prayers were answered, for they were afraid that such an unexpected favor might be a ruse, an attempt on the part of God to mislead them.

A prayer that will always be granted is the prayer for others. The formula of blessing and prayer for the Prophet was part of the prescribed ritual and has often been elaborated as a prayer to be recited a number of times on every occasion. One has to pray for one's parents, for those whom one loves, and for those who have aided, wittingly or unwittingly, in one's progress—even the highway robber who may have been a cause for one's repentance should be included in the mystic's prayer (M 4:81–99). Thus, many Persian, Turkish, and Urdu epic poems and numerous prose works end with an invitation to the reader to recite a prayer for the author and for the scribe. And one should remember the words of a mystic who longed for solitude with God but was constantly asked to teach people some steps on the mystical Path: "O God, whosoever distracts me from Thee, distract him from me by Thyself!" (N 54)—a prayer that would involve two noble goals.

It is understood that the Sufi should implore God not for worldly goods but only for spiritual bounty. For the advanced mystics, only God Himself—increase in His love, His vision—should be the object of all prayer. Nevertheless, we read and hear many legends about Sufi masters who were *mustajāb ad-duʿā*, "whose prayers were heard" so that "if he would ask for something God would certainly grant it." In illness and danger, in times of dearth and need, they would utter an effectual prayer for themselves or their fellow townsmen, and they were capable of punishing those who disagreed with them. The stories told about the miraculous powers of praying saints sometimes approach the realm of fairy tales and sheer magic—one sheikh was so powerful in his prayers that he was able to help restore a fallen angel to his place in the celestial hierarchy (N 379).

Some of the prayers practiced by certain Sufis—mainly in later periods—are in fact very close to magical incantation: the master played with the letters of the Arabic alphabet, he composed prayers by deriving every possible word from a particular Arabic root—for example, the root underlying a specific divine name—or wrote prayers in alphabetical order, filling them with certain words and letters that are considered powerful and impressive. The names of God, with their practical implications, were used according to the wish and need of the person praying; the number of repetitions required to make these names efficient is dependent upon the numerical value of the name (thus, *ar-raḥmān,* "the Merciful," has the numerical value of 229 and should be repeated that many times). Illness could be cured by applying the appropriate divine name; and to strengthen the power of prayers, strange-sounding words of non-Arabic origin and intricate names of angelic beings were added.

But true mystical prayer is the one in which trust in God, love, and longing are reflected. Not to ask for Paradise nor to express the hope of being saved from Hell—that is the ideal of the selfless love that should underlie every thought of the Sufi. The only reason a mystic might ask for Paradise would be his hope for the *visio beatifica,* but even that would not be accepted by the Sufis of later times. Bāyezīd Bisṭāmī expressed this absoluteness of the mystical quest—God spoke: "Everybody wants something from Me, only Bāyezīd wants Me Myself" (T 1:152).

Many centuries later, the mystical poet of Delhi, Mīr Dard (d. 1785) poetically described the true mystic's state in prayer: "The hand of the gnostic's prayer turns over the leaves of the booklet of involuntariness, similar to the leaves of the plane tree whose object is not to grasp the skirt of the rose of wish. They must follow the blowing of destiny's wind; in what manner it moves them they are moved."[54] The essence of mystical prayer is neither asking nor petitioning; its essence is everlasting praise and adoration. Daqqāq,

54. Dard, "Shamᶜ-i maḥfil," no. 118, *Chahār risāla.*

Qushayrī's master, classified prayer in the usual threefold way: "There are three degrees: to ask, to pray, to praise. Asking belongs to those who wish this world, praying to those who wish the other world, and praising to those who wish the Lord" (T 2:195). That corresponds to Qushayrī's enumeration of the stages of gratitude, culminating in "thanking for the thanking."

The Prophet's word—"I cannot reckon up Thy bounties and the infinite praise and thanksgiving due to Thee from me"—is the core of mystical piety. Even though the Sufi could feel in consonance with everything created in his constant adoration, he knew that neither his words of praise nor his silent worship was sufficient to express the gratitude and adoration that he owed to his creator.

> The darkness of the night and the brightness of the day, the beams of the sun and the light of the moon, the murmuring of the waters and the whispering of the leaves, the stars of the sky and the dust of the earth, the stones of the mountains, the sands of the desert and the waves of the oceans, the animals of water and land praise Thee.[55]

This is the feeling out of which the prayers of Dhūʾn-Nūn developed. In prayers of hymnic praise or calm admiration the mystical feeling of the Sufis found its most natural outlet. Out of this feeling, poetical prayers were written. The monorhymed forms of Arabic, and consequently Persian, Turkish, and Urdu poetry, are ideal vehicles for mystical experience, whether it be in the long *qaṣīda* (mainly a praise poem) or in the short *ghazal* (love poem). Outside the Arabic-speaking world, the rhyme was often extended by the addition of a *radīf*, an additional rhyme word or even a whole sentence that is repeated. Thus, the mystical poet can go on reiterating one of the divine names in the *radīf*, or by carefully chosen words emphasize his main goal. His longing seems to be more eloquent if repeated dozens of times in the same poetical utterance. The whole poem turns around one central idea, which is, by the different rhyme words, reflected from different angles, broken up, brought into a new pattern, at times uprising, at other times becoming a monotonous hammering. The constant call to God, the intense yearning and longing, fear and hope, are most impressively heard in the poetical prayers written in the Muslim world. A hybrid form, which became typical of later Persian poetry, combines love poem

55. [Jalāluddīn Rūmī?], *Aurād-i Maulānā* (Istanbul Universitesi Kütüphanesi, Arab. 148), fols. 25 ff.; see T 2:295.

and prayer so that it is often difficult to judge which level of experience the poem reveals. Rūmī's *ghazals* are wonderful specimens of this ambiguous style, which was refined by Ḥāfiẓ, in whose poems it achieved a fascinating iridescence. The poetical elaborations of classical prayers as found in the great mystical epics, like ʿAṭṭār's work or Rūmī's *Mathnawī*, are some of the finest examples of religious poetry in the Persian-speaking world.

A special genre, developed primarily in Iran and the countries under its cultural influence, is the *qaṣīda* in honor of the divine creator, which became in the course of time a sort of vehicle for the author's display of eloquence and erudition, filled with strange allusions and complicated antitheses. Most of the great writers of Iran and Indo-Pakistan have composed such praise hymns, in which they dwelt, in impressive, sometimes unexpected, images, upon the mystery of God's beauty and majesty, His grace and wrath, and the marvels of creation. And the more eloquent they were, the more they were inclined to confess in ever new forms their utter inability to correctly and aptly express their praise and adoration.

Persian, Turkish, and Urdu epics alike usually begin with a poem of invocation, which discloses the theme of the poem. When the poet sings about the love of Majnūn and Laila, he will praise God as the creator of love and beauty in his introductory hymn. When he intends to write a heroic epic, he may speak, first, of God's majesty, power, and wrath. In many hymns that begin as poetical descriptions of the divine glory and power, the poet becomes so enraptured by his own laudatory words that he turns from the impersonal "He" of description to the personal address "Thou" and ends in a prayer full of enthusiasm and love.

The perfect way of interpreting true mystical prayer was shown by Rūmī. He was asked: "Is there any way to God nearer than the ritual prayer?" In his work *Fīhi mā fīhi*, he answered:

> No, but prayer does not consist in forms alone. . . . Prayer is the drowning and unconsciousness of the soul, so that all these forms remain without. At that time there is no room even for Gabriel, who is pure spirit. One may say that the man who prays in this fashion is exempt from all religious obligations, since he is deprived of his reason. Absorption in the Divine Unity is the soul of prayer. (MC 1:371)

But Rūmī knew well that it is impossible to reach this mystical union by means of contemplation, and it is impossible by human effort even to utter any word of true prayer: everything is divine grace. All human thought, all human longing to reach God, is nothing but God's work.

The idea of the *oratio infusa*, the God-given prayer, can be understood in three different ways, according to the conception of *tauḥīd* the Sufi practices:

1) God the creator has preordained every word of prayer;
2) God, dwelling in the heart of man, addresses him and inspires him to answer; or
3) God, the unique existent, is both the object of prayer and recollection and the praying and recollecting subject.

God addressed mankind first by the address of love that was manifested on the Day of the Covenant—"Am I not your Lord?"—in order that man might praise Him and adore Him as the only object of worship. Abū Isḥāq al-Kāzarūnī is right in his prayer: "O God, Thy kindness toward us is without end, and it is of Thy kindness that Thou hast given us the grace to recollect Thee with the tongue and to thank Thee with the heart" (T 2:299). The Sufis' familiarity with this idea is indicated by an alleged *ḥadīth* that speaks of the prayer of Moses: "O Lord, Thou hast commanded me to be grateful for Thy blessing, and my very gratitude is a blessing from Thee."[56] This is, surely, a typical Sufi prayer. Centuries later, Ibn ʿAṭāʾ Allāh (d. 1309) prayed in the same manner: "O God, if Thou dost not give us faith, we have no faith, and if Thou dost not loosen our tongue for prayer, we do not pray."[57] For all human action depends upon God, is decreed by Him, and is performed in executing His eternal and everlasting will. Ibn Qayyim al-Jauziyya (d. 1350), known as an orthodox Muslim, says in his small *Kitāb asrār aṣ-ṣalāt*: "And He is the Most High who praises Himself through the tongue of the praising one; for it is He who brought the praise upon his tongue and into his heart and moved it with His praise. And it is man's duty to acknowledge that the praise he gives, God has given him by an act of grace and when he praises Him on account of this gift his praise demands another praise."[58]

The feeling that prayer was indeed inspired by God must have

56. Abu Bakr al-Kharrāz, *"Kitāb aṣ-ṣidq": The Book of Truthfulness*, ed. A. J. Arberry (Oxford, 1937), Arabic, p. 47; English, p. 38.

57. Aḥmad Ibn ʿAṭāʾ Allāh al-Iskandarī, *Munājāt* (Istanbul Universitesi Kütüphanesi, Arab. 1574), fol. 6b.

58. Ibn Qayyim al-Jauziyya, *Kitāb asrār aṣ-ṣalāt* (Istanbul Universitesi Kütüphanesi, Arab. 2347), fol. 14a.

been vivid among the first generations of Sufis. Abū Bakr al-Kattānī told his disciples: "He never loosens man's tongue for prayer nor makes them busy beseeching forgiveness of sins, without opening the door of forgiveness" (T 2:123). And Niffarī, the greatest theologian of prayer in the tenth century, was addressed by God: "To Me belongs the giving: if I had not answered thy prayer, I should not have made thee seeking it."[59] God, dwelling between the cortex of the heart and the heart, as Ḥallāj said in one of his prayer-poems, converses with His friends in a secret tongue, and they silently answer His speech.

Ḥallāj's lyrical prayers are the most sublime colloquies between man and God, the mystic's answer to God's eternal call: "I call Thee, no, Thou callest me unto Thee!"[60] God is the source of seeking, and the mystics knew what Rūmī expressed in one unforgettable verse:

> Not only the thirsty seek the water,
> the water as well seeks the thirsty.
>
> (M 1:1741)

Every love relation is mutual, inspired by the beloved and answered by the lover. The idea of prayer as a gift of divine grace, found in early Sufism just as in Christian theology, has been described by Rūmī in a poem that became famous at the very outset of oriental studies in Europe.[61] For many historians of religion it constitutes the most exquisite expression of Muslim mystical life. The poet tells the story of a man who

> cried "Allah" till his lips grew sweet with praising Him.
> The Devil said: O man of many words, where is the response "Here am I" to all this "Allah"?
> Not a single response is coming from the Throne—how long will you say "Allah" with grim face?
> He was broken-hearted and lay down to sleep; in a dream he saw Khiḍr amidst the verdure,
> Who said: Hark! You have held back from praising God: why do you repent of calling unto Him?
> He answered: No "Here am I" is coming to me in re-

59. Niffarī, *Mukh.*, no. 42.10.

60. Al-Ḥallāj, *Dīwān*, qaṣīda no. 1, verse 2; see also *Muqaṭṭaʿāt*, no. 59.

61. Annemarie Schimmel, "Maulānā Rūmī's Story on Prayer," *Yādnāme Jan Rypka*, ed. Jiří Bečka (Prague, 1967).

sponse; I fear that I am turned away from the Door.
Said Khiḍr: Nay; God saith: That "Allah" of thine is My "Here am I," and that supplication and grief and ardour of thine is My messenger to thee.
Thy fear and love are the noose to catch My favour,
Beneath every "O Lord" of thine is many a "Here am I" from Me.

(M 3:189–98)

Although this story has been criticized by Tholuck as leading to immanentism and self-contemplation, it seems that such a danger is out of the question if one compares the numerous verses of the *Mathnawī* that reveal the same idea, i.e., that prayer springs from God's presence in the heart and is answered even before it has been uttered.

Rūmī asked God:

Teach us to pray (M 2:2206).

Thou hast given and taught this prayer:
otherwise how could a rose garden grow out of the dust?

(M 2:2443)

Since prayer is given by God, He will respond in a mysterious way.

Both the prayer and the answer are from Thee.
At first Thou givest desire for prayer,
and at the last Thou givest likewise the recompense for prayers.

(M 4:3499)

A long list of similar prayers could be drawn from the *Mathnawī*. Rūmī often symbolizes the idea of *oratio infusa* through the image of man as the instrument on which God plays: he is the harp, touched by His hands so that it may give forth sound; he is the flute, which sings only when the divine breath first fills it. From whatever side one looks, prayer is always an answer to the divine address.

It is only natural that these ideas should have been elaborated and theoretically supported by Ibn ʿArabī and his followers. Henri Corbin has shown how the idea of prayer (prayer as the typical form of mystical experience) permeates the work of Ibn ʿArabī. Since the great master of Sufi theosophy has greatly impressed later Sufi thought and poetry, it would be easy to find hundreds of verses in Persian or Turkish poems like that of Ibn ᶜArabī's faithful interpreter Maghribī (d. ca. 1406), who expresses the theories of transcendental unity of being in prayer form:

> And if I send Thee greetings, Thou art the greeting,
> and if I speak, Thou art the prayer.[62]

Dhikr[63]

Ritual and free prayer are aspects of Muslim spiritual life shared by mystics and nonmystics alike. But the distinctive worship of the Sufi is the *dhikr* (*théomnémie*, as Nwyia calls it with a term borrowed from Byzantine Christianity),[64] the remembrance or recollection of God—a recollection that can be performed either silently or aloud (cf. K 95–97). Defenders of both practices found Koranic sanction: "Be not loud-voiced in thy worship, nor yet silent therein, but follow a way between" (Sūra 17:110). The Sufi practices of *dhikr* were founded upon a Koranic order, "and recollect God often" (Sūra 33:40), for, as another word attests, "the recollection of God makes the heart calm" (Sūra 13:28).

"*Dhikr* is a strong pillar in the path toward God, nay rather the most important pillar" (Q 35), for nobody can reach God without constantly remembering Him. Indeed, "life without the thought (*yād*) of Him is altogether wind (*bād*)" (S 94). In modern terminology one may say that concentrated recollection sets free spiritual energies that provide help in the progress on the Path.

The particularly attractive aspect of *dhikr* is that—in its primary form (not in its later, highly developed phase)—it is permitted in any place and at any time; its practice is restricted neither to the exact hours of ritual prayer nor to a ritually clean place. God can be remembered anywhere in His world. Whenever the adept finds difficulties on the Path, "*dhikr* is the sword by which he threatens his enemies, and God will protect him who remembers Him constantly in the moment of affliction and danger" (Q 37). Only in exceptional cases might a Sufi feel that it is a sign of reverence not to

62. Edward G. Browne, *A Literary History of Persia*, 4 vols. (1902; reprint ed., Cambridge, 1957), 3:336.

63. Louis Gardet, "La mention du nom divin, *dhikr*, dans la mystique musulmane," *Revue Thomiste*, 1952–53; G.-C. Anawati and Louis Gardet, *Mystique musulmane* (Paris, 1961), pp. 187–234. The main *dhikr* formulae are found in G 1:302 ff.

64. Paul Nwyia, *Ibn ᶜAṭāʾ Allāh et la naissance de la confrèrie šāḏilite* (Beirut, 1972), p. 251.

mention God's name too often, lest it be misused (Q 38). On the whole, the Sufis would agree that the heart of the faithful must be "perfumed with the recollection of God." Recollection is the spiritual food of the mystic. A disciple of Sahl at-Tustarī became hungry and, after days of starvation, asked: "O master, what is the food? And Sahl answered: The recollection of God the Immortal" (T 1:259). The heart could be compared to Jesus, who was nurtured by Mary's milk, to which the *dhikr* corresponds (L 116). It leads to a complete spiritualization, and "he who remembers God permanently is the true companion (*jalīs*) of God" (B 638), for God has promised in a *ḥadīth qudsī: "anā jalīsu man dhakaranī,"* "I am the companion of him who recollects Me."

Dhikr is the first step in the way of love; for when somebody loves someone, he likes to repeat his name and constantly remember him. Therefore the heart of him in whom the love of God has been implanted will become a dwelling place of constant *dhikr* (A 10:44). It is, as ʿAṭṭār shows with a slightly amusing image, one of the four elements by which the perfect Sufi is formed:

> The soul needs warm love, the *dhikr* should keep the tongue wet,
> dry asceticism and piety are required,
> and a cold sigh from the coolness of Certitude will be added:
> these are the four elements to constitute a well balanced human being.
>
> (U 11)

The mystics have credited Muhammad himself with the praise of *dhikr*:

> He who recollects God among the negligent
> is like a fighter in the midst of those who flee,
> like a green tree in the midst of dry trees.
>
> (G 1:265)

This last verse has contributed to the imagery of popular mystical folk poetry. The poets of Turkey (following Rūmī and Yūnus Emre) and of Muslim India often compared the heart to a tree, which lives and moves only by the breeze of love and is nourished by the water of the *dhikr*; it is the jasmine tree watered by the *lā* and *illā* (the two parts of the profession of faith, which was frequently used in *dhikr*), as Sulṭān Bāhū of the Punjab sang. His younger contemporary, Shāh ʿAbduʾl-Laṭīf in Sind (d. 1752), devoted a whole chapter of his poetical work to the dry tree that needs the water of recollection to be revived.

The mystics who urged their disciples to "teach the nightingale of the tongue the *dhikr*"[65] constructed, as in the case of the mystical stations and states, a progression of various degrees of recollection. It must be remembered that the *talqīn adh-dhikr*, the teaching of the formula of recollection, was one of the most important aspects of mystical initiation and was later developed into a complicated art. Only a *dhikr* properly inspired by the spiritual director, and constantly controlled by him, was effective, and we may well believe the story told about Sahl at-Tustarī (who had learned the first simple formulae as a child from his uncle):

Sahl said to one of his disciples: Strive to say continuously for one day: "O Allah! O Allah! O Allah!" and do the same the next day and the day after that—until he became habituated to saying those words. Then he bade him to repeat them at night also, until they became so familiar that he uttered them even during his sleep. Then he said: "Do not repeat them any more, but let all your faculties be engrossed in remembering God!" The disciple did this, until he became absorbed in the thought of God. One day, when he was in his house, a piece of wood fell on his head and broke it. The drops of blood which trickled to the ground bore the legend "Allah! Allah! Allah!" (H 195)

This growing presence of the divine in the heart has been explained theoretically by a number of later Sufis. Shāh Walīullāh devotes a whole paragraph of his *Saṭaʿāt* to this phenomenon (no. 39).

The *dhikr* could be learned, if not from a living master, then from Khiḍr, the mysterious guide of the wayfarers; but it had to be a proper initiation. The formula has to be transmitted through the chain of spiritual leaders that goes back to the Prophet himself or to an angelic inspirer of Muhammad. Sometimes the different techniques of *dhikr* were traced back to the first caliphs: the Prophet allegedly taught Abū Bakr the silent *dhikr* when he was with him in the cave during his emigration to Medina, whereas ʿAlī was granted the loud *dhikr*.[66]

Since the ninth century the rosary (*tasbīḥ, subḥa*) has been used to count the repetitions of the formulae, yet a true mystic would regard this medium as a toy "to attract heedlessness" (N 79). A Sufi

65. *Sanāʾīʾābād*, line 391.
66. Joseph Fletcher, *The Old and New Teachings in Chinese Islam* (forthcoming).

performing the true recollection would scarcely use it, for being lost in his prayer. Still, sometimes "heedlessness" was needed as relaxation from the mental stress of constant, intense *dhikr* (N 71). There is no reason to doubt stories according to which Sufis were completely drowned in sweat when uttering the *shahāda* (N 166) or were able to melt the snow around them because of the heat of their meditation (N 138)—the same is said about the *tapas*, the ascetic "heat" of the Hindu ascetics, and about Christian saints. A later handbook orders the Sufi to drink water after performing the *dhikr* to cool down the internal heat that he has produced.[67] Some ascetics among the Indian Sufis added to the difficulty of their task by sitting in front of a fire on a summer day so that the heat was, in fact, intolerable for anybody—a custom inherited from Hindu ascetics.[68] This is an exaggeration of *dhikr* practices.

Even though the general recollection of God is licit anywhere and at any time, the "official" *dhikr* should be executed after performing some preliminary acts. According to Simnānī (d. 1336), the mystic should sit cross-legged, the right hand on the left, and the left hand keeping the right leg in position on top of the left leg (CL 115).[69] Even if the sitting style might vary according to the orders, the correct position was considered of great importance for the success of the *dhikr,* and the manuals carefully explain the relevant rules. The adept must not only purify himself inwardly and outwardly before entering the cell to perform his *dhikr,* but should keep the image of his sheikh before his eyes for spiritual help during the recollection. This practice is, apparently, not of very early origin, but was elaborated by the orders.

The mystical leader had to decide, first, which kind of *dhikr* was fitting for the spiritual stage of his disciple. "The recollected object is one, but the recollections are variable, and the places of the heart of those who recollect are different" (X 286), says Ibn Khafīf. The wayfarer who lives in the station of hope will need a formula different from that used by a mystic in the station of renunciation or of complete trust in God.

67. Shaʿrānī, *Risāla fi talqīn adh-dhikr* (Istanbul Universitesi Kütüphanesi, Arab. 3531).

68. Muḥammad Aʾẓam Tattawī, *Tuḥfat aṭ-ṭāhirīn,* ed. Badr-i ʿAlam Durrānī (Karachi, 1956), p. 166.

69. Fritz Meier, *Die "fawāʾiḥ al-ǧamāl wa fawātiḥ al-ǧalāl" des Naǧmuddīn al-Kubrā* (Wiesbaden, 1957), p. 202; and Johann Karl Teufel, *Eine Lebensbeschreibung des Scheichs ʿAli-i Hamaḏānī* (Leiden, 1962), pp. 80 ff.

As has been mentioned, *dhikr* is generally divided into two branches: recollection with the tongue (*dhikr jalī, jahrī, ʿalanīya, lisānī*) and recollection in the heart (*dhikr khafī, qalbī*). The latter is usually recognized as superior to the former—there is even a *ḥadīth* to underscore its high rank (L 42); the spoken *dhikr*, however, plays an important role in the common ritual of the dervishes: "A man asked Abū ʿUthmān al-Ḥīrī: 'I recollect with the tongue, but my heart does not become friends with the recollection.' He answered: 'Be grateful that one of your limbs obeys and one of your parts is led aright: maybe later your heart too will come into accord' " (T 2:59). Even he who offers the *dhikr* with his tongue only polishes the mirror of his heart so that it becomes pure enough to reflect God's beauty. But, as one Sufi has said, it is the mirror itself that should be cleaned, not its handle or its back—if the disciple does not realize the implications of this thought, the danger is that he performs his silent *dhikr* "with his stomach, not with the heart" (N 390).

Dhikr has also been classified according to the traditional tripartition: "a recollection with the tongue, that is reckoned for ten good works, with the heart, that is reckoned for 700 good works, and a recollection the reward of which can neither be reckoned nor weighed—that is, to be filled with His love and awe of His nearness" (L 219). Or, as Kharrāz has defined it:

> a recollection with the tongue not felt by the heart—that is the usual recollection; a recollection with the tongue in which the heart is present—that is a recollection seeking reward, and a recollection when the heart is wandering in recollection and lets the tongue be silent, and the worth of such a recollection is known only to God. (T 2:44)

The *dhikr* should permeate the mystic's whole being, so that in constant *dhikr* he forgets the recollection of everything else; "everybody who forgets to recollect the [created] things in recollecting God, is guarded by all things, since God has become a substitute for all things" (T 1:321). That sentence was written by Yūsuf ibn Ḥusayn ar-Rāzī, who may have gotten this idea from his part-time master Dhūʾn-Nūn, to whom similar words are ascribed. The complete reliance upon God and absolute love of Him that both cause *dhikr* and result in *dhikr* make the mystic independent of this world, even make him the sovereign of the world.

The Sufis began to ponder the meaning of *dhikr* very early. They recognized its superior qualities as spiritual exercise and accepted it as the form of worship peculiar to those who strove to wander on the path leading toward God. They therefore tried to discover why the *dhikr* should yield such wonderful results in the spirits of the adepts. Kalābādhī gives an answer to this question that may well reflect the general feeling among the early Sufis: "People heard their first *dhikr* when God addressed them, saying *alastu birabbikum* 'Am I not your Lord?' This *dhikr* was secreted in their heart, even as the fact was secreted in their intellects. So when they heard the [Sufi] *dhikr,* the secret things of their hearts appeared" (K 166). The *dhikr* goes back to the primordial covenant, and the initiative goes back to God's activity; man responds with his *dhikr* to the eternal words that made him truly man. Thus his *dhikr,* performed now in time and space, brings him back to the moment of the divine address, when spiritual nourishment was granted to him at the "banquet of *alast,*" as the Persian poets would call it. And man answers with words of adoration and glorification, until in permament recollection he may reach the stage in which the subject is lost in the object, in which recollection, recollecting subject, and recollected object become again one, as they were before the Day of *Alast.* What has been created disappears, and the only true subject, the everlasting God, is as He had been and will be.

This is the goal of *dhikr,* as formulated by Junayd (T 2:32); centuries later the Naqshbandiyya would teach that the end of *dhikr* without words is contemplation (*mushāhada*), in which subject and object are, eventually, indiscernible (N 404). "True *dhikr* is that you forget your *dhikr*" (L 220), says Shiblī. Since even the word or thought "O God!" implies the consciousness of subject and object, the last mystery of recollection is complete silence.

"Worshipping has ten parts, of which nine are silence."[70] Sincere recollection is beyond letter and thought; rosary and beads are, for the advanced Sufis, "like the lion painted in the batnroom" (B 509), i.e., dead, without meaning and value. Baqlī's lofty meditations about the *dhikr,* which—if genuine—is the recollection of the non-created primordial God Himself, deserve special study (B 164). He who has reached the last stage no longer speaks, for "when the tongue speaks, the heart is silent" (N 396); the poets may compare him to the lily, breathless with adoration and silent with ten tongues. Even the syllable *hū,* "he," or the letter *ha,* the last sound of the word "Allah," the last sigh in *dhikr,* becomes meaningless.

70. Braune, "*Futūḥ al-ġaib,*" p. 98.

In the increased proximity brought about by the *dhikr* of the heart the seeker becomes, eventually, completely heart; every limb of his is a heart recollecting God. Qushayrī describes this state very well in his *Tartīb as-sulūk*, which contains an impressive description of the overwhelming experience of *dhikr* by which the mystic is completely beyond sleep and rest and lives exclusively in his *dhikr*, which he does not want to miss for a second. The limbs partake in such *dhikr*: first they move, and then their movements grow stronger until they become voices and sounds; these voices, uttering words of *dhikr*, can be heard coming from the mystic's whole body, except from his tongue.[71]

We may place here the grotesque stories told about several Sufis of India. Their limbs became separated from them during the *dhikr* and recollected God each in its own way. This experience is known from Shamanism, but was apparently not rare among later Sufis, mainly in the Subcontinent.[72]

The Sufis—at least since Bāyezīd Bisṭāmī—were well aware that *dhikr* is still a veil (T 2:159), that the "homeland of recollection is separation"[73]—a leitmotif of Niffarī's prayer theology. Niffarī's contemporary Abū Bakr al-Wāsiṭī said, in the same vein: "Those who remember His recollection are more negligent than those who forget His recollection" (cf. N 144). For, as Hallāj put it, "recollection is the most precious pearl, and recollection hides Thee from my eye."[74]

Dhikr in its developed forms is usually connected with some sort of breath control. Sahl expressed the idea that "the breaths are counted; every breath that goes out without remembering Him is dead, but every breath that goes out in recollecting the Lord is alive and is connected with Him."[75] One cannot determine the exact dates when different methods of breath control were adopted into Sufism; but everyone who has practiced *dhikr* in one religious tradition or the other—be it the Jesus prayer of the Greek monks,

71. See the analysis by Fritz Meier, "Qušayrīs Tartīb as-sulūk," *Oriens* 16 (1963); and QR 70–71. See also Walīullāh, *Saṭaᶜāt*, p. 57, no. 39.

72. Dārā Shikōh, *Sakīnat al-auliyāʾ*, p. 207; Aᶜẓam Tattawī, *Tuḥfat*, p. 159, no. 146; Khwāja Mīr Dard, *ᶜIlm ul-kitāb* (Bhopal, 1309 h./1891–92), p. 505. Even in the strange, modern syncretistic book by Francis Brabazon, *Stay with God: A Statement in Illusion on Reality* (Woombye, Queensland, 1959), p. 40, the author speaks of a certain ᶜAbdul Qādir Jīlānī Tanjore: "He was a 'ghous'-like *mast*—one who can separate his limbs from his body."

73. Niffarī, *Maw.*, no. 49/2.

74. Al-Ḥallāj, *Diwan*, muq. no. 18.

75. Al-Khānqāhī, *Guzīda*, p. 53.

or the *Namu Amida Butsu* of Amida Buddhism—knows that concentration without control of breathing is scarcely possible. Jāmī preserved the teachings of his own master in the early Naqshbandī tradition—Khwāja ʿAṭṭār said: "The purpose in *dhikr* is not to speak much; one says in one breath three times *lā ilāh illā Allāh,* beginning from the right side, and brings it down to the heart, and brings forth *Muḥammad rasūl Allāh* from the left side. A ninefold or eighteenfold repetition in one breath is also possible" (N 390–91). In the later Middle Ages, especially in Afghanistan and India, the *ḥabs-i dam,* holding the breath for a very long time, was practiced—a disputed technique that may show influence from Indian asceticism.

The peculiarities of *dhikr* were explained theoretically in later times. Thus Shaʿrānī, who is a good interpreter of Sufism in the Near East in the sixteenth century,[76] speaks of a sevenfold *dhikr*: *dhikr al-lisān,* with the tongue; *dhikr an-nafs,* which is not audible but consists of inner movement and feeling; *dhikr al-qalb,* with the heart, when the heart contemplates God's beauty and majesty in its inner recesses; *dhikr ar-rūḥ,* when the meditating mystic perceives the lights of the attributes; *dhikr as-sirr,* in the innermost heart, when divine mysteries are revealed; *dhikr al-khafiy,* the secret recollection, which means the vision of the light of the beauty of essential unity; and, finally, the *dhikr akhfā al-khafī,* the most secret of secret, which is the vision of the Reality of Absolute Truth (*ḥaqq al-yaqīn*).

The Naqshbandī tradition has taught the *dhikr* of the five *laṭāʾif,* five subtle points in the body upon which the mystic has to concentrate his recollection until his whole being is transformed. A clear description of these theories as practiced in the late eighteenth century is given by Mīr Dard (IK 112, 637). He speaks of the *dhikr qalbī,* located in the heart at the left side of the breast, pronounced in love and longing; the *dhikr rūḥī,* performed at the right side of the breast in quietude and tranquillity; the *dhikr sirrī,* pronounced in intimacy, close to the left side of the breast; the *dhikr khafawī,* performed close to the right corner of the breast and connected with absence and extinction of the self; and the *dhikr akhfawī,* in the center of the breast, which is the sign of annihilation and consummation. The *dhikr* is, then, extended to the brain in perfect con-

76. Ash-Shaʿrānī, *Bayān al-asrār* (Istanbul Universitesi Kütüphanesi, Arab. 248), fols. 88b ff.

tentment (*dhikr nafsī,* connected with the *nafs qaddīsa,* the "sanctified soul") and eventually permeates the whole being, body and soul, when man attains perfect recollectedness and peace—that is the *dhikr sulṭānī,* the royal recollection. Like many of the Sufis, Dard insists that constant practice is required; the *dhikr* is a medicine for the soul, and the physician must learn his art by practice rather than from books (IK 161).

A peculiar method of concentration, connected with the *dhikr,* is the contemplation of the word *Allāh,* written in the mystic's heart, until he is surrounded by the loop of the *h,* ه, in perfect lucidity (see Appendix 1).

The Naqshbandī masters considered it useful to visit the tombs of deceased saints and to concentrate upon the spirit of particular departed Sufis in order to increase their spiritual strength. By directing one's thought to the spirit of this or that mystic—instead of concentrating upon one's sheikh exclusively—a mystic might achieve a greater sublimation of the spirit, according to the power of the saint in question.

The problem of whether the true *dhikr* should be hidden or spoken aloud caused a major split in the Naqshbandī order in Central Asia in the sixteenth and seventeenth centuries; it had grave political consequences resulting in religious wars in Sinkiang. Yet the tradition was always divided; although silent *dhikr* was preferred by most of the Naqshbandī leaders, one of the fourteenth-century masters had answered the question whether loud *dhikr* was licit by quoting the example of the *talqīn,* the loud recitation of the profession of faith in a dying person's ear, "and for the dervish, every breath is his last breath" (N 391). In retrospect, one claimed that another forerunner of the order defended the loud *dhikr* as praiseworthy "so the sleeping may be awakened and the inattentive may be made aware, and that by the *dhikr* he may come into the path."[77] The loud *dhikr* was almost a war cry against infidelity and heedlessness, but it was to be used only by those whose tongues and hearts were free from falsehood and slander.

The mystics who opposed the loud *dhikr* relied upon the Prophet's word: "You do not call upon a Deaf one and not an Absent one, but you call unto a Hearing one who is with you wherever you are!" They also held that the loud *dhikr* pronounced by a small group

77. Fletcher, *Old and New Teachings,* app. 6, from ᶜAlī ibn Ḥusayn Wāᶜiẓ-i Kāshifī's *Rashaḥāt ᶜayn al-ḥayāt* (Kanpur, 1912), p. 38.

could disturb the people in the mosque who were absorbed in silent meditation. In many cases, however, the loud *dhikr* was thought of as a means of bringing a larger group into an ecstatic or quasi-ecstatic state. The repetition of the word *Allāh,* or of the rhythmical formula *lā ilāh illā Allāh,* accompanied by certain movements, could easily induce a state of trance. The word *Allāh* would be shortened until only its last letter, *h,* remained; pronounced *ha,* it was spoken toward the left shoulder, then *hu* was spoken toward the right shoulder, and *hi* was pronounced with a lowering of the head. Often the Sufis would join in a *ḥalqa,* a circle formed around a *quṭb,* "pivot"; they would put right hands on the left hands of their neighbors and with closed eyes repeat the *shahāda* until it consisted merely of the last *h.*[78] Anyone who has had the opportunity to attend such a rhythmical *dhikr,* with its increasing tempo and its reduction of words until a kind of permanent sighing is reached, knows that even a noncommitted listener is easily carried away by the strength of the experience. Unfortunately, in some Muslim countries *dhikr* sessions of this type have been used lately as tourist attractions.

Among the different types of loud *dhikr,* that of the Rifāʿī dervishes is best known in the West—they are called the Howling Dervishes because of the strange sounds they produce during their *dhikr* meetings. One may also mention the *dhikr-i arra,* the "sawing *dhikr,*" practiced primarily among Central Asian and Turkish orders. The heavy sounds that come from the larynx are indeed reminiscent of a crosscut saw. The "sawing *dhikr*" began, allegedly, with Aḥmad Yasawī and was, perhaps, "the Yesewīya answer to the ecstatic Shamanist dances."[79]

Besides being an excellent means of inducing a sort of ecstatic state, the *dhikr* was also recommended to the faithful as a means of obtaining heavenly reward. Manuals of piety, like Ghazzālī's *Iḥyāʾ ʿulūm ad-dīn,* teach a number of *dhikr* formulae, along with exact prescriptions as to how often each of these formulae should be repeated in order to bear fruit in Paradise (G 1:265, 302 ff). Sūra 112, the confession of God's Unity, is considered especially powerful for producing bliss in the otherworld. Reciting the profession of faith seven thousand times can save the mystic himself

78. Émile Dermenghem, *Le culte des saints dans l'Islam Maghrebin* (Paris, 1954), p. 321.
79. Fletcher, *Old and New Teachings,* p. 16.

or any other person from hellfire (N 531). These ideas were, and still are, widely accepted by the masses. Many a pious old woman will never get up from her ritual prayer without adding to it a number of *dhikr* formulae, and many a Muslim has found consolation in the frequent repetition of a sacred sentence or a divine name from which he experiences comfort and strength.

The *dhikr* of the divine names is extremely important in this connection. The fact that God has been described in the Koran as possessing the most beautiful names forms the basis for a whole theology of the divine names (*al-asmāʾ al-ḥusnā*)[80]—though the mystics knew that these names were not proper names applicable to God, but derivative (M 4:217). The usual collection of these names of glorification comprises ninety-nine names. The Greatest Name is hidden, but many a mystic has claimed that he possesses it and that it enables him to perform every kind of miracle. Others have stated that the Greatest Name differs according to the wayfarer's station.[81]

The rosary, with its thirty-three or ninety-nine beads, is used for counting the names. They may be repeated one by one, beginning with *Yā Raḥmān yā Rahīm,* "O Merciful, O All-compassionate," and ending with *Yā Ṣabūr,* "O Patient." The Sufis have written repeatedly about the qualities of these divine names, which are divided into *luṭfiyya,* connected with God's beauty and lovingkindness, and *qahriyya,* connected with His wrath and majesty. These two categories constantly work together to produce the whole fabric of the world and are mysteriously connected with human beings. Even the differences between mystical teachers have been ascribed to the various divine names they reflect.

The rules for the use of this or that divine name at a certain moment have been carefully laid down by the Sufi leaders. The name *al-Hādī,* "the Guiding One," must work upon the adept when he turns to God in his *dhikr* (N 410). The name *al-Laṭīf,* "The Subtle," "the Kind," should be used by the mystic in seclusion to make his nature subtle. *Al-Ḥāfiẓ,* "The Preserver," should be used when one tries to preserve one's mystical state. *Al-Wadūd,* "The Loving-Beloved," makes the mystic loved by all creatures, and when it is

80. See Abū Ḥāmid al-Ghazzālī, *Al-Maqṣad al-asnāʾ fī sharḥ maʿānī asmāʾ Allāh al-Ḥusnā,* ed. Fadlou Shéhadi (Beirut, 1971), on the meaning of the divine names. Mohammad al-Gawhary, *Die Gottesnamen im magischen Gebrauch in den al-Būnī zugeschriebenen Werken* (Bonn, 1968), discusses the magical use of the divine names in the works of a thirteenth-century Egyptian author.

81. Johann Karl Teufel, *Hamaḏānī,* p. 87.

constantly recited in seclusion, intimacy and divine love will increase. The name *al-Fā᾽iq*, "The Overpowering," should never be used by the beginner, but only by the gnostic in a high station.

These are a few examples given by Ibn ᶜAṭā᾽ Allāh, the great teacher of the Shādhiliyya order in Egypt (d. 1309).[82] A wrong application of a divine name was considered to produce grave consequences for the person who used it or for those close to him. It is in this field of the *dhikr* of the names that the wisdom of the mystical guide is particularly needed to instruct and supervise the disciple who may, otherwise, be exposed to serious spiritual and mental dangers.

In addition to the *dhikr* formulae proper, the master could also give his disciples, or those who called upon him, rather long formulae to be recited after the ritual prayer or in case of special need (*wird, aurād,* or *ḥizb*). Many of these prayers are credited with supernatural powers, and the most famous one is probably the *ḥizb al-baḥr,* attributed to ash-Shādhilī and used mainly during travel as a protective charm.

Samāᶜ

The goal of the mystic attained, sometimes, through constant meditation is *fanā*, annihilation, and subsequent perseverance in God. This final experience is always regarded as a free act of divine grace, which might enrapture man and take him out of himself, often in an experience described as ecstatic. In Sufism, the term generally translated as "ecstasy" is *wajd,* which means, literally, "finding," i.e., to find God and become quiet and peaceful in finding Him. In the overwhelming happiness of having found Him, man may be enraptured in ecstatic bliss. Nwyia has proposed (W 254) calling this state "instasy" instead of "ecstasy" since the mystic is not carried out of himself but rather into the depths of himself, into "the ocean of the soul," as the poets might say.[83]

"Ecstasy is a flame which springs up in the secret heart, and appears out of longing, and at that visitation (*wārid*) the members are stirred either to joy or grief" (K 106). ᶜAṭṭār also employed the image of the flame:

82. Aḥmad Ibn ᶜAṭā᾽ Allāh al-Iskandarī, *Miftāḥ al-falāḥ wa miṣbāḥ al-arwāḥ* (Cairo, 1961).

83. See Nwyia, *Ibn ᶜAṭā᾽ Allāh,* pp. 276 ff.

What is *wajd*? To become happy thanks to the true
morning,
to become fire without the presence of the sun.

(U 41)

In this ecstatic state, the Sufi might become absolutely senseless and lose consciousness even for years, during which he would be exempt from the prescribed rites (B 576). In this respect, the term *wajd* is the true equivalent of ecstasy; the sixth form of the verb *wajada*, "to find,"—*tawājud*, "to attempt to reach an ecstatic state by outward means"—has been derived from it. It was this attempting to find freedom from one's self by indulging in singing, dancing, and drugs that was often connected with Sufi practices and was criticized both by the orthodox and by the moderate mystics themselves.

The problem of *samāᶜ*, "hearing," was a major cause of differences among the schools. There were complicated problems as to whether "listening to music" and "dancing movement" are genuine utterances of mystical states or illegitimate attempts to gain by one's own effort a state that can only be granted by God; the views of the authorities are clearly divided.

The *samāᶜ* is, no doubt, the most widely known expression of mystical life in Islam. This mystical dance was noted by the first European visitors to the convents of the Mevlevis, the Whirling Dervishes. For the Mevlevi *ṭarīqa* is the only order in which this whirling movement has been institutionalized, though it has been practiced throughout the world of Islam from early times.[84]

In fact, dancing and whirling belong to the oldest religious acts of all. Dance is the "absolute play" and was considered, in ancient Greece, the movement of the gods—both Apollo and Dionysius have dancing movements that suit their particular characters. In primitive societies, dance had a magical character—rituals to produce rain or ensure victory were usually connected with dance. The encircling of a sacred object—or a person, as sometimes in the *samāᶜ*—means to partake of its magical power or to endow it with power. The rap-

84. Duncan Black Macdonald, "Emotional Religion in Islam as Affected by Music and Singing, Being a Translation of a Book of the *Iḥyāʾ ᶜUlūm ad-Dīn* of al-Ghazzālī," *Journal of the Royal Asiatic Society*, 1901. Fritz Meier, "Der Derwisch-Tanz," *Asiatische Studien* 8 (1954), on the development and forms of the dance. Marijan Molé, "La dance exstatique en Islam," *Sources orientales* 6 (1963), an excellent study of mystical dance in Islam.

ture caused by dance was well known to the Christian church fathers, who strictly prohibited it. "Where there is dance, there is Satan," said St. Chrysostom, and this could as well have been the verdict of an orthodox Muslim theologian.

The handbooks of Sufism are filled with discussions as to whether the *samāᶜ* is permitted or not. The conclusions differ according to the mystical theologians and the orders. Orthodoxy would ban every musical and rhythmical movement, and some of the sober orders, like the Naqshbandiyya, followed their example. Others saw in *samāᶜ* an outlet for the religious feeling of the pious—and it was this musical side of some of the fraternities that attracted large masses. Those who longed for an emotional kind of worship that ritual prayer could not really provide might find it by listening to music or by participating in the dance movement.

The beginning of *samāᶜ* is probably that the mystics were enchanted by a beautiful voice or even by a casual word that fitted into their current state of mind and thus engendered a spiritual uplifting. It is well known how strongly the Arabs respond to sound and the rhythmical wording of a sentence; the recitation of the Koran as performed by a good *ḥāfiẓ* can move large audiences to tears. There is no reason to doubt the stories told by the classical authors that a moving recitation of a line from the scripture or a worldly verse could cause people to faint, even to die from excitement. One should not forget that in the Middle Ages in Islam nervous diseases and mental illness were often treated by applying music, as Ibn Sīnā recommended. The basin in the asylum attached to the Great Mosque in Divrigi (Anatolia, built in 1228), where the water produced a sweet, enthralling sound, or the Bayezit Külliyesi in Edirne (built 1370), with its concert-hall arrangement in the asylum, are good examples of the way music was used in medical treatment.

It is said of al-Ḥaddād, a blacksmith who became a leading Sufi in the late ninth century: "One day he was sitting in his shop listening to a blind man who was reciting the Koran in the bazaar. He became so absorbed in listening that he put his hand into the fire, and without using the pincers, drew out a piece of molten iron from the furnace" (H 124). Stories of this kind are frequently found in Islamic hagiography, and many miracles are, in fact, explained by a state of absolute unconsciousness caused by listening to the Koran or by performing any kind of mental prayer. The mystic would no longer feel any pain, and any surgical operation could be performed upon him without his being aware.

The question was posed, however, as to whether the listener—who had to be wholly occupied (*ḥāḍir*, "present") with his Lord—should allow himself to be enraptured by the music or by any sound. He might start turning and whirling around, sometimes rending his garments, sometimes gaining supernatural strength. Some have died in ecstasy (N 195); others are said to have just disappeared in the air in a flight produced by their spinning movement (N 146); or, as the legends tell, a negro would turn white as long as his ecstatic state continued (N 102, 164, 37).

Was this the state a Sufi should try to reach? Or was it rather the complete self-control of the masters that deeply impressed the historians? Junayd's answer to the enthusiastic Nūrī, who objected to his sitting quietly while the Sufis performed their whirling dance, is famous: "You see the mountains—you think them firm, yet they move like clouds" (Sūra 27:90; N 188).

This episode must have occurred about the year 900. *Samā*ᶜ*khāna*s, houses in which the Sufis could listen to music and let themselves be drawn into ecstatic states, were founded in Baghdad as early as the second half of the ninth century. The orthodox were scandalized by the sight of what took place there. They very much objected, among other things, to the rending of the garments that frequently happened in *samā*ᶜ. The theoreticians of Sufism have discussed this topic particularly when—as in later times—charming young boys took part in the *samā*ᶜ and added to the spiritual joy. It is said of Auḥaduddīn Kirmānī, a Sufi of the first half of the thirteenth century, that "he rent the shirts of the 'unbearded' when he got excited, and danced breast to breast with them" (N 590)—certainly not an act of which lawyer divines could approve.

The authors of the tenth and eleventh centuries devoted long chapters to the dangers inherent in *samā*ᶜ:

> Dancing has no foundation in the religious law or in the path. . . . But since ecstatic movements and the practices of those who endeavour to induce ecstasy resemble it, some frivolous imitators have indulged in it immoderately and have made it a religion. I have met with a number of common people who adopted Sufism in the belief that it is this dancing and nothing more. . . .
>
> It is more desirable that beginners should not be allowed to attend musical concerts lest their natures become depraved. (H 416, 430)

This last sentence would be subscribed to by all spiritual directors in the moderate orders, for the beginner might experience merely a sensual, not a spiritual, pleasure by listening to music or whirling around his own axis. Abū Ḥafṣ Suhrawardī has defined the standpoint of the classical Sufi theologians well:

Music does not give rise, in the heart, to anything which is not already there: so he whose inner self is attached to anything else than God is stirred by music to sensual desire, but the one who is inwardly attached to the love of God is moved, by hearing music, to do His will. What is false is veiled by the veil of self and what is true by the veil of the heart, and the veil of the self is a dark earthy veil, and the veil of the heart is a radiant heavenly veil.

The common folk listen to music according to nature, and the novices listen with desire and awe, while the listening of the saints brings them a vision of the Divine gifts and graces, and these are the gnostics to whom listening means contemplation. But finally, there is the listening of the spiritually perfect to whom, through music, God reveals Himself unveiled.[85]

For the perfect, every sound becomes heavenly music; the true Sufi feels that every sound brings him glad tidings from his beloved, and every word serves as a revelation from God. Rūzbihān Baqlī tells a story typical of this attitude: "A certain mystic saw a group of thieves who drank wine and played tambour. He went and sat with them and listened to that music as if it were a *samā*ᶜ. The thieves enjoyed his attitude so much that all were converted" (B 597).

Rūzbihān himself was a lover of *samā*ᶜ and—following Ibn Khafīf's example (X 214)—taught that for perfect spiritual enjoyment three things were required: fine scents, a beautiful face to look at, and a lovely voice (N 256)—the beauty of the singer is a prerequisite for spiritual happiness. Rūzbihān even symbolized the state of mystical union as "a dance with God."[86]

Ancient authors had seen, in dance, the movement of the deities or of the spheres.[87] Medieval Christians sometimes regarded eternal life as an eternal dance of beatitude—reflected so charmingly in some of Fra Angelico's paintings. *Geistliche Tanzliedchen*, "spiritual dancing verses," were a well-known genre in medieval German

85. Smith, *Readings*, no. 100.

86. See Louis Massignon, "La vie et les oeuvres de Rūzbehān Baqlī," in *Studia Orientalia Ioanni Pedersen dicata septuagenario* (Copenhagen, 1953), p. 238; Henri Corbin, "Quiétude et inquiétude de l'âme dans le soufisme de Rūzbihān Baqlī de Shiraz," *Eranos-Jahrbuch* 27 (1958), p. 101.

87. For the whole complex see Friedrich Heiler, *Erscheinungsformen und Wesen der Religion* (Stuttgart, 1961), pp. 239 ff., with an extensive bibliography. Heiler's book is indispensable for the student of phenomenology of religion.

mystical literature and are echoed, in this century, in some of the *rondas* of Gabriela Mistral, the Chilean poetess. The Muslim mystics composed such "spiritual dancing verses" as well—Yaḥyā ibn Muᶜādh, the "preacher of hope" from Rayy, is credited with one of the earliest known examples of such songs:

> The truth we have not found;
> so dancing, we beat the ground!
> Is dancing reproved in me
> who wander reproved from Thee?
> In Thy valley we go around
> and therefore we beat the ground![88]

The movement of the soul in its approach to God is sometimes, though rarely, described as a heavenly dance.

In the poetry of Jalāluddīn Rūmī this enthusiastic dance has found its most eloquent expression. His verses often echo the strong rhythm of the dancing movement later institutionalized by the order of the Whirling Dervishes.[89] Rūmī sees that "the House of Love is made completely of music, of verses and songs" (D 332), and that the heavenly beloved circumambulates this house, carrying his rebab with him and singing intoxicating tunes (D 2395). For Rūmī, music was the sound of the doors of Paradise, as a lovely legend tells: "A certain man objected to Rūmī's statement and said that he disliked the sound of scratching doors. Whereupon the master replied: 'You hear the doors when they close—I hear them when they are opened' " (N 462).

The *samāᶜ* is, for him, nourishment of the soul (just as the *dhikr* was previously described)—this expression forms part of the last Turkish poem in the Mevlevi ritual, in which it is repeated several times. Wherever the lover touches the ground with his dancing feet, the water of life will spring out of the darkness,[90] and when the name of the beloved is uttered, "even the dead start dancing in their shrouds" (D 1978). Rūmī has compared the whirling movement of the dervishes to workers treading on grapes, an act that brings the spiritual wine into existence (D 624). The dancing lover

88. A 10:61; trans. A. J. Arberry, in *Sufism: An Account of the Mystics of Islam* (London, 1950), p. 62.

89. Hellmut Ritter, "Der Reigen der 'Tanzenden Derwische,'" *Zeitschrift für Vergleichende Musikwissenschaft,* 1 (1933); Ritter, "Die Mevlânafeier in Konya vom 11–17. Dezember 1960," *Oriens* 25 (1962), is a detailed description of the ritual.

90. Maulāna Jalāladdin Rūmī, *Rubāᶜiyāt,* ms. Esat Ef. no. 2693, fol. 322 a 5.

is higher than the spheres, for the call to *samā*ᶜ comes from Heaven (M 2:1942); he may be compared to the particle of dust that spins around the sun and thus experiences a strange sort of union, for without the gravitation of the sun it would not be able to move—just as man cannot live without turning around the spiritual center of gravity, around God.

Once the fetters of the body are broken by means of enthusiastic dance, the soul is set free and realizes that everything created takes part in the dance—the spring breeze of love touches the tree so that the branches, flower buds, and stars start whirling in the all-embracing mystical movement.

True *samā*ᶜ is also "a dance in blood"—an allusion to the legend that Ḥallāj danced in his fetters on the way to the place of execution; the last step of spiritual freedom has often been described as a dance in fetters (M 3:96). The *samā*ᶜ means to die to this world and to be revived in the eternal dance of the free spirits around a sun that neither rises nor sets. *Fanā* and *baqā*, annihilation and eternal life in God, can thus be represented in the movement of the mystical dance as understood by Rūmī and his followers:

> Sound drum and mellow flute, resounding Allah Hu!
> Dance, ruddy dawn, in gladness bounding Allah Hu!
> Sound exalted in the centre, o thou streaming light!
> Soul of all wheeling planets rounding Allah Hu!
>
> . . . .
>
> Who knows love's mazy circling, ever lives in God,
> For death, he knows, is love abounding: Allah Hu![91]

The preeternal covenant of the Day of *Alastu* is represented, by Rūmī, by the image of *samā*ᶜ:

> A call reached Not-Being; Not-Being said : "Yes [*balā*], yes,
> I shall put my foot on that side, fresh and green and joyful!"
> It heard the *alast*; it came forth running and intoxicated,
> It was Not-Being and became Being [manifested in] tulips and willows and sweet basil.
>
> (D 1832)

91. William Hastie, *The Festival of Spring from the "Divan" of Jeláleddin* (Glasgow, 1903), no. 6.

The nonexistent possibilities were endowed with existence by the divine address; this sound enraptured them into a dance that led into the beautiful world full of flowers and scents, just as the sound of the divine voice as heard through the medium of music uplifts the soul to previously unknown worlds of spiritual happiness.

Rūmī's imagery is almost unlimited when he talks about the beauty and force of *samā*^{c}. In ever new images he described this movement induced by the vision of the beloved, who himself may dance on the screen of the lover's heart in the hour of ecstasy. Other poets and mystics have followed his example both in applying the symbolism of music and dance to their poetry and by practicing *samā*^{c} with their disciples. Notwithstanding the orthodox aversion to this aspect of mystical life, it was too attractive to be stopped. Even a sober mystic of the Naqshbandiyya in Delhi like Mīr Dard felt compelled to write a book in defense of music and used to gather musicians once or twice a week to play melodies for him and his followers—without the dancing movement, however, and in strict discipline.

In India, *samā*^{c} was advocated by the Chishtī order. Others followed their example, and one of the saints of Thatta in Sind, ^{c}Isā Jund Allāh, in the seventeenth century even dared to equate *samā*^{c} with ritual prayer.[92] Others would call the *samā*^{c} the "ascension of the saints."[93] When one mystic got a negative answer to his question whether there would be *samā*^{c} in Paradise, he sighed: "What, then, have we to do with Paradise?"[94]

The activities of the Mevlevi dervishes in Turkey, along with those of the other orders, were banned by Atatürk in 1925; since 1954 they have been allowed to perform the *samā*^{c} on the occasion of the anniversary of Rūmī's death on December 17 in Konya, though not in the central sanctuary (they have even performed outside the country). Still, the admiration for this ritual is deeply rooted in many Turkish families, and a modern Turkish poem reflects the feeling of ecstasy that is so typical for the Sufis and that has been echoed in so many verses and hymns. Asaf Halet Çelebi

92. I^{c}jāzul Ḥaqq Quddūsī, *Tadhkira-yi ṣūfiya-yi Sind* (Karachi, 1959), p. 156.

93. Bēdil Rohrīwārō, *Dīwān*, ed. ^{c}Abdul Ḥusayn Mūsawī (Hyderabad, Sind, 1954), p. 297.

94. Qāni^{c}, *Tuḥfat al-kirām*, p. 436; see H. T. Sorley, *Shah Abdul Latif of Bhit: His Poetry, Life, and Times* (1940; reprint ed., Oxford, 1966).

(d. 1958) is, to my knowledge, the last poet to genuinely interpret this feeling:[95]

The trees, donning their dancing gowns
supplicate in love
Mevlâna

The image in me
is a different image
how many stars fall
into my interior dance!
I whirl and I whirl
the skies whirl as well
roses blossom out of my face

The trees in the garden, in sunshine
"He created Heaven and earth"
the serpents listen to the song of the reed
in the trees donning their dancing gowns

The meadow's children, intoxicated
Heart
they call you

I look, smiling, at suns
which have lost their way . . .
I fly, I fly
the skies fly . . . .

95. Asaf Halet Çelebi, *He* (Istanbul, 1951).

4. MAN *and* HIS PERFECTION

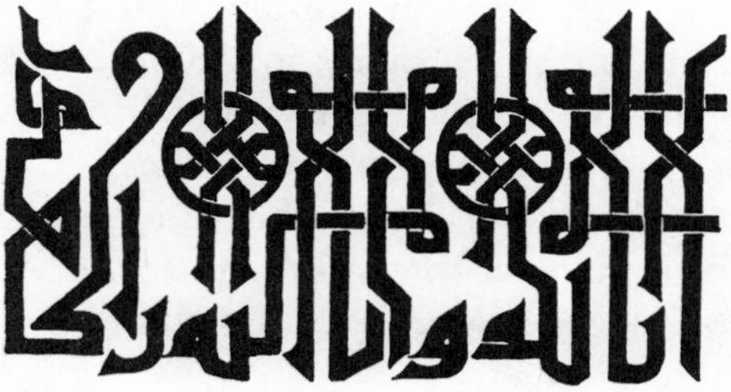

SOME NOTES ON SUFI PSYCHOLOGY

The position of man in Islam, and especially in Sufism, has been a subject of controversy among Western scholars. Some of them have held that man, as "slave of God," has no importance whatsoever before the Almighty God; he almost disappears, loses his personality, and is nothing but an instrument of eternal fate. The concept of "humanism" of which European culture is so proud is, according to these scholars, basically alien to Islamic thought. Others have sensed in the development of later Sufism an inherent danger that might result in an absolute subjectivism, because the human personality is, so to speak, "inflated" to such an extent that it is considered the microcosm, the perfect mirror of God. The doctrine of the Perfect Man (see chapter 6) seemed, to some orientalists, extremely dangerous for Islamic anthropology—no less dangerous than the allegedly humiliating role of man as "slave of God."

It is, in fact, not easy to give an account of mystical anthropology in Islam,[1] since it is as many-sided as Islam itself; the differences

1. Nicholas Heer, "A Sufi Psychological Treatise," *Moslem World* 51 (1961), a translation of a text by al-Ḥakīm at-Tirmidhī that was edited in Cairo in 1958. For later times see J. M. S. Baljon, "Psychology as Apprehended and Applied by Shāh Walī Allāh Dihlawī," *Acta Orientalia Neerlandica*, 1971.

between the earliest and the later mystical currents are considerable. It is possible, therefore, to point to only a few facets of the problem that seem important for the understanding of "man" in Sufism, without even attempting to sketch most of the lines in the picture.

According to the Koran, man was created "by God's hands" (Sūra 38:75), an idea that the tradition elaborated: God kneaded Adam's clay forty days before He gave him life and spirit by breathing into him with His own breath (Sūra 15:29; 38:72). "That means, His Presence was operative 40,000 years upon him" (B 545), as Baqlī interprets this tradition. And he continues: "The form of Adam is the mirror of both worlds. Whatever has been put into these two kingdoms, was made visible in human form. 'And we will show them Our signs in the horizons and in themselves' " (Sūra 41:53; B 437).

This creation myth assigns an extremely high position to man: he is in every respect God's perfect work, living through His breath, and is, thus, almost a mirror reflecting God's qualities. As the tradition says, "He created Adam in His image" (*ʿalā ṣūratihi*). Adam, seen from this angle, is the prototype of the Perfect Man; he was blessed with the special grace of knowledge: "He taught Adam the names," says the Koran (Sūra 2:31). To know a thing's name means to be able to rule it, to use it for one's self: by virtue of his knowledge of the names, Adam became master over all created things. Yet the simple Koranic statement was sometimes explained to imply that God had granted Adam the knowledge of the divine names reflected in creation, which he might "use" in his prayers. Adam became, thus, the *ʿallamaʾl-asmāʾ-bēg*, as Rūmī says, with a remarkable combination of Arabic and Turkish components (M 1:1234), "the prince of He taught the names." God made Adam his *khalīfa*, his vicegerent, on earth and ordered the angels to prostrate themselves before him—man is superior to the angels (cf. H 239), who have not been given the secret of the names and who do nothing but worship God in perfect obedience, whereas man enjoys—or suffers from—the choice between obedience and rebellion (though this choice may be limited by predestination). Man was entrusted with the *amāna*, the "trust" (Sūra 33:72) that Heaven and earth refused to carry—a trust that has been differently interpreted: as responsibility, free will, love, or the power of individuation. Yet the Sufis often longed for their true home, for the time and place of their lofty primeval state:

> We were in heaven, we were the companions of angels—
> when will we return there again?
>
> (D 463)

This remembrance of the paradisiacal days accompanies them in this vale of tears and leads them back from their worldly exile. In man, creation reaches its final point. One Bektashi poet wrote:

> This universe is a tree—man became its fruit.
> That which was intended is the fruit—do not think it
> is the tree!
>
> (BO 118)

Later tradition ascribed to God the words *kuntu kanzan makhfiyan,* "I was a hidden treasure, and I wanted to be known, so I created the world." God, in His eternal loneliness, wanted to be known, so he created a world in which man is the highest manifestation. Man is the microcosm and is created—again according to a *ḥadīth qudsī*—for God's sake, who in turn created everything for man's sake.

The Koran has, indeed, assigned a very high place to man, without entering into detailed discussion. The Sufis, however, dwelt intently upon the different aspects of man. The operations of divine omnipotence are carried out on man; he is, as Rūmī says in a poignant image, "the astrolabe of the qualities of highness" (M 6:3138–43). The mystics have found numerous allusions in the Koran to prove man's lofty rank. One of their favorite verses in this respect is: "And we shall show you our signs on the horizons and in yourselves—do you not see?" (Sūra 41:53), a verse that they interpreted as God's order to look into their own hearts to find the source of knowledge and, eventually, the divine beloved, who is "closer than the jugular vein" (Sūra 50:16).

From this feeling the *ḥadīth "man ʿarafa nafsahu faqad ʿarafa rabbahu,"* "who knows himself knows his Lord," must have developed; it may originally have been an adaptation of the Delphic *gnotí theauton,* "know yourself." The mystical theorists have relied heavily upon this tradition: to know one's innermost heart means to discover the point at which the divine is found as the *dulcis hospes animae,* the meeting point of the human and the divine. The *ḥadīth* has been interpreted differently. One of the finest allegories ever written is by Rūmī, who tells the story of Ayāz, Maḥmūd of Ghazna's favorite slave, who looked every morning at the outworn shoes and shabby clothes he wore before Maḥmūd elected him for himself; it was necessary for him to remember his former lowly state so that he could appreciate the bounty that his lord had bestowed upon him (M 5:2113). Thus, concludes Rūmī, man should likewise remember how weak he was created, and then he will recognize his nothingness before God, who gives him everything out of grace.

Most mystics, however, would interpret the *ḥadīth* as a condensation of the basic experience of the mystical path as a way inward, an interiorization of experience, a journey into one's own heart (CL 93). This has been beautifully described by ʿAṭṭār in the *Muṣībatnāma,* where the hero eventually finds his peace in the ocean of the soul.

That God resides in the loving heart is expressed by another favorite tradition: "Heaven and earth contain Me not, but the heart of my faithful servant contains Me." The heart is the dwelling place of God; or it is, in other terminology, the mirror in which God reflects Himself. But this mirror has to be polished by constant asceticism and by permanent acts of loving obedience until all dust and rust have disappeared and it can reflect the primordial divine light.

Another image often used to show how man has to prepare for this state of "finding" is that of "breaking." One *ḥadīth qudsī* attests: "I am with those whose hearts are broken for My sake." The theme of breaking for the sake of construction is in full accord with ascetic practices as a preparatory stage. Junayd's statement that "God is affirmed more by Not-being than by Being" (P 1:45) led Massignon to the conclusion that the general tendency of Islamic theology is "to affirm God rather through destruction than through construction" (P 2:631). The *nafs* has to be broken, the body has to be broken, and the heart, too, has to be broken and everything in it naughted so that God can build a new mansion for Himself in it. For the ruined house contains treasures—such treasures can only be found by digging up the foundation (as the story of Khiḍr in Sūra 18 tells).

Wherever there is a ruin, there is hope for a treasure—
why do you not seek the treasure of God in the wasted
heart?

(D 141)

ᶜAṭṭār often spoke of "breaking" as a means of attaining peace and unity—be it the broken millstone, which no longer turns in endless restlessness (U 149), or the puppet-player in the *Ushturnāme*, who breaks all the figures he has used and puts them back into the box of unity (V 137). In later Sufi poetry, mainly in the Indo-Persian style around 1700—when all the leading poets were under the influence of the Naqshbandiyya *ṭarīqa*—the word *shikast*, "broken," became a favorite term. Perhaps, in a period in which Muslim India broke down completely, they hoped to find some consolation in the idea that breaking is necessary for a new beginning.

The mystic may find the figure of the friend who dwells within the heart emptied of everything, may find in its ruin the hidden treasure and discover, in a jubilant experience, "What I have never found, I found in man!" (Y 79). The utterances of a number of enthusiastic mystics who had reached this state have often opened the way to a boundless feeling of all-embracing unity, which, along with the theories of Ibn ᶜArabī, could easily lead to a state in which the boundary between man and God seemed forgotten. However, the Lord remains Lord, the slave, slave—this is the generally accepted viewpoint of moderate Sufism.

Sufi psychology, like everything else in Sufism, is based on Koranic ideas—the ideas on the *nafs*, the lowest principle of man, have already been mentioned. Higher than the *nafs* is the *qalb*, "heart," and the *rūḥ*, "spirit."[2] This tripartition forms the foundation of later, more complicated systems; it is found as early as the Koranic commentary by Jaᶜfar aṣ-Ṣādiq. He holds that the *nafs* is peculiar to the *ẓālim*, "tyrant," the *qalb* to the *muqtaṣid*, "moderate," and the *rūḥ* to the *sābiq*, "preceding one, winner"; the *ẓālim* loves God for his own sake, the *muqtaṣid* loves Him for Himself, and the *sābiq* annihilates his own will in God's will (W 17). Bāyezīd Bisṭāmī, al-Ḥakīm at-Tirmidhī, and Junayd have followed this tripartition. Kharrāz, however, inserts between *nafs* and *qalb* the element *ṭab*ᶜ, "nature," the natural functions of man (W 240–42).

2. See Louis Massignon, "Le 'coeur' (*al-qalb*) dans la prière et la méditation musulmane," *Études carmélitaines* 9 (1950).

At almost the same time in history, Nūrī saw in man four different aspects of the heart, which he derived in an ingenious way from the Koran:

Ṣadr, "breast," is connected with Islam (Sūra 39:23);
qalb, "heart," is the seat of *īmān,* "faith" (Sūra 49:7; 16:106);
fuʾād, "heart," is connected with *maʿrifa,* "gnosis" (Sūra 53:11); and
lubb, "innermost heart," is the seat of *tauḥīd* (Sūra 3:190) (W 321).

The Sufis often add the element of *sirr,* the innermost part of the heart in which the divine revelation is experienced. Jaʿfar introduced, in an interesting comparison, reason, *ʿaql,* as the barrier between *nafs* and *qalb*—"the barrier which they both cannot transcend" (Sūra 55:20), so that the dark lower instincts cannot jeopardize the heart's purity (W 163).

Each of these spiritual centers has its own functions, and ʿAmr al-Makkī has summed up some of the early Sufi ideas in a lovely myth:

God created the hearts seven thousand years before the bodies and kept them in the station of proximity to Himself and He created the spirits seven thousand years before the hearts and kept them in the garden of intimate fellowship (*uns*) with Himself, and the consciences—the innermost part—He created seven thousand years before the spirits and kept them in the degree of union (*waṣl*) with Himself. Then he imprisoned the conscience in the spirit and the spirit in the heart and the heart in the body. Then He tested them and sent prophets, and then each began to seek its own station. The body occupied itself with prayer, the heart attained to love, the spirit arrived at proximity to its Lord, and the innermost part found rest in union with Him.[3]

Later Sufis have elaborated these comparatively simple teachings into a minute system of correspondences in which every spiritual experience is connected with its respective recipient part.

In the same way, the different kinds of revelations (*kashf*) that are granted to the Sufis have been classified on the basis of the different levels of consciousness on which they occur and whether they lead to intellectual or intuitive knowledge of the divine. A late mystic, relying upon the traditional terminology, classifies the revelations as follows:

a) *Kashf kaunī,* revelation on the plane of the created things, is a result of pious actions and purifications of the lower soul; it becomes manifest in dreams and clairvoyance.
b) *Kashf ilāhī,* divine revelation, is a fruit of constant worship and polishing of the heart; it results in the knowledge of the world of spirits

3. Margaret Smith, *Readings from the Mystics of Islam* (London, 1950), no. 29.

and in cardiognosy ["soul-reading"] so that the mystic sees the hidden things and reads the hidden thoughts.
c) *Kashf ʿaqlī,* revelation by reason, is essentially the lowest grade of intuitive knowledge; it can be attained by polishing the moral faculties, and can be experienced by the philosophers as well.
d) *Kashf īmānī,* revelation through faith, is the fruit of perfect faith after man has acquired proximity to the perfections of prophethood; then he will be blessed by direct divine addresses; he talks with the angels, meets the spirits of the prophets, sees the Night of Might and the blessings of the month of Ramaḍan in human form in the *ʿālam al-mithāl.* (IK 443–44)

On the whole, these last specifications belong to a later development of Sufism; however, the different degrees of nonrational revelation of supernatural realities have been accepted by all the mystics from early times. They clearly distinguished the *ilm ladunnī* (cf. Sūra 18:65), the "wisdom that is with and from God" and is granted to the gnostic by an act of divine grace, from normal knowledge. They "tasted" *(dhauq)* in this experience new levels of revealed wisdom that were not to be attained by a scientific approach or by theological reasoning.

GOOD AND EVIL: THE ROLE OF SATAN

One of the most fascinating aspects of mystical psychology in Islam is the way in which the Sufis have dealt with Satan, the power of evil. Satan, according to the Koran either a fallen angel or a jinn created from fire, plays a dominant role in the story of creation as told in the Koran (Sūra 2:28–34). According to some mystics, he was the teacher of the angels and in this role was even made the subject of a Bengali Muslim poem of the early seventeenth century, the *Iblīsnāme* by Sayyid Sulṭān.[4] The author says that the angels were ordered to honor Iblis even after God had cursed him, since he had been their teacher—the same applies to the disciple who has to honor and obey his sheikh, even if the sheikh is a veritable satan.

A well-known tradition says that Satan sits in the blood of Adam's children (cf. S 471), and thus he could be equated with the *nafs,* the lower principle, the "flesh." But never in the history of Islam has Satan been given absolute power over men: he can tell them lies and seduce them as he did with Adam, but they have the possibility to resist his insinuations (Iqbal's Satan sadly complains that

4. Enamul Haqq, *Muslim Bengali Literature* (Karachi, 1957), p. 119.

it is much too easy for him to seduce people). Iblis never becomes "evil as such"; he always remains a creature of God and, thus, a necessary instrument in His hands.

In some mystical circles something like a rehabilitation of Satan was attempted. It seems that this idea was first formulated by Ḥallāj: Satan boasts of having served God for thousands of years before Adam's creation, and his pride in being created from fire makes him refuse God's order to prostrate himself before Adam, newly created from clay. Ḥallāj recognizes only two true monotheists in the world, Muhammad and Satan—but Muhammad is the treasurer of divine grace, whereas Iblis has become the treasurer of divine wrath. In Ḥallāj's theory, Satan becomes "more monotheist than God Himself" (R 538). For God's eternal will is that no one should be worshiped except Him, and Satan refuses to fall down before a created being, notwithstanding God's explicit order. As Ḥallāj translates his outcry in a famous quatrain: "My rebellion means to declare Thee Holy!" Iblis was kept between will and order, and

> He was thrown in the water, his hands tied to his back,
> and He said to him: "Beware lest you become wet."

This tragic situation of Satan has inspired a number of poets to express their sympathies with him whose predicament, in a certain sense, foreshadowed the difficulties man would have to undergo in this world. The most beautiful poem in this respect is that by Sanāʾī (SD 871)—a first great "Lament of Satan," in which the fallen angel, whose "heart was the nest for the Sīmurgh of love," complains of God's ruse: He had intended from eternity to condemn him and made Adam the outward cause for his fall:

> He put the hidden snare into my way—
> Adam was the corn in the ring of this snare.
> He wanted to give me the mark of curse—
> He did what He wanted—the earthen Adam was but an
> excuse.

To be sure, Satan had read on the Well-preserved Tablet that one creature would be cursed by God—but how could he, with his thousands of treasures of obedience, expect that it would be he himself? There are few poems that show the tragic greatness of Iblis better than this little-known *ghazal* by the master of Ghazna.

Sanāʾī may have been influenced in his thought by his elder contemporary Aḥmad Ghazzālī (d. 1126), the classical representative of Satan's rehabilitation, who dared to say: "Who does not learn *tauḥīd* from Satan, is an infidel"[5]—a remark that infuriated the orthodox but found an echo in many later Sufi writings. ʿAṭṭār follows him in his approach—he too sees in Iblis the perfect monotheist and lover, who, once cursed by God, accepts this curse as a robe of honor; for (in the true Ḥallājian tradition), "to be cursed by Thee, is a thousand times dearer to me than to turn my head away from Thee to anything else" (cf. MT 217). Iblis becomes here the model of the perfect lover, who obeys every wish of the beloved and prefers eternal separation willed by the beloved to the union for which he longs. Centuries later Sarmad, the Jewish convert to Sufism (executed 1661) in Mogul India, shocked the orthodox with a quatrain in which he called men to imitate Satan:

> Go, learn the method of servantship from Satan:
> Choose one *qibla* and do not prostrate yourself before
> anything else.
>
> (AP 238)

Even the poetry of the eighteenth-century mystic Shāh ʿAbduʾl-Laṭīf in the remote province of Sind calls the reader to admire Iblis as the one true lover and to follow his example—a verse that has caused considerable puzzlement to the commentators.[6]

Other mystics, however, have seen in Iblis's refusal to fall down before Adam not only an act of disobedience—the prototype of all disobedience in the world—but an act resulting from lack of love. Iblis was, as Rūmī has repeatedly asserted, one-eyed: He saw only Adam's form, made of dust, and therefore boasted, "I am better than he," fire being superior to clay. But he overlooked the decisive fact that God had breathed His breath into man and formed him according to His image (M 4:1617). He is, thus, a representative of one-eyed intellectualism, lacking in that divine love that is Adam's heritage, as Rūmī (M 4:1402) and, following him, Iqbal have shown.

Satan becomes a tragic figure, lost, hopeless, and lonely, some-

5. Merlin S. Swartz, *Ibn al-Jawzī's "kitāb al-quṣṣās waʾl-mudhakkirīn"* (Beirut, 1971), 221.

6. *Sur Yaman Kalyan*; see Annemarie Schimmel, "Schah ʿAbdul Laṭīf's Beschreibung des wahren Sufi," in *Festschrift für Fritz Meier*, comp. Richard Gramlich (Wiesbaden, 1974).

times visualized by the mystics in a sad attire or playing melancholy songs of separation. The manifold aspects of Satan developed throughout the centuries by the Sufis have been echoed, in our day, in the work of Muhammad Iqbal, whose multicolored picture of Satan is quite unusual.[7] He sees in him the lover as well as the intellectual, the monotheist and the spirit of evil who longs to be overcome by the perfect man (faithful to the Prophetic tradition, "My *shayṭān* has become Muslim") and to be broken in order to find salvation. Thus, he will eventually prostrate himself before man, who proves stronger than he. On the other hand, Iqbal has also employed the more common image of Satan the seducer, the materialist, and the destroyer.

The problems of Satanology are closely connected with those of good and evil and, thus, with predestination and free will. These problems constituted the subject of the first theological discussions in early Islamic thought and have never ceased to puzzle the minds of the pious. For if there is no agent but God, what is the role of man? To what extent can his deeds and actions be attributed to him? What is the derivation of evil? To what extent is man caught, like the mythical Satan, between divine will and divine order?

"Predestination (*qadar*) is the secret of God with which neither a close angel nor a sent messenger is acquainted." It is, as Rūzbihān Baqlī says, quoting this alleged *ḥadīth*, "the divine mystery from the time before creation, which nothing created in time can ever hope to solve" (B 175). The mystics knew well that an unquestioned acceptance of all-embracing predestination could produce dangerous consequences for human activities and faith. The early ascetics, though, were never certain about their fate. In spite of their supererogative prayers, vigils, and fasts, they constantly dreaded the Day of Judgment that might lead them to Hell, according to God's eternal decree: "These to Hell, and I do not care, and those to Paradise, and I do not care"— this *ḥadīth* is quoted even by Ghazzālī to point to the inscrutability of the divine will.

Later mystics tried to solve the problem by the introduction of the principle of love: the will of someone who has reached annihilation through asceticism, suffering, and love persists in God's will. Then man no longer attributes any actions to himself but lives and

7. Alessandro Bausani, "Satan nell'opera filosofico-poetica di Muhammad Iqbal," *Rivista degli Studi Orientali* 30 (1957); Annemarie Schimmel, "Die Gestalt des Satan in Muhammad Iqbal's Werk," *Kairos*, 1963, fasc. 2.

works, so to speak, out of the divine will, thus experiencing the *jabr maḥmūd,* "agreeable constraint."

More outspoken than other Sufis, Rūmī pondered the incompatibility of piety and the acceptance of a blind predestination. He charmingly told the story of a man who climbed a tree and ate the fruit, assuring the gardener that "this is God's garden, and I am eating from God's fruit given by Him." The gardener, thereupon, nicely thrashed him "with the stick of God" until the thief had to acknowledge that the transgression was done by his own will, not by God's order (M 5:3077–100).

In the same line of thought, Rūmī refuses to believe in the generally accepted explanation of the *ḥadīth "qad jaffa'l-qalam,"* "the pen has dried up," which means that nothing once decreed and written on the Well-preserved Tablet can ever be changed. This *ḥadīth,* he thinks, says that God has ordered once and for all that the good deeds of the faithful shall never be lost, but not that good and evil actions are of equal value (M 5:3131–53).

> Dress in that material which you yourself have woven,
> and drink the product of what you have planted.
>
> (M 5:3181)

This *ḥadīth* is not an invitation to laziness but rather a charge to work harder and to act in perfect sincerity so that one's service becomes purer and thus more acceptable (M 5:3113). For,

> One beats a cow when it refuses to carry the yoke,
> but not because it does not put on wings!
>
> (M 5:3110)

One may also argue that man's acting in accordance with his God-given nature constitutes, in itself, an identification with the divine purpose in creation: whatever God brings into existence and allows to be done must be useful for some good end, even though man may not be able to see the final goal of his own action. Man is, as the tradition says, "between the two fingers of the Merciful." That means that each action has two faces, each state of constraint has in itself an extension, just as in the very act of breathing extension and compression are united. In the same way, God manifests Himself through His different and contradictory attributes and names, and the manifestation of the attribute of majesty is as necessary as that of kindness for the maintenance of the current of creation. Man sees only the outward phenomena and takes them at face value but rarely thinks of the hidden power that brings them into existence. He sees—to use Rūmī's favorite comparison—the dust but not the wind; he looks at the foam but not at the bottom of the sea. The divine is the *coincidentia oppositorum,* but in order to become known it has to show itself in contrasting forms and colors, for the absolute light is too strong to be perceived and must be broken through material media. Through the opposite of light one recognizes the light (M 1:1133). Thus, the mystic can understand that God's wrath is mercy in disguise, and that the pain and punishment that He inflicts upon those who love Him are necessary for their spiritual growth—just as bitter medicine is necessary for the sick. How often is man misled by the delusion of outward appearances:

> How many enmities were friendship,
> how many destructions were renovation!
>
> (M 5:186)

For God hides His grace in wrath and His wrath in grace. And everything created shows this double face:

> The cold wind became a murderer for the people of ʿĀd,
> but for Solomon it served as a porter.
>
> (M 6:2660)

Poison is the life element for the serpent, but it carries death to others (M 5:3295). The figure of Khiḍr, whose seemingly illogical actions had a deep meaning, can be understood from this viewpoint.

On the other hand, the Sufi should not only accept good and evil as coming from God and therefore equally welcome, he should also be careful that no ruse be hidden in grace. Constant watchfulness is required to keep the soul safe.

The great theosophists of later centuries have devoted detailed studies to the will and knowledge of God, discussing minutely the relation of the human to the divine will. A good example is Jīlī's thought, as explained so excellently by Reynold A. Nicholson. But even the most learned systems could not eliminate the painful dilemma of predestination and free will; for this problem cannot be solved by intellect but only, if at all, by love. Ḥallāj, Rūmī, and their followers understood that the *jabr maḥmūd,* the "higher predestination," as Iqbal calls it, can be achieved not simply by accepting a given situation but by actively conforming with God's will through love and prayer. Once such a change of human will is achieved by absolute and loving surrender, the mystic can hope for new doors to open before him on his spiritual path into the depths of God—

> And if He closes before you all the ways and passes,
> He will show a hidden way which nobody knows.
>
> (D 765)

SAINTS AND MIRACLES

"You must know that the principle and foundation of Sufism and knowledge of God rest on saintship" (H 210), says Hujwīrī, and three centuries after him Jāmī opened his discussions about the history of Sufism with a paragraph on saintship. In fact, the theories of saintship, *wilāya,* have formed one theme that has been discussed by the Sufis since the late ninth century, when Kharrāz, Sahl at-Tustarī, and al-Ḥakīm at-Tirmidhī wrote their essays on this subject.

The word usually translated as "saint," *walī,* means "someone who is under special protection, friend"; it is the attribute given by the Shiites to ʿAlī, the *walī Allāh* par excellence. The word is, as Qushayrī points out, both active and passive: a *walī* is one whose affairs are led (*tuwulliya*) by God and who performs (*tawallā*) worship and obedience (cf. N 6). The *auliyāʾ Allāh,* the "friends of God," are mentioned in the Koran several times, the most famous occasion being Sūra 10:63: "Verily, the friends of God, no fear is upon them nor are they sad."

The concept of *wilāya* developed during the early centuries of Sufism. An authority of the early tenth century, Abū ʿAbdallāh as-Sālimī, defined the saints as "those who are recognizable by the loveliness of their speech, and fine manners, and submission, and generosity, showing little opposition, and accepting the excuse of everyone who excuses himself before them, and perfect mildness towards all creatures, the good as well as the bad" (N 121). Thus, the ideal Sufi is here called a *walī.*

The *wilāyat ʿāmma,* the "general saintship" common to all the sincere faithful (and it is to that *wilāya* that Sālimī's statement points), is usually distinguished from the *wilāya khāṣṣa,* that of the advanced mystics, "who have become annihilated in God and remain through Him, and the *walī* is he who has been annihilated in Him and lives in Him" (N 5). From among those perfect mystics, a whole hierarchy of saints has evolved since at least the time of Tirmidhī. The highest spiritual authority is the *quṭb*, "axis, pole," or *ghauth*, "help." He is surrounded by three *nuqabā*ʾ, "substitutes," four *autād*, "pillars," seven *abrār*, "pious," forty *abdāl*, "substitutes," three hundred *akhyār*, "good," and four thousand hidden saints. Some authorities, e.g., Ibn ʿArabī, claim that there are seven *abdāl*, one for each of the seven climates;[8] Rūzbihān Baqlī expressed similar ideas. The *quṭb* is the virtual center of spiritual energy upon whom the well-being of this world depends (CL 80). Henri Corbin has shown, in a penetrating study, the importance of the orientation toward the Pole, the place where the celestial revelation, "the sun at midnight," will appear to the pilgrim on the mystical Path. The *quṭb* rests in perfect tranquillity, grounded in God—that is why all the "minor stars" revolve around him.

One may assume a close structural relationship between the concept of the *quṭb* as the highest spiritual guide of the faithful and that of the hidden *imām* of Shia Islam. Not a few mystics claimed to be the *quṭb* of their time, and quite a number of them assumed the role of the Mahdi, the manifestation of the hidden *imām* at the end of time. The veneration shown to the *imām* and the *quṭb*, as manifested in the mystical preceptor, is common to Sufism and Shiism. The Shia teaches: "Who dies without knowing the *imām* of his time, dies as an infidel." And Jalāluddīn Rūmī, though a relatively moderate Sufi, said: "He who does not know the true sheikh—i.e., the Perfect Man and *quṭb* of his time—is a *kāfir*, an infidel" (M 2:3325). The world cannot exist without a pole or an axis—it turns around him just as a mill turns around its axis and is otherwise of no use (U 63).

In later Iranian theosophy, the *quṭb* is considered the locus of Sarosh, the old Zoroastrian angel of obedience, hearing, and inspiration who corresponds, in Sufi mythology, either to Gabriel or to Isrāfīl, the angel of resurrection. In light of this, the claim of a modern thinker like Iqbal that he would "call a people to spiritual resurrection" gains special significance; he assumes, in a sense,

8. Muḥyīuddīn Ibn ʿArabī, *Al-futūḥāt al-makkiyya*, 4 vols. (Cairo, 1329 h./1911), chap. 198, faṣl 31.

A scene from Jāmī's Nafaḥāt ul-uns:
Abū'l-Adyān passing through the pyre.

British Museum, Or. 1362

the role of the *quṭb*. In fact, the three angelic figures Sarosh, Isrāfīl, and Gabriel occur very frequently in his poetry.

A very peculiar theory—or rather an elaboration of the abovementioned ideas—was invented by Rūzbihān Baqlī, who speaks of a hierarchic structure of three hundred persons whose hearts are like Adam's heart, forty whose hearts are like Moses's heart, seven whose hearts are fashioned after Abraham's heart, five whose hearts correspond to Gabriel's heart, three whose hearts correspond to that of Michael, and one, the *quṭb*, whose heart is equal to Isrāfīl's. He adds to this group of saintly persons the four prophets who have been lifted up to Heaven alive—Idrīs, Khiḍr, Ilyas, and Jesus—and thus reaches the cosmic number of 360, the pleroma of saints (CL 83).

Among the groups in the hierarchy the Forty have gained special prominence in Islam. Numerous stories are told about them, and there are local names in the Near East connected with their presence, such as *Kĭrklareli*, "the county of the Forty," in the European province of Turkey. The word *abdāl*, usually connected with the Forty, seems to have assumed this high spiritual meaning only gradually. In a number of early Sufi texts—in Sanāʾī's poetry, for example—the *abdāl* are usually mentioned together with the ascetics. Later, the word was used to designate a saint who after his death would be "substituted" for (*badal*) by another person. In Turkey, mainly in the Bektashi tradition, it has become a sort of sobriquet for a certain group of mystics, like Kaygusuz Abdāl, Pīr Sulṭān Abdāl.

The Seven are mentioned in some towns as the spiritual guardians of a sacred place—Marrakesh, for instance, claims to be protected by the Seven. Often, seven saintly persons or virgins are treated as a single unit in veneration (that can be the case with the Forty as well). A connection between the veneration of the Seven and that of the Seven Sleepers—mentioned in the Koran (Sūra 18)—is possible.[9]

The saints are supposed to know each other. Though they are veiled from the eyes of the common people, they recognize fellow saints without ever having met them, and many stories are told about secret meetings of saints on certain mountains in which, sometimes, an adept is allowed to partake. But on the whole it is

9. Émile Dermenghem, *Le culte des saints dans l'Islam Maghrebin* (Paris, 1954), is the best study in this field, written with a deep understanding of mystical Islam.

held that God veils His friends from the world. "Out of jealousy, God puts a veil upon them and keeps them concealed from the public" (N 442), says Simnānī, following Bāyezīd's idea that "the saints are God's brides whom only the close relatives can behold" (MC 1:43). The *ḥadīth qudsī,* "verily my saints are under my domes, and only I know them," is often cited to support this idea.

The saints are the governors of the universe:

Every night the *autād* must go round the whole universe, and if there should be any place on which their eyes have not fallen, next day some imperfection will appear in that place, and they must then inform the *Quṭb,* in order that he may fix his attention on the weak spot and that by his blessing the imperfection may be removed. (H 228)

It is through the blessings of the saints that rain falls from heaven; on the places touched by their sacred feet plants spring up, and thanks to their help the Muslims will gain victory over the unbelievers. They are, as Rūzbihān put it, "the eyes which regard God, since they are the eyes through which He regards the world" (CL 82). These ideas of saintship have lived among the mystics for centuries and were extremely popular among the masses. They are expanded in the theories of the great Naqshbandī reformer Aḥmad Sirhindī (d. 1624), who claimed for himself and three of his descendants the rank of the *qayyūm,* which is even superior to that of the *quṭb.*

Tirmidhī distinguished between two types of saints, the *walī ṣidq Allāh* and the *walī minnat Allāh,* the first one reaching the state of saintship through faithful adherence to every detail of the *sharīʿa* and the *ṭarīqa,* the second one by God's grace through the act of loving (MM 16). This differentiation points to the different spiritual and psychological attitudes of the faithful in pursuing the Path; divine grace, however, is always required to reach the last illumination and true saintship. Tirmidhī devoted a large part of his discussions to the topic that gave his book its title, the *khatm al-wilāya,* the "seal of saintship"; for just as the prophets have their "seal," their closing and most perfect manifestation of the prophetic spirit, in Muhammad, the saints have a "seal" as well.

The problem of whether the saint or the prophet is endowed with a higher spiritual rank has been discussed often from the time of Tirmidhī onward; and the traditional Sufi schools have always agreed upon the superiority of the prophet. The end of saintship is only the beginning of prophethood. Every prophet possesses the aspect of saintship in himself, but only rarely will the saint worship—which are scarcely compatible with the basic teach-mystic may strive to attain higher and higher degrees of proximity, the highest level he can reach is spiritual ascension, which corresponds to the ascension that the Prophet performed in body. Thus "in the last stage of saintship the spirit of the saint becomes similar to the body of the Prophet" (N 443), says Simnānī. Certainly, some mystics of the intoxicated type—symbolized, for example, by the love-enraptured merchant of Rūmī's *Mathnawī*—have declared the mystical intoxication of the saint superior to the sobriety of the prophet; for the prophet is not lost in the vision of God but turns back to his people to teach them the will of God, being forever united with the divine. The difference between what N. Söderblom and Friedrich Heiler have defined as "mystical" and "prophetic" religiosity has been very clearly understood and expressed by the saints of medieval Islam, whom Iqbal follows in the fifth chapter of his *Reconstruction of Religious Thought in Islam* (1930).

The role of the *walī* in Islamic piety does not correspond exactly to that of the saint in the Christian faith. It is closely connected with the mystery of initiation and progress on the spiritual path and leads through a well-established hierarchy, the members of which surpass each other according to the degree of their love and gnosis. The initiation of the adept through Khiḍr, the prototype of a saint among the prophets, belongs, therefore, to this discussion.

Some theories could lead to a deterioration of saintship in practical life if applied in the wrong way. A saying like *ḥasanāt al-abrār sayyiʾāt al-muqarrabīn* (L 44)—"the good deeds of the pious are the bad deeds of those who are brought near," i.e., the saints—could lead, and in fact led, to the "saint" abolishing the religiously prescribed norms. He might consider himself *jenseits von Gut und Böse*, beyond good and evil, claiming to be united with the divine will in such a mysterious way that those dwelling on lower levels of the path—let alone the common people— are incapable of understanding and appreciating his actions. Once more Khiḍr, with his three mysterious, outwardly destructive actions (Sūra 18), comes to mind. Even though the claim may be true for some saints endowed with powerful personalities and acting in perfect sincerity, it could easily induce pretenders to sanctity to actions that are by no means useful for their fellow mystics, to say nothing of the majority of the population. It is because of these darker sides of Muslim saint worship—which are scarcely compatible with the basic teaching of Islam—that Sufism has come into disrepute among many Muslim modernists, who see only the negative aspects as they are manifested at the lower levels of popular piety.

One factor that led people to believe in the spiritual capacity of a Sufi leader was his ability to work miracles. Numerous stories of saints say that "he was heard when he prayed," or "such as he said would definitely come true," or "when he became angry God Almighty would quickly take revenge for his sake" (N 506). There is no doubt that many Sufis indeed had extraordinary powers to perform acts that seemed to supersede natural laws.

One of the main traits of Sufi hagiographical works is that they tell about the *firāsa*, "cardiognosia" (soul-reading), of a master. "Beware of the *firāsa* [discernment] of the faithful," it was said, "for he sees by God's light" (B 588). Innumerable stories are told about a sheikh's insight into his disciple's heart; he was able to tell his secret wishes, hopes, and dislikes, to understand signs of spiritual pride or hypocrisy the very moment the adept entered his presence. There were even some who claimed to be able to discern whether a person was destined for Heaven or Hell (N 439).

The saint was able to disappear from sight, to become completely invisible, and to practice *burūz*, exteriorization, i.e., he could be present at different places at the same time. According to legend, Rūmī attended seventeen parties at one time and wrote a poem at each one![10] The saint was capable of coming to the aid of his disciples wherever they were through the faculty of *ṭayy al-makān*, of being beyond spatial restriction, which is often attested to in hagiography. In cases of danger the sheikh might suddenly appear in the midst of a band of robbers to drive them away or assume the shape of the ruler in order to protect a disciple who called for help, or—as I was told several times in Turkey—the master might appear, in spiritualized form, at a sick person's bed in order to cure him or at least relieve him temporarily from his pain. "To enter under the burden of the sick" (N 397) was a miracle often performed by Sufis. A very strong *tawajjuh*, the concentration of two partners on

10. Johann Karl Teufel, *Eine Lebensbeschreibung des Scheichs ʿAlī-i Hamadānī* (Leiden, 1962), p. 108.

each other, is necessary to produce such an effect; it is taken for granted that the sheikh and his disciple are, so to speak, on the same wave length.

This unity between master and *murīd* can manifest itself in vicarious suffering: when the disciple is hurt, the master's body shows the traces. Or, as in the story of Bāyezīd Bisṭāmī, when his disciples tried to kill him, the wounds appeared on their own bodies. Distance has no meaning for the saints: "To traverse distance is child's play: henceforth pay visits by means of thought; it is not worth while to visit any person, and there is no virtue in bodily presence" (H 235), as one of Hujwīrī's masters told his disciple.

The theologians carefully discussed the theories of miracles: the saint's miracles are called *karāmāt*, "charismata," whereas the prophet's miracles are classified as *muᶜjizāt*, "what renders others incapable to do the same," and the two types must never be confused (K 59–61). The general term for anything extraordinary is *khāriq ul-ᶜāda*, "what tears the custom" (of God); i.e., when God wants to disrupt the chain of cause and result to which we are accustomed, since He usually acts in this or that way, a *khāriqa* may be performed and change the course of life. The mystics have also argued, in lengthy deliberations, about whether miracles are performed in the state of sobriety or in that of mystical intoxication. They have classified the miracles under different headings—Subkī distinguishes twenty-five main types—and whole collections have been composed to show the various kinds of miracles performed by Muslim saints.[11]

Islamic hagiography is filled with legends, and the same miracle is often attributed to Sufis in distant parts of the Muslim world (and even outside it). Motifs known from folklore and fairy tales are woven into this fabric—such as the idea that a saint can grant a hundred-year-old couple three sons only to call them back when the parents do not behave decently. Fertility miracles are one of the most popular aspects of saint worship, and the hopes of barren women are expressed all over the world—not only in Islamic lands—by the same magical means: by binding little cradles at the gate of the saint's abode, by taking vows, by "selling" the child to the saint (in Turkey many boys are called *Satïlmïsh*, "sold," or girls

11. Tājuddīn as-Subkī, *Ṭabaqāt ash-shāfiᶜiyya al-kubrā*, 12 vols. (Cairo, 1324 h./1906), 2:59ff. The comprehensive study is Yūsuf an-Nabahānī, *Jāmiᶜ karāmāt al-auliyā*ʾ (Bulaq, 1329 h./1911). See also Hans Joachim Kissling, "Die Wunder der Derwische," *Zeitschrift der Deutschen Morgenländischen Gesellschaft* 107 (1957).

Satī, because they were granted by a living or dead saint to whose threshold they were "sold" by the parents).

Other miracles frequently mentioned in Islamic sources are connected with food: a buck gives milk so that unexpected guests can be entertained; food and drink are mysteriously provided in the middle of the desert. Even a great mystic like Ḥallāj is credited with this kind of display. For people famous for their hospitality and accustomed to traveling long distances through uninhabited areas, the miraculous production of food and water and, very often, sweetmeat would certainly be one of the most coveted powers of a saint. The traveler would also appreciate the saint about whom it was told: "When one remembers him when a lion turns toward you, the lion will turn away, and when one remembers him in a place where bedbugs abound, the bedbugs will disappear with God's permission" (N 513). Many tales are concerned with miraculous rescues from danger or escapes from death. Such a story is told of a Sindhi saint who fell in love with a beautiful boy and was thrown, by the boy's father, into the Indus, a millstone fastened around his neck; he was seen, later, calmly riding on the stone on the waves of the river.

Whosoever obeys God completely, everything created is bound to obey him—that is an old Sufi maxim that has been illustrated by miracle stories. In wrath a saint can turn a flower into an alligator (as happened in Mango Pir near Karachi) or live among wild animals, who serve him, as the charming story of Ibrāhīm Raqqī relates:

In my novitiate I set out to visit Muslim Maghribī. I found him in his mosque, acting as preceptor. He pronounced *al-ḥamd* (Praise be God) incorrectly. I said to myself: "My trouble has been wasted." Next day when I was going to the bank of the Euphrates to perform the religious ablution I saw a lion asleep on the road. I turned back, and was faced by another lion which had been following me. Hearing my cry of despair, Muslim came forth from his cell. When the lions saw him, they humbled themselves before him. He took the ear of each of them and rubbed it, saying: "O dogs of God, have not I told you that you must not interfere with my guest?" Then he said to me: "O Abū Isḥāq, thou hast busied thyself with correcting the exterior for the sake of God's creatures, hence thou art afraid of them, but it has been my business to correct my interior for God's sake, hence His creatures are afraid of me." (H 233–34)

The later books about Muslim saints, particularly Yāfiʿī's *Rauḍat ar-riyāḥīn*, abound with stories—similar to the legends of medieval Christian saints, and the numerous Buddhist tales—that show the warm, pleasant relationship between the man of God and the animals. A number of Indian and Persian miniatures show the saint sleeping or sitting among the beasts, the lions tamed and obedient, the birds at his service, the shy gazelle conversing with him. For the Muslim mystic, this close relationship with the animal world is not at all amazing, since every creature praises God in its own voice and he who has purified his soul understands their praise and can join them. Once the mystic has subdued the "dog of the lower soul," every creature becomes obedient to him. He can, then, sanctify a dog by a mere glance (N 419); even the frogs may talk to him, and the crocodile, with tears in its eyes, is willing to surrender its prey to him.[12] The saint would consider it a severe setback on the spiritual journey if the animals become silent and see in him "something else," so that he has to repent.[13]

Not only animals, but plants and stones, too, obey the friend of God. He may even be blessed by the appearance of the months in human form, as happened, according to the legend, to ʿAbduʾl-Qādir Gīlānī: every month would present itself to him as a beautiful or ugly youth, according to the events that were to take place in the coming four weeks (N 512).

Many miracles point to the capacity of the Sufi saint to spread the true Islamic doctrines. Even as a baby he will not drink his mother's milk in the daytime during the month of Ramaḍan, but only after sunset. In the desert he is provided with facilities to perform his ablutions correctly. That illnesses are cured by means of religious formulae is well known—the story of the deaf girl who was cured by the saint's whispering the call to prayer into her ear is only one example from a long list of miracles in which the Sufis used prayer and *dhikr* formulae for healing purposes. Even today the recitation of a *Fātiḥa* or similar prayer, together with "breathing upon" (*damīdan, üflemek*) the sick, is common in the Muslim world (cf. N 352)—and the faith in a religious formula pronounced by an alleged saint is often, in rural areas, much greater than the trust in a Western-trained physician.

In many miracle stories the issue at stake is that of conversion. These stories were frequently told in the classical period of Islam, when "materialists" or those who denied the basic tenets of Islam

12. Annemarie Schimmel, "Sufismus und Heiligenverehrung im spätmittelalterlichen Agypten," in *Festschrift für W. Caskel*, ed. Erich Gräf (Leiden, 1968), p. 282.

13. Mīr ʿAlī Shīr Qāniʿ, *Tuḥfat al-kirām* (Hyderabad, Sind, 1957), p. 419.

were convinced by the Sufis. A famous example is the story of Abūʾl-Adyān in the tenth century (X 179). He argued with a Zoroastrian that he could walk through a fire without being hurt, since fire has the capacity to burn only by God's permission. He indeed passed through the pyre and proved to the stunned Persian the truth of the Ashʿarite doctrine that there is no real causality, but that God gives or withholds the capacities of the elements to which mankind is accustomed: He creates these qualities and capacities anew every moment. A comparable story is related by Ibn ʿArabī about a philosopher who expressed similar views about whether fire could burn him; his frock was filled with fire, but it did not hurt him (N 552).

The first version of the miracle can be explained by the end of the story: at night the Sufi saint discovered a blister on his foot. He told his servant that this happened the very moment he awoke from his trance, as he was emerging from the fire, "and if I had come to myself in the midst of the fire, I would have been burnt completely." He was safeguarded by the power of his trance. In the same way, the Aissawiyya dervishes in North Africa dance with burning coals in their hands without feeling any pain.[14] Similar events are often attested to in the history of religions, and particularly in Sufism. The pious one becomes so transported in his prayers or meditation that he feels no pain when one of his limbs is amputated, or he is so out of himself that he is oblivious to the bites of scorpions or serpents. One may think, on a lower level, of the Rifāʿī dervishes and many pretenders to Sufism who injure themselves by gashing themselves with a sword or by eating glass.

In the case of Abūʾl-Adyān, as well as in the parallel story told by Ibn ʿArabī, the purpose was the conversion of an infidel to Islam: that is why these stories have been told and retold. There are numerous examples of this type of miracle in later times. In Sind, a Hindu physician was converted when he examined a saint's urine.

Even animals played a part in the conversion of non-Muslims. Cats, especially, are often associated with miracles, and some convents had cats as guardians. In a religion in which, according to popular belief, even the *sakīna* (divine presence) is supposed to appear in the form of a white cat, it is not surprising that the strange

14. Dermenghem, *Culte des saints*, p. 314; see René Brunel, *Essai sur la confrérie religieuse des Aissaouwa au Maroc* (Paris, 1926).

beggars' order of the Heddāwa in Morocco explicitly venerates cats[15] (was not the Prophet a great lover of these gentle animals?), and even the novices are called *quēṭāṭ*, "little tomcats." The following story—told in fifteenth-century India about a miraculous cat—is a typical example in which different trends of miracle telling are blended together. The story itself goes back to earlier sources (cf. N 148).[16]

It had occurred to a disciple of Shaikh Ashraf Jahāngīr, Qāḍī Rabīᶜaddīn by name and an inhabitant of Awadh, that in former times there were *shaikhs* whose glance had power over animals and birds; but he did not know whether such people existed at the present day. The *shaikh* when he learnt of this, smiled and said "Perhaps." Now Kamāl the Jogi had a cat which sometimes used to pass in front of the *shaikh*. He ordered the cat to be brought to him and began a discourse on a holy topic. The *shaikh*'s face gradually assumed such expression that all present were struck with fear. The cat also listened to the discourse and was so affected that it fell down unconscious; when it came to its senses again, it began to rub the feet of the *shaikh* and then those of the other companions. After this it became a habit that when the *shaikh* was talking upon divine mysteries, the cat never left the holy gathering. When travellers were about to come to the *khānqāh*, it used to indicate their number by mewing; from this the servitors of the *khānqāh* would know for how many guests to lay the cloth for the meal. At the time when food was served, the cat also was given a portion equal to that of others who were present, and sometimes it was sent to bring members of the company who had been summoned. It would go to the room of the person who had been called and by mewing insistently or banging at the door would make the person understand that the *shaikh* had summoned him.

One day a party of dervishes had arrived at the *khānqāh*. The cat mewed as usual but when the food was sent it appeared that it was short by one portion. The *shaikh* returned to the cat and said: "Why have you made a mistake today?" The cat immediately went away and began to sniff at each of the dervishes of the party. When it came to the head of the band it jumped upon his knee and made a mess. When the *shaikh* saw what had happened he said: "The poor cat has done nothing wrong: this man is a stranger." The head of the band immediately cast himself at the feet of the *shaikh* and said "I am a *dahriyya* [materialist]. For twelve years I have travelled through the world wearing the garments of Islam. It was my intention that if it should so befall that some Sufi recognized me, I would accept Islam. Up to now none has known my secret: but that cat has revealed it. Today I accept Islam . . . ."

The cat remained alive until after the death of the *shaikh*. One day the successor of the *shaikh* had put a pot of milk upon the fire in order

15. René Brunel, *Le monachisme errant dans l'Islam, Sīdī Heddī et les Heddawa* (Paris, 1955), one of the most lovable books on a little known aspect of Sufism.

16. Quoted from Simon Digby, "Encounters with Jogis in Indian Sufi Hagiography," mimeographed, School of Oriental and African Studies (London, January 1970). For the story see Fritz Meier, ed., *Die "fawāʾiḥ al-ǧamāl wa fawātiḥ al-ǧalāl" des Naǧmuddīn al-Kubrā* (Wiesbaden, 1957), p. 28.

to cook milk rice and it chanced that a snake fell into the pot. The cat saw this and circled around the pot: he would not budge from the place and he mewed several times, but the cook did not understand and drove him out of the kitchen. When the cat saw that there was no way of making the cook understand, he leapt into the boiling liquid and surrendered his life. The rice had of course to be thrown away, and with it a black snake was discovered. The Sufi remarked that the cat had sacrificed his own life for the sake of the dervishes, and a tomb should be built for him.

In connection with the manifestation of spiritual power, contests (*munāqara*) were held to prove which saint was more powerful and could work more exciting miracles. These contests—which go back at least to Shiblī—are usually ascribed to the popular saints, who could easily turn their enemies into stones or wither trees with their curses. One of the most charming stories in this otherwise rather unpleasant and, basically, un-Sufi field of spiritual contests has been told by Émile Dermenghem about a North African saint who came riding on a lion to visit another saint. He was told to put his lion in the stable where the host's cow was tethered. Reluctantly, he entered the house and saw his host surrounded by beautiful dancing girls, which made him doubt his mystical qualities. But the next morning he found that his lion had been devoured by the cow.[17]

There was, however, one problem behind all the miracle stories that so delighted the crowds. To what extent was it legitimate for a mystic to perform miracles at all?

It is said that Junayd criticized Nūrī when the latter swore that he would drown himself in the Tigris unless he could catch a fish of a certain weight (which he succeeded in catching). Apprehensive of this kind of miracle, Junayd said that he would have preferred a viper to come out of the river and punish the impudent mystic (L 327).

Junayd's view is typical of the sober, high-ranking mystics throughout history; they regard interest in miracles as one of the three "veils" that can cover the hearts of the elect (the two others being too much attention to works of obedience and hope for heavenly reward).[18]

A beautiful story is attributed to Abū Saʿīd ibn Abīʾl-Khayr. Someone told him about a mystic who walked on water, and he

17. Dermenghem, *Culte des saints*, p. 12.

18. A. Ṭāhir al-Khānqāhī, *Guzīda dar akhlāq ū taṣawwuf*, ed. Iraj Afshar (Tehran, 1347 sh./1968), p. 19.

said: "Frogs and waterfowl do that as well!" When the person said, "and so-and-so flies in the air!" he replied: "So do birds and insects!" And when the narrator told him that somebody went from one town to the other in one minute, he answered: "Satan goes in one moment from the East to the West!" (NS 67). On another occasion he reproached somebody who asked what kind of miracles a certain Sufi had to his credit by drawing his attention to the life story of the saint in question: Is it not the greatest miracle that a butcher, who was also a butcher's son, should be attracted to the mystical Path, talk to Khiḍr, and be visited by innumerable people who want to obtain his blessings (N 288)?

The great masters considered miracles snares on the way toward God. The adept who has reached a certain stage on the Path will certainly gain the power of working some extraordinary feats, and these will probably keep him from further progress on the Path. It is so much easier to perform miracles and attract the interest of the masses than to pursue the hard path of spiritual training and constant struggle with the subtlest ruses of the lower self. This aversion of the spiritually advanced mystics for the kind of miracle-mongering that constituted part of the activities of the "shopkeeper sheikhs" and pseudo-mystics has found its crudest expression in an alleged *ḥadīth*: "Miracles are the menstruation of men" (IK 449). This saying, which seems to belong to the Indian, or at least eastern, part of the Muslim world, indicates that miracles come between man and God. Just as the husband avoids intercourse with his wife during the days of her impurity, so God denies mystical union to those who perform miracles. A different explanation of this oft-quoted saying may be found in another sentence—also current among the Indian Muslims since the thirteenth century—that juxtaposes the *ṭālib ad-dunyā*, "who seeks the world," the *ṭālib al-ākhira*, "who seeks the otherworld," and the *ṭālib al-maulā*, "who seeks the Lord." Only the last one is masculine, the second being equal to a eunuch indulging in passive pederasty (a classification that ᶜAṭṭār ascribed to Shiblī); and he who seeks the world is as low as a female and, we may conclude, therefore also afflicted with female impurities. The performance of miracles is a sign that a person's intention is still directed toward worldy approval, not exclusively toward God.[19]

19. Syed Muhammad Naguib al-Attas, *The Mysticism of Ḥamza al-Fanṣūrī* (Kuala Lumpur, 1970), p. 414; "lust" and even "poetry" have been called the "menstruation

There is no doubt that many of the miracles wrought by Sufi saints were true and real. These mystics had the power to bring down into the world of phenomena events that were still in the *ʿālam al-mithāl* and could, by virtue of their spiritual purity, help their disciples on the difficult path. But the danger of using certain extraordinary gifts for impure, or at least for less worthy, spiritual purposes was always present. And the saint was right who said: "It is better to restore one dead heart to eternal life than to restore to life a thousand dead bodies."[20]

THE VENERATION OF THE PROPHET

In his *Mathnawī* Rūmī tells how the infant Muhammad got lost and his nurse Ḥalīma, dissolved in tears, was consoled with the words:

> Do not grieve: he will not become lost to thee;
> nay, but the whole world will become lost in him.
> (M 4:975)

This was certainly a perfect expression of the feelings of every Muslim in the thirteenth century. A few centuries later, the Turkish Sufi poet Eshrefoghlu happily addressed the Prophet:

> In Muhammad's gathering I put on the trousers of faith
> and came, strutting like a peacock.[21]

From earliest times, Muhammad, the messenger of God, had been the ideal for the faithful Muslim. His behavior, his acts, and his words served as models for the pious, who tried to imitate him as closely as possible even in the smallest details of outward life—be it the form of dress, the style of the beard, the performance of the tiniest particulars of ablution, and even his preference for certain kinds of food.

A new dimension was added by the introduction of much legendary lore into the Prophet's biography. He himself had rejected legends and forbade any personality cult, claiming to have only one

---

of men." The classification of *ṭālib al-maulā, ṭālib al-ākhira,* and *ṭālib ad-dunyā* seems to have been invented by Jamāluddīn Hānswī, the Chishtī saint of the late thirteenth century; see Zubaid Ahmad, *The Contribution of Indo-Pakistan to Arabic Literature,* 2d ed., (Lahore, 1968), p. 82. It was used by almost every Indo-Muslim mystic.

20. H. T. Sorley, *Shah Abdul Latif of Bhit: His Poetry, Life, and Times* (1940; reprint ed., Oxford, 1966), p. 248.

21. William Hickman, "Eshrefoghlu Rumi: Reconstitution of his *dīwān*" (Ph.D. diss., Harvard University, 1972). no. M 7.

miracle to his credit, that of having transmitted the words of the Koran to his people. Yet he was surrounded by miracles: the gazelle spoke to him, the palm-tree trunk sighed when he no longer leaned against it while preaching, the poisoned sheep warned him not to eat it, the handkerchief with which he had wiped his mouth and hands would not burn in a furnace. All the noble qualities of his body and his soul were described in terms of marked admiration. Since Muslim tradition forbids figural representation, one finds, instead, accounts of Muhammad's lofty qualities (*ḥilya*) written in exquisite calligraphy hanging on the walls of the houses; such *ḥilya*s are still sold in the courtyards of some Turkish mosques.

The personality of the Prophet became the medium of religious experience, although, phenomenologically speaking, the center of Islam is the Koran as direct divine revelation, not the messenger who brought it. But the Muslims felt that the figure of the Prophet was necessary for the maintenance of the Muslim faith in its "legal" aspect (as indicated in the second phrase of the profession of faith). The Prophet, as Rūmī says (M 3:801), is a divine test for man; in contrast to Iblisian *tauḥīd*, which will bow only before God, the Prophet is put in between to destroy this temptation, which may lead, ultimately, toward pantheism and confusion of all religious creeds. Muhammad constitutes a limit in the definition of Islam and sets it off from other forms of faith. Mystics who used the first half of the profession of faith exclusively, without acknowledging the special rank of Muhammad, were prone to fall into a sweeping pantheistic interpretation of Islam.

Some of the early mystics might have claimed that their love of God did not leave any room for a specialized love of the Prophet. "One night I saw the Prophet in my dream. He said: 'Do you love me?' I said: 'Forgive me, but the love of God has kept me busy from loving thee.' He said 'Whosoever loves God, loves me' " (T 2:41). Others might have been reluctant to mention his name together with God's name in the call to prayer (Q 17). But the beginning of a genuine Muhammad mysticism dates back to the early eighth century. Muqātil idealized the person of Muhammad in his work; and it was this mystic who interpreted the second sentence of the *āyat an-nūr*, the "Light verse" of the Koran (Sūra 24:35), as pertaining to Muhammad, whose light shines through the other prophets (W 93–94). Kharrāz elaborated upon these ideas, and Ḥallāj devotes much of his *Kitāb aṭ-ṭawāsīn* to the praise of the Prophet: he is the first created being, his light precedes everything and is part of God's light. As ᶜAṭṭār says, in the same vein,

> The origin of the soul is the absolute light, nothing
> else,
> That means it was the light of Muhammad, nothing else.
> (U 358)

The Prophet is, in Ḥallāj's hymn, both the cause and goal of creation. To give this idea more authority, it was couched in a *ḥadīth qudsī: laulāka mā khalaqtuʾl-aflāka*—"if thou hadst not been (but for thee), I would not have created the heavens." The world was created for the primordial love that manifested itself in the Prophet Muhammad. The Prophet himself was credited with words that highlight his extraordinary position: "The first thing God created was my spirit." "I was a prophet when Adam was still between clay and water."

The idea of the "Muhammadan light" seems to have been fully developed about 900—Sahl at-Tustarī speaks of the three lights of God, the first one being Muhammad, his special friend: "When He wanted to create Muhammad He showed a light from His light which illuminated the whole kingdom."[22] The most famous prayer ascribed to Muhammad is a prayer for light, which has been treasured by the mystics of Islam. Abū Ṭālib al-Makkī quotes it; Ghazzālī taught it; and the eighteenth-century Indian mystic Mīr Dard wrote it down as his last orison before his death:

> O God, give me light in my heart and light in my tongue and light in my hearing and light in my sight and light in my feeling and light in all my body and light before me and light behind me. Give me, I pray Thee, light on my right hand and light on my left hand and light above me and light beneath me. O Lord, increase light within me and give me light and illuminate me!

Makkī continues his quotation: "These are the lights which the Prophet asked for: verily to possess such light means to be contemplated by the Light of Lights."[23] Sanāʾī takes up the tradition that hellfire is afraid of the true believer's light, connecting it with the Muhammadan light:

22. ᶜAlī ibn Aḥmad Daylamī, *Kitāb ᶜaṭf al-alif al-maʾlūf ilaʾl-lām al-maᶜṭūf*, ed. Jean-Claude Vadet (Cairo, 1962), p. 33, § 123.

23. Smith, *Readings*, no. 47.

When your heart has become filled with the Light of
Aḥmad,
then know with certitude that you are safe from the Fire.
(S 202)

Even without any knowledge of these high speculations on the Prophetic light, which were to develop into complicated mystical systems, the faithful simply loved the Prophet. For love of the Prophet leads to love of God. This idea was expressed, in later Sufism, by the theory of the *fanā fi᾽r-rasūl.* The mystic no longer goes straight on his Path toward God: first he has to experience annihilation in the spiritual guide, who functions as the representative of the Prophet, then the *fanā fi᾽r-rasūl,* "annihilation in the Prophet," before he can hope to reach, if he ever does, *fanā fi Allāh.* In a masterful study Tor Andrae has shown how this veneration of the Prophet grew during the first six centuries of Islamic religious history, until the Muhammad mysticism was fully systematized by Ibn ᶜArabī and his followers.[24]

As early as the late eleventh century, and generally from the twelfth century on, the veneration of the Prophet assumed a visible form in the celebration of the *maulid,* his birthday, on 12 *Rabīᶜ ul-awwal,* the third month of the Muslim lunar year. This day is still celebrated in the Muslim world.[25] The number of poems written for this festive occasion in all Islamic languages is beyond reckoning. From the eastern end of the Muslim world to the west the *maulid* is a wonderful occasion for the pious to show their warm love of the Prophet in songs, poems, and prayers. Nowhere has the simple trust in the grace of the Prophet and his intercession at Doomsday been expressed more beautifully than in Turkey, where Süleyman Çelebi of Bursa (d. 1419) told the story of Muhammad's birth in his *Mevlûd-i şerif,* a *mathnawī* in touchingly unsophisticated Turkish verse of the simplest possible meter, to which is added a sweet melody.[26] This poem is still recited on special occasions in many Turkish families: at the anniversaries, or at the fortieth day, of a bereavement or in fulfilment of a vow. Parallels to the central

24. Tor Andrae, *Die person Muhammads in lehre und glauben seiner gemeinde* (Stockholm, 1918), the outstanding study of the development of the veneration of Muhammad from the seventh to the thirteenth century.

25. Ibn Kathīr, *Maulid rasūl Allāh,* ed. Salāḥuddīn al-Munajjid (Beirut, 1961).

26. F. Lyman McCallum, trans., *The Mevlidi Sherif by Suleyman Chelebi* (London, 1943). See Irmgard Engelke, *Sulejman Tschelebis Lobgedicht auf die Geburt des Propheten* (Halle, 1926).

part of Süleyman Çelebi's *Mevlûd*, the great *Merḥaba*, "Welcome," chapter, have been found as far away as India, where Abū ᶜAlī Qalandar, in the fourteenth century, greeted the new-born Prophet:

> Welcome, o Nightingale of the Ancient Garden!
> Speak to us about the lovely Rose!
> Welcome, o Hoepoe of happy augury,
> Welcome, you sugar-talking Parrot . . . !
>
> (AP 109)

In the hearts of the masses, Muhammad is primarily the intercessor at Doomsday; as the only prophet, he will intercede for his community, as the Koran has promised. It is this trust in his help at the terrible Day of Judgment that has largely colored the popular veneration of Muhammad. He was sent as "mercy for the worlds," *raḥmatan lilᶜālamīn* (Sūra 21:107). As such, he may be compared, as Shāh ᶜAbduʾl-Laṭīf of Sind has done, to the cloud that sends down the life-giving rain to the thirsty fields, quickening what seemed to be dead. The rain is, in fact, called *raḥmat*, "mercy," by the villagers in Turkey and Iran. And the image of the "jewel-carrying cloud," which stretches from Istanbul to Delhi, shedding its gems over the hearts of the Muslims, is not uncommon among the Indian poets when they sing of the Prophet (cf. Sūra 7:55).[27]

It was only natural that the faithful saw their beloved Prophet in the light of the Koranic revelation and that those expressions from the Koran that point to his high rank were repeated over and over again in mystical piety and in poetry. Thus, the beginning words of Sūra 54—"and the moon was split"—are taken to allude to Muhammad's supernatural powers: he was able to split the moon. They are also meant for the faithful who has annihilated himself in him and works through the Muhammadan light; as Rūmī says, "I split the moon with the light of Mustafa" (D 2967). *Muṣṭafā*, "the Elect," is one of the names by which the Prophet is commonly known.

The problem of the *baraka*, the blessing power of the Prophet's name, has often been discussed,[28] and the Turkish usage of calling boys by his name, but pronouncing the consonant skeleton with

27. Annemarie Schimmel, "Der Regen als Symbol in der Religionsgeschichte," in *Religion und Religionen: Festschrift Gustav Mensching* (Bonn, 1966).

28. August Fischer, "Vergöttlichung und Tabuisierung der Namen Muhammads," in *Beiträge zur Arabistik, Semitistik und Islamkunde*, ed. Helmuth Scheel and Richard Hartmann (Leipzig, 1944).

a different vocalization—namely, *Meḥmed* instead of *Muḥammad*—is part of the respect due to the blessed name of the Prophet. Many poets sang: "Thy name is beautiful, you are beautiful, Muhammad!" Or they have alluded to the high names bestowed upon him by Allah.

> I addressed the wind: "Why do you serve Solomon?"
> He said: "Because Aḥmad's [i.e., Muhammad's] name
> was engraved on his seal."
>
> (SD 167)

Thus Sanāʾī explains the miraculous power of a previous prophet. Expressions from the Koranic *sūra*s are used to describe the Prophet's marvelous beauty and majesty:

> "By the Sun" is a story of Muhammad's face,
> "By the Night" is a metaphor for Muhammad's hair.[29]

Thus, the oath formulae that form the beginning lines of Sūra 91 and 92 were fitting allusions to Muhammad's eternal loveliness, his sunlike radiant face, and his black hair; and the most commonly used Koranic allusion is "by the morning light" (Sūra 93), which is usually applied to his face. An exquisite example of this kind of interpretation is Sanāʾī's hymn on Muhammad, which is a poetical commentary on Sūra 93 (SD 34).

The fact that Muhammad is called *ummī* in the Koran (Sūra 7:157), a word usually translated as "illiterate," was considered to have a special mystical implication. Only a man whose heart was not spoiled by outward intellectual achievement and learning, but was as pure a vessel as Mary's virgin body, could be a worthy receptacle for the divine word. When later mystics boasted of their alleged or real illiteracy, which permitted them to read only the letter *alif*, the symbol of divine unity and uniqueness, they had the Prophet's example always before their eyes—the model of pure love and surrender, as opposed to cold reasoning.

The main object of mystical meditation, however, was Muhammad's night journey, the *miʿrāj*, his ascent through the spheres—a topic only touched upon in the introductory verse of Sūra 17, but lavishly elaborated upon in later legends. The connection of the *miʿrāj* with daily prayer—which was experienced by Muhammad as a repetition of the joy of ascension (H 302)—made such an

29. Cited in Muḥammad Nāṣir ʿAndalīb, *Nāla-yi ʿAndalīb*, 2 vols. (Bhopal, 1309 h./1891–92), 2:818.

ascension into the divine presence possible for every sincere Muslim. The mystics applied the ascension terminology to their own experiences in the rapture of ecstasy. Bāyezīd Bisṭāmī was the first to use this imagery in describing his mystical flight through the heavens, and he was followed by many others.[30] Enrico Cerulli has shown that the literary genre of the *Libro della scala*, the "Book of *miʿrāj*," was so well known in the medieval Mediterranean world that possible influences on Dante's *Divina Commedia* cannot be excluded.[31] In the twentieth century, Muhammad Iqbal has chosen the type of the heavenly journey in the company of the spiritual preceptor (in his case the spirit of Rūmī) for his most intriguing literary work, the *Jāwīdnāme* (1932).[32]

It is the experience of love that manifests itself in the ascension of God's specially elected friend Muhammad Muṣṭafā. Rūmī expressed it this way:

> Love is ascension toward the roof of the Prince of
> Beauty,
> Read the story of the ascension from the cheek of the
> beloved.
>
> (D 133)

According to the tradition, not even Gabriel could accompany the Prophet beyond the ultimate lotus tree, *as-sidrat al-muntahā*. "If I would go one step further, my wings would get burned," is the archangel's sigh, as the poets and mystics interpreted it. For Rūmī, this answer describes the weakness of discursive reason when it draws nearer to the mystery of divine love:

> Reason speaks, like Gabriel: O Aḥmad,
> If I advance one step, He will burn me.
>
> (M 1:1066)

30. Many articles have been devoted to the Prophet's ascension, e.g., Bernhard Schrieke, "Die Himmelsreise Muhammads," *Der Islam* 6 (1916); Joseph Horovitz, "Muhammads Himmelfahrt," *Der Islam* 9 (1919); Richard Hartmann, "Die Himmelsreise Muhammads und ihre Bedeutung in der Religion des Islam," in *Vorträge der Bibliothek Warburg* (Hamburg, 1928–29); Geo Widengren, *Muhammad, the Apostle of God, and His Ascension* (Uppsala, 1955).

31. Enrico Cerulli, *Il "Libro della Scala" e la questione delle fonti arabo-spagnole della "Divina Commedia"* (Vatican City, 1949).

32. *Jāwīdnāme* (Lahore, 1932); English translations, Shaikh Mahmūd Aḥmad (Lahore, 1961) and A. J. Arberry (London, 1966); German verse translation, Annemarie Schimmel (1957); Italian translation, Alessandro Bausani (1955); French translation, Eva Meyerovitch (1962); Turkish translation, Annemarie Schimmel (1958). Annemarie Schimmel, *Gabriel's Wing: A Study into the Religious Ideas of Sir Muhammad Iqbal* (Leiden, 1963), contains a detailed bibliography on prophetology and ascension.

It was at this moment that the Prophet was left alone in the loving encounter with God that he describes with the words, "I have a time with God in which no created being has access, not even Gabriel who is pure spirit." For Gabriel is still a veil between the lover and the beloved.

The Prophet's expression "I have a time with God" (*lī maᶜa Allāh waqt*) is often used by the Sufis to point to their experience of *waqt*, "time," the moment at which they break through created time and reach the Eternal Now in God, when everything created (including the archangel) remains outside and is, in their experience, annihilated. Iqbal, in his modern interpretation of mystical symbols, understands this tradition as a reference to the moment at which "the infidel's girdle," namely, "serial" time, is torn and the mystic establishes direct contact with God in a person-to-person encounter.

This emphasis on the person-to-person encounter in the mystical interpretation of the *miᶜrāj* seems particularly revealing. The Prophet, although created as the most perfect being, still remains a creature and is not united with God. The opening words of Sūra 17—"praised be He who traveled with His servant at night"— indicate that even in the moment of rapture the Prophet is still called *ᶜabduhu*, "His servant." That implies that "servant" is the highest possible name for a human being, who, however, is able to speak to God without being extinguished.

The poets and artists of the Persian- and Turkish-speaking lands have lovingly embellished the story of the *miᶜrāj*. Almost every great Persian epic contains a special chapter, after the general praise of the Prophet, in which the poet indulges in imaginative description of the heavenly journey, performed on the handsome steed *Burāq*, with its peacock tail and human face. In ever new images the poets describe how Muhammad passes through the spheres of sun and moon and along the Milky Way, talking with the prophets, surrounded by colorful angels, until he reaches the divine presence, when Gabriel remains behind, "lonely, like a nightingale who is separated from the rose."[33] And miniatures from the fourteenth and fifteenth centuries show the Prophet in a wonderful aura of overwhelming splendor.[34]

33. Ghanizade, "Miᶜrajiyye," in *Eski Şairlerimiz*, ed. Mehmet Fuat Köprülü (Istanbul, 1931), p. 356.

34. Richard Ettinghausen, "Persian Ascension Miniatures of the 14th Century," *Publicazione delle Academia dei Lincei*, 1957.

Another Koranic passage upon which the mystics meditated is Sūra 53, *an-Najm,* "The Star," which describes Muhammad's vision. The fact that "his sight did not rove" is, for the mystic, the symbol of Muhammad's absolute concentration upon God. In his motionless and steadfast contemplation, the Prophet is superior to Moses, who had asked for vision and could not even look at the divine manifestation through the burning bush without fainting. As Jamālī Kanbōh put it in fifteenth-century India:

> Moses went out of his mind by a single revelation of
> the Attributes—
> Thou seest the essence of the Essence and still smilest.
> (AP 158)

The expression *qāba qausayn,* "two bows' length," found in the same Sūra, designates for the mystics the highest degree of proximity the heart can reach.

The different Koranic dicta about Muhammad as the Seal of Prophets, after whom no prophet will ever appear on earth, have shaped the Muslim faith in general and have provided the Sufis with almost infinite possibilities for meditating on the mysteries hidden behind the person of the Prophet.

Since a close imitation of the Prophet's actions was binding for every faithful Muslim, one of the occupations that pious Sufis would undertake was the collection of Prophetic traditions, and more than one well-known Sufi's name is noted in the chain of transmitters of *ḥadīth.* Among them is Ibn Khafīf, the saint of Shiraz, who collected traditions from more than thirty masters—yet the Hanbalite theologian Ibn al-Jauzī (d. 1200) calls him "not trustworthy."[35] And he may be right in his criticism—for it cannot be denied that many of the traditions that are favorites with the later Sufis have no basis in the "canonical" collections of *ḥadīth* completed in the last third of the ninth century. As time passed, mystical thinkers and poets made use of certain traditions that cannot be verified before the tenth or even the eleventh century. At the same time, the number of the so-called *ḥadīth qudsī*—traditions that contain some extra-Koranic divine revelations—grew along with the Sufi influence on Muslim piety.

As worthy of reward as the occupation with *ḥadīth* might have been in itself, it was objected to by many Sufis, who believed more

35. Ibn al-Jauzī, *Talbīs Iblīs* (Cairo, 1340 h./1921–22), p. 358.

in direct experience than in copying words. As Kharaqānī, himself illiterate, says: "The heir of the Prophet is he who follows the Prophet with his actions, not he who blackens the face of paper" (N 299)—to "blacken the face" of something means to disgrace it, and here the term is cleverly adapted to the art of writing seemingly useless texts.

In the course of time, Muhammad was surrounded by many charming stories, which reached the common people through the *qiṣaṣ al-anbiyāʾ*, "The Stories of the Prophets," and through Sufi interpretation of the Koran and *ḥadīth* and shaped their ideas about Muhammad. The development of Persian mystical poetry, with its language so permeated by allusions to Koranic and *ḥadīth* material, contributed to this process of popularization. The Prophet's *hijra* from Mecca to Medina became the prototype of the mystical Path, the journey from home and back (and thus a microcosmic picture of the way of the soul from God and back to God). Only such a journey can bring man to perfection. Muhammad's poverty became the model of mystical poverty; his way of educating his *shayṭān*, the base faculties, prefigured the Sufi's constant struggle with his *nafs*. Romantic trends are not lacking in this new picture of Muhammad painted by his community. There is the lovely story produced by later Persian Sufis to explain their love of roses: "When the Prophet saw a rose, he kissed it and pressed it to his eyes and he said: 'The red rose is part of God's glory' " (BA 77). Or, in a different tradition, which is widely accepted: the rose was created from the Prophet's perspiration and is therefore the most beautiful and precious flower in the world (cf. U 28; D 1348). The Prophet's love for roses may have induced the poets to call him "the nightingale of the Eternal Garden," for he discloses to the faithful some of the mysteries of God, the Everlasting Rose. And when the mystics were so overwhelmed by God's greatness, beauty, and majesty that they no longer knew how to articulate their longing and their admiration, they remembered Muhammad's simple words of thanks—*lā uḥṣī thanāʾan ʿalaika*, "I cannot reckon the praise due to Thee"—thus acknowledging that God's bounty exceeds the thanks that man can render.

A distinguished role was given to Muhammad's family as well—the Sufi *khirqa* was sometimes interpreted as inspired by the mantle in which the Prophet had wrapped his family members, and the Sufis thus became "members of his family." The veneration of the

Prophet's family, common in Shia Islam, can be found in Sufi circles as well, and the reverence shown to the *sayyids,* his descendants, is part of this veneration.[36]

The strong faith in Muhammad, about whom the Koran says, "who obeys the Messenger, obeys God" (Sūra 4:82), might lead to the thought that Muhammad had said: "Who has seen me, has seen Allah."[37] Words like that must be understood in connection with the speculations about Muhammad's cosmic function, his unique place among men and among the prophets. Even an orthodox mystic like Ghazzālī, in his *Mishkāt al-anwār,* spoke of the *muṭāᶜ*, the "one who is obeyed," whom he defines as Allah's *khalīfa* or vicegerent, the supreme controller of the whole universe. Indeed, according to the Koran, Muhammad was he who has to be obeyed, and thus one may assume that the great mystic had in mind the equation *muṭāᶜ*=Muhammad, though this cannot be absolutely proved. The relation between Allah and the *muṭāᶜ* is likened to the relation of the impalpable essence of light to the sun, or of the elemental fire to a glowing coal, an equation that would lead the mystic, once more, to the concept of the Muhammadan light as "light from God's light."

The question has been posed whether or not this *muṭāᶜ* is a personification of the *amr,* the divine command, or, as W. H. Temple Gairdner holds, of the *rūḥ,* the spirit—in fact, in Jīlī's (d. after 1408) theosophy the *amr* (which corresponds roughly to the *logos* of Greek philosophy) is equated with the *ḥaqīqa muḥammadiyya,* the reality of Muhammad or the archetypal Muhammad. That would lead one to see the *muṭāᶜ* as the cosmic Muhammad who becomes the working principle in the world. The absolute transcendence of God has removed Him, so to speak, into the situation of a *deus otiosus,* one and absolutely aloof from the movement of the world. As Reynold A. Nicholson puts it:

God indeed remains the creator of the world, but He is no longer in any direct sense its ruler. He is absolutely transcendent, and since the moving of the heavenly spheres would be incompatible with His unity, that function is assigned to One by whose command the spheres are moved,

36. See Marijan Molé, "Les Kubrawiyya entre Sunnisme et Shiisme," *Revue des études islamiques,* 1961, p. 73. A typical example is Mīr Dard, who derived his whole approach to his own family and to mystical experience from the fact that he was a *sayyid* from both sides, hence closest to the Prophet.

37. Badīᶜuz-Zamān Furūzānfar, *Aḥādīth-i mathnawī* (Tehran, 1334 sh./1955), no. 62; see Farīduddīn ᶜAṭṭār, *Dīwān-i qaṣāʾid wa ghazaliyāt,* ed. Saᶜīd Nafisi (Tehran, 1339 sh./1960), p. 50.

i.e., to the *muṭāʿ*. The *muṭāʿ* is not identical with God: he must therefore be a created being . . . [He] represents the archetypal Spirit of Muhammad, the Heavenly Man created in the image of God and regarded as a Cosmic Power on whom depends the order and preservation of the Universe.[38]

This leads to the role of Muhammad as fully worked out by Ibn ʿArabī. There Muhammad assumes the place of the Perfect Man. God created a microcosmic being, the Perfect Man, *insān kāmil*, through whom His consciousness is manifested to Himself. The Perfect Man is the spirit in which all things have their origin; the created spirit of Muhammad is, thus, a mode of the uncreated divine spirit, and he is the medium through which God becomes conscious of Himself in creation. It would be correct to compare the *nūr muḥammadī*, the Muhammadan Light, or the *ḥaqīqa muḥammadiyya* to the active intellect of Hellenistic philosophy. One can say in this context that the whole world is created from the light of Muhammad: Isrāfīl, the angel of Doomsday, is created from his heart; Gabriel becomes equivalent to the First Intelligence; Muhammad's intelligence corresponds to the heavenly Pen; and his soul to the Well-preserved Tablet.

To point out this unique rank of Muhammad—quite a while before Ibn ʿArabī's systematizing attempts and Jīlī's speculations about Muhammad as the *insān kāmil*—the Sufis invented the *ḥadīth qudsī, anā Aḥmad bilā mīm,* "I am Aḥmad (= Muhammad) without the letter *m*," i.e., *Aḥad,* "One." Only the letter *m*—the letter of creatureliness and trial, of discontinuity and limitation, of death (being the initial letter of *maut,* "death"), and of the illusory aspect of everything besides God—separates the Prophet—announced as Aḥmad, the Paraclete (Sūra 61:6)—from God, the One, the Eternal and Everlasting. The numerical value of the letter *m* is forty, and it thus corresponds to the forty stages through which man, having descended into the depths of created beings, can ascend again to God, eventually throwing off the "shawl of humanity," as a Punjabi poet has called the letter *m*.

Almost every poet in the eastern Islamic world, beginning with ʿAṭṭār, has used this *ḥadīth qudsī*—the Uzbeg ruler Shaibani in the sixteenth century, the Chishtī saint Gīsūdarāz in India (d. 1422), Jalāluddīn Rūmī in thirteenth-century Konya, Ghālib in nineteenth-century Delhi, and many folk poets of Turkey and north-

38. Reynold A. Nicholson, *The Idea of Personality in Sufism* (Cambridge, 1923), p. 44.

western India. "The two worlds are created from the two *m*'s of his name" (U 20), says ʿAṭṭār, and later mystics invented lengthy, but not always very persuasive, explanations of the meaning of Muhammad's name. Aḥmad Sirhindī even built his whole system for the renovation of Islam after the first millenium upon speculations on the two *m*'s of Muhammad (see chapter 8).

The Sufis found that Adam, created by God "in His image" and thus the perfect copy of the divine creator, is nothing but Muhammad: "surely the head of Adam is a *m* م, and his hand is a *ḥ* ح and his middle part is a *m* م; the remaining part is a *d* د. Thus it was that the name Muhammad محمد was written in the old script."[39] The form of Adam, and therefore of every human being, bears in itself the name of Muhammad. The same thirteenth-century Egyptian mystic who first proposed this idea had another, much more complicated system to prove that in the very letter value of the word Muhammad are contained the 313 messengers who possess the qualifications of prophecy, plus one messenger of the station of sainthood. Other mystics would claim that the Prophet is the manifestation of the divine name *ar-Raḥmān*, "the merciful," which is usually considered the most important and essential name after the name Allāh.

One of the finest expressions of the mystically deepened love of Muhammad with all its implications is the famous *Burda*, the ode written by the Egyptian poet al-Būṣīrī toward the end of the thirteenth century. Būṣīrī composed this long poem during an illness of which he was miraculously cured by the Prophet, who cast his mantle (*burda*) upon him, just as he had done during his lifetime to the Arab bard Kaʿb ibn Zuhayr when he recited his *qaṣīda* before him, imploring his forgiveness and mercy.[40] The *Burda*, written in the high style of classical Arabic, soon became a favorite with all Arabic-speaking Muslims and was early translated into Persian, and later into Turkish and Urdu. Copies are still being sold in the shops of Lahore and elsewhere. The *Burda* was translated into and imitated in Swahili as well, in which language a remarkable literature has grown up around the Prophet's powerful personality. Twentieth-century Arabic poetry, which contains

39. Edward Jabra Jurji, ed. and trans., *Illumination in Islamic Mysticism* (Princeton, 1938), pp. 84 ff.

40. al-Būṣīrī, *Die Burda*, ed. C. A. Ralfs (Vienna, 1860), with Persian and Turkish translations. The standard translation is René Basset, *La Bordah du Cheikh al Bousiri* (Paris, 1893).

"modern" versions of such praise *qaṣīda*s, reflects the love of the Prophet in different styles.

The poets of the non-Arab Muslim world have never tired of inventing new and wonderful epithets for Muhammad, and the prose pieces by Rūzbihān Baqlī almost defy translation in their subtlety. Most Persian or Turkish *dīwān*s contain, after the initial orison, an invocation of the Prophet and often a description of the *miᶜrāj*.[41] In their *qaṣīda*s, the poets often did not dare to express more than their utter bewilderment when praising God—the all-embracing and loving, the incomprehensible and fathomless who reveals Himself in contrasting colors and forms of life—but they would sing about their hearts' sorrows, their hopes and griefs, in poems addressed to the Prophet. Khāqānī and ᶜUrfī, Sanāʾī and Ghālib, to mention only a few outstanding Persian writers, gave their best in their *naᶜt* poetry (*naᶜt* is the term applied to praise of the Prophet); the personality of Muhammad looms large in Rūmī's lyrics and in his *Mathnawī*. In India even a number of Hindu poets joined the Muslims in the composition of *naᶜt* in honor of the Prophet[42] (strangely enough, the first historical approach to Muhammad's life, written in Sindhi in 1911, was composed by a Hindu, not by a Muslim).[43] They wrote in Urdu and Persian, completely adopting the terminology of the Sufis.

In fact, the *qaṣīda*s written in Turkey, Iran, Afghanistan, and India in the name of the leader of mankind, the best of creatures, the preeternal light, the helper of his community, reflect more of the true feeling of the Muslim communities than many learned discourses about mystical prophetology.[44] This is even more true of the small prayer books, like the *Dalāʾil al-khairāt* by al-Jazūlī (d. ca. 1465), which were composed in moderate Sufi style to teach people trust in God and the Prophet. And Ghazzālī devoted the central chapter of his *Iḥyāʾ ᶜulūm ad-dīn* to Muhammad's personality. The love of the Prophet, as it was profoundly experienced by the mystics, is and was the strongest binding force of Muslims everywhere, be they peasants or high officials. Children first learned

41. Ghulam Dastagir Rasheed, "The Development of Naᶜtia Poetry in Persian Literature," *Islamic Culture*, 1965.

42. Fānī Murādābādī, *Hindu shuᶜarā kā naᶜtiya kalām* (Lyallpur, 1962).

43. Lalchand A. Jagtiani, *Muḥammad rasūl Allāh* (Hyderabad, Sind, 1911).

44. Annemarie Schimmel, "The Veneration of the Prophet Muhammad, as Reflected in Sindhi Poetry," in *The Savior God*, ed. Samuel G. F. Brandon (Manchester, Eng., 1963).

his miracles from unpretentious poems in their mother tongue, and simple villagers could sing of their trust and hope in the Prophet in tender verses.[45] Allusions to the mystical traditions about the Prophet's light or to the well-known legends are found on every level of literature, down to lullabies and bridal songs in remote provinces of the Muslim world. Muhammad Iqbal stressed the importance of the Prophet in his daring statement: "You can deny God, but you cannot deny the Prophet."[46]

It is Muhammad who makes Islam a distinct religion, and it is typical that, in a time when Islam was defeated everywhere in the political field, and when the Western powers encroached practically and spiritually upon the Muslim world, those mystics who founded new orders and fraternities called them *ṭarīqa Muḥammadiyya,* "the Muhammadan path." The figure of Muhammad became, for them, the center of strength, whether they struggled against the non-Muslims or British in India (like Mīr Dard and Aḥmad Brelwī in the late eighteenth and early nineteenth century) or against the French, like the Sanūsiyya in North Africa. Muhammad was their helper, and in him they trusted when they thought of the future of the Muslims. This is one of the most important contributions of Sufism to Muslim life.

45. See also Enno Littmann, *Mohammad in Volksepos* (Copenhagen, 1950), on popular epics dealing with the Prophet.

46. Iqbal, *Jāwīdnāme,* verse 608; see Annemarie Schimmel, "The Place of the Prophet in Iqbal's Thought," *Islamic Studies* 1, no. 4 (1962); Raīs Aḥmad Jaᶜfrī, *Iqbāl aur ᶜashq-i rasūl* (Lahore, 1956).

5. SUFI ORDERS *and* FRATERNITIES

COMMUNITY LIFE[1]

Al-muʾmin mirʾāt al-muʾmin, "the faithful is the mirror of the faithful"—that is a Prophetic tradition that the Sufis considered an excellent maxim for social intercourse. They see in the behavior and actions of their companions the reflection of their own feelings and deeds. When the Sufi sees a fault in his neighbor, he should correct this very fault in himself; thus the mirror of his heart becomes increasingly pure.

The practical application of this maxim is clearly visible in the history of Sufism and leads to one of the most pleasing aspects of the movement, namely, to the fraternal love that first came into existence among the Sufis of one group and was then extended to include humanity in general. It was a behavior quite different from that of the early ascetics, who stressed individual salvation through austerity and supererogative works of piety.[2] Although the case of Nūrī, who offered his life for the sake of his Sufi breth-

1. J. Spencer Trimingham, *The Sufi Orders in Islam* (Oxford, 1971), is the first comprehensive book on the development and the situation of Islamic orders; it contains an extensive bibliography.

2. See the examples in Tor Andrae, *Islamische Mystiker* (Stuttgart, 1960), pp. 75 ff.

ren, is certainly an exception, one of the main rules valid for the Sufi is to do good for one's brother's sake, to prefer others to himself (*īthār*), to give up one's prestige for the sake of one's fellow beings. The Sufi should break his fasting if he sees a member of the community who needs or wants food, since the joy of a brother's heart is more valuable than the reward for fasting (N 124); he should accept a gift without qualms because it would be impolite not to acknowledge gratefully the trouble the donor has taken in preparing it. To make one of the faithful happy is to make the Prophet happy, as one tradition asserts.[3]

Service to men has always been one of the first stages in the preparatory steps of the Path, but it remains the true Sufi's duty throughout his life. For, "whoever excuses himself from the service of his brethren, God will give him a humiliation from which he cannot be rescued" (N 268).

The Sufi must care for the sick, even when he is extremely weary. A typical story is told of Ibn Khafīf, who nursed an aged visitor who was suffering from diarrhea. Even the curse *laʿanaka Allāh,* "God curse you," which the old man flung at his host, became in his ears a word of blessing and spurred him on in his ministrations. For, as the visitor grumbled: "If you cannot serve your human companions properly, how could you serve God?" (X 167). The Sufi must even be careful about brushing away the flies from his face, as they might disturb others in the room (N 277).

A somewhat strange anecdote illustrates the tenderness of heart every Sufi should possess. It too belongs to the legends about Ibn Khafīf, the master of Shiraz, whose practical piety has lived in an institutionalized form in the order founded by his spiritual pupil Kāzarūnī (d. 1035),[4] who was noted for his social activities.

Ibn Khafīf was once invited to the house of his neighbor, a poor weaver who offered him some meat. Ibn Khafīf would not touch it, for it was too rotten, and his host felt ashamed. He then set out for the pilgrimage to Mecca; the caravan lost its way in the desert. After days of hunger the last resort for the pilgrims was to kill a dog—unclean, and therefore to be eaten only in times of dire straits! Distributed among them, the head fell to Ibn Khafīf as his portion to eat. Then he sensed that this was his punishment for his callous attitude towards the destituted neighbor. [In a later version of the legend, the dog's head speaks and reproaches

3. Tor Andrae, *Die person Muhammads in lehre und glauben seiner gemeinde* (Stockholm, 1918), p. 369.

4. For the Kāzerūniyya see Fritz Meier, ed., *"Firdaus al-muršidīya fī asrār aṣ-ṣamadīya": Die Vita des Scheich Abū Isḥāq al-Kāzarūnī* (Leipzig, 1948).

the poor mystic for his misbehavior!] Thus he returned and asked his neighbor's forgiveness, and only then was able to perform the pilgrimage. (X 44)

This story may sound exaggerated to the modern reader, but it shows how the Sufi was expected to behave—"truthful in his mystical states and correct in his transactions with men" (N 312). The manuals of Sufism are replete with stories illustrating correct behavior (*adab*) in the presence of the sheikh and the brethren. Whole books were devoted to this topic—an attitude that has resulted in a wholly admirable social sensitivity that has persisted in the Muslim world throughout the centuries, "correct behavior" being one of the basic rules of social life. "Everything has a servant, and correct behavior is the servant of religion" (N 91).

The Sufi should always excuse the brethren and act with them so that they need not excuse themselves (N 96); and he should extend his love to every created thing. If God is content with weak human beings as His servants, the Sufi should be content with them as brethren (N 115).

The Sufis were sure that they belonged to each other. They had no secrets from each other and might even practice a kind of communism comparable to that of the first Christians. A dervish must never say "my shoes" or "my so-and-so"—he should have no private property (N 216, 109). If one possesses anything, he should give it to the brethren; otherwise he will lose his spiritual rank (N 169). How can one say "mine" when he knows that everything belongs to God? This feeling and the proverbial oriental hospitality have worked together in shaping the ideal of the Sufi who will offer everything to his guests, leaving nothing for himself or even for his family.

The Sufis—especially those who followed the same spiritual master—felt that they had known each other since preeternity; they constituted a spiritual family. A lovely story told by ʿAṭṭār suggests that they are in reality a corporate entity:

A man brought a Sufi as witness with him before the judge; the judge, however, did not accept the witness. So he continued bringing some more Sufis until the judge exclaimed that this was useless, for:

> Every Sufi whom you bring with you—
> they are all one, even though you bring a hundred.
> For this group has become *one* body,
> and between them the form of I and We has vanished.
> (U 31)

The love of the Sufis did not end with love of man; it extended to the animals as well. The legends tell how lions become tamed in the presence of the soft-hearted saint, or how a dog is surprised when a Sufi beats it. A dog can be sent as a substitute for a guest into a Sufi's cell (U 137), and one Sufi even offered the reward for his seventy pilgrimages to the person who would bring water to a thirsty dog in the desert (N 77).

Out of this social activity of the expanding Sufi groups, a new attitude seems to have developed that transformed Sufism from the religion of the elite into a mass movement, spreading its tenets to all levels of the population. Just as the Sufis wanted to share their worldly property with their fellow human beings, they may have felt that they should share with them the best they had as well—namely, the way leading to salvation.

Gradually, the preaching of the Sufis began to attract wider groups of people. The basic rules of mystical education were elaborated during the eleventh century, and in a comparatively short span of time—beginning in the early twelfth century—mystical fraternities that included adepts from all strata of society were emerging. How the crystallization process itself worked is difficult to explain; it must have been a response to an inner need of the community that was not being met spiritually by the scholasticism of orthodox theologians; people craved a more intimate and personal relationship with God and with the Prophet. One cannot exclude the possibility that the orders came into existence as a movement to counter the strong Ismaili-Bāṭinī influence against which Ghazzālī had fought so relentlessly. The esoteric interpretation of Islam, which threatened its very structure, was, thus, replaced by an interiorization of orthodox Muslim teaching.

At the time that the fraternities came into existence, the center of mystical activity was no longer the private house or shop of the master. A more institutional structure proved to be necessary to cope with the growing number of disciples and adepts. These new centers were usually called *khānqāh* in the eastern Islamic world; the same term was used in medieval Egypt, where the Sufi *khānqāh*s formed cultural and theological centers and were subsidized by the government or endowed by influential benefactors. The word *zāwiya,* literally "corner," was used for smaller units, like the solitary dwelling place of a sheikh. The Turks would call the Sufi convent *tekke*. The term *ribāṭ,* essentially connected with the frontier castles of the soldiers who defend Islam and expand it, could also be used to refer to the center of a fraternity. Often the expression *dargāh* "door, court," is used. The history of Islamic art can contribute more to the history of the construction of such Sufi buildings, which were sometimes isolated but more frequently were connected with a mosque, a large kitchen for both the disciples and the guests, and sometimes a school. The tomb of the founder was usually located in the same compound—unless the compound was built later around the sacred place where the first saint of the order or subgroup was buried.

In some *khānqāh*s, the dervishes lived in small cells—the Mevlâna Müzesi in Konya is a fine example of this type; other convents had only one large room in which all the dervishes lived, studied, and worked.

> The *khānqāh* is the nest for the bird "purity,"
> it is the rosegarden of pleasure and the garden of
> faithfulness,

Sanāʾī could already say shortly after 1100.[5]

The organization of the *khānqāh* was not everywhere alike. Some *khānqāh*s lived on *futūḥ*, unsolicited gifts or donations, whereas others enjoyed regular stipends. Orders like the Chishtīs in India were extremely hospitable, and foreign visitors were always admitted; in others, strict rules were enforced about visiting times and the types of visitors who were allowed to see the master. Arrangements for occasional and for long-term visitors were found in almost every *khānqāh*. The sheikh himself would live, with his family, in one quarter of the compound and see his disciples at fixed hours to supervise their spiritual progress; he would generally lead the five prayers in the congregation.

We have exact accounts of the Sufi *khānqāh*s in Egypt during the Mamluk period. The *khānqāh Saʿīd as-Suʿadāʾ*, founded by the Ayyubid Sultan Saladin in 1173, was most revered, and "in order to get blessings," people liked to watch the three hundred dervishes who lived there when they went out for the Friday prayer. The sultans gave rich endowments to the inhabitants of "their" *khānqāh*—daily rations of meat, bread, and sometimes sweetmeat, soap, new clothing for the two Muslim festivals, and some cash. The *khānqāh*s also enjoyed some tax privileges. They were controlled

5. Abūʾl-Majd Majdūd Sanāʾī, *Sanāʾiʾābād*, line 289.

Rembrandt's copy of a Mogul miniature, showing the founders of the four great mystical orders.

British Museum

by the *amīr majlis,* one of the highest ranking members of the military government (comparable to the Home Minister).[6]

Some of the rules for a person who wanted to enter the service of a sheikh have already been mentioned. The formerly more individual regulations became stricter, the larger the number of adepts was, but the main object remained the same for most of the orders—to break and train the lower soul. Only a few orders laid more emphasis upon the purification of the heart than upon ascetic preliminaries. The Mevlevis, to mention a prominent example, trained the novice in different kitchen functions; at the same time he had to study Rūmī's *Mathnawī* and its correct recitation and interpretation, as well as the technique of the whirling dance. This training continued for 1001 days.[7] Each adept, of course, had to learn the *silsila,* the spiritual lineage that leads from his master back through past generations to the Prophet; the pivotal figure in most *silsila*s is Junayd. The proper knowledge of the affiliations, difficult as it may be for an uninitiated person, is absolutely necessary for an understanding of the mystical tradition.[8]

During the initiation ceremony—a festive day in the dervish community—the adept had to pronounce the *bay*ᶜ*a,* the oath of allegiance, and was invested with the *khirqa,* the Sufi frock. An essential part of the ceremony consists of the novice's putting his hand into the sheikh's hand so that the *baraka* is properly transmitted. Another important act is the bestowing of the *tāj,* the dervish cap. Headdresses differed from order to order both in shape and in color, and the number of their parts—twelve, according to the twelve imāms, or nine, or seven—has symbolic meaning. The *tāj* and *khirqa* constitute such important parts of the initiation of the Sufi that even in early times some poets perceived the danger of fossilization. Yūnus Emre exclaimed: "Dervishhood consists not of frock and headdress" (Y 176). "Dervishhood is in the head, not in the headdress" (Y 520). And in the eighteenth century Shāh Abdu'l-Laṭīf of Sind advised the true Sufi to throw his cap into the fire instead of boasting with it.

6. Annemarie Schimmel, "Sufismus und Heiligenverehrung im spätmittelalterlichen Ägypten," in *Festschrift für W. Caskel,* ed. Erich Gräf (Leiden, 1968); Schimmel, "Some Glimpses of the Religious Life in Egypt during the Later Mamluk Period," *Islamic Studies* 4, no. 4 (1965); Virginia Vacca, "Aspetti politici e sociali dei 'sufi' musulmani," *Oriente moderno* 35, no. 1 (1955).

7. Abdülbâki Gölpınarlı, *Mevlâna'dan sonra Mevlevilik* (Istanbul, 1953).

8. The only Western work about this problem is the fundamental study by Richard Gramlich, *Die schiitischen Derwischorden Persiens, Teil I, Die Affiliationen* (Wiesbaden, 1965).

The investiture brought the Sufi formally into a close community of people with whom he felt like a single body. The remark of one person, who "wanted to sit with the dervishes in a *khānqāh* because 120 mercies rain from heaven upon the dervishes, particularly during the time of their siesta at noon" (N 294), shows the admiration that ordinary people felt for this close-knit community. In fact, a *ḥadīth* was coined at that time that promised: "Who wants to sit with God should sit with the Sufis" (M 1:1529). And Ruwaym is credited with saying that "when someone sits with the Sufis and contradicts them in anything they have realized, then God will tear away the light of faith from his heart" (N 95).

The rules of behavior among the Sufis became more and more detailed—every limb had its own etiquette.[9] Abū Saᶜīd, who may be regarded as a forerunner of organized dervishhood, went so far as to refuse a man who had entered the mosque with his left foot first, for that showed want of etiquette. The Prophet had explicitly commanded that one should enter the Friend's house with the right foot first (N 6).

When a Sufi decided to wander through the Muslim lands to visit other communities of friends, or to find a master who would instruct him further and perhaps invest him with the *khirqa-yi tabarruk*, the "frock of blessing," he was to take with him a stick and a beggar's bowl. Other Sufis were supposed to receive him well, feed him, bring him to the hot bath, and, if possible, provide him with new clothes, or at least wash his frock—according to the legends, people who neglected these duties were severely punished.

In spite of the numerous rules for correct behavior, a considerable number of indulgences, *rukhaṣ*, existed along with them; these are exemptions from duties under certain circumstances. Earlier Sufis were apprehensive of the dangers of such laxities; but the larger the orders grew, the more frequently disciples found recourse in indulgences when they were too weak to live under the constant stress of obligations.

The dervish would be invested with different offices in the *khānqāh* according to his progress on the spiritual path; the hierarchical chain in such offices was carefully maintained, but it was a hierarchy of virtue, not of power. The most sincere dervish could gain the rank of *khalīfa*, "successor"; he would either stay in the monastery to direct it after the sheikh's death or would be sent to

9. ᶜAbdur Raḥmān as-Sulamī, *Kitāb ādāb aṣ-ṣuḥba*, ed. Meir J. Kister (Jerusalem, 1954), p. 85.

foreign countries to preach and extend the order. In the *khilāfatnāme,* the document given to him at the occasion of his investiture, he was sometimes assigned a special area in which his spiritual influence was needed. In cases in which a successor was elected who had not previously excelled in spiritual qualities, the sheikh could transfer his lofty qualities to his successor at the moment of his death (*intiqāl-i nisbat*) and thus endow him with the necessary spiritual power.

In her highly interesting book *Istanbul Geceleri,* "Nights of Istanbul," Samiha Ayverdi gives a lively description of the investiture of a *khalīfa* in the Rifāᶜī *ṭarīqa* in Istanbul in the early part of this century. One can assume that the ceremony was not very different in other orders.[10] All friends of the order were invited, candles were lit according to a prescribed ritual, recitation of the Koran and mystical music alternated, and after the candidate had kissed the sheikh's hand four dervishes held a veil over the two persons so that the master might introduce the *khalīfa* into the secrets of the office. The whole night was spent in recitations, music, and prayer.

Sometimes a dying sheikh elected as *khalīfa* a member of the dervish community whom nobody had suspected of possessing the necessary spiritual virtues, but whom the order was obliged to accept. Legends then tell that a green bird descended upon the head of the elect, and the dervishes had no choice but to believe this sign (N 574)—a motif that is also known from tales about medieval papal elections. The *khalīfa* inherited the carpet (*sajjāda*) or the deerskin or sheepskin (*pōst*), which was the sheikh's ritual place—hence the expression *pōst-nishīn* or *sajjāda-nishīn,* "he who sits on the carpet," for the successor. Later, the office of *khalīfa* in the main convent often became hereditary. This led to a deterioration of the office and to an accumulation of power and wealth in the hands of certain *pīr* families, in whom, in the course of time, not too many traces of true spirituality were left.

Execessive importance was attributed to the sheikh or *pīr* in the course of time.[11] As early as about 1200, ᶜAṭṭār said:

> The *Pīr* is the red sulphur, and his breast the green
> ocean,

10. *Istanbul Geceleri* (Istanbul, 1952), pp. 174ff. About the author, a remarkable representative of modern Sufism, see Annemarie Schimmel, "Samiha Ayverdi, eine Istanbuler Schriftstellerin," *Festschrift Otto Spies,* ed. Wilhelm Hoenerbach (Wiesbaden, 1967).

11. Fritz Meier, "Ḫurāsān und das Ende der klassischen Sufik," in *La Persia nel medioevo* (Rome, 1971), shows these problems with great clarity.

> Who does not make collyrium for his eyes from the dust of the *pīr*, may die pure or impure.
>
> (U 62)

The sheikh is the master of spiritual alchemy (*kibrīt aḥmar*, red sulphur, was the mysteriously working substance in the alchemistic process); thus he can transform the base material of the novice's soul into pure gold. He is the sea of wisdom. The dust of his feet gives the blind eye of the beginner sight, just as collyrium enhances the power of seeing. He is the ladder toward heaven (M 6:4125), so completely purified that all the virtues of the Prophet are visible in him as in a mirror. Likewise he becomes the mirror whom God puts before the adept and who teaches him right behavior—just as one puts a mirror before a parrot so that he may learn how to talk (M 5:1430–40).

While the earlier Sufis had quoted the Prophetic tradition that the sheikh in his group is like the prophet in his nation, later Sufis developed—in connection with the overwhelming veneration of the Prophet—the stage of *fanā fīʾsh-shaykh* (AD 347), annihilation in the master, which leads to annihilation in the Prophet. According to some orders, on the higher levels of his path the mystic ascends through the stations of the Islamic prophets, from Adam to Jesus; many Sufis remain in one of these stages, but the perfect sheikh is he who has become annihilated in the Prophet Muhammad. United with the *ḥaqīqa muḥammadiyya*, he becomes the Perfect Man and thus leads his disciples with a guidance granted directly by God (cf. N 411).

The strong relationship between sheikh and *murīd* is exemplified in the technique of *tawajjuh*, concentration upon the sheikh, which later orders, mainly the Naqshbandiyya, considered necessary for the successful performance of the *dhikr*. One speaks in Turkish of *rabıta kurmak*, "to establish a tie" between master and disciple. The sheikh, too, would practice *tawajjuh* and thus "enter the door of the disciple's heart" to watch him and to guard him every moment. Endowed with knowledge of things that exist potentially in God's eternal knowledge, he is able to realize certain of these possibilities on the worldly plane.

Faith in these powers of the mystical leader—which, however, often belong to the magical sphere rather than to the mystical—is still strong. But the implications of such a faith are dangerous in times of degeneration. Some dervishes would resort to spectacular forms of asceticism and miracle-mongering and all kinds of eccentricities in order to attract interest and gain disciples for their orders or suborders. This allowed the development of one of the darker aspects of Sufism in the later period: the sheikh often took advantage of the veneration offered him by his followers, most of whom were illiterate. The history of the political role assumed by mystical leaders in Islamic countries has still to be written. And one enigma remains to be resolved: how so many of those who preached poverty as their pride became wealthy landlords and fitted perfectly into the feudal system, amassing wealth laid at their feet by poor, ignorant followers. It seems that by the early thirteenth century some sheikhs were spending enormous amounts of money for the maintenance of their followers: Jāmī speaks of 20,000 gold dinar a year in the case of Majduddīn Baghdādī (N 442). Others put their inherited property into a *waqf*, a tax-exempt endowment, bequeathed for the living expenses of their disciples.

The influence of such "saints" upon the population, who saw in them true guides to eternal salvation as well as to happiness in this world, reached an almost incredible extent. Only after studying this phenomenon carefully can one understand why Atatürk, in 1925, abolished the dervish orders in Turkey and why, though mystically minded, a modernist like Iqbal considered Pirism one of the most dangerous aspects of Islam, a wall that closes off large groups of Muslims from a new and vital interpretation of Islamic values. Even if one does not fully agree with John K. Birge's statement about the Bektashi order—"social progress, even the highest moral progress of the individual, was impossible under the dervish system" (BO 202)—one has to admit that "even if the *sheikh* is well meaning but ignorant, his influence is certain to count for evil." The mystical fraternities that grew out of a need for spiritualizing Islam became, in the course of time, the very cause contributing to the stagnation of the Islamic religion. People would flock around the *khānqāh* or *dargāh*, waiting for help for all their needs, hoping that the sheikh, or his *khalīfa*, would give them some amulets or teach them some useful prayer formulae. Indeed, the fabrication of amulets was one of the major occupations of mystical leaders in later times.

Even greater than the veneration offered to the living sheikh was that shown to the deceased masters. All over the Muslim world small sanctuaries indicate the places where holy people are buried. In many cases, sacred places of pre-Islamic religions were taken over, and, according to the assertion that people always pray at the same places, Christian or Hindu places of worship were transformed into Muslim sanctuaries, and legends connected with the former place were often applied to the new saint. Many stories—often rather awkward—are told, especially in Pakistan, in the Baloch and Pathan areas, about the necessity of having at least one saint's tomb in the village so that life can properly continue with his blessing.[12] These tombs are often found close to strangely formed stones, to wells, fountains, or caves; in many cases they are pseudotombs. Several *maqāms* (places) may bear the name of the same saint—a few years ago a *maqām* of Muhammad Iqbal (who is buried in Lahore) was erected in the garden of Jalāluddīn Rūmī's tomb in Konya. At these tombs, or sacred enclosures (which give sanctuary to the persecuted), people take their vows, make the circumambulation three or seven times, hang pieces of cloth around the windows or on nearby trees. Women praying for children will go to one place (and, incidentally, make of such a visit at a *ziyāra*, "visiting place," a pleasant occasion of a rare outing); men longing for success in worldly matters will go to see another saint; children will visit a certain shrine before their examinations—all of them sure that the *baraka*, the spiritual power of the saint, will help them.[13]

The orders have contributed to converting Sufism into a mass movement—a movement in which the high ambitions of the classical Sufis were considerably watered down. However, the rank and file of the faithful have been given an emotional outlet for their feelings of veneration for the holy man and the opportunity for participation in festivities with music and often with whirling dancing. The corporate pursuit of the Way was easier for most people than the lonely spiritual struggle of the mystical seeker; the common prayer meetings gave them strength and warmed their faith. It is interesting to see how the *ṭarīqas* developed collective methods of spiritual education that could uplift the followers into a sort of ecstatic state—the danger was, however, that this rapture induced by more or less mechanical means might be confused with the ecstatic

12. See Sir Thomas Arnold, "Saints, Muhammadan, in India," in *Encyclopedia of Religion and Ethics*, ed. James Hastings, 13 vols. (1908–27), 11:67–73.

13. Among the general works dealing with popular Islam are Edward William Lane, *The Manners and Customs of the Modern Egyptians* (London, 1860); Rudolf Kriss and Hubert Kriss-Heinrich, *Volksglaube im Bereich des Islam*, 2 vols. (Wiesbaden, 1960–61), with an extensive bibliography; and César E. Dubler, *Über islamischen Grab- und Heiligenkult* (Zurich, 1960).

loneliness of the true mystical experience, which is and remains an act of divine grace with which only a few are ever blessed.

The *ṭarīqa*s usually had a large number of lay members. One may even speak of a kind of "third order." Such persons would stay in the convent for a couple of days every year to participate in exercises and in the festivities of the order, like the *maulid*, the birthday of the Prophet and the saint, or the *ʿurs*, "wedding," the anniversary of the saint's death.[14] In many cases the orders assumed, thus, a function similar to that of associations (*Verein*) or sodalities in the modern world; many are the interrelations of the dervish orders proper and the artisans' lodges, the guilds, and the *futuwwa* groups.

The orders were adaptable to every social level as well as to the several races represented in Islam. Orders are found in the strangely mystically oriented Indonesian archipelago and in Black Africa as a civilizing and Islamicizing force, though the mystical life manifests itself quite differently in each setting. It should not be forgotten—as Dermenghem has emphasized—that in North Africa the mystical groups formed a very important source of spiritual life for the black slaves, who saw in the Prophet's *muezzin*, the Abyssinian Bilāl, the black confidant of Muhammad, a prototype of their own situation. In the rituals performed in a saint's presence, they could express their feelings in music and dance, and their contribution in these activities can be seen as comparable to the religious fervor of the former black slaves in America expressed so movingly in the spirituals.[15]

Their adaptability made the orders ideal vehicles for the spread of Islamic teachings. It is a well-established fact that large parts of India, Indonesia, and Black Africa were Islamicized by the untiring activity of Sufi preachers who manifested in their lives the basic obligations of Islam: simple love of and trust in God, and love of the Prophet and their fellow creatures, without indulging in logical or juridical hairsplitting.[16] These preachers also used the local languages instead of the Arabic of the learned and are, thus, largely responsible for the early development of languages like Turkish, Urdu, Sindhi, and Panjabi as literary vehicles. They taught the veneration of the Prophet, and thanks to them the founder of Islam,

14. Joseph Williams McPherson, *The Moulid of Egypt* (Cairo, 1941).

15. Émile Dermenghem, *Le culte des saints dans l'Islam maghrebin* (Paris, 1954), p. 260.

16. Sir Thomas Arnold, *The Preaching of Islam* (1896; reprint ed., Lahore, 1956), is still the outstanding introduction.

surrounded by a veil of mystical and mythical tales, not as a historical person but as a transhistorical power, is deeply venerated from Indonesia to East and West Africa, as innumerable folk songs prove.

Most of the Sufi orders are identified with certain strata of the population. Even in modern Turkey after the prohibition of religious activities in 1925, the old allegiances can still be felt: the Shādhiliyya order was attractive primarily to the middle classes; the Mevleviyya—the order of the Whirling Dervishes—was close to the house of the Ottoman emperors and, at the same time, the order of artists, inspiring music, poetry, and the fine arts; whereas the rustic Bektashis were connected with the Janissaries and produced a typically Turkish folk literature (see chapter 7). The noble Suhrawardiyya can be contrasted with the Heddāwa, a beggars' order in Morocco, which claims descent from the Qādiriyya and practices absolute poverty.[17] Suborders and small fractions of orders are found everywhere—J. Spencer Trimingham speaks of the *ṭāʾifa* system; each of these suborders jealously tried to preserve the special teaching and the *baraka* of the founder sheikh or the family *baraka*. North Africa, primarily Morocco, is a good example of this development. It is natural that under these circumstances the orders could rarely maintain the high level of spirituality with which their founders were credited. But even in our day one witnesses now and then personalities who, in the established tradition of their respective orders, rise to great spiritual heights and have been instrumental in awakening among Western scholars and laymen a new interest in the best tradition of the *ṭarīqas*.

ABŪ SAᶜĪD IBN ABĪʾL-KHAYR[18]

The first Sufi to draw up a preliminary monastic rule for his disciples was one of Sulamī's followers, Abū Saᶜīd ibn Abīʾl-Khayr, born in 967 in Mayhana (Mihna) in Khurasan, a place peopled with Sufi saints. After theological studies in Merw and Sarakhs, he was introduced to the mystical path; the tradition tells that he devoted himself completely to the word "Allāh" and for seven years underwent very difficult ascetic practices—among them, the *ṣalāt maqlūba*, hanging by the feet into a well or a similar dark place

17. René Brunel, *Le monachisme errant dans l'Islam, Sīdī Heddī et les Heddāwa* (Paris, 1955), deals with an outwardly rather repellent beggars' order in North Africa.

18. See Reynold A. Nicholson, *Studies in Islamic Mysticism* (1921; reprint ed., Cambridge, 1967), chap. 1; hence the quotations.

while reciting the Koran and prayer formulae. This practice was performed by some later Indo-Muslim saints as well, which has led to the suggestion of a yoga origin; but as early a witness as Abū Saᶜīd in Khurasan seems to contradict such an idea.[19] Abū Saᶜīd showed extreme zeal in asceticism, primarily in ablutions; his self-abasement in the service of his Sufi brethren had no limits. People first admired him and then deserted him; at the legendary age of forty he reached perfect illumination. From the age of forty onward he no longer practiced austerities but spent all the money he was given in entertaining his Sufi friends; the emaciated ascetic enjoyed good food and became rather corpulent. He was immersed in an intense spiritual joy and tried to share his radiant gratitude with his brethren.

Abū Saᶜīd never performed the pilgrimage. A saying ascribed to him claims that the Kaaba would come several times a day to visit him, performing the circumambulation above his head—such a claim is also ascribed to other Sufis who no longer considered the outward rites absolutely binding on one who has reached perfection. According to Abū Saᶜīd, "Sufism is glory in wretchedness and riches in poverty and lordship in servitude and satiety in hunger and clothedness in nakedness and freedom in slavery and life in death and sweetness in bitterness. . . . The Sufi is he who is pleased with all that God does in order that God may be pleased with all that he does" (NS 49). Such a state is, of course, attained only when the Sufi ceases regarding his own self, the greatest source of all trouble, and is filled with love and longing for God. In the typical anecdotal framework into which Sufi sayings are put, he heard a peasant sigh:

> If God, when He created the world, had created no creatures in it; and if He had filled it full of millet from East to West and from earth to heaven; and if then He had created one bird and bidden it eat one grain of this millet every thousand years, and if, after that, He had created a man and kindled in his heart this mystic longing and had told him that he would never win to his goal until this bird left not a single milletseed in the whole world, and that he would continue until then in this burning pain of love—I have been thinking, it would still be a thing soon ended! (NS 18)

God reveals Himself as the loving and affectionate one to the Sufi, who, in turn, ought to put away whatever keeps him apart from God

19. For the *ṣalāt maqlūba* see Khaliq Ahmad Nizami, *The Life and Times of Farīd Ganj-i Shakar* (Aligarh, 1955), p. 179. Johann Karl Teufel, *Eine Lebensbeschreibung des Scheichs ᶜAlī-i Hamaḏānī* (Leiden, 1962), writes of Hamadhānī standing on his head while meditating.

and bring comfort to his brethren. And Abū Saʿīd did not think much of miracles; he felt that "whosoever belongs entirely to the Giver (*karīm*), all his acts are *karāmāt*, 'gifts of grace' " (NS 66). That is the same attitude that made him say about the perfect saint: "The true saint goes in and out amongst the people and eats and sleeps with them and buys and sells in the market and takes part in social intercourse, and never forgets God for a single moment" (NS 55). This ideal was defined later by the Naqshbandī mystics as *khalwat dar anjuman*, complete absorption in proximity to God in the midst of a crowd; the perfect mystic's concentration can no longer be disturbed or altered by any external event or occupation.

Gathering his disciples, Abū Saʿīd founded a convent, though he did not organize an order as such. For his disciples he set up ten rules, which were imitated by many later founders of fraternities since they embrace the ideals of Muslim community life.

1) The disciple should keep his garments clean and be always in a state of ritual purity. [This rule applies, basically, to every Muslim, for the state of ritual impurity prohibits him or her from reciting the Koran and from any religious action; should he or she die in this state, punishment in the other world would be exacted.]
2) One should not sit in a holy place for gossiping. [The mosques had often been used as congregational meeting places, where people would sit and converse; the womanfolk love to go to the graveyards not only to perform pious acts but to sit there and chat.]
3) The prayer should be performed in the congregation, particularly by the beginner. [Although the obligation for congregational prayer is valid only for the Friday noon prayer, the Muslims have always considered it more rewarding to pray in a group.]
4) Much night prayer is recommended [following the Koranic injunctions, and according to the practice of the early ascetics. In later times, meditation after prayer was usually practiced in the small hours of the night, which is merely an extension of this rule.]
5) At dawn, the disciple should pray for forgiveness. [The so-called *istighfār* formula has been used for *dhikr* since early days.]
6) Then, in the early morning, he should read the Koran, abstaining from talk till sunrise.
7) Between the two evening prayers, he should be occupied with his recollection (*dhikr*) and the specially litany (*wird*) which is given to him by his master.
8) The Sufi should welcome the poor and needy, and look after them.
9) He should not eat without another person participating—to eat alone is considered unpleasant and unlawful; to offer even the smallest morsel to a brother who may be hungrier than the host is highly appreciated.
10) The disciple should not absent himself without permission. (NS 46)

Abū Saʿīd was well aware of the dangers inherent in the mystical path if the disciple was not directed carefully (hence the last rule). In his time, the practice of *samāʿ* to incite ecstasy was apparently very popular, but for him the *samāᶜ* was mainly a practical device to dissipate the lust of the dervishes, which might otherwise find other, more dangerous ways of distraction.

Abū Saᶜīd's name is, or rather was, usually connected with the first examples of Persian mystical poetry. He is the alleged author of a number of poems in which the *rubāᶜī*, quatrain, with its rhyme scheme *a a x a*, is used as a vehicle for mystical thought. We can be quite sure that none of the quatrains formerly attributed to him are actually his; according to his own statement, his love-intoxicated teacher Bishr ibn Yāsīn was the author of such verses—a genre that later became very popular.[20]

A true representative of early Sufi poetry in quatrains, though in a popular meter and vernacular speech, is Bābā Ṭāhir, who died in Khorramābād in the first part of the eleventh century.[21]

Abū Saᶜīd passed away in 1049. It is said that on his deathbed he bestowed his *khirqa* to Aḥmad-i Jām Žandapīl, who was just about to be born. Aḥmad-i Jām was a Persian saint who was the opposite of Abū Saᶜīd in almost every respect: stern, proud of his mystical power, drawing people to repentance, not to love, and often using his spiritual strength for revenge and punishment.[22]

Abū Saᶜīd's tomb was destroyed when the wild Ghuzz tribes conquered Mayhana about 1180. By that time, the first real Sufi fraternities had come into existence—namely, the Suhrawardiyya and the Qādiriyya, which even today are influential in large areas of the Muslim world.

THE FIRST ORDERS

ᶜAbduᵓl-Qāhir Abū Najīb as-Suhrawardī (d. 1168),[23] the founder of the Suhrawardiyya, was a disciple of Aḥmad Ghazzālī,

20. Hermann Ethé, "Die *Rubāᶜīs* des Abū Saᶜīd ibn Abūlchair," *Sitzungsberichte der bayrischen Akademie der Wissenschaften, philologisch-historische Klasse,* 1875, 1878.

21. See Jan Rypka, *History of Iranian Literature* (Dordrecht, 1968), p. 234, on Bābā Ṭāhir.

22. Vladimir Ivanow, "A Biography of Shaykh Aḥmad-i Jām," *Journal of the Royal Asiatic Society,* 1917; Fritz Meier, "Zur Biographie Ahmad-i Ǧām's und zur Quellenkunde von Ǧāmī's *Nafaḥātuᵓl-uns,*" *Zeitschrift der Deutschen Morgenländischen Gesellschaft* 97 (1943); Heshmat Moayyad, *Die "Maqāmāt" des Ġaznawī, eine legendäre Vita Aḥmad-i Ǧāms, genannt Žandapīl, 1049–1141* (Frankfurt, 1958).

23. Hellmut Ritter, "Philologika IX: Die vier Suhrawardī," *Der Islam* 24–25 (1935–36), deals with the two Suhrawardīs mentioned here and the *shaykh al-ishrāq*; see chapter 6 of this book.

Imām Ghazzālī's younger brother. Suhrawardī is the author of one of the most widely read handbooks of mystical education, *Ādāb al-murīdīn,* "The Manners of the Adepts," a classic that has been translated into the different Islamic languages and has often been imitated.

Even more influential than he was his brother's son, Shihābuddīn Abū Ḥafṣ ᶜUmar as-Suhrawardī (1145–1234), who studied under him and whose treatise on Sufi theories, *ᶜAwārif al-maᶜārif,* was—partly in the Arabic original, partly in translation—even more widely read than his uncle's book and became one of the standard works taught in Indian *madrasa*s in courses on Sufism.[24] It certainly enhanced the influence of the Suhrawardiyya order, which soon spread into India.

Abū Ḥafṣ ᶜUmar entered upon a political career as well; he became *shaykh ash-shuyūkh,* the official Sufi master of Baghdad, under the caliph an-Nāṣir at a time when this last enterprising member of the Abbasid dynasty dreamed of reviving the stagnant spiritual life throughout the Islamic lands and was trying to unite Islamic rulers in defense against the Mongol threat. Abū Ḥafṣ served as the caliph's ambassador to the Ayyubid rulers of Egypt and Syria as well as to the Seljukids of Rum, whose power had just reached its apex in their flourishing capital of Konya—the place that was to become a new center of mystical and religious life in the years following Suhrawardī's visit. Abū Ḥafṣ ᶜUmar's friendly relations with the ruling classes also determined the attitude of his followers in India in later centuries; they were usually more open to the exigencies of the world and more willing to accept political participation than their brethren in other orders.

Abū Ḥafṣ ᶜUmar helped the caliph propagate his ideas of renewing the *futuwwa* ideals; it has even been suggested that an-Nāṣir organized the *futuwwa* order, in part, to diffuse Suhrawardī's teachings.[25] For all practical purposes, the caliph had institutionalized the so-called *futuwwa* movement, which was closely connected with Sufism. He took the investiture ceremony of neighboring Muslim rulers with the "*futuwwa* trousers" and headgear as a sign of their allegiance to him.

24. *ᶜAwārif al-maᶜārif* (Bulaq, 1289 h./1892–93), at the margin of Ghazzālī's *Iḥyāʾ*. H. Wilberforce Clarke, trans., *The "ᶜAwārifʾul-Maᶜārif" written in the thirteenth century by Shaikh Shahābuʾd-Din Umar bin Muhammad-i Suhrawardi* (1891; reprint ed., New York, 1970), from a Persian translation of the Arabic text.

25. Herbert Mason, *Two Medieval Muslim Statesmen* (The Hague, 1971), p. 124.

Essentially, the idea of *futuwwa* goes back to early Sufism. The *fatā* is "the young man," "the brave youth," generous and faithful. The Koran had called the Seven Sleepers *fityan* (plural of *fatā*; Sūra 18:10). Ḥallāj used the term for those who excel by their absolute faithfulness and loyalty to treaties, including, particularly, Iblis and Pharaoh, who remained faithful to their claims. But generally the term was connected with ʿAlī ibn Abī Ṭālib, as the sentence goes: "There is no *fatā* but ʿAlī, and no sword but Dhūʾl-Fiqār."[26]

The term *jawānmard*, the Persian translation of *fatā*, is used in the hagiographies for many Sufis, often for those who are classified among the sincere *malāmatīs*. This connection is quite likely; and Sulamī, who had composed a treatise about the *Malāmatiyya*, devoted a treatise to the *futuwwa* as well, in which he enumerated 212 definitions of the true *fatā*. Qushayrī followed him by treating the *futuwwa* in a special chapter of his *Risāla*. "The *fatā* is he who has no enemy, and who does not care whether he is with a saint or an infidel; and Muhammad was the perfect *fatā*, for at Doomsday everybody will say 'I,' but he will say 'My community' " (Q 103). On the whole, one may accept Ibn ʿArabī's definition that a *fatā* is he who honors those senior to him, who shows mercy to those junior or inferior to him, and prefers those who are his equals to himself. The Sufi ideal of *īthār*, to prefer others to oneself, is brought to its perfection in the *futuwwa* concept. In the early thirteenth century, an-Nāṣir tried once more to revive these ideas, but without much success. Yet *futuwwa* groups existed in several parts of the Near East, where they constituted an important factor in the social life. In Turkey, the related groups of the *akhi*, in which only blameless men of respectable profession were accepted as members, maintained the *futuwwa* ideals throughout the next centuries; the North African traveler Ibn Baṭṭūṭa (d. 1368) has told, in his travel account, how well he was received by these hospitable sodalities in Anatolia. Out of them associations like the "socialist" movement of Akhi Evrān in the fourteenth century came into existence; the relations between *futuwwa* groups and the guilds have been studied several times, though with different conclusions.

At the same time that the elder Suhrawardī laid the foundation

26. Franz Taeschner, "Das futūwa-Rittertum des islamischen Mittelalters," in *Beiträge zur Arabistik, Semitistik und Islamkunde*, ed. Richard Hartmann and H. Scheel (Leipzig, 1944), and numerous other articles about this topic. See Taeschner's article *futuwwa* in *Encyclopedia of Islam*, 2d ed., with additions by Claude Cahen. Abdülbâki Gölpınarlı, *Islam ve Türk Illerinde Fütuvvet Teşkilatı ve Kaynakları* (Istanbul, 1952).

of his order, a Hanbalite preacher in Baghdad was attracting large crowds of faithful by his sermons and exhortations, though his works reveal but little of the lofty mystical states of which his contemporaries spoke. This ascetic preacher was ʿAbduʾl-Qādir al-Gīlānī (1088–1166) from the Caspian Sea, probably the most popular saint in the Islamic world, whose name is surrounded by innumerable legends that scarcely fit the image of the stern, sober representative of contrition and mystical fear.[27] He had studied Hanbalite law with Ibn ʿAqīl and had received the *khirqa* from his teacher's colleague al-Mukharrimī, the builder of the first Hanbalite *madrasa,* which his disciple inherited from him.

ʿAbduʾl-Qādir's tomb in Baghdad is still a place of pilgrimage for pious Muslims, mainly from the Indo-Pakistani Subcontinent, where the order was introduced in the late fourteenth century. These pilgrims, who often stay for weeks, silently walk around with little brooms, cleaning the sanctuary—to sweep the threshold of a saint is considered very rewarding work. A poet may sing that he sweeps the floor of his beloved with his eyelashes, or a modern Turkish woman, modernizing and simplifying the original act of sweeping, may offer a broom at the door of Ankara's local saint Ḥājjī Bayram.

ʿAbduʾl-Qādir's fame soon reached incredible heights. He is called *Muḥyī ud-dīn,* "the reviver of religion." A charming legend tells how the pious man helped a weak and destitute person who was lying, completely exhausted, on the road; after he had given him some sustenance and almost revived him, that person revealed himself to ʿAbduʾl-Qādir as "the religion of Islam," and hence he gained this honorific title (N 519). Strange as the story sounds, it reveals the admiration of ʿAbduʾl-Qādir's followers for their master. A number of sayings are attributed to him in which he claims the highest mystical rank possible. The author of the *Nafaḥāt al-uns* highly praises the great saint, who was, according to Yāfiʿī, the sheikh of the east, Abū Madyan of Tlemcen being the sheikh of the west. Yet Abū Madyan spiritually heard, and immediately obeyed, Gīlānī's famous saying, "My foot is on the neck of every saint" (N 527), admitting the superiority of the Baghdad saint.

A satisfactory explanation of the transition from the sober Han-

27. Walter Braune, *Die "futūḥ al-ġaib" des ʿAbdul Qādir* (Berlin and Leipzig, 1933), contains a translation of Gīlānī's main work; English translation of the *fūtūḥ* by M. Aftāb ud-Dīn Aḥmad (Lahore, n.d.).

balite preacher (that he was not a pure ascetic is clear from the fact that he had forty-nine sons!) to the prototype of saintliness venerated all over the Muslim world is still lacking. The poems in honor of ᶜAbduᵓl-Qādir, which are sung at his anniversary in the fourth month of the Muslim lunar year, reveal the tremendous admiration of the people for this mystical leader, who, as a sixteenth-century Turkish song attests, "recited the complete Koran every night, standing on one leg."[28] He is the *ghauth-i aᶜẓam,* "the Greatest Help," and the *pīr-i dast-gīr,* "the *Pīr* who keeps one's hand" for support. Turkish folk poets boast:

> I am the honey of his bee,
> I am the rose of his garden,
> I am the nightingale of his meadow—
> of my sheikh ᶜAbduᵓl-Qādir![29]

Old Sindhi songs describe how his spiritual realm extends from Istanbul to Delhi, town by town, country by country being blessed by him. Sir Richard Burton, writing about 1850, says that there were about a hundred large trees in Sind, all called after Gīlānī.[30] Each had a pole and a flag hung upon it to fulfill some vow made in adversity or sickness. Sweetmeats were distributed to the poor in honor of the saint, and the fruit and leaves of the trees were not allowed to be touched even by cattle. Proper names like *Ghauth Bakhsh,* "gift of the help," in Sind and Balochistan point to his popularity. Indeed, in folk piety Gīlānī has become the master of the *jinn,* and many haunted caves and sacred places in the Maghreb are devoted to his cult. He has also had a decisive influence in the Islamization of West Africa.

Almost contemporary with ᶜAbduᵓl-Qādir al-Gīlānī, and also living in Iraq, was Aḥmad ar-Rifāᶜī, founder of an order that appears more eccentric than the Qādiriyya—the Rifāᶜiyya dervishes, known as the Howling Dervishes because of their loud *dhikr.* They are notorious for performing strange miracles, like eating live snakes, cutting themselves with swords and lances without being hurt, and taking out their eyes. "But this is something the sheikh did not know, nor did his pious companions—we seek refuge from

28. William Hickman, "Eshrefoghlu Rumi: Reconstitution of His *dīwān*" (Ph.D. diss., Harvard University, 1972), no. Y 21*.

29. Ibid., no. K 9*.

30. Sir Richard Burton, *Sind and the Races That Inhabit the Valley of the Indus* (London, 1851), p. 177.

Satan with God!" (N 532), exclaims Jāmī when speaking of these "aberrations."

One century later—when the Muslim culture of Iraq had been swept away by the Mongols—Egypt became a center for mystical orders. Aḥmad al-Badawī from Tanta (d. 1278)[31] founded a fraternity that drew most of its adherents from the rural population of Egypt, but was able to attract some members of the ruling Mamluk house during the late Middle Ages. The wife of Sultan Khushqadam was buried, in 1466, covered with the red flag of the Badawiyya,[32] and during the fifteenth century the festivals in Tanta were often attended by Mamluk officers and soldiers (which sometimes led to disturbances when the excitement grew). A recent novel by the young Egyptian writer ᶜAbduʾl-Ḥakīm Qāsim centers around the veneration of Sīdī Aḥmad in Tanta and gives a vivid picture of the social and psychological background of this deep-rooted cult.[33] The most remarkable representative of the order is ash-Shaᶜrānī, the last great Muslim mystic in Egypt (d. 1565), whose literary legacy is interesting as a typical expression of later Sufi thought.[34]

The Badawiyya is a rustic order that has adopted a considerable number of pre-Islamic customs. Its festivities are held according to the solar Coptic calendar and thus are connected with the Nile and its flood; signs of old fertility rites are therefore assimilated into the cult. That is why the Badawiyya never crossed the borders of its homeland, as was also the case with an order founded by Aḥmad's contemporary Aḥmad ad-Dasūqī in the same country.

Another order that came into existence in Egypt at about the same time, however, expanded widely and attracted large numbers of followers—first in the western part of the Muslim world and more recently among Europeans as well. It is the Shādhiliyya, which manifests one important aspect of mystical life, though the attitude of its masters differs considerably from the more emotional approach found in at least some of the orders that emerged in the eastern part of the Muslim world (with the exception of the Naqshbandiyya, which is, in some respects, close to the Shādhiliyya). This

31. See Ignaz Goldziher, "Aus dem muhammedanischen Heiligenkult in Aegypten," *Globus* 71 (1897); Enno Littmann, *Aḥmed il-Bedawī, Ein Lied auf den ägyptischen Nationalheiligen* (Mainz, 1950).

32. Abūʾl-Maḥāsin Ibn Taġrībirdī, *An-nuğūm az-zāhira fi mulūk Miṣr waʾl-Qāhira*, ed. William Popper, 8 vols. (Berkeley, 1908–36), 7:809. See Schimmel, "Sufismus," in *Festschrift für W. Caskel*, ed. Gräf, p. 277.

33. ᶜAbduʾl-Ḥakīm Qāsim, *Ayyām al-insān as-sabᶜā* (Cairo, 1971).

34. See Trimingham, *Sufi Orders*, pp. 220–25, on ash-Shaᶜrānī.

more sober attitude of the Sufis in the Islamic West is probably the reason for Maqqarī's (d. 1631) somewhat unfair statement: "Faqirhood as it is current in the East which discourages its followers from work and encourages them to beg, is considered by us as an extremely hideous matter."[35] The order crystallized around Abū'l-Ḥasan ʿAlī ash-Shādhilī, a disciple of ʿAbdu's-Salām ibn Mashīsh, the Moroccan mystic whose teachings survive in a number of Maghrebi orders, including the beggars' order of the Heddāwa. Through him the tradition goes back to Abū Madyan, the patron saint of Tlemcen (d. 1126).

Abū'l-Ḥasan went from Spain, via Tunis, to Alexandria, where he settled and eventually died in 1258, the year of the destruction of Baghdad and the end of the Abbasid caliphate. Although he was apparently by no means an intellectual, he had an extraordinary insight into the souls of men and a deep mystical fire, which he transmitted to the members of the fraternity. Unlike other mystical leaders (and similar to the later Naqshbandiyya), Shādhilī did not emphasize the necessity of monastic or solitary life, nor did he encourage specific forms of vocal *dhikr*. Every member of the *ṭarīqa* was supposed to realize the spirit of the order in his own life and his own environment, in the midst of his duties. The Shādhiliyya Sufis were not expected to beg or espouse poverty; on the contrary, the Egyptian sources of the fourteenth and fifteenth centuries tell how members of this order excelled in their tidy attire, quite in contrast to some of the other Sufis who filled the streets of Cairo. The Shādhiliyya does not even have a fully developed system of mystical theories. Their most distinctive feature is that a Shādhilī is sure to be predestined as a member of this *ṭarīqa* from preeternity and believes that the *quṭb*, the head of the spiritual hierarchy, will always be a member of this order.[36]

Abū'l-Ḥasan left little written material; his tendency to write letters of spiritual instruction, however, was emulated by some of his illustrious followers. The great prayer that he composed under the title *Ḥizb al-baḥr* has become one of the most popular devotional

35. *Analecta* 1:135, cited in Ignaz Goldziher and Joseph de Somogyi, "The Spanish Arabs and Islam," *Moslem World* 4, no. 1 (1964): 37.

36. Some books have been published in Arabic about the Shādhiliyya, one by ʿAbdu'l-Ḥalīm Maḥmud about the order and one by ʿAlī Ṣafī Ḥusayn about the poetry of fourteenth-century mystics in Egypt. On the theories of the Shādhiliyya, see Edward Jabra Jurji, ed. and trans., *Illumination in Islamic Mysticism* (Princeton, 1938), and Jurji, "The Illuministic Sufis," *Journal of the American Oriental Society*, 1937 (the way from Ibn Masarrā via the Ishrāqiyya school to ash-Shādhilī).

texts—Ibn Baṭṭūṭa used it during his long voyages, apparently with success.

The student of Sufism used to the florid and enrapturing songs of Persian mystical poets will find in the Shādhilī writings a certain sobriety—the Baghdadian trend. That is understandable from the sources upon which the members of this order drew: Muḥāsibī's *Kitāb ar-riᶜāya*, the fine psychological treatise of early Islam; Makkī's *Qūt al-qulūb*; and Ghazzālī's *Iḥyā ᶜulūm ad-dīn*. This sobriety also distinguishes the writings of the two masters of the order, two of the outstanding figures in the history of later Sufism, Ibn ᶜAṭāʾ Allāh al-Iskandarānī and Ibn ᶜAbbād of Ronda.

When Abūʾl-Ḥasan ash-Shādhilī died, Abūʾl-ᶜAbbās al-Mursī became his *khalīfa* (d. 1287); he was succeeded by Tājuddīn Ibn ᶜAṭāʾ Allāh (d. 1309). Ibn ᶜAṭāʾ Allāh provided the Shādhiliyya with their classical literature, the *Laṭāʾif al-minan* and, even more, the *Ḥikam*, a collection of 262 short sayings—a genre not uncommon in twelfth- and thirteenth-century Sufism—followed by four short treatises and a few prayers. These sentences are regarded as the finest expressions of Shādhiliyya ideals, and pious followers have uttered the opinion that, if it were permitted to recite any text other than the Koran in the ritual prayer one would surely recite the *Ḥikam*. As Père Nwyia says so poignantly about Ibn ᶜAṭāʾ Allāh: "His *ḥikam* are without contest the last Sufi miracle worked on the shores of the Nile, and this miracle belongs to the Shādhiliyya and was one of the instruments for their expansion."[37]

Numerous commentaries on the comparatively small book are extant; its influence extends through the western and central part of the Islamic world, but is rather less in the Persian-speaking lands. Yet one of the leading scholars of sixteenth-century India, ᶜAlī al-Muttaqī (d. 1556)—otherwise known as the author of a widely accepted anthology of *ḥadīth*, the *Kanz al-ᶜummāl*—has reworked the *Ḥikam*, as well as its major commentaries, classifying the sayings according to their contents. The concise Arabic style, the short and poignant sentences of the *Ḥikam*, enthrall every lover of Arabic lan-

37. Paul Nwyia, *Ibn ᶜAṭāʾ Allāh et la naissance de la confrèrie šāḏilite* (Beirut, 1972), contains the best introduction to Shādhiliyya thought and also an annotated translation of the *ḥikam*, which is most welcome to Western scholars. The first English translation of the *ḥikam* appeared in Singapore in 1937: R. le R. Archer, "Muhammadan Mysticism in Sumatra," *Journal Malayan Branch of the Royal Asiatic Society* 15, no. 2. A new English translation of the *ḥikam*, though interpreted from a peculiar mystical viewpoint, is offered by Victor Danner, *Ibn ᶜAṭāʾillāh's Ṣūfī Aphorisms* (Leiden, 1973).

guage. The wisdom conveyed in them is, to a certain extent, an elaboration of the sayings of the great masters of classical Sufism—one finds similarities not only with aphorisms of Junayd, but also with those of Ḥallāj, of Niffarī (whose work was studied in Egypt), and, of course, of Ghazzālī. Nwyia has defined the main content of the *Ḥikam* as a "dialectic of the mystery of God Who is both obscure and transparent." Sentences like the following conform exactly to the classical meditations: "If there were not the spaces of the soul, there would not be a mystical way, for there is no distance between you and Him that your foot could traverse"—an interiorization of the concept of the Path, reminiscent of sayings about the state of *qurb*, "proximity," in earlier sources. "What veils God from you is His excessive nearness." He veils Himself because He is too transparent and becomes invisible by the very intensity of His light—a favorite idea with the Persian Sufis as well, and one often repeated in Rūmī's work.

The Shādhiliyya soon extended itself to North Africa, where, in the fourteenth century, six differently named orders existed, about which little is known. In any case, Sufism in the Maghreb developed under the sign of the *Iḥyā*ᵓ, as Père Nwyia has correctly stated, and the final victory of Shādhilī ideas was brought about by Ibn ᶜAbbād ar-Rondi, a contemporary of the great North African philosopher of history Ibn Khaldūn (d. 1406). Ibn ᶜAbbād's *Sharḥ al-ḥikam* made Ibn ᶜAṭāᵓ Allāh's work widely known in the western Muslim countries and exerted a tremendous influence upon the different branches of Maghrebi Sufism.[38]

Ibn ᶜAbbād was born in Ronda in Spain in 1332. He studied in Tlemcen and Fez, a city that flourished under the Merinid rulers. After a period of solitude and meditation under Ibn ᶜAshīr in Salé, he eventually became a preacher and *imām* in the famous Qarāwiyīn *madrasa* in Fez. There he died in 1390. According to the sources, Ibn ᶜAbbād was a silent man who adhered strictly to the tenets of Ghazzālī's and Abū Najīb Suhrawardī's mystical works; he seems to have led a celibate life. Although he acted as a preacher in the leading mosque of Morocco for many years, his sermons, as far as they have been preserved, lack brilliance and emotional fire. It is through his writings—the *Sharḥ al-ḥikam* and the two collections of

38. Paul Nwyia, *Ibn ᶜAbbād de Ronda* (Beirut, 1961), a penetrating analysis of the great Shādhilī master, whose letters Nwyia has also edited: *"As-rasāᵓil aṣ-ṣugrā," Lettres de direction spirituelle* (Beirut, 1958).

letters (fifty-four in all)—that one gains some insight into his soul as well as into his method of psychological guidance. He modestly admits that he never enjoyed real *dhauq*, mystical experience, or rapture and immediate "tasting" of the ineffable joy; nor was he granted any ecstatic experience—nothing "but the study of some Sufi works" brought him to his state. We do not find, in his expressions, that overwhelming love that inspired the intoxicated songs of many mystics, whose yearning grows after every fulfillment. His is the unquestioning faith that eventually becomes deeply rooted in the soul and turns into unshakable certitude, *yaqīn*. He always saw himself as *ʿabd*, a slave who constantly feels his nothingness before God's majesty—not as a lover craving for union. The "vigilant fear of God's ruse (*makr*)" looms large in his devotion—"if God gives you something good He may want to punish you"; therefore one has to be on one's guard and not neglect obedience and prayer for a single moment. It is natural that Ibn ʿAbbād should give a prominent place in his system to the constant struggle against the *nafs*: "There is no arrival to God but by God, as well as there is no veil between the servant and the Lord but his *nafs*. One does not fight the *nafs* by the *nafs* but fights it by God."

Asín Palacios, the first Western orientalist to draw attention to Ibn ʿAbbād's work, in 1933, has seen in him "un precourseur hispano-musulman de San Juan de la Cruz."[39] His main point of comparison was the concept of the Dark Night of the Soul: he had found in Ibn ʿAbbād—influenced by Junayd as well as by the school of Abū Madyan[40]—a certain predilection for the state of *qabḍ*, the constraint in which God reveals His graces better than in outward gifts and spiritual consolation. IbnʿAbbād, following his predecessors in the Path, compares the *qabḍ* to the night out of which great things will be born. It is considered higher than *basṭ*, since man is completely passive, renouncing his own will and acting only to the extent that God makes him act. In this more than in any other mystical state, he feels his absolute dependence upon God, his nothingness, and thus is prepared for the highest possible attitude a servant can reach, that of uninterrupted *shukr*, "giving thanks," "rendering grace." The problem of *ṣabr* and *shukr*, patience and gratitude, is solved here, and, following the traditional Sufi tripartition, Ibn ʿAbbād teaches man to thank God first with his tongue, then with

39. M. Asín Palacios, "Šā̠dilies y alumbrados," *Al-Andalus* 9 (1944), 16 (1951).
40. Dermenghem, *Culte des saints*, p. 71.

his heart, until his whole being is transformed into gratitude and every moment of life consists of gratitude toward the Lord: "Our whole occupation and only practice should be to consider God's kindness toward us, and to think that our might and power is nothing, and to attach ourselves to God in a feeling of intense need for Him, asking Him to grant us gratitude." This is the conclusion of Shādhiliyya teaching, a teaching that, in its subtlest expressions, is directed not to a large community but to each individual, inspiring him to cultivate his heart until he knows himself to be completely in the hands of God, thanking him with every breath for His kindness—even though it may be outwardly hidden—uplifted by the mental prayer during which the heart forgets itself in the divine presence and is confirmed in its certitude.

This teaching appealed neither to the lower classes, who needed more exciting means of getting onto the Path, nor to the poets, but is primarily connected with the middle class, the officials and civil servants who were trained in the Shādhiliyya method to fulfill their duties carefully. It is revealing that one of the few modern orders that still attracts new disciples in Egypt, and gives them a thorough training in spiritual education, is an offshoot of the Shādhiliyya, an order that inspired man to a sanctification of his daily life.[41]

The Shādhiliyya mystics are credited with having invented the use of coffee as a way of staying awake during their litanies and vigils. Many mystics of the sober orders still rejoice in coffee as a useful means of attaining spiritual wakefulness and strictly refuse alcoholic beverages or drugs that would produce a spiritual intoxication and thus preclude clear contemplation.

To show the wide range of mystical experiences in the Sufi orders, we may turn to an order that was founded in the eastern part of the Muslim world approximately half a century before the Shādhiliyya —the Kubrāwiyya. Its founder is Abū'l-Jannāb Aḥmad, surnamed *at-ṭāmmat al-kubrā*, "the greatest affliction" (cf. Sūra 79:34), which is shortened to Najmuddīn Kubrā. He was born in 1145 in Khiva in Central Asia. During his training as a traditionalist, he traveled widely throughout the Muslim world, returned to Khwarizm about 1185, and was killed during the Mongol invasion in 1220. His tomb is located in Uzgen.

Kubrā was a prolific writer; his Arabic commentary on the Koran

41. See Michael Gilsenan, *Saint and Sufi in Modern Egypt* (Oxford, 1973), an excellent study of the contemporary Ḥāmidiyya-Shādhiliyya.

in nine volumes was continued by his disciple Najmuddīn Dāyā Rāzī and then by another prominent member of the order, ʿAlāʾud-daula Simnānī. Kubrā's mystical treatises on the ten stages for the novices have been translated and commented on in several of the Islamic languages; he followed the example of Sulamī and Suhrawardī in composing a book on the etiquette of the disciples.

Kubrā's main work is the *Fawāʾiḥ al-jamāl wa fawātiḥ al-jalāl*, which has been thouroughly analyzed by Fritz Meier in his excellent edition.[42] The work contains Kubrā's mystical psychology and gives an account of the visions and ecstatic experiences the mystic may attain. There is no doubt that Kubrā himself experienced these heavenly journeys and traversed the cosmic ranks in his visions. He agrees with other Sufi theoreticians insofar as he sees man as a microcosmos, containing everything that exists in the macrocosmos; man can be qualified with God's qualities, with the exception of the rank *Allāh ar-Raḥmān ar-Raḥīm*. But he regards God's qualities as located in special places in heaven, and the mystic who reaches these points during his spiritual ascension can incorporate them in himself. These acts are regarded by him as perfectly real, for the "heart" is a fine body that ascends through the heavens. However, such experiences can be realized only after the strictest adherence to the rules of the tenfold Path, some conditions of which are to abstain from food as much as possible and to give complete surrender to the sheikh by giving up one's own will completely. Included in the path, too, is the so-called "way of Junayd": constant ritual purity, constant fasting, constant silence, constant retreat, constant recollection of God, and constant direction of a sheikh who explains the meaning of one's dreams and visions. Finally, one must give up resistance to God's decree and refrain from prayer for reward in the otherworld. This is the theoretical foundation of the Kubrawī order.

Permanent concentration upon the divine names in the retreat leads to mystical awareness. Najmuddīn Kubrā gives an exact description of the revelations of colored lights that occur to the initiate during his spiritual training: there are dots and spots and circles;

42. Najmuddīn al-Kubrá, *Die "fawāʾiḥ al-ǧamāl wa fawātiḥ al-ǧalāl" des Naǧmuddīn Kubrā*, ed. Fritz Meier (Wiesbaden, 1957), is one of the indispensable books for the student of Sufism, mainly because of Meier's detailed introduction to the thought of Kubrā. See also Fritz Meier, "Stambuler Handschriften dreier persischen Mystiker: ʿAin al-Quḍāt al-Hamaḏānī, Naǧm ad-dīn al-Kubrā, Naǧm ad-dīn ad-Dājā," *Der Islam* 24 (1937).

the soul passes through periods of black color and of black and red spots until the appearance of the green color indicates that divine grace is near—green has always been considered the highest and heavenly color.[43]

The Kubrāwiyya developed an elaborate color symbolism. Kubrā's disciple Najmuddīn Dāyā speaks of white as connected with Islam, yellow with *īmān,* "faith," dark blue with *iḥsān,* "beneficence," green with *iṭmiʾnān,* "tranquillity," light blue with *īqān,* "true assurance," red with *ʿirfān,* "gnosis," and black with *hayamān,* "passionate love and ecstatic bewilderment." Black is the light of the essence, the "Divine Ipseity as revealing light that cannot be seen but makes see"; it is the color of *jalāl,* the unfathomable divine majesty, whereas God's *jamāl,* His beauty, reveals itself in other colors. But beyond the Black Light—the experience of which has been equated with the experience of *fanā* as well—is the "mountain of emerald," the color of Eternal Life (CL 153, 160).

There are other sequences of colors as well, and Kubrā admits that the colors and forms seen by the disciples can have different meanings and imports. They may even be of different origins—for Kubrā, good psychologist that he is, knows that the *khawāṭir,* the ideas occurring to the heart in the state of retreat, may be of divine or satanic origin, may stem from the human heart or from the lower soul, may come from angels or from *jinns.* Therefore, the disciple is always in need of a master to instruct him carefully in the deeper meaning of this or that color, form, or thought.

In the state of elevation, the mystic may be able to read heavenly books in languages and characters previously unknown to him and learn the heavenly names of things and beings, including his own eternal name, which is different from his worldly name.

The Kubrāwiyya chose as *dhikr* the profession of faith, which, when practiced under the stern conditions of the initial retreat, should work not only on the breath but even on the blood and permeate the disciple's entire being. Then the adept will learn that the Greatest Name of God is Allāh, or rather the *h* at the end of this word.

One of the unusual aspects of Najmuddīn Kubrā's psychology is the concept of the *shāhid al-ghaib,* the *Doppelgänger* in the otherworld, who may appear to the mystic at certain stages of the Path

43. Johann Leberecht Fleischer, "Uber die farbigen Lichterscheinungen der Sufis," *Zeitschrift der Deutschen Morgenländischen Gesellschaft* 16 (1862).

and is reminiscent, in a certain way, of Suhrawardī Maqtūl's angelic half of the soul, which lives outside the body. The Mazdaist idea of the personification of one's thoughts and actions may underlie the concepts of both mystics.

It is natural that a mystic who attributed such great importance to otherworldly realities should also have developed a theory of *himmat* and *taṣarruf*. Kubrā, like his contemporaries, held that the mystic is capable of bringing certain events to pass by directing his spiritual energy toward the sphere of possibilities, just as his spiritual energy allows him to work upon other human beings, forming their hearts according to the exigencies of the mystical Path.

Kubrā implanted his mystical theories in the Central Asian areas, from which they spread to Turkey and India. His disciple Najmuddīn Dāyā Rāzī left Khwarizm before the Mongols invaded it and migrated to Anatolia; in Sivas he wrote his *Mirṣād ul-ᶜibād*, which he dedicated to the Seljukid ruler of Konya, ᶜAlāʾuddīn Kaykobad —the same sultan who gave shelter to Jalāluddīn Rūmī and his family during those same years. The *Mirṣād ul-ᶜibād* became one of the favorite books of mystics throughout the Persian-speaking world and was soon translated into Turkish.[44] It was frequently used in India, so much so that in one of the strange and fanciful apologies of Islam against Hinduism, the *Ḥujjat al-Hind*, the clever parrot who instructs the princess in Islamic doctrine quotes long paragraphs from the *Mirṣād ul-ᶜibād*.[45] A good translation of this book into a Western language is one of the desiderata in the field of Sufi studies.

Another Kubrāwī, ᶜAlāʾuddaula Simnānī (d. 1336), who had spent his youth at the Ilkhanid court, was an excellent mystical psychologist and philosopher and is often cited because of his statements that question the truth of Ibn ᶜArabī's concept of *waḥdat al-wujūd* (see chapter 6). He thus became a favorite saint of the later Naqshbandiyya.[46]

44. Najmuddīn Dāyā Rāzī, *Mirṣād ul-ᶜibād* (Tehran, 1312 sh./1933).

45. Ibn ᶜUmar Miḥrābī's *Ḥujjat al-Hind*, not yet published, was probably written in 1645. See D. N. Marshall, *Mughals in India: A Bibliography* (Bombay, 1967), nos. 221, 1809.

46. On Simnānī, see Hermann Landolt, "Simnānī on Waḥdat al-Wujūd," in *Collected Papers on Islamic Philosophy and Mysticism*, ed. Mehdi Mohaghegh and Hermann Landolt (Tehran, 1971); Landolt, ed. and trans., *Correspondence spirituelle, échangé entre Nouroddin Esfarayeni (ob. 717/1317) et son disciple ᶜAlāoddawleh Semnānī (ob. 736/1336)* (Tehran and Paris, 1972), a highly interesting document; and Marijan Molé, "Un traité de ᶜAlāʾud-dawla Simnānī sur ᶜAlī ibn Abī Ṭālib," *Bulletin de l'Institut Français de Damas* 16 (1958–60). On the later Kubrawiyya in general, see

The Kubrāwiyya became the most important order in Kashmir in the latter part of the fourteenth century, when, according to the legend, Sayyid ʿAlī Hamadhānī migrated to that country with seven hundred followers.[47] Coming from a high-ranking family, Hamadhānī underwent Sufi education as a young boy and wandered through the eastern Islamic lands, including Ceylon, until he reached Kashmir in 1371. He is the author of several commentaries—including a commentary on the *Fuṣūṣ al-ḥikam*—and numerous other books in Arabic and Persian. His influence did much to shape Muslim mystical thought in the Kashmir valley, which had only recently been Islamized. Hamadhānī died in 1385 in Swat, but his order remained active in the Subcontinent, though it lost some of its initial strength in the course of time and was eventually superseded by orders like the Chishtiyya, Suhrawardiyya, Qādiriyya, and, since about 1600, the Naqshbandiyya in India. Still, the works of Kubrāwī saints have deeply influenced Indo-Muslim mysticism.[48]

Molé, "Les Kubrawiyya entre Sunnisme et Shiisme," *Revue des études islamiques*, 1961; and Molé, "Professions de foi de deux Kubrawis," *Bulletin de l'Institut Français de Damas* 17 (1961–63).

47. Teufel, *ʿAlī-i Hamadānī*, contains a biography of the saint. For his mystical theories see Fritz Meier, "Die Welt der Urbilder bei ʿAlī Hamadānī," *Eranos-Jahrbuch* 18 (1950).

48. On another leading mystic of the Kubrawiyya, ʿAzīz an-Nasafī, see Fritz Meier, "Die Schriften des ʿAzīz-i Nasafī," *Wiener Zeitschrift für die Kunde des Morgenlandes* 52 (1953); and Meier, "Das Problem der Natur im esoterischen Monismus des Islams," *Eranos-Jahrbuch* 14 (1946). See also Marijan Molé, ed., *Le livre de l'homme parfait* (Paris and Tehran, 1962).

6. THEOSOPHICAL SUFISM

SUHRAWARDĪ MAQTŪL, THE MASTER OF ILLUMINATION

The main current of moderate orthodox Sufism had been systematized by Ghazzālī, yet his own works contain views that were to develop in full in that stream of Islamic theosophy against which he had fought so relentlessly. His *Mishkāt al-anwār*, "The Niche for Lights," is the book from which most of the later Sufis start. The clearest expression of the light mysticism that had been known to the Sufis from early times and was first set forth explicitly in this work of Ghazzālī's is found in the mystical theories of Shihābuddīn Suhrawardī.[1]

Suhrawardī was born in 1153 in the same place in northwestern Iran from which the founder of the Suhrawardiyya order came. After initial studies he wandered through the central Islamic countries until he was drawn to Aleppo by the Ayyubid ruler al-Malik aẓ-Ẓāhir, who was fond of Sufis and scholars. But the lawyer divines,

1. Henri Corbin, *Sohrawardi d'Alep, fondateur de la doctrine illuminative (ishrāqī)* (Paris, 1939), was the first of Corbin's numerous studies devoted to the *shaykh al-ishrāq*. Suhrawardī Maqtūl, "Le bruissement de l'aile de Gabriel," ed. and trans. Henri Corbin and Paul Kraus, *Journal asiatique*, 1935, is an analysis of an important short Persian treatise. See the Bibliography for further works, and Hellmut Ritter, "Philologika IX: Die vier Suhrawardi," *Der Islam* 24–25 (1935–36).

afraid of the brilliant young philosopher-mystic, eventually persuaded the king, with the help of his father Saladin—the hero of the Crusades—to imprison Suhrawardī; he died in prison at the age of thirty-eight in 1191. That is why he is often called *al-maqtūl,* "he who was killed," to avoid confusion with the two other Suhrawardīs who played decisive roles in the formation of Sufi orders and the systematization of mystical thought.

Suhrawardī is the *shaykh al-ishrāq,* the master of the philosophy of illumination. "What is conceived metaphysically as existence (*wujūd*) coincides with what is grasped in terms of the root experience as Light (*nūr*). In this context existence *is* light."[2] The teachings pertaining to the philosophy of light were laid down by Suhrawardī in nearly fifty Arabic and Persian books. They show influences and criticism of peripatetic philosophy, of Ibn Sīnā, and a somewhat surprising, yet wonderful combination of Iranian, Hellenistic, and ancient oriental elements. His four large didactic and doctrinal works culminate in the *Ḥikmat al-ishrāq,* "The Philosophy of Illumination"; shorter, and easier to comprehend, are a number of Arabic and Persian writings of which the *Hayākil an-nūr,* "The Altars of Light," has gained special fame. Written originally in Arabic, it is also extant in Persian; numerous commentaries in the Islamic languages exist, and a Turkish version was produced by Ismāʿīl Anqarawī, the seventeenth-century scholar who wrote a commentary on Rūmī's *Mathnawī* as well. The *Hayākil,* like some other works by the *shaykh al-ishrāq,* has been read in Muslim India throughout the centuries.

The most fascinating of Suhrawardī's writings are some symbolic tales and mystical narratives in which he describes the journey of the soul and his angelology in strange and beautiful symbols, such as *ʿAql-i surkh,* "The Red Intellect," *Awāz-i par-i Jibrīl,* "The Sound of Gabriel's Wing," *Lughat-i mūrān,* "The Language of the Ants" (alluding to the Koranic story, often elaborated upon by the Sufis, of Solomon and the complaining ants), or *Ṣafīr-i Sīmurgh,* "The Whistling of the Sīmurgh," that mystical bird that, according to Islamic tradition, lives on the world-encircling mountain Qāf and that became the symbol of the divine in the work of Suhrawardī's contemporary, Farīduddīn ʿAṭṭār. Suhrawardī's treatise on love

2. Toshihiko Izutsu, "The Paradox of Light and Darkness in the Garden of Mystery of Shabastari," in *Anagogic Qualities of Literature,* ed. Joseph P. Strelka (University Park, Pa., 1971), p. 299.

is based primarily on Avicenna's book on the same subject. His *wāridāt* and *taqdīsāt,* prayers and sanctifications, different types of mystical invocations, reflect the whole range of his mythical and religious ideas.

Suhrawardī took his inspiration from different Islamic sources, among which the theology of Ḥallāj must certainly be mentioned. In fact, one may detect similarities between the two mystics not only in their violent deaths but also in the "divine fire that devoured Suhrawardī's soul."[3] At the same time Suhrawardī considered himself a continuer of the traditions of old Iran and ancient Egypt. He derives the wisdom of which he considers himself the true representative from Hermes (Idrīs in Islamic sources). Through the Greek philosophers, culminating in Plato, this spiritual stream reached Dhū'n-Nūn and Sahl at-Tustarī; through the Persian priest-kings it was transmitted to Bāyezīd Bisṭāmī and Kharaqānī, and to Ḥallāj. Suhrawardī's attempt to unite the two major trends of pre-Islamic theosophical tradition makes his work extremely important for the student of the history of religion.

Suhrawardī's main theories can be summed up in the following quotation:

> The Essence of the First Absolute Light, God, gives constant illumination, whereby it is manifested and it brings all things into existence, giving life to them by its rays. Everything in the world is derived from the Light of His essence and all beauty and perfection are the gift of His bounty, and to attain fully to this illumination is salvation.[4]

The ontological status of a being depends on the degree to which it is illuminated or veiled. The light radiates through longitudinal and latitudinal orders of angels who stand in well-defined relations to each other. Suhrawardī's angelology is perhaps the most attractive aspect of his work. He sees angels everywhere; they are as numerous as the fixed stars, i.e., innumerable. In one group of these angels, each angel dominates a species; they are often called by Zoroastrian names, since many of their features are inherited from the Iranian tradition. Gabriel is the archetype of humanity, the *rabb an-nauᶜ al-insānī;* he can be equated with the Holy Spirit and, as such, with the preexistent spirit of Muhammad, the prototype

3. Paul Nwyia, *Ibn ᶜAṭāʾ Allāh et la naissance de la confrérie šāḏilite* (Beirut, 1972), p. 10.

4. Seyyed H. Nasr, *Three Muslim Sages* (Cambridge, Mass., 1963), p. 69; a fine study of Avicenna, Suhrawardī, and Ibn ᶜArabī.

and model of humanity. All things are brought into existence by the sound of Gabriel's wings, which extend over the whole world. In addition to this general guardian angel of humanity, each soul has its own guardian angel. For the soul has a previous existence in the angelic world and "upon entering the body [it] . . . is divided into two parts, one remaining in heaven and the other descending into the prison or 'fort' of the body."[5] That is why the soul is unhappy in this world; it searches for its other half and must be reunited with its heavenly prototype in order to become perfected and to become itself again.

The archangels are located in the Orient *(sharq)*, which is conceived as the world of pure light devoid of matter, whereas the Occident is the world of darkness and matter; the two regions are separated by the heaven of fixed stars—which means that Orient and Occident should be understood in the vertical rather than in the horizontal sense. Man lives in the *ghurbat al-gharbiyya*, the "western exile": fallen into a well in the city of Qairuwan, he longs for home—for Yemen, *Arabia felix*, the Orient of light—and tries to find this radiant place during his sojourn on earth.

The choice of Yemen, the country connected with the right side, is not accidental—did not Muhammad feel the *nafas ar-Raḥmān*, the "breath of the Merciful," come from Yemen, where Uways al-Qaranī lived? Later Ishraqi philosophers would confront the *ḥikmat-i yūnāni*, "Greek philosophy," with the *ḥikmat-i yamanī*, "Yemenite wisdom," which is mystical knowledge granted by immediate gnosis.

When reading Suhrawardī's description of the "Orient of the soul," it is difficult not to think of the dreams of German romantic poets and philosophers, who saw in the *Morgenland* the mythical Orient, the true home of mankind, the lost Paradise, the goal of the spiritual pilgrimage (symbolized, in our day, by Hermann Hesse's *Morgenlandfahrt*). And the symbolism of Yemen has reached even the Rosicrucians.

It is clear that the condition of the soul after death depends upon the degree of illumination and purification it has reached during this life; life is a constant process of striving to attain that primordial light in its purity. The perfect state is granted only to the elect few, yet it should be everybody's goal.

Suhrawardī's philosophy was taken up mainly by Shia philoso-

5. Ibid., p. 73.

phers and constituted a very important element in Persian philosophical thought in the later Middle Ages. Mollā Ṣadrā of Shiraz (d. 1640) was deeply influenced by Suhrawardian ideas, and the Iranians who migrated to India took the philosophy of *ishrāq* with them and taught it in Indian mystical circles, so that even an orthodox mystic like Mīr Dard in the eighteenth century equates God with light—an idea that finds a faint echo in some sentences of Iqbal as well.

IBN ᶜARABĪ, THE GREAT MASTER[6]

Whereas Suhrawardī's spiritual legacy remained, for the most part, restricted to the Persian world, the influence of Ibn ᶜArabī—*ash-shaykh al-akbar*, "the greatest master"—on the general development of Sufism can scarcely be overrated. For most of the Sufis after the thirteenth century, his writings constitute the apex of mystical theories, and the orthodox have never ceased attacking him.

A correct interpretation of Ibn ᶜArabī's thought is difficult. The traditional Western view is that he is the representative of Islamic pantheism, or monism, and that because of such monist theories, he destroyed the Islamic idea of God as a living and active force and was largely responsible for the decay of true Islamic religious life. On the other hand, modern mystical thinkers, such as Seyyed H. Nasr, see in Ibn ᶜArabī's work a full explanation of what was already understood by earlier Sufis. In fact, it is surprising to find how many formulations attributed to him are already found in the so-called "classical" period. It may be that the very fact that he was more a genius of systematization than an enraptured mystic proved helpful for the generations to come, who found, thanks to him, a comprehensive system at their disposal. As even Aḥmad Sirhindī—usually considered Ibn ᶜArabī's antagonist—had to admit: "The Sufis who preceded him—if they spoke about these matters at all—only hinted at them and did not elaborate. Most of those who came after him chose to follow in his footsteps and used his terms. We latecomers have also benefited from the blessings of that great man and learned a great deal from his mystical insights. May God give him for this the best reward."[7]

6. See Osman Yaḥyā, *Histoire et classification de l'oeuvre d'Ibn ᶜArabī*, 2 vols. (Damascus, 1964). See also the review by Joseph van Ess in *Erasmus* 17, nos. 3–4 (1965).

7. Yohanan Friedmann, *Shaykh Ahmad Sirhindī: An Outline of His Thought and a Study of His Image in the Eyes of Posterity* (Montreal, 1971).

Ibn ʿArabī was born in 1165 in Murcia, Spain, and was educated by two women saints, one of them Fāṭima of Cordova (see Appendix 2). It is said that, during his stay in Cordova, he met Averroes, the philosopher and court physician of the Berber dynasty of the Almohads of Marrakesh. In Tunisia, Ibn ʿArabī studied Ibn Qasyi's *Khalʿ an-naʿlayn,* "The Taking Off of Both Shoes," a book of which Ibn Khaldūn said, 150 years later, that it should be burned or washed off because of its heterodox ideas.[8] The author of this questionable work had been the founder of a mystico-political group, the *murīdūn,* that was involved in an insurrection against the Almoravid rulers in Algarve in southern Portugal about 1130.

Ibn ʿArabī certainly studied the works of Ibn Masarrā of Cordova, who, about 900, had spoken about the purifying illumination and who has been classified among the philosopher-mystics. Perhaps the western Muslim world was generally more inclined toward a more philosophical or theosophical interpretation of religion, as contrasted to the enthusiastic, enraptured attitude of many of the mystics in the eastern countries—trends that can be observed in the peculiarities of some of the mystical fraternities as well.

In 1201 Ibn ʿArabī was inspired to perform the pilgrimage to Mecca. It was there that he met a highly accomplished young Persian lady. Enraptured by her beauty and intelligence, he composed the *Tarjumān al-ashwāq,* "The Interpreter of Longing," graceful verses written in the best tradition of classical Arabic poetry.[9] He himself later interpreted the booklet in a mystical sense, a device common to many Sufi poets. Further journeys led the mystic—who claimed to have received the *khirqa* from Khiḍr—to Cairo and to Konya, the capital of the Rum Seljukids. Young Ṣadruddīn Qōnawī was to become his foremost interpreter (d. 1274). The sheikh visited Baghdad and eventually settled in Damascus, where he died in 1240; his tomb is a goal for pious pilgrims.

Ibn ʿArabī has produced an enormous number of works, among which *Al-futūḥāt al-makkiyya,* "Meccan Revelations," in 560 chapters,[10] and the *Fuṣūṣ al-ḥikam,* "Bezels of Divine Wisdom," have

8. Ibn Khaldūn, *Shifāʾ as-sāʾil li-tahdhīb al-masāʾil,* ed. M. ibn Tavit at-Tanci (Istanbul, 1957), p. 110; Ibn Khaldūn's *fatwā* against the heretic Sufis.

9. *The "Tarjumān al-ashwāq": A Collection of Mystical Odes by Muḥyiuʾddīn ibn al-ʿArabī,* ed. Reynold A. Nicholson (London, 1911), with translation, is still the best available introduction.

10. *Al-Futūḥāt al-makkiyya,* 4 vols. (Cairo, 1329 h./1911).

gained the greatest popularity."[11] The fifteenth-century Naqshbandī mystic Muḥammad Pārsā compared the *Fuṣūṣ* to the soul and the *Futūḥāt* to the heart (N 396); later Naqshbandīs would be more reserved in their judgment, if they did not condemn outright the theories contained in these books.

The *Futūḥāt* were, as the author claims, dictated by God through the angel of inspiration, whereas the *Fuṣūṣ*, a small volume of twenty-nine chapters dealing with prophetology, were inspired by the Prophet. Each "bezel" speaks of the human and spiritual nature of a certain prophet; this serves as a vehicle for the particular aspect of divine wisdom revealed to that prophet. The book became so popular that the poets could play with its title, as did Jāmī, a great admirer of Ibn ᶜArabī, when he addressed his beloved:

> If the author of the "Bezels" had seen your lip,
> he would have written hundred "bezels" about the
> wisdom of the Messiah.[12]

The lip of the beloved is, in the traditional image, as life-bestowing as Jesus' breath and at the same time resembles the ruby-signet in shape and color. The verse assumes that every reader would be familiar with the contents of the *Fuṣūṣ al-ḥikam*.

A translation of the *Fuṣūṣ* into a western language is extremely difficult; the style is so concise that it reads very elegantly in the original but needs a detailed commentary for the non-Muslim reader. The influences of gnosticism, Hermetism, and Neoplatonic thought make Ibn ᶜArabī's works look very complicated and often

11. *Fuṣūṣ al-ḥikam*, ed. Abūʾl-Alāʾ Affifi (Cairo, 1946); translated into German by Hans Kofler as *Das Buch der Siegelringsteine der Weisheit* (Graz, 1970), which is not very satisfactory. More congenial is the part translation by Titus Burckhardt, *La sagesse des prophètes* (Paris, 1955). Burckhardt has built his *Introduction to Sufi Doctrines* (Lahore, 1959), an English version of his German book *Vom Sufitum* (Munich, 1953), upon the teachings of Ibn ᶜArabī. Ibn ᶜArabī's *fuṣūṣ* were even translated into Urdu verse by a pious Indian Muslim in the late eighteenth century; see Maulānā ᶜAbdas Salām Nadwī, *Shiᶜr al-Hind* (Azamgarh, ca. 1936), 2:209. The first scholarly introduction to Ibn ᶜArabī's work in Europe was Hendrik Samuel Nyberg, *Kleinere Schriften des Ibn ᶜArabī* (Leiden, 1919), an excellent edition and evaluation of the thought of Ibn ᶜArabī, unfortunately too little known among the students of Sufism. See also Arthur Jeffery, "Ibn al-ᶜArabī's *Shajarat al-Kawn*," *Islamic Studies*, nos. 10 and 11 (1959). One aspect of Ibn ᶜArabī's thought is discussed by Manfred Profitlich, *Die Terminologie Ibn ᶜArabīs im "Kitāb wasāʾil as-sāʾil" des Ibn Saudakīn* (Freiburg, 1973).

12. Maulānā ᶜAbdurraḥman Jāmī, *Dīwān-i kāmil*, ed. Hāshim Riżā (Tehran, 1341 sh./1962), p. 470.

seem to present insurmountable difficulties to the translator. That is why the interpretations of his work vary so greatly.

In the first thesis devoted to Ibn ᶜArabī's mystical system,[13] A. A. Affifi holds that he is a pure pantheist and supports this by discussing his theory of love:

> Ibnul ᶜArabi's pantheism is clear, when he says that the ultimate goal of love is to know the reality of love and that the reality of love is identical with God's Essence. Love is not an abstract quality superadded to the Essence. It is not a relation between a lover and an object loved. This is the true love of the "gnostics" who know no particular object of love . . . .
>
> When my Beloved appears,
> With what eye do I see Him?
> With his eye, not with mine,
> For none sees Him except Himself.[14]

Ibn ᶜArabī sees the revelation of God out of the pure being, *ᶜamā*, the absolute inwardness, in the world of created things: "We ourselves are the attributes by which we describe God; our existence is merely an objectification of His existence. God is necessary to us in order that we may exist, while we are necessary to Him in order that He may be manifested to Himself."

> I give Him also life, by knowing Him in my heart.[15]

This last sentence is reminiscent of verses by the seventeenth-century German mystic Angelus Silesius or the twentieth-century poet Rainer Maria Rilke.[16] A verse in the *Tarjumān al-ashwāq* says:

> He praises me, and I praise Him,
> and He worships me and I worship Him.
> How can He be independent,
> When I help Him and assist Him?
> In my knowing Him, I create Him.[17]

13. Abūʾl-ᶜAlāʾ Affifi, *The Mystical Philosophy of Muḥyid'Dīn Ibnul-ᶜArabī* (Cambridge, 1936).

14. Ibid., p. 172.

15. Henri Corbin, "Imagination créatrice et prière créatrice dans le soufisme d'Ibn Arabi," *Eranos-Jahrbuch* 25 (1956): 182.

16. Angelus Silesius (d. 1677), *Der Cherubinische Wandersmann*:

Ich weiss, dass ohne mich Gott nicht ein Nu kann leben;
Werd ich zunicht, muss er sogleich den Geist aufgeben.

See also some of Rilke's poems in *Das Stundenbuch* (1903), especially:

Was wirst du tun, Gott, wenn ich sterbe?
Ich bin dein Krug—wenn ich zerscherbe . . . .

17. Affifi, *Ibnul-ᶜArabī*, p. 13.

Reynold A. Nicholson interprets these theories with the conclusion that "correlative terms are merely names for different aspects of the same Reality, each aspect logically necessitating the other and being interchangeable with it. According to the point of view God (actually) is man and man is God, or God (conceptually) is not man and man is not God" (MC 121). Creator and creation are like water and ice, the same being in different modes or manifestations (NS 99)—an image that later poets lovingly employed.

Ibn ʿArabī's entire system is generally designated by the term *waḥdat al-wujūd*, "unity of being." The correct translation of this expression provides the key to most of his other theories. His concepts have evoked numerous discussions about the "pantheistic" or "monist" trend in later Islam. Marijan Molé has put his finger on the difficulty of translating *wujūd* correctly (MM 59–62): Arabic, like other Semitic languages, has no verb to express "to be." The term *wujūd*, which is usually translated as "being," "existence," means, basically, "finding," "to be found," and is, thus, more dynamic than mere "existence." "At the end of the Path only God is present, is 'found.' " Thus, *waḥdat al-wujūd* is not simply "unity of being," but also the unity of existentialization and the perception of this act; it sometimes becomes quasi-synonymous with *shuhūd*, "contemplation," "witnessing," so that the terms *waḥdat al-wujūd* and *waḥdat ash-shuhūd*, which were so intensely discussed by later mystics, especially in India, are sometimes even interchangeable (MM 61; cf. N 408).

Everything gains its *wujūd*, its existence, by "being found," i.e., perceived, by God, and "only their face that is turned to God is real, the rest is pure not-Being" (MM 97). That would imply that terms like pantheism, panentheism, and even Louis Massignon's term "existential monism"[18] would have to be revised, since the concept of *waḥdat al-wujūd* does not involve a substantial continuity between God and creation. In Ibn ʿArabī's thought a transcendence across categories, including substance, is maintained. God is above all qualities—they are neither He nor other than He—and He manifests Himself only by means of the names, not by His essence. On the plane of essence, He is inconceivable (transcending concepts) and nonexperiential (transcending even nonrational cog-

18. Louis Massignon, "L'alternative de la pensée mystique en Islam: monisme existentiel ou monisme testimonial," *Annuaire de Collège de France* 52 (1952). Massignon has always maintained that "monisme testimonial" is typically Islamic and compatible with orthodoxy.

nition). That means that in their actual existence the creatures are not identical with God, but only reflections of His attributes.

The main problem of interpretation seems to lie in the use of the term "transcendent," which in Western philosophy would scarcely be applicable when speaking of Ibn ᶜArabī's God in words like these: "By Himself He sees Himself . . . . None sees Him other than He, no sent Prophet, nor saint made perfect, nor angel brought nigh know Him. His Prophet is He, and His sending is He, and His Word is He. He sent Himself with Himself to Himself."[19] This does not sound like a description of a "transcendent" God.

Both Henri Corbin and Seyyed H. Nasr have repeatedly dwelt upon the nonpantheistic interpretation of Ibn ᶜArabī's thought; they have tried to show the importance of the theophanies and the decisive role of what Corbin calls the "creative imagination."[20] Then the relationship between God and creatures can be condensed, very roughly, approximately this way: The Absolute yearned in His Loneliness, and according to the tradition, "I was a hidden treasure and I wanted to be known, so I created the world," produced creation as a mirror for His *tajalliyāt*, His manifestations.

The "pathetic God" brought into existence the named things for the sake of the primordial sadness of the divine names. The infinite thirst of the pathetic God is, in a certain way, reflected in the infinite thirst of his creatures, who long for home— the concept of *khamyāza*, literally "yawning," i.e., "infinite longing" (the longing of the shore to embrace the whole ocean), which plays such an important role in later Indo-Muslim poetry, may have its roots in these concepts of the mutual yearning of Creator and creatures. Creation is "the effusion of Being upon the heavenly archetypes";[21] it is as if glass pieces of a mirror were hit by light so that their iridescence becomes visible through this coloring. Or creation may be compared to articulation—did not the Koran speak of the *nafas*, the "breath" of the Lord, which is infused into Adam or into Mary to create a new being? The pure Essence was as if it had held its "breath" until it could no longer do so—and the world appeared as *nafas ar-Raḥmān*. As in breathing, so the universe is created and

19. Nasr, *Three Muslim Sages*, p. 107.

20. Henri Corbin, *L'imagination créatrice dans le soufisme d'Ibn ᶜArabi* (Paris, 1958); trans. Ralph Manheim as *Creative Imagination in the Sufism of Ibn Arabi* (Princeton, 1969), a thought-provoking study.

21. Nasr, *Three Muslim Sages*, p. 107.

The pious sheikh Ṣanᶜān tending the swine of his beloved. This story, found in ᶜAṭṭār's Manṭiq uṭ-ṭayr *and here reworked by the Chagatay poet Mīr ᶜAli Shīr Nawāʾī, is one of the most famous Sufi tales.*

Bibliothèque Nationale, Ms. suppl. Turc. 996

annihilated every moment; it is taken back into its transcendent origin just as breath is taken back into the lungs. And the great movement of going forth and returning is symbolically manifested in the two parts of the profession of faith—*lā ilāh* points to the emanation of "things other than He," and *illā Allāh* indicates their return to Him, to the everlasting unity.[22]

This creation can be seen in various cosmic orders, which are veiled from each other. The divine essence itself is called *hāhūt* (derived from the *h*, the letter of the essence), and Ibn ʿArabī is said to have experienced the vision of the highest divine essence in the shape of the word *hū*, "He," luminous between the arms of the letter *h* ه.[23] The divine nature revealing itself is called *lāhūt*; the spiritual existence, beyond form, is *jabarūt*, where the divine decrees and spiritual powers are located. This plane is followed by the *malakūt*, the angelic world, whereas the place of humanity and creation is *nāsūt*. Ibn ʿArabī and his followers insert between *jabarūt* and *malakūt* a sphere called *ʿālam al-mithāl*, where the existentialization takes place; this is the sphere into which the high ambition (*himma*) and prayers of the saints reach in order to set spiritual energies free and bring the possibilities into actual being.[24]

The most fascinating aspect of Ibn ʿArabī's theories is the constant correlation between the names and the named ones. Not only is each of the twenty-eight degrees of emanation connected with a divine name (thus, the divine throne is the manifestation place of *al-Muḥīṭ*, "the comprehensive"; the vegetable world that of *ar-Rāziq*, "the nourisher," etc.),[25] but each divine name is the *rabb*, the "Lord," of a created being, which is, in turn, its *marbūb*. The names may be compared to the archetypes, molds through which the creative energy was channeled to produce particular beings. The *rabb*, in His manifestation, remains Lord, and the *marbūb* remains servant, "who has a Lord," but "God becomes the mirror in which the spiritual man contemplates his own reality and man

22. Cyprian Rice, *The Persian Sufis*, 2d ed. (London, 1969), p. 64.

23. Corbin, "Imagination créatrice," p. 171.

24. Fazlur Rahman, "Dream, Imagination, and ʿālam al-mithāl," *Islamic Studies* 3, no. 2 (1964–65); Rahman's article is also in *The Dream and Human Societies*, ed. Gustave E. von Grunebaum and R. Caillois (Berkeley, 1966), pp. 409ff.

25. S. A. Q. Husaini, *The Pantheistic Monism of Ibn al-Arabi* (Lahore, 1970), a sober collection of texts with translation.

in turn becomes the mirror in which God contemplates His Names and Qualities."[26]

The idea of the relation between the name and the named one may have contributed to the formation of one of the favorite symbols of later Persian mystical poetry, that of the bezel (the connection with the "Bezels of Wisdom" may have contributed as well). The heart of the sheikh was considered a signet ring on which the divine names and attributes are imprinted, which he, in turn, would imprint upon his disciple, who might be compared to the piece of sealing wax (cf. MC 287). Rūmī compares the mystic who has lost himself completely in God to the signet that bears God's name, and Indo-Persian Sufi poets carried this idea to the conclusion that "the mind becomes blank like the stone upon which the name of God will be engraved," so that no name and trace remain from the worthless stone, but everything is filled with His names.

> Do not seek anything from us but the name of
> somebody,
> like the bezel we are the place of the manifestation
> of the names,

sang Mīr Dard in the mid-eighteenth century, though he, on the whole, rejected many of Ibn ʿArabī's ideas.[27]

The theory of the names and the named also implies that a certain form of faith is designated for every human being. The faithful can have vision only of the form of faith he professes; the Muslim will see it differently from the Christian or Jew. We are reminded of the Indian myth of the *gopis*, each of whom saw Krishna as the beloved in the form in which she had imagined him and which, in a certain sense, belonged to her. For name and named one are mutually interdependent, united through a *unio sympathetica.*

Ibn ʿArabī is usually praised as the advocate of religious tolerance, and everyone who tries to underline the "mystical ideal of tolerance" and indifference to exterior forms and rituals quotes his verses:

> My heart is capable of every form,
> a cloister of the monk, a temple for idols,

26. Nasr, *Three Muslim Sages*, p. 116.

27. Khwāja Mīr Dard, *Dīwān-i fārsī* (Delhi, 1310 h./1892–93), pp. 7, 56, 84, 147; Dard, *Urdu Diwan*, ed. Khalīl ur-Raḥmān Dāʾūdī (Lahore, 1962), p. 118.

a pasture for gazelles, the votary's Kaaba,
the tables of the Thora, the Koran.
Love is the creed I hold: wherever turn
His camels, love is still my creed and faith.[28]

But this seemingly tolerant statement contains, rather, a statement about the author's own lofty spiritual rank: "The form of God is for him no longer the form of this or that faith exclusive of all others, but his own eternal form which he encounters at the end of his *ṭawāf*."[29] It is highest self-praise, acknowledgment of an illumination that is far beyond the "illumination of the names," but not tolerance preached to the rank and file.

One aspect of Ibn ᶜArabī's theories deserves special mention: it is the role attributed to the female element (the word for essence, *dhāt,* being feminine in Arabic, he could speak of the "woman creator," the secret of the compassionate God through which God is revealed [see Appendix 2]). His modern critics define such interpretations as "para-sexual symbolism which abound in his thought";[30] even Adam is, so to speak, "female," since Eve was born from him. And indeed, it is quite embarrassing for an uninitiated person to read, in the *Fuṣūṣ,* the final chapter on Muhammad, the seal of prophets and saints, where the meditation centers around the *ḥadīth*: "God has made dear to me three things: perfume and women, and my heart's consolation is in prayer."

One of the pillars of Ibn ᶜArabī's system is the veneration of Muhammad, who assumes, in his theories, the role of the Perfect Man. He is the total theophany of the divine names, the whole of the universe in its oneness as seen by the divine essence. Muhammad is the prototype of the universe as well as of man, since he is like a mirror in which each sees the other. The Perfect Man is necessary to God as the medium through which He is known and manifested. He is "like the pupil in the eye of 'humanity' " (MC 300, 117). The Muhammadan reality, *ḥaqīqa muḥammadiyya,* bears in itself the divine word that reveals itself in its particulars in the different prophets and messengers until it reaches, once more, its fullness in the Prophet of Islam. A modern French follower of Ibn ᶜArabī has condensed the master's theories about prophetology

28. Ibn ᶜArabī, *Tarjumān,* ed. Nicholson, no. 11, lines 13–15.
29. Corbin, "Imagination créatrice," p. 180.
30. Fazlur Rahman, *Islam* (London, 1966), p. 146.

as laid down in his *Risālat al-Aḥadiyya,* "About Divine Unicity," as follows:

> In the Absolute, the Messenger is no longer the Sent One but the Absolute, he is at the same time the receptacle of the effusions of the Absolute, His Gift; as far as he is a relative being, he is the Illiterate Prophet and receptive of his own aspect of being the Sent one, of Descent or Divine Revelation; eventually, the Prophet is the active revealer before the world which accepts, by his mediation, the highest message.[31]

The Perfect Man is he who has realized in himself all the possibilities of being; he is, so to speak, the model for everybody, for, in fact, every being is called to realize his innate possibilities in accordance with the divine name that is his particular *rabb.* However, only the prophets and saints reach that level. Iqbal's ideas of the Perfect Man as he who has developed his individual possibilities to the fullest bloom are derived from these theories rather than from the Nietzschean superman.

Even though Ibn ᶜArabī may have claimed not to have created any system, his sharp and cool intellect certainly brought him to systematize his experiences and thoughts, and the influence of his terminology upon later Sufis seems to show that they accepted his thoughts as a handy systematization of what formed, in their view, the true essence of Sufism. There is no doubt that this theosophical mysticism is attractive because it gives an answer to most of the questions of being and becoming, of creation and return.

This system is the very reverse of the teachings of orthodox Islam, as a modern Muslim thinker like Fazlur Rahman holds, following the leading medieval Hanbalite theologian, Ibn Taymiyya (d. 1328):[32] "A thoroughly monistic system, no matter how pious and conscientious it may claim to be, can not, by its very nature, take seriously the objective validity of moral standards."[33] For here, both good and evil are from God, and as much as Muhammad is the manifestation of the name *al-Hādī,* "who guides right," so much is Satan the manifestation of the name *al-Muḍill,* "who leads astray." Everything is in perfect order—that is the meaning of God's *raḥma,* "mercy."

Has the easy formulation of "unity of being" contributed to the

31. Léon Schaya, *La doctrine soufique de l'unité* (Paris, 1962), p. 68.

32. Ibn Taymiyya, "Ar-radd ᶜalā Ibn ᶜArabī waʾṣ-Ṣūfiyya," *Majmūᶜa rasāʾil shaykh al-Islām Ibn Taymiyya* (Cairo, 1348 sh./1929–30).

33. Rahman, *Islam,* p. 146.

decline of Islam, especially in its simplified and dangerous condensation as *hama ūst,* "everything is He," which left no room for the subtle distinctions maintained by Ibn ᶜArabī himself? Was the transformation of classical Sufism with its stress on *ᶜamal,* "religious work," "activity," not completely superseded by *ᶜirfān,* "gnosis," theosophical knowledge as provided by an ingenious system? Hans Heinrich Schaeder has, in his thought-provoking article on the Perfect Man, written in 1925, contrasted Ḥallāj and Ibn ᶜArabī by saying:

> The fulfillment of Islamic revelation through complete loving surrender to God, as inherent in original Islam, and raised onto the level of full consciousness by Ḥallāj who realized it in his life and in his martyrdom, was replaced, by Ibn ᶜArabī, with a systematization of *Weltdeutung* [explanation of the world] which is no longer concerned with active but only with contemplative piety.[34]

One may achieve a profounder understanding of the system of Ibn ᶜArabī now than was possible fifty years ago; but the discussion about his role—positive or negative—will probably never end as long as there are two different approaches to the mystical goal—by activity and conformity of will, or by contemplation and gnosis.

IBN AL-FĀRIḌ, MYSTICAL POET

It has become customary to mention the name of Ibn ᶜArabī along with that of his contemporary Ibn al-Fāriḍ—as different as the two great thirteenth-century masters of Arabic Sufism were.[35] On the one hand, there was the powerful personality of the Spanish-born theosophist who poured out his knowledge and mystical experiences in a few poems and in an almost inexhaustible stream of prose works. On the other hand, there was the delicate poet and scholar from Cairo, who lived a solitary life first on the Muqattam Hill and then, for fifteen years, in the Hijaz, eventually returning to his hometown and dying there in 1235—five years before Ibn ᶜArabī died in Damascus.

34. Hans Heinrich Schaeder, "Die islamische Lehre vom Vollkommenen Menschen, ihre Herkunft und ihre dichterische Gestaltung," *Zeitschrift der Deutschen Morgenländischen Gesellschaft* 79 (1925), p. 237.

35. Reynold A. Nicholson, "The Lives of ᶜUmar Ibnuʾl-Fāriḍ and Muḥiyyuʾddin Ibnuʾl-ᶜArabī," *Journal of the Royal Asiatic Society,* 1906. The third chapter of Nicholson's *Studies in Islamic Mysticism* (1921; reprint ed., Cambridge, 1967), is still the best introduction to Ibn al-Fāriḍ's art and thought. See also Muḥammad Muṣṭafā Ḥilmī, *Ibn al-Fāriḍ waʾl-ḥubb al-ilāhī* (Cairo, 1945).

Ibn al-Fāriḍ reduced his mystical experiences to a small number of Arabic odes of exquisite beauty in the style of classical Arabic poetry, but he wrote no prose at all. Reynold A. Nicholson, his masterful interpreter, writes about his poetry: "His style and diction resemble the choicest and finest jewel-work of a fastidious artist rather than the first fruits of divine inspiration" (NS 167). When reading his intricate verses, one wonders how they could have been produced, as the tradition has it, in a state of rapture. Both in form and in content these poems are perfectly Arabic: they display the Arabs' joy in wordplays, puns, and diminutives and speak of the love of the Absolute in terms taken from the pre-Islamic tradition, calling the beloved by the names of the heroines of old Arabic poetry, like Laila or Salma.

Ibn al-Fāriḍ's poetry has attracted the interest of the European scholars of Arabic from the very beginning of oriental studies. The French orientalists took up the task of explicating his highly sophisticated mystical poetry. In 1828 Grangeret de Lagrange published some of his poems; he was followed by the master of Arabic studies, Silvestre de Sacy. Joseph von Hammer-Purgstall even dared to translate Ibn al-Fāriḍ's greatest poem, the *Tāʾiyya,* into what he thought was German poetry;[36] but the meaning is only rarely captured, and Nicholson ironically says that the *Tāʾiyya* "had the misfortune of being translated by Hammer." Italian scholars turned to the same poem in the early twentieth century—I. di Matteo in 1917, and Nallino in 1919. A resolution of the literary feud occasioned by their different interpretations was reached by Nicholson, who has written the most penetrating article on Ibn al-Fāriḍ. Finally, the mystic's work was once more the subject of investigation by A. J. Arberry in the 1950s.[37]

Out of Ibn al-Fāriḍ's small *Dīwān* two poems have gained special popularity. One of these is the *Khamriyya,* the "Wine Ode"; it is a description of the wine of divine love, which the lovers have quaffed before the grapes were created (i.e., on the Day of the Covenant), and which intoxicates the whole world, cures the sick, makes the blind see and the deaf hear, and leads man like the

36. Joseph von Hammer-Purgstall, *Das arabische Hohe Lied der Liebe, das ist Ibnol Faridh's Taije in Text und Übersetzung zum ersten Male herausgegeben* (Vienna, 1854), a beautifully printed and illuminated book.

37. A. J. Arberry, ed. and trans., *The Mystical Poems of Ibn al-Fāriḍ,* Chester Beatty Monographs, no. 4 (London, 1954); Arberry, ed. and trans., *The Mystical Poems of Ibn al-Fāriḍ* (Dublin, 1956).

North Star toward his eternal goal.[38] This ode, relying upon a symbolism common to the poets of the Arabic and Persian worlds alike, can be understood and translated without major difficulties—much more easily than many of his pure love poems, with their complicated diction and subtle imagery. At times, Ibn al-Fāriḍ achieves such a tenderness of feeling, and such a purity of images, that his verses instantly touch the reader's heart, as in the following lyrical passage from the poem rhyming in *j*:

> Every limb [of my body] sees him, even if he be absent
> from me, in every delicate, clear, joyous essence,
> In the tune of the melodious lute and flute when they
> blend together in trilling strains,
> And in luxurious pasturage of gazelles in the coolness
> of twilight and in the first rays of dawning,
> And in misty rains falling from a cloud on a carpet woven
> of flowers,
> And where the breeze sweeps her train, guiding to me
> most fragrant attar at sweet dawn,
> And when I kiss the lip of the cup, sipping the clear
> wine in pleasure and joy.
> I knew no estrangement from my homeland when he was
> with me: My mind was undisturbed where we were—
> That place was my home while my beloved was present;
> where the sloping dune appeared, that was my halting-
> place.[39]

These verses, expressing the feeling of the lover in the constant recollection of the beloved, are among the tenderest lines in classical Arabic poetry and, though studded with rhetorical ornamentation, convey a highly romantic air.

But the poem to which the orientalists—as well as the oriental commentators—have devoted most of their attention is the so-called *Tāʾiyyat al-kubrā*, "The Greater Poem Rhyming in T," a poem of 756 verses. Massignon called it "a heavy tapestry in gold-brocade," a "sort of *kiswa* for the spiritual pilgrimage"[40]—just as the Egyptian pilgrims to Mecca used to take with them a gold-embroidered black

38. Émile Dermenghem, trans., *L'éloge du vin (al-Khamrīya), poème mystique de Omar ibn al-Faridh, et son commentaire par Abdalghanī an-Nabolosi* (Paris, 1931).
39. Translated privately by Wheeler M. Thackston.
40. Louis Massignon, *La cité des morts au Caire* (Cairo, 1958), p. 64.

velvet cover to be hung over the Kaaba, the Egyptian mystic offers the spiritual pilgrims a *kiswa* woven of words and symbols, weaving and embroidering into it the different phases of mystical life, of stations and stages, and—to quote Massignon once more—finally reaching an *"esthétique transcendantale."*

The poet himself declared that in a dream he saw the Prophet, who asked him the name of this *qaṣīda*; when Ibn al-Fāriḍ mentioned a high-sounding title, the Prophet bade him to call it simply *Naẓm as-sulūk*, "Order of the Progress," and that is what he did (N 542). Poetical inspiration is sometimes stronger than logic and theory, and disentangling the different parts of the *Naẓm as-sulūk* is no easy task. A number of passages are of special interest for mystical psychology, such as the description of the change in the senses during esctasy:

> I knew for sure that we are really One, and the sobriety
> of union restored the notion of separation,
> And my whole being was a tongue to speak, an eye to see,
> an ear to hear, and a hand to seize.

This idea is elaborated upon in the following verses (580–88); it goes back to the *ḥadīth an-nawāfil*, in which God promises his loving servant to become the eye through which he sees and the ear through which he hears, as well as to the experience in *dhikr* in which very limb is engaged in its own recollection and the parts of the body become, so to speak, interchangeable.

One of the most inspiring and frequently quoted scenes in the *Tāʾiyya* is that of the shadow play (lines 680–706):

> Lo from behind the veil mysterious
> the forms of things are shown in every guise,
> of manifold appearance . . . .

Life is seen in terms of the image of the shadow play, and eventually the mystic discovers:

> All thou beholdest is the act of One.
> In solitude, but closely veiled is He.
> Let him but lift the screen, no doubt remains:
> The forms are vanished, He alone is all;
> And thou, illumined, knowest by His light
> Thou find'st His actions in the senses' night.

The showman remains invisible, but the mystic knows: "Everything you see is the action of the One."

Ibn al-Fāriḍ was not the first to use the imagery of the shadow play; similar allegories are found rather frequently in Persian and Turkish mystical poetry, for the shadow play, adopted from China, was a well-known form of entertainment in the eastern lands of the caliphate and was enjoyed in Baghdad as early as the tenth century. In early Persian poetry, the puppets are often called "Chinese puppets." It was left to the Sufi poets to see in this play the image of divine actions in the world. ʿAṭṭār, who once compared the stars to the puppets and the sky to the veil, made a Turkish puppet-player the hero of this *Ushturnāme* several decades before Ibn al-Fāriḍ wrote his *Tāʾiyya*. The play master leads the adept through the seven veils and eventually destroys all his puppets: people accuse him—just as Omar Khayyam accuses the potter—of producing beautiful things and then of breaking them in pieces and throwing them away; but the master explains that he breaks them to free them from their outward forms and bring them back into the "box of Unity," where there is no distinction between the manifestations of different attributes and names (V 131 ff.; R 42). The closest source for Ibn al-Fāriḍ's imagery is, no doubt, his contemporary Ibn ʿArabī, who described the shadow play of his world in a touching passage of his *Futūḥāt al-makkiyya*. Rūmī also spoke of the shadow play, though he rarely used it as elaborately as ʿAṭṭār and Ibn al-Fāriḍ. The motif was then taken up in later Persian and Turkish mystical poems;[41] in eighteenth-century India the same image was used, though in more sophisticated language, to describe the apparent contradictions of life in this created world:

> Now the intelligent people and the traditionists know: all these puppets of the contingent existences are not more than the manifestation-places of the Active Creator Who Does What He Wants, and the whole beauty of the forms of the worldly creatures is nothing but the opening of the screen "And they want only what He wants." Praised be God, even though good and evil are both from Him, but yet evil is evil and good is good, and the thief comes to the rewards of the theft and the police master strives to watch, and the string of predestination is hidden from the view of all, and the player [is hidden] in the screen, and the puppets are visible.[42]

41. Samiha Ayverdi, *Istanbul Geceleri* (Istanbul, 1952), pp. 79ff. See Georg Jacob, *Geschichte des Schattenspiels* (Hannover, 1925).

42. Khwāja Mīr Dard, "Dard-i dil," no. 267, in *Chahār risāla* (Bhopal, 1310 h./1892–93).

Thus Ibn al-Fāriḍ stands here, as he does in all his poetry, wholly in the tradition of the mystical imagery of medieval Islam. His poetry has often been understood as a witness to the pantheistic interpretation of Islam, but, as with many other mystical poets, one must not forget that poetry is not to be equated with theoretical discussions about theological problems. When Ibn al-Fāriḍ saw the transcendent unity of all things, and felt in every movement of his life the hand of the great play master, who calls the puppets into existence and puts them again into the dark box, he uses the language of the heart rather than that of the head. His love relation with God, the beloved who is veiled behind the beautiful forms of Salma and Laila, is personal, and the mystic's soul, leaving behind it every trace of self-will, reaches conformity with the divine will and becomes, thus, as Nicholson puts it, "the beloved of God."

THE DEVELOPMENT OF IBN ᶜARABĪ'S MYSTICISM OF UNITY

The ideas of Ibn ᶜArabī soon spread throughout the world of Islam and gained innumerable followers, mainly in the Persian- and Turkish-speaking areas. It is as if the tremendous political changes of the thirteenth century—when the Mongols overrode most of Asia and penetrated deep into Europe, thus breaking up long-established political orders and destroying large areas of highly developed cultures—produced, in marked contrast to this destruction, an upsurge of mystical activity, ideas, feeling, and poetry not only in the Islamic world but throughout Europe and Asia. In the Islamic world the greatest mystical writers came out of the thirteenth century—ᶜAṭṭār and Najmuddīn Kubrā both died about 1220, and their disciples, like Najmuddīn Dāyā Rāzī, continued their traditions; Jalāluddīn Rūmī represents the pinnacle in the achievements of Persian mystical poetry, and in the country where he spent the greater part of his life, Anatolia, mystics like Ṣadruddīn Qōnawī transmitted and publicized Ibn ᶜArabī's ideas;[43] later, a Turkish poet, Yūnus Emre, produced the first truly Turkish mystical poetry. The orders acquired a firm footing in India, where the names of Muᶜīnuddīn Chishtī, Bahāʾuddīn Zakariya Multānī, Farīd Ganj-i Shakar, Niẓāmuddīn Auliyā, Fakhruddīn ᶜIrāqī, and many others tell of the spiritual glory of the thirteenth

43. Nihat Keklik, *Sadreddin Konevi'nin Felsefesinde Allah, Kâinat, ve Insan* (Istanbul, 1967), the first Turkish study of Ṣadruddīn's highly interesting work.

century. In Egypt, too, several orders, from the Badawiyya to the Shadhiliyya, came into being. These are only the most important mystical trends during a time when the Muslim world, mainly in its central and eastern parts, was exposed to an almost fatal disaster on the political front.

It may be that the activity of Ibn ᶜArabī and his followers was needed to give this widespread mystical upsurge a framework into which its main ideas could be put: a fixed vocabulary and a comparatively simple theology. From the fourteenth century on even those mystics who did not accept Ibn ᶜArabī's theories remained spellbound by his terminology and used it very freely.

Two smaller theoretical works have contributed in important ways to making the great master's major ideas known to a wider public—one is Shabistarī's *Gulshan-i rāz*, the other is ᶜAbduʾl-Karīm Jīlī's *Al-insān al-kāmil*.

In 1311 Shabistarī, who lived not far from Tabriz, wrote a Persian poem called *Gulshan-i rāz*, "Rose Garden of Mystery," as a reply to eighteen questions posed to him by a Sufi friend.[44] This poem is the handiest introduction to the thought of post-Ibn ᶜArabī Sufism; it deals with the Perfect Man, the stages of development, and mystical terminology, among other things. Shabistarī describes the divine beauty that is hidden under the veil of every single atom, because "the Absolute is so nakedly apparent to man's sight that it is not visible"[45]—an idea often expressed by the mystics: overwhelming nearness blinds the eye, just as unveiled light becomes invisible, "black." The Perfect Man is, in Shabistarī's definition, he who goes the twofold way: down into the world of phenomena, then upward to the light and divine unity. This idea continued as the central theory of most of the Sufi orders; it was developed before Ibn ᶜArabī and his followers, but it had not yet been couched in terminology that would enable it to be understood by the average Sufi. The mystics generally experienced this movement as divided into forty steps—twenty downward from the First Intelligence to earth, and then the twenty-step "arc of ascent" toward the Perfect Man. These ideas—derived from Neoplatonic speculations—became so common in the mystical fraternities that even a rather unsophisticated order like the Turkish Bektashis

44. Muḥammad Lāhījī, *Mafātīḥ al-iᶜjāz fī sharḥ gulshan-i rāz*, ed. Kaiwān Samīᶜī (Tehran, 1337 sh./1958).

45. Izutsu, "Paradox of Light and Darkness," in *Anagogic Qualities of Literature*, ed. Strelka, p. 297.

dwelt, in its so-called *devriye* poems, on the circles describing the "outward track" and the "homeward track" (BO 116).

Shabistarī's *Gulshan-i rāz* gave impetus to the spread of these ideas, especially when it was used with Lāhījī's excellent commentary, composed in the second half of the fifteenth century. For the Niᶜmatullāhī dervishes in Iran, the book "served (and perhaps still serves) as a traditional manual for all those men or women (instructed in separate groups) who came under their direction in a kind of Third Order."[46] Its popularity in the East made it interesting to Western scholars as well. It is one of the first books on Sufism that was translated into Western languages: into German by Hammer-Purgstall in 1838 (almost as unsuccessfully as his translations from Ibn al-Fāriḍ), and into English by E. H. Whinfield in 1880.[47] Its form and content inspired Muhammad Iqbal to compose his *Gulshan-i rāz-i jadīd,* "The New Rose Garden of Mystery," published in 1927; in this poem he follows Shabistarī's notions and offers his own solutions to the questions of the Perfect Man (one of his central ideas), of God, and of destiny.

In the field of mystical theory, Jīlī (d. after 1408)—a descendant of the founder of the Qādiriyya order—did his utmost to systematize the thoughts of Ibn ᶜArabī, though at certain points he differed from him.[48] His book *Al-insān al-kāmil,* "The Perfect Man," has been carefully analyzed by Reynold A. Nicholson. Jīlī discussed thoroughly the different levels of divine manifestations and the revelations of the divine—from the plane of essence to the plane of the attributes, the plane of actions, the plane of similitude, and the plane of sense and color vision, thus distinguishing the different levels of mystical revelation (*tajallī*). The illumination of the actions is followed by that of the names, then by that of the attributes, and eventually every experience is terminated in the illumination of the essence, which only the Perfect Man can reach.

46. Rice, *Persian Sufis,* p. 28. On the Niᶜmatullāhi see Richard Gramlich, *Die schiitischen Derwischorden Persiens, Teil I, Die Affiliationen* (Wiesbaden, 1965); on their founder, see Jean Aubin, *Matériaux pour la biographie de Shāh Niᶜmatullāh Walī Kermānī* (Tehran and Paris, 1956).

47. Maḥmūd Shabistarī, *The Rose-Garden of Mysteries,* ed. and trans. Edward Henry Whinfield (London, 1880). Shabistarī, *The Dialogue of the Gulshan-i Rāz* (London, 1887); Shabistarī, *The Secret Garden,* trans. Juraj Paska (New York and London, 1969).

48. The best introduction is still the second chapter of Nicholson's *Studies.* Ernst Bannerth, "Das Buch der 40 Stufen von ᶜAbd al-Karīm al-Ǧīlī," *Österreichische Akademie der Wissenschaften, philologisch-historische Klasse* 230, no. 3 (1956). ᶜAbdul Karīm al-Jīlī, *Al-insān al-kāmil,* 2 vols. (Cairo, 1340 h./1921–22).

In theories like this, the central concept of Sufism, and of Islam in general, *tauḥīd,* is eventually understood as "the extinction of the ignorance of our essential and unmovable identity with the only Real."[49] It is no longer a unity of will, but a lifting of the veils of ignorance: a decisive difference in the whole approach to the problems of God and the world—even though Jīlī admits that the Lord remains Lord, and the slave remains slave.

The longing for the Perfect Man, theoretically explained in Ibn ᶜArabī's and Jīlī's work, is much older than these theories[50]—the veneration offered to the Prophet shows this. It seems typical that Ibn ᶜArabī's younger contemporary, Jalāluddīn Rūmī, twice took up in his poetry the story of Diogenes, who searched with a lantern for "man" (M 5: 2887; D 441). Rūmī probably did not think of the implications of a cosmic power embodied in this ideal man or of the possible relations between this perfect human being and gnostic concepts of the Primordial Man (*Urmensch*). When reading his statements, one should remember that the Sufis frequently regarded the common people as something "like animals" (*kaʾl-anᶜām*), relying upon Koranic statements like that in Sūra 7:178 about those who do not hear or see the signs of divine power and grace. Only the true "man" can experience the vision of God through and behind His creation.

The elaboration of these theories could lead to the consequences reflected in the utterances of some Persian and Turkish mystical poets who combined the feeling of all-pervading unity with the boast of having reached the station of the Perfect Man themselves. The verses of writers like Maghribī and similar poets of fifteenth-century Iran show this tendency very clearly: the mystic feels that he embraces everything in himself; he experiences not only a cosmic consciousness but also a unity with all those who have lived before him and are living together with him, with Moses and with Pharaoh, with Jonah and with the whale, with Ḥallāj and with his judge. This is the general trend in much of the later popular mystical poetry that has led the interpreters to see here nothing but immoderate pantheism.

Orthodox Sufis would speak here of the *kufr-i ṭarīqat,* a state of intoxication in which the mystic is no longer aware of anything

49. Schaya, *Doctrine soufique,* p. 38.

50. Louis Massignon, "L'homme parfait en Islam et son originalité eschatologique," *Eranos-Jahrbuch* 15 (1947).

except God and in which he sees everything as one; but this is not the last stage he can reach. The classical distinction of "intoxication" as preceding the "second sobriety" remains valid, although most of the later Sufis remained in the "lower" state.

For these poets, the whole world was filled with God—whether or not they thought of the theoretical implications. The phrase *hama ūst*, "everything is He," can be found as early as ᶜAṭṭār's poetry, even before Ibn ᶜArabī (cf. U 223). In the late fifteenth century Jāmī was to exclaim:

> Neighbor and associate and companion—everything
> is He.
> In the beggar's coarse frock and in the king's silk—
> everything is He.
> In the crowd of separation and in the loneliness of
> collectedness
> By God! everything is He, and by God! everything is He.[51]

For some mystics the faith in God's manifestation in every shape led to strange excesses. Some of them would experience an ecstatic state when they heard the sound of the wind or a bird (L 495); they might even answer a sheep's bleating with the words, "Here, at Thy service!" (B 355); they might run after a camel in which they saw a manifestation of God, or touch a snake because "there is nothing but God." In the latter case, the sheikh wisely told his disciple not to do such things any more, for the snake shows God under the veil of wrath, and the disciple is still too weak to draw close to this divine manifestation (N 261).

The feeling that God is everywhere, inherent in everything, is beautifully expressed in many of Jāmī's verses, which summarize the mystical feeling of his time:

> Sometimes we call Thee wine, sometimes goblet,
> Sometimes we call Thee corn, and sometimes snare,
> There is no letter save Thy name on the tablet of the
> world—
> Now: by which name shall we call Thee?[52]

51. Maulānā ᶜAbdurraḥmān Jāmī, *Lawāʾiḥ* (Tehran, 1342 sh./1963), chap. 21; see the English translation by Edward Henry Whinfield and Mirza Muhammad Kazwini (London, 1914).

52. Maulānā ᶜAbdurraḥmān Jāmī, *Dīwān-i kāmil*, ed. Hāshim Riżā (Tehran, 1341 sh./1962), p. 810.

Two centuries later, Dārā Shikōh would take up this thought in his mystical poetry, when he changed the formula "in the name of God the Merciful the Compassionate" into the words:

> In the name of Him Who has no name,
> Who appears by whatever name you will call Him.

The feeling of the essential unity of God and man, theoretically underlined by Ibn ʿArabī and his followers, has been expressed by the poets through different symbols; they like to speak of the ocean, the billows, the foam, and the drop, which in each instance look different and yet are the same water. Niffarī seems to have been the first to use the symbolism of the divine ocean. Ibn ʿArabī had visualized the divine essence as a large green ocean out of which the fleeting forms emerge like waves, to fall again and disappear in the fathomless depths.[53] Rūmī emulated him in many of his poems, which speak of the ocean of God. But the image is found much earlier: everyone who meditated upon the similarities and differences between God and the world and wanted to illustrate their basic unity and temporal differentiation, would use the image of the ocean, which, psychologically, symbolizes so perfectly the longing of the individual for union and annihilation in the whole.[54] Later poetry abounds in ocean imagery. Even those poets who did not accept Ibn ʿArabī's *waḥdat al-wujūd* have used it, though in their imagery the drop does not vanish in the sea but becomes a precious pearl (according to oriental folklore, pearls are raindrops, preferably drops of April rain, that rest in the oyster to mature); the pearl gains its value by its journey from the sea through the cloud and the drop back to its home, changed into a jewel, unable to live without the ocean and yet distinct from it. Those who equated the divine essence with dynamic love could easily extend the image of the ocean of love, of which intellectual knowledge is only the dry shore. It is an ocean filled with dangerous beasts, alligators and whales, which threaten the loving soul, or it is made of consuming fire (MT 222). God's majesty and His power, as well as His beauty, are revealed in this ocean.

The ocean and the drop of water offered themselves as apt sym-

53. See Reynold A. Nicholson, *Selected Poems from the Divan-i Shams-i Tabriz* (1898; reprint ed., Cambridge, 1961), no. 9.

54. Toshihiko Izutsu, "The Basic Structure of Metaphysical Thinking in Islam," in *Collected Papers on Islamic Philosophy and Mysticism*, ed. Mehdi Mohaghegh and Hermann Landolt (Tehran, 1971), p. 67.

bols for the relationship of the individual soul to the divine, but other images as well were used to point to this insoluble paradox of unity and multiplicity: glass pieces that are from the same substance and yet show different shapes and colors (V 137); chess figures that are carved from the same piece of wood (as the Taoists would compare the Tao to a block of uncarved wood) and yet fight against each other seemed to be a fitting symbol for unity of being, as seen by a sixteenth-century Malayan Sufi.[55] But long before him, the image of God as the great chess player, who moves the figures in inexplicable ways so that the pawn may become a king, was widely used in Iran—small wonder in a culture in which chess has played a central role since early times.

The imagery of chess and the *nard* play (a kind of backgammon in which the most hopeless position is called *shashdar*, "six doors," and could thus be used by the Sufis to allude to those who are imprisoned in the "six walls" of the created world) still leaves room for a differentiation between the play master and the figures, and such differentiation is also often maintained in Jāmī's poetry. Though a great admirer of Ibn ʿArabī, he could not deny his affiliation with the Nayshbandiyya school (see chapter 8). Where the strict Ibn ʿArabī school sometimes speaks of the mutual dependence of God and His creatures, Jāmī states:

> We and Thou are not separate from each other,
> but we need Thee, whereas Thou doest not need us.[56]

For "that which is fettered in created forms is in need of the Absolute, but the Absolute is independent of the relative." In spite of this important difference from Ibn ʿArabī's position, Jāmī has often praised the all-embracing unity; and the poets, who were rarely aware of the fine, but decisive distinctions, continued singing of this all-pervading unity behind the various forms: a unity in which lover, beloved, and love are one, so that neither separation nor union has any meaning.

Sanāʾī addressed God, in the proem of his *Ḥadīqa*, with the words:

> Infidelity and faith both wander along thy Path saying:
> "He alone, without any associate!"
>
> (S 60)

55. Al-Attas, *Ḥamza al-Fanṣūrī*, p. 412.
56. Jāmī, *Lawāʾiḥ*, no. 20.

And he expressed the view that:

> What is intended with manliness (virtue) is the
> action of a free man,
> be it a man connected with the mosque or with the
> church.
>
> (SD 1097)

In the course of time this view gained acceptance among the Sufis. For as the Sufis gained more knowledge of God (or thought they had), their religious prejudices diminished, and they understood that "the ways to God are as many as the breaths of men." They knew that he who enters the flaming ocean of love is no longer capable of discerning Islam from unbelief (MT 222). Nevertheless, they would formally cling to their own religion as the last and most comprehensive revelation of divine truth, and even though some of them might allegorize the rites of Islam, they did not abolish them.

Although Sufism, and especially the theories of *waḥdat al-wujūd*, has certainly contributed to a blurring of borders between the external religious forms, the images that juxtapose the sheikh and the *brahmin*, the Kaaba and the idol temple as contrasting manifestations of the one true reality soon became fossilized, and one should not draw far-reaching consequences from their constant use in poetry. These images express the predominance of love over law, of the spirit over the letter, but they were used even by the most law-bound poets to flavor their verses. One has to distinguish carefully between poetic language and metaphysical systems.

7. THE ROSE *and the* NIGHTINGALE: *Persian and Turkish Mystical Poetry*

IMMORTAL ROSE

One of the questions that has been discussed frequently in connection with Persian lyrical poetry is whether this literature should be interpreted as mystical or as erotic.[1] The defenders of

1. Every history of Persian, Turkish, and Pakistani literature contains information about Sufi poetry. The student should consult these books to get acquainted with the different viewpoints of Western authors concerning the phenomenon of mystical love and the influence of Sufi thought on the development of poetry. The following are particularly important: Hermann Ethé, "Neupersische Literatur," in *Grundriss der Iranischen Philologie*, ed. Wilhelm Geiger and Ernst Kuhn (Strasbourg, 1895–1901), gives an excellent survey of the historical development and the genres. Edward G. Browne, *A Literary History of Persia*, 4 vols. (1902; reprint ed., Cambridge, 1957), is a valuable introduction to the problems, with many fine translations from classical poetry. A. J. Arberry, *Classical Persian Literature* (London, 1958), contains a useful introduction. Jan Rypka, *History of Iranian Literature* (Dordrecht, 1968), is very informative, with exhaustive notes and an extensive bibliography, including Tajik and Indo-Persian literatures, unfortunately without examples. Antonio Pagliaro and Alessandro Bausani, *Storia della letteratura persiana* (Milan, 1960), is, like Bausani's *Persia Religiosa* (Milan, 1959), very thought-provoking and contains interesting remarks about poetical technique and imagery. Elias John Wilkinson Gibb, *A History of Ottoman Poetry*, 6 vols. (1901–1909; reprint ed., London, 1958–63), gives an excellent introduction to the problems of mystical poetry and its roots.

the purely mystical meaning of Ḥāfiẓ's *ghazal*s are as vehement in their claims as those who find in his poetry only sensual love, earthly intoxication by "the daughter of the grape," and sheer hedonism. Yet both claims are equally wide of the mark.

It is typical of Persian lyrics that certain religious ideas that form the center of Islamic theology, certain images taken from the Koran and the Prophetic tradition, or whole sentences from the Holy Writ or the *ḥadīth* can turn into symbols of a purely aesthetic character. Thus poetry provides almost unlimited possibilities for creating new relations between worldly and otherworldly images, between religious and profane ideas; the talented poet may reach a perfect interplay of both levels and make even the most profane poem bear a distinct "religious" flavor. The profanation of certain Koranic words may often shock the Western reader, but it opens surprising new vistas. There is scarcely a verse in the poetry of the greatest masters of Persian, Turkish, and Urdu poetry that does not reflect, in some way, the religious background of Islamic culture; it is like the pools in the courtyards of the mosques, in which the grandeur of the huge building is mirrored, its beauty enhanced by the strange effects of tiny waves or of verdure springing forth from the shallow water.

It seems futile, therefore, to look for either a purely mystical or a purely profane interpretation of the poems of Ḥāfiẓ, Jāmī, or ʿIrāqī—their ambiguity is intended, the oscillation between the two levels of being is consciously maintained (sometimes even a third level may be added), and the texture and flavor of the meaning of a word may change at any moment, much as the color of the tiles in a Persian mosque varies in depth according to the hour of the day. One cannot derive a mystical system out of Persian or Turkish poetry or see in it an expression of experiences to be taken at face value. The opalescence of Persian poetry has caused much misunderstanding in the West, for no translation can reflect the closely interwoven, glittering symbolism that lies behind each word of a hemistich or a verse.

Persian lyrics would never have acquired their peculiar charm without the Sufi theories; these are the background upon which this poetry develops, and the tension between the worldly and the religious interpretation of life is resolved, in the poems of the outstanding masters of this art, in a perfect harmony of the spiritual, psychic, and sensual components. Confronted with the supreme beauty in his love experiences, the poet was able to create works of art that reflect this glory in small, lucid, prismatic fragments, which, taken together, may be able to convey an idea of the original brightness of this glorious beauty.

> Rose and mirror and sun and moon—what are they?
> Wherever we looked, there was always Thy face,[2]

says the Urdu poet Mīr in the late eighteenth century, to cite but one of the hundreds of poets who realized this ineffable experience of love in its fullness and tried to sing of it in the imagery of roses and nightingales.

The phenomenon of mystical love that underlies this development is one of the most fascinating aspects of Sufism: a transcendent and absolute object is made the goal of every thought and feeling, so that love gains absolute primacy in the soul and mind of the lover. The spiritual life becomes so highly intensified, so delicately differentiated, that it almost develops into an art of its own. The expression of these subtle and basically ineffable feelings of mystical love forms the content of some of the finest books on love ever written in the Persian language. Sometimes such a refined and deepened love would find its object in a human being, in which the fullness of divine beauty and radiant glory seemed to be reflected, and out of this attitude the hybrid Persian mystical-erotic poetry developed.

Such speculations seem to take us far away from the love mysticism advocated by the early Sufis, who would never have accepted a human medium for the feeling of love, but concentrated exclusively upon divine love. They were aware that the inclusion of a human object of love could lead to consequences that were more than objectionable and that threatened to pollute purity of feeling (B 347). It is well known that the company of the "unbearded" young men constituted a danger for the mystics—living as they did in a society in which the feminine element was largely excluded from communal life, they directed their admiration to young boys, disciples, or foreigners, and the books from the Abbasid period abound with love stories of this kind. The handsome boy of fourteen, "radiant like the full moon," soon became the ideal of human beauty and as such is often praised in later Persian and Turkish poetry. That many Sufis could not keep their feeling in

2. Dr. Syed Abdullah, *Naqd-i Mīr* (Lahore, 1958), p. 117.

check is understood from the complaints about such tendencies in Sufi circles. Kharrāz—at the end of the ninth century—even had a dream about Satan joyfully boasting that he had at least one noose to ensnare the Sufis, namely their "love for the unbearded" (Q 9).[3] This feeling of danger is by no means unique to Kharrāz. Hujwīrī devoted a weighty paragraph to the practice of *naẓar ilā᾽ l-aḥdāth,* the "looking toward the young men":

> Looking at youth and associating with them are forbidden practices and anyone who declares this to be allowable is an unbeliever. The traditions brought forward in this matter are vain and foolish. I have seen ignorant persons who suspected the Sufis of the crime in question and regarded them with abhorrence, and I observed that some have made it a religious rule. All the Sufi *shaykhs,* however, have recognized the wickedness of such practices, which the adherents of incarnation (*ḥulūlīyat*)—may God curse them!—have left as a stigma on the saints of God and the aspirants to Sufism. (H 549)

The traditions to which Hujwīrī refers here claim that Muhammad had seen his Lord "in the most beautiful form" and that he beheld Gabriel in the form of Daḥyā al-Kalbī, a handsome young man from Mecca. Another tradition, according to which three things are pleasant to look at—verdure, a beautiful face, and running water—does not go beyond the limits of a perfectly normal admiration of beauty; but the alleged *ḥadīth* in which Muhammad attests, "I saw my Lord in the shape of a beautiful young man, with his cap awry," was suspect in orthodox circles. Nevertheless, it was this very *ḥadīth* that so strongly impressed Persian poets: the expression *kaj-kulāh,* "with his cap awry," is found in poetic description of, or addresses to, the beloved as early as ᶜAṭṭār's lyrics (AD 26) and is commonplace with later poets of Iran and India. *Naẓar,* "looking," becomes, then, one of the central topics of mystical love experience. The mystic who is completely absorbed in his love contemplates in the human beloved only the perfect manifestation of divine beauty, which is as distant from him as God Himself. Gīsūdarāz says:

> You look at the beautiful one and see figure and stature—
> I do not see anything between save the beauty and art of
> the creator.[4]

3. For this phenomenon see Adam Mez, *Die Renaissance des Islam* (Heidelberg, 1922), pp. 275, 337; Hellmut Ritter, *Das Meer der Seele. Gott, Welt und Mensch in den Geschichten Farīduddin ᶜAṭṭārs* (Leiden, 1955), pp. 459 ff., about the problem of *naẓar* and "love of the unbearded."

4. Muhammad Gīsūdarāz, *Dīwān anīs al-ᶜushshāq* (n.p., n.d.), p. 67.

Although God has no likeness and none like him (*mithl*), He has a *mithāl*, "image," in this world, as Lāhījī writes in his much-read commentary on Shabistarī's *Gulshan-i rāz* (CL 178).

The term *shāhid*, "witness," is used for the beautiful beloved, for he is the true witness of divine beauty (R 549). To look at him, to adore him from a distance, may induce the Sufi to truly religious ecstasy, and to contemplate his face is worship. Wherever beauty is revealed, there out of necessity love must grow. Beauty and love are interdependent, and many Persian, Turkish, and Urdu romances deal with the eternal story of *ḥusn ū ʿishq*, "beauty and love." As a late Indo-Persian poet has put it:

> Wherever there is an idol,
> a Brahmin was created.
>
> (AP 258)

The beloved is usually called an "idol" in Persian poetry, worthy of worship, a sensual image of the divine, which is hidden by its very brightness. Beauty would be meaningless if there were no love to contemplate it—we may think, once more, of the concept of God as the hidden treasure who wanted to be known: the treasure of beauty (for "God is beautiful and loves beauty") reveals itself in order to kindle love in the human heart.

The great masters of love mysticism, like Aḥmad Ghazzālī, Jalāluddīn Rūmī, and Fakhruddīn ʿIrāqī, have regarded this worldly love as a pedagogical experience, a training in obedience toward God, since the human beloved, like God, has to be obeyed absolutely. "When the soul is educated by human love and has become firm-footed in the innermost secret of love, and the heart is polished by the fire of love from the satanic and base insinuations, then the 'soul which commands evil' becomes 'peaceful' beneath the strokes of the violent wrath of love" (BA 203), says Baqlī in his book on love. Rūmī compares it to the "wooden sword that the hero gives his child" (D 27) so that the child may learn the technique of fighting.

Lover and beloved are unthinkable without each other—the lover's actions consist completely of *niyāz*, "asking and petitioning," whereas the beloved is made of perfect *nāz*, "coquetry"; beyond this contrast lies the unity in love. Beauty, though basically a static concept, has no full meaning without admiration and love, and the beloved needs the lover for his own perfection. The story of

Maḥmūd and Ayāz is a typical expression of this kind of love and shows, at the same time, how the poets of Iran used historical facts to point out eternal truth. Maḥmūd of Ghazna, the warrior king of Afghanistan (d. 1030), famous in political history as the conqueror of northwest India, becomes in literary tradition the model of the lover, because of his inclination toward his slave Ayāz.[5] The complete surrender of the Turkish officer Ayāz, for whom only Maḥmūd exists, results in perfect love of the king, who becomes, in a wonderful transformation, the slave of his slave. Ayāz is the symbol of the loving soul. One day the Humā bird passed over Maḥmūd's army, and everybody rushed to be touched by the Humā's shade, which, in Persian tradition, conveys kingdom. Only Ayāz went into Maḥmūd's shade (U 176), for here was his true kingdom: he is like the faithful, who does not seek glory and power from anything created but only from his eternally rich, beloved Lord.[6]

The other model of mystical love is Majnūn, the hero of the old Arabic tale, who lost his senses in his love of Laila. This woman, who was not even particularly beautiful, was for him the paragon of beauty, and thus, as interpreted by the Sufi poets, became the manifestation of divine beauty seen through the eyes of love.

It is in this world of intense spiritual passion that Persian poetry grew. When Rūzbihān Baqlī holds that the love of a human being is the ladder toward the love of the Merciful (BA 183; B 571), he alludes to the classical Arabic saying that the metaphor is the bridge toward reality—hence, human love is generally called, in the Persian tradition, *ʿishq-i majāzī*, "metaphorical love." Jāmī sums it up this way: "Beholding in many souls the traits of Divine beauty, and separating in each soul that which it has contracted in the world, the lover ascends to the highest beauty, to the love and knowledge of the Divinity, by steps of this ladder of created souls."[7]

The unsurpassable master of love and passion in the highest sense was, no doubt, Jalāluddīn Rūmī, whose work will be discussed

5. See Gertrud Spies, *Maḥmūd von Ghazna bei Farīd udʾdīn ʿAṭṭār* (Basel, 1959); several epics have been devoted to this topic, and lyrics abound in allusions to Ayāz.

6. Another typical example of this kind of mystical love is Hilālī's *Shāh ū gadā*; see Hermann Ethé, *König und Derwisch, Romantisch-mystisches Epos vom Scheich Hilali, dem persischen Original treu nachgebildet* (Leipzig, 1870). This poem was criticized by the Mogul emperor Babur, who found it highly immoral. Another expression of mystical surrender is ʿĀrifī, *"Gū ū jaugān," The Ball and the Polo-Stick, or Book of Exstasy*, ed. and trans. Robert Scott Greenshields (London, 1932).

7. Reynold A. Nicholson, *The Mystics of Islam* (1914; reprint ed., Chester Springs, Pa., 1962), p. 110.

later. For him, as for many of his predecessors and followers, love was the power innate in everything, working through everything and directing all things toward unification. Avicenna has expressed ideas of this kind in his *Risāla fīʾl-ʿishq*, and poets like the romantic Niẓāmī had described the magnetic force of this love:

> If the magnet were not loving, how could it attract the
> iron with such longing?
> And if love were not there, the straw would not seek
> the amber.

In the great hymn on love in *Khosrau Shīrīn*, to which these lines belong, Niẓāmī claims that "the heaven has no *miḥrāb* save love." This cosmological role of love was emphasized by Rūmī: love is, for him, like an ocean on which the skies are only foam, agitated like Zulaykhā in her love for Joseph; the whirling movement of the skies is the result of the wave of love—if there were no love, the world would be frozen (M 5:3854–58).

> If this heaven were not in love, then its breast would
> have no purity,
> and if the sun were not in love, in his beauty would be
> no light,
> and if earth and mountain were not lovers, grass would
> not grow out of their breast.
>
> (D 2674)

It is only for the sake of the lovers that the sky revolves and the spheres turn, not for the sake of the baker and the blacksmith, nor for the sake of the magistrate and pharmacist (D 1158).

More than any other poet, Rūmī stresses the dynamic character of love—it makes the ocean boil like a kettle (M 5:2735), as he says repeatedly, and it is the power that changes everything for the better, purifying it and quickening it:

> From love bitterness became sweet, from love copper
> became gold,
> from love the dregs became pure, from love the pains
> became medicine,
> from love the dead become alive, from love the king is
> made a slave.
>
> (M 2:1529–31)

For love turns the dead matter of bread into soul and then makes the perishable soul eternal (M 5:2014). It is poison, but:

> Sweeter than this poison I did not see any drink,
> Lovelier than this illness I did not see any health.
> (M 6:4599)

Love is fire, it burns everything. First of all it burns the station of patience: "My patience died the night that love was born" (M 6:4161). And the poor lover is in the hand of love "like the cat in the bag, one moment high, one moment low" (M 6:908).

Carried away by this love that manifests God's beauty as well as His majesty—since it is fascinating and frightening, killing and reviving at the same time—the mystics have seen love as "a flame that burns everything save the Beloved" (N 408). The classical definition of love that leads to true *tauḥīd,* extinguishing and consuming everything that is other than God, is expressed here in poetical language that was taken over by almost all the Muslim poets writing in Persian, Turkish, or Urdu. The fire symbolism that abounds in the work of a nineteenth-century Urdu poet like Ghālib has its roots in this concept of absolute love.

Only out of such experiences can the fascinating works of some of the early Persian mystics be understood.[8] Three of them have gained popularity primarily because of their love theories and their subtle interpretation of the mystical states; they are Aḥmad Ghazzālī (d. 1126), his disciple ʿAynuʾl-Quḍāt Hamadhānī (executed 1132), and Rūzbihān Baqlī of Shiraz (d. 1209).

There is little doubt that Abū Ḥāmid al-Ghazzālī, the great reviver of religious sciences, appealed to the average Muslim and is largely responsible for forming the moderately mystical outlook of Islamic society in the later Middle Ages, but neither in depth of experience nor in beauty of language can he compete with his younger brother Aḥmad. In fact, the "Muslim intellectual" Abū Ḥāmid is reported to have acknowledged his brother's superiority in the path of love. Aḥmad Ghazzālī was a successful preacher and director of souls with a number of disciples, who carried on his teachings; some members of his mystical lineage became important representatives of Sufi orders. The orthodox—shocked by his views

8. The best introduction to this literature is given by Hellmut Ritter, "Philologika VII: Arabische und persische Schriften über die profane und die mystische Liebe," *Der Islam* 21 (1933).

about the justification of Satan and his love theories—disliked him thoroughly, and even one of his own colleagues could not help calling him "one of the marvels of God in lying, gaining access to worldly possession through his preaching."[9]

Aḥmad composed a number of mystical treatises, among them one about the problem of *samāᶜ*; but even if he had written only the small treatise called *Sawāniḥ*, "Aphorisms on Love," it would have been enough to establish him as one of the greatest mystics in the Muslim world.[10] In those short paragraphs, interspersed with verses, we recognize him as the master of chaste love, who puts between himself and the beautiful beloved a rose, contemplating now the rose, now the beloved. The *Sawāniḥ* are written in a Persian style that looks, at first glance, simple and unassuming; but the language has reached such a degree of refinement, the words and the sentences are so fragile, that any attempt to render them into a Western language and keep their flavor intact would be futile. The author speaks of the mystery of the mutual relationship between lover and beloved, who are like mirrors to each other, lost in contemplating each other, one being "more he than he." Aḥmad touches the secret of suffering in love, of hope in hopelessness, of inexplicable grace. The eternal theme of the interaction of love and beauty forms the continuum beneath the delicate melodies of this booklet, which should be read aloud to enjoy its softly swinging rhythm. Its words about lover, beloved, and love need to be meditated upon again and again; each time one reads them, they disclose a new aspect, as if veils were taken off the meaning and again replaced by new veils of different color.

It is in the spiritual chain of Aḥmad Ghazzālī that a *ḥadīth qudsī* was transmitted that tells how God answered the question of a Sufi who asked Him the meaning and wisdom of creation: "The wisdom of My creating you is to see My vision in the mirror of your spirit, and My love in your heart" (N 370) .

The *Sawāniḥ* inspired one of the works of Aḥmad Ghazzālī's beloved disciple, ᶜAynu'l-Quḍāt Hamadhānī, the *Tamhīdāt*.[11] This book—in spite of its delicate language, more accessible than the

9. Merlin S. Swartz, *Ibn al-Jauzi's "kitāb al-quṣṣāṣ waᵓl-mudhakkirīn"* (Beirut, 1971), # 221.

10. Aḥmad Ghazzālī, *Sawāniḥ. Aphorismen über die Liebe*, ed. Hellmut Ritter (Istanbul, 1942).

11. ᶜAynuᵓl-Quḍāt Hamadhānī, *Lawāᵓiḥ*, ed. Rahīm Farmānish (Tehran, 1337 sh. /1958); ᶜAynuᵓl-Quḍāt Hamadhānī, *Aḥwāl ū āthār*, ed. ᶜAfīf ᶜUsayrān (Tehran, 1338 sh./1959).

Sawāniḥ—has often been copied. ᶜAynuʾl-Quḍāt's talent for explaining even the deepest and most serious thoughts in poetical language was greater than his master's. Because it was easy to understand, therefore, the *Tamhīdāt* was widely read in the Muslim world; it was one of the favorite books of the Delhi Chishtī mystics in the late thirteenth century. The south Indian Chishtī saint Gīsūdarāz wrote a commentary on it about 1400, and later a saint of Bijapur, Mīrān Ḥusain Shāh (d. 1669), translated the book into Dakhni Urdu, an idiom that was just beginning to emerge as a literary language.

Like his master, ᶜAynuʾl-Quḍāt was consumed by burning divine passion. Jāmī said about him: "Only few people made such disclosures of realities and explanations of subtle points as he did, and miracles like killing and reviving became manifest in him" (N 414–15). The talented young man was, however, imprisoned in Baghdad for some alleged heresy and executed in 1132 in the bloom of youth. His apology, written in Arabic like some of his other works, proves that he did not feel at all guilty of the heresies that the orthodox claimed to have discovered in his very personal interpretation of Sufism. Rather, he felt that he was in perfect agreement with the tenets of Islam.[12] We may suspect, therefore, that a matter of personal envy or revenge precipitated his premature death.

The third name in the chain of the great love mystics of Iran is that of Rūzbihān Baqlī, who died at an advanced age in 1209 in his hometown of Shiraz.

> That elder of Shiraz, famed Rūzbihān,
> whose like in all the earth was never seen
> for purity and truth, the bezel was
> bejewelling the ring of saints, a man
> learned in spirit, life of all the world;
> of lovers all and gnostics he was king,
> captain of every heart that hath attained
> his spirit gladdening beauty.[13]

That is how ᶜIrāqī, another of the great lovers in the history of Sufism, described him poetically.

12. A. J. Arberry, *A Sufi Martyr* (London, 1969), a translation of ᶜAynuʾl-Quḍāt's apology. See Fritz Meier's review in *Der Islam* 49, no. 1 (1972).

13. Fakhruddīn ᶜIrāqī, *The Song of the Lovers*, ed. and trans. A. J. Arberry (Oxford, 1939), p. 57.

Rūzbihān's numerous works are not only an important source for mystical love theories; his *Sharḥ-i shaṭḥiyāt* gives us a key to the understanding of the theopathic utterances of early mystics. These paradoxes, which have always been a stumbling block for the orthodox and even for moderate Sufis, in many cases defy rational explanation and can only be understood by reaching the same state as the mystic who uttered them. Baqlī's main concern is the writings and sayings of Ḥallāj, which makes the *Sharḥ* indispensable for an understanding of Ḥallāj's work. In this area Rūzbihān's interpretations are unquestionably correct, for the Shirazi Sufis had generally been favorable to the martyr-mystic of Baghdad; Ibn Khafīf of Shiraz (d. 982) had been one of the few admirers of Ḥallāj who remained faithful to him until his death, and Rūzbihān saw himself in this tradition.[14]

Overwhelmed by love and longing, Baqlī laments over the lost greatness of Sufism and, calling upon the different cosmic powers, cries out (enumerating the masters of the Path before he reaches the praise of him to whom every mystical chain goes back—of Aḥmad al-Hāshimī, i.e., the Prophet Muhammad):

> O Time that causes misfortune! Where is the outcry of
> Shiblī? Where is Ḥuṣrī's calling?
> O Epoch [or: afternoon] of the world! Where is Abūʾl-
> Ḥasan Nūrī's singing? Where Abū Ḥamza-yi
> Ṣūfī's Ah?
> O shadow of the skies! Where is Sumnūn's age and
> Dhūʾn-Nūn's love and Sumnūn's sigh and Buhlūl's
> complaints?
> O carpet of the earth! Where is Junayd's steadfastness
> and Ruwaym's mystical concert?
> O limpid green water! Where are the melodies of
> Subbūhi and the handclapping of Abū ʿAmr Zujjājī?
> And the dance of Abūʾl-Ḥusayn Sīrwānī?

14. Rūzbihān Baqlī, "*ʿAbhar al-ʿāshiqīn,*" *Le jasmine des fidèles d'amour,* ed. Henri Corbin (Tehran and Paris, 1958); Rūzbihān Baqlī, "*Sharḥ-i shaṭḥiyāt,*" *Les paradoxes des Soufis,* ed. Henri Corbin (Tehran and Paris, 1966). Louis Massignon, "La vie et les oeuvres de Rūzbehān Baqlī," in *Studia Orientalia Ioanni Pedersen dicata septuagenario* (Copenhagen, 1953), is the first biography of this fascinating mystic. Henri Corbin, "Quiétude et inquiétude de l'âme dans le soufisme de Rūzbihān Baqlī de Shīrāz," *Eranos-Jahrbuch* 17 (1948); Corbin, "Sympathie et théopathie chez les fidèles d'amour en Islam," *Eranos-Jahrbuch* 24 (1955).

O light of the sun! Where is the breath of Kattānī, and the fervent passion of Naṣrābādhī?
O sphere of Saturn! Where is the realm of Bāyezīd Bisṭāmī's *tauḥīd*?
O crescent of the sky! Where is Wāsiṭī's unrest, and Yūsuf ibn Ḥusain's elegance?
O drops of the cloud in the air! Where are the moanings of Abū Mazāḥim-i Shīrāzī? Where is the changing color of Jaᶜfar-i Ḥaddā?
O color of Saturn, o shame of Venus, o letter of intelligence! Where is the bloodshed of Ḥusayn ibn Manṣūr in "I am the Truth"?
Where is the strutting of the strange scholar in unfamiliar fetters in the place of execution in the midst of friends and enemies?
O Time and Space! Why are you without the beauty of Sheikh ᶜAbdullāh ibn Khafīf?

(B 377–78)

What so profoundly impresses the reader in Rūzbihān's writings, both in his commentary on the *Shaṭḥiyāt* and his *ᶜAbhar al-ᶜāshiqīn* —"*Le Jasmin des fidèles d'amour,*" as Henri Corbin translates its title—is his style, which is at times as hard to translate as that of Aḥmad Ghazzālī and possesses a stronger and deeper instrumentation. It is no longer the scholastic language of the early exponents of Sufism, who tried to classify stages and stations, though Baqlī surely knew these theories and the technical terms. It is the language refined by the poets of Iran during the eleventh and twelfth centuries, filled with roses and nightingales, pliable and colorful. Who else would describe love in such words: "Look well, for the heart is the marketplace of His love, and there the rose of Adam on the branch of Love is from the color of manifestation [*tajallī*] of His Rose. When the nightingale 'spirit' becomes intoxicated by this rose, he will hear with the ear of the soul the song of the bird of *Alast* ['Am I not your Lord?'] in the fountainplace of preeternity" (B 396). Or who would invite his beloved, to whom the *Jasmin* is dedicated, to enter his heart to see the manifestation of pure love in the rose petals of his soul, where thousands of nightingales have burned the wings of their high ambition in the fire of love (BA 47)? Divine beauty is revealed in human beauty:

The vision of the cosmos is the *qibla* of the ascetics,
the vision of Adam is the *qibla* of the lovers.
(BA 79)

Without any wish or hope of even touching the beloved's skirt, this love is absolutely pure: "The antinomy of the eyes of the lovers who travel in Reality is the dust of the village of the Divine Law" (BA 112).

Rūzbihān finds the proof for this lawbound and chaste love in the Koran itself. Did not God say in his revelation: "We tell you the most beautiful story"? And this is the story of lover and beloved, of Yusuf and Zulaykhā, the story of chaste and, therefore, lawful love as revealed in Sūra 12 (BA 19). Thus, he can feel that at the Day of the Primordial Covenant, "the soul flew in the world of Divine love with the wings of human love" (BA 4).

It was Rūzbihān Baqlī who highlighted the prophetic tradition according to which Muhammad declared the red rose to be the manifestation of God's glory (B 265). He thus gave the rose—loved by poets throughout the world—the sanction of religious experience; his vision of God is a vision of clouds of roses, the divine presence fulgent as a marvelous red rose. Since this flower reveals divine beauty and glory most perfectly, the nightingale, symbol of the longing soul, is once and forever bound to love it—and the numberless roses and nightingales in Persian and Turkish poetry take on, wittingly or unwittingly, this metaphysical connotation of soul-bird and divine rose.

Rūzbihān becomes enraptured when he speaks of his own experiences, of his suffering, his yearning for beauty. The *iltibās*, the concealment of preeternal beauty in created forms, is the theme of his meditations; faithful to the classical Sufi tradition, he sees in love the effort to break once more through the limits of the created world in order to reach the state of true *tauḥīd*, as it existed at the Day of the Covenant. In this experience, the passage from human love to transcendental love and thus to true *tauḥīd* is, as Corbin—following Rūzbihān's mystical flights—has stated (CV 135), a metamorphosis of the subject: the lover, finally, is transformed into sheer love and thus reaches the state in which lover and beloved are one and in which the beloved can speak through the lover (B 57). More than five centuries later, this transformation of the loving soul into pure love was expressed in a remote corner of the Islamic world, in Sind, by Shāh ᶜAbdu'l-Laṭīf, whose heroine, lost in the desert in search of her beloved, cries out her longing. But the poet understands:

> O voice in the desert—as if the grouse were crying . . .
> cry from the water's depths—it is the sigh of love.
>
> O voice in the desert, like sound of a violin—
> It is the song of love—only the people unaware took it
> to be a woman's song.[15]

This mystery of transformation from chaste human love to the summit of divine love remains one of the central themes of great poetry in Iran and its neighboring countries, and the lover understands:

> Everything is the beloved, and the lover a veil,
> Living is the beloved, and the lover is dead.
>
> (M 1:30)

The ambiguity of the experience of love, as it emerges from these mystical theories and practices, resulted in the use of erotic symbolism by the mystics and of mystical terms by the profane poets. The true, pure mystics have sometimes tried to explain the symbolism of earthly love and wine as completely allegorical—even Ibn ᶜArabī used this method in his interpretation of his own *Tarjumān al-ashwāq*. This trend became even stronger in later Persian, Turkish, and Urdu poetry, and the mystics drew up whole charts to explain the simplest words in a mystical sense. A glance at the list by Muḥsin Fayḍ Kāshānī, a seventeenth-century Persian author, suffices to illustrate this tendency:

rukh (face, cheek): the revelation of Divine Beauty in Attributes of grace, e.g., the Gracious, the Clement, the Life-giving, the Guide, the Bountiful, Light, Divine Reality.

zulf (tress): the revelation of Divine Majesty in Attributes of Omnipotence, e.g., the Withholder, the Seizer . . . phenomena as veil concealing Divine Reality.

kharābāt (tavern): Pure Unity, undifferentiated and unqualified . . . .[16]

Other poets have used even more abstract methods of allegorizing,

15. Shāh ᶜAbduʾl-Laṭīf, "Sur Maᶜdhūrī," in *Shāha jō risālō*, ed. Kalyan B. Adwānī (Bombay, 1958), 1:lines 21–22.

16. A. J. Arberry, *Sufism: An Account of the Mystics of Islam* (London, 1950), pp. 113 ff.

in which, eventually, the charm of a quatrain is lost in the heavy chains of a terminology stemming from Ibn ᶜArabī. It is doubtful whether the great masters of mystical love, like Rūzbihān Baqlī, would have appreciated this exaggerated "mystical" explanation—they knew that the word in itself is like a fan, veiling and unveiling at the same time.

THE PILGRIMAGE OF THE BIRDS: SANĀʾĪ AND ᶜAṬṬĀR

Persian mystical poetry, especially mystical didactic poetry, seems to have originated in the eastern part of Iran. One of its early centers was Herat, where ᶜAbdullāh-i Anṣārī's *Munājāt* ushered in a new period of religious literature in Persian. These short orisons have never been surpassed, in prayer literature, in their stylistic simplicity, which combines an easy-flowing rhythm with material for long meditations. Y. E. Bertels has traced the course of Sufi didactic poetry,[17] of which some of Anṣārī's books constitute a first stage, but which found its first master, half a century later, in Anṣārī's compatriot Abūʾl-Majd Majdūd Sanāʾī (d. ca 1131).[18]

As a court poet of the later Ghaznawids in Ghazna itself, Sanāʾī began his career with highly elaborate and skillful *qaṣīda*s. He visited several places in Khurasan, most importantly Balkh and Sarakhs. He then turned to mystical, or rather ascetic, poetry. Although there is a charming anecdote about his repentance, the true reason for this change of attitude is not clear. He says in one of his *ghazal*s:

> First I wrote books with great painstaking care—
> Eventually I broke my pens in complete bewilderment.
> (SD 801)

Sanāʾī's major work, which laid the foundations of mystical didactic poetry, is a *mathnawī*, a poem written in rhyming hemistiches, a form that was developed in Iran for epic purposes and in which only a certain group of rather short meters is applicable. This book, the *Ḥadīqat al-ḥaqīqa*, "Orchard of Truth," shows traces of the author's past as court poet; it is dedicated to Sultan

17. Y. E. Berthels, "Grundlinien der Entwicklungsgeschichte des sufischen Lehrgedichtes," *Islamica* 3, no. 1 (1929).

18. Abūʾl-Majd Majdūd Sanāʾī, *The First Book of the "Ḥadīqatuʾl-Ḥaqīqat" or the Enclosed Garden of the Truth of the Ḥakīm Sanāʾī of Ghazna*, ed. and trans. Major John Stephenson (1908; reprint ed., New York, 1971). For editions of Sanāʾī's works see the Bibliography.

Bahrāmshāh, to whom the entire tenth chapter is devoted. Western scholars usually consider the *Ḥadīqa* a rather boring book; in fact, it lacks the flowing delicacy of many later mystical poems. Written in a slightly jumping meter, the book is divided into ten chapters, most of which deal with different aspects of the mystical and the practical life. The style is, at times, rather dry; yet the *Ḥadīqa* contains a number of famous stories that were known in Sufi circles in the early twelfth century and may have been adapted partly from Qushayrī's *Risāla,* partly from Ghazzālī's *Iḥyāʾ ʿulūm ad-dīn,* both of which were familiar to the author. The anecdotes of earlier Sufis and meditations on mystical sentences show which aspects of the tradition were alive during Sanāʾī's time in the eastern fringe of the Muslim world.

The reader eventually comes to enjoy the way in which Sanāʾī sets forth his ideas of God and the world, of piety and of false Sufism in his matter-of-fact style, not hesitating to insert stories and images of an avowedly unmystical, sometimes obscene character. The same can be said of Sanāʾī's smaller *mathnawī*s, like the satirical *Kārnāma-yi Balkh,* with its very crude tenor. Some of its expressions have, however, been taken over almost word for word by Sanāʾī's most distinguished spiritual disciple, Jalāluddīn Rūmī, who came from Balkh. Medieval Christian mystics and theologians also used very straightforward and unrestricted language when explaining their ideas or attacking the enemies of the true religion. On the whole, Sanāʾī's imagery is clear and frank (except when he indulges in highly rhetorical devices); it is not as elaborate and oscillating as the language of later mystics, but it captures the reader by its simplicity, which is well suited to the topics he usually treats. The *Ḥadīqa* has become a model for all the later *mathnawīs* written for mystical didactic purposes.

Western orientalists have admired Sanāʾī's lyrics much more than the *Ḥadīqat;* they are fluent, fresh, and sensitive, for the most part, and for the first time the *ghazal* form is used for mystical thought. One of the finest pieces in his *Dīwān* is the "Lament of Satan," in which the sober language rises to a height not often found in Persian mystical poetry. Among his *qaṣīda*s, the numerous skillfully wrought eulogies on the Prophet must be mentioned, along with the charming "Litany of the Birds," in which each bird is assigned a special way of praising God (SD 30–35).

Among Sanāʾī's smaller *mathnawī*s, the *Sayr al-ʿibād ilāʾl-maʿād,*

"The Journey of the Servants toward the Place of Return," is highly revealing. In it the poet describes the mystical theories of the return of the soul through the different stages of life to its original source—ideas expressed by Sanāʾī's compatriot Avicenna a century earlier, but here brought for the first time into a poem, in which the poet displays all his knowledge of philosophy and Sufi theories. Reynold A. Nicholson and others have considered this *mathnawī* the model for ʿAṭṭār's *Manṭiq uṭ-ṭayr*; Nicholson has even spoken of it as prefiguring the theme of the *Divine Comedy*.[19] It is only one expression of the idea of traveling and ascension that was so dear to the Muslim mystics and that found its most beautiful poetic expression in the works of Farīduddīn ʿAṭṭār.

> Out of the ocean like rain clouds come and travel—
> for without traveling you will never become a pearl!
>
> (AD 707)

Thus says ʿAṭṭār, who is regarded by many scholars as the greatest of the *mathnawī*-writers in the history of Persian mystical poetry.

> Sanāʾī was the spirit, and ʿAṭṭār his two eyes—
> we have come after Sanāʾī and ʿAṭṭār,

says Jalāluddīn Rūmī, acknowledging his indebtedness to the two great masters. In his work he follows quite closely the patterns established by these two mystics of eastern Iran, his own homeland.

While Sanāʾī was sober and told short, poignant, and sometimes even biting allegories, ʿAṭṭār, a century later, was a born storyteller. One can imagine him, sitting in his druggist's shop—as his surname ʿAṭṭār indicates—talking to people, curing them, meditating upon mystical subjects, and then writing down his meditations in his inimitable style, in beautiful and clear language.

Farīduddīn was born in Nishapur and died there, most likely in 1220 at an old age. Later mystical tradition includes him in the list of the martyrs of love, slain by the orthodox or, in his case, by the infidels because of his excessive divine love. Whether he was indeed killed by the invading Mongols is uncertain, but the story indicates the rank he was given in the spiritual tradition of Iran.

Both in lyrics and in his numerous epic works ʿAṭṭār shows a fascinating talent as narrator; this trait is also evident in his collection of biographies of the saints, the *Tadhkirat al-auliyāʾ*. Hagiogra-

19. Reynold A. Nicholson, *A Persian Forerunner of Dante* (Towyn-on-Sea, 1944).

phy was, for him, another medium for telling stories about his venerated masters; his narrative, and even dramatic, talent is beautifully displayed in the *Tadhkirat*. For factual details, this book should be supplemented with other, more sober sources. Many anecdotes from the *Tadhkirat al-auliyā*ʾ have been inserted into ʿAṭṭār's poetic work as well. All his books are, indeed, storehouses of anecdotes and of lively tales.

One remarkable aspect of his epics is his stern criticism of temporal rulers. The old Sufi ideals of poverty become, in his work, a practical device—is not the dervish much richer and higher than the king? The king begs everywhere for money; the dervish does not beg from anybody. Social criticism is often put into the mouth of a lunatic—ʿAṭṭār has a whole group of these mentally deranged persons, who struggle both with God and with the earthly rulers; an old woman is another instrument by which a tyrannical ruler is called to reason. The stories about right government are sometimes reminiscent of similar anecdotes found in the "Mirrors for Princes," a literary genre that enjoyed great popularity in Iran in the late eleventh century. ʿAṭṭār does not merely tell stories; he often interprets them as well without leaving that to the reader.

Hellmut Ritter, who devoted his masterful book *Das Meer der Seele* to ʿAṭṭār's mysticism and poetic art, discerns three stages in the poet's life.[20] In the first period he is the master of storytelling; it was in this period that he must have composed his masterpiece, the *Manṭiq uṭ-ṭayr*, "The Birds' Conversation," his *Ilāhīnāme*, "The Story of the King and His Six Sons," and the *Muṣībatnāme*, "The Book of Affliction." In the second period the external forms are fading away and the anaphoras become longer and longer: ʿAṭṭār is often so enraptured while writing that he tries to describe the divine mysteries in long chains of repeated exclamations or identical words; his intoxication carries him away from logical reasoning. It is typical of this period that the hero of the *Ushtur-*

20. Hellmut Ritter, *Das Meer der Seele*, is the comprehensive work about ʿAṭṭār and, at the same time, about the problems of Sufi thought and poetry; it is indispensable for every serious student. See also Hellmut Ritter, "Philologika X," *Der Islam* 25 (1936), and "Philologika XIV–XVI," *Oriens* 11–14 (1961), for the philological background. M. Joseph Héliodore Garcin de Tassy, *La poésie philosophique et religieuse chez les persans d'après le "Manṭiq uṭ-ṭair"* (Paris, 1857–60); Fritz Meier, "Der Geistmensch bei dem persischen Dichter ʿAṭṭār," *Eranos-Jahrbuch* 13 (1946); Wolfgang Lentz, "ʿAṭṭār als Allegoriker," *Der Islam* 35 (1960); A. J. Arberry, *Muslim Saints and Mystics* (London, 1960), select translations from the *Tadhkirat al-auliyā*ʾ. For editions of ʿAṭṭār's works see the Bibliography.

nāme—a poem centering around the figure of the puppet player—commits suicide in mystical rapture. The once widely held idea that ʿAṭṭār became a pious Shiite in the third period of his life can no longer be maintained; the works that show a strong Shia inclination and were once thought to be his can now be ascribed to another poet by the same name.

ʿAṭṭār's poems, especially the *Manṭiq uṭ-ṭayr*, have become standard works of Sufi literature, from which generations of mystics and poets have taken their inspiration. His influence on related literature remains to be discussed. It is sufficient to mention here the story of Sheikh Ṣanʿān, who fell in love with a Christian maiden and "changed the rosary for the infidel's girdle" (MT 77 ff.). This story has found its way even into Kashmiri and Malay literature. ʿIrāqī sings:

> Upon this path, for love of a gazelle
> the holiest man shrinks not from tending swine.[21]

Ṣanʿān's name occurs in popular Turkish mystical poetry as often as in Sindhi Sufi songs. He has become one of the best-known symbols of true loving surrender, regardless of religious traditions, reputation, name, or fame.

One of the most fascinating aspects of ʿAṭṭār's mysticism—as of that of his elder contemporary Rūzbihān—is his relation to Ḥallāj. The spiritual Ḥallāj initiated him into the mystical path. His biography of the martyr-mystic is among the most touching parts of the *Tadhkirat al-auliyāʾ* and has shaped the image of Ḥallāj for all subsequent generations. From him ʿAṭṭār learned the mysticism of suffering, constant pain as remedy:

> The pain of love became the medicine for every heart,
> The difficulty could never be solved without love.
>
> (U 346)

More than any other mystical poet of Iran, ʿAṭṭār can be called "the voice of pain" (MT 287), the voice of longing and of searching. His works treat the perpetual movement of the soul toward its origin and goal in different allegories. The *Muṣībatnāme* is the story of the Sufi's quest for the absolute: in an objectification of the experience of the forty days' seclusion, the mystic wanders through the world of created beings, from the divine spirit down

21. ʿIrāqī, *Song of the Lovers*, p. 17.

to the lowliest of creatures. The wayfarer listens to the *lisān ul-ḥāl,* the "tongue of the state" of wind and earth, of fire and sea, and hears the endless yearning of all creatures, who in a state of confusion long for their original home. The experiences that result from discussions with the forty created beings are submitted, one by one, to the *Pir,* who explains them. Finally, under the guidance of the Prophet Muhammad, the seeker finds his way into the ocean of his own soul, where all longing ends. But even the union with the ocean of the soul is not final—when the soul has finished its journey to God, the journey in God will begin—the state that the mystics call *baqā,* subsistence in God—and the soul will traverse ever new abysses of the fathomless divine being, of which no tongue can speak.

ᶜAṭṭār knew—like Sanāʾī and Rūmī—that this constant movement is not peculiar to the human soul; it goes through the whole created world (U 63). Endless periods of development are necessary before the one beautiful flower, the one Perfect Man, can come into existence—periods marked by the death and annihilation of hundreds of thousands of lower existences, which, in turn, may one day reach the state from which their upward movement can start (cf. MT 234), for

> Everyone's journey is toward his perfection—
> Everyone's proximity is according to his "state."
>
> (MT 232)

This restlessness of creation has been echoed often in later Persian poetry—among the post-medieval poets, Bēdil, the Indian mystical poet (d. 1721), must be mentioned; in our time, it was Muhammad Iqbal, who never tired of describing the long way of development from a drop to the ocean, from sperm to man, and eventually to the Perfect Man, the crown and apex of creation.

The motif of this journey is fully developed in ᶜAṭṭār's most famous epic poem, "The Birds' Conversation" (a title alluding to the Koranic figure of Solomon, representative of the mystical leader who was able to converse with the soul birds in a secret tongue). This epic is the most perfect poetic introduction to the mystical path, with its seven valleys, in which are described all the difficulties the soul will encounter on the road. The equation soul=bird is popular all over the world. It appeared in many primitive religions and is still to be found today. In Turkey one still hears the expression *can kuşu uçtu,* "his soul bird has flown away," when someone has died. Persian poetry abounds in this imagery. Avicenna had used it, and Ghazzālī wrote a *Risālat aṭ-ṭayr,* a "Birds' Treatise," of similar contents. ʿAṭṭār, however, invented the mystical end to the story: the thirty birds who have undertaken the painful journey in search of the Sīmurgh, the king of birds, realize finally that they themselves—being *sī murgh,* "thirty birds"—are the Sīmurgh. This is the most ingenious pun in Persian literature, expressing so marvelously the experience of the identity of the soul with the divine essence.

The imagery of the birds was elaborated more and more after ʿAṭṭār's *Manṭiq uṭ-ṭayr* became one of the favorite story books of Persian literature.[22] Everyone who has read Persian poetry, if only in translation, knows of the nightingale who yearns for the rose—it is, in mystical language, the soul longing for eternal beauty, as Rūzbihān defined it. The nightingale infinitely repeats the praise of the rose without tiring, tells of its longing, sings hymns from the Koran of the rose (i.e., its petals), suffers without complaint the stings of the thorns. Iqbal has interpreted the song of the nightingale in the context of his philosophy of unfulfilled union and longing—only longing gives the soul bird the capacity to sing, inspiring it to create lovely melodies. Longing is the highest state the soul can reach, for it results in creativity, whereas union brings about silence and annihilation.

One of the birds described in the *Manṭiq uṭ-ṭayr* is the falcon, the white royal bird who longs to return to his master's fist. The falcon, or white hawk, as beautifully described in ʿAṭṭār's *Ushturnāme,* was to become one of Rūmī's favorite symbols—he often spoke of the soul as a falcon, exiled in the company of black crows, or as a nightingale surrounded by ravens, or as a gazelle in the donkey stable (M 5:833–38). And just as ʿAṭṭār invented a pun on the name of the Sīmurgh, Rūmī used a pun on the word falcon, *bāz*—the bird is called by this name because he longs to come back, *bāz,* to his sultan's breast. How touching is his imagery when he describes the noble bird, returning at the sound of the falcon's drum from his earthly exile; he perches on his master's forearm, rubbing his head on his breast: thus the once lost and bewildered soul returns, at peace, to the Lord (D 1353). Every bird, every animal, has its place in this wonderful cosmos of ʿAṭṭār and his follow-

22. Annemarie Schimmel, "Rose und Nachtigall," *Numen* 5, no. 2 (1968).

ers in the mystical Path. Sanā'ī had invented the Litany of the Birds. The dove constantly repeats *kū kū* because it is asking the way toward the beloved, repeating the question *kū kū*, "Where, where?" And the stork, *lak-lak*, gets his name from his pious attestation, *al-mulk lak, al-amr lak, al-ḥamd lak*, "Thine is the kingdom, Thine is the order, Thine is the praise." The duck symbolizes the human being, half bound to earth, half living in the ocean of God; and the crow is always connected with the ugly winter landscape of this worldly existence.

The camel becomes the symbol of the faithful person who fulfills, in perfect patience, the orders of his master (M 4:3389); even the unclean dog can become a model for the Sufi since, keeping faithful company with the Seven Sleepers, he became purified and sanctified, just as the lower soul becomes elevated and purified in the company of saintly people.

One of the finest images in Persian poetry—used by Khāqānī, Niẓāmī, and ʿAṭṭār in the late twelfth century, and then often by Rūmī and his imitators—is that of the elephant who dreamed of India. The elephant, an animal invariably connected with India, may be captured and carried away from his homeland to foreign lands, but when he sees his home in a dream, he will break all his chains and run there. This is a perfect image of the mystic's soul, which, in the midst of worldly entanglements, is blessed with the vision of its eternal homeland and returns to the primordial Hindustan, for "the ass does not dream of Hindustan at all!" (M 4:3067). As Kipling expressed it in his poem "The Captive's Dream," the elephant thinks:

> I will remember what I was, I am sick of rope and chain.
> I will revisit my lost loves, and playmates masterless.

Every flower in the garden becomes, for the mystic poets of the late twelfth century, a tongue to praise God; every leaf and petal is a book in which God's wisdom can be read, if man will only look. God has put signs on the horizon and in man's soul (Sūra 41:53); man has only to look at them. The lily praises God, silently, with ten tongues; the violet sits modestly in its dark blue Sufi garb, its head on the "knee of meditation." Red tulips with their dark scars in their "hearts" may grow out of the burned hearts of lovers, or they may remind the mystic of black-hearted hypocrites. The narcissus looks, with languid eyes, toward the creator or makes the lover think of the friend's half-closed eyes, and the purple, curly hyacinth resembles the tresses of the beloved.

Behind all created beauty the mystic sees a witness to the source of eternal beauty—the ruby is the heart of the stone, which has been transformed into a priceless jewel through patience and shedding its blood;[23] the emerald is powerful like the mystical leader, blinding the eyes of the serpents or the enemies of faith. The millstone turns in its restless journey like the Sufi, and the waterwheel sighs like the lover who is separated from his home and his friend. Rain is God's mercy, which revives the heart that has become lowly as dust; sun is His glory, to be contemplated through the multicolored prisms of created things. The breeze of His loving-kindness makes the growing boughs and buds dance, and the storm of His wrath uproots the dried-up bushes and trees that lack the sap of love.

The eye of the mystic who is enraptured in love sees traces of eternal beauty everywhere and listens to the mute eloquence of everything created. Whatever he mentions, his goal is the essence of the beloved—like Zulaykhā, who, longing for Joseph's beauty, applied to him "the name of every thing, from rue-seed to aloes-wood."

> If she piled up a hundred thousand names—
> her meaning and intention was always Joseph.
> (M 6:4022–37)

Persian poetry—from its very beginning conducive to precious, gemlike images—was the ideal vehicle to express these feelings. The subtle harmony and ultimate equilibrium between the different spheres of being is best maintained in the poetry of Ḥāfiẓ, whose verses are the perfect flower of the gardens of Shiraz, transparent as the air of that town, and fragrant as rose oil distilled from the centuries-old tradition of love of the divine revealed in visible forms.

MAULĀNĀ JALĀLUDDĪN RŪMĪ.

No mystic of Islam is as well known in the West as Jalāluddīn Rūmī, called by his followers Maulānā, "our master" (Turkish pronounciation Mevlâna), or Maulawī. The order inspired by him, the Mevlevis, known in the West as the Whirling Dervishes, early attracted the interest of European visitors to the Ottoman

23. Annemarie Schimmel, "The Ruby of the Heart," in *Zakir Husain Presentation Volume*, ed. Malik Ram (New Delhi, 1968).

Empire, and the first orientalists interested in Persian literature chose his poetry for translation.

Joseph von Hammer-Purgstall (1774–1856), the indefatigable translator of Persian, Turkish, and Arabic literature, dedicated many pages to Rūmī in his classical *Geschichte der schönen Redekünste Persiens* (1818). His rather dry translations from parts of the *Dīwān* inspired his one-time disciple Friedrich Rückert (1788–1866) to create *ghazal*s in Rūmī's style—the first attempt to adapt the *ghazal* form to German poetry. Rückert's book (1819) is a collection of wonderful mystical poems; they are free adaptations, yet they convey more of Maulānā's genius than most of the later, more literal, translations do. Rückert's translations have been a major force in shaping Rūmī's image in German literary history—more so than the translations by Vincenz von Rosenzweig-Schwannau (1838). It was through Rückert's book that Hegel became familiar with the enthusiastic mystical poet whom he praised in his *Encyclopaedie der philosophischen Wissenschaften.* A century later—to mention only one example—Constantin Brunner relied partially on Rūmī (in Rückert's translation) for his philosophical ideas about the genius. In 1903 Rückert's *ghazal*s were even translated into English *ghazal*s by the Scottish theologian William Hastie—as an antidote to the cult of Omar Khayyam, as the translator says. The intense study of Rūmī's work by British orientalists—like E. H. Whinfield and James W. Redhouse—culminated in the magnificent edition by Reynold A. Nicholson of Rūmī's *Mathnawī*, together with a translation and commentary (1925–1940).[24] Both Nicholson, whose *Selections from the "Dīvān-i Shams-i Tabrīz"* (1898) is still one of the finest introductions to Maulānā's work, and A. J. Arberry have translated many of Rūmī's poems and stories into English.[25] Yet a

24. Maulānā Jalāladdīn Rūmī, *Mathnawī-i maᶜnawī*, ed. and trans. Reynold A. Nicholson, 8 vols. (London, 1925–40). Among other English translations two should be mentioned: that of the first volume by James W. Redhouse (London, 1881), and that by Edward Henry Whinfield (London, 1857). Georg Rosen, *Mesnevi oder Doppelverse des Scheich Mevlāna Dschalālad-Dīn Rumi* (1843; rev. ed., Munich, 1913). See Reynold A. Nicholson, *Tales of Mystic Meaning* (London, 1931); A. J. Arberry, *Tales from the Mathnawi* (London, 1961) and *More Tales from the Mathnawi* (London, 1963).

25. Reynold A. Nicholson, *Selected Poems from the "Divan-i Shams-i Tabriz"* (1898; reprint ed., Cambridge, 1961), was the first European edition and translation of forty-eight ghazals, with a fine introduction. Reynold A. Nicholson, *Rumi: Poet and Mystic* (London, 1950); A. J. Arberry, *The "Rubāᶜīyāt" of Jalāluddin Rumi* (London, 1959); Arberry, *Mystical Poems of Rumi* (Chicago, 1968); William Hastie, *The Festival of Spring from the "Divan" of Jeláleddin* (Glasgow, 1903); Annemarie Schimmel, *Dschelaladdin Rumi, Aus dem Diwan* (Stuttgart, 1964). The 700th anniversary of

truly comprehensive study of Rūmī in a Western language is still lacking. It will be difficult to do full justice to his work without making an extensive study of the Persian originals and the large number of Persian and Turkish works written about him, as well as the enormous amount of material composed in the Indo-Pakistan Subcontinent.[26]

It is probably legend that young Jalāluddīn—who was born in 1207 in the city of Balkh—was blessed by Farīduddīn ᶜAṭṭār about 1219, when he and his family were wandering through Iran after his father had left Balkh before the advancing hordes of Genghis Khan. Yet the story underlines the spiritual affinity between the two great masters of mystical poetry: Jalāluddīn never failed to acknowledge his indebtedness to both ᶜAṭṭār and Sanāʾī. His elegy on Sanāʾī's death (D 996)—based on a line of the Ghaznawid mystic himself (DS 1059)—is one of his most touching poems, and there are a number of literal allusions to Sanāʾī's poetry in Rūmī's lyrics and in the *Mathnawī*.

The interest in theological and mystical problems came naturally to Jalāluddīn; his father, Bahāʾuddīn Walad, was a noted theologian with mystical inclinations. The influence of his ideas, as set forth in his *Maᶜārif*, on the formation of Jalāluddīn's thought still remains to be analyzed in full. After long migrations, the family eventually reached Anatolia, where the dynasty of the Rum Seljukids was ruling in comparative peace. In Laranda (modern Karaman) Jalāluddīn's mother died and his first son, Sultan Walad, was born (1226). It was in that year that Najmuddīn Dāyā Rāzī, Ku-

---

Rūmī's death in December 1973 resulted in a remarkable output of writing about him and translations from his work, particularly in Turkey. Very useful is Mehmet Önder's *Mevlâna bibliografyasi*, vol. 1 (Ankara, 1973), which contains the previously published books and articles about Rūmī. The second volume gives a survey of the manuscripts. A collection of papers read at the Biruni-Rūmī Conference at New York University in January 1974 was published under the title *Biruni/Rumi, the Scholar and the Saint*, edited by Peter Chelkowski (New York, 1975). Rūmī, *Licht und Reigen, Gedichte aus dem Diwan*, trans. Johann Christoph Bürgel (Bern, 1973). A fine introduction to the *Mathnawī*, and indeed the first one in a Western language, is Joseph von Hammer-Purgstall, *Bericht über den zu Kairo im Jahre 1835 erschienenen türkischen Kommentar des Mesnewi Dschelaleddin Rumi's* (Vienna, 1851); it also appears in *Zwei Abhandlungen zur Mystik und Magie des Islam von Josef Hammer-Purgstall*, ed. Annemarie Schimmel (Vienna, 1974).

26. Afzal Iqbal, *The Life and Thought of Rumi* (Lahore, ca. 1956); Eva Meyerovitch, *Mystique et poésie en Islam, Djalal-ud Din Rumi et l'ordre des dervishes tourneurs* (Paris, 1972). An extensive study of Rūmī's poetry and thought in English by the present author is in preparation (to be published in the Persian Heritage Series, Abaris Books, New York).

brā's disciple, finished his *Mirṣād ul-ᶜibād* in Sivas, in the northern province of the Rum-Seljukid kingdom; in later years, he met Jalāluddīn as well as Ṣadruddīn Qōnawī in the capital (N 435).

Bahāᵓuddīn Walad was called to Konya in 1228. There Sultan ᶜAlāᵓuddīn Kaykobād had just built the magnificent mosque in the center of the town. Numerous smaller mosques and *madrasas* surrounded the castle; two of them, built during Rūmī's lifetime, are still standing: the Ince Minareli (1258) and the Karatay Medrese (1251). The exquisite turquoise blue tile work of the dome of this rather small building is a perfect illustration of Rūmī's poetry: Out of the four times five "Turkish triangles"—which bear in squared Kufi the names of the Prophet and the four righteous caliphs, as well as those of other prophets—rises the tambour, decorated with Koranic verses in sophisticated plaited Kufi script. The dome itself is covered with intricately interlaced stars in turquoise, blue, black, and white tiles, each of them separate and yet all interwoven in an almost inexplicable way. The top of the dome is open, so that the sky, and at night the stars, are reflected in the little pool in the center of the *madrasa*.

In Rūmī's time scholars, artists, and mystics from all over the eastern Islamic world sought shelter in Konya, one of the few safe places during this period when the Mongol onslaught devastated large parts of the Muslim world. The intellectual and religious life of Konya was, therefore, intensely stimulating. Persian continued to be used as a literary language, but the population spoke partly Greek—there being a strong Christian substratum in the former city of Iconium—and partly Turkish. Rūmī used both languages in some of his verses.

Bahāᵓuddīn Walad died after a few years of teaching, and his son Jalāluddīn succeeded him in his chair. His interest in mystical problems was strengthened by the instruction of his father's disciple and friend Burhānuddīn Muḥaqqiq, who introduced him to the deeper secrets of mystical thought. Burhānuddīn left Konya about 1240 and is buried in Kaisari, where his modest tomb is still venerated. Jalāluddīn probably went once, or perhaps twice, to Syria in search of knowledge and wisdom—unless his relations with the Syrian mystics go back to his earlier stay in that country. In Damascus, he may have met Ibn ᶜArabī, who died there in 1240. Even if he had no personal relationship with the great theosophist, Ibn ᶜArabī's foremost commentator Ṣadruddīn Qōnawī lived in Konya and was connected with Rūmī "by special friendship and acquaintance" (N 55), though Jalāluddīn was not fond of theosophical speculations. He may also have met Shamsuddīn Tabrīzī in Syria for the first time, but we do not know anything about their relations.

The sources describe Shams as an overpowering person of strange behavior who shocked people by his remarks and his harsh words. He claimed that he had reached the station of being the beloved, no longer the lover. The favorite story told about him describes his meeting with Auḥaduddīn Kirmānī, one of those mystical poets who contemplated absolute beauty in limited forms. He told Shams: " 'I see the moon in a vessel filled with water.' Shams rebuked him with the words: 'If you have no boil on your neck, why don't you look at it in the sky?' " (N 59), thus ridiculing him for "looking at the unbearded." This dervish, whose spiritual affiliation is as unknown as his family, was to become the decisive influence in Jalāluddīn's life. At the end of October 1244, he met Shams in the streets of Konya, and it was this strange, demanding mystic who kindled in him the fire of mystical love—that love described by mystics like Aḥmad Ghazzālī, ʿAynuʾl-Quḍāt, and Rūzbihān Baqlī—an absolute love that completely enraptured him, causing him to neglect his family and his disciples for months at a time. At last they rebelled and demanded that Shams leave town. He left indeed, but after a while he was brought back from Syria by Sultan Walad, for Rūmī found separation unbearable.

We have a description of their meeting after Shamsuddīn's return: they embraced each other and fell at each other's feet, "so that one did not know who was lover and who was beloved." The intensity of their relationship grew once more and became so overwhelming that some of Rūmī's disciples, with the cooperation of Rūmī's son ʿAlāʾuddīn, "the pride of professors," decided to send Shams to the place from which there is no return. One night they called him out of Jalāluddīn's house, which was opposite his son's house, and, after stabbing him, they threw him into the nearby well. Sultan Walad tried to allay his father's fears, telling him that everybody was in search of Shams; the chronicles, however, relate that during his father's sleep, he quickly buried Shams's body, which he had taken out of the well, covering the tomb with a hurriedly prepared plaster. This very tomb was discovered a few years ago by the then director of the Mevlâna Müzesi, Mehmet Önder; it is located beneath the memorial erected for Shams some time after the event.

As the sun moving clouds behind him run,
All hearts attend thee, O Tabriz's sun!

(D 310)

In the experience of this consuming love, Rūmī became a poet. He who had searched for Shams, the "Sun of Truth," in vain outside the country eventually discovered that he was united with him and "found him in himself, radiant like the moon," as Sultan Walad says. The lyrical poetry born out of this experience is written from a feeling of complete identification; instead of using his own pen name, Jalāluddīn used his friend's name as *nom de plume* at the end of most of the poems in which he sings of his love, longing, happiness, and despair in verses that have never been surpassed in their sincerity. It was this experience that he described in a famous passage of the *Mathnawī*:

A certain man knocked at his friend's door: his friend asked: "Who is there?"
He answered "I." "Begone," said his friend, "tis too soon! at my table there is no place for the raw.
How shall the raw be cooked but in the fire of absence? What else will deliver him from hypocrisy?"
He turned sadly away, and for a whole year the flames of separation consumed him;
Then he came back and again paced to and fro beside the house of his friend.
He knocked at the door with a hundred fears and reverence lest any disrespectful word might escape from his lips.
"Who is there?" cried the friend. He answered: "Thou, O charmer of all hearts."
"Now," said the friend, "since thou art I, come in, there is no room for two I's in this house." (M 1:3056–64)

Despite his poetical exuberance and despite his grief and sorrow, Jalāluddīn remained a highly esteemed member of Konya society; he was on friendly terms with Muʿīnuddīn Parwāne, the minister, and his presence was sought by theologians, mystics, and government officials alike. Not too long after Shamsuddīn's death, he experienced another mystical love relationship with Burhānuddīn Muḥaqqiq's spiritual successor, the modest goldsmith Ṣalāḥuddīn

Zarkūb, whose daughter became Sultan Walad's wife. Eventually, Rūmī's disciple Ḥusāmuddīn Çelebī inspired him to write his *Mathnawī*, that mystical didactic poem that Jāmī called "the Koran in Pahlavi," i.e., in the Persian tongue. Jalāluddīn often referred to the act of inspiration through Ḥusāmuddīn, who had asked the master to compose a work that his disciples could read instead of Sanāʾī's and ʿAṭṭār's mystical epics. Ḥusāmuddīn was charged with writing down the verses that would flow from Rūmī's lips, whether he was walking on the street or even sitting in the bath.

Both Ṣalāḥuddīn and Ḥusāmuddīn were, for Jalāluddīn, nothing but reflections of the same divine beauty and power he had seen in the person of Shams, and in many cases he addresses Ḥusāmuddīn in terms that show that he too was considered a "light of the sun," another manifestation of the Sun of Tabriz.

When Rūmī died, on 17 December 1273, Ḥusāmuddīn succeeded to the leadership of his disciples. But the formation of the order of the Whirling Dervishes, the organization of the dancing ritual and the establishment of a true hierarchy, was left to Sultan Walad (d. 1312), Rūmī's son, who took over his office after Ḥusāmuddīn's death in 1284. Sultan Walad's literary legacy—the *Maʿārif* and the three *Mathnāwī*s: *Ibtidāʾnāme*, "Book of the Beginning," *Intihāʾ-nāma*, "Book of the End," and *Rabābnāme*, "Book of the Rebec"—are considered the only authentic commentaries on Rūmī's work and contain most of the trustworthy information about his life and teaching—more than the numerous books composed by pious devotees.[27]

It seems that Jalāluddīn's position among the mystics in Konya was uncontested, even if we do not take literally the story that the great masters of mystical thought and poetry—like Ṣadruddīn Qōnawī, Fakhruddīn ʿIrāqī, Shamsuddīn Ikī, Saʿīd Farghānī, and others—gathered after his death. Asked about Maulānā, Ṣadruddīn said: "If Bāyezīd and Junayd had lived in this time, they would have seized his mantle and would have felt indebted to him; he is the majordomo of Muhammadan poverty, and we taste it thanks to him" (N 464).

Rūmī's literary output was great: more than 30,000 verses of lyric

27. See Farīdūn Aḥmad Sipahsālār, *Risāla dar aḥwāl-i Maulānā Jalāluddīn Rūmī*, ed. Saʿīd Nafisi (Tehran, 1325 sh./1946). Shamsaddīn Aḥmad al-Aflākī, *Manāqib al-ʿārifīn*, ed. Tahsin Yazıcı, 2 vols. (Ankara, 1959–61); this book was translated into French, though not fully satisfactorily, by Clemens Huart as *Les saints des derviches tourneurs* (Paris, 1918–22).

poetry, more than 26,000 verses in the *Mathnawī*; besides his "table talks," called *Fīhi mā fīhi*, which "substitute poetic imagination for logical argument," but are not comparable to his poetry,[28] a number of letters are also extant.[29] Like ʿAṭṭār, Rūmī liked storytelling, but he lacked the sustained narration that distinguishes ʿAṭṭār's mystical epics. He often begins a story—even in lyrical poems—and then is distracted by an association, by the sound or the meaning of one word, which sets him on a completely different course until he admonishes himself to return to the original story. The actors in the *Mathnawī*, as well as the symbols and images used there, have an almost protean versatility, and the *Mathnawī*—"the shop of unity" (M 6:1528)—contains almost every conceivable mystical theory known in the thirteenth century. It is, however, next to impossible to build up a mystical system from its tales and parables; every interpreter has found whatever he sought, from pantheism to personal mysticism, from enraptured love to law-bound orthodoxy. The *Mathnawī* is without end, "even if the forests were pens and the ocean ink" (M 6:2247), as Rūmī says, alluding to the Koranic claim that God's words are without end (Sūra 18:109).

If there was ever an inspired writer among the Muslim mystics, it was certainly Jalāluddīn. It is said that for the most part he dictated his verses in a state of rapture or even trance.[30] The birth of such inspired poetry—not rare among Muslim mystics—can be witnessed in Rūmī's enthusiastic lyrics as well. Their rhythms often suggest the turning and whirling movement out of which they came. It is said that the hammering of the goldsmiths in the bazaar of Konya inspired him to dance and to recite verses, as did the sound of the watermills in the gardens of Meram. There are probably many more occasions when a mere word or sound struck a responsive chord in him and set him to reciting a new poem. The rhythmical patterns

28. See A. J. Arberry, *Discourses of Rumi* (London, 1961), a translation of *Fīhi mā fīhi*.

29. See Reynold A. Nicholson, "The Table-talk of Jalāluʾddin Rūmī," *Journal of the Royal Asiatic Society*, 1924; the letters have been translated into Turkish, with an excellent commentary, by Abdülbâki Gölpınarlı, *Mevlâna'nin Mektupları* (Istanbul, 1964).

30. See Hellmut Ritter, "Philologika XI: Maulānā Ǧalāluddīn Rūmī und sein Kreis," *Der Islam* 26 (1942); Ritter, "Neue literatur über Maulanā Calāluddin Rumi und seinen orden," *Oriens* 13–14, no. 1 (1960), a review of recent publications about Rūmī and the Mevlevis. For Rūmī's style see Gustav Richter, *Dschelaladdin Rumi. Eine Stildeutung in drei Vorträgen* (Breslau, 1932); Annemarie Schimmel, *Die Bildersprache Dschelaladdin Rumis* (Walldorf, 1949); on some of his religious ideas see Alessandro Bausani, "Il Pensiero religioso di Maulānā Gialāl ad-Dīn Rūmī," *Oriente moderne* 33 (April 1953).

of his lyrics have not yet been analyzed in detail, but even at first glance they reveal a predilection for comparatively simple patterns. The meters often chosen have a strong hiatus so that the two hemistiches are divided into four parts, sometimes with internal rhyme, thus resulting in something very similar to Turkish folk songs. In many cases one has the feeling that his poems need to be read according to word stress rather than by quantitative meter. Whether they are written in short, light meters or in long, heavy lines, one often feels that they should be sung.

It is small wonder that Rūmī, expressing the inner song of his soul, should have used the imagery of music and dance more frequently than any other poet before him. The most famous example is the introductory poem of the *Mathnawī*, the "Song of the Reed." The reed flute, complaining that it has been cut from the reedbed and longs for home, tells the secrets of divine union and eternal happiness to all who have ears to hear.[31] This simile was not invented by Rūmī. He often relied upon stories and legends handed down from time immemorial, endowing them with new spirit, as he says:

> You may have read it in Kalīla,
> but that was the husk of the story—this is the kernel of the soul.
>
> (M 4:2203)

The reed story was taken over from Sanāʾī (S 484). He spoke of the confidant of a king who became ill because he had been forbidden to tell his ruler's secret to anyone; the physician sent him to a lonely lake, where he gave utterance to his heart's secret, but the reed growing at the shore of the lake was later made into a flute and revealed the secret to the world. This was, originally, the story of "King Midas with the donkey's ears" (and Midas's old residence, Gordion, is not far from Konya). A similar story is also told about ʿAlī, Muhammad's cousin and son-in-law, who revealed the divine secrets that the Prophet had entrusted to him to the lake. This example shows how, in Rūmī's poetry, age-old traditions are blended with the mystic's personal experience.

In a country in which the sound of the Phrygian flute had been

31. Hellmut Ritter, "Das Proömium des Maṯnawī-i Maulawi," *Zeitschrift der Deutschen Morgenländischen Gesellschaft* 93 (1932), is a study of the sources of Rūmī's introductory verses to the *Mathnawī*.

famous since Greek times, he himself, cut off from his beloved, began complaining like a flute, telling the secrets of union and longing. Touched by the breath of the friend, he is able to declare what would otherwise remain secret and hidden, just as the *rabāb* or the harp can only tell its pain when touched by the fingers of the beloved. All of Rūmī's poetry abounds with symbols taken from music and mystical dance; for him, the dance was a life-giving movement, part of the heavenly dance in which the stars and the angels take part.

Attempts have been made to trace much of Rūmī's theology back to Neoplatonic influences, but it is almost as impossible to disentangle the colorful strands of the fabric of his feeling (and, rarely, his thought) as it is to analyze one of the colorful brocades of which he sometimes speaks in his poetry. That there are Neoplatonic themes in the *Mathnawī* cannot be doubted. On the one hand, he was acquainted with Ibn ᶜArabī's teachings through Ṣadruddīn Qōnawī, while on the other, Hellenistic traditions were always alive in the Near East, particularly in the "country of the Romans" (*Rūm*, hence his surname *Rūmī*), Anatolia. Arabic scientists and philosophers had carefully preserved the teachings of the Greeks, and even some of Plato's parables found their way into the *Mathnawī*. Popular tradition in the province of Konya has it that Plato lived for many years in this region and that he was a great sorcerer; close to the lake of Beyshehir south of Konya, a Hittite monument at a fountainhead is called *Eflâtun Pınarı*, "Plato's Spring," for it was here that the great magician transformed the country into its present shape.

Greek and Christian traditions were very much alive in Konya in the thirteenth century. The old centers of Cappadocian Christianity and the large monastic settlement in the caves near Göreme were only a few days' journey from the capital. Thus images alluding to Jesus and Mary occur more frequently in Jalāluddīn's poetry than in any other comparable poetical work, though such allusions are common in Muslim poetry. Rūmī even quotes Biblical passages otherwise rarely mentioned in Islamic poetry. On the whole, however, his work can be explained without difficulty from the Koran and the Prophetic tradition.

Rūmī's imagery, both in the lyrics and in the *Mathnawī*, reflects the complete tradition of his time. There is not a single poetical or rhetorical form that he does not use skillfully, though sometimes he tires of thinking of elegant rhyming words and fills a line with a jubilant *tirilala,* or with the catchwords for the metrical schemes, *mufāʿilun fāʿilātun.* Jalāluddīn was usually in high spirits, uplifting his listeners in order to show them the secrets of love. It would be wrong to imply that the reader wearies of the constant repetitions of high-soaring religious ideas. On the contrary, there are few poets, especially among the mystics, whose repertoire in vocabulary and imagery is as rich as his.

Rūmī often employs the simplest situations of life to catch his reader's interest—"Did you hear? Our neighbor was ill. And what kind of medicine did they apply?" Of course, it is the illness of love, as we discover from a thorough description of the not very heavenly symptoms. There was noise at night? The "vessel fell from the roof" and a lover's secret was revealed (or will be revealed to the neighbors after nine months). And what happened yesterday? The *lūlīs* (Gypsies) came; we all admired their ropedancing and joked with them, "but thine image teaches my soul ropedancing on thy black tresses" (D 886, 1198). The cat in the bag, jumping restlessly up and down, reminds the poet of the way the lover is carried in the hand of love. The hearts and heads of the lovers are piled up in front of the beloved as in the shop of a butcher who specializes in heads and intestines (D 1600). The dream figure of the friend comes into the hot bath of his tears, where the poet's pupil ("the little man of the eye") sits as watchman (D 3037).

There is a certain sense of humor in many of these verses, and Rūmī does not refrain from using extremely coarse expressions to shock, perhaps to awaken, his listeners. He even wrote parodies of traditional modes of expression.

Jalāluddīn describes his longing in dramatic images. He is thirsty like the sand (D 1200); his is the eternal thirst of the lover for more and more love, the thirst of the dunes, which absorb the water as soon as it reaches them. Does the lover ever sleep? No, sleep just looks at him and goes away (D 1444) and sits near someone else; or the poor fellow dies when he tastes the poisonous tears in Rūmī's eyes (D 779); or sleep finds his heart tasteless, is mistreated by the fists of love, and eventually runs away, full of sadness (D 500).

Folk tales, known mainly from the Naṣruddīn Khwāja tradition, are filled with mystical meaning. Obscene scenes, mainly in the fifth book of the *Mathnawī,* turn suddenly into mystical allegory, for "my dirty jokes (*hazal*) are not dirty jokes but instruction" (M

5:2497). At times, the imagery becomes weird, sinister, awkward. The subconscious reminiscence of Shamsuddīn's blood before his door inspired some of the darkest and yet most impressive poems in the *Dīwān*. There are, for instance, the lines, remarkable for their initial alliteration:

> *kūh kun az kalla-hā, baḥr kun az khūn-i mā.*
> Make a mountain from skulls, make an ocean from our blood.
>
> (D 1304)

Or, in a similar context:

> This soil is not dust, it is a vessel full of blood, of the blood of the lovers.
>
> (D 336)

And there are poems in soft meters, full of tenderness:

> Open the veil and close our door—
> You are and I, and empty the house.
>
> (D 2728)

> Without your speech the soul has no ear,
> Without your ear the soul has no tongue.
>
> (D 697)

These verses contain unforgettable images, which, though taken in large part from the traditional stock of Persian poetry, convey a completely different feeling with the change of a single accent or the addition of an adjective.

The masters of early Sufism become, in Rūmī's work as in Sanā'ī's and even more in ʿAṭṭār's, symbols for the different spiritual stages and states. Numerous allusions to Ḥallāj, the martyr of love, permeate both Rūmī's *Dīwān* and the *Mathnawī*. Ḥallāj's verse, "Kill me, o my trustworthy friends," becomes a key word for Rūmī's thought. One of the central motifs in his poetry is that of dying and thus gaining a new life, faithful to the Prophetic tradition, "die before ye die." To prove the truth of this *ḥadīth*, and of Ḥallāj's related poem, Rūmī sometimes combines very strange images. Even the chickpea becomes the symbol of the human situation (M 3: 4158):[32] put in boiling water, the vegetable complains and tries to

32. Annemarie Schimmel, "Zu einigen Versen Dschelāladdīn Rūmīs," *Anatolica* 1 (1967).

jump out of the kettle. But the poet tells it that since it grew by the rain and sunshine of divine grace, it now must learn to suffer in the fire of divine wrath in order to mature. The person who cooks the chickpeas is comparable to Abraham, who was willing to slaughter his beloved son; "the eternal goal is your surrender." Only by such willing surrender can the vegetable reach the stage of animal life and be endowed with spirit and thought.

Not-being is necessary for becoming and being. All the masters seek not-being and breaking, because only then can God work upon them (M 6:1467–74). ʿAṭṭār had already spoken of the necessity of "being eaten," and Rūmī, with his remarkable fondness for images taken from the kitchen, imitated him. Life is a constant movement, and no stage can be reached until the previous stage has been fulfilled. The caravan has to be ready for the sound of the bell that calls it to journey toward new stations (D 1789). And out of the dust grow plants, which in turn are transformed into a higher form of life through annihilation. Rūmī sometimes used the commercial terminology found in the Koran:

> With God is the best bargain: he buys from you your dirty fortune and gives in exchange light of the soul,
> He buys the ice of the perishable body and gives a kingdom beyond imagination.
>
> (M 6:880–81)

Rūmī's description of this upward movement of the soul—usually explained as a poetic version of the Neoplatonic idea of the return of the soul to its divine origin—interested Western scholars from the very beginning of their acquaintance with Rūmī. More than 150 years ago, Rückert translated a passage from the *Mathnawī* (M 3:3901–6) into German, without, however, translating the last, decisive, line:

> I died as mineral and became a plant,
> I died as plant and rose to animal.
> I died as animal and I was Man.
> Why should I fear? When was I less by dying?
> Yet once more I shall die as Man, to soar
> With angels blest; but even from angelhood
> I must pass on: all except God doth perish.
> When I have sacrificed my angel-soul,

I shall become what no mind e'er conceived.
O let me not exist! For Non-existence
Proclaims in organ tones "To him we shall return!"

Nonexistence, *ᶜadam,* is the ineffable divine essence, which has been seen in this way by some of the mystics, and particularly by Rūmī, because it is beyond every possible mode of expression or imagination—it is like the *neti neti* of the Upanishads. A little later in his work, Rūmī took up the same idea (M 4:3637–60), ending, however, by likening the world to a dream and death to morning light—another common image among the Sufis. Even in his lyrics, the development from dust to plant and then to animal is mentioned, sometimes with an emphasis on the humility and poverty of dust. When man becomes as lowly as dust—and only under that condition—plants may grow out of him, and a heart will be given to him. To be broken and low is the condition for development toward higher stages of life.

Islamic modernists have seen in Rūmī's poem "I died as mineral" a perfect expression of Darwin's theories; this interpretation was probably originated by the Indian scholar Maulānā Shiblī in his Urdu biography of Rūmī (1903), which deeply influenced Iqbal's ideas. Some Pakistani scholars have found evidence for the idea of evolution already anticipated in the Middle Ages, a proof of the scientific strength of medieval Muslims (such as Khalīfa ᶜAbdul Ḥakīm);[33] others regard Rūmī's verses as pointing to the free development of the ego, which rises to ever higher levels of consciousness (such as Afzal Iqbal), or as the eternal striving for more and more freedom and individualization (Muhammad Iqbal), or as an expression of the struggle for survival inherent in creation (Abdûlbâki Gölpınarlı). But the quotation of Ḥallāj's verses at the turning point of the chickpea story, where the vegetable calls out,

Kill me, o my trustworthy friends,
for in my being killed is my life,[34]

lends itself to a purely mystical interpretation and seems to exclude a pseudoscientific understanding of such verses. To gain a higher life through death and spiritual resurrection is the goal of the lovers; it is the constant interplay of *fanā* and *baqā,* as expressed even

33. See Khalīfa ᶜAbdul Ḥakīm, *The Metaphysics of Rumi* (Lahore, ca. 1954).
34. Ḥusayn ibn Manṣūr al-Ḥallāj, *Dīwān,* ed. Louis Massignon, *Journal asiatique,* January–July, 1931, qaṣīda 10.

through the ritual of the enrapturing dance. And the mystics know that this first dying implies more and more acts of spiritual surrender, each of which ends on a higher level of spiritual life—the Goethean *"Stirb und Werde."*

The idea of constant development even after death has been maintained by a number of Sufis, as well as by some modern Western philosophers and theologians. In the Muslim world, Muhammad Iqbal gave this idea of constant development a new interpretation in his poetical works, which appeared from 1915 until 1935. This goal can be symbolized in terms of the most diverse aspects of life; the images offered themselves to everybody who had eyes to see.

> Only when man becomes deprived of outward being like winter,
> there is hope for a new spring to develop in him.
> (M 5:552)

William Hastie was quite right to call his adaptations of Rūmī's poetry *Festival of Spring*. The same themes of death and resurrection that are reflected in those verses by Rūmī just mentioned permeate his spring poetry.

Spring has always been a favorite subject for Persian and Turkish poets, but the exuberance of Rūmī's numerous spring poems can be fully appreciated only by those who have experienced how, in a sudden outburst, the vast plain of Konya is covered with green after a spring thunderstorm, which makes the roses blossom and the *iğde* open and fills the air with strong fragrance. This spring is really a *qiyāmat*, a day of resurrection, which calls forth from the dark dust flowers and leaves. Enchanted by the spring breeze of love, the leaves dance and the flowers praise God in their own silent language. Rūmī had heard this praise and taken part in it, translating it into melodious lines; he had seen the loveliness of the heavenly beloved in roses, hyacinths, and running brooks, each of them reflecting it and yet forming a colorful veil for that beauty that is too radiant to be seen unveiled. He knew the fragrance of an Anatolian morning in May; in his verses he alludes often to the scents that are still characteristic of an Anatolian town. He has experienced divine beauty and majesty with all his senses: in the sight of the gardens of Konya, in the sound of the thunder or of the meaningful prayer of the birds, in the soft touch of the silks or the carpets manufactured in Konya, in the fragrance of the *iğde*, as well as in the taste of the delicious food, especially the sweetmeat for which Konya has always been famous. Sensual experiences are reflected strongly in his poetry; one of the reasons why these verses never fade or lose their charm is that the balance between sensual experience and divine love is maintained. Rūmī has transformed even the roughest, most ordinary aspect of life; and the symbol of the transforming power of the sun, which he uses so often in connection with Shamsuddīn, can be applied to his poetic touch as well.

Rūmī's strength came from his love, a love experienced in human terms but completely grounded in God. No one has disclosed the deepest secrets of mystical prayer as he did; he felt that every prayer was in itself an act of divine grace, and he left himself open to this divine grace. United in love with the divine will, he found solutions for the enigma of predestination and was able to rise to the zenith of joy from the deepest depressions of separation. He himself summed up his life in two lines:

> And the result is not more than these three words:
> I burnt, and burnt, and burnt.
>
> (D 1768)

Shortly after Rūmī's death, his works, especially his *Mathnawī*, were known all over the Persian-speaking world, and his fame reached the eastern fringes of the Muslim lands. In East Bengal, in the fifteenth century, its impression was so great that a chronicler said: "The holy Brahmin will recite the *Mathnawī*."[35] The first major contributions to an understanding of his poetry were made in Turkey itself. The Mevlevi order, which had been institutionalized by Sultan Walad and whose ritual was later elaborated, spread Rūmī's word and music through the just-emerging Ottoman Empire; and in later times the head of the Mevlevi order was so closely connected with the Ottoman court that he had the privilege of girding the Sultan with the sword.

The center of the order was always in Konya; the leader was called by the honorific titles Mollâ Hunkâr and Çelebi. Many smaller *tekke*s of the Mevlevis were found all over the Ottoman Empire, as far away as Egypt and Syria, although the order never crossed the Ottoman borders. Nor did Rūmī's poetry become as popular with the Arabic-speaking Sufis as with the Persian-speaking mystics; the imagery used was too different, and even the few Arabic translations

35. Enamul Haq, *Muslim Bengali Literature* (Karachi, 1957), p. 42.

made in classical times did not help much toward a deeper understanding of Rūmī's ideas.

At the occasion of the ceremonial *samā*ᶜ, usually held on Friday at noon after the congregational prayer,[36] the dervishes used to wear their typical dress: a *tennure,* a white sleeveless frock, the *destegül,* a jacket with long sleeves, a belt, and a black *khirqa,* used as an overcoat but cast aside before the ritual dance started. The head was covered by a high felt cap around which a turban cloth might be wound. The cap, *sikke,* became the typical sign of the Mevlevis, and many inscriptions composed of words of prayers or blessings have been written in the shape of the dervish hat.

The *samā*ᶜ is regulated by very strict rules. The sheikh stands in the most honored corner of the dancing place, and the dervishes pass by him three times, each time exchanging greetings, until the circling movement starts. This is to be performed on the right foot, with accelerating speed. If a dervish should become too enraptured, another Sufi, who is in charge of the orderly performance, will gently touch his frock in order to curb his movement. The dance of the dervishes is one of the most impressive features of the mystical life in Islam, and the music accompanying it is of exquisite beauty, beginning with the great hymn in honor of the Prophet (*na*ᶜ*t-i sharīf,* written by Jalāluddīn himself) and ending with short, enthusiastic songs, sometimes sung in Turkish.

The intense love for music that the Mevlevis inherited from their master Jalāluddīn has inspired many classical musicians and composers in the Ottoman Empire. In fact, the best pieces of Turkish classical music, such as those by ᶜIṭrī (seventeenth century), were composed by artists who were either members of, or at least loosely connected with, the order. The same is true of the calligraphers and miniaturists, many of whom belonged to the Mevlevis. The order furnished Turkish society with some of the finest examples of Muslim art ever created.[37]

The Turks were deeply attached to their *Hazret-i Mevlâna,* and Turkish scholars and mystics have contributed a great deal to a better understanding of the *Mathnawī.*[38] In the late sixteenth and early

36. See the literature mentioned in chapter 3, notes 87–94.

37. Şehabettin Uzluk, *Mevlevilikte Resim, Resimde Mevleviler* (Ankara, 1957).

38. Mehmet Önder, *Mevlâna* (Ankara, 1971); Önder, *Mevlâna Şiirleri Antolojisi,* 2d ed. (Konya, Turkey, 1956, 1957). The best introduction to the personality and the survival of Rūmī has been written by the Turkish scholar Abdülbâki Gölpınarlı in his two books *Mevlâna Celâleddin, hayati, felsefesi, eserlerinden seçmeler* (Istanbul,

seventeenth centuries three famous commentaries on the *Mathnawī* were written in Turkey. The one by Ismāʿīl Rüsūḥī Ankarawī (d. 1631) is still considered the best commentary available. A century later, another commentary was written by Ismaʿīl Ḥaqqī Burṣalī, himself a fine mystical poet (d. 1724), and about the same time Süleyman Nahīfī (d. 1738) translated the entire work into Turkish verse, faithfully preserving the meter and the form. This seems to be the first complete translation into a foreign language in which concern for the meter was paramount; in later times we find similar attempts in the Subcontinent, where Urdu, Panjabi, and Sindhi translations have been produced in the same style.[39]

Most of the Turkish poets, from Gulshanī in the fifteenth century on, have paid tribute to Mevlâna. Among the successful artists of the Mevlevi order, the name of Ghālib Dede (d. 1799), the sheikh of the convent in Galata, should be mentioned. He was an excellent poet, perhaps the last true master of classical Turkish poetry, and his verses express the inward fire that enabled the dervishes to spin around their axes and become transported in ecstatic flights. The nineteenth century, too, had poets who sang in honor of Rūmī, and in recent years an amazing number of verses have been written in his honor by members of divergent groups; from very orthodox preachers to leftist politicians, from representatives of surrealistic art to satirists. And if the long list of names that could easily be drawn up were not sufficient to show the love of the Turks for "their" Mevlâna (for they will never admit that he was not a Turk), the thousands of visitors who come to pay their respect at his shrine in Konya and the large crowds that throng there for the festivities in commemoration of his death in December would prove how deeply this love is rooted even forty-five years after Atatürk closed the dervish lodges and strictly prohibited any activity of mystical fraternities.

Rūmī's work was widely read in Iran up to the Safawid period, when the interest in Sufi literature was curbed. A number of commentaries and imitations of the *Mathnawī* have been preserved from

1951; 3d ed., 1959), and *Mevlâna'dan sonra Mevlevilik* (Istanbul, 1953), a history of the order. Gölpınarlı has also translated most of Rūmī's lyrics into Turkish and contributed to the study of rare manuscripts concerning the Mevlevis.

39. Annemarie Schimmel, *Mevlâna Celâlettin Rumi'nin şark ve garpta tesirleri* (Ankara, 1963); Schimmel, "Rumi's Influence on Muslim Literature," in *Güldeste* (Konya, Turkey, 1971), a collection of papers on Rūmī.

the fifteenth century, and Jāmī attests that the early Naqshbandī master Khwāja Pārsā "took omen from the *Dīvān-i Shams-i Tabrīz*" (N 393). The activities of Persian scholars in our day aimed toward producing an authentic text of the *Dīwān*—as it was done by Badīʿuz-Zamān Furūzānfar—is matched only by Reynold A. Nicholson's edition of the *Mathnawī*.[40]

Rūmī's work had its largest influence in the Indo-Pakistan Subcontinent, where his poetry has been popular since the early fourteenth century. The Chishti saints of Delhi, beginning with Niẓāmuddīn Auliyā, studied the *Mathnawī* (for they permitted mystical dance and were, thus, prone to give expression to the enthusiastic spirit of Rūmī's verses). Shams-i Tabrīz became a legendary figure in India and was often counted among the martyrs of love. The interest in Rūmī's work seems to have been common to all classes of society—the Mogul emperors (especially Akbar) were as fond of him as the simple villagers in Sind and Punjab. Aurangzēb shed tears when listening to a beautiful recitation of the *Mathnawī*, as did his brother, the mystically minded Dārā Shikōh. During the time of their father, Shāh Jihān, a number of commentaries on the *Mathnawī* were composed in Muslim India, as well as glossaries, indexes, anthologies, and imitations.[41] Even Aurangzēb's daughter, Zēb un-Nisāʾ, herself a talented poetess, ordered her poet friends to compose a *Mathnawī* imitating Rūmī's work. A glance through Indo-Persian poetry reveals many lines inspired by Rūmī's thoughts and expressions. That is true even in our day; Iqbal was deeply influenced by Maulānā and inserted many of his lines into his own works, mainly into his *mathnawī*s, which he wrote in the same meter as that of his master's *Mathnawī*. It is said that some mystics in Sind—and it may be true for other provinces as well—kept only three books for spiritual nourishment: the Koran, the *Mathnawī*, and the *Dīwān* of Ḥāfiẓ.[42] Quotations from Rūmī permeate the Sindhi verses of the eighteenth-century poet Shāh ʿAbduʾl-Laṭīf, and it would be easy to draw up an inventory of all the verses used in Indo-Pakistani

40. Maulānā Jalāluddīn Rūmī, *Dīwān-i kabīr ya Kulliyāt-i Shams*, ed. Badīʿuz-Zamān Furūzānfar, 10 vols. (Tehran, 1336 sh./1957); see the Bibliography under Furūzānfar for his other studies.

41. See Ethé, "Neupersische Literatur," in *Grundriss*, ed. Geiger and Kuhn, 2:301. A useful analytical index, to mention only one example from the immense production, is Tilmīdh Ḥusayn, *Mirʾāt al-mathnawī* (Hyderabad, Deccan, 1352 h./1933–34).

42. Ghulām Muṣṭafā Qāsimī, "Hāshimīya Library," in *Mihrān jā Mōtī* (Karachi, 1959), p. 309.

literature written in the vernaculars that are inspired by the great mystic's work.

Most of the poets of the Subcontinent—as in Turkey—saw in Rūmī a representative of the pantheistic trend that had colored most Sufi expressions after Ibn ʿArabī's time. He was interpreted as a mouthpiece of Ibn ʿArabī's ideas, and only toward the beginning of the twentieth century were new approaches made toward a better understanding. Muhammad Iqbal, no doubt, understood best the dynamic force behind Rūmī's experiences, though he highlights only one of the numerous aspects of the great lover. But in many respects his interpretation appeals more to the modern mind than many of the traditional interpretations, which try to tie the free-roaming spirit to a theosophical system.[43]

It is good to see that there are still many possibilities for understanding Rūmī's enrapturing poetry in ever fresh ways, and that both oriental and Western scholars are continuing their study of his inexhaustible treasure of poetry.

TURKISH POPULAR MYSTICISM

Jalāluddīn Rūmī's influence had been a living force in the development of Turkish mysticism, literature, and fine arts. But there are other, perhaps even more typical, expressions of the Sufi experience in the area of the late Seljukid and expanding Ottoman Empire.[44]

A folk tale tells how the city of Konya got its name (a name that is, of course, derived from Iconium): "Two saints came from Khurasan, gently flying and spreading their wings until they saw the summits of the two hills that bound the Konya plain. They liked the view, and the one asked the other: *Konalım mı?* 'Shall we dwell there?' And the other replied: *Kon ya!* 'Certainly, alight and dwell!' " This story, with its simple pun, shows that the Anatolian people were well aware that the strongest influence upon the formation of mystical thought came from Khurasan, the eastern part of Iran, a country in which Sufism had always flourished and which

43. Annemarie Schimmel, *Gabriel's Wing: A Study into the Religious Ideas of Sir Muhammad Iqbal* (Leiden, 1963), pp. 353 ff. and bibliography.

44. Speros Vryonis, Jr., *The Decline of Medieval Hellenism in Asia Minor and the Process of Islamization from the Eleventh through the Fifteenth Century* (Berkeley, 1971), deals, among other things, with the Mevleviyya and the other orders and their role in the Islamization of Turkey.

became, in popular geography, almost coterminus with "the eastern and northern lands of Islam." In fact, that area had produced a number of outstanding mystics.

The first great representative of "Turkish" mystical literature is Aḥmad Yasawī (d. 1166), a disciple of Yūsuf Hamadhānī, thus springing from the same spiritual root as the Naqshbandiyya, who were to become so powerful in the Turkish areas of Central Asia and in Southeast Asia. Aḥmad Yasawī's *Ḥikam* are the first known sentences of mystical wisdom written in the Turkic language of the area of Yassi in present Uzbekistan.[45]

Jalāluddīn Rūmī on occasion played with a few Turkish words in his poetry, and his son, Sultan Walad, used Turkish very skillfully in his *Dīwān*. But it was Sultan Walad's contemporary Yūnus Emre in central Anatolia who transformed his Turkish mother tongue into a vehicle for mystical expression; he left Turkey a treasure of his simple, deep-felt, touchingly memorable poems, which are still known today by school children.[46] Those who have had the opportunity of listening to the Turkish composer Adnan Saygun's *Yunus Emre Oratoryusu* will have realized, to their surprise, how traditional dervish melodies and modern musical technique can be blended into an impressive work of art. The most typical and almost haunting passage of the *Oratorio* is that moment when the chorus repeats, as *basso ostinato,* the refrain of one of Yūnus's poems—*aşkın ver, şevkin ver,* "give Thy love, give longing for Thee" (Y 584). The modern composer aptly chose this expression of everlasting love, of never-ending yearning, as a central motif of his composition. Yūnus stands with these words in the tradition of classical Sufism.

Not much is known about Yūnus Emre's life. He seems to have grown up in the circles of Turkish Sufis that had slowly emerged after the Seljukid conquest of eastern and central Anatolia (i.e., after 1071). These Sufi groups partly continued the tradition of Aḥmad Yasawī and were also probably inspired by those mystics who left eastern Iran on the arrival of the Mongols in the early thirteenth century. Yūnus was, as he says, a disciple of a mystic called Tapduq Emre for forty years (the number of perseverance).

45. Mehmet Fuat Köprülü, *Türk edebiyatında ilk mutesavvıflar,* 2d ed. (Ankara, 1966).

46. Yūnus Emre, *Divan,* ed. Abdülbâki Gölpınarlı (Istanbul, 1948); see also Yūnus Emre, *Risalat an-nushiyye ve Divan,* ed. Abdülbâki Gölpınarlı (Istanbul, 1965). Gölpınarlı, *Yunus Emre, Hayatı* (Istanbul, 1936); Sofi Huri, "Yunus Emre: In Memoriam," *Moslem World* 49, no. 2 (1959); Annemarie Schimmel, "Yunus Emre," *Numen* 8, no. 1 (1961); Yves Regnier, *Le "dīvān" de Yunus Emre* (Paris, 1963).

Those called *Emre* probably formed a subgroup of mystics in Anatolia, where the system of loosely affiliating oneself with a spiritual guide was apparently still in use; the major orders had not yet developed a "missionary" activity. The mystical poet wandered through the country—he may even have met Rūmī during the latter's last years. According to the most recent research, he died in 1321 at the age of 72; numerous places in Turkey claim to house his real tomb.

Just as his tomb will probably never be certainly identified, it is almost impossible to select those poems that are really his. The different editions of his *Dīwān* brought out by the indefatigable Turkish scholar Abdülbâki Gölpınarlı show the learned author's increasing skepticism as to the authenticity of Yūnus's poems. At present it seems impossible to establish a reliable text—a fact that holds true for many other popular Turkish poets. Their collections have been augmented by additions from later poets, and many of them reflect rather a whole tradition—that of poems sung in the *tekke*s, the centers of Sufi life—than the original work of a single poet. The genre of *ilâhî*, a mystical poem in popular meter meant to be sung in the meetings of the dervishes, is the typical expression of this tradition.

It is a comfortable working hypothesis to accept as Yūnus Emre's the poems collected by Gölpınarlı in his 1943 edition, though many of them are now considered spurious. Yet, they reveal who Yūnus might have been and how he might have felt. Numerous other poets could not help writing in exactly the same strain of thought, with the same images and puns.

Yūnus Emre often used the classical quantitative Persian meters in his poetry, preferring the easiest ones; Rūmī, too, had often chosen meters in which each hemistich can be split by a caesura into two parts to produce the so-called *musammaṭ* form. Using this device, both Rūmī and Yūnus get close to the simple forms of Turkish folk songs, with their four-line verses rhyming in *a a a a, b b b a.* Yūnus skillfully applied the classical meters to his own simple mother tongue, but his best poems are written in Turkish popular meters, in which syllable counting is the essential requirement (e.g., 8+7, 8+8, 6+6 syllables).

Yūnus was a master of description; his images were inspired not only by the stock of tradition but by the daily life of Anatolia as well. One has to know the endless roads through the Anatolian highlands to really enjoy the freshness of Yūnus's verses. Like many mystics before him and even more after him, he talks to the water-wheel, whose wailing sound, so typical of Near Eastern countries, makes him understand that it is cut off from its roots and relates the pangs of separation from its forest as eloquently as Rūmī's reed flute tells of its longing for its reedbed home. The stone-breasted mountain ranges are Yūnus's personal enemies, since they try to separate him from his beloved master; but the cloud, hanging like black tresses from the head of the snow-covered hills, loosens her hair and weeps for him (Y 252). His heart turns to a torrent, and his whole body is reduced to dust in the summer heat, moved by the wind of love, which carries it to an unknown destination. "Look, what love has made of me!" is the refrain of one of his most popular poems (Y 124).

Yūnus faithfully follows the patterns set by classical Sufism. Meditating upon death and the Last Judgment, he describes the horror of the day when man "has to wear a shirt without collar and sleeves" and the "negro," i.e., the questioning angel, interrogates him (Y 133). His faith is firmly grounded in the Koran:

> Whoever does not know the Koran
> is as if he were never born.
>
> (Y 508)

The five ritual prayers are fundamental, but almost as important as ritual prayer is the *dhikr* that is uttered by all nature. Yūnus is one of those mystics who listen to and join in the constant *dhikr* of everything created:

> With the mountains, with the stones
> Will I call Thee, Lord, o Lord!
> With the birds in early dawn
> Will I call Thee, Lord, o Lord!
>
> With the fishes in the sea,
> With gazelles in deserts free,
> With the mystics' call "O He!"
> Will I call Thee, Lord, o Lord!
>
> (Y 552)

The profession of faith, used as *dhikr* formula, is

honey for those who are bees,
a rose for those who are nightingales.

(Y 534)

As shown with great insight by John R. Walsh,[47] a number of Yūnus's poems, repeating *al-ḥamdulillāh*, "praise be to God," or other pious sentences at the end of each verse, were probably meant to be recited as *dhikr* formulae in the dervish communities. Yūnus's most subtle poem, which sings of the constant remembrance of God in Paradise, is still memorized in Turkish schools:

Şol cinnetin ırmakları . . .

The rivers all in Paradise
Flow with the word Allah, Allah,
And ev'ry longing nightingale
He sings and sings Allah, Allah.

(Y 477)

Everything in Paradise, be it voice, scent, breeze, or growing and loving, is nothing else than "Allah," since everything is lost in Him. This is the paradise of the mystic who does not care for a house and a few houris who are thousands of years old: the vision of the divine beloved is Paradise, and those who are deprived of this vision experience Hell in every place.

Like his fellow mystics, Yūnus was an ardent lover of the Prophet Muhammad, and when modern Turkish interpreters of his poetry tend to regard him as a representative of unorthodox "Turkish national piety," they forget how deeply rooted in the Muslim tradition is his mystical approach. The Prophet is the intercessor, the goal of creation; his name is beautiful, as is he himself:

Every bee that enters the beehive
speaks a thousand and one blessings over Muhammad.

(Y 524)

Yūnus's poetry reflects the different stages of the mystic—asceticism, loneliness in this world, and uncertainty, until he is safe and at peace in the company of his sheikh: "Yūnus was a falcon, perched on Tapduq's arm" (Y 179). He firmly believes in the power of the men of God (*erenler*), but he also knows that even the sheikh can

47. John R. Walsh, "Yunus Emre: A Medieval Hymnodist," *Numen* 7, nos. 2–3 (1960).

only prepare man for union, which depends solely upon grace (cf. Y 516).

Like other Sufi poets, Yūnus once rebelled in a long poem (Y 353) against the eschatological descriptions contained in the Koran and expanded by later theologians and writers. He began:

> O God, should you once ask me [on the Day of Judgment],
> then I will tell you this: . . .

He then goes on to ridicule the idea of the eschatological bridge: Why should it be only a hair's breadth when men are accustomed to building bridges wide enough to cross without endangering life? Why should God put up scales for weighing the sordid sins of man? He discusses the various aspects of Doomsday until he finally resigns himself to the inscrutable will of God and asks forgiveness. This subject has been repeated by a number of Turkish mystical poets; Kaygusuz Abdāl in the fifteenth century invites God Himself to pass over such a useless bridge, and the Bektashi poet ʿAzmī in the late sixteenth century asks the Lord:

> What have you to do with this hellfire?
> Are you the owner of a hot bath, or are you a *külhanbeyi?* [i.e., one who sits in the ashes of the bath house to keep himself warm; hence, a destitute person].[48]

Such teasing of God is an exception with Yūnus, but is not rare in later Bektashi poetry.

Yūnus Emre's verses, particularly those in classical meters, often reflect the all-embracing "cosmic consciousness." The same poet who cried in fear of Hell and trembled under the burden of his sins feels that this world and the next are filled with the grandeur of God and, at the same time, that the beloved is hidden in his own innermost heart. This may lead him to identify his heart and the All and make him sing in jubilant verses:

> I am the First and the Last . .
> I am he who gave Noah the flood . .
> I am the Seer, I am the Taker and the Giver.

Or he may identify himself with all the prophets, with all the lovers and those who suffered for their love, like Jonah or Manṣūr Ḥallāj.

48. Vasfı Mahir Kocatürk, *Tekke Şiiri Antolojisi* (Ankara, 1955), p. 219.

These poems are in form and content almost identical with later Sufi poetry written in the several languages of the Indian Subcontinent.

One of Yūnus's poems has attracted the interest of both Turkish mystics and Western historians of literature. It is a so-called *tekerleme,* a genre typical of Turkish folk poetry, comparable to nonsense verses and nursery rhymes in European languages (Y 131). This poem begins with the lines:

> I climbed upon the plum tree,
> To pluck grapes there—
> The master of the garden asked me:
> Why do you eat my walnut?

And a later line, "The fish climbed upon the poplar tree to eat there pickled pitch," has become proverbial: "When the fish climbs on the poplar tree" means "never," or "when the pig flies"—the same expression is, incidentally, also found in the mystical poetry of Kabīr in India.[49]

Yūnus's *tekerleme,* which is by no means unique in Turkish mystical poetry, has been commented upon by many Turkish mystics. The commentary of Niyāzī Miṣrī (d. 1697), himself a fine poet and advanced spiritual leader, gives a good introduction to the traditional method of interpretation:[50]

> With this verse the poet wants to show that every tree of deeds has a special kind of fruit. Just as in the external world every fruit has a tree of its own, thus every deed has an instrument of its own by which it can be reached: thus, for example, the instruments for acquiring external sciences are language, grammar, syntax, logic, literature, scholastics, rhetoric, jurisprudence, the study of Prophetic traditions and of the commentaries of the Koran, philosophy and astronomy. To acquire the internal sciences, however, the instruments are permanent sincere submission and constant recollection of God and the "inner leader," little food, little speech, little sleep, keeping away from human beings. And to attain Reality, the instrument is the renunciation of the world, renunciation of the otherworld, and the renunciation of existence.
>
> Now, the most venerable master hints with "prune," "grape," and "nut" at the Divine law, *sharīᶜa,* the mystical Path, *ṭarīqa,* and Divine Reality, *ḥaqīqa.* For one eats the outer parts of the prune, but not its interior. Whatever is like the prune, corresponds to the outward side of actions.
>
> As for the grape, it is eaten, and many delicious things are made of it:

49. Charlotte Vaudeville, *Kabir Granthvali (Doha)* (Pondicherry, 1957), no. 12.

50. Ḥamza Ṭāhir, "At-taṣawwuf ash-shaᶜbī fiʾl-adab at-turkī," *Majalla Kulliyat al-ādāb* 12, no. 2 (Cairo, 1950).

sausage, thick juice, pickles, vinegar and similar edibles and many other good things. But since still a few kernels of hypocrisy, fame, vanity, and ostentation exist in it, it is called "interior acts," but not "Reality."
The nut, now, is completely a symbol of Reality. In the interior of the nut there is nothing that must be thrown away. Its interior is completely edible, and for how many illnesses is it a remedy!
The master of the garden is the perfect mystical leader. One can discern the different fruits only with his help and eventually reach reality . . . .

This interpretation may or may not be correct, but it shows how commentators in later centuries discovered the tenets of mystical truth even in a *tekerleme*.

Turkish mystics were apparently fond of such simple poems, and here mention must be made of Kaygusuz Abdāl, a Bektashi mystic who lived in the fifteenth century, probably in the European provinces of the Ottoman Empire. He is said to have settled in Cairo to found a Bektashi convent; according to tradition, his tomb is on the Muqattam Hill, where many saints of Cairo are buried.[51] Kaygusuz may have been one of the *abdālān-i Rūm*, dervishes who wandered through the Ottoman Empire covered with animal skins and wearing a silver earring. A model case of this kind of dervish was a certain Barak Baba in the fourteenth century, who went around shouting like a bear and dancing like a monkey, according to the sources. The *abdālān-i Rūm* were also notorious for their use of opium. One finds reminiscences of these groups in the paintings ascribed to the fifteenth-century painter known as Siyāh Kalam, which show strange, wild people who form almost perfect illustrations for the poetry of Kaygusuz.[52]

Kaygusuz's poetry is among the strangest expressions of Sufism. He does not hesitate to describe in great detail his dreams of good food—God is asked to grant him hundreds of plates, filled with halvah, roast lamb's leg, all kinds of soups, vegetables, and even roast pork! Nor does he shrink from singing about his love adventures with a charming young man, who tries to get rid of this crude dervish with his old fur cap and his stick, this nuisance who

51. *Kayğusuz Abdal, Hatayî, Kul Himmet* (Istanbul, 1953); Annemarie Schimmel, "Drei türkische Mystiker: Yunus Emre, Kayğusuz Abdal, Pir Sultan Abdal," *Mitteilungen der Deutsch-Türkischen Gesellschaft,* no. 48 (1962). See also the German verse translations of all the mystics mentioned, and others as well, in Annemarie Schimmel, *Aus dem goldenen Becher. Türkische Poesie vom 13. bis 20. Jahrhundert* (Istanbul, 1973).

52. About this artist see Emel Esin, "The Turkish Bakši and the Painter Muhammad Siyāh Kalam," *Acta Orientalia* 32 (1970). A number of studies of Siyāh Kalam have been published both in Turkey and in the West in the last fifteen years.

wants to kiss his peachlike face and his honey lips—a lively parody of the numberless love lyrics praising the attractive youth as a manifestation of divine beauty. Most amusing is Kaygusuz's poem on the goose that he tries to cook with the help of the Seven and the Nine (groups of the mystical hierarchy): "I cooked it forty days, and yet it was not done," and even the bulghur that he throws into the broth says "Allah" and flies away, while the goose lifts its head from the pan and grins. This stubborn, die-hard animal is probably the lower soul, which the poet found difficult to tame.

A *tekerleme* by Kaygusuz sounds like a perfect translation of a nursery rhyme:

kaplu kaplu bağalar kanatlanmiş uçmağa

The turturturtles have taken wings to fly

It is difficult to decide whether verses like this contain some deeper mystical wisdom or whether they belong to a secret language known to exist in certain dervish circles. Hellmut Ritter has discovered a Turkish vocabulary in which kitchen expressions are equated with mystical terms—"martyr son of a martyr" is lamb, *biryanı*, the "Highest Judge" is *halvah*, etc.[53] These verses may also express a simple joy in nonsensical poetry, which is, in a way, closer to the mystical reality than other poetical forms, the paradox being the most legitimate form of guiding the seeker toward the goal. Such poems may as easily be interpreted as results of "trips," and this possibility, at least in the case of Kaygusuz Abdāl, cannot be excluded, since the word *kayğusuz*, "*sans souci*," has been used as a secret name for hashish, as Gölpınarlı has shown. The use of drugs was—and still is—quite common in the lower levels of some mystical fraternities, particularly among the musicians.

One may ask how the poetry of Yūnus and Kaygusuz can be explained in the framework of Sufism. One feels in their—and in many of their fellow mystics'—poetry "that there is vast unleashed power," as an art historian has so poignantly described Turkish art.[54] Only a few of these poems are the products of learning and school wisdom; many of them are "inspired" in one way or the other. Even in contemporary Turkey similar cases of inspiration

53. Hellmut Ritter, "Philologika IX: Die vier Suhrawardī," *Der Islam* 25 (1938); the manuscript is Aya Sofia 2052, fol. 53b.

54. Stuart Cary Welsh, "Islamic Art in the Metropolitan Museum," *Metropolitan Museum Bulletin*, 1972, p. 291.

can be observed. The case of *Yeni Yunus Emre*, the "New Yūnus Emre," seems to shed some light on this phenomenon. Ismail Emre (d. 1973) is a blacksmith from Adana who can read no more than a few words.[55] Since 1940 he has produced a large number of mystical songs in traditional forms, which he recites in a state of trance. During the so-called "birth" (*doğuş*) of two of these songs in an unheated car between Ankara and Konya in December 1958, when the temperature outside was about 25 degrees Fahrenheit (—3 degrees centigrade), the inner heat of the singing mystic warmed up the car to such an extent that the windows became fogged and those of us traveling with him felt no discomfort from the cold throughout the last hour of our journey. Cases of automatic writing are known from different levels of Turkish society; the contents vary according to the intellectual level of the recipients, who, however, proved capable of jotting down verses in languages not even known to them (like Persian).[56]

It is typical of the development in Turkey that after the closing of the dervish orders in 1925, the former mystical tradition, at least on the higher strata of society, sometimes merged into spiritualism and was cultivated in spiritualist seances.

One should also not overlook another unexpected development of Turkish popular mysticism. Gershom Scholem has shown that the outwardly Islamized Jewish converts, the *dönme* (the followers of Sabbatay Zwi in the seventeenth century), had close connections with mystical groups and used Sufi poetry in their meetings.[57]

Yūnus Emre and Kaygusuz Abdāl are among the foremost masters of Bektashi poetry as it developed in Anatolia from the fourteenth century. And a treatise attributed to Kaygusuz Abdāl is one of the major religious books of this order. Bektashi poetry has maintained, in most cases, the popular syllable-counting meters. Some of the touching and appealing verses in this tradition are remarkable for their comparatively fresh imagery, though they show a somewhat "peasantish" crudity, which now and then contrasts not unfavorably with the overrefined classical Turkish court poetry.

55. Ismail Emre, *Yeni Yunus Emre ve Doğuşları* (Istanbul, 1951); Ismail Emre, *Doğuşlar* 2 (Adana, 1965).

56. Two examples are Turgut Akkaş, *Özkaynak* (Ankara, 1957), a collection of "inspired" poems, some of which had been published previously in his journal *Içvarlık*; and Ömer Fevzi Mardin, *Varidat-i Süleyman şerhi* (Istanbul, 1951), a commentary by a noted modern mystic on the "inspired" poems of a Turkish civil servant.

57. See Gershom Scholem, "Die krypto-jüdische Sekte der Dönme (Sabbatianer) in der Türkei," *Numen* 7, no. 1 (1960).

Muhammad, ʿAlī, and the twelve Imams of Shia Islam figure prominently in this literature, as in the whole fabric of Bektashi thought, in which Allah, Muhammad, and ʿAlī even constitute a sort of trinity. The Bektashis have always maintained strong relations with the Imamiya-Shia in Iran. The founder of the Safawid rule in Iran, and thus the archenemy of the Ottomans, Shah Ismail (d. 1524), is even regarded by the Bektashis as one of their own leading poets. He wrote in Turkish (at a time when the Ottoman sultan Selim Yavuz wrote in Persian!), and the poetry that he composed under the pen name Khaṭāʾī is in fact very much in tune with traditional Bektashi verses.[58]

One of the few major poets in this line was Pīr Sulṭān Abdāl, who was executed in Sivas about 1560 because of alleged treasonous relations with the Persian Safawids.[59] Pīr Sulṭān's imagery was inspired by the austere landscape of the eastern Anatolian highlands: the lover suffers in separation like the ewe that has lost her lamb; he talks to the cranes that fly over the hills; the yellow mountain flower in its modesty and patience resembles a perfect dervish. Like so many Bektashi poets, Pīr Sulṭān stands in the tradition of the martyr-mystic Ḥallāj. In one poem he alludes to the rose that made Ḥallāj sigh when his friend Shiblī flung it at him, while the common people were throwing stones at him. Pīr Sulṭān, imprisoned by the Ottoman authorities, must have felt that the faithlessness of his former friends hurt more than the enemies' attacks. His few poems are outstanding models of Bektashi poetry at its best, a poetry the results of which are often difficult to classify or even attribute to this or that poet, since the imagery soon became as standardized as the imagery of traditional court or learned poetry, the verse forms allowing even less variation than the "classical" tradition did.

What kind of Sufis were these Bektashis, who inspired a long line of popular Turkish poets, who were politically influential because of their long-standing relations with the Janissaries, and who are still remembered for their jokes, which indicate their apparently rather antinomian way of life?[60]

The alleged founder of the order, Ḥājjī Bektāsh, is said to have

58. Sadettin Nüzhet Ergun, *Bektaşi Edebiyatı Antolojisi* (Istanbul, 1944), gives a good survey of the most famous poems.

59. *Pir Sultan Abdal* (Istanbul, 1953).

60. John K. Birge, *The Bektashi Order of Dervishes* (1937; reprint ed., London, 1965), is the best study of this order, which was first studied in Europe by Georg Jacob, in his *Beiträge zur Kenntnis des Derwisch-Ordens der Bektaschis* (Berlin, 1908).

come to Anatolia in the thirteenth century from Khurasan. The date of his birth is given—typical of Bektashi thought—by the numerical value of the word *murawwat*, "virtue," which is 648/1247, and his death is dated, by a similar device, in 738/1338. The traditions about his activities vary: the *vilāyetnāme*s, books on saintliness that favor miraculous evidence, speak of some of the miracles he performed. The order, or fraternity, that crystallized around his personality soon established relations with the military corps of the Janissaries. From the fifteenth century on, Bektashi leaders (*bābā*) lived close to the Janissary barracks to give spiritual guidance to the soldiers. Thus they were, logically, involved in the fall of the Janissaries in 1826, when this corps was uprooted because of its increasingly destructive role in Ottoman society.

The order claims as its second master a certain Bālim Sultan, who was born about 1500 in Rumeli. The European part of the Ottoman Empire was then apparently hospitable to Bektashi influences, and the order is still very much alive today in Albania, where it was introduced prior to the seventeenth century.[61]

It seems that the Bektashiyya became a receptacle for all kinds of non-Sunnite currents, though the Khurasanian spiritual chain of Ḥājjī Bektāsh would have required a strict Sunnite ideology. However, not only did "normal" Shia ideas strongly permeate the *ṭarīqa* and grow there into strange forms that are sometimes reminiscent of popular developments of the Ismailiyya in India, but one of the strangest offsprings of Shia thought, the Ḥurūfīs, had an influence on the Bektashis. Faḍlullāh of Asterabad in Khurasan had received a revelation according to which God was revealed in the word and developed theories of kabbalistic speculations about the letters, their values and their interior meaning (see Appendix 1). The greatest Ḥurūfī poet, Nesīmī (who was flayed alive in Aleppo in 1417), has left a deep imprint upon Turkish poetry, with his glowing and passionate mystical hymns. The Ḥurūfī influence is visible

61. Hans Joachim Kissling, "Zur Frage der Anfänge des Bektaschitums in Albanien," *Oriens* 15 (1962); Kissling, "Zum islamischen Heiligenwesen auf dem Balkan," *Zeitschrift für Balkanologie*, 1963. Kissling and his students have contributed many articles and books toward a better understanding of Turkish dervish orders. It is worth noting that the influence of Sufism in the Balkans has even led to the development of Serbo-Croatian mystical folk songs, as Hamid Algar has recently shown in his fine article, "Some Notes on the Naqshbandi Ṭarīqat in Bosnia," *Die Welt des Islam*, n.s. 13, nos, 3–4 (1971). See also B. G. Martin, "A Short History of the Khalwati Order of Dervishes," in *Scholars, Saints, and Sufis: Muslim Religious Institutions since 1500*, ed. Nikki R. Keddie (Berkeley, 1972).

in the pictures that sometimes adorned Bektashi convents: the faces of ʿAli, Ḥasan, and Ḥusayn, or of others, are drawn by combining the letters of their names.

In addition to the Shia trend, which is one of the peculiarities of the Bektashi order, Christian influences have been seen in the ritual (which would not be astonishing, in view of the strong Christian substratum in Anatolia). There are, in fact, certain similarities, like penitence or the sacramental meal of bread and wine, but one should not press these similarities too far. The communal meal is much older than the Christian sacrament. In modern, nationalistic Turkish research, a certain "shamanist" aspect of Bektashism has been emphasized; this would connect the order with old Turkish, Central Asian forms of mystical life.

Many trends known from other mystical fraternities can be found in the Bektashiyya as well. The Bektashis speak of the four gateways: divine law, *sharīʿa,* whose adherent is the *ʿābid,* "worshiper"; the mystical path, *ṭarīqa,* traveled by the *zāhid,* "ascetic"; the *maʿrifa,* "gnosis," held by the *ʿārif,* "gnostic"; and the *ḥaqīqa,* "reality,' which the *muḥibb,* "lover," reaches. Each of these four gateways is founded upon ten obligations (very much like those taught in other orders), and the sacred number of forty is attained once more. The head of the order is the *dede,* "grandfather," in the village of Hacci Bektaş, where a second leader, the Çelebi, used to reside as well. The next position is that of the *bābā,* who is in charge of teaching and of the pastoral work; *bābā*s were located all over the Ottoman Empire. The intermediate station is that of the dervish who, like the *bābā,* may be married or lead a celibate life, and the regular initiated member is called *muḥibb,* "lover."

The initiation ceremony is replete with symbolic acts, among which the "hanging" of the initiate on the *dār-i Manṣūr,* "the gallows of Manṣūr Ḥallāj," plays a special role. Many *ʿāshiq,* "ardent lovers," are affiliated with the order as lay members; they have not taken their "part" (*nasīb*) in the initiation but are bound by loyalty to the order. Certain peculiar prayer formulae are used, such as the *gulbāng* and the *tercemān,* which contain Turkish prayers. Muharram and New Year are celebrated in good Shia and Persian form. On ʿAshūrā Day, the day of Ḥusayn's martyrdom in Kerbela, a special dish called *ʿāşūre* is cooked; this reminds the pious of the last meal of the martyrs of Kerbela, which were prepared from leftovers. Even today many Turkish families—most of them non-

Bektashis—prepare this sweetish, delicious dish on the tenth of Muharram.

One of the outstanding features of the Bektashi order—unique in Islam—is that women are treated as equals; they participate in all ceremonies and freely converse with the men. This aspect of the order has, of course, given rise to monstrous stories about the moral, or rather immoral, life of the Bektashis—stories that are, in most cases, greatly exaggerated. The fact that the Bektashis kept their doctrines as secret as possible, especially after the extinction of the Janissaries, has excited the imaginations of orthodox defenders of the pure faith, as is the case with most secret societies.

In their theoretical approach, the Bektashis have added nothing to the teachings of the Ibn ʿArabī school. They believe in the forty degrees of descent and ascent, culminating in the Perfect Man. In some of their best-known and most frequently recited poems (*devriye*), they have tried to describe their participation in the ascending circles of existence, which leads their poets to claim that they are one with the great masters of all religions.

The problem of Bektashi practices was laid before the Turkish intellectuals in 1922, when Yakup Kadri Karaosmanoğlu published his novel *Nur Baba*. The well-known Turkish diplomat and novelist described in piquant details how a society lady from Istanbul became involved in the order through an attractive young Bektashi *Pīr*, Nur Baba, "Father Light." Karaosmanoğlu gave a good, though highly satirical, introduction to some of its rituals, for instance, the *ayın-i cem*, the initiation ceremony. One may assume that *Nur Baba* was, at least to a certain extent, instrumental in convincing Kemal Atatürk of the necessity of abolishing the dervish orders. However, one should not read *Nur Baba* without complementing it with Yakup Kadri's small book *Erenlerin Bağından*, "From the Garden of the Wise," which contains twelve meditations in simple, but highly refined and musical language, and which makes the reader understand at least a few values of mystical life.[62]

Erenlerin Bağından reminds one of the works of the great masters of Turkish mystical poetry who, throughout the centuries, tried to console the people with their delicate, warm verses. Many of them did not belong to the Bektashi order, but to other fraternities that

62. German translation of *Nur Baba* by Annemarie Schimmel, *Flamme und Falter* (Gummersbach, 1948); Schimmel, "Aus dem Garten der Weisen," in *Das Geisterhaus*, ed. Otto Spies (Kevelaer, 1949).

had developed on Turkish soil in the course of time, growing, splitting up into suborders, and covering the country in a widespread network of centers of spirituality. We may think of Eshrefoğlu Rūmī, a Qādirī mystic who lived in Iznik in the fifteenth century and whose poems have often been sung in dervish communities—simple verses, filled with allusions to mystical wine and eternal love and always keeping the figure of Manṣūr Ḥallāj before the eyes of his followers. Even though the following lines from his *Dīwān* were probably written not by himself but by one of his later admirers, they are charming examples of Turkish dervish diction, alluding to the custom of opening a sacred book for fortune-telling:

> They had told me: "Do not read the book of love!"
> "Look for an omen," I said—and this very page opened again!
> I ordered the tailor to make an ascetic's garment for me—
> He did not keep to my word, and again a lover's dress was cut.[63]

Niyāzī Miṣrī has already been mentioned as the commentator of Yūnus Emre's enigmatic poem. A leading member of the influential Khalvetiyya order, he was a remarkable poet in his own right, reflecting in subtle verses the search of the soul and the peace that he finally found after leaving himself and surrendering completely to the beloved:

> I thought that in the world no friend was left for me—
> I left myself, and lo, no fiend was left for me.[64]

Even the Turkish rulers, defenders of orthodox Sunni Islam, were sometimes inclined to mystical thought. The role of Aq Shamsuddīn in the life of Mehmet the Conqueror is well known; and the frequently quoted poem of Sultan Murād III (d. 1595), who wants "to awake from the sleep of heedlessness," shows the extent to which Sufi terminology had been absorbed into the language even of the highest circles, in spite of the strained relations between the orthodox and the dervish orders that, from the time of Mehmet the Conqueror, frequently resulted in friction and even political

63. William Hickman, "Eshrefoghlu Rumi: Reconstitution of His *dīwān*" (Ph.D. diss., Harvard University, 1972), no. H 20*.

64. Niyāzī Miṣrī, *Dīvān* (Istanbul, 1955).

upheaval.[65] The large masses remained under the influence of the orders and found consolation in the simple songs and sermons of the dervishes, and in verses like that of Ibrāhīm Ḥaqqı Erzerumlu, the eighteenth-century Sufi writer:

Görelim Hak ne eyler,
N'eylerse güzel eyler.

Let us see what God will do—
Good is ev'rything He'll do.

This kind of unquestioning trust in God taught by the Sufis has to a great extent shaped the faith of the population in the dazzling capital of Istanbul and even more in the half-forgotten villages of Anatolia. It has given them strength to endure the hardships of life.[66]

In the course of time, however, the institutions found themselves unable to respond to the need for modernization and changed outlook. Instead of fulfilling their centuries-old function as centers of spiritual education, they became headquarters of obscurantism and backwardness. That is why Atatürk abolished the orders in 1925—a step that some of the leading personalities in the mystical hierarchy even approved of. They felt that the spiritual values of Sufism as taught by the poets of Anatolia would survive without the ruined framework of the orders—perhaps even in a more genuine way. And these values are, indeed, still alive.

65. Franz Babinger, "Schejch Bedr ad-din, der Sohn der Richters von Simawna," *Der Islam* 2 (1912); Hans Joachim Kissling, "Das Menaqybname Scheich Bedr ad-Dins," *Zeitschrift der Deutschen Morgenländischen Gesellschaft* 101 (1950).

66. A pleasant introduction is Nezihe Araz, *Anadolu Evliyaları* (Istanbul, 1958); for other aspects of Turkish popular mysticism see Annemarie Schimmel, "Das Gelübde im türkischen Volksglauben," *Die Welt des Islam*, n.s. 6, nos. 1–2 (1959).

8. SUFISM IN INDO-PAKISTAN

THE CLASSICAL PERIOD

The western provinces of the Indo-Pakistan Subcontinent had become part of the Muslim Empire in 711, the year in which the Arabs conquered Sind and the adjacent provinces northward up to Multan.[1] The Muslim pious in these areas were, in the early centuries, apparently interested mainly in the collection of *ḥadīth* and in the transmission to the central Muslim countries of scientific information from India (mathematics, the "Arabic" numbers, astronomy and astrology, medicine), but their religious feel-

1. General surveys of the cultural life of Muslim India contain much information about mystical trends. See, for example, Ishtiaq Husain Qureshi, *The Muslim Community of the Indo-Pakistan Subcontinent* (The Hague, 1962), from a strict Pakistani viewpoint; Mohammed Mujeeb, *The Indian Muslims* (Montreal and London, 1969), from an Indian standpoint; Aziz Ahmad, *Studies in Islamic Culture in the Indian Environment* (Oxford, 1964); Aziz Ahmad, *An Intellectual History of Islam in India* (Edinburgh, 1969); Yusuf Husain, *L'Inde mystique au moyen âge* (Paris, 1929); Yusuf Husain, *Glimpses of Medieval Indian Culture,* 2d ed. (London, 1959). An extensive bibliography is D. N. Marshall, *Mughals in India: A Bibliography* (Bombay, 1967). Zubaid Ahmad, *The Contribution of Indo-Pakistan to Arabic Literature,* 2d. ed. (Lahore, 1968), contains many mystical works; Alessandro Bausani, *Storia delle letterature del Pakistan* (Milan, 1958), gives a good survey of high and popular literatures; Annemarie Schimmel, "The Influence of Sufism on Indo-Muslim Poetry," in *Anagogic Qualities of Literature,* ed. Joseph P. Strelka (University Park, Pa., 1971).

ings may sometimes have reached the heights of mystical experience. Spiritual contacts between the Muslims and the small Buddhist minority, as well as with the large group of Hindus (who were slightly outside the main current of orthodox Hinduism), may have existed, though earlier European theories that tried to explain Sufism as an Islamized form of Vedanta philosophy or of Yoga have now been discarded. In 905, a mystic like Ḥallāj traveled extensively throughout Sind and probably discussed theological problems with the sages of this country.[2]

The second wave of Muslim conquest in India, that of the Ghaznawids about the year 1000, brought into the Subcontinent not only scholars like al-Bīrūnī (d. 1048), who made a careful study of Hindu philosophy and life, but theologians and poets as well. Lahore became the first center of Persian-inspired Muslim culture in the Subcontinent—the name of Hujwīrī, who composed his famous Persian treatise on Sufism in this town, has already been mentioned; his tomb still provides a place of pilgrimage for the Panjabis.

The full impact of Sufism, however, began to be felt in the late twelfth and early thirteenth centuries, after the consolidation of the main Sufi orders in the central provinces of Islam. The most outstanding representative of this movement is Muʿīnuddīn Chishtī, born in Sistan and part-time disciple of Abū Najīb Suhrawardī. He reached Delhi in 1193,[3] then settled in Ajmer, when the Delhi kings conquered this important city in the heart of Rajputana. His dwelling place soon became a nucleus for the Islamization of the central and southern parts of India. The Chishtī order spread rapidly, and conversions in India during that period were due mainly to the untiring activity of the Chishtī saints, whose simple and unsophisticated preaching and practice of love of God and one's neighbor impressed many Hindus, particularly those from the lower castes, and even members of the scheduled castes. The fact that the Chishtī *khānqāh*s avoided any discrimination between the disciples and practiced a classless society attracted many people into their fold. Muʿīnuddīn reduced his teaching to three principles, which had been formulated first by Bāyezīd Bisṭāmī (T 1:164):

2. For a modern approach to mysticism by an Indian Muslim see Syed Vahiduddin, *Indisch-Moslemische Werterlebnisse* (Leipzig, 1937).

3. Zahur U. Sharib, *The Life and Teachings of Khawaja Moinud-din Hasan Chishti* (Ajmer, India, 1959). Mirza Wahiduddin Begg, *The Holy Biography of Hazrat Khwaja Muinaddin Chishti* (Ajmer, 1960). A scholarly study of Muʿīnuddīn is still needed.

a Sufi should possess "a generosity like that of the ocean, a mildness like that of the sun, and a modesty like that of the earth." Although the type of the soldier-Sufi, the fighter for the true religion, is sometimes found in the frontier provinces of India, as it is in other border areas between Islam and the land of the infidels,[4] the Islamization of the country was achieved largely by the preaching of the dervishes, not by the sword.[5]

When Muᶜīnuddīn died in 1236—not far from the beautiful mosque Quṭbuddīn Aybek of Delhi had erected in Ajmer—he was succeeded by a large number of *khalīfa*s, who made his ideals known all over India. To a certain extent, the sphere of influence of a *khalīfa* was designated by the master, who determined the areas where the *baraka* of this or that disciple should become active—a territorial distribution of spiritual power frequently found in Indian Sufism.

Even today the tomb of Quṭbuddīn Bakhtiyār Kākī from Farghana, who came to India together with Muᶜīnuddīn, is frequently visited. This saint, who died in 1235, was highly venerated by Iltutmish, the first king of the Slave Dynasty of Delhi, and the rather modest compound in Merauli near the Qutb Minar in Delhi is usually filled with pious pilgrims, who recite and sing their devotional poetry. The beautiful marble sanctuary of Muᶜīnuddīn (erected by the Mogul Emperor Jihangir) is also still a center of religious inspiration for thousands of faithful Muslims.

Bakhtiyār Kākī's successor was Farīduddīn (d. 1265), but because of the politically confused situation he left the capital and settled in the Punjab on the river Sutlej.[6] His home has been known, ever since, as Pakpattan, "the ferry of the pure." Farīd had been influenced in his early religious life by his pious mother. He performed extremely difficult ascetic practices, among them the *chilla maᶜkūsa*, hanging upside down in a well and performing the prescribed prayers and recollections for forty days. His constant fasting was miraculously rewarded—even pebbles turned into sugar, hence

4. Richard M. Eaton, "Sufis of Bijapur: Some Social Roles of Medieval Muslim Saints" (Paper delivered at the Conference of South East Asian Studies, New York, 29 March 1972).

5. Sir Thomas Arnold, *The Preaching of Islam* (1896; reprint ed., Lahore, 1956); see the same author's "Saints, Muhammadan, in India," in *Encyclopedia of Religion and Ethics*, ed. James Hastings, 13 vols. (1908–27), 11:68–73, the most illuminating short survey of the subject.

6. Khaliq Ahmad Nizami, *The Life and Times of Shaikh Farīd Ganj-i Shakar* (Aligarh, 1955), gives a good introduction to the problems.

his surname *Ganj-i shakar*, "sugar treasure." Whether this charming legend is true or not, it shows the extreme importance Farīd placed on ascetic exercises, and we may well believe that "no saint excelled him in his devotions and penances." Even his family life suffered under the restrictions he placed upon himself. He did not care for his wives or children, eight of whom survived. When he was informed that a child had died—so legend has it—he said: "If fate has so decreed and he dies, tie a rope around his feet and throw him out and come back!" This tradition reminds the historian of the attitude of some of the early ascetics, who rejoiced at the death of their family members. But as a consequence of this inhuman attitude, most sons of early Chishtī saints turned out to be worldly people, some even drunkards, who had no disposition at all for the religious, let alone mystical, life.[7]

The maintenance of Farīduddīn's *khānqāh*—and he is mentioned here as an outstanding example of the early Chishtī way of life—was difficult, since the sheikh relied exclusively upon gifts (*futūḥ*), and the *khānqāh* did not own or cultivate land from which the dervishes might draw their living. No *jāgīr*s (endowments of land) or grants from the rulers were accepted by the Chishtīs, for they refused to deal with the worldly government. One of their poets said:

> How long will you go to the doors of Amirs and sultans?
> This is nothing else than walking in the traces of Satan.

This mistrust of government, familiar from early Sufi literature, became more outspoken with these Chishtī saints, who considered everything in the hands of the rulers to be unlawful.

The dervishes in the *khānqāh* regarded themselves as "guests of God," living and working in one large room; visitors were always welcome, and the table always spread for unexpected guests—if there was any food available. The residents had to serve the sheikh and the community, and their main occupations were prayer, worship, and the study of books of devotion and the biographies of saints. Farīduddīn and his fellow saints in the order, however,

7. Khaliq Ahmad Nizami, *Some Aspects of Religion and Politics in India during the 13th Century* (Bombay, 1961), p. 204; Nizami, "Some Aspects of Khānqāh Life in Medieval India," *Studia Islamica* 8 (1957). Nizami has published numerous books and articles, both in English and in Urdu, on medieval Indian intellectual history. He has also edited the *Khayr al-majālis*, by Chirāgh-i Dehlawi (Aligarh, 1959), one of the most important sources for early Chishtī life.

recommended a good education for the disciples and were interested in poetry and music. It is possible that Farīduddīn composed a few lines of poetry in the local dialect, which would place him in the chain of those mystics who helped disseminate Sufi teachings in popular songs, thus influencing the population, particularly the women, who used to sing these simple verses while doing their daily work.

Farīduddīn invested seven *khalīfa*s with spiritual power; among his disciples, Jamāl Hānswī and Niẓāmuddīn must be counted as his special friends. The poet Jamāl Hānswī (d. 1260) wrote moving mystical songs in Persian—unsophisticated and sometimes slightly didactic, but attractive. Farīduddīn's outstanding *khalīfa,* however, was Niẓāmuddīn, whom he met in 1257, only a few years before his death.

Niẓāmuddīn was one of the well-known theologians of Delhi; then, with his master, he studied Suhrawardī's *ᶜAwārif al-maᶜārif,* the guidebook of almost all the Indo-Muslim mystics in the thirteenth and fourteenth centuries. After his third visit to Pakpattan, he was appointed *khalīfa* in Delhi. The name of Niẓāmuddīn *Auliyāʾ*, "Saints," as he came to be known out of respect, marks the high tide of mystical life in Delhi. The saint was a strict follower of the Prophetic *sunna,* a student of and commentator on the Prophetic traditions, and, at the same time, a friend of poets and musicians. Baranī, the Indo-Muslim historiographer of the early fourteenth century, claims that it was Niẓāmuddīn's influence that inclined most of the Muslims in Delhi toward mysticism and prayers, toward remaining aloof from the world. Books on devotion were frequently sold. No wine, gambling, or usury was to be found in Delhi, and people even refrained from telling lies. It became almost fashionable, if we are to believe Baranī, to purchase copies of the following books: Makkī's *Qūt al-qulūb* and, quite logically, Ghazzālī's *Iḥyāʾ ᶜulūm ad-dīn;* Suhrawardī's *ᶜAwārif al-maᶜārif* and Hujwīrī's *Kashf al-maḥjūb;* Kalābādhī's *Kitāb at-taᶜarruf* and its commentary; and the *Risāla* of Qushayrī. Also in Baranī's list are Najmuddīn Dāyā's *Mirṣād ul-ᶜibād,* the letters of ᶜAynuʾl-Quḍāt Hamadhānī, and, the only book written by an Indian Muslim, Ḥamīduddīn Nagōrī's *Lawāmiᶜ*, a treatise by one of the early Chishtī saints (d. 1274) noted for his poverty and his vegetarianism. These books may have given succor to the population in the confused

A saint with his tame lions,
Indian, early seventeenth century.

Staatliche Museen, East Berlin

political situation. Niẓāmuddīn Auliyā (d. 1325), tenderly called by his followers *Maḥbūb-i ilāhī*, "God's beloved,"[8] outlived seven kings, and constant intrigues, bloodshed, and rebellions took place in Delhi and its environs during his life.

During Niẓāmuddīn's time, Sufism became a mass movement in northwestern India, and the moral principles laid down by the early Chishtī saints did much to shape the ideals of the Muslim society in that part of the Subcontinent. A number of Punjabi tribes still claim to have been converted by Farīduddīn Ganj-i Shakar.

Close to Niẓāmuddīn's tomb in Delhi—still the most frequently visited sanctuary in Delhi—is the tomb of his closest friend and disciple, Amīr Khosrau (1254–1325), the best-known poet of the early Muslim period in India. Versatile and witty, he composed lyrics and epics, historical poetical novels, and treatises on epistolography, but almost no mystical poetry. He was, however, the founder of the Indo-Muslim musical tradition; he was a composer and a theoretician, and this talent of his certainly developed in connection with his Chishtī affiliation. Austere as they were in their preparatory stage of life, the Chishtiyya allowed the *samā*ᶜ, the spiritual concert and dance; this predilection is reflected in many of their sayings and in their poetry. They have contributed a great deal to the development of the Indo-Muslim musical tradition, of which Amīr Khosrau—lovingly styled "the parrot of India" and "God's Turk"—was the first great representative.

Khosrau's friend Ḥasan Sijzī Dihlawī (d. 1328)—the disciple of Niẓāmuddīn who collected his master's sayings—is less well known as a poet, but his verses convey more of the truly mystical spirit than Khosrau's. They are winsome in their lyrical wording, replete with love and tender emotion. About the same time, a beautiful poem in honor of the Prophet Muhammad was composed by a third poet of the Chishtiyya, Bū ᶜAlī Qalandar Panīpatī (d. 1323), whose verses

8. See the lovely story in Ahmad Ali, *Twilight in Delhi* (Oxford, 1966), p. 146, in which a pious inhabitant of Delhi tries to explain the breakdown of Indo-Muslim glory as a result of acting against Niẓāmuddīn's spirit: "The real causes of the loss of the Mughal Empire were some mistakes committed by the elders of that king, and the biggest of them all was that they had separated lover and beloved from each other by burying Mohammad Shah between the graves of Hazrat Mahboob Elahi and Hazrat Amir Khusro. . . ." Indeed, one of the most artistic poems by Amīr Khosrau (who often praised his master Niẓāmuddīn) is the ghazal no. 291 in his *Dīwān-i Kāmil*, ed. Mahmūd Derwish (Tehran, 1343 sh./1964), in which the master is praised as the one "through whose existence the world is kept alive in the same manner as the forms are kept alive by the spirit."

were the first of the many eulogies for the Prophet written in the Subcontinent. The same mystic who wrote charming lines about the all-embracing power of love—"Were there not love and the grief of love—who would say, who would hear so many sweet words?" (AP 112)—wrote some remarkable letters to the Delhi kings criticizing their way of life.

From Niẓāmuddīn Auliyā the spiritual chain goes to Chirāgh-i Dehlī, the "Lamp of Dehli" (d. 1356) and then to Muhammad Gīsūdarāz, "he with the long tresses," who migrated to the Deccan and enjoyed the patronage of the Bahmani Sultans. This saint, who died in 1422 and is buried in Gulbarga near present-day Hyderabad, was a prolific writer of both poetry and prose in Arabic and Persian. He also composed a book on the Prophet of Islam, *Miᶜrāj al-ᶜāshiqīn,* for the instruction of the masses, in Dakhni, the southern branch of Urdu. He was the first Sufi to use this vernacular, which was elaborated upon by many other saints in southern India in the next two centuries. Gīsūdarāz was probably the first author in the Subcontinent who tried to introduce the classical works of Sufism on a broad scale; he commented upon Ibn ᶜArabī's *Fuṣūṣ al-ḥikam* as well as upon Suhrawardī's *Ādāb al-murīdīn* and wrote numerous treatises and books on mystical life and on Prophetic traditions. Thanks to him, both the refined love mysticism of ᶜAynuᵓl-Quḍāt's *Tamh̲īdāt* and the fundamental work of Ibn ᶜArabī were made accessible to Indian Sufis and came to influence the development of mystical thought in later centuries. Gīsūdarāz's Persian poetry gracefully translates the feelings of his loving heart—intoxicated by divine love, he feels himself to be beyond separation and union. The true lovers, who quaffed the wine of love at the Day of the Covenant,

> are the first page (*dibāja*) of the book of existence
> and have become the preeternal title of endless eternity.
> (AP 152)

The Chishtiyya remained for centuries the most influential order in the Subcontinent, but it never went beyond its borders.

Another important order was the Suhrawardiyya, the tradition from which Muᶜīnuddīn Chishtī had drawn his first inspiration. Several of Abū Ḥafṣ ᶜUmar Suhrawardī's disciples reached India at the beginning of the thirteenth century. Among them was Jalāluddīn Tabrīzī, who went to Bengal, where he died in 1244. The order still flourishes in this area and has produced a number of mystics and political figures among the Bengali Muslims.

An even greater Suhrawardiyya impact on Muslim religious life was made by Bahāʾuddīn Zakariya Multānī (d. ca. 1262), a contemporary of Farīduddīn Ganj-i Shakar. It is revealing to compare the style of life of these two mystics, who were separated by only a few hundred miles—the stern ascetic Farīd, who gave no thought to any worldly needs and refused all governmental grants for his family and his disciples, and the well-to-do landlord Bahāʾuddīn, who looked after the needs of his family and never failed to keep a supply of grain in his house. His accumulation of wealth was sufficient to make him the target of accusations by other Sufis, but his sons, unlike the sons of most of the early Chishtī saints, followed in his path; the succession in the Suhrawardiyya became, generally, hereditary. As opposed to the open table in the poor Chishtī *khānqāh*s, Bahāʾuddīn was more formal and had fixed hours for visitors who were invited to partake in meals. And he was willing to mix freely with members of the ruling classes—just as Abū Ḥafṣ ʿUmar Suhrawardī himself had served the caliph an-Nāṣir.[9] This contrasting attitude toward the world, and toward its most dangerous representative, the government, has survived through the centuries. It is interesting to compare the theories of the sixteenth-century Egyptian mystic Shaʿrānī about the relations between the Sufis and the government with the utterances of the Indian saints of either tradition.

It may be that Bahāʾuddīn Zakariya would not have been so well known if a noted love poet had not lived in his entourage for nearly twenty-five years. This poet was Fakhruddīn ʿIrāqī (d. 1289).[10] He had fallen in love with a certain youth and had followed him and a group of dervishes who went to India. In Multan he attached himself to Bahāʾuddīn, to whom he dedicated some impressive *qaṣīda*s. The story goes:

> The saint set him in a cell. For ten days ʿIrāqī sat therein admitting nobody. On the eleventh day, overcome by his emotion, he wept aloud and sang:
>
> The wine wherewith the cup they first filled high,
> was borrowed from the *sāqī*'s languorous eye.

9. Aziz Ahmad, "The Sufi and the Sultan in Pre-Mughal Muslim India," *Der Islam* 38 (1963).

10. Fakhruddīn ʿIrāqī, *Dīwān*, ed. Saʿīd Nafīsī (Tehran, 1338 sh./1959); ʿIrāqī, *The Song of the Lovers ('Ushshāqnāme)*, ed. and trans. A. J. Arberry (Oxford, 1939).

The inmates of the hospice ran and told the saint what was passing. Now this order followed the rule of Shihābuddīn Suhrawardī whose favoured pupil Bahāʾuddīn was, and Suhrawardī's rule was that the devotee should occupy himself only with the recitation of the Koran and the expounding of tradition. The other brothers therefore viewed ʿIrāqī's behavior with disapproval, and complained to the saint. He however replied that this was prohibited to them, but not to him.

Some days later, ʿImāduddīn, passing through the bazaar, observed that this poem was being recited to the accompaniment of music. Visiting the taverns he found the same thing there. On his return, he reported this to the saint recounting what he had heard as far as the lines:

> Why should they seek to hurt ʿIrāqī's fame,
> since they themselves their secrets thus proclaim!

"His affair is complete," said the saint, and arising he went to the door of ʿIrāqī's cell.

"ʿIrāqī," he called, "do you make your prayers in taverns? Come forth!"

The poet came out of his cell, and laid his head at the saint's feet, weeping. The latter raised his head from the ground, and would not suffer him to return to his cell, but taking off the mystic robe set it upon him.[11]

Bahāʾuddīn, with the spiritual insight of a true saint, acknowledged ʿIrāqī's greatness and true love. The tender and intoxicating love poems that the Persian poet composed are still being sung by Pakistani musicians at the door of the master's tomb in Multan.

ʿIrāqī's poetic interpretation of a classic Arabic verse about the wine and the glass, indistinguishable in the light of the sun, is one of the favorite quotations of later Sufis:

> Cups are those a-flashing with wine,
> Or suns through the clouds a-gleaming?
> So clear is the wine and the glass so fine,
> that the two are one in seeming.
> The glass is all and the wine is naughted,
> Or the glass is naught and the wine is all.[12]

For the history of Sufi thought, his *Lamaʿāt*, "Flashes," inspired by Ibn ʿArabī's theories, are highly important. He dealt in the traditional Persian form of mixed poetry and prose with a number of problems of mystical life in general and of his own life in particular: with love revealed through the medium of human beauty. For ʿIrāqī, love is the only thing existing in the world (*lamʿa* 7), and lover, beloved, and love are one—union and separation no

11. ʿIrāqī, *Song of the Lovers*, no. 15; cf. N 602.
12. Edward G. Browne, *A Literary History of Persia*, 4 vols. (1902; reprint ed., Cambridge, 1957), 3:130.

longer pertain (*lamᶜa* 2). The light of the cheek of the beloved is the first thing the eye sees, His voice the first thing the ear hears (*lamᶜa* 18), and the separation that the beloved wishes is a thousand times better and more beautiful than the union desired by the lover (*lamᶜa* 22). Thus he goes beyond the early formulation that love means staying at the friend's door even if sent away.

ᶜIrāqī sees God, the eternally beautiful beloved, everywhere and is in love with everything the beloved does and orders. Why should he himself wish anything? Heart and love are one; love sometimes grows out of the heart like flowers, and the whole world is nothing but an echo of love's eternal song. Although the lover is bound to secrecy, the beloved himself makes the secret of love manifest. Why, then, was a lover like Ḥallāj punished for his disclosure of the secret of divine love?

Soon after Bahāʾuddīn Zakariya's death, ᶜIrāqī left Multan for Konya, where he met Ṣadruddīn Qōnawī and perhaps Jalāluddīn Rūmī. ᶜIrāqī is buried in Damascus, close to the grave of Ibn ᶜArabī, whose thoughts he had transformed poetically. ᶜIrāqī's influence on later Persian and Indo-Persian poetry can scarcely be overrated; the *Lamaᶜāt* were often commented upon, and Jāmī popularized his thoughts.

In the history of the Suhrawardiyya in India the intensity of ᶜIrāqī's experience, the splendor of his radiating love, has rarely been repeated. One of Zakariya's disciples, Sayyid Jalāluddīn Surkhpūsh ("Red-dressed," d. 1292) from Bukhara, settled in Ucch, northeast of Multan, and is the forefather of a long line of devout mystics and theologians. Ucch was, for a while, the center of the Suhrawardiyya, thanks chiefly to the active and pious Jalāluddīn Makhdūm-i Jahāniyān, "whom all the inhabitants of the world serve" (d. 1383), a prolific writer in almost all religious fields. It was in Ucch that the first missionaries of the Qādiriyya settled in the late fifteenth century; from there this order spread into the Subcontinent, where it soon gained a firm footing and was carried to Indonesia and Malaysia.[13]

Another aspect of mystical life developed in the same period during which Muᶜīnuddīn Chishtī and Bahāʾuddīn Zakariya were preaching divine love and union: its representative is Lāl Shahbāz,

13. A typical example of the spread of the Qādiriyya is given by Syed Muhammad Naquib al-Attas, *The Mysticism of Ḥamza al-Fanṣūrī* (Kuala Lumpur, 1970). This mystic made the order popular in Malaysia.

"the Red Falcon," Qalandar. From Marwand in Sistan, he was the saint of Sehwan, who lived in the mid-thirteenth century in Sind, at the site of the old Shiva sanctuary at the west bank of the lower Indus. Lāl Shahbāz was an intoxicated mystic who considered himself a member of the spiritual lineage of Ḥallāj, as some of his Persian verses seem to show. Around his sanctuary strange groups of *bī-sharᶜ*, "lawless," Sufis (*malang*) gathered, dressed in black, and the mystical current connected with Sehwan often shows Sufism in its least attractive aspects. The "fair" of Sehwan—celebrated between Shawwal 18 and 20—has become notorious for its rather illicit events.[14] A *lingam* close to the actual tomb proves the Shivait background of some of the rites.

The orders grew in India in the following centuries, and new suborders emerged, among which the Shaṭṭāriyya in the sixteenth century deserves special mention. The main representative of this order—which is restricted to India and Indonesia—was Muhammad Ghauth Gwaliori (d. 1562), for whom Akbar built a magnificent tomb. This Muhammad Ghauth is the author of an interesting book, *Al-jawāhir al-khamsa*, "The Five Jewels," which deals with manners and practices of Sufism and also connects the meditation of the most beautiful names with astrological ideas. This book deserves a detailed study both in its original Persian and in its widely read Arabic translation.[15] Another member of the Shaṭṭāriyya, Muhammad Ghauthī (d. after 1633), composed a voluminous work about the Indo-Muslim, especially Gujrati, saints that contains biographies of 575 Sufis. As time passed, the mystics became ever more preoccupied with collecting biographical notes and making compilations of second- and often third-hand information.

The early Indian Sufis had already displayed an amazing literary activity. Although the mystics often expressed their aversion to intellectual scholarship and writing, most of them were quite eager to

14. Peter Mayne, *Saints of Sind* (London, 1956), gives a vivid and often ironical account of the customs of so-called saints; yet his brilliantly written book contains much valuable information about little-known facts of saint worship and mystical thought in the Indus Valley.

15. See Marshall, *Mughals in India*, no. 1169, and Zubaid Ahmad, *The Contribution of Indo-Pakistan*, pp. 94ff. Muḥammad Ghauth's book has been very popular, as may be understood from the number of commentaries on it. About some of the commentators, and about Sufism in South Arabia as well as the relationships between Indian mystics (mainly Naqshbandis) and the scholars and saints of Yemen and Hadramaut, see the little-known, but very useful, study by Ferdinand Wüstenfeld, "Die Çufiten in Süd-Arabien im XI. (XVII) Jahrhundert," *Nachrichten von der Gesellschaft der Wissenschaften zu Göttingen, Philologisch-historische Klasse* 30, no. 1 (1883).

put down their knowledge in books and treatises. In India, a special literary genre became very popular—the so-called *malfūẓāt*, collections of sayings of the spiritual preceptors. This was not an Indian invention—the classical handbooks of Sufism consist to a large extent of apothegmata and random sentences of the masters of old. The Indian Sufis, however, carefully collected the dicta of their masters from day to day, and, as Khaliq Ahmad Nizami has rightly pointed out, these "diaries" constitute a valuable source for our knowledge of life outside the court circles. They are a necessary corrective of the official historiography; they allow us interesting glimpses into social and cultural problems that the official authors wittingly or unwittingly overlooked.

The first important example of this genre is the *Fawāʾid al-fuʾād*, Niẓāmuddīn Auliyā's conversations compiled between 1307 and 1322 by his disciple Amīr Ḥasan Sijzī Dihlawī, the poet. Only after a year had passed did he let his master know of his scheme. From then on Niẓāmuddīn himself helped him in filling the lacunae in the manuscript. Most of the fourteenth-century mystics, whether they lived in Delhi—like Chirāgh-i Delhi (*Khayr al-majālis*)—or settled in central India—like the grandson of Ḥamīduddīn Nagōrī, who compiled his ancestor's sentences (*Surūr aṣ-ṣudūr*)—had their sayings recorded. In later times, collections of *malfūẓāt* were fabricated with more or less pious intent.[16]

Some other mystics set out to write histories of their orders. Mīr Khurd, a disciple of Niẓāmuddīn and friend of Ḥasan Dihlawī, like him and like many leading intellectuals of Delhi forced by Muhammad Tughluq to leave Delhi for the Deccan in 1327, felt guilty about deserting his master's sanctuary, and, as expiation for this impiety, he undertook to write a history of the Chishtī order, the *Siyar al-auliyāʾ*. This book is still the most trustworthy account of the Chishtī *silsila* and of medieval Chishtī *khānqāh* life.

Another literary activity was the writing of letters, partly private, partly for circulation. The collections of the letters of Muslim Indian Sufis from the thirteenth century on are an extremely important source of our knowledge of the age and movement and, as in the case of Aḥmad Sirhindī, have played a remarkable role even in politics. Sufi thought permeated all fields of poetry, and even poets who are classified primarily as court poets could reach mystical

16. For the whole problem see Khaliq Ahmad Nizami, "Malfūẓat kī tārīkhī ahammiyat," in *Arshi Presentation Volume*, ed. Malik Ram (Delhi, 1961).

heights of expression. An example is Jamālī Kanbōh (d. 1535), Iskandar Lodi's court poet, whose famous lines on the Prophet have already been quoted (p. 221).

By the fourteenth century, the works of Sufis of the classical period were being continuously read and explained. Though the interest was at first concentrated upon the representatives of moderate Sufism, the theosophy of Ibn ʿArabī and his disciples soon became popular in India. The number of commentaries written on the *Fuṣūṣ al-ḥikam*, and the number of books that were composed to explain the theories of the Great Master, are myriad. From the late fifteenth century on, Ibn ʿArabī's ideas became influential everywhere. ʿIrāqī's and Jāmī's poetry, which were a poetical elaboration of these ideas, made them even more popular, since many people who would not read theoretical Sufi works certainly enjoyed these lovely poems. The name of ʿAbduʾl-Quddūs Gangōhī (d. 1538), a leading saint and prolific writer, is an outstanding example of Sufism tinged by the theories of the *waḥdat al-wujūd*. It should, however, be emphasized that ʿAbduʾl-Quddūs strictly observed the Muslim law, as did most of the influential spiritual preceptors.[17]

Under the influence of the theory of "Unity of Being," some mystics might see points of correspondence between Sufi thought and the Vedanta system of Hindu philosophy and attempt to bring about an approximation between Muslim and Hindu thought—a current that was viewed with great distrust by the orthodox.

The question of the probability and extent of mutual influences of Muslim and Hindu mysticism has been discussed often by Oriental and Western scholars. India had, indeed, been known as the country of magical practices—Ḥallāj even went there "in order to learn magic," according to his detractors. It is small wonder, then, that Sufi hagiography in India describes magic-working contests between Sufi saints and yogis or mysterious conversions of Indian yogis by Sufis.[18] The Muslim saints and theologians discussed the question of the extent to which the experiences of the yogis were real, or whether they relied upon a satanic, or at least a magical, basis. They would usually admit the possibility of certain miracles performed

17. Iʿjāzul Ḥaqq Quddūsī, *ʿAbdul Quddūs Gangōhī* (Karachi, 1961). ʿAbduʾl-Quddūs's *Rushdnāme*, in which Hindi poetry is inserted and which seems to be influenced by Hindu thought, still deserves careful study. Khaja Khan, *Studies in Tasawwuf* (Madras, 1923), contains an appendix, "Sufi Orders in the Deccan," which is fairly useful.

18. Simon Digby, "Encounters with Jogis in Indian Sufi Hagiography," mimeographed, School of Oriental and African Studies (London, 1970).

by the yogis but would maintain the importance of following the Islamic Path for the performance of true miracles. The *sharīʿa* is the divine secret, as Gīsūdarāz said, and as late as the eighteenth century the view was expounded that even the greatest ascetic practices and the resulting miracles of a yogi could not properly be compared to even the smallest sign of divine grace manifested in a faithful Muslim.

Another question has to do with the extent to which the ascetic practices of Indo-Muslim saints developed under the influence of Yoga practices. It has been claimed that the strict vegetarianism of some of the Indian Sufis, like Ḥamīduddīn Nagōrī and others, might be attributed to contact with Hindu ascetics. But a story about Rābiʿa al-ʿAdawiyya told by ʿAṭṭār (T 1:64) makes it clear that this saint was credited with complete abstinence from animal products so that the animals no longer fled from her. Similar legends are told of North African saints, and from very early times some ascetics even avoided killing insects—a trend found in the Maghreb as well, where no Hindu or Jain influence can possibly have been present.[19]

To what extent the breath control advocated by early Sufis in their *dhikr* developed under the influence of Indian practices cannot be judged properly. It existed, like the "inverted *chillah,*" among the Sufis of eastern Iran before Sufism spread to India. For the later period, however, we may assume that a deepened interest in the ascetic practices of their Hindu neighbors might have colored some aspects of Indian Sufi life. Some theoretical works about Yoga practices were composed by Indo-Muslim scholars, and a few outstanding Sanskrit works in this field were translated into Persian during the Mogul period.[20]

On the whole, the boundaries between Muslim and Hindu saints remained quite well defined during the first five centuries of Muslim rule over large parts of India, though there were syncretistic movements, like that of Kabīr in the fifteenth century. The situation changed somewhat with the arrival of the Moguls in India. Babur, from the dynasty of Timur, who established the rule of his house over northwestern India with the decisive Battle of Panipat in 1526, was accustomed to showing reverence to the Sufis in his

19. Émile Dermenghem, *Le culte des saints dans l'Islam Maghrebin* (Paris, 1954), p. 100.

20. Aziz Ahmad, "Sufismus und Hindumystik," *Saeculum* 15, no. 1 (1964). See also Hellmut Ritter, "Al-Bīrūnī's übersetzung des Yoga-Sutra des Patanjali," *Oriens* 9 (1956).

Central Asian homeland. In his lively and informative Turkish memoirs he tells some interesting stories about the connections between the Timurid princes and some of the mystical leaders of Central Asia. The influence of the Naqshbandiyya on Central Asian politics in the late fifteenth century and after will be discussed later. Babur himself translated into Turkish the *Risāla-yi wālidiyya* of ʿUbaydullāh Aḥrār, the leading Naqshbandī master of Central Asia (d. 1490), and in one of his poems called himself "the servant of the dervishes." After his arrival in India, Babur turned his interest to the Chishtī order, which in the following decades became closely connected with the Mogul house.

It was Babur's grandson Akbar (1556–1605) who, during the half century of his reign, tried to establish a religious eclecticism in which the best elements of all religions known to him would be contained. It seems that his ideas were, to some degree, influenced by the teaching of the Mahdawiyya, the chiliastic movement of Muhammad of Jaunpur, who at the beginning of the sixteenth century had declared himself to be the promised Mahdi.[21] Akbar's two most faithful friends, the court poet Fayżī and the historiographer Abūʾl-Fażl, were the sons of a mystic connected with the Mahdi movement; thus an influence cannot be completely excluded. The ideal of a golden age and restoration of peace all over the world, so typical of chiliastic movements, was in Akbar's mind, and the "lying together of the lamb and the lion" in the peaceful reign of the Moguls was often represented in Mogul painting of the early seventeenth century.[22] Akbar's religious tolerance was, in its practical consequences, scarcely compatible with Muslim law, and the orthodox became highly suspicious of the *dīn-i ilāhī*, the Divine Religion invented by the Emperor. Badāūnī's chronicle reflects the unalloyed hatred of the orthodox theologian who, because of his talents, had been one of the leading translators at Akbar's court and was forced to translate into Persian "the books of the infidels," i.e., the Sanskrit

21. See A. S. Bazmee Ansari, "Sayyid Muhammad Jawnpuri and His Movement," *Islamic Studies* 2 (1963).

22. See Richard Ettinghausen, "The Emperor's Choice," *Festschrift E. Panofsky* (New York, 1961); Emmy Wellecz, *Akbar's Religious Thought as Reflected in Moghul Painting* (London, 1952). The "drinking together of the wolf and the lamb," inherited from Old Testament prophecies, occurs as a sign of the ruler's perfect justice in early Ismaili propaganda; see Tilman Nagel, *Frühe Ismailiya und Fatimiden im Lichte der risālat iftitāḥ ad-daʿwā* (Bonn, 1972), p. 14. It also forms part of Rūmī's imagery, in which it is applied to the mystical beloved, under whose spell the differences between men and animals disappear.

epics that were at such variance with the monotheistic ideals of the basically exclusive Muslim mind.

Akbar's attempts could not bring forth a perfect solution of the problems confronting a large, multireligious country; on the contrary, they evoked much resistance in all segments of the population. Yet they are reflected in the poetry and the fine arts of his time. Persian poetry written at the Mogul court and throughout Muslim India, including Bengal, was dominated by the imagery developed in Iran—most of the leading poets between 1570 and 1650, in fact, came from Iran. Their verses revealed the same mystical feeling as the best poems of their motherland. The constant oscillation between worldly and divine love, the symbolism of roses and nightingales continued; now the vocabulary was enriched by allegorical stories from Indian sources and allusions to the newly discovered European world. But the general tenor of poetry remained by and large the same: endless longing for a beloved who can never be reached, unless the lover undertakes very difficult tasks and gladly offers his life on the thorny path toward the eternal goal. The nostalgia and melancholy so often found in classical Persian poetry was more pronounced in India, hidden under a dazzling exterior, and the later Mogul period once more produced great and truly touching mystical poetry.

It was in the house of a Chishtī saint that Akbar's heir apparent Salīm, whose throne name was Jihangir, was born. In gratitude for the blessings of this saint, Akbar erected a wonderful Sufi *dargāh* in his new capital Fathpur Sikri. When Jihangir grew up, he adorned Ajmer, Muᶜīnuddīn Chishtī's city, with beautiful buildings of white marble. The close association of the Chishtiyya with the Moguls, so alien to their previous antigovernment attitude, is reflected in many stories about Akbar and his successors.

The mystical movement aiming at the unification of Hindu and Muslim thought, inaugurated by Akbar, reached its culmination in the days of Dārā Shikōh (1615–59), his great-grandson, the heir apparent of the Mogul Empire.[23] This talented prince was the first-born son of Shāh Jihān and Mumtaz Mahal, whose monumental

23. Kalika-Ranjan Qanungo, *Dara Shukoh* (Calcutta, 1935); Bikrama Jit Hasrat, *Dara Shikuh: Life and Works* (Calcutta, 1953). Many of Dārā Shikōh's works have been edited and translated; see Louis Massignon and Clemens Huart, eds., "Les entretiens de Lahore," *Journal asiatique* 209 (1926); and Louis Massignon and A. M. Kassim, "Un essai de bloc islamo-hindou au XVII siècle: l'humanisme mystique du Prince Dara," *Revue du monde musulman* 63 (1926).

tomb, the Taj Mahal, symbolizes the ruler's deep love for the mother of his fourteen children. Dārā became interested in mystical thought very early. It was not the "official" Chishtī order to which he was attracted, but rather the Qādiriyya, represented in Lahore by Miān Mīr, who had come there from Sind, together with his mystically inclined sister Bībī Jamāl. Miān Mīr's disciple and successor, Mollā Shāh Badakhshī, introduced the prince to the saint. Instead of involving himself actively in politics and military affairs, Dārā indulged in literary activities, to say nothing of his exquisite calligraphy. Widely read in classical works of Sufism, including Rūzbihān Baqlī's writings, he showed ready ability at compiling biographical studies on the earlier Sufis and collecting their sayings (*Ḥasanāt al-ʿārifīn*). The *Sakīnat al-auliyāʾ* is a fine biography of Miān Mīr and the Qādiriyya in Lahore. The admiration with which his collection of biographies of the saints, the *Safīnat al-auliyāʾ*, was accepted in Indian Sufi circles is evident from the fact that the book was translated into Arabic by Jaʿfar al-ʿAydarūs in Bijapur during the prince's lifetime. Dārā's *Risāla-yi ḥaqnumā* was planned as a completion of Ibn ʿArabī's *Fuṣūṣ*, Aḥmad Ghazzālī's *Sawāniḥ*, ʿIrāqī's *Lamaʿāt*, Jāmī's *Lawāʾiḥ*, and other short mystical works, but it lacks the stature of these treatises, just as his mystical poetry, though it shows great skill in the use of words, is somewhat dry. In letters and short treatises Dārā tried to find a common denominator for Islam and Hinduism, and his disputations with a Hindu sage, Bābā Lāl Dās, show his keen interest in the problem of a common mystical language.

Dārā's great work was the translation of the Upanishads into Persian—a work that he completed with the help of some Indian scholars, but that unmistakably bears the stamp of his personality.[24] For him, the Upanishads was the book to which the Koran refers as "a book that is hidden" (Sūra 56:78); thus it is one of the sacred books a Muslim should know, just as he knows the Torah, the Psalms, and the Gospel. Dārā Shikōh's translation, called *Sirr-i akbar*, "The Greatest Mystery," was introduced to Europe by the French scholar Anquetil Duperron, who in 1801 issued its Latin translation under the title *Oūpnekʾat, id est secretum tegendum.* Neither Dārā Shikōh nor his translator could have foreseen to what

24. Dārā Shikōh, *Sirr-i akbar*, ed. Tara Chand and M. Jalālī Nāʾinī (Tehran, 1961). See Erhard Göbel-Gross, " 'Sirr-i akbar,' Die Upanishad-Ubersetzung Dārā Shikōhs" (Ph.D. diss., University of Marburg, 1962).

extent this first great book on Hindu mysticism would influence the thought of Europe. German idealistic philosophers were inspired by its contents and praised its eternal wisdom in lofty language. Throughout the nineteenth century the Upanishads remained one of the most sacred textbooks for many German and German-influenced thinkers. Its mystical outlook has, to a large extent, helped to form in the West an image of India that has little in common with the realities.

Dārā Shikōh despised the representatives of Muslim orthodoxy. In the same tone as many earlier Persian poets, he could write: "Paradise is there, where there is no *mollā*." In the true mystical spirit, he emphasized the immediate experience as contrasted with blind imitation: "The gnostic is like the lion who eats only what he himself has killed, not like the fox who lives on the remnants of other animals' booty." The feeling of *hama ūst*, "everything is He," permeates all of his work. Dārā practiced his ideas of unity and was surrounded by a number of poets and prose writers who did not fit into the framework of orthodox Islam. There is the very strange figure of Sarmad, a highly intellectual Persian Jew.[25] After studying Christian and Islamic theology, he converted to Islam; later, he came as a merchant to India, fell in love with a Hindu boy in Thatta, became a dervish, and eventually joined Dārā's circle. It is said that he walked around stark naked, defending himself with the lines:

> Those with deformity He has covered with dresses,
> To the immaculate He gave the robe of nudity.

Sarmad is one of the outstanding masters of the Persian quatrain. Many of his mystical *rubāʿīyāt* are extremely concise and vigorous, revealing the deep melancholy of a great lover. Several of the traditional themes of Persian poetry have found their most poignant expression in his verses. He followed the tradition of Ḥallāj, longing for execution as the final goal of his life:

> The sweetheart with the naked sword in hand
> approached:
> In whatever garb Thou mayst come—I recognize Thee!

25. Bashir Ahmad Hashmi, "Sarmad," *Islamic Culture*, 1933–34, is a good translation of his quatrains. See also Walter J. Fischel, "Jews and Judaism at the Court of the Moghul Emperors in Medieval India," *Islamic Culture*, 1951.

This idea goes back at least to ᶜAynuʾl-Quḍāt Hamadhānī. Sarmad was, in fact, executed not long after Dārā (1661).

Another member of the circle around the heir apparent was Brahman (d. 1661), his private secretary, a Hindu who wrote good Persian descriptive poetry and prose. There was also Fānī Kashmīrī, the author of mediocre Persian verses to whom a book on comparative religion, the *Dabistān-i madhāhib*, is, probably wrongly, attributed. (Kashmir, the lovely summer resort of the Moguls, had been a center of mystical poetry since the Kubrāwī leader Sayyid ᶜAlī Hamadhānī had settled there, with seven hundred followers, in 1371.)[26]

Dārā's attitude was regarded with suspicion by the orthodox, and his younger brother ᶜAlamgir Aurangzeb, coveting the crown, took advantage of Shāh Jihān's illness to imprison his father and persecute his elder brother. After a series of battles, Dārā was eventually betrayed to Aurangzeb, who had him executed in 1659, to become himself the last great ruler of the Mogul Empire (1659–1707). It is worth noting that Dārā's and Aurangzeb's eldest sister, Jihānārā, was also an outstanding mystic and a renowned author of mystical works. Her master Mollā Shāh thought her worthy to be his successor, though this did not materialize.

One other member of the Qādiriyya order in Mogul India deserves mention—the great traditionist ᶜAbduʾl-Ḥaqq Dihlawī (d. 1642), founder of the traditionist school in Indian Islam. In addition to a great many works devoted to the revival of *ḥadīth* and to the interpretation of the Koran, to hagiography and Islamic history, he is also credited with mystical treatises. As a member of the Qādiriyya, he commented upon and interpreted famous sayings of the eponym of his order. In a famous letter he expressed his disapproval of some of the claims a leading mystic of his time had made. The mystic in question was Aḥmad Sirhindī, with whose name the "revival of orthodoxy," or the "Naqshbandī reaction," is closely connected.

THE "NAQSHBANDĪ REACTION"

It is typical of the situation in Islamic countries, and particularly in the Subcontinent, that the struggle against Akbar's

26. See Muḥammad Aṣlaḥ, *Tadhkira-yi shuᶜarā-yi Kashmīr*, ed. Sayyid Hussamuddin Rashdi, 5 vols. (Karachi, 1967–68); Girdhari L. Tikku, *Persian Poetry in Kashmir, 1339–1846: An Introduction* (Berkeley, 1971).

syncretism and against the representatives of emotional Sufism was carried out by a mystical order: the Naqshbandiyya.[27] "The Naqshbandiyya are strange caravan leaders / who bring the caravan through hidden paths into the sanctuary" (N 413). So said Jāmī, one of the outstanding members of this order in its second period. The Naqshbandiyya differed in many respects from most of the medieval mystical fraternities in the central Islamic countries. The man who gave it his name, Bahāʾuddīn Naqshband, belonged to the Central Asian tradition, which traced its lineage back to Yūsuf Hamadhānī (d. 1140). He was "the *imām* of his time, the one who knew the secrets of the soul, who saw the work" (MT 219).

Hamadhānī's spiritual affiliation went back to Kharaqānī and Bāyezīd Bisṭāmī; these two saints remained highly venerated in the order. According to the tradition, it was Hamadhānī who encouraged ʿAbduʾl-Qādir Gīlānī to preach in public. Two major traditions stem from him; one is the Yasawiyya in Central Asia, which in turn influenced the Bektashiyye in Anatolia. Hamadhānī's most successful *khalīfa*, besides Aḥmad Yasawī, was ʿAbduʾl-Khāliq Ghijduwānī (d. 1220), who propagated the teachings of his master primarily in Transoxania. The way he taught became known as the *ṭarīqa-yi Khwājagān*, "the way of the Khojas, or teachers." It is said that he set up the eight principles upon which the later Naqshbandiyya was built:

1) *hūsh dar dam*, "awareness in breathing,"
2) *naẓar bar qadam*, "watching over one's steps,"
3) *safar dar waṭan*, "internal mystical journey,"
4) *khalwat dar anjuman*, "solitude in the crowd,"
5) *yād kard*, "recollection,"
6) *bāz gard*, "restraining one's thoughts,"
7) *nigāh dāsht*, "to watch one's thought," and
8) *yād dāsht*, "concentration upon God."

Although Bahāʾuddīn Naqshband (d. 1390) had a formal initiation into the path, he was blessed with an immediate spiritual succession from Ghijduwānī and soon became an active leader of the Khwājagān groups. His main activities were first connected with Bukhara, of which he became the patron saint. Even today, the sellers of wild rue in Afghanistan may offer their merchandise, which is to be burned against the evil eye, with an invocation of

27. Madeleine Habib, "Some Notes on the Naqshbandi Order," *Moslem World* 59 (1969); Marijan Molé, "Autour du Daré Mansour: l'apprentissage mystique de Bahāʾ al-Dīn Naqshband," *Revue des études islamiques* 27 (1959).

Shāh Naqshband.[28] His order established connections with the trade guilds and merchants, and his wealth grew parallel to the growth of his spiritual influence, so that he and his followers and friends controlled the Timurid court and carefully watched over religious practices there. At almost the same time the order became highly politicized.

It may be true that as early as the twelfth century a ruler of Kashgar had been a disciple of Ghijduwānī. The Naqshbandīs had taken an active role in the constant internal feuds among the Timurid rulers. But it was not until Khwāja Aḥrār (1404–90) assumed leadership of the order that Central Asia was virtually dominated by the Naqshbandiyya. His relations with the Timurid prince Abū Saᶜīd, as well as with the Shibanid Uzbegs, proved decisive for the development of Central Asian politics in the mid-fifteenth century. When Abū Saᶜīd settled in Herat, most of the area toward the north and the east was under the influence of Khwāja ᶜUbaydullāh Aḥrār, who even had disciples in the country of the Mongols, where Yūnus Khān Moghul, Babur's maternal uncle, belonged to the order. Their leaders were, and still are, known as *Īshān*, "they." It was the Khwāja's conviction that "to serve the world it is necessary to exercise political power"[29] and to bring the rulers under control so that the divine law can be implemented in every part of life.

The Naqshbandiyya is a sober order, eschewing artistic performance—mainly music and *samāᶜ*. Nevertheless, the leading artists at the court of Herat belonged to this order, among them Jāmī (d. 1492), who devoted one of his poetical works to ᶜUbaydullāh Aḥrār (*Tuḥfat al-aḥrār*, "The Gift of the Free"),[30] though his lyrical poetry in general reveals little of his close connection with the Naqshbandiyya. His hagiographic work, the *Nafaḥāt al-uns*, however, is an important account of the fifteenth-century Naqshbandiyya, as well as a summary of classical Sufi thought. The main source for our knowledge of Khwāja Aḥrār's activities is the *Rashaḥāt ᶜayn al-ḥayāt*, "Tricklings from the Fountain of Life," composed by ᶜAlī ibn Ḥusayn Wāᶜiẓ Kāshifī, the son of one of the most artistic prose writers at the Herat court. Jāmī's friend and colleague, the vizier,

28. Pierre Centlivres, *Un bazar de l'Asie Centrale: Tashqurgan* (Wiesbaden, 1972), p. 174.

29. Joseph Fletcher, *The Old and New Teachings in Chinese Islam* (forthcoming).

30. F. Hadland Davis, *The Persian Mystics: Jami* (ca. 1908; reprint ed., Lahore, n.d.); Jiří Bečka, "Publications to Celebrate the 550th Anniversary of the Birth of ᶜAbdur Raḥmān Jāmī," *Archiv Orientálni* 34 (1966). For Jāmī's works see the Bibliography.

poet and Maecenas of artists, Mīr ʿAlī Shīr Nawāʾī (d. 1501), was also an initiate of the Naqshbandiyya. He is the greatest representative of Chagatay Turkish literature, which he encouraged at the court. Thus the order had among its early members two outstanding poets who deeply influenced Persian and Turkish literatures and who, like Nawāʾī, actively participated in political life.[31] More than two centuries later members of the "anti-artistic" Naqshbandiyya played a similar role in the Indian Subcontinent.

The center of Naqshbandī education is the silent *dhikr*, as opposed to the loud *dhikr*, with musical accompaniment, that attracted the masses to the other orders. The second noteworthy characteristic is *ṣuḥbat*,[32] the intimate conversation between master and disciple conducted on a very high spiritual level (cf. N 387). The close relation between master and disciple reveals itself in *tawajjuh*, the concentration of the two partners upon each other that results in experiences of spiritual unity, faith healing, and many other phenomena (cf. N 403).

It has been said that the Naqshbandiyya begin their spiritual journey where other orders end it—the "inclusion of the end in the beginning" is an important part of their teaching, though it is an idea that goes back to early Sufi education. It is not the long periods of mortification but the spiritual purification, the education of the heart instead of the training of the lower soul, that are characteristic of the Naqshbandiyya method. " 'Heart' is the name of the house that I restore," says Mīr Dard. They were absolutely sure, as many of their members expressed it, that their path, with its strict reliance upon religious duties, led to the perfections of prophethood, whereas those who emphasized the supererogatory works and intoxicated experiences could, at best, reach the perfections of sainthood.

The order was extremely successful in Central Asia—successful enough to play a major role in Central Asian politics during the

31. Vasilij V. Barthold, *Herat zur Zeit Husain Baiqaras*, trans. Walter Hinz (1938; reprint ed., Leipzig, 1968). Russian scholars have published a considerable number of studies about Nawāʾī during recent years.

32. Typical of contemporary Turkish Naqshbandī approach is the title of an unfortunately short-lived journal, *Sohbet Dergisi* (Istanbul, 1952–53). See Hasan Lutfi Şuşut, *Islam tasavvufunda Hacegân Hanedanı* (Istanbul, 1958), selections from the *Rashaḥāt ʿayn ul-ḥayat* about the early Naqshbandī masters; Şuşut, *Fakir sözleri* (Istanbul, 1958), mystical thoughts and aphorisms. An excellent short survey of Naqshbandī thought and practice is given by Hamid Algar, "Some Notes on the Naqshbandi Ṭarīqat in Bosnia," *Die Welt des Islam*, n.s. 13, nos. 3–4 (1971).

seventeenth and early eighteenth centuries. In India, the Naqshbandiyya gained a firm footing shortly before 1600, i.e., near the end of Akbar's reign. At that time, Khwāja Bāqī billāh, a sober but inspiring teacher, attracted a number of disciples who were interested in a law-bound mystical life and opposed the sweeping religious attitude that prevailed in the circles surrounding Akbar.

It was Bāqī billāh's disciple Aḥmad Farūqī Sirhindī (1564–1624) who was destined to play a major role in Indian religious and, to some extent, political life.[33] Aḥmad had studied in Sialkot, one of the centers of Islamic scholarship during the Mogul period. In Agra he came in touch with Fayżī and Abū'l-Fażl, Akbar's favorite writers and intimate friends, who were, however, disliked by the orthodox because of their "heretical" views. Aḥmad Sirhindī, like a number of his compatriots, had an aversion to the Shia, to which persuasion some of the southern Indian rulers belonged and which became more fashionable at the Mogul court in the late days of Akbar's rule and in the reign of Jihangir (1605–27), whose intelligent and politically active wife, Nūr Jihān, was herself Shia. The constant influx of poets from Iran to India during the Mogul period considerably strengthened the Shia element, and it was against them that Aḥmad Sirhindī wrote his first treatise, even before he was formally initiated into the Naqshbandiyya, i.e., before 1600. For a while, he was imprisoned in Gwalior, but he was set free after a year, in 1620. Four years later he died.

Although Aḥmad Sirhindī composed a number of books, his fame rests chiefly upon his 534 letters, of which 70 are addressed to Mogul officials. They were, like many letters by mystical leaders, intended for circulation, with only a few of them meant for his closest friends. He gave utterance to ideas that shocked some of the defenders of orthodoxy, as can be seen from some treatises published against his teachings in the late seventeenth century. The letters have been translated into Arabic, Turkish, and Urdu from the original Persian, and from them Aḥmad gained the honorific titles *mujaddid-i alf-i thānī*, "the Renovator of the Second Millenium" (after the *hijra*), and *imām-i rabbānī*, "the Divinely Inspired Leader."

In modern times, Aḥmad Sirhindī has usually been depicted as

33. Yohanan Friedman, *Shaikh Ahmad Sirhindi: An Outline of His Thought and a Study of His Image in the Eyes of Posterity* (Montreal, 1971), is the first comprehensive study of his mysticism; see the review by Annemarie Schimmel in *Die Welt des Islam*, n.s. 14 (1973).

the person who defended Islamic orthodoxy against the heterodoxy of Akbar and his imitators, the leader whose descendants supported Aurangzeb against his mystically inclined brother Dārā Shikōh. Yohanan Friedman has tried to show that this image developed only after 1919, in Abūʾl Kalām Azād's work, and that it has been eagerly elaborated by many Indo-Muslim, particularly Pakistani, scholars. It may be true that Sirhindī's direct influence upon Mogul religious life was not as strong as his modern adherents claim, but the fact remains that the Naqshbandiyya, though a mystical order, has always been interested in politics, regarding the education of the ruling classes as absolutely incumbent upon them. We may safely accept the notion that Aḥmad's successor in the order had a hand in the political development that followed his death and that this situation continued until about 1740.

Aḥmad Sirhindī has been praised primarily as the restorer of the classical theology of *waḥdat ash-shuhūd*, "unity of vision," or "testimonial monism," as opposed to the "degenerate"—as the orthodox would call it—system of *waḥdat al-wujūd*.[34] However, the problem can scarcely be seen in such oversimplified terms. Marijan Molé has interpreted Aḥmad's theology well (MM 108–10); he explains the *tauḥīd-i wujūdī* as an expression of *ʿilm al-yaqīn*, and *tauḥīd-i shuhūdī* as *ʿayn al-yaqīn*. That means that the *tauḥīd-i wujūdī* is the intellectual perception of the Unity of Being, or rather of the nonexistence of anything but God, whereas in *tauḥīd-i shuhūdī* the mystic experiences the union by the "view of certitude," not as an ontological unity of man and God. The mystic eventually realizes, by *ḥaqq al-yaqīn*, that they are different and yet connected in a mysterious way (the Zen Buddhist experiences *satori* exactly at the same point: at the return from the unitive experience, he realizes the multiplicity in a changed light).

Sirhindī finds himself in full harmony with the great Kubrāwī mystic ʿAlāʾuddaula Simnānī, who had criticized Ibn ʿArabī's theories. As a good psychologist, he acknowledges the reality of the state of intoxicated love, in which the enraptured mystic sees only the divine unity. But as long as he complies to the words of the divine law, his state should be classified as *kufr-i ṭarīqa*, "infidelity of the Path," which may lead him eventually to the sober state in

34. Bashir Ahmad Faruqi, *The Mujaddid's Conception of God* (Lahore, 1952); Faruqi, *The Mujaddid's Conception of Ṭauhīd* (Lahore, 1940); Aziz Ahmad, "Religious and Political Ideas of Shaikh Aḥmad Sirhindi," *Rivista degli studi orientali* 36 (1961).

which he becomes aware, once more, of the subjectivity of his experience. Such a reclassification of theories elaborated by the Sufis of old was perhaps necessary in a society in which the mystically oriented poets never ceased singing of the unity of all religions and boasted of their alleged infidelity. This "intoxication" is—and here again classical ideas are developed—the station of the saint, whereas the prophet excels by his sobriety, which permits him to turn back, after the unitive experience, into the world in order to preach God's word there: prophecy is the way down, is the aspect of reality turned toward creation.

One of Sirhindī's most astounding theories is, in fact, his prophetology. He spoke about the two individuations of Muhammad, the bodily human one as contrasted to the spiritually angelic one—the two *m*'s in Muhammad's name point to them. In the course of the first millennium, the first *m* disappeared to make room for the *alif*, the letter of divinity, so that now the manifestation of *Aḥmad* remains, purely spiritual and unconnected with the worldly needs of his community. In a complicated process, the new millennium has to restore the perfections of prophethood. It is no accident that the change from *Muḥammad* to *Aḥmad* coincides with the very name of Aḥmad Sirhindī and points to his discretely hidden role as the "common believer" called to restore these perfections.

That fits well with certain theories about the *qayyūm*, the highest representative of God and His agent (Aḥmad wrote, in one of his letters: "My hand is a substitute for the hand of God"). It is through the *qayyūm* that the world is kept in order; he is even higher than the mystical leader, the *quṭb*, and keeps in motion everything created. Shāh Walīullāh, in the eighteenth century, seems to equate him sometimes with "the breath of the merciful," sometimes with the "seal of the divine names" or with the universal soul.[35] The *qayyūm* has been elected by God, who bestowed upon him special grace, and, if we believe the Naqshbandiyya sources and especially the *Rauḍat al-qayyūmiyya*, Aḥmad Sirhindī claimed that this highest rank in the hierarchy of beings was held by him and three of his successors, beginning with his son Muhammad Maʿṣūm.[36] The

35. Shāh Walīullāh, *Lamaḥāt*, ed. Ghulam Muṣṭafa Qāsimi (Hyderabad, Sind, n.d.), no. 5. An interesting introduction to the thought of Shah Walīullāh is given in J. M. S. Baljon, trans., *A Mystical Interpretation of Prophetic Tales by an Indian Muslim: Shāh Walī Allāh's "Taʾwīl al-aḥādīth"* (Leiden, 1973).

36. Abūʾl Fayḍ Iḥsān, "Rauḍat al-qayyūmīya," 1751, manuscript, Library of the Asiatic Society of Bengal. Only an Urdu translation has been published. Sheikh Mu-

Rauḍat al-qayyūmiyya is certainly not a solid historical work. Written at the time of the breakdown of the Mogul Empire (after 1739), it reflects the admiration of a certain Naqshbandī faction for the master and his family; yet it must certainly rely upon some true statements of Sirhindī and shed light, if not on Naqshbandī history, at least on mystical psychology. The theories about the *qayyūmiyya* have only begun to be explored by the scholars of Sufism. The role of the four *qayyūms* in Mogul politics has still to be studied in detail. It is a strange coincidence that the fourth and last *qayyūm*, Pīr Muhammad Zubayr (Aḥmad's great-grandson) died in 1740, only a few months after Nadir Shah's attack on Delhi. The Persian invasion in northwest India had virtually destroyed the Mogul rule,[37] and now, the "spiritual guardian," too, left this world.

Pīr Muhammad Zubayr was the mystical leader of Muhammad Nāṣir ʿAndalīb, the father of Mīr Dard, to whom Urdu poetry owes its earliest and most beautiful mystical verses. Once more, the Naqshbandiyya played a decisive role in the development of a field in which the founders of the order were not at all interested. Members of this order are closely connected with the growth of Urdu literature in the northern part of the Subcontinent.

Urdu, in its early forms, such as Dakhni, had been used first as a literary medium by Gīsūdarāz, the Chishtī saint of Golconda in the early fifteenth century.[38] It was developed by mystics in Bijapur and Gujerat in the late fifteenth and sixteenth centuries. In addition to popular poetry to be remembered by the villagers and the women, several poetical works on mystical theories were composed in this language, which soon became fashionable for profane poetry as well. The first classic to be translated into Dakhni Urdu in the seventeenth century was ʿAynuʾl-Quḍāt's *Tamhīdāt*.

Later, the greatest lyrical poet of the South, Walī, went to Delhi in 1707. It was the year of Aurangzeb's death—a date that marks the end of the glory of the Moguls. Twilight fell on the political scene. The inherited values were scattered, the social order changed,

---

hammad Ikram, *Rūd-i kauthar*, 4th ed. (Lahore, 1969), discusses the work critically. The only extensive account in a Western language is that in John A. Subhan, *Sufism: Its Saints and Shrines*, 2d ed. (Lucknow, India, 1960), a book that contains much previously neglected material about later Indian Sufism.

37. See W. Cantwell Smith, "The Crystallization of Religious Communities in Mughal India," in *Yādnāme-ye Īrān-e Minorsky* (Tehran, 1969).

38. Maulvi Abdul Haqq, *Urdu ki nashw ū numā meñ Ṣūfiya-i kirām kā kām* [The Contribution of the Sufis to the Development of Urdu] (Karachi, 1953), a most valuable study.

and even the traditional forms of language and literature were no longer preserved. Walī attached himself to the Naqshbandī master Shāh Saᶜdullāh Gulshan, a prolific poet in Persian who was fond of music and was apparently a lovable and soft-hearted person who played a definite role in the poetry- and music-loving society of Delhi. Gulshan was also a friend of Bedil (d. 1721), the lonely poet whose humble tomb in Delhi does not reflect the influence his poetry had upon Afghan and Central Asian, mainly Tajik, literature. Bedil, though not a practicing member of any order, was steeped in the traditions of mystical Islam.[39] His numerous *mathnawīs* deal with philosophical and mystical problems and show a remarkable dynamism along with dark hopelessness. His favorite word is *shikast*, "broken, break"—an attitude the mystics had always favored for describing their hearts' state. Bedil's works of mixed poetry and prose, and his lyrics, offer the reader severe technical difficulties. The vocabulary, the conceits, the whole structure of his thought is unusual, but extremely attractive. His stylistic difficulties are surpassed only by his compatriot Nāṣir ᶜAlī Sirhindī (d. 1697), who later became a member of the Naqshbandiyya and considerably influenced the style of some eighteenth-century poets in India without, however, adding anything to the mystical teachings of his masters.

This tradition of highly sophisticated, almost incomprehensible Persian poetry was the breeding ground from which Shāh Saᶜdullāh Gulshan came. He quickly discovered the poetical strength of his new disciple Walī. After a few years, it became fashionable in Delhi to use the previously despised vernacular, *rekhta* or Urdu, for poetry, and in an amazingly short span of time, perfect works of poetry were written in this language, which was now generally used instead of the traditional Persian. The breakdown of the Mogul Empire was accompanied by a breakdown of poetical language. Not only did Urdu grow in the capital, but Sindhi, Panjabi, and Pashto developed literatures of their own during the last decades of Aurangzeb's reign and continued to flourish during the eighteenth century.

This background must be kept in mind to properly understand

39. Bedil's works have been published in four volumes of approximately 1100 large folios each: Mirza Bedil, *Kulliyāt*, 4 vols. (Kabul, 1962–65). Alessandro Bausani, "Note su Mirzā Bedil," *Annali dell Istituto Universitario Orientale Napoli*, n.s. 6 (1957); Jiří Bečka, "Tajik Literature," in *History of Iranian Literature*, ed. Jan Rypka (Dordrecht, 1968), pp. 515ff.

the role of the Naqshbandīs in Delhi. Two of the "pillars of Urdu literature" belonged to this order: Maẓhar Jānjānān, the militant adversary of the Shiites, who was killed by a Shia at the age of eighty-one in 1782,[40] and Mīr Dard, the lyrical poet of Delhi whose mystical poetry is sweeter than anything written in Urdu. These two men belong as much to the picture of eighteenth-century Delhi as the figure of Shāh Walīullāh (1703–62), the defender of the true faith, initiated into both Qādiriyya and Naqshbandiyya, a scholar and mystic whose works still await serious study in the West. (That he was attacked by a disciple of Maẓhar shows the manifold currents inside eighteenth-century Naqshbandī theology.)[41] It was Walīullāh who tried to bridge the gap between the *tauḥīd-i shuhūdī* and the *tauḥīd-i wujūdī,* just as he tried to explain the differences between the law schools as historical facts with no basic difference of importance. Shāh Walīullāh also ventured to translate the Koran into Persian so that the Muslims could read and properly understand the Holy Book and live according to its words—an attempt that was continued by his sons in Urdu. He was also instrumental in inviting the Afghan king Ahmad Shah Durrani Abdali to India to defend the Muslims against the Sikh and Mahratta. From Shāh Walīullāh the mystical chain extends to his grandson Shāh Ismāʿīl Shahīd, a prolific writer in Arabic and Urdu, and Sayyid Aḥmad of Bareilly, both known for their brave fight against the Sikh, who had occupied the whole of the Punjab and part of the northwestern frontier.[42] The Urdu poet Momin (1801–51), related through marriage with Mīr Dard's family, sided with the two reformers. The political impact of Shāh Walīullāh's work helped to form the modern Indo-Muslim religious life and attitude toward the British. It has survived in the school of Deoband to our day, though without the strong mystical bias of Shāh Walīullāh's original thought.

40. Marshall, *Mughals in India,* no. 800. Maẓhar's poetical work and his letters have been published. A number of hagiographical works about him and his branch of the Naqshbandiyya may be found in Charles Ambrose Storey, *Persian Literature* (London, 1953), 1: no. 1375; and Marshall, *Mughals in India,* no. 1357.

41. Alessandro Bausani, "Note su Shah Walīullāh di Delhi," *Annali dell Istituto Universitario Orientale Napoli,* n.s. 10 (1961); Aziz Ahmad, "Political and Religious Ideas of Shāh Walīullāh of Delhi," *Moslem World* 50, no. 1 (1962). The Shāh Walīullāh Academy in Hyderabad, Sind, under the presidency of Maulānā Ghulām Muṣṭafā Qāsimī, has published a number of Walīullāh's works, as well as studies about him.

42. *A History of Freedom Movement* (Karachi, 1957), 1:556; Aziz Ahmad, *Studies,* pp. 210ff. See also J. Spencer Trimingham, *The Sufi Orders in Islam* (Oxford, 1971), p. 129. The most comprehensive biography is by Ghulām Rasūl Mehr, *Sayyid Aḥmad Shahīd* (Lahore, ca. 1955), in Urdu.

It would be interesting to follow the relations between the great mystical leaders of Delhi during the eighteenth century. Although Shāh Walīullāh was, no doubt, the strongest personality among them, we would prefer to give here some notes about Mīr Dard's work, since he is an interesting representative of fundamentalist Naqshbandī thought, combined with a deep love of music and poetry. He was a poet of first rank, as well as a pious Muslim, who elaborated some of the Naqshbandī ideas in a quite original way.

KHWĀJA MĪR DARD, A "SINCERE MUHAMMADAN"

. . . and I was brought out of this exciting stage by special grace and particular protection and peculiar blessing to the station of perfect unveiling and to the Reality of Islam, and was granted special proximity to the plane of the Pure Essence Most Exalted and Holy, and became honored by the honor of the perfection of Prophethood and pure Muhammadanism, and was brought forth from the subjective views of unity, unification and identity toward complete annihilation, and was gratified by the ending of individuality and outward traces, and was exalted to "remaining in God"; and after the ascent I was sent toward the descent, and the door of Divine Law was opened to me . . . .

Thus wrote Khwāja Mīr Dard of Delhi (1721–85), describing the mystical way that led him from his former state of intoxication and poetic exuberance to the quiet, sober attitude of a "sincere Muhammadan."[43]

This spiritual way is not peculiar to Mīr Dard; it reminds us of the traditional Naqshbandī theories. Even Aḥmad Sirhindī had spoken in his letters about his former state of intoxication before he was blessed with the second sobriety, the "remaining in God." And the "way downward" is, as we saw, connected with the prophetic activities and qualities. Yet in the case of Dard such a statement is worth quoting, since he was usually known as the master of short, moving Urdu poems, as an artist who composed the first mystical poetry in Urdu. Scarcely anyone has studied his numerous Persian prose works, interspersed with verses, in which he unfolds the doctrines of the *ṭarīqa Muḥammadiyya*, of which he was the first initiate.

Dard was the son of Muhammad Nāṣir ʿAndalīb (1697–1758),

43. Annemarie Schimmel, "Mir Dard's Gedanken über das Verhältnis von Mystik und Wort," in *Festgabe deutscher Iranisten zur 2500-Jahrfeier Irans*, ed. Wilhelm Eilers (Stuttgart, 1971); Schimmel, "A Sincere Muhammadan's Way to Salvation," in *Memorial Volume S. F. G. Brandon*, ed. Eric J. Sharpe and John R Hinnels (Manchester, 1973); Haydar Akhtar, *Khwāja Mīr Dard, taṣawwuf aur shāʿirī* (Aligarh, India, 1971).

a *sayyid* from Turkish lands and a descendant of Bahāʾuddīn Naqshband. His mother claimed descent from ʿAbduʾl-Qādir Gīlānī. Muhammad Nāṣir gave up the military service to become a dervish; his master was Saʿdullāh Gulshan, "rose garden," whose role in the development of Urdu poetry has already been mentioned. It was in honor of his master that Muhammad Nāṣir chose *ʿAndalīb,* "nightingale," as a pen name, just as Gulshan had selected his nom de plume in honor of his master ʿAbduʾl-Aḥad Gul, "rose," a member of Aḥmad Sirhindī's family. Gulshan spent his later life in Nāṣir ʿAndalīb's house, where he died in 1728. ʿAndalīb's second master was Pīr Muḥammad Zubayr, the fourth and last *qayyūm* from the house of Aḥmad Sirhindī, and it was after Pīr Zubayr's death that he composed his *Nāla-yi ʿAndalīb,* "The Lamentation of the Nightingale," which he dictated to his son Khwāja Mīr, surnamed Dard, "Pain."[44] It is a strange mixture of theological, legal, and philosophical discourses in the framework of an allegorical story, the thread of which is often lost. Now and then, charming anecdotes and verses, dissertations on Indian music or on Yoga philosophy, can be found, and the ending—in which the hero "Nightingale" is recognized as the Prophet himself—is one of moving tenderness and pathetic beauty. Mīr Dard considered this book the highest expression of mystical wisdom, second only to the Koran. It was the source book for teaching the Muhammadan Path.

Muhammad Nāṣir had been blessed about 1734 by a vision of the Prophet's grandson Ḥasan ibn ʿAlī, who had introduced him to the secret of the true Muhammadan Path (*aṭ-ṭarīqa al-Muḥammadiyya*). (Ḥasan ibn ʿAlī was considered by the Shādhiliyya to be "the first Pole," *quṭb.*)[45] Young Dard became his father's first disciple and spent the rest of his life propagating the doctrine of "sincere Muhammadanism," which was a fundamentalist interpretation of Islam, deepened by the mystical and ascetic techniques of the Naqshbandiyya. Dard succeeded his father in 1758 and never left Delhi, despite the tribulations that befell the capital during the late eighteenth century. Dard instructed a number of Urdu poets, who would gather in his house for *mushāʿiras*, and he was a prolific writer in Persian. His greatest work, the voluminous *ʿIlm ul-kitāb* (1770), gives a detailed account of his religious ideas

44. Muhammad Nāṣir ʿAndalīb, *Nāla-yi ʿAndalīb,* 2 vols. (Bhopal, 1309 h./1891–92).

45. Paul Nwyia, *Ibn ʿAṭāʾ Allāh et la naissance de la confrèrie šāḏilite* (Beirut, 1972), p. 31 (quotation from Mursī).

and of his mystical experiences. It is a kind of spiritual autobiography, which bears an amazing similarity to that of the sixteenth-century Egyptian mystic Shaʿrānī. Essentially, Dard's *ʿIlm ul-kitāb* was conceived as a commentary on the 111 *wāridāt*, short poems and prose pieces that "descended" upon him about 1750; it then grew into a work of 111 chapters, each headed by the words *Ya Nāṣir*, "O Helper," alluding to his father's name. Whatever he wrote was connected with his father, with whom he had reached perfect identification. Between 1775 and 1785 he composed the *Chahār Risāla*, four stylistically beautiful spiritual diaries; each of them is divided into 341 sections, corresponding to the numerical value of the word *Nāṣir*.[46]

When Dard finished his last book, he had reached the age of sixty-six lunar years, and since his father had died at that age and God had promised him that he would resemble his father in every respect, he was sure that he would die very soon. In fact, he died shortly afterward, on 11 January 1785.

Dard's close relationship with his father is the strangest aspect of his life. His love for his family meant, at the same time, love for the Prophet, since both parents claimed *sayyid* lineage and thus special proximity to the Prophet. His father was, for Dard, the mystical guide par excellence. Traditional Sufi theories regard the sheikh as the father of the disciple; for Dard the two functions actually coincided in Muhammad Nāṣir. This led him to interpret the theory of ascent and descent in a peculiar way. He begins, naturally, with the *fanā fīʾsh-shaykh*, annihilation in the sheikh, which leads to annihilation in the Prophet and annihilation in God; from there, the descent begins. This descent, usually called *baqā billāh*, was explained by Dard:

> *fanā* in God is directed toward God, and *baqā* in God is directed toward creation, and one calls the most perfect wayfarer him who comes down more than others, and then again becomes firmly established in the *baqā* in the Prophet, and he who is on this descendent rank is called higher and more exalted than he who is still in ascent, for the end is the return to the beginning.
>
> But higher than he who has reached this stage is he who has found *baqā* in his sheikh, for he has completed the whole circle. This is the terminating rank which God Almighty has kept for the pure Muhammadans whereas the others with all their power cannot be honored by it. (IK 115–16)

46. Khwāja Mīr Dard, *ʿIlm ul-kitāb* (Bhopal, 1310 h.). Dard's *Chahār risāla* (Bhopal, 1310 h./1892–93), contains the *Nāla-yi Dard, Āh-i sard, Dard-i dil,* and *Shamʿ-i maḥfil.*

This experience was born out of Dard's relationship with his own father-sheikh and could not be shared by anybody else.

Many of the chapters in the *ʿIlm ul-kitāb* and the *Risālas* are devoted to the problems of unity and multiplicity; true "Muhammadan *tauḥīd*" meant, for him, "immersion in the contemplation of God along with the preservation of the stages of servantship" (IK 609). Dard frequently attacks those "imperfect Sufis" who claim "in their immature minds" to be confessors of unity, but are entangled in a sort of heresy, namely, believing in *waḥdat al-wujūd*. The vision of the all-embracing divine light—and "Light" is the most appropriate name for God—is the highest goal the mystic can hope for: a vision in which no duality is left and all traces of distinction and self-will are extinguished, but which is not a substantial union. Constant *dhikr*, fasting, and trust in God can lead man to this noble state. Creation is seen through the image of giving light to pieces of glass—an image known to the earlier mystics: "Just as in the particles of a broken mirror the One form is reflected, thus the beauty of the Real Unity of Existence is reflected in the different apparent ranks of beings. . . . God brings you from the darknesses to the Light, i.e., He brings you who are contingent quiddities from nonexistence into existence" (IK 217). But Dard was well aware that the "pantheistic" formulation so dear to the poets—"everything is He"—was dangerous and incorrect. In common with the elders of his order, he saw that "everything is from Him" and, as the Koran attests, "whithersoever ye turn, there is the Face of God" (Sūra 2:109). "From every form in this worldly rosebed pluck nothing except the rose of the vision of God."[47] He does not shun the traditional imagery of Persian poetry when he addresses the Lord in his prayer: "We, beguiled by Thy perfect Beauty, do not see in all the horizons anything but Thine open signs . . . . The light of faith is a sign of coquetry from the manifestation of Thy face, and the darkness of infidelity is dressed in black from the shade of Thy tresses."[48]

Dard elaborated the theories of the divine as they are reflected in the different levels of creation, a creation that culminates in man, the microscosm reflecting the divine attributes. It is man who is

> the seal of the degrees of creation, for after him no species has come into existence, and he is the sealing of the hand of Omnipotence, for God

47. *Āh-i sard*, no. 192.
48. *Āh-i sard*, no. 96.

Most Exalted has said: "I created him with My hands" [Sūra 38:75]. He is, so to speak, the divine seal that has been put on the page of contingency, and the Greatest Name of God has become radiant from the signet of his forehead. The *alif* of his stature points to God's unity, and the *tughrā* of his composition, i.e., the absolute comprehensive picture of his eyes, is an *h* with two eyes, which indicates Divine Ipseity [*huwiyya*]. His mouth is the door of the treasure of Divine mysteries, which is opened at the time of speaking, and he has got a face that everywhere holds up the mirror of the Face of God, and he has got an eyebrow for which the word "We honored the children of Adam" [Sūra 17:72] is valid. (IK 422)

In fact, as he says in one of his best-known Urdu lines:

> Although Adam had not got wings,
> yet he has reached a place that was not destined even
> for angels.[49]

It is this high rank of man that enables him to ascend through the stages of the prophets toward the proximity of Muhammad and thus toward the *ḥaqīqa Muḥammadiyya,* the first principle of individuation.

Like a number of mystics before him, Dard went this way, and his spiritual autobiography (IK 504–5) gives an account of his ascent–in Arabic, as always when he conveys the highest mysteries of faith.

> And He made him his closest friend [*ṣafī*] and His vicegerent on earth by virtue of the Adamic sanctity [see Sūra 3:30].
> And God saved him from the ruses of the lower self and from Satan and made him His friend [*nājī*] by virtue of the Noachian sanctity.
> And God softened the heart of the unfeeling before him and sent to him people of melodies by virtue of the sanctity of David.
> He made him ruler of the kingdom of his body and his nature, by a manifest power, by virtue of the sanctity of Solomon.
> And God made him a friend [*khalīl*] and extinguished the fire of wrath in his nature so that it became "cool and peaceful" [Sūra 21:69] by virtue of the Abrahamic sanctity.
> And God caused the natural passions to die and slaughtered his lower soul and made him free from worldly concern so that he became completely cut off from this world and what is in it, and God honored him with a mighty slaughtering [Sūra 37:107] in front of his mild father, and his father put the knife to his throat in one of the states of being drawn near to God in the beginning of his way, with the intention of slaughtering him for God, and God accepted him well, and thus he is really one who has been slaughtered by God and remained safe in the outward form as his father gave him the glad tidings: "Whoever has not

49. Khwāja Mīr Dard, *Urdu Dīwān,* ed. Khalīl ur-Raḥmān Dāʾūdī (Lahore, 1962), p. 9.

seen a dead person wandering around on earth may look at this son of mine who lives through me and who moves through me!" In this state he gained the sanctity of Ishmael.

God beautified his nature and character and made him loved and accepted by His beloved [Muhammad]. He attracted the hearts to him and cast love for him into his father's heart—a most intense love!—and he taught him the interpretation of Prophetic traditions by virtue of the sanctity of Joseph [Sūra 12:45].

God talked to him in inspirational words when he called: "Verily, I am God, put off thy shoes! [Sūra 20:12] of the relations with both worlds from the foot of your ascent and throw away from the hand of your knowledge the stick with which you lean on things besides Me, for you are in the Holy Valley" [by virtue of] the sanctity of Moses.

God made him one of His complete words and breathed into him from His own spirit [Sūra 15:29, 38:72], and he became a spirit from him [Sūra 4:169] by virtue of the sanctity of Jesus.

And God honored him with that perfect comprehensiveness which is the end of the perfections by virtue of the sanctity of Muhammad, and he became according to "Follow me, then God will make you loved by His beloved," and he was veiled in the veil of pure Muhammadanism and annihilated in the Prophet, and no name and trace remained with him, and God manifested upon him His name The Comprising [*al-jāmi*ᶜ] and helped him with angelic support.

And he knows through Gabriel's help without mediation of sciences written in books, and he eats with Michael's help without outward secondary causes, and he breathes through Israfil's breath and loosens the parts of his body and collects them every moment, and he sleeps and awakes every day and is drawn toward death every moment by Azrail's attraction.

God created him as a complete person in respect to reason, lower soul, spirit and body, and as a place of manifestation of all His names and the manifestation of His attributes, and as He made him vicegerent of earth in general for humanity generally, so He also made him the vicegerent of His vicegerent on the carpet of specialisation, especially to complete His bounty in summary and in detail, and He approved for him of Islam outwardly and inwardly [Sūra 5:5], and made him sit on the throne of vicegerency of his father, as heritage and in realisation, and on the seat of the followers of His prophet by attestation and Divine success.

This description shows the steady ascent of Dard until he reaches the closest possible relation to the Prophet through his father.

Many mystics considered themselves to be united with the spirit of a particular prophet, but just as the Muhammadan Reality embraces the spirits of all prophets, Dard realized all their different stages in himself. The name *al-jāmi*ᶜ, "the Comprising," which was given to him, is, in fact, the divine name specialized for man as the last level of emanation, as Ibn ᶜArabī claimed.[50]

50. S. A. Q. Husain, *The Pantheistic Monism of Ibn al-Arabi* (Lahore, 1970), p. 58.

Dard's list is not as comprehensive as the list of twenty-eight prophets shown by Ibn ᶜArabī as the loci of particular divine manifestations, nor does it correspond with the list his father mentions: there, Adam manifests the Divine Will or Creativity; Jesus, Life; Abraham, Knowledge; Noah, Power; David, Hearing; Jacob, Seeing; and Muhammad, Existence—the seven basic attributes of God. One may also recall the list developed by the Kubrāwī mystic Simnānī, who connects the seven prophets with the seven *laṭāʾif or* spiritual centers of man: the Adam of man's being, connected with black color, is the *qalabiyya,* the outward, formal aspect; Noah (blue color), the aspect of the *nafs,* the lower soul; Abraham (red color), the aspect of the heart; Moses (white color), the aspect of the *sirr,* the innermost core of the heart; David (yellow color), the spiritual (*rūḥī*) aspect; Jesus (luminous black), the innermost secret (*khafī*); and Muhammad (green color), the *ḥaqqiyya,* the point connected with the divine reality (CL 182). According to these theories, the mystic who had reached the green after passing the luminous black is the "true Muhammadan" (CL 193).

Dard did not propound a color mysticism, but his claims are revealing. He was blessed with auditions, and he records, again in Arabic (for God speaks to His servant in the language of the Koran):

> And he said: "Say: If Reality were more than that which was unveiled to me, then God would verily have unveiled it to me, for He Most High has completed for me my religion and perfected for me His favor and approved for me Islam as religion, and if the veil were to be opened I would not gain more certitude—verily my Lord possesses mighty bounty." (IK 61)

After this report of an experience in which Dard was invested a the true successor of the Prophet, he goes on to speak of the names by which God has distinguished him. He gives a long list of his "attributive and relative" names: ninety-nine names have been bestowed upon him, corresponding to the ninety-nine most beautiful names of God. We cannot judge whether these names point to a veiling of his real personality or whether they are an expression of the search for identity reflected in his poetry and prose. It may be remembered that his father was predisposed to surrounding the heroes of his books with long chains of high-sounding names.

Only a few people probably knew these secret names of Dard or the comprehensive theological system hidden behind the short verses he wrote, which became the favorite poetry of the people of Delhi,

> Delhi which time has now devastated—
> Tears are flowing now instead of its rivers:
> This town has been like the face of the lovely,
> and its suburbs like the down of the beloved ones![51]

He prayed for the unhappy population that God might not allow foreign armies to enter the town—as happened time and again during his lifetime. He was certainly being idealistic when he expressed the thought that it would be better for the poverty-stricken and destitute inhabitants of the capital "to follow the path of God and the Muhammadan Path, so that they may pluck the roses of inner blessings from the rose garden of their company and listen to the 'Lamentation of the Nightingale' and understand his works."[52]

One of his biographers writes that "the mountain of his patience would have made Sheikh Farīd Ganj-i Shakar bite his fingers from amazement like sugarcane," for he never left Delhi, and apparently did not even leave the compound that had been given to him and his father by one of Aurangzeb's daughters. "Why should I go out? It means just a loss of time; for everywhere there is nothing apparent but annihilation in annihilation, and at every place the lustre of 'Everything is perishing except His Face' [Sūra 55:26] becomes visible."[53] Dard's life was sternly ascetic. Later biographers emphasize mainly the long periods of fasting he kept; even his family, whom he loved dearly, took part in the constant fasting.

There were only two things other than purely religious activities that Dard enjoyed, both of which were contrary to the strict Naqshbandī practice: poetry and music. He was well versed in classical Indian music, and in his own defense he had written a book on music (*Ḥurmat-i ghinā*). The *samā*ᶜ meetings that he arranged twice a month were famous in Delhi, and even the ruler, Shah ᶜAlam II, with the pen name Aftāb, sometimes attended them. The candid logic by which Dard defends his love for music is somewhat amusing:

> My *samā*ᶜ is from God, and God is witness that the singers come from themselves and sing whenever they want; not that I would call them and would consider it a sort of worship when I listen to them, as others do; but I do not refuse such an act. However, I do not do it myself, and my creed is that of the masters [i.e., the Naqshbandiyya]. But since I am imprisoned in this affliction according to the Divine Assent—what can

51. *Nāla*, no. 140.
52. *Dard-i Dil*, no. 154.
53. Ibid., no. 33.

I do? God may absolve me for I have not given a *fatwā* to my friends that this should be licit; and I have not built the mystical path upon *samā*ᶜ so that the other masters of the Path who have absolutely no idea of the way of modulation should have become dissonant and sing about me all those melodies which one should not sing, and open the lip of reproach without reason in my absence.[54]

Dard must have been attacked by other Sufis for his love of music, and it is regrettable that we still know so little about his relationships with Shāh Walīullāh and Maẓhar Jānjānān, the two great Naqshbandī leaders of Delhi. His mystical poetry was apparently also misunderstood by some of his colleagues, as we can guess from some sad remarks scattered in his later works. But he loved writing; the capacity of logical and clear speech was, for him, the divine trust offered to heaven and earth, but accepted only by man (Sūra 33:72)—a trust that has been explained differently in the course of Islamic theology. Dard thought that "a gnostic without a book is like a man without children, and a work that is absurdly unconnected is like a child of bad character" (IK 592). His books were, indeed, his beloved children, and he was grateful that God had granted him both external and internal children of whom he could boast. His son, with the pen name *Alam*, "Pain," was a poet in his own right, and so was Dard's youngest brother, Athar, who was connected with him by a very close love and was virtually his alter ego.

As soft-spoken as Dard may appear from some of his poems, he was quite certain that his literary activity was superior to that of many other mystics and poets. He felt that he had been granted, "like the candle, the tongue of clear speech." He often asserted that he never wrote poetry on commission but that it came to him by inspiration, so that he simply wrote it down without personal effort. His whole work is, in fact, an interpretation of those lines that had been revealed to him, and the way that he explained the simplest and most charming verses in the framework of mystical philosophy, with a terminology borrowed from Ibn ᶜArabī, is surprising and, quite frankly, not very uplifting. His Persian poetry followed the traditional patterns and the inherited imagery, and is good and readable, but his fame rests primarily on the small Urdu *Dīwān* of some 1200 verses, most of which are of unsurpassable beauty. He sings of the unity of the created beings experienced by the mystic:

54. *Nāla*, no. 38.

> In the state of collectedness the single beings of the world are one:
> all the petals of the rose together are one.[55]

The garden imagery is taken up, not as brilliantly as in classical poetry, but somewhat veiled in melancholy:

> We are unaware of our own manifestation in this garden:
> the narcissus does not see its own spring with its own eye.[56]

He speaks of the footprint in the desert or in the street of the beloved and compares life to an imprint in water. He uses the image of the "fairy in the bottle" as much as the "dance of the peacock," but his favorite image is that of the mirror. The whole creation is one great mirror, or a large number of mirrors, reflecting God's overwhelming beauty. He knew that the world of matter is needed to show the radiance of the pure light:

> My turpitude is the place of manifestation for the lights of purity;
> as much as I am iron, I can become a mirror.[57]

Constant recollection polishes the mirror of the heart to show God's hidden beauty, that "hidden treasure" that wanted to become manifest. And yet the "sacred valley of absolute existence" remains concealed behind the sand dunes of various individuations, which change their forms every moment, and the weary wayfarer becomes aware that the desert of absoluteness is caught in new limitations.

What is all this life? It is real only as far as God has shed His light upon it, but it is like a puppet play, like a dream. Dard's famous line says this:

> Alas, O ignorant one: at the day of death this will be proved:
> A dream was what we saw, what we heard, a tale.[58]

Dard takes up the Prophetic tradition, "men are asleep, and when they die, they awake"—a *ḥadīth* that had been popular with the

55. Dard, *Urdu Dīwān*, p. 57.
56. *Dīwān-i Fārsī*, p. 45.
57. Dard, *Urdu Dīwān*, p. 49.
58. Ibid., p. 2.

mystics throughout the centuries. Rūmī had often warned people not to worry about the facts of this life—why should we worry about a pain we feel in a dream that will end as soon as the morning of eternal life—the *Morgenglanz der Ewigkeit*—dawns upon us? But Rūmī is more optimistic than later poets: he speaks of the joyful apprehension of all the possibilities that will open up before man once he returns to his original home (like the elephant who dreamed of India). In Dard's verses, the feeling of the dreamlike state is filled with hopelessness—what could an inhabitant of eighteenth-century Delhi expect from life? It is a nightmare, unreal; and the use of the word "tale" in the verse just mentioned reminds the reader of the usual connection of fairy tales, which were told at evening time to put children to bed. "Tale" and "sleep" have been invariably—since the days of Omar Khayyam—connected in Persian poetry.

Dard's verses, which look so fragile and have yet lasted longer than most poems written in the eighteenth century—verses that are veritable gems—reflect the situation in Delhi very well: dream, footprints or shifting sand dunes, a reflection in flowing water, and again the hope for the vision of the beloved, which the mystic should find behind all these fading individual existences, whose face does not perish like them. Then, he will realize:

> Pain and happiness have the same shape in this world:
> You may call the rose an open heart, or a broken heart.[59]

MYSTICAL POETRY IN THE REGIONAL LANGUAGES—SINDHI, PANJABI, PASHTO

The visitor who stays in a Panjabi village will certainly find somebody to sing for him the old romance of *Hīr Ranjhā* in the classical form given it by Wārith Shāh in the late eighteenth century. When he proceeds, then, to Sind, to the lower Indus valley, he will enjoy listening to the moving mystical songs of Shāh ʿAbduʾl-Laṭīf of Bhit (1689–1752) or the ardent poems of Sachal Sarmast (d. 1826), whose melodies and words are almost as popular today as they were 150 years ago. The Punjab and the Indus valley have a common tradition of mystical folk literature.[60] At approximately

59. Ibid., p. 41.
60. Lajwanti Ramakrishna, *Panjabi Ṣūfī Poets* (London and Calcutta, 1938), is the only introduction to the subject, but see the review by Johann Fück in *Orientalistische*

the same time, in the thirteenth century, the fertile areas of present Pakistan became the seat of mystics who had migrated from the central lands of the Muslim world, partly because of the threat of the approaching Mongols. Farīduddīn Ganj-i Shakar of Pakpattan is credited with having used a kind of Old Panjabi for his mystical songs. Reliable tradition traces the use of the native language for mystical poetry both in Sind and in the Punjab back to the fifteenth century. The name of a sixteenth-century Panjabi Sufi, Mādhō Lāl Ḥusayn, is mentioned by Dārā Shikōh in his *Ḥasanāt al-ᶜārifīn.* This Mādhō Lāl (1539–93) had sung of his love for a Hindu boy in simple Panjabi verses, and his poems contain the traditional mystical vocabulary of longing and hope for annihilation. He also alluded to popular motifs, like the stories of *Hīr* and of *Sohnī Mehanwal,* and thus seems to inaugurate (or perhaps even continue from unknown beginnings) a tradition typical of the religious poetry of the two provinces: the insertion of folk tales into the context of mystical thought. Mādhō Lāl's anniversary, still celebrated in Lahore near the Shalimar Garden on the last Saturday in March, is famous as *Mēlā Chirāghān,* the "Fair of Lamps."

Also in the sixteenth century, a group of mystics migrated from Sind to Burhanpur in central India, where they founded a new branch of the Qādiriyya *ṭarīqa;* they are reported to have used Sindhi verses during their *samāᶜ* sessions.[61] From that time on the indigenous Sindhi tradition contains innumerable stories of saints, mainly of those who are buried on Makli Hill near Thatta. Makli Hill, one of the most fascinating sites of Indo-Muslim architecture, is the last resting place for 125,000 saints, according to the tradition. An interesting Persian book written in the late eighteenth century, Mīr ᶜAlī Shīr Qāniᶜs *Maklīnāme,* retells the numerous legends surrounding this graveyard, which stretches over miles, where mystical concerts and dances were performed on almost any day of the week.[62]

Literaturzeitung 43 (1943); he rightly criticized the overall Hindu interpretation. Lionel D. Barnett, *Panjabi: Printed Books in the British Museum* (London, 1961). A good survey in Urdu is Shafīᶜ ᶜAqeel, *Panjab rang* (Lahore, 1968). Iᶜjāzul Ḥaqq Quddūsi, *Tadhkira-yi Ṣūfiyā-yi Sindh* (Karachi, 1959); Quddūsi, *Tadhkira-yi ṣūfiyā-yi Panjāb* (Karachi, 1962); Jethmal Parsram, *Sufis of Sind* (Madras, 1924). Annemarie Schimmel, "Sindhi Literature," in *History of Indian Literature,* ed. Jan Gonda (Wiesbaden, 1974).

61. Rāshid Burhānpūrī, *Burhānpūr ke Sindhī auliyā* (Karachi, 1957).

62. Mīr ᶜAlī Shīr Qāniᶜ, *Maklīname,* ed. Sayyid Hussamuddin Rashdi (Karachi, 1967).

The Punjab and Sind show close similarities in the types of mystical literature that flourished there. The more rustic, very idiomatic Panjabi and the complicated, musical Sindhi—both strong, expressive languages—were excellent media to express mystical feelings, though not mystical theories. The mystical works center around the endless yearning of the soul, burning love, longing for pain, which is the very blessing of God. These themes were sung time and again in forms inherited from the Indian past—*dhōra*s, *kāfī*s, *wāy*—not in the Persian form of *ghazal* in quantitative meters, but in Indian poetical forms that were closely connected with indigenous musical modes. The tunes were partly adapted from the Indian tradition, partly invented by the mystical poets themselves on the basis of classical and folk music.

The old accusations against the dry-as-dust theologians, the *mollā,* which form a standard motif of Persian and Turkish mystical and quasi-mystical poetry, were taken up again by the mystics in the northwest part of the Subcontinent.

> Reading and reading knowledge, the muftis give
>   judgment,
> but without love they have remained ignorant, Sir!
> By reading knowledge the secret of God is not known,
> only one word of love is efficient, Sir!

an eighteenth-century Panjabi poet sings.[63] Such verses appealed particularly to the peasants and the illiterate, who understood that even they—though not learned like the hairsplitting *mollā*s—might attain a higher level of spiritual life through surrender in love.

The imagery in this poetry is generally taken from the daily life of the villagers, from gardening and planting. Though the verses of the first great Panjabi mystical poet, Sulṭān Bāhū (who got his surname because each line of his *Sīḥarfī,* "Golden Alphabet," ends with the exclamation *hū,* "He") do nothing but develop ideas well known to earlier Sufis, his approach is worth mentioning as typical of the way rural mystics spread the ideas of Sufism.[64] The first verse of Sulṭān Bāhū's (d. 1691) poem goes:

> *Alif*: Allah is like the jasmine plant which the preceptor
>   planted in my heart—o Hū!
> By water and the gardener of negation and positive

63. Ramakrishna, *Panjabi Sufi Poets,* p. xxx.
64. Sulṭān Bāhoo, *Abyāt,* trans. Maqbool Elahi (Lahore, 1967).

statement it remained near the jugular vein
and everywhere—o Hū!
It spread fragrance inside when it approached the
time of blossoming—o Hū!
May the efficient preceptor live long, says Bāhū,
who planted this plant—o Hū!

These lines point to the recollection of the divine name, planted in the mystic's heart by his Pir. The water of negation and affirmation, the *lā* and *illā* of the profession of faith in the *dhikr*, is combined with the allusion to Sūra 50:16—"He is nearer to you than your jugular vein"—in the context of plant life. This verse is a fine example of the kind of Panjabi and Sindhi imagery that could easily be understood by everybody in the village.

In both provinces, a preference for the motif of spinning and weaving can be observed, a natural propensity in a cotton-growing country; the *dhikr* could therefore be compared to the act of spinning (the aptness of the image is enhanced by the similarity of the humming sounds). Such "spinning" can turn the heart into fine, precious thread, which God will buy at Doomsday for a good price.

Both provinces have also produced hymns extolling the great masters of the mystical orders, particularly ʿAbduʾl-Qādir Gīlānī, whose glorious deeds are often celebrated. One of the first "geographical" poems in Sindhi was composed in his honor. His blessings are described as extending to a long series of cities and countries nicely enumerated in alliterative form.[65] Allusions to the fate of Manṣūr Ḥallāj are very common.[66] Some of the mystical poets expressed their feelings of all-embracing unity with amazing audacity—the Sufi is no longer Arab, Hindu, Turk, or Peshawari; eventually Ḥallāj and the judge who condemned him, the lover and the theologian, are seen as nothing but different manifestations of the one divine reality. Such verses have led a number of authors, particularly the Hindus who studied this aspect of Indo-Muslim

65. The author, Jaman Charan, lived in the eighteenth century. His poem was often imitated. See Dr. Nabi Bakhsh Baloch, ed., *Madaḥūn ayn munājātūn* (Karachi, 1959), no. 1.

66. On the whole literary complex see Annemarie Schimmel, "The Activities of the Sindhi Adabi Board," *Die Welt des Islam*, n.s. 4, nos. 3–4 (1961); Schimmel, "Neue Veröffentlichungen zur Volkskunde von Sind," *Die Welt des Islam*, n.s. 9, nos. 1–4 (1964); Schimmel, "The Martyr-Mystic Ḥallāj in Sindhi Folk-Poetry," *Numen* 9, no. 3 (1962).

religious life, to believe that here Indian *advaita* mysticism gained a complete victory over Islamic monotheism. The love for the sheikh and the attempt at becoming annihilated in him, which is a peculiar feature of Sufi practices, has also been explained as the typical Hindu love for the *guru*.

There is no doubt that the Indian Sufis were inclined to take over images and forms from their Hindu neighbors; however, none of the Panjabi or Sindhi mystics neglected the love of the Prophet, whose miracles are told and retold in poetry throughout the country. Even on the level of simple folk songs, riddles, or bridal songs the traditional wordplays on *Aḥmad* and *Aḥad* were repeated, and the poetry of Shāh ᶜAbduʾl-Laṭīf contains a fine description of the Prophet through the image of the rain cloud, the symbol of divine mercy, whose help is implored for the Day of Judgment. Exalted descriptions of Muhammad as the Perfect Man, who is like the dawn between the divine light and the darkness of human existence, can be read in the theoretical works of some Sindhi Sufis, for example, the eighteenth-century Suhrawardī mystic ᶜAbduʾr-Raḥīm Girhōrī, who paid with his life for his missionary zeal.[67] The popular veneration of the Prophet was grounded theoretically in such a way that the historical person of the Prophet was almost totally eclipsed behind the veil of light that the Sindhi Sufis wove about him.

A strange fact—more visible in Sind than in the Punjab—is the way Hindus shared in the Muslim orders. Some saints were claimed by both communities, like Sheikh Ṭāhir, who was called Lāl Udērō by the Hindus.[68] This sixteenth-century mystic was one of the most ardent defenders of the unity of being; he saw God "even in a camel." Hindu writers wrote mystical poems in which they used the imagery of the Muslims; they composed poems in honor of the Prophet and even wrote *taᶜzīya* for the Muḥarram mourning of the Shia community of Sind; or they devoted ballads to the fate of famous Sufi martyrs.[69] They played a prominent part in the study of Sufism as well, though, as pointed out earlier, they usually lacked a true understanding of the Koran and the founda-

67. Umar Muhammad Daudpota, *Kalām-i Girhōrī* (Hyderabad, Sind, 1956).
68. Mīr ᶜAlī Shīr Qāniᶜ, *Tuḥfat al-kirām* (Hyderabad, Sind, 1957), p. 389.
69. Mīr ᶜAlī Shīr Qāniᶜ, *Maqālāt ash-shuᶜarā*, ed. Sayyid Hussamuddin Rashdi (Karachi, 1956), p. 867.

tions of Muslim faith and tried to explain everything in the light of Hindu philosophy.

A feature common to Panjabi and Sindhi mysticism is the use of folk tales as vehicles for the expression of mystical experiences. The first known representative of this trend, Mādhō Lāl Ḥusayn, has already been mentioned. The theme of *Hīr Ranjhā* was used by Bullhē Shāh, as well as by his younger contemporary Hāshim Shāh of Amritsar, for their mystical meditations.

Bullhē Shāh (1680–1752) is considered the greatest of the Panjabi mystical poets; he lived near Lahore.[70] Like his contemporaries Shāh ʿAbduʾl-Laṭīf in Sind and Shāh Walīullāh, Mīr Dard, and Maẓhar Jānjānān in Delhi, he was a witness of the epoch of great political disasters that occurred, with only brief interruptions, in the northwestern part of the Subcontinent after Aurangzeb's death in 1707. Like these mystics, he found peace in the inner world of love and surrender, singing his mystical songs in order to console himself and his friends in the times of external sufferings and afflictions. His poetry was so highly esteemed that he was surnamed "the Rūmī of Punjab." In addition to being the leading poet of Panjabi Sufism, he also composed a number of Persian prose treatises, comparable to those of Mīr Dard.

The story of *Hīr Ranjhā* probably goes back to an historical event in the sixteenth century. Ranjhā, the son of a landlord of the Sargodha district, falls in love with Hīr, the daughter of the ruler of Djang. Despite her father's prohibition, the lovers meet in the fields, until Hīr's uncle catches them. Hīr is first imprisoned in her father's house and then married to a Rajput, but she manages to send a letter to her beloved. After numerous tribulations, the luckless lovers die. According to one version, they are poisoned by Hīr's family; in another version they die from thirst in the desert during their pilgrimage to Mecca and are eventually united in death (or, by drinking the water of life, in eternal life).

This story has been told by nearly a hundred poets in Panjabi, Persian, Urdu, and Sindhi and has been translated several times into English. It was given its classical form by Wārith Shāh (completed around 1794). Since the tale was known to everybody, the poet has the heroes recite short verses, which are commonly interpreted in a mystical sense. Mohan Singh Diwāna, the best authority

70. Bullhē Shāh, *Dīwān*, ed. Faqir M. Faqir (Lahore, 1960).

on Panjabi literature and a mystic in his own right,[71] has translated the mystical interpretation given by Wārith Shāh:

Our soul is the tragic heroine Hīr,
Our body is the lover Ranjhā,
Our spiritual preceptor is the Yogi Balmath,
  the five helpful saints are our five senses
  who support us in our adventures' dread.
Truth is the judge.
Our deeds, good and bad, are the two boat-women
  who lust for us.
The shepherds in the forest are the recording angels
  who at our shoulders invisible sit.
The secret chamber is the grave,
Saida Khera is the angel of death.
The lame uncle, Kaido, is the reprobate and renegade
  Satan who delights to introduce into disobedience and
  disgrace.
The girl friends of Hīr are our relationships
  and loyalties that bind us fast.
Reason is the flute
  that to us the music of Divine wisdom conveys.
Wārith Shāh says: Those alone cross over
  who have silently prayed to the Lord,
  and ever devotedly recited His glorious Name.

"Hīr is our soul"—one of the characteristics of Sindhi and Panjabi poetry is that the longing soul is always depicted as a woman; this typical aspect of Indian Sufi poetry was inherited from Hinduism (see Appendix 2).

The most outstanding master of popular Sufi poetry in Pakistan is, no doubt, Shah ʿAbduʾl-Laṭīf of Bhit. He is not the first in the long line of Sindhi mystical poets. Attempts at expressing mystical experiences in the Sindhi tongue go back at least to the sixteenth century. A prominent master was Qāḍī Qāḍan (d. 1546), of whose work only a few verses have been preserved; they distinctly show, however, all the peculiarities of later poetry. The poems of ʿAbduʾl-

71. Mohan Singh Diwāna, *An Introduction to Panjabi Literature* (Amritsar, 1951). The best translation is Charles Frederick Usborne, *Hir Ranjha*, ed. Mumtaz Hasan (Karachi, 1966). On the subject in Indo-Persian literature see Ḥafeeẓ Hoshyārpūrī, *Mathnawiyāt-i Hīr Rānjhā* (Karachi, 1957).

Laṭīf's ancestor Shāh ʿAbduʾl-Karīm[72] or those of Shāh ʿInāt[73] in the seventeenth century are closely related to Laṭīf's poetry. Their language is extremely compact, since the Sindhi grammar allows very intricate combinations of words. Each group of poems, which rhyme according to particular rules of popular Indian prosody, usually contains an alternation between the recitation of the main verses by a solo voice and the repetition of a so-called *kāfī* or *wāy* by a chorus; the *wāy* usually sums up the contents of the whole group of verses.

Shāh ʿAbduʾl-Laṭīf was born into a family of mystics in 1689 in Hala, near present-day Hyderabad-Sind,[74] where mystical leaders of the Suhrawardiyya had settled—the name of Makhdūm Nūḥ in the seventeenth century is best known. In his early years Laṭīf wandered through the country in the company of a group of yogis and perhaps reached the sacred mountain Hinglaj in Balochistan, which is often mentioned as "the goal" in Sindhi mystical poetry. He then settled down in Bhit, not far from his hometown, and gathered a number of disciples around him. His tomb in Bhit Shah is one of the loveliest sanctuaries in the Muslim world. The building, covered with blue and white tiles (typical of Hala), with exquisite ornaments, exudes serenity and peace. The pillar bases are almost suggestive of large flowers just opening, and delicate tilework decorates the ceiling.

We do not know much about Shāh Laṭīf's external life; his personality is reflected in the poems collected under the title *Shāha jō risālō,* "The Book of Shāh," and published for the first time by the German missionary Ernest Trumpp in 1866. The *Risālō* contains thirty chapters (*sur*), named according to their musical modes; in addition to traditional Indian *raga*s like *Kalyān* and *Kabōdh,* Shāh ʿAbduʾl-Laṭīf invented a number of new modes. Some dervishes who live at the threshold of his tomb perform this music in their gatherings on Thursday nights, and the melodies are well known all over Sind.[75]

72. Motilal Jotwani, *Shāh ʿAbdul Karīm* (New Delhi, 1970).

73. *Miyēn Shāh ʿInāt jō kalām,* ed. Dr. Nabi Bakhsh Baloch (Hyderabad, Sind, 1963).

74. H. T. Sorley, *Shah Abdul Latif of Bhit: His Poetry, Life, and Times* (1940; reprint ed., Oxford, 1966), is an excellent study, although it underscores the political and social background slightly too much. Motilal Jotwani, "Shah Latif: Man and Poet," *Indian Literatures* 6, no. 2 (1963); Annemarie Schimmel, "Schah Abdul Latif," *Kairos,* 1961, fasc. 3–4.

75. The best edition of the *Risālō* is that by Kalyan B. Adwani (Bombay, 1958). An Urdu verse translation was made by Sheikh Ayāz (Hyderabad, Sind, 1963). The English

Some of the *surs* are related to folk ballads of the Indus valley, like those dealing with Sassuī Punhun, Sohnī Mehanwal, ᶜUmar Maruī, and Līlā Chanēsar. Others describe the mystical moods or the ideal lover in traditional terminology, like *Asā* and *Yaman Kalyān*. Still others sing of the camel, the symbol of the base faculties that become trained during the long journey toward the beloved, or of the seafarer's wife waiting for her husband to return from Ceylon; of the dry tree in the desert, or of the wild grouse. Or the poet describes a group of yogis to whom he applies Koranic verses: their knees are like Mount Sinai, places of revelation; their faces shine in the divine light.

The last chapter (*Sur Ramakālī*) is one of the most interesting parts of the *Risālō* in terms of mystical syncretism, but it should be read together with the praise of the Prophet in *Sur Sārang*, or with the bitter laments for Ḥusayn's death in Kerbela in *Sur Kēdārō*.

For the Sindhi, however, the favorite poems are those in which Shāh ᶜAbduʾl-Laṭīf relies upon folk tales. Everybody knew the contents of these tales, so that the poet did not need to dwell on the preliminaries; he could begin his poems with the most dramatic moment and then elaborate the feeling of the heroine and the different shades of the soul's movements—hope, longing, fear, annihilation. Shāh Laṭīf translated into poetry the cries of Sohnī, whose beloved Mehanwal grazes cattle on an island in the Indus and who slips away from her husband every night to swim across the river to meet Mehanwal, guided by the starlike eyes of the soft cows, though surrounded by alligators and all kinds of danger. Finally, one night, Sohnī's sister-in-law discovers her adventures and replaces the baked jar that she uses as a kind of life vest with an unbaked vessel, so that the loving woman is drowned on her way.

And there is Sassuī, a washerman's daughter whose beauty attracts people from all parts of the country; even Punhun, the prince of Kecch in Balochistan, falls in love with her and stays with her. His father sends some relatives to make the couple drunk and carry away Punhun; Sassuī, awakening at dawn from the "sleep of heedlessness," finds herself alone. She decides to follow the caravan to Kecch, but perishes in the desert after her voice, no longer the voice of a woman or a bird, has been transformed into the voice of

---

selection by Elsa Kazi, *Risalo of Shah Abdul Latif* (Hyderabad, Sind, 1965), gives a good impression of style and contents.

love itself. Sassuī is, in a certain sense, the feminine counterpart of Majnūn in the Arabo-Persian tradition.

There is the shepherd girl Maruī, kidnapped by the mighty ruler ʿUmar of Omarkot. Confined in his castle, she refuses to look after herself and tries to become as unattractive as possible, waiting every day for a letter from her family, until the ruler sends her back to her homeland. Or there is Nūrī, the fisher maid who wins the heart of Prince Tamāchī by her obedience and sweetness—a story that can be historically located in the late fifteenth century, but that bears the distinct flavor of the Indian tale of "the maid with the fish-smell." Nūrī is the model of the obedient soul blessed by the love of the mighty Lord for her constant devotion. And there is the Hindu tale of Sorathi, in which the king offers even his head to the minstrel who enthralls him with heartrending verses about divine love and surrender.[76] Rūmī, in common with many tales of initiation through death, sang: "What is beheading? Slaying the carnal soul in the Holy War" (M 3:2525).

In the description of the female characters Shāh ʿAbduʾl-Laṭīf made every posible effort to depict even the slightest feelings and every change of mood. Sassuī wanders through the desert, lonely and hopeless, and eventually discovers—with a verse translated from Rūmī's *Mathnawī* (M 1:1741)—that

> Not only the thirsty seek the water,
> but the water seeks the thirsty as well.

Or, in the midst of her painful wandering, the poet suddenly turns to the "interior journey," that journey by which she will find the lost beloved in her own heart—as Majnūn did, no longer needing the "real" Laila because he had become one with her, or as Rūmī discovered the lost Shamsuddīn in himself. Sassuī reaches the higher unitive stage by dying before she dies. Maruī, in turn, is compared to the oyster, which would rather die from thirst than drink the salty water that surrounds it; one day it will open to receive the raindrop that will become a pearl in its womb.

The verses of the *Risālō* are often repetitious. Some critics have considered them rather unpolished in terms of classical (i.e., "Per-

76. Ernst Trumpp, "Sorathi. Ein Sindhi-Gedicht aus dem grossen Divan des Sayyid ʿAbd-ul-Laṭīf," *Zeitschrift der Deutschen Morgenländischen Gesellschaft* 17 (1863); Trumpp, "Einige Bemerkungen zum Sufismus," *Zeitschrift der Deutschen Morgenländischen Gesellschaft* 16 (1862).

sianized") metrics and vocabulary, or thought they were too full of jingling rhymes and puns (thus Trumpp, who thoroughly disliked Sufism). Shāh ᶜAbduʾl-Laṭīf did use the inherited language of the Sufis; he himself acknowledged his indebtedness to Rūmī, and his work cannot be fully appreciated without a thorough knowledge of the different currents of Sufism in Iran and India. This is the point at which most of the Hindu interpreters, and even an excellent British scholar like Herbert Tower Sorley, have not done full justice to him.

Shāh ᶜAbduʾl-Laṭīf, in spite of his intense mystical feeling and his poetic talent, still maintained a certain reluctance in unveiling the mysteries of divine love. He usually speaks in allusions, in difficult and opaque words, in oblique expressions. This tendency makes his style as complicated as it is attractive; it always induces the reader, or rather the listener, to meditate upon a verse that is repeated several times with slight yet meaningful variations. One may best characterize these verses as sighs, as heartbeats of a longing soul.

There is a story that once when a boy came to his convent, the mystic immediately recognized that he would one day "open the lid from those things" that he had kept secret. The young man was Sachal Sarmast (1739–1826), destined to become a Sufi poet second only to Shāh ᶜAbduʾl-Laṭīf. The anecdote may have been derived from the pen name Sachal used in his Persian poetry, namely, *Ashikār*, "Open." His name *Sachal*, a diminutive of *sach*, "truth," seems to be an allusion to the word *Ḥaqq*, "truth," as found in Ḥallāj's sentence *anāʾl-Ḥaqq*; and the name *Sarmast* indicates that he was an "intoxicated" Sufi—and intoxicated he was indeed![77]

Sachal Sarmast was a versatile mystic who led a solitary life; he wrote in Sindhi, Siraiki (the northern dialect of Sindhi), Urdu, and Persian, uttering whatever came into his heart with no thought for the consequences. Like his predecessors, he relied upon folk tales and made Sassuī and Sohnī his heroines; he did not, however, elaborate the subjects as much as Shāh ᶜAbduʾl-Laṭīf did. His Persian and Urdu poetry is traditional and conventional in style and expression, but in his mother tongue his feeling overpowers him. In short, jubilant verses he reveals the secrets of divine union, and in hymnlike poems he describes the unity of being in daring words

77. Sachal Sarmast, *Risālō Sindhī*, ed. ᶜOthmān ᶜAlī Anṣāri (Karachi, 1958). See the Bibliography for other editions.

that are often reminiscent of the way Yūnus Emre and other Turkish folk poets sang of their unitive experience.

I do not know, o sisters, what I really am?
Perhaps I am a puppet, perhaps the thread on which
it hangs,
perhaps a ball in the hand of the Beloved,
perhaps a yoke with heavy burden,
perhaps the castle where the king sits and thinks
and talks about many things to get new information.
Perhaps I am a horse which some rider guides,
perhaps a wave of the ocean which drowns the outward
being,
perhaps a henna-flower with red coloring,
perhaps a rose, the head full of scent.
Perhaps I am a fountain, filled by a cloud,
in which the sun is reflected and the moon as well.
Perhaps I am the mirror of God since pre-eternity
which is beyond all words . . .
perhaps I am not at all! [78]

Chains of anaphora are used, often in the form of questions: "Who is . . . who is . . . who is . . .?" Like all the Sufis, Sachal was fond of contrasting pairs of concepts that reveal the basic unity of being:

He is Abū Ḥanīfa and He is Hanuman,
He is the Koran and He is the Vedas,
He is this and He is that,
He is Moses, and He is Pharaoh.

Like many mystics before him, Sachal sighed about the afflictions brought about by love; he enumerated the names of those who have had to suffer for their love of God:

Welcome, welcome Thou art—to which place wilt
Thou bring me? Thou wilt again cut off
a head!
Giving a kick to Sarmad Thou has killed him;
Thou hast brought Manṣūr on the gallows,
cut off Sheikh ʿAṭṭār's head—
Now Thou art asking the way here!

78. Ibid., p. 110.

Thou hast split Zakariya with a saw, thrown Joseph into
a well,
Thou hast made Shams to be killed at the hand of the
mollas, Thou usest to afflict the lover.
Thou hast made Ṣanᶜān bind the brahmins' thread,
Thou hast made to be slaughtered Bullhē Shāh, Jaᶜfar to
be drowned in the sea,
In misfortune hast Thou pressed Bilāwal, hast killed
ᶜInāyat in the fighting arena, hast sentenced
Karmal . . . .[79]

This poem gives a good idea of the historical information on which a mystic in a distant province of the Muslim world could rely, though some of the charges cannot be verified. The form itself is traditional; Rūzbihān Baqlī had devoted a whole paragraph in his *Sharḥ-i shaṭḥiyāt* to the enumeration of the afflictions of the Sufis, beginning with the words: "Did you not see what the people of the exterior meaning did to Ḥārith al-Muḥāsibī and Maᶜrūf and Sarī?" (B 37). He then went through a long list of Sufis who were attacked, persecuted, or even killed by the theologians and the "establishment." At about the same time, ᶜAṭṭār enumerated long lists of prophets as models for the suffering of those who love God most (MT 12; V 6). Rūmī accuses God of drawing Jonah and Abraham into water and fire; Yūnus Emre and the Bektashi poets of Turkey echo similar accusations in recounting the stories of the martyrs of love in their poetry. Long lists of Sufi names in the litanies of some orders, with allusions to their fates, are sometimes found in North Africa as well; the poets established their spiritual genealogy with all the lovers who had been afflicted or tried by God throughout the ages.[80]

Sachal has been called "the ᶜAṭṭār of Sind," and in fact the influence of ᶜAṭṭār's imagery is clearly visible in his poetry. This

79. Ibid., p. 377. Sarmad was executed in 1661; Manṣūr Ḥallāj's fate is well known; but it is unlikely that ᶜAṭṭār was killed. According to Islamic legend, which is based on Christian apocrypha, Zakariya (Zacharias) was persecuted by his enemies, and when he sought shelter in a hollow tree, the tree was sawed and he as well. Joseph in the well is a standard motif in poetry. It has been proved that Shams-i Tabrīzī was indeed murdered by Rūmī's entourage. Shaykh Ṣanᶜān is the figure from ᶜAṭṭar's *Manṭiq uṭ-ṭayr*. ᶜInāyat is the martyr-mystic of Jhok. The traditional sources say nothing about the martyrdom of Bullhē Shah. Jaᶜfar may be the Prophet's cousin Jaᶜfar aṭ-Ṭayyār, who was killed in one of the first battles of the Muslims in 630; his hands and feet were cut off, and he "flew to Paradise," hence his surname aṭ-Ṭayyār, "the flying." He is frequently a subject of Sufi poetry. Karmal and Bilawal have not yet been identified.

80. Dermenghem, *Culte des saints*, p. 309.

implies his ardent love for Ḥallāj, whose name occurs hundreds of times in his verses. Shāh ʿAbduʾl-Laṭīf, too, had alluded to Ḥallāj's fate, seeing in every tree and plant the vision of the suffering mystic, proclaiming *anāʾl-ḥaqq* and therefore doomed to death. The generations of mystics who followed Sachal took over this practice, except for the members of the Naqshbandiyya, who have little sympathy for the martyr-mystic. But none of the later mystical poets can match Sachal's intense glow; he is a vigorous poet, and the rhythms and energy, the intense yearning and love, give his verses an almost magical quality.

In the Punjab, the literary heritage of Panjabi was rarely continued by Muslims after 1800, though in the twentieth century a number of mystical treatises have been written and published in Panjabi, including a part translation of Rūmī's *Mathnawī.* The language was used almost exclusively by the Sikhs as their literary medium,[81] whereas the Panjabi Muslims resorted to Urdu to express their more sophisticated thoughts, though they enjoyed and still enjoy listening to the simple mystical verses and ballads in their spoken mother tongue.

Sindhi continued to flourish after the British occupation in 1843. With the introduction of a new Arabic alphabet in 1852, a considerable literature grew up that included mystical poetry and prose. The country had always been proud of its mystical heritage. Did not Dīwān Gidumal, the minister, give the invading Nadir Shah (1739) the most precious treasure Sind had to offer, some of the dust of its saints? The province continued to produce mystics who wrote either in Persian or in their mother tongue. Among them Bēdil of Rohri (d. 1872) should be mentioned as a prolific, though not very outstanding, writer in five languages.[82]

The attitude of some mystical leaders in the lower Indus valley in the late nineteenth and early twentieth centuries, notably between the two world wars, proved quite decisive in the political arena. One may think of the activities of the *ḥurr,* the "Free," the loyal and absolutely obedient disciples of the Pīr Pagarō who were gathered first to support Aḥmad Brelwī's struggle against the Sikh (1829–31) and later actively joined in the struggle against the British by acts that cannot be called mystical or even religious. The

81. Mohan Singh Diwāna, *Sikh Mysticism* (Amritsar, 1964).

82. See the numerous examples in H. I. Sadarangani, *Persian Poets of Sind* (Karachi, 1956).

ḥurr even played a minor role in the Indian-Pakistani war in 1971.[83]

This was not the first time that mystical leaders in Sind, or in other parts of the Muslim world, were engaged in politics or in social reforms. An interesting case in Sind is that of Shāh ʿInāyat Shahīd of Jhok, which is not far from Hyderabad (his name occurs in Sachal's litany).[84] His way of life, spirituality, and justice attracted a large number, not only of Sufi adepts, but also, according to the sources, of slaves and husbandmen from the neighboring villages. The Sufi sheikhs and the feudal lords in the country lost large numbers of disciples and workers, whereas the *dargāh* in Jhok flourished. A considerable amount of land was distributed among Shāh ʿInāyat's followers after an unjustified attack on Jhok, led by the Sayyids of Bulrri. To what extent Shāh ʿInāyat really aimed at something like a land reform in the modern sense of the word cannot be detected from the sources, which are mostly unfriendly to him; positive evaluations, on the other hand, are strongly mixed with legends. Whatever his movement was, the pious mystic was accused of conspiracy against the Mogul throne, the easiest method of blackmail, since the throne was in constant danger after Aurangzeb's death. Large armies were sent to Jhok, which surrendered after four months' siege; Shāh ʿInāyat was executed in January 1718. Both Muslim and Hindu admirers have composed songs extolling him or describing his martyrdom; among them is the Suhrawardī mystic Jānullāh of Rohri, one of the outstanding Persian poets of Sind from the second half of the eighteenth century.

Mystical speculation flourished in the Indus valley as it did elsewhere. A strong Naqshbandiyya influence in the beginning of the eighteenth century, however, changed the spiritual climate of southern Sind to a certain extent; at that time, Makhdūm Muhammad Hāshim of Thatta and his relatives undertook to attack all those Sufis who defended the emotional side of religion as exemplified in the dancing practices on Makli Hill. Through their literary activities, this Naqshbandī group contributed to promoting a more sober mystical piety. During the same years when Shāh ʿAbduʾl-Laṭīf was singing his moving verses, commentaries on the Koran and legends of the Prophet were being written in the Sindhi language by

83. See Mayne, *Saints of Sind*; Herbert Feldman, *From Crisis to Crisis: Pakistan 1962–1969* (London, 1972), p. 165.

84. Annemarie Schimmel, "Shah ʿInāyat of Jhok: A Sindhī Mystic of the Early 18th Century," in *Liber Amicorum in Honor of C. J. Bleeker* (Leiden, 1969).

the learned Naqshbandī families of Thatta.[85] One of their members, Mīr ᶜAlī Shīr Qāniᶜ (d. 1789), who was to become the leading historian of Lower Sind, left Persian works, mostly still unexamined, that are mines of information about the mystical and cultural life of his homeland.[86]

With or without the Naqshbandī reform, however, the majority of the masses continued, and partly still continue, in the veneration of their saints, which is echoed in hundreds of simple folk songs and popular verses. The exaggerated veneration of a saint's tomb has been made the target of some of the best modern Sindhi short stories.[87] The discrepancy between the wealth of the shrines and their guardians and the poverty of the masses indeed provides an impressive theme for social and religious criticism. That holds true not only for Sind, but for other parts of the Muslim world as well.

The neighboring peoples in the Subcontinent also produced mystical literature in their own tongues. The most important period of Pashto mystical poetry coincided with the time of Aurangzeb, slightly earlier than the heyday of Sindhi and Panjabi Sufi poetry.[88]

There had been a mystical movement in the days of Humayun and Akbar, the Roshaniyya, so called after its founder Bāyezīd Anṣārī, Pīr-i Rōshan, "Radiant Master" (d. 1585).[89] He was the first to apply Persian metrics to his mother tongue, and his *Khayr ul-bayān,* a treatise in rhymed prose, can be regarded as the beginning of Pashto literature proper. Pīr-i Rōshan's mystical theories—a full-fledged pantheism—were vehemently attacked by Akhūnd Darwāza, the orthodox preacher, and Pīr-i Rōshan's sons were drowned in the Indus near Attock. Yet his mystical movement seems to have survived beneath the surface of religious life, and one of the leading mystical poets of the later Aurangzeb period in the beginning of the eighteenth century was Mīrzā Khān Anṣārī,

85. Annemarie Schimmel, "Translations and Commentaries of the Qurān in the Sindhi Language," *Oriens* 15 (1963).

86. Some of Mīr ᶜAlī Shīr Qāni's books have been edited by Sayyid Hussamuddin Rashdi; others are still in manuscript, including those specializing in Sufi topics.

87. Jamāl Abrō, *Munhun kārō,* trans. Annemarie Schimmel as "Geschwärzten Gesichtes," in *Aus der Palmweinschenke. Pakistan in Erzählungen seiner zeitgenössischen Autoren* (Tübingen, 1966). An English translation of this translation by E. Mohr Rahman was published in *Mahfil,* 1969.

88. Iᶜjāzul Ḥaqq Quddūsi, *Tadhkira-yi ṣūfiyā-yi Sarḥad* (Lahore, 1966); Abdul Ḥayy Ḥabibi, *D pashtō adabiyātō tārīkh* (Kabul, 1342 sh./1964), a good introduction to Pashto literature.

89. Syed Athar Abbas Rizvi, "The Rawshaniyya Movement," *Abr-Nahrain* 6 (1965–66), 7 (1967–68).

a descendant of Bāyezīd Anṣārī. In many ways his poetry resembles that of the poets in Sind and Punjab; like them, he used the *ṣīḥarfi*, "Golden Alphabet," to teach his theories, and one of his poems could have inspired the lines of Sachal quoted earlier:

> How shall I define what thing I am?
> Wholly existent, and non-existent, I am.
> . . . Sometimes a mote in the disc of the sun,
> At others, a ripple of the water's surface.
> Now I fly about on the wind of association,
> Now I am a bird of the incorporeal world . . . .
> I have enveloped myself in the four elements.
> I am the cloud on the face of the sky . . . .
> In the lot of the devoted, I am the honey,
> In the soul of the impious, the sting.
> I am with every one, and in all things;
> Without imperfection—immaculate I am.[90]

On the whole, the imagery of the early Pathan mystics shows a strong inheritance from Persian poetry. That is particularly clear in the case of ʿAbduʾr-Raḥmān, lovingly called Raḥmān Bābā, a mystic of the Chishtī order who lived during the Aurangzeb period (d. 1709) and is usually regarded as the best mystical poet in Pashto. As legend has it, he led a life of withdrawal and seclusion, and his poetry reflects a sadness and ascetic feeling that are not too frequent in the mystical poets of this period. His anniversary at the end of April is usually celebrated in a solemn manner. Sometimes it seems as if ʿAbduʾr-Raḥmān had carefully studied the works of his great compatriot Sanāʾī; his ascetic verses, his mourning over the transitoriness of the world—a theme frequently found in Pashto mystical writing—have much in common with the didactic, slightly dry, and yet very attractive style of the great medieval poet of Ghazna. Thus his lines about the resurrection and the necessity to prepare for that day:

> Since to-morrow he will rise again with the same
> qualities,
> Let not God give any one an evil nature, in this world!
> That will, verily, be unto him a harvest after death,
> Whatever he may have sown in the field of this world.[91]

90. H. G. Raverty, *Selections from the Poetry of the Afghans* (London, 1862), p. 75.
91. Ibid., p. 16.

With an image typical of an inhabitant of Afghanistan, ʿAbduʾr-Raḥmān compares the passing of life to the *rēg-i rawān*, the shifting sand dunes. He was probably acquainted with Omar Khayyam's verses, or numerous poems written in the same vein; in that mood he complains:

> Fortune is like unto a potter—it fashioneth and
> breaketh:
> Many, like unto me and thee, it hath created and
> destroyed.
> Every stone and clod of the world, that may be looked
> upon,
> Are all skulls, some those of kings, and some of beggars.[92]

Again in full harmony with the traditions of the early Sufis—listening to the psalms of the created beings without identifying themselves with everything—ʿAbduʾr-Raḥmān praises God, whose creative power can be witnessed in this world and all its marvels:

> The earth hath bowed down its head in His adoration,
> And the firmament is bent over in the worship of Him.
> Every tree, and every shrub, stand ready to bend before
> Him:
> Every herb and blade of grass are a tongue to utter His
> praises.
> Every fish in the deep praiseth and blesseth His name,
> Every bird, in the meadows and in the fields, magnifieth
> Him . . . .
> No one hath lauded Him equal unto His just deserts;
> Neither hath any one sufficiently resounded His praise.[93]

The Persianization of Pashto poetry became even more conspicuous after ʿAbduʾl-Qādir Khattak translated some of the works of Saʿdī and Jāmī into his mother tongue. ʿAbduʾl-Qādir's father, Khushḥāl Khān Khattak (d. 1689), the great warrior poet of the Pathans, sometimes wrote lovely verses of mystical flavor. The other Afghan ruler known as a poet was Ahmad Shah Abdali Durrani. The successor of Nadir Shah of Iran, he invaded northwestern India several times, called in to help against the Sikhs and Mahrattas. It

92. Ibid., p. 9.
93. Ibid., pp. 47ff.

was probably in his time that a remarkable poet tried to express mystical teachings in Pashto. This poet was Khwāja Muhammad Bangash, like ʿAbduʾr-Raḥmān a member of the Chishtī order, whose poems breathe almost the same atmosphere as those by ʿAbduʾr-Raḥmān, though he also alluded to the *dhikr* and the breath regulation that is so important for the advanced Sufi:

> Thy every breath is a pearl and coral of inestimable
> price:
> Be careful, therefore, and guard every respiration well![94]

A deeper study of Pashto mystical poetry would be worthwhile, and it would probably strengthen the impression that the inhabitants of the Afghan hills rarely indulged in the exuberant, fanciful love songs and poetical sighs that the Sindhi or Panjabi mystics did, but followed, on the whole, a more sober line in Sufism that was fully consistent with the tradition developed earlier in Ghazna.

A large body of mystical poetry is found in East Bengal,[95] and here once more the folk songs—so-called *marifati*—are of exquisite beauty, delicate and full of music. They were sung on the rivers, and Muhammad, the mystical leader, appears as the boatsman who brings the soul safely to the other shore. The imagery is that of a country where water is plentiful and has a soft, melodious quality—the soul may be compared to the water hyacinths, which constantly move on the surface of the rivulets and canals, and the heart resembles the tiny waves on the surface of the water, moved by changing winds.

Mystical theories were also expressed in the Bengali language as early as the seventeenth century, when a mystic called Ḥājjī Muhammad described, in his *Nūrnāma*, "The Book of Light," the problems of *waḥdat al-wujūd* and *waḥdat ash-shuhūd* and the different types of light mysticism.[96] However, the higher mystical literature was usually composed either in Arabic or Persian, and many of the *maulūd*s in honor of the Prophet are written in one of these languages.

In Bengal as in Sind, the Naqshbandiyya and some more militant

94. Ibid., p. 337.
95. Iʿjāzul Ḥaqq Quddūsi, *Tadhkira-yi ṣūfiyā-yi Bengal* (Lahore, 1965).
96. Enamul Haq, "Sufi Movement in Bengal," *Indo-Iranica* 3, nos. 1–2 (1948). His *Muslim Bengali Literature* (Karachi, 1957) contains interesting material about Sufi poetry in Bengali.

mystically inspired groups tried to curb the overflowing emotionalism expressed in the lovely folk songs. As a defense against syncretism, the later Naqshbandiyya has played a remarkable role in all parts of Muslim India.

9. EPILOGUE

Khwāja Mīr Dard is a typical example of later Sufi life and thought: poet and mystic, fundamentalist and follower of both Ibn ʿArabī and Aḥmad Sirhindī, fighter against all kinds of innovation and lover of music and art, he is the *complexio oppositorum*.

It is symptomatic of the development of Sufism in the nineteenth century that the emphasis was placed once more upon the person of Muhammad. The Indian orders of Mīr Dard and of Aḥmad Brelwī, the fighter for freedom, are called *ṭarīqa muḥammadiyya*. Indeed, Sayyid Aḥmad Brelwī had taken pledge from the classical Sufi orders and also in the Muhammadan way as founded by Nāṣir Muhammad ʿAndalīb. The North African fraternities, like the Sanūsiyya and the Tijaniyya, who tried to revive the concept of the Muslims confronting the "infidels," have placed the person of the Prophet in the center of their teachings and meditations.

In the course of this study we have seen how much criticism was directed against Sufism from the early tenth century on. The complaint about the decay of mysticism becomes stronger from century to century. This may be one reason why the later forms of Sufism have attracted comparatively little interest on the part of the scholars. Another reason is certainly the indebtedness of the majority of later Sufis to the system of Ibn ʿArabī, which apparently left very little room for independent theological thought. Although a sixteenth-century mystic like Shaʿrānī in Egypt has been studied by a number of European scholars, a full evaluation of his various contributions to the history of Sufism and cultural life is still lacking. The same thing is true for ʿAbduʾl-Ghanī an-Nābulusī (d. 1728), the Syrian scholar and mystic whose commentaries have been used by many students of Sufism for a better understanding of classical sources.

In recent years the interest in the militant orders in North and West Africa has grown considerably. Here one finds—as in Dard's *ṭarīqa muḥammadiyya*—a strong fundamentalism tinged by the mystical theories of the previous centuries and the use of technical devices (like common *dhikr*) by the orders to gain control over larger circles of the community. The success of the Tījāniyya[1] and Sanūsiyya[2] in the political field indicates that their approach is attractive for many of the pious. It is worth mentioning in this connection that some of the fundamentalist Muslim leaders in our century, like Ḥasan al-Bannāʾ, the founder of the Muslim Brethren, came from a background of strong connections with Sufi orders: it was from the Sufis that he learned his methods of channeling the enthusiasm of people into religious activities.

The discussion about the validity of the orders and about the whole cultural role of Sufism has extended over many years. The general view is that most of the orders, in their present forms, appeal to the lower instincts of the people and can be classified as either un-Islamic or antimodern. There are still many orders alive—the High Sufi Council of Egypt enumerated not less than sixty orders a few years ago;[3] they were, however, losing followers because of urbanization, though some of them were able to attract new members. It is typical that among the successful ones is a subbranch of the Shādhiliyya, which teaches the punctual fulfillment of man's duties rather than a way to ecstasy that can be achieved only through ascetic practices.

The fact that the orders were banned in Turkey in 1925 has

1. M. Jamil Abun Nasr, *The Tijaniya: A Sufi Order in the Modern World* (Oxford, 1965). A careful introduction to the life and work, and particularly the mystical language, of a nineteenth-century mystical teacher in North Africa is: Jean-Louis Michon, *Le Soufi Marocain Ahmad ibn ʿAjība et son miʿrāj* (Paris, 1973).

2. N. A. Ziadah, *Sanusiyah: A Study of a Revivalist Movement in Islam* (Leiden, 1958).

3. Michael Gilsenan, "Some Factors in the Decline of the Sufi Orders in Modern Egypt," *Moslem World* 57, no. 1 (1967).

curbed only their external activities; they were, and are, very much alive beneath the surface.[4] The loving, venerating attitude toward truly saintly persons and the interpretation of Islam in terms of mystical experience still play an important role. Almost everyone who has lived in the East would agree with the example cited by Dermenghem from North Africa: a modern man may violently deny miracles and saint worship in rational debate and is highly critical of mysticism in any form, but he will show veneration at a sacred place or respect to a person who is reported to be a saint, or who comes from a noted family of mystics. A number of mystical leaders in modern Turkey have attracted followers who, silently and intensely, preach and practice the message of all-embracing love to their friends. Some interesting mystical poetry has been produced in these circles.[5] The situation is similar in other Muslim countries, though in some of them the influence of the "village sheikh" or the mystical leader is still strong enough even to influence political decisions. Other spiritual masters—mainly in North Africa—have been sufficiently powerful to attract a number of Europeans as disciples. Martin Lings's book *A Sufi Saint of the Twentieth Century* gives a vivid impression of this spiritual activity; similar biographies could be written about a number of mystics in the area between Istanbul and Delhi.[6] An interesting example is the faith movement in India, founded by Maulānā Ilyās in the 1920s, which combines strict fundamentalism with mystical practices. Popular mystical movements can be found in different parts of the Muslim world.[7]

More than once Muhammad Iqbal attacked the "Pirism" and backwardness of the so-called "spiritual leaders" of the Indo-

4. There is a great deal of material about modern mystical currents in Islam in A. J. Arberry, ed., *Religion in the Middle East*, vol. 2 (Cambridge, 1969). Clifford Geertz, *Islam Observed: Religious Development in Morocco and Indonesia* (New Haven, 1968), gives a very interesting analysis of Indonesian and Moroccan Islam. Morroe Berger, *Islam in Egypt Today: Social and Political Aspects of Popular Religion* (Cambridge, 1970), has some useful statistics and general information.

5. For Turkey see Samiha Ayverdi, Nezihe Araz, Safiye Erol, and Sofi Huri, *Kenan Rifai ve yirminci asrın ışıgında Müslümanlık* (Istanbul, 1951).

6. Martin Lings, *A Sufi Saint of the Twentieth Century*, 2d ed. (London, 1971); see also ad-Darqawi, *Letters of a Sufi Master*, trans. Titus Burckhardt (London, 1961).

7. See A. A. M. Mackeen, "The Sufi-Qawm Movement," *Moslem World* 53, no. 3 (1963); H. B. Barclay, "A Sudanese Religious Brotherhood: Aṭ-ṭarīqa al-hindīya," *Moslem World* 53, no. 2 (1963), about a nineteenth-century "sober" order. M. Anwarul Haq, *The Faith-Movement of Mawlānā Ilyās* (London, 1972), is very interesting on Indian popular mysticism.

Pakistani Subcontinent;[8] yet a close study of his work makes it clear that he himself follows quite closely the Sufi thought of the classical period. As a thinker, Iqbal turned from a Hegelian-Ibn ʿArabī pantheism to what seemed to him true Islam. In fact, he relied heavily upon the heritage of the great masters of early Sufism; and his treatment of Ḥallāj, with whose work he became acquainted through Louis Massignon's books, shows an extraordinary insight into the phenomenon of the enthusiastic mystic who has achieved an experience that every faithful person is entitled to reach, but which is denied by most of the common believers, who cling only to the word of the revelation, not recognizing the spirit. The tension between the traditional Sufi thought and the fresh, and very authentic, interpretation of some of the most exciting sentences in early Sufism is one of the truly fascinating aspects of Iqbal's thought. His imagery, like that of most Turkish, Persian, or Urdu poets, is largely colored by Sufi symbolism: as much as he detested the kind of enthralling, "otherworldly" mysticism that he thought was hidden behind Ḥāfiẓ's beautiful verses, he himself used the whole fabric of Sufi imagery in his poetry, though he often reinterpreted it.

That statement could describe almost every great poet of the Islamic world, especially those under the influence of Iran. Even the work of those who are often considered to be frivolous, or pagan, or unreligious, cannot be properly interpreted without a thorough knowledge of the Sufi heritage. One prominent example will suffice: Ghālib (d. 1869), who is usually labelled as a free thinker or "half-Muslim" (according to his own joking words), is deeply steeped in the traditions of the Delhi school of Sufism (just as was true of the reformer of Indian Islam, Sir Sayyid Ahmad Khan, d. 1898).

It seems to be a promising sign for the survival of the best traditions of Sufism—far removed from stale theosophy, from dangerous Pirism, from stagnating pantheism—that there is now a growing interest in the figure of al-Ḥallāj in the whole Muslim world. It is, no doubt, Massignon's monumental work that has aroused this interest; but the Ḥallājian tradition had been kept alive in Sufi poetry throughout the centuries. Ghālib's poetic statement that the

8. Muhammad Iqbal, *The Development of Metaphysics in Iran* (Cambridge, 1908); Iqbal, *Six Lectures on the Reconstruction of Religious Thought in Islam* (Lahore, 1930). See the Bibliography in Annemarie Schimmel, *Gabriel's Wing: A Study into the Religious Ideas of Sir Muhammad Iqbal* (Leiden, 1963), and in Hafeez Malik, ed., *Muhammad Iqbal: Poet-Philosopher of Pakistan* (New York, 1971).

place where the secret of love can be divulged is not the pulpit but the gallows can be traced back to Sanāʾī and has been imitated many times by Persian and Urdu writers. His description of the lovers who gladly suffer from gallows and rope—again a traditional image—became, during the Indian freedom movement and even after World War II, the symbol of those who suffer for their ideals, be they religious or ideological.

The mysticism of love and suffering—which teaches man to live and to die for a goal outside himself—is perhaps the most important message of Sufism today. For some seekers, the theosophical approach may be easier to combine with a modern intellectual world view. Others will find the small, outward signs of devotion, the emotional aspects of Sufism, more attractive. Fayżī, Akbar's court poet, said:

> Do not destroy the Kaaba of the pilgrims,
> for the travellers on the path will rest there for a
> moment.

And a modern French interpreter of Sufism concludes that it would be cruel "to destroy the *qubba,* the sanctuary of the village,"[9] where so many simple souls have found spiritual help.

One may agree with this idea or reject it in favor of a modernized world view without the whole firmament of saints, which, like the stars at dawn, is naughted when the sun of reality appears. But those who have experienced the dark night of the soul know that the sun at midnight will one day appear and the world will gain new beauty once more.

These experiences cannot be communicated properly, as Ibn ʿAṭāʾ says:

> When men of common parlance question us,
> we answer them with signs mysterious
> and dark enigmas; for the tongue of man
> cannot express so high a truth, whose span
> surpasses human measure. But my heart
> has known it, and has known of it a rapture
> that thrilled and filled my body, every part.

9. Émile Dermenghem, *Le culte des saints dans l'Islam Maghrebin* (Paris, 1954), p. 331.

Seest thou not, these mystic feelings capture
the very art of speech, as men who know
vanquish and silence their unlettered foe.

(K 78)

And "when you see the Sufi conversing with men, know that he is empty" (K 149).

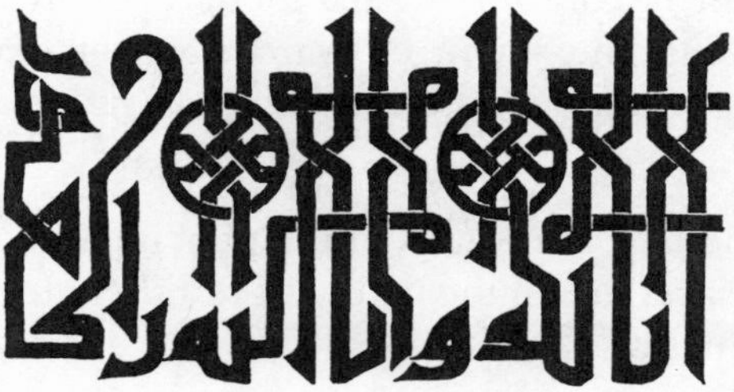

APPENDIXES
BIBLIOGRAPHY
INDEXES

APPENDIX 1

LETTER SYMBOLISM IN SUFI LITERATURE

One aspect of Sufi imagery and symbolism that is extremely important for a proper understanding of many writings is the symbolism of letters, the emphasis laid on the mystical meaning of single letters and on the art of writing in general.[1]

Every Muslim admits the importance of the Arabic alphabet—those letters in which God's eternal word was revealed. The Koran itself declares that, even if all the seas were ink and the trees pens, they would never be sufficient to write down the words of the Lord (Sūra 18:109). This Koranic statement was frequently repeated by the mystics in their attempts to describe the greatness, beauty, and perfection of the divine being. Learning the Arabic letters is incumbent upon everybody who embraces Islam, for they are the vessels of revelation; the divine names and attributes can be expressed only by means of these letters—and yet, the letters constitute something different from God; they are a veil of otherness that the mystic must penetrate. As long as he remains bound to the letters—as Niffarī put it—the mystic is in some sense fettered by idols; he commits idolatry instead of reaching the place in which there are no more letters and forms (W 363–65).

At a very early stage of Sufism the mystics detected the secret meaning hidden within the different letters, and the detached groups of letters found at the beginning of twenty-nine Koranic *sūra*s inspired them to produce amazing allegorical explanations. Most of the great Sufis have dwelt upon the topic, and even in distant parts of the Muslim world, like Indonesia, manuscripts containing speculations about letter mysticism have come to light.[2] Out of this mystical interpretation of the letters of the Arabic alphabet the Sufis developed secret languages in order to hide their thoughts from the common people. The so-called *balabailān* language, which has long attracted the interest of the orientalists, is a good example of this inventiveness.[3] Even a highly sophisticated thinker like Suhrawardī Maqtūl speaks of his initiation into a

1. See Ernst Kühnel, *Islamische Schriftkunst* (Berlin, 1942; reprint ed., Graz, 1972); Annemarie Schimmel, *Islamic Calligraphy* (Leiden, 1970); Schimmel, "Schriftsymbolik im Islam," in *Festschrift für Ernst Kühnel*, ed. Richard Ettinghausen (Berlin, 1959).

2. Bibliothèque Nationale, *Catalogue des mss. Indiens-Malais-Javanese* (Paris, 1910), 65:191.

3. Edgard Blochet, *Catalogue des mss. Persans de la bibliothèque nationale* (Paris, 1905 f.), 2: no. 1030. See Ignaz Goldziher, "Linguistisches aus der Literatur der muhammadanischen Mystik," *Zeitschrift der Deutschen Morgenländischen Gesellschaft* 26 (1872): 765. Alessandro Bausani, "About a Curious Mystical Language," *East and West* 4, no. 4 (1958).

secret alphabet in order to understand the deeper meaning of the Koranic word.[4]

Even in pre-Islamic times, the poets of Arabia had compared different parts of the body, or of their dwellings, with letters—comparisons that were inherited and elaborated upon by Islamic poets throughout the world. It is scarcely possible to fully understand and enjoy the poetry of the Muslim world, mainly of Iran and the neighboring countries, without a thorough knowledge of the meaning given to the letters.

The mystics felt that "there is no letter that does not praise God in a language" (W 165), as Shiblī said, and they tried, therefore, to reach deeper layers of understanding in order to interpret the divine words correctly. "When God created the letters, he kept their secret for Himself, and when He created Adam, He conveyed this secret to him, but did not convey it to any of the angels."[5] The Sufis not only played with the shapes and appearances of the letters but often indulged in cabalistic speculations. Such tendencies are visible in comparatively early times; they are fully developed in Ḥallāj's poetry in the early tenth century.

The technique of *jafr* is thought to have been used first by Jaᶜfar aṣ-Ṣādiq, the sixth Shia *imām*, whose role in early Sufi thought has been mentioned (W 164–66). *Jafr* is a speculation about events, present and future, from certain combinations of words; it has often deteriorated into a kind of prognostication.[6] By counting the words on a page of the Koran and computing their numerical values—for every letter of the Arabic alphabet has a numerical value—one could figure out names and places, dates and events, in the same way as some Christian Cabalists detected historical events in the words and numbers of the Bible, mainly in Revelation.

This trend in Sufism and early Shia was developed by a Shia group known as the *Ḥurūfī*,[7] "those who deal with the letters." Their founder was Faḍlullāh Astarābādī, who was executed for his heretical ideas in 1398; he had followers among the Turkish and Persian poets and writers, among whom Nesīmī deserves special mention. This Turkish poet expressed the Ḥurūfī ideas—blended with extravagant Sufi teachings and an interesting imitation of Ḥallāj—in his highly enthusiastic poems and, like his master, was cruelly put to death in 1417.

For the Ḥurūfī, the word is the supreme manifestation of God himself; it is also revealed in the human face, which becomes the Koran par excellence, the writing through which God's secrets were made visible. Faḍlullāh taught that Adam had been given nine letters; Abraham, fourteen; Muhammad, twenty-eight; and that he himself was honored with the knowledge of 32 letters (the four additional letters of

4. Suhrawardī Maqtūl, *Oeuvres persanes* (Paris, 1970), p. 216.

5. See Gustav Flügel, *Die arabischen, persischen und türkischen Handschriften in der K. K. Hofbibliothek zu Wien* (Vienna, 1865–67), 1:192.

6. Louis Massignon, *Essai sur les origines du lexique technique de la mystique musulmane* (Paris, 1928), pp. 37, 98.

7. Hellmut Ritter, "Die Anfänge der Hurufisekte," *Oriens* 7 (1954).

the Persian version of the Arabic alphabet). In many cases it is difficult to decipher the correct meaning of his sayings, since his interpretation of the letters varies. His most interesting theory is that of the letters as reflected in the human face; *alif* forms the *khaṭṭ-i istiwā*, the equator that, like the nose, divides the human face and corresponds not, as usual, to Allah, but to ᶜAlī; the *b* points to the fourteen innocent martyrs of Shia Islam and is manifested on the left side of the nose. A number of pictures, mostly used in the Bektashi convents, show a tendency toward representing the names of the *imāms* or similar combinations of sacred names in the shape of a human face (see BO, Supplement 2). Even in India it was said: "ᶜAlī is written twice on the face."[8]

The idea that the face of the beloved is like a marvelously written manuscript of the Koran is widely accepted even outside Ḥurūfī circles. The pretty face is a fine illuminated copy of the Holy Book. Man is the perfect copy of the Well-preserved Tablet, in which all wisdom and beauty take shape—a notion whose development shows the change in consciousness of a late poet like Bedil (d. 1721), whose contacts with Indian Sufi circles are well known; he describes man no longer as the copy of the heavenly Koran, but as "a manuscript of nothingness."

On the whole, the poets would agree with a late Indo-Persian writer:

> Your face is like a Koran copy, without correction and mistake,
> which the pen of Fate has written exclusively from musk.
> Your eyes and your mouth are verses and the dot for stopping, your
> eyebrows the *madda* [for lengthening the *alif*],
> the eyelashes the signs for declension, the mole and the down
> letters and dots.[9]

The comparisons used here are familiar. The curved eyebrows were usually compared to a beautifully written *ṭughrā*, as found at the beginning of official letters. Shah Ismail, the Safawid ruler who wrote Turkish mystical poetry, likened them to the *basmala*, the formula "in the name of God."[10] The narrow, small mouth is constantly represented as a *mīm*, the narrowest ringlet in the alphabet م: the eyes by the letters *ṣād* (according to their shape ص), or ᶜ*ayn* ع (which means both "eye" and the name of the letter). Curls and tresses are the long, winding letters like *dāl*, or *jīm*. Every poet could write a whole poem on the letters as revealed in his beloved's face. Among these puns are some that may be almost repulsive to modern taste. One of these is the comparison of the down on the upper lip with a dark line of writing; the word *khaṭṭ* has this twofold meaning. Even the greatest mystics have not hesitated to see in the black *khaṭṭ* of their beloved the divine writing; they may even claim that the beauty of this *khaṭṭ*, which appears on the cheek of the

8. Muḥammad Nāṣir, *Nāla-yi ᶜAndalīb* (Bhopal, 1309 h./1891–92), 2:344.

9. Mīr ᶜAlī Shīr Qāniᶜ, *Maqālāt ash-shuᶜarāʾ*, ed. Sayyid Hussamuddin Rashdi (Karachi, 1956), p. 44.

10. Quoted in Fakhrī Harawī, *Rauḍat as-salāṭīn*, ed. Sayyid Hussamuddin Rashdi (Hyderabad, Sind, 1968), p. 85.

youthful beloved, is comparable to the Seal of Prophecy, which eliminates all writing that had been valid before his time (AD 283).

Rūmī once spoke of the Koran copy of the heart, the *muṣḥaf-i dil.* When the beloved looks once at this manuscript, "the signs for declension begin to dance, and the parts start stamping with their feet" (in ecstatic dance) (D 2282). This play with letters has produced some of the most charming verses in Islamic poetry, and the field is almost inexhaustible.

A central theme of Koranic mythology is the concept of the *lauḥ al-maḥfūẓ,* the Well-preserved Tablet, on which the destinies of men have been engraved since the beginning of time; the Pen that has written these verdicts is often mentioned together with it. In fact, the primordial pen has become a standard expression in Islamic poetry in general and in Sufism in particular, for everything that happens is written with this instrument and cannot be changed, since, as the *ḥadīth* says, "the pen has already dried up." The poet could imagine that the Pen had written the fate of the lovers in black (*bakht-i siyāh, karabaht*; "black luck" means, in Persian and Turkish respectively, "misfortune"). He might say that the Pen of Power had selected only the figure of the beloved from the anthology of beauties and drawn his shape in the lover's heart at the very moment of creation.[11] The poets would complain, in hundreds of variations, that the writing of their destiny was crooked, because the Pen was cut the wrong way.

It is from the idea that fate is written down forever on the Well-preserved Tablet that the Islamic expressions for "fate" are derived—*maktūb,* "written," in Arabic; *sarniwisht* or *alın yazısı,* "what is written on the forehead," in Persian and Turkish respectively. Fate is also seen as recorded on man's face, and the Sufis have been credited in many a verse with the ability to read the book of a man's fate from the title that is visible on his face. The lines engraved on the forehead gave an excellent illustration for this image. The poets might praise the beloved who could decipher the contents of the closed letter from the complicated lines on the forehead.

> The true men of God are those
> who already in this world
> read the script of the heart
> from the tablet of the forehead,[12]

said the Pathan warrior Khushḥāl Khān Khattak in a quatrain. This imagery is very widely used in eastern Islamic areas.

The Koran speaks not only of the Pen of Destiny and the Tablet, but also of man's sinful deeds, which blacken the book that will be given into his hand on Doomsday. But there is one way to clean the record of one's sins, and that is to weep: Oriental ink is soluble in water, and a page could easily be washed off, if necessary. The water of tears, so

11. Fuzuli, *Divanı,* ed. Abdulbâki Gölpınarlı (Istanbul, 1948), no. 30, verse 6.
12. Khushḥāl Khān Khattak, *Muntakhabāt* (Peshawar, 1958), Rubāʿī no. 88.

often praised by the ascetics and mystics, can, similarly, wash off all the ink of black sins; "God loves the weeping of human beings" (N 299). Repentance cleans the book of actions: that idea is repeated in different words by hundreds of pious poets in the Muslim world.

The feeling that nothing created is worth looking at once man has found God is expressed in the same image of "washing off the pages" by Niẓāmī, as quoted by Jāmī (N 608):

> Whatever exists from the subtleties of the stars,
> or the different hidden sciences—I read it, and searched every paper:
> When I found Thee, I washed off the pages.

To indulge in writing and reading nonreligious books, or even in the subtleties of intricate law cases or hairsplitting grammar, was, for the Sufis, to add to the blackness of the book of deeds; it was to sin.

The mystics have dwelt on another aspect of pen symbolism as well. There is a famous *ḥadīth*: "The heart of the faithful is between the two fingers of the All-compassionate, and He turns it wherever He wants."

This *ḥadīth* suggests the activity of the writer with his reed pen, who produces intelligible or confused lines; the pen has no will of its own, but goes wherever the writer turns it. Rūmī told a story of some ants walking on a manuscript, looking at the writing, which resembled hyacinths and narcissus, until they slowly discovered that this writing was not done by the pen itself but by the hand, in fact, by the mind that set the pen in motion (M 4:3722–29)—an argument for divine activity, which is made manifest through secondary causes and then seems to become man's own activity. Ghazzālī had put forth a similar argument. The *ḥadīth* of the pen has inspired the poets of Iran and other countries —they saw man as a pen that the master calligrapher uses to bring forth pictures and letters according to His design, which the pen cannot comprehend. Mirzā Ghālib, the great poet of Muslim India (d. 1869), opened his Urdu *Dīwān* with a line that expresses the complaint of the letters against their inventor, for "every letter has a paper shirt."[13] In traditional poetic language, that means that each letter wears the garment of a complainant at court. Since a letter becomes visible only after it is written on some solid medium, mainly paper, it wears, so to speak, a paper shirt and complains, so the poet thinks, about the inventiveness of the creator, who has combined it with ugly or meaningless letters, or has written it in an unusual way or on brittle or coarse paper.

The heart, like a pen, is bound to write every calligraphic style, to turn left and right without resistance. One of the qualities required in a pen is that its tongue, or even its head, be cut off: the pen becomes the symbol of the mystic who must not divulge the secret, who "speaks without tongue." ʿAṭṭār, like many other mystical and nonmystical

13. Annemarie Schimmel, "Poetry and Calligraphy," *Pakistan Quarterly* 17, no. 1 (1969).

poets, dwelt upon this aspect of the pen, "turning on the tablet of annihilation with cut-off tongue" (AD 603).

> When you say "I shall cut off your head,"
> I shall run on my head like the pen out of joy.
>
> (AD 508)

Other poets might compare themselves to a pen that, owing to its "black fate"—i.e., being immersed in black ink—weeps the whole day.

In one of ʿAṭṭār's ghazals (AD 601) the pen, *qalam,* is connected with the letter *nūn* (*n*), alluding to the introductory words of Sūra 68: "*nūn waʾl-qalam,* N, and By the Pen!" The poet wants to walk with his head cut off and his hands and feet cast away like the rounded letter *nūn. Nūn* also means "fish," and the relation between the several meanings, together with the mystical interpretation of the beginning of the *sūra,* has often occupied mystically minded writers. One of the most amusing versions is that by Rūmī:

> I saw a Jonah sitting at the shore of the ocean of love.
> I said to him: "How are you?" He answered in his own way
> And said: "In the ocean I was the food of a fish,
> then I became curved like the letter *nūn,* until I became
> Dhūʾn-Nūn himself.
>
> (D 1247)

The mystic who, like the Prophet Jonah, has been swallowed by the "fish annihilation" (as Jāmī puts it) and is thrown back on the shore of separation feels, after his experience in the fish (*nūn*), like the letter *nūn* without head and tail and becomes, therefore, identical with Dhūʾn-Nūn, the leading mystic of medieval Egypt.

The detached letters at the beginning of twenty-nine *sūras* of the Koran have inspired the Sufis with many strange and amazing ideas—the *a-l-m* (*alif lām mīm*) at the beginning of Sūra 2 has particularly puzzled the interpreters. Read as one word, it means *alam,* "pain," as the later poets would hold; but there are several ways of explaining the three letters in a mystical sense, e.g.: *alif* is Allah, *m* Muhammad, and *l* the symbol of Gabriel, the mediator through whom the Koran was brought down to the Prophet. "These letters *a-l-m-* and *ḥ-m* are like the rod of Moses," says Rūmī (M 5:1316–30); they are filled with mysterious qualities for him who understands their secrets. The same can be said about the *ṭāhā* at the beginning of Sūra 20, which Sanāʾī interprets as follows:

> He has seen from the *ṭā* all the purities [*ṭahāra*],
> He has made from the *hā* all the buildings.
>
> (S 235)

The detached letters *ṭā-sīn* at the beginning of Sūra 27 point to purity and lordship, according to some mystics. They are incorporated in the title of one of the most intriguing books of early Sufism, Ḥallāj's *Kitāb aṭ-ṭawāsīn* (in the plural); the title has been imitated, in our time, by Muhammad Iqbal, who in his account of his spiritual journey, the *Jāwīdnāme,* invented the "*ṭawāsīn* of the Prophets," dwelling places of the prophetic spirits in the Sphere of Moon.

While some of the mystics spoke about human activities as comparable to the movements of the pen, later Persian Sufis saw the mystery of all-embracing unity revealed in the relation of the ink and the letters. Thus says Ḥaydar Amulī (as quoted by Toshihiko Izutsu):

> Letters written with ink do not really exist *qua* letters. For the letters are but various forms to which meanings have been assigned through convention. What really and concretely exists is nothing but the ink. The existence of the letters is in truth no other than the existence of the ink which is the sole, unique reality that unfolds itself in many forms of self-modification. One has to cultivate, first of all, the eye to see the selfsame reality of ink in all letters, and then to see the letters as so many intrinsic modifications of the ink.[14]

Most of the meditations of the mystics were directed toward the letter *alif, ā,* the first letter of the alphabet, a slender vertical line (ا) often used as a comparison for the slender stature of the beloved.

> There is on the tablet of the heart nothing but the *alif* of my friend's stature—
> What shall I do?—My teacher gave me no other letter to memorize!

That is how Ḥāfiẓ expresses an idea common to all poets. And his verses can be interpreted mystically as well; for the *alif,* with the numerical value one, isolated and yet active, became the divine letter par excellence. To know the *alif* meant, for the Sufis, to know the divine unity and unicity; he who has remembered this simple letter need no longer remember any other letter or word. In the *alif,* all of creation is comprehended; it is as Sahl at-Tustarī says, "the first and most majestic letter and points to the *ālif,* i.e., Allah, who has connected (*allafa*) all things and is yet isolated from the things" (L 89). Before him Muḥāsibī had pointed out: "When God created the letters he incited them to obey. All letters were in the shape [*ʿalā ṣūrat*] of *alif,* but only the *alif* kept its form and image after which it has been created" (W 166). This idea was expanded by Niffarī, who saw all the letters except *alif* as ill (W 166). The expression "in the shape of" in Muḥāsibī's dictum seems to allude to the tradition according to which God created Adam *ʿalā ṣūratihi,* "in his image"; *alif* was the divine letter, and the other letters were similar to it and lost their shape by disobedience, just as Adam, formed in God's image, lost his original purity by disobedience.

ʿAṭṭār took up the idea and showed how the different numbers grew out of the *alif* with the value one and how the letters emerged from it: when it became crooked, a *d* (د) came into existence; then, with another

14. Toshihiko Izutsu, "The Basic Structure of Metaphysical Thinking in Islam," in *Collected Papers on Islamic Philosophy and Mysticism,* ed. Mehdi Mohaghegh and Hermann Landolt (Tehran, 1971), p. 66.

kind of bend, an *r* (ر) became visible; when its two ends were bent, a *b* ب came forth; and made into a horseshoe, the *alif* became like a *nūn* ن. In the same way, all the various created beings in the different shapes have emerged from the divine unity (V 95).

Alif is the letter of *aḥadiyya,* unity and unicity, and at the same time the letter of transcendence. Therefore,

> The meaning of the four sacred books
> is contained in a single *alif.*
>
> (Y 308)

There is scarcely a popular poet in the Muslim world, from Turkey to Indonesia, who has not elaborated this topic, attacking the bookish scholars who forget the true meaning of the most important letter and instead blacken the pages of their learned books. For Rūzbihān Baqlī, the *alif* points to the absolute, uncreated unicity and informs the mystic about the *ᶜayn-i jamᶜ*, the perfect union (B 94). Since the *alif* is pure and free from qualification (M 5:3612), it can become the symbol of the spiritually free, the true mystics who have reached union with God —the *erenler,* the Turkish expression for advanced Sufis, are "like *alifs,* signs of witness" (Y 524).

Other interpretations of the *alif* are possible; it has even been regarded as the letter of Satan, because it has refused to prostrate itself before any but God. As Rūmī says:

> Do not be an *alif,* which is stubborn,
> Do not be a *b* with two heads—be like a *jīm.*
>
> (D 1744)

A particularly strange chapter on the meaning of *alif,* which is composed of three letters (the *a, l,* and *f,* which constitute its Arabic name), is found in a book on mystical love written in the mid-tenth century by Abūʾl-Ḥasan ad-Daylamī. Its very title clearly shows the role of letter symbolism: *Kitāb ᶜaṭf al-alif al-maʾlūf ilāʾl-lām al-maᶜṭūf,* "The Book of the Inclination of the Tamed *alif* toward the Inclined *l.*"[15] In paragraphs 38–40 the author proves that *alif* is both one and three, and that therefore Christian ideas of trinity are much closer to Sufism than dualist ideas as defended by the Iranians—a somewhat surprising result, which can, however, be understood, since Sufi terminology is very fond of threefold groupings or of proving the basic unity of lover, beloved, and love, or of him who recollects, the object recollected, and the recollection, etc.

Speculations of this kind have never lacked in Sufism. Suffice it to mention a modern expression of these interpretations of the *alif* by a Sindhi Shia author who has counted up the numerical values of the three letters that constitute the name of *alif*: $a=1$, $l=30$, $f=80=111$; these, in turn, point to the threefold allegiance of the pious Shia Muslim,

15. ᶜAlī ibn Aḥmad ad-Daylami, *Kitāb ᶜaṭf al-alif al-maʾlūf ilāʾl-lām al-maᶜṭūf,* ed. Jean-Claude Vadet (Cairo, 1962).

which is expressed by the letters *a*=1, "Allah," *m*=40, "Muhammad," and *ʿayn*=70, "ʿAlī"—the sum of which is, once more, 111.[16]

These plays, which may seem strange to a modern Westerner, constitute an important aspect of Sufi poetry and can be studied even in comparatively modern mystical works; classical poetry abounds in them. Special importance is attributed to the connection *lām-alif, l-ā,* which, if read as one word, means *lā,* "no," and is thus the first word of the profession of faith. The *lām-alif,* though combined of two letters, was often regarded as a single letter and endowed with special mystical meaning. It is most commonly a metaphor for the closely embracing lovers who are two and one at the same time. Because of its shape, the letters *lām-alif* or the word *lā* لا has often been compared to a sword, particularly the *dhūʾl-fiqār,* ʿAlī's famous two-edged sword, or to scissors: "I made mute the tongue of speaking with the scissors of *lā*" (B 196). The believer is expected to cut all but God with the sword of *lā,* i.e., with the first word of the *shahāda,* "there is no deity but God." Whatever is created should be destroyed by the powerful sword of *lā,* "no." That is, however, only the first step in the path of the Muslim mystic—he has to go upward (*bā lā*), to reach the *illā,* "save God," which is achieved, in Arabic writing, by putting an *alif* before the *lā* الا. Ghālib, who was not a mystic but was deeply influenced by the mystical traditions of the Subcontinent, speaks of the *alif-i ṣayqal,* the "*alif* of polishing" (which is a specially high level of polishing steel): once man has polished the sword of *lā* so intensely that it shines with the *alif-i ṣayqal,* he has reached the positive value *illā Allāh,* "save God." Puns of this kind are very frequent in Persian, Turkish, and Urdu literature both in mystical and nonmystical circles.

Another combination of which the Sufis were extremely fond, and which was mentioned briefly in the chapter on Prophetology, is the connection of *alif* and *mīm*:

> Put a *mīm* into your soul,
> and an *alif* in front of it,

says Shāh ʿAbduʾl-Laṭīf.[17] The *mīm* points to Muhammad's name, the *alif,* once more, to Allah. *M,* with the numerical value of forty, is, as a Punjabi Sufi had said, the "shawl of createdness" by which God manifests Himself through the person of the Prophet. A *ḥadīth qudsī* attests: *Anā Aḥmad bilā mīm,* "I am Aḥmad without *m,* namely *Aḥad,* One." The letter *mīm* is the only barrier between God, the One, and Aḥmad, the Prophet Muhammad. It is understood as an expression of the forty grades of divine emanation from universal reason to man and back and of the forty days spent in seclusion, which are connected with the experience of the forty degrees. From ʿAṭṭār's time on, the mystics have loved the *Aḥmad bilā mīm* tradition, and it has been repeated in high

16. *Makhzan Shāh ʿAbdul Laṭīf Bhitāʾī* (Hyderabad, Sind, 1954), p. 63.

17. *Shāh jō risālo*; see Annemarie Schimmel, "Shah ʿAbdul Laṭīf's Beschreibung des wahren Sufi," in *Festschrift für Fritz Meier* (Wiesbaden, 1974).

literature as much as in popular mystical poetry, be it among the Turkish Bektashis or among the mystical bards of Sind and the Punjab. The Bektashis practiced a special *mīm duası,* a prayer of the letter *m,* which is said to point to the manifestation of the light of Muhammad (BO 268). Aḥmad Sirhindī's daring interpretation of the two *ms* in Muhammad's name should not be forgotten.

The letter *b,* the second in the alphabet, is connected in mystical understanding with the created world. It symbolizes the first act of creation; the *b* stands at the beginning of the *basmala,* the formula "in the name of God," which opens the Koran. Not only the *b* but the dot beneath it could be regarded as the point from which the movement of the created universe starts: it is the differentiating power after the perfect unity of the *alif* and has often been used as a symbol either of the Prophet or of ʿAlī, who claimed, as Shia tradition maintains, "I am the dot beneath the *b.*" Its shape ب shows that "when God created the letters, the *b* prostrated itself," as Sarī as-Saqaṭī thought. As the letter of creatureliness, it prostrates itself at the side of the unqualified divine unity of Allah.

Sanāʾī found a lovely explanation for the all-embracing greatness of the Koran: it begins with the letter *b* and ends with the letter *s*—that makes *bas,* "enough" (in Persian), and this word shows that the Koran is enough once and forever (SD 309).

Among the other letters, one may mention that the *w*—which also means "and"—symbolizes the relation between God and creation.[18] It is the favorite letter of Turkish calligraphers, who even invented a Prophetic tradition, "Trust in the *wāw*'s."

A special role is attributed to the *h,* the last letter of the word Allah and the beginning of *huwa,* "He." According to Baqlī (B 95), the *lām* is the beloved, turned into a lover through its own love in its own love; here the symbolism of the word Allah, with its two *l*s, becomes even more poignant. Rūmī may have been thinking of speculations of this kind when he said, in a wonderfully simple image:

> I made my sides empty from both worlds,
> like the *h* I was seated beside the *l* of Allah.
>
> (D 1728)

It is typical of Sufism that Ibn ʿArabī, whose *Kitāb al-mabādiʾ waʾl-ghāyāt* deals with the mysteries of the letters, visualized the divine ipseity, *huwiyya,* in the shape of the letter *h,* in brilliant light, on a carpet of red, the two letters *hu* shining between the two arms of the *h,* which sends its rays in all four directions.[19] Such a vision of the divine in the form of a letter is characteristic of a religion that prohibits representation, particularly representation of the divine. The letter is,

18. Johann Karl Teufel, *Eine Lebensbeschreibung des Scheichs ʿAlī-i Hamad̲ānī* (Leiden, 1962), p. 87n.

19. Henri Corbin, "Imagination créatrice et prière créatrice dans le soufisme d'Ibn Arabi," *Eranos-Jahrbuch* 25 (1965):171.

in fact, the highest possible manifestation of the divine in Islamic thought. Ibn ᶜArabī's vision conforms, to a certain extent, to a description of the degrees of meditation by the eighteenth-century Naqshbandī Sufi Nāṣir Muhammad ᶜAndālīb in Delhi:

He sees the blessed figure of the word Allah in the color of light written on the tablet of his heart and the mirror of his imagination. . . . Then he will understand himself opposite to this form or beneath it or at its right or left side, and he should strive to bring himself towards this light . . . . And whenever he finds himself in the middle of the rank of *alif* and *lām*, he must proceed and take his place between the two *lāms*, and then walk away from there, and bring himself between the *lām* and the *h*, and with high ambition he leaves this place too and sees himself in the middle of the ringlet of the *h*. At the beginning he will find his head in this ringlet, but eventually he will find that his whole self has found repose in this house and will rest there free from all affliction and perilous calamities.[20]

Thus, the highest stage the mystic can reach is to be surrounded by the light of the letter *h*.

The mystics and poets have used a peculiar way of expressing their ideas by playing with the first letters of those concepts of which they wanted to convey the deeper meaning to their readers. When they speak, in early times, of the *l* of *luṭf*, "grace," and the *q* of *qahr*, "wrath," this type of allusion is still very primitive. But rather soon meaningful combinations were invented, like those with the letter *q* (*qāf*), the meaning of which is also "Mount Qāf," the mythical mountain that surrounds the world, on which the Sīmurgh or ᶜAnqā has its dwelling place. The *q* is mainly connected with the concept of *qurb*, "proximity," and the *qāf-i qurb*, the "first letter," or "Mount Qāf," of proximity, becomes a rather common expression—especially since this mountain is regarded as the station at the end of the created world, the place where man can find true proximity, *qurb*, on his way toward God (who, since ᶜAṭṭār, has sometimes been symbolized by the Sīmurgh). Another combination is that of *q* with *qanāᶜat*, "contentment": the perfect Sufi lives, like the mythological bird, in the Mount Qāf of *qanāᶜat*. The letter *ᶜayn* was used in similar ways; its meaning is manifold: "eye," "source," "essence"—the word *ᶜayn-i ᶜafw* means not only the letter *ᶜayn* with which the word *ᶜafw*, "forgiveness," begins, but also "the essence of forgiveness."

Such speculations and wordplays served the Sufis even in defending highly difficult mystical definitions and philosophical positions. It is said that Saᶜduddīn Ḥamūya regarded *wilāya*, "saintship," as superior to *nubuwwa*, "Prophetship," because of the different ranks of the letters *w* and *n* with which the respective words begin.[21] But Simnānī opposed this view, which was in contrast to the general Sufi attitude, again on the basis of a letter speculation. It became a custom to seek deep meaning in each letter of the words designating mystical states and stations.

20. Muḥammad Nāṣir, *Nāla-yi ᶜAndalīb*, 1:270.

21. Marijan Molé, "Les Kubrawiyya entre Sunnisme et Shiisme," *Revue des études islamiques*, 1961, p. 100.

If we can believe the sources, the tenth-century Sufi Abūʾl-Qāsim Ḥakīm Samarqandī liked this kind of interpretation and explained the word *namāz*, "ritual prayer," as consisting of:

> n=*nuṣrat*, "victory"
> m=*milkat*, "reign"
> a=*ulfat*, "intimacy"
> z=*ziyādat*, "increase."[22]

Later the Bektashis found secrets in the word *ṭarīqat*, "mystical Path":

> t=*ṭalab-i ḥaqq ū ḥaqīqat*, "seeking of Reality and Truth"
> r=*riyāḍat*, "ascetic discipline"
> i=*yol u din kardeşi*, "to be faithful in every respect toward 'a brother of the way' "
> q=*qanāʿat*, "contentment"
> t=*taslīm-i tāmm*, "complete submission."
>
> (BO 100 ff.)

In the word *ḥaqīqat*, the *q* might mean *qāʾim billāh*, "subsistent through God," and the *t* might point to *tarbiya*, "education"—it was unimportant to the simple Turkish dervishes if they confused Arabic and Turkish words and spellings.

It is not surprising to learn that the Sufis, chiefly the theosophists, found similar secrets in the divine names. The name *ar-Raḥmān*, "the Merciful," points to God's life, knowledge, power, will, hearing, seeing, and word—the seven basic qualities of Allah, as Jīlī had seen them and as they were usually accepted in later Sufism. The name *Allāh* was, of course, interpreted in a similar way:

> *alif*: the Only Real,
> *l*: His pure Knowledge of Himself,
> *l*: His Knowledge of Himself through His all-embracingness, which comprehends the illusionist appearances that seem to be other than He,
> the double *l* plus *al* is, then, the self-negation of every negation,
> the *h*: *huwa*, the absolutely unmanifested Essence in His Ipseity, and the vowelling *u*, the not-manifested world in the Nonmanifestation of the Only Real.[23]

These are ideas elaborated by the school of Ibn ʿArabī. Much more attractive is the simple way in which Turkish friends explained to me the secret of the tulip and the crescent, both typical of Turkish Muslim culture: tulip, *lāle*, and crescent moon, *hilāl*, are formed from the same letters as the word *Allāh* (one *alif*, two *lām*, and one *h*) and have, like the divine name, the numerical value of 66.

22. A. Tahir al-Khānqāhī, *Guzīda dar akhlāq u taṣawwuf*, ed. Iraj Afshar (Tehran, 1347 sh./1968), p. 47; see ibid., p. 69, for *ḥikmat*.

23. Léon Schaya, *La doctrine soufique de l'unité* (Paris, 1962), pp. 47, 83.

Sometimes the mystics joked about the attempts to understand the real meaning of a word from the letters that made it up—*g-l* does not make a *gul*, "rose," and the pain, *dard*, of true lovers is not expressed by *d-r-d* (S 330); nor is it love that is written *ʿshq*. These letters are nothing but a skin, a husk to veil the interior meaning from the human eye.

The same interest in the mystical meaning of letters that led to the strange explanations of mystical words and of divine names is evident in a poetical form known in Ancient Eastern literature and throughout the Muslim world, mainly in later times. This was the Golden Alphabet, in which each verse begins with the following letter of the Arabic alphabet. There is no rule for the verse form; the verses may be written in long or short meters, with two or five or any number of rhyming lines. Sometimes, when the poet chooses short verses, all the lines of a single verse may begin with the same letter.[24] It was a form that could easily be memorized by anybody who tried to learn the alphabet itself, and that is why Turkish, Sindhi, Panjabi, and Pashto poets loved to explain their mystical doctrines and the mysteries of faith in the form of Golden Alphabets—the pupils would know forever that *kh* stands for *khūdī*, "selfishness," *s* for *sālik*, "wayfarer," *ṣād* for *ṣirāṭ al-mustaqīm*, "the straight path," for *Ṣūfī*, and for *ṣāfī*, "pure." Sometimes words beginning with the same letters were combined in a single verse, since alliteration was a frequently used poetical device, particularly in Sind. We may even find, in Muslim India, Golden Alphabets in honor of certain religious figures—a fine example is the *Alif-name* by the most skillful Persian poet at the Mogul court in the late sixteenth century, Maulānā Qāsim Kāhī (d. 1582). This poem is composed in honor of ʿAlī ibn Abī Ṭālib and abounds in puns and witty combinations.[25] In this kind of poetry, the imaginative power of religious and intellectual people found an outlet that, though sometimes appearing too playful, still conveys a feeling of very serious concern with the mystical and magical qualities of the Arabic letters.

The Sufis themselves, as much as they boasted of their disinterest in worldly affairs, were usually very fond of letter-writing. The letters of the great masters of old, collected by their disciples, form a valuable source for our knowledge of mystical thought and practice. Even today mystical instruction through letters is practiced by some Sufi leaders. Junayd's letters are a famous example of the cryptic density of early Sufi writing. Of special interest are the letters written by Ḥallāj and received by him from his followers; they were beautifully written, as the tradition asserts, on precious material, illuminated and colored, not unlike the artistically decorated books of the Manichaeans in Cen-

24. A good Turkish example is Abdülbâki Gölpınarlı, *Melâmilik ve Melâmiler* (Istanbul, 1931), p. 200. For Pashto, see H. G. Raverty, *Selections from the Poetry of the Afghans* (London, 1862), pp. 61 ff. Sindhi Golden Alphabets have been collected by Dr. Nabi Bakhsh Baloch in *Tih akaryūn* (Hyderabad, Sind, 1962).

25. Hadi Hasan, "Qasim-i-Kahi, His Life, Times and Works," *Islamic Culture* 27 (1953): 99–131, 161–94; *alif*-name, pp. 186–89.

tral Asia. But Ḥallāj also knew that the true correspondence is spiritual, not by exchange of letters; he expressed that in his famous lines to his faithful friend Ibn ᶜAṭāʾ:

> I wrote [to you], but I did not write to you, but
> I wrote to my spirit without letter.[26]

The imagery of letter-writing was used frequently by the Sufis—they wrote with the water of tears and the fire of the heart, and the tears washed off what the hand had written (L 249). These are the true letters that the knowing people understand; as Shiblī says:

> My tears wrote lines on my cheeks,
> which someone has read who does not read well.
>
> (L 50)

The language of tears is clearer than that of the written word; and the red tears—mixed with blood from constant weeping—form a commentary to the topic of "longing" on the parchmentlike yellow cheeks of the mystic.

The complaint about friends who do not write is commonplace in Persian and related poetry. Even in an environment in which illiteracy prevailed, particularly among women, the motif of letter-writing and waiting for letters is used with amazing frequency. In the folk poetry of Sind the heroines always complain that no letter from the beloved has reached them—these letters are symbols for the signs of grace that the longing soul of the lonely mystic expects from God, which inspire him with new hope for union. It is natural that, in a civilization in which pigeon post was widely used, allusions to birds as letter-carriers are often found: the pigeon that is supposed to bring the letter from the beloved is often connected with the pigeons that live in the central sanctuary in Mecca. Thus the connection of the letter with the prayer sent by the faithful in the direction of the Kaaba in Mecca is understood, and the pigeon of the sanctuary may also convey the "letter" of divine grace to the patiently waiting Sufi. The traditional connection of the soul with the bird, and the designation of the mystical language as "language of the birds," gives this imagery another overtone.

The Sufi influence can be seen clearly in the field of calligraphy. The mystics who loved to enter into the deeper levels of meaning when looking at the letters of the alphabet indulged in inventing surprising forms from letters that seemed to be particularly meaningful. Arabic calligraphy is the typical expression of a culture that outlawed the representation of living beings, and the artists created very intricate patterns of floriated and lacelike plaited Kufi script on domes, minarets, and objects of minor art. In the later Middle Ages the calligraphers devised figures in which the verses of the Koran or words of mystical import were represented in a suitable form. They were written in mirror script,

26. Louis Massignon, "Le *diwan* d'al-Ḥallāj, essai de reconstitution," *Journal asiatique*, January–July 1931, muqaṭṭaᶜa no. 6.

reflecting one central truth of the Koran twice or fourfold. Or the artist created animals—horses, amusing little birds—from the words of the *basmala* or the Throne verse (Sūra 2:256). In Turkey, the calligraphers —who were often members of the Mevlevi order—liked to shape the *basmala* as stork, a bird praised in Turkish, Persian, and Arabic folklore for its piety in performing the pilgrimage to Mecca. Sentences connected with ʿAlī, the "lion of God," could be worked into the shape of a lion—a figure often found in Bektashi convents and all over the Shia world. A beautiful example of the living force of this mystical calligraphy may be seen in a recent painting by the young Pakistani artist Sadiquain, who has, in the course of his new calligraphic representation of the Koran, written the words *kun fayakūn*—"Be! and it becomes"—the words with which God created the world, in the shape of a spiral nebula of great spiritual power.

A thorough study of the relations between calligraphy and Sufi thought would doubtless yield interesting results and contribute to a better understanding of some of the basic Sufi ideas as well as of Islamic art.

APPENDIX 2

THE FEMININE ELEMENT IN SUFISM

"A pious woman is better than a thousand bad men" (S 271), says Sanāʾī, the Persian mystical poet who is, on the whole, not too favorably disposed toward the weaker sex. It was he who wrote that the constellation of *ursa maior,* called in Arabic *banāt an-naʿsh,* "daughters of the bier," points by its very name to the fact that daughters are better on a bier than alive (S 658).

Sanāʾī was not the only Sufi poet who expressed his aversion toward women. The ideal of the Sufi was always the "man" (Persian *mard,* Turkish *er*) or the "virtuous young man" (*fatā* or *jawānmard*). In these figures the high ambition of Sufism was best expressed.

The attitude of Sufism toward the fair sex was ambivalent, and it can even be said that Sufism was more favorable to the development of feminine activities than were other branches of Islam. The sympathy of the Prophet for women, his numerous marriages and his four daughters, excluded that feeling of dejection so often found in medieval Christian monasticism. The veneration of Fāṭima in Shia circles is indicative of the important role that could be assigned to the feminine element in Islamic religious life.

The very fact that the first true saint of Islam was a woman—the great lover Rābiʿa al-ʿAdawiyya[1]—certainly helped to shape the image of the ideal pious woman who can be praised in the most glowing terms (just because of her difference from the ordinary representatives of her sex!): "When a woman walks in the way of God like a man, she can not be called a woman" (T 1:59). To call a virtuous woman "a second Rābiʿa" was, and still is, quite common among the Muslims.

History shows, however, that Rābiʿa was no exception, though she was credited with introducing the concept of pure love into the austere ascetic outlook of early Sufism. Margaret Smith has collected the material about the lives of some of Rābiʿa's contemporaries, saintly women who lived in the late eighth century in Basra and in Syria. Among them are Maryam of Basra and Rīḥāna, "the enthusiastic" (*al-wāliha*), and many others who were known as "ever weeping, fearful, and who make others weep" (N 61). They might even become blind from constant weeping, so that their hearts' eyes might see better.

Some of the female descendants of the Prophet, like Sayyida Nafīsa

1. Margaret Smith, *Rabiʿa the Mystic and Her Fellow-Saints in Islam* (Cambridge, 1928), gives much information about the role of women saints in Islam.

(d. 824), excelled by their virtue and piety; her tomb in Cairo is still visited by the faithful. The same holds true for Sayyida Zaynab, whose sanctuary in Cairo is visited so often that it even provides the setting for two modern Egyptian novels, as Muhammad Mustafa Badawi has shown in a fine study.[2]

Apparently women were allowed to attend the meetings of Sufi preachers. The daughter of Abū Bakr al-Kattānī, the mystic, expired during a session in which Nūrī, the enraptured Sufi, spoke about love, and three men died with her (N 623). A considerable number of women of the ninth and tenth centuries are mentioned in the Arabic and Persian sources for their extraordinary achievements in piety and mysticism. And there were even women mystics who were guided by Khiḍr himself and received spiritual instruction from him (N 332).

In addition to these ascetics and mystics, in addition to these women who excelled as traditionalists, as calligraphers, or as poets, mention must be made of those who were married to the leading Sufis of their time. The pious Rābiʿa the Syrian, wife of Aḥmad ibn Abīʾl-Ḥawārī (N 617), was noted for her constantly changing mystical states, which she expressed in lovely verses. In later times, the wife of al-Qushayrī—daughter of his mystical master Abū ʿAlī ad-Daqqāq—is noted for her piety and learnedness; she was also a well-known transmitter of Prophetic traditions.

In the formative period of Islam, the most impressive figure among the married Sufi women is, no doubt, Aḥmad Khiḍrūya's wife Fāṭima of Nishapur (d. 849). She consorted with Dhūʾn-Nūn and Bāyezīd Bisṭāmī and seems to have guided her husband in religious and practical matters (cf. T 1:285; H 120). It is said that Dhūʾn-Nūn once refused a gift sent by her because it was given by a woman; she informed him that the true Sufi is he who does not look at the secondary causes—in this case a female—but at the Eternal Giver (N 620). The most famous story told about her is that she used to discuss mystical subjects freely with Bāyezīd Bisṭāmī; during the discussion she would lift her veil without restriction, until the day came that the great saint remarked that her hands were stained with henna. From that moment onward free spiritual conversation was no longer possible between the two mystics, for "the world" had interfered. This story has often been told in different contexts, and it may well be that a legendary motif was applied to Fāṭima, whose figure is, in any case, rather oscillating. Sanāʾī tells a similar story: a man crossed the Tigris every night in order to see his beloved until, one night, he became aware of a mole on her cheek; that night she warned him not to swim back lest he drown, because he had left the realm of pure spiritual love (S 331).

Other Sufis were not as lucky as Aḥmad Khiḍrūya. In fact, the historians enjoy telling stories about saints who were married to perfectly dreadful women, the prophet Jonah being the first example of this group

2. Muhammad Mustafa Badawi, "Islam in Modern Egyptian Literature," *Journal of Arabic Literature* 2 (1971), pp. 154 ff.

(Job is also sometimes cited).[3] These stories are more or less explicit illustrations of the much-discussed problem of whether or not a Sufi should lead a celibate life, and the authorities in favor of celibacy indulge in describing the horrors and dangers of married life. Some of the mystics were absolutely antagonistic to or disinterested in women, even to the point that they would not touch food cooked by a woman (N 576). Thus, married life could be considered, by some, as a substitute for the hellfire the saint may escape when patiently enduring the afflictions brought upon him by a nasty, misbehaving, or talkative spouse (even now some spiritual directors will tell their disciples to get married, for "the afflictions that wait for you will certainly lead you on the way toward God"). Rūmī tells, tongue in cheek, the story of Kharaqānī and his wife (M 6:2044–129): An adept wanted to join the disciples of this great Persian saint, but when he reached the saint's house, Kharaqānī's wife treated him very badly and told him all kinds of stories about her good-for-nothing husband. The young man, disillusioned, went into the forest and found the sheikh, riding on a lion and using a snake as a whip. That is how he was rewarded for the patience he had shown under his railing wife's constant pressures.

The women in stories like this remind the reader of a tendency found in both classical Sufism and medieval Christianity, the tendency to equate the "world" with a woman. This world is like an old hag who paints her ghastly and toothless face, even putting some scraps from a torn, illuminated Koran upon it to hide her wrinkles. Thus she tries to seduce men (M 6:1222–36, 1268–92) and is like "a stinking crooked old female who kills every day thousands of husbands" (U 39), a lecherous prostitute, faithless and mean, a mother who devours her children. That idea was expressed first in the sermons of the austere preacher Ḥasan al-Baṣrī, but it was frequently used by later authors like Ghazzālī, ʿAṭṭār (R 46), and even Rūmī. On the other hand, a later saying attests, "He who seeks the world is female," i.e., he suffers from all the impurities of a woman, which make union with the beloved impossible.

The ascetic should not care for this woman "world" but "throw the stone 'Poverty is my pride' into her mouth and divorce her thrice" (B 472). Essentially, the world is not even worth looking at: "This world is a bride: whosoever loves her, adorns her and combs her hair. The ascetic blackens her face. But he who has attained to mystical knowledge is completely possessed by God and does not care at all for her," says Yaḥyā ibn Muʿādh (L 39), who is a good translator of the mystical attitude toward the things "outside God."

The *nafs*, the lower soul, which is, so to speak, the individual representative of the world and its temptations, is also sometimes compared to a woman who, by her ruses, tries to ensnare the pure spirit and thus bring him down into the trap of worldly life. Rūmī illustrates this idea amusingly in his story of the enamored she-mouse who tries to seduce a

3. See Tor Andrae, *Islamische Mystiker* (Stuttgart, 1960), pp. 55 ff.

frog (M 6:2665 ff.). The fact that the word *nafs* is feminine in Arabic makes this comparison both easy and apt. The "animal quality" prevails in woman (M 5:2465); the *nafs* can be regarded as the mother, the intellect as the father, of man (M 6:1436). Many a Sufi would join Rūmī's hero in his exclamation: "First and last my fall is through woman" (M 6:2799), which sounds almost like a medieval Christian monk's sigh. Though some of the sayings about women found in the Islamic tradition are anything but friendly (even a woman's dream is considered less true than a man's dream because of her lower intellectual capacities) (M 6:4320), the Muslims scarcely reached the apogee of hatred displayed by medieval Christian writers in their condemnation of the feminine element. Eve was never made responsible for the fall of Adam, and the often repeated Christian accusation that "woman has no soul according to Islam" has no basis in the Koran or in the classical tradition.

The Sufis were well aware of the positive aspects of womanhood. Some of the Koranic tales could serve as beautiful illustrations of the role of women in religious life. The most famous example is that of Potiphar's wife as told in Sūra 12: the woman completely lost in her love of Joseph is a fine symbol for the enrapturing power of love, expressed by the mystic in the contemplation of divine beauty revealed in human form. The ecstasy of love leads everyone who experiences it into the same state as the women at Zulaykhā's table who cut their hands when gazing at the overwhelming beauty of her beloved. Thus, Zulaykhā has become, in Sufi poetry, the symbol of the soul, purified by ceaseless longing in the path of poverty and love. Her story was given its classical poetic form by Jāmī; a very fine example in the Turkish-speaking world is the epic written by Ḥamdī (d. 1503), in which Zulaykhā sings her longing in profoundly moving verses, having lost every trace of self-will in the hands of this primordial and eternal love.

The Sufis particularly loved Mary, *Maryam*, the immaculate mother who gave birth to the spiritual child Jesus. She is often taken as the symbol of the spirit that receives divine inspiration and thus becomes pregnant with the divine light. Here the purely spiritual role of the female receptacle is fully accepted, and few stories can compete in tenderness with Rūmī's description of the annunciation as told in the *Mathnawī* (M 3:3700–85). The veneration shown to Mary's alleged tomb near Ephesus proves that the deep love for the model of purity who is so often invoked in mystical poetry is still a living force in Islamic countries.

The strong, untiring faith of Muslim women has played, and still plays, an important role in the formation of the Muslim community. The Koran speaks repeatedly of the *muslimūn wa muslimāt, muʾminūn wa muʾmināt*, the "Muslim men and women," "the faithful men and women." The same religious injunctions are valid for both sexes, and one may assume that even in our day women are usually more concerned with ritual prayer and fasting than the average man in a Turkish or Pakistani household.

Many stories are told about pious sons who carried their aged mothers on their shoulders to enable them to partake in the pilgrimage to Mecca. It would be worthwhile to study the role of the mothers in the biographies of the Sufis. Although the energetic mother of Majduddīn Baghdādī, herself an accomplished physician (N 424; see p. 101), is certainly an exception, many religious leaders admitted that they received not only their first religious instruction but also their preliminary training in the mystical path from their mothers. Did not the Prophet say: "Paradise lies at the feet of the mothers"? A nice story that illustrates this point is that of Ibn Khafīf, whose devout mother was blessed with the vision of the *laylat ul-qadr*, the Night of Might in the end of Ramadan, during which heavenly light fills the world and becomes visible to the elect who have reached the highest illumination (X 205). In spite of his perpetual ascetic practices, her son was not graced with such a vision. Whether it be Farīd Ganj-i Shakar's mother in India or ʿAbduʾl-Qādir Gīlānī's mother and aunt (N 628), there is no doubt that many elderly women in the families contributed to the spiritual formation of some of the great Sufi leaders.

In this context one should not forget the role assigned by Sufi legends to the "old woman" who suddenly appears and warns or instructs the adepts in some mystical problems (cf. MT 243). And she may be praised for her high ambition, which induces her to bid when Joseph is sold, for

> It is enough for me that foe and friend should say:
> This woman is among those who would buy him—

she has at least attempted to reach the beautiful beloved (MT 17), though she knows that her case is hopeless in the eyes of men.

The same tendency is seen in the old woman—particularly the poor widow—who becomes the prototype of the oppressed in Persian mystical and mystically tinged poetry. Her prayer can stop armies, her complaint can change a ruler's mind (S 557), and her appeals to the religious law are always heard, since the Koran teaches respect and affection for widows and orphans. The "faith of the old women of the Muslim community" is often favorably contrasted with the hairsplitting discussions of intellectual theologians. Many a simple soul among them found salvation through sheer love and faith. How touching is the legend of Lallā Mīmūnah in the Maghreb! She was a poor negro woman who asked the captain of a boat to teach her the ritual prayer, but she could not remember the formula correctly. To learn it once more, she ran behind the departing boat, walking on the water. Her only prayer was: "Mīmūnah knows God, and God knows Mīmūnah." She became a saint, greatly venerated in North Africa.

Quite different from this simple soul is another woman saint of the western Islamic world, a mystical leader who educated one of the greatest mystical thinkers of Islam for two years. This was a certain Fāṭima of Cordova, who, in spite of her age of ninety-five years, was beautiful and fresh like a young girl (N 629), completely transformed by divine love.

A first and decisive meeting with a woman who radiated divine beauty as if she were transparent may have prepared the ground for Ibn ᶜArabī's inclination to perceive the divine through the medium of female beauty and to see the female as the true revelation of God's mercy and creativity. He composed his love lyrics in Mecca under the spell of a young Persian lady. The closing chapter of the *Fuṣūṣ al-ḥikam*, that on the Prophet Muhammad, centers around the famous tradition according to which the Prophet was given a love for perfumes and women and joy in prayer. Thus, Ibn ᶜArabī could defend the idea that "love of women belongs to the perfections of the gnostics, for it is inherited from the Prophet and is a divine love" (R 480). Woman reveals, for Ibn ᶜArabī, the secret of the compassionate God. The grammatical fact that the word *dhāt*, "essence," is feminine offers Ibn ᶜArabī different methods to discover this feminine element in God. His viewpoint has been condensed by Reynold A. Nicholson in commenting upon a relevant passage by Rūmī, who attested that the creative activity of God reveals itself best in women and that one might even say that "she is not created but creator" (M 1:2437). Ibn ᶜArabī thinks:

> God can not be seen apart from matter, and He is seen more perfectly in the human *materia* than in any other, and more perfectly in woman than in man. For He is seen either in the aspect of *agens* or in that of *patiens* or as both simultaneously. Therefore when a man contemplates God in his own person in regard to the fact that woman is produced from man, he contemplates God in the aspect of *agens*, and when he pays no regard to the production of women from himself he contemplates God in the aspect of *patiens*, because as God's creature he is absolutely *patiens* in relation to God, but when he contemplates God in woman he contemplates Him both as *agens* and *patiens*. God manifested in the form of woman is *agens* in virtue of exercising complete sway over man's soul and causing man to become submissive and devoted to Himself, and He is also *patiens* because inasmuch as He appears in the form of women He is under the man's control and subject to his orders: hence to see God in woman is to see Him in both these aspects, and such vision is more perfect than seeing Him in all the forms in which He manifests Himself. (MC 1:155–56)

Ibn ᶜArabī did not hesitate to admit the possibility that woman may be found among the *abdāl*, the Forty (or Seven) in the hierarchy of saints (N 615).

Ibn ᶜArabī's contemporary, the Egyptian poet Ibn al-Fāriḍ, used the feminine gender in his mystical odes when talking of the divine beloved. The names of his heroines—Layla, Salma, and many others—become, in his verses, symbols of divine beauty and perfection.

In Persian literature, the contemplation of the divine in the form of woman has been symbolized best in the originally Arabic story of Layla and Majnūn: Majnūn, completely absorbed in his love of Layla, becomes demented; the equation of love with loss of intellect, the substitution of rapture for reasoning was, as we have seen, a typical aspect of mystical experience. Majnūn sees in Layla the absolute beauty, even though the caliph may tell him that there are thousands of women more beautiful in the world. The eye of love, nevertheless, sees only one beauty, in contrast to the eye of intellect, which cannot perceive divine beauty in created forms (this is the case with Satan, who refused to fall down before Adam because he failed to recognize the divine spark in him). Majnūn sees Layla everywhere; every brick of her house is sacred, he kisses the paws of the dogs that have passed through her lane, and eventually he becomes so completely united with her that he is afraid of bloodletting because "it may hurt Layla" when the needle touches his skin. This complete unification leads to an absolute isolation—he no longer wants to see her, because her corporeal appearance might disturb the absoluteness of his heart's vision. Majnūn, becomes, thus, the mystical lover who sees God everywhere and has found him not outside himself but in the innermost corner of his own heart.

The other classic example of the role of women in mystical love theories is that of the story of Sheikh Ṣanʿān told by ʿAṭṭār. The pious mystical leader falls in love with a Christian maiden, leaves everything connected with Islam, and herds his beloved's pigs (but is eventually brought back into his old state of piety through the constant prayer of his aggrieved disciples). Here, the rapture is produced by a beloved object that should, essentially, be repellent to the pious ascetic. The story of Sheikh Ṣanʿān symbolizes that frenzy of love that is beyond all bounds, be they religious, social, or communal, a frenzy that defies logical reasoning and carries the lover into a state that he himself would never have anticipated. Historical cases of such love occur occasionally in Muslim mysticism, the object usually being a Christian or a Hindu boy, persons who have become stereotypes in Persian poetry as well. But in ʿAṭṭār's story the eternal beauty reveals itself once more in feminine form, and the experience of Sheikh Ṣanʿān is so deep as to change the whole course of a "normal" orthodox life into sheer surrender in love. That is why Ṣanʿān exchanging the rosary for the infidel's girdle became a favorite symbolic figure in later Persian and related poetry whenever the power of love needed to be adequately described.

To turn from the field of high mystical speculations and classical literature back to everyday life: Sufism, more than stern orthodoxy, offered women a certain amount of possibilities to participate actively in the religious and social life. In the later Middle Ages, the chronicles tell about convents where women could gather in pursuit of the mystical path or of religious life in general. In Mamluk Egypt, these convents had a *shaykha* who led the congregation in service and prayer. One of those convents was a refuge for divorced women, who could stay there until they found an opportunity for remarrying.

A number of Sufi orders had women attached to them as lay members. Although some of them do not allow women inside the sanctuaries, the The order that granted the greatest opportunities to women was the love and enthusiasm of the female adherents is, as a rule, very ardent. Bektashi in Ottoman Turkey. Here, they were absolutely equal with men; they had to undergo the same ceremony of initiation and joined in the common festive meals and gatherings—a custom that has lent itself to accusations of immorality against the Bektashis.

From the earliest times on, wealthy women are mentioned as benefactors of Sufi masters or institutions or of whole groups of dervishes. They would endow the *khānqāh*s with food and money (the faithful Bībī Fāṭima supported Abū Saʿīd ibn Abīʾl-Khayr and his disciples in the early eleventh century, and one of Aurangzeb's daughters offered a whole complex of buildings to Mīr Dard in eighteenth-century Delhi). The role of women sponsoring Sufi activities deserves special attention, and its importance should be underlined; it was in this field that pious, well-to-do women found an outlet for their energies and could do much good in social service, in founding *khānqāh*s, or in contributing to the growth of extant facilities for the dervish community. As a reward for their help, they might find consolation and spiritual uplift in the gatherings of the mystics. These kinds of feminine activities—such as looking after individual mystics, inviting Sufi gatherings to their homes—can still be witnessed in some parts of the Muslim world.

Names of women saints are found throughout the world of Islam, though only few of them have been entered into the official annals. But the popular imagination often invented tender legends that eventually resulted in the emergence of a new woman saint. Anatolia can boast of a large number of small shrines where more or less historical women are buried—simple village girls and noble virgins, whose very names often suggest sad or romantic stories. They are visited by women to express special wishes connected with conjugal life, children, and similar problems. The same is true in Iran. North Africa is also rich in sanctuaries devoted to women saints; but the area in which women saints flourished most is probably Muslim India. Suffice it to mention Shāh Jihān's eldest daughter Jihānārā who, together with her luckless brother Dārā Shikōh, joined the Qādiriyya and was highly praised by her master Mollā Shāh. Her writings prove her deep understanding of mystical problems. The sister of Jihānārā's and Dārā's first mystical guide Miān Mīr, Bībī Jamāl Khātūn (d. 1639), was one of the outstanding saints of the Qādiriyya order during its formative period in the Punjab.

In all the provinces of Muslim India and Pakistan one may see shrines of women saints to which men are not admitted (which is true for other parts of the Islamic world as well). I vividly remember my visit to one such small shrine in Multan, decorated with lovely blue and white tiles; the cheerful women in charge of the tomb were no less greedy than the guardians in many other sacred places.

The province of Sind, generally famous for its saint worship, is particularly rich in legends connected with women saints, as the critical observer Richard Burton long ago observed: "To the credit of the Sindhi it must be said that they do not refuse to admit the religious merits of the softer sex."[4] He speaks of the *faqīrāṇī* (feminine for *faqīr*): "a few of them occasionally rise to the high rank of a *murshid*"; and his remarks

4. Sir Richard Burton, *Sind and the Races That Inhabit the Valley of the Indus* (London, 1851), p. 230.

about one of the most famous saints in the province, Bībī Fāṭima Hajrānī, a *ḥāfiẓa* who performed many miracles, are corroborated by the numerous books devoted by Sindhi scholars to the religious life of their country. As elsewhere in the Muslim world, we find in Sind whole groups of women saints, like the *haft ᶜafīfa*, "the Seven Chaste," who escaped a group of attacking soldiers and were swallowed by the earth before their virtue could be touched, or the *mukhaddarāt-i abdāliyya*, "the veiled women in the rank of *abdāl*," and countless others.[5]

In the province of Sind, as well as in Punjab, a special aspect of mystical appreciation of women can be observed that is rarely encountered in other parts of the Muslim world, i.e., the representation of the longing soul in the form of a woman. Now and then, as has been pointed out, the image of love between two men—so frequent in Persian poetry—was changed into a love of the divine as symbolized in woman; but a representation of the longing soul in the image of a woman occurs only rarely, as in the Koranic cases of Zulaykhā and Mary. In the western part of Muslim India, however—from Sind to Kashmir—the poets followed the Hindu tradition, which describes the soul as the longing girl, a faithful wife, or a loving bride. The classical example in Hinduism is the legend of Krishna and the *gopi*s, the cowherd-girls (not to mention the whole complex of Shakti mysticism in Indian tradition). Sikh mysticism, too, has adopted this imagery. The *ginan*—sacred songs of the Ismaili community of Indo-Pakistan—also depict the soul as a loving female. The earliest Urdu-writing Sufi poets—like Sayyid Muhammad Jīw Jān in the seventeenth century—knew this bridal symbolism; but it is used mostly in the mystically interpreted folk tales of Sind and the Punjab.

The tragic heroines of the Sindhi and Panjabi folk tales—like Hīr, Sassuī, Sohnī, and many others—represent the human soul in search of the beloved, a beloved to whom she can be united only by endless suffering and eventually through death on the Path. The disobedient woman—the lower soul—sits in her lowly hut, covered with rags, waiting for her husband to come and veil her once more in his inexhaustible mercy and lovingkindness; the faithful wife expects His return from distant islands, to bring precious gifts and spices, i.e., the graces He bestows upon those who love Him to the exclusion of everything else. Even in the popular poetical genre of the *bārāmāsa*, poems dealing with the peculiarities of the twelve months and the feeling of the lover in each of these months, or in the "Golden Alphabets" composed by Sindhi and Panjabi folk poets, the soul is the bride and God—or the Prophet Muhammad—the longed-for bridegroom. This symbolism allows the poet to give delicate expression to those sentiments of love, yearning, fear, and hope that constitute the main topics of classical Sufi poetry in a language that overflows with tenderness and intense, genuine longing. The Western reader—used to the imagery of the "Song of Songs" and to medieval Christian bridal mysticism—can more easily appreciate and en-

5. Iᶜjāzul Ḥaqq Quddūsī, *Tadhkira-yi ṣufiyā-yi Sind* (Karachi, 1959), p. 334; see Aᶜẓam Tattawi, *Tuḥfat aṭ-ṭāhirīn*, ed. B. A. Durrani (Karachi, 1956), pp. 91, 138, 175.

joy these expressions of Sufi experience than he can the usual symbolism of Persian and Turkish mystical poetry.

It is interesting to note how one of the Indo-Persian mystics, Mīr Dard's father, Muhammad Nāṣir ᶜAndalīb, used this bridal symbolism in his Persian prose work *Nāla-yi ᶜAndalīb*. Nāṣir ᶜAndalīb thought very highly of pious women, some of whom "have surpassed many men in learning and mystical knowledge and love and charity."[6] He is sure that they, too, will be blessed with the vision of God in the otherworld. But he, too, held that the wife should regard her husband as the representative of the Lord, and he quotes the alleged Prophetic tradition: "If it were permissible to prostrate oneself before anyone but God, I would say that the wives should prostrate themselves before their husbands"[7]—a sentence that is reminiscent of the Hindu ideals of marriage, according to which the husband is, indeed, the representative of divine power. In an allegory, Muhammad Nāṣir confronts his readers with this idea. Dwelling upon the traditional theory of man as the place of manifestation of the various divine names and as microcosmos, he uses these ideas in the context of bridal mysticism: in the moment of the consummation of marriage, the virgin recognizes in her husband the qualities of tremendous majesty instead of the mercy she had seen in him before; but he explains to her that this seeming cruelty of his of wounding her body is nothing but the proof of highest love and "naked union."[8] Here, the Indian tradition of the bridal soul and the Muslim tradition of union through complete surrender in suffering are blended in a strange way.

It is remarkable that in modern times Sufi teaching is, to a large extent, carried on by women again. Not only does the interest in the mystical path—modernized as it may be—apparently appeal more to women, who hope to find a more "romantic" or poetic expression of religious feeling than that offered by traditional religious forms, but some of the most genuine representatives of mystical tradition, directors of souls, in Istanbul and Delhi (and probably in other places as well) are women, who exert a remarkable influence upon smaller or larger groups of seekers who find consolation and spiritual help in their presence.

The verse about Rābiᶜa quoted by Jāmī (N 615)—who was, in general, not too favorably inclined to women—is still valid in this respect:

> If all women were like as the one we have mentioned,
> then women would be preferred to men.
> For the feminine gender is no shame for the sun,
> nor is the masculine gender an honor for the crescent moon.

6. Muhammad Nāṣir, *Nāla-yi ᶜAndalīb* (Bhopal, 1309 h./1891–92), 1:832.
7. Ibid., 1:578.
8. Ibid., 1:560.

BIBLIOGRAPHY

ʿAbduṣ-Ṣabūr, Ṣalāh. *Maʾsāt al-Ḥallāj.* Beirut, 1964. In Arabic. Translated by K. J. Semaan as *Murder in Baghdad.* Leiden, 1972.

Abd el-Ḥaqq el-Badīsī. *El-Maqṣad (Vies des saints du Rif).* Translated by Gabriel S. Colin. Paris, 1926.

Abd El-Jalil, J. M. "Autour de la sincérité d'al-Gazzali." In *Mélanges Louis Massignon.* Vol. 1. Damascus, 1956.

Abdel Kader, A. H. *The Life, Personality and Writings of al-Junayd.* Gibb Memorial Series, n.s. 22. London, 1962.

Abdullah, Dr. Syed. *Naqd-i Mīr.* Lahore, 1958. In Urdu.

ʿAbdul Ḥakīm, Khalīfa. *The Metaphysics of Rumi.* Lahore, n.d.

ʿAbdul Ḥaqq, Maulvi. *Urdū kī nashw ū numā meñ Ṣūfiyā-i kirām kā kām.* Karachi, 1953. In Urdu.

ʿAbdul Qādir al-Jīlānī. *Al-fatḥ ar-rabbānī.* Cairo, 1960. In Arabic.

———. *Futūḥ al-ghayb.* Translated by M. Aftab ud-Din Ahmad. Lahore, n.d.

ʿAbdul Qādir Tattawī, Sayyid. *Ḥadīqat al-auliyā.* Edited by Sayyid Hussamuddin Rashdi. Hyderabad, Sind, 1967. In Persian.

Abṛō, Jamāl. *Munhun kārō.* In Sindhi. Translated by Annemarie Schimmel as "Geschwärzten Gesichts." In *Aus der Palmweinschenke: Pakistan in Erzählungen seiner zeitgenössischen Autoren.* Tübingen, 1966. English translation by E. Mohr Rahman in *Mahfil: A Quarterly of South Asian Literature,* 1969.

Abun Nasr, Jamil M. *The Tijaniya: A Sufi Order in the Modern World.* Oxford, 1965.

Abū Nuʿaym. See Iṣfahānī, Abū Nuʿaym al-.

Affīfī, Abūʾl-ʿAlāʾ. *Al-malāmatiyya waʾṣ-ṣūfiyya wa ahl al-futuwwa.* Cairo, 1945. In Arabic.

———. *The Mystical Philosophy of Muḥyid'Dīn Ibnul-ʿArabī.* Cambridge, 1936.

———. *At-taṣawwuf: ath-thaurat ar-rūḥiyya fīʾl-Islām.* Cairo, 1963. In Arabic.

Aflākī, Shamsaddin Ahmad al-. *Manāqib al-ʿārifīn.* 2 vols. Ankara, 1959–61. In Persian. Turkish translation: *Ariflerin menkibeleri.* Edited by Tahsin Yazıcı. Ankara, 1964.

Ahmad, Aziz. *An Intellectual History of Islam in India.* Edinburgh, 1969.

———. "Political and Religious Ideas of Shāh Walīullāh of Delhi." *Moslem World* 52, no. 1 (1962).

———. "Religious and Political Ideas of Shaikh Aḥmad Sirhindi." *Rivista degli studi orientali* 36 (1961).

———. *Studies in Islamic Culture in the Indian Environment*. Oxford, 1964.

———. "The Sufi and the Sultan in Pre-Mughal Muslim India." *Der Islam* 38 (1963).

———. "Sufismus und Hindumystik." *Saeculum* 15, no. 1 (1964).

Ahmad, Zubaid. *The Contribution of Indo-Pakistan to Arabic Literature*. 2d ed. Lahore, 1968.

Ahuya, Yog Dhyan. "Iraqi in India." *Islamic Culture*, 1958.

Aini, Mehmed Ali. *Un grand saint de l'Islam: Abd al-Kadir Guilani*. 2d ed. Paris, 1967.

Akhtar, Ḥaydar. *Khwāja Mīr Dard, taṣawwuf aur shāʿirī*. Aligarh, 1971. In Urdu.

Akkaş, Turgut. *Özkaynak*. Ankara, 1957. In Turkish.

Aktay, Salih Zeki. *Hallac-ı Mansur*. Istanbul, 1942. In Turkish.

Algar, Hamid. "Some Notes on the Naqshbandi Ṭarīqat in Bosnia." *Die Welt des Islams*, n.s. 13, nos. 3–4 (1971).

Ali, Ahmad. *Twilight in Delhi*. Oxford, 1966.

Ali, Meer Hassan. *Observations on the Mussulmauns of India*. 2 vols. London, 1832.

ʿAlī ibn Ḥusayn Wāʿiẓ-i al-Kāshifī. *Rashaḥāt ʿayn al-ḥayāt*. Kanpur, 1291 sh./1912. In Persian. Much more in use is the Turkish translation: *Rashaḥāt ʿayn ʿal-ḥayāt*. Istanbul, 1291 h./1874–75. It contains many other Naqshbandī treatises at the margin.

Amedroz, Henry Frederick. "Notes on Some Sufi Lives." *Journal of the Royal Asiatic Society*, 1912.

Amīr Khūrd. *Siyar al-auliyāʾ*. Delhi, 1309 h./1891–92. In Persian.

Amīr Khusrau. *Dīwān-i kāmil*. Edited by Mahmūd Derwish. Tehran, 1343 sh./1964. In Persian.

Anawati, G.-C., and Gardet, Louis. *Mystique musulmane*. Paris, 1961.

ʿAndalīb, Muḥammad Nāṣir. *Nāla-yi ʿAndalīb*. 2 vols. Bhopal, 1309 h./ 1891–92. In Persian.

Andrae, Tor. *Die person Muhammads in lehre und glauben seiner gemeinde*. Stockholm, 1918.

———. *I Myrtenträdgården*. Uppsala, 1947. In Swedish. Translated into German by Hans Helmhart Kanus as *Islamische Mystiker*. Stuttgart, 1960.

———. "Zuhd und Mönchtum." *Le monde oriental* 25 (1931).

Andrée, P. J. *Confréries religieuses musulmans*. Algiers, 1956.

Anṣārī, ʿAbdullāh-i. *The Invocations of Shaikh Abdullah Ansari*. Translated by Jogendra Singh. 3d ed. London, 1959.

———. *Manāzil as-sāʾirīn*. Edited and translated by Serge de Laugier de Beaureceuil. Cairo, 1962. In Arabic.

———. *Munājāt ū naṣāʾiḥ*. Berlin, 1925. In Persian.

Anṣārī, A. S. Bazmee. "Sayyid Muhammad Jawnpuri and His Movement." *Islamic Studies* 2 (1963).

Antes, Peter. *Das Prophetenwunder in der frühen Ašʿarīya bis al-Ġazālī*. Freiburg, 1970.

———. *Zur Theologie der Shia. Eine Untersuchung des Ġāmi^c al-asrār wa manba^c al-anwār von Sayyid Ḥaidar Amolī.* Freiburg, 1971.
ᶜAqueel, Shafiᶜ. *Panjab rang.* Lahore, 1968. In Urdu.
Araz, Nezihe. *Anadolu Evliyaları.* Istanbul, 1958. In Turkish.
Arberry, A. J. *Aspects of Islamic Civilization.* Ann Arbor, 1967.
———. *Classical Persian Literature.* London, 1958.
———. *An Introduction to the History of Sufism.* London, 1942.
———. "Junaid." *Journal of the Royal Asiatic Society,* 1935.
———. *Sufism: An Account of the Mystics of Islam.* London, 1950.
———, ed. *The Mystical Poems of Ibn al-Fāriḍ.* Chester Beatty Monographs, no. 4. London, 1954.
———. *The Mystical Poems of Ibn al-Fāriḍ.* Dublin, 1956.
———. *Pages from the "Kitāb al-Lumaᶜ."* London, 1947. From the Bankipore manuscript.
———. *Religion in the Middle East.* 2 vols. Cambridge, 1969.
———, trans. *Discourses of Rumi.* London, 1961.
———. *The Doctrine of the Sufis.* Cambridge, 1935. Translation of Kalābādhī's *Kitāb at-taᶜarruf.*
———. *More Tales from the Mathnawi.* London, 1963.
———. *Muslim Saints and Mystics.* London, 1964. Excerpts from ᶜAṭṭār's *Tadhkirat al-auliyā.*
———. *Mystical Poems of Rumi.* Chicago, 1968.
———. *The "Rubāʾīyāt" of Jalāluddīn Rūmī.* London, 1959.
———. *A Sufi Martyr.* London, 1969. Translation of ᶜAynuʾl-Quḍāt's Apology.
———. *Tales from the Mathnawi.* London, 1961.
Archer, J. C. *Mystical Elements in Mohammad.* New Haven, 1924.
Ardalan, Nader, and Laleh Bakhtiar. *The Sense of Unity: The Sufi Tradition in Persian Architecture.* Chicago, 1973.
ᶜĀrifī. *"Gū ū jaugān," The Ball and the Polo-Stick, or Book of Exstasy.* Edited and translated by Robert Scott Greenshields. London, 1932.
Arnaldez, Roger. *Hallaj ou la religion de la croix.* Paris, 1964.
Arnold, Sir Edwin. *Pearls of the Faith, or Islam's Rosary.* London, 1882.
Arnold, Sir Thomas. *The Preaching of Islam.* 1896. Reprint. Lahore, 1956.
———. "Saints, Muhammadan, India." In *Encylopedia of Religion and Ethics,* edited by James Hastings, vol. 11, pp. 68–73. 1908–27.
Aṣlaḥ, Muḥammad. *Tadhkira-yi shuᶜarā-yi Kashmīr.* Edited by Sayyid Hussamuddin Rashdi. 5 vols. Karachi, 1967–68. In Persian.
Ateş, Süleyman. *Sülemi ve tasavvufi tefsiri.* Istanbul, 1969. In Turkish.
ᶜAṭṭār, Farīduddīn. *The Conference of the Birds.* Translated by C. S. Noth. 1954. Paperback. Berkeley, 1971.
———. *Dīwan-ī qaṣāʾid wa ghazaliyāt.* Edited by Saᶜīd Nafisi. Tehran, 1339 sh./1960. In Persian.
———. *Ilāhīnāme, Die Gespräche des Königs mit seinen sechs Söhnen.* Edited by Hellmut Ritter. Leipzig, 1940. In Persian.

———. *Manṭiq aṭ-ṭayr*. Edited by M. Jawād Shakūr. Tehran, 1962. In Persian.

———. *Muṣībatnāme*. Edited by N. Fiṣāl. Tehran, 1338 sh./1959. In Persian.

———. *Pandname*. Edited by Silvestre de Sacy. Paris, 1819.

———. *Tadhkirat al-auliyā*ʾ. Edited by Reynold A. Nicholson. 2 vols. 1905–7. Reprint. London and Leiden, 1959. In Persian.

———. *Ushturnāme*. Edited by Mahdi Muḥaqqiq. Tehran, 1339 sh./1960. In Persian.

Attas, Syed Muhammad Naguib al-. *The Mysticism of Ḥamza al-Fanṣūrī*. Kuala Lumpur, 1970.

Aubin, Jean. *Matériaux pour la biographie de Shah Niʿmatullāh Walī Kermānī*. Tehran and Paris, 1956.

Aurād-i Maulānā. Istanbul Universitesi Kütüphanesi, Arab. 148. In Arabic. A collection of prayers ascribed to Jalāluddīn Rūmī.

ʿAynuʾl-Quḍāt Hamadhānī. *Aḥwal ū āthār*. Edited by ʿAfīf ʿUsayrān. Tehran, 1338 sh./1959. In Persian.

———. *Lawāʾiḥ*. Edited by Rahīm Farmānish. Tehran, 1337 sh./1958. In Persian.

Ayverdi, Samiha. *Istanbul Geceleri*. Istanbul, 1952. In Turkish.

Ayverdi, Samiha; Araz, Nezihe; Erol, Safiye; and Huri, Sofi. *Kenan Rifai ve yirminci asrın ışığında Müslümanlık*. Istanbul, 1951. In Turkish.

Aʿẓam Tattawī, Muḥammad. *Tuḥfat aṭ-ṭāhirīn*. Edited by Badr-i Alam Durrani. Karachi, 1956. In Persian.

Bābā Ṭāhir. *The Lament of Baba Tāhir, Being the "Rubāʿiyat" of Baba Tahir Hamadani ʿUryān*. Edited and translated by Edward Heron-Allen and Elizabeth Curtis Brenton. London, 1902.

Babinger, Franz. "Schejch Bedr ad-din, der Sohn des Richters von Simawna." *Der Islam* 2 (1912).

———. "Zur Frühgeschichte des Naqschbendi-Ordens." *Der Islam* 13 (1923), 14 (1925).

Badawi, Abdur Rahman. "Les points de rencontre de la mystique musulmane et de l'existentialisme." *Studia Islamica* 27 (1967).

———. *Shāhidat al-ʿishq al-ilāhī, Rābiʿa alʿAdawiyya*. Cairo, 1946. In Arabic.

———. *Shaṭaḥāt aṣ-ṣūfiyya, juzʾ 1: Abū Yazīd al-Bisṭāmī*. Cairo, 1949. In Arabic.

Badawi, Muhammad Mustafa. "Islam in Modern Egyptian Literature." *Journal of Arabic Literature* 2 (1971).

Badīsī, el-. See ʿAbd el-Ḥaqq el-Badīsī.

Bagley, R. R. C., trans. *Ghazālī's Book of Counsel for Kings (naṣīḥat al-mulūk)*. Oxford, 1964.

Bahāʾuddīn Walad. *Maʿārif*. Edited by Badīʿuz-Zamān Furūzānfar. Tehran, 1338 sh./1959. In Persian.

Bakharzī, A. M. Yaḥyā al-Kubrawī al-. *Aurād al-aḥbāb wa fuṣūṣ al-ādāb*. Edited by Iraj Afshar. Tehran, 1347 sh./1968. In Persian.

Baljon, J. M. S. "Psychology as Apprehended and Applied by Shah Walī Allāh Dihlawī." *Acta Orientalia Neerlandica,* 1971.

———, trans. *A Mystical Interpretation of Prophetic Tales by an Indian Muslim: Shāh Walī Allāh's "taʾwīl al-aḥādīth."* Leiden, 1973.

Baloch, Dr. Nabi Bakhsh, ed. *Madaḥūn ayn munājātūn.* Karachi, 1959. In Sindhi.

———. *Tih akaryūn.* Hyderabad, Sind, 1962. In Sindhi.

Bannerth, Ernst. "Das Buch der 40 Stufen von ᶜAbd al-Karīm al-Ǧīlī." *Sitzungsberichte der Oesterreichischen Akademie der Wissenschaften, philologisch-historiche Klasse* 230, no. 3. Vienna, 1956.

———. "La Khalwatiyya en Egypte." *Mélanges de l'institut dominicaine d'études orientales du Caire* 8 (1964–66).

———, trans. *Der Pfad der Gottesdiener.* Salzburg, 1964. Al-Ghazzālī's *Minhāj al-ᶜābidīn.*

Baqlī, Rūzbihān. *"ᶜAbhar al-ᶜashiqīn," Le jasmin des fidèles d'amour.* Edited by Henri Corbin. Tehran and Paris, 1958. In Persian.

———. *"Sharḥ-i shaṭḥiyāt," Les paradoxes des soufis.* Edited by Henri Corbin. Tehran and Paris, 1966. In Persian.

Barclay, Harold B. "A Sudanese Religious Brotherhood: At-ṭarīqa al-hindīya." *Moslem World* 53, no. 2 (1963).

Barnett, Lionel D. *Panjabi: Printed Books in the British Museum.* London, 1961.

Barthold, Vasilij V. *Herat zur Zeit Husain Baiqaras.* Translated by Walter Hinz. Leipzig, 1938.

Bauer, Hans. *Islamische Ethik.* 4 vols. Halle, 1916. Translated from al-Ghazzālī's *Iḥyā.*

Bausani, Alessandro. "About a Curious Mystical Language." *East and West* 4, no. 4 (1958).

———. "Il Gulšan-i rāz-i ǧadīd di Muhammad Iqbal." *Annali del Istituto Universitario Orientale di Napoli,* n.s. 8 (1959).

———. "Il pensiero religioso di Maulānā Gialāl ad-Dīn Rūmī." *Oriente moderno* 33 (April 1953).

———. "Note su Mirzā Bedil." *Annali del Istituto Universitario Orientale di Napoli,* n.s. 6 (1957).

———. "Note su Shah Waliullah di Delhi." *Annali del Istituto Universitario Orientale di Napoli,* n.s. 10 (1961).

———. *Persia religiosa.* Milan, 1959.

———. "Satana nell'opera filosofico-poetica di Muhammad Iqbal." *Rivista degli studi orientali* 30 (1957).

———. *Storia delle letterature del Pakistan.* Milan, 1958.

Bausani, Alessandro, and Pagliaro, Antonio, *Storia della letteratura persiana.* Milan, 1960.

Bečka, Jiří. "Publications to Celebrate the 550th Anniversary of the Birth of ᶜAbdur Raḥmān Jāmī." *Archiv Orientální* 34 (1966).

Bedil, Mirza. *Kulliyāt.* 4 vols. Kabul, 1962–65. In Persian.

Bēdil Rohrīwārō. *Dīwān.* Edited by ᶜAbdul Ḥusayn Mūsawī. Karachi, 1954. In Sindhi.

Begg, Mirza Wahiduddin. *The Holy Biography of Hazrat Khwaja Muinaddin Chishti.* Ajmer, 1960.

Bel, Alfred. "Le sufisme en occident musulman au XIIe et au XIIIe siècle de J. C." *Annales de l'institut des études orientales* 1 (1934–35).

Bercher, Leon, and Bousquet, G. H. *Le livre des bon usages en matière de mariage.* Paris, 1953. Translation of a chapter of Ghazzālī's *Iḥyā*ʾ.

Berger, Morroe. *Islam in Egypt Today: Social and Political Aspects of Popular Religion.* Cambridge, 1970.

Berthels, Y. E. "Grundlinien der Entwicklungsgeschichte des sufischen Lehrgedichtes." *Islamica* 3, no. 1 (1929).

Bhatti, M. Salih. *Manṣur Ḥallāj.* Hyderabad, Sind, 1952. In Sindhi.

Birge, John K. *The Bektashi Order of Dervishes.* 1937. Reprint. London, 1965.

Bīrūnī, al-. *Kitāb al-Hind.* Edited by Eduard Sachau. London, 1887. Translated by Eduard Sachau as *Al-Biruni's India: An Account of the Religion, Philosophy, Literature, Geography, Chronology, Astronomy, Customs, Laws and Astrology of India, about AD 1030.* London, 1881.

Blochet, Edgard. *Catalogue des Mss. persans de la bibliothèque nationale.* Paris, 1905ff.

Bousquet, G. H. *Ih'ya ʿouloum ad-dīn, ou vivification des sciences de la foi.* Paris, 1955.

Bouyges, Maurice. *Essai de chronologie des oeuvres d'al-Ghazālī.* Edited by Michel Allard. Beirut, 1959.

Brabazon, Francis. *Stay with God: A Statement in Illusion on Reality.* Woombye, Queensland, 1959.

Braune, Walter. *Die "Futūḥ al-ġaib" des ʿAbdul Qādir.* Berlin and Leipzig, 1933.

Bremond, Henri. *Histoire du sentiment religieux en France.* Vol. 9. Paris, 1928.

Brögelmann, Emil. *Die religiösen Erlebnisse der persischen Mystiker.* Hannover, 1932.

Brown, John P. *The Dervishes.* 1868. Reprint. London, 1968.

Browne, Edward G. *A Literary History of Persia.* 4 vols. 1902–21. Reprint. Cambridge, 1957.

———. "Notes on the Literature of the Ḥurūfis and Their Connection with the Bektashi Dervishes." *Journal of the Royal Asiatic Society,* 1907.

Brugsch, Mohammed. *Die kostbare Perle im Wissen des Jenseits.* Hannover, 1924. A translation of Ghazzālī's eschatological treatise.

Brunel, René. *Essai sur la confrèrie religieuse des Aissouwa au Maroc.* Paris, 1926.

———. *Le monachisme errant dans l'Islam, Sīdī Heddī et les Heddāwa.* Paris, 1955.

Bukhari, al-. *Kitāb ğāmi ʿaṣ-ṣaḥīḥ.* Edited by L. Krehl and W. Juynboll. 4 vols. Leiden, 1862–1908.

Bullhē Shāh. *Dīwān*. Edited by Faqir M. Faqir. Lahore, 1960. In Panjabi.

Burckhardt, Titus. *Introduction aux doctrines esotériques de l'Islam*. Algiers and Lyon, 1955.

———. *Introduction to Sufi Doctrines*. Lahore, 1959.

———. *La sagesse des prophètes*. Paris, 1955.

———. *Vom Sufitum*. Munich, 1953.

Burhānpūrī, Rāshid. *Burhānpūr kē Sindhi auliyā*. Karachi, 1957. In Urdu.

Burton, Sir Richard. *Sind and the Races That Inhabit the Valley of the Indus*. London, 1851.

Būṣīrī, al-. *La Bordah du Cheikh al Bousiri*. Edited and translated by René Basset. Paris, 1894.

———. *Die Burda*. Edited by C. A. Ralfs. Vienna, 1860. In Arabic with Persian and Turkish translations.

Calverley, Edwin Elliot. *Worship in Islam, Being a Translation, with Commentary and Introduction of al-Ghazzālī's Book of the "Iḥyā᾽" on the Worship*. Madras, 1925.

Çelebi, Asaf Halet. *HE*. Istanbul, 1951. Turkish poetry.

———. *Lām-Alif*. Istanbul, 1953. Turkish poetry.

Centlivres, Pierre. *Un bazar de l'Asie Centrale: Tashqurgan*. Wiesbaden, 1972.

Cerulli, Enrico. *Il "Libro della scala" e la questione delle fonti arabo-spagnole della "Divina Commedia."* Vatican City, 1949.

Chelkowski, Peter, ed. *Biruni/Rumi, the Scholar and the Saint*. New York, 1975.

Chirāgh-i Dehlawī. *Khayr al-majālis*. Edited by Khaliq Ahmad Nizami. Aligarh, 1959. In Persian.

Corbin, Henri. *Avicenna and the Visionary Recital*. New York and London, 1960.

———. *L'imagination créatrice dans le soufisme d'Ibn ᶜArabi*. Paris, 1958. Translated by Ralph Manheim as *Creative Imagination in the Sufism of Ibn ᶜArabi*. Princeton, 1969.

———. "Imagination créatrice et prière créatrice dans le soufisme d'Ibn Arabi." *Eranos-Jahrbuch* 25 (1956).

———. "Quiétude et inquiétude de l'âme dans le soufisme de Rūzbihān Baqlī de Shiraz." *Eranos-Jahrbuch* 27 (1958).

———. *Sohrawardi d'Alep, fondateur de la doctrine illuminative (ishrāqī)*. Paris, 1939.

———. "Sympathie et théopathie chez les fidèles d'amour en Islam." *Eranos-Jahrbuch* 24 (1955).

Crapazano, Vincent. "The Mamadsha." In *Scholars, Saints, and Sufis: Muslim Religious Institutions since 1500*, edited by Nikki R. Keddie. Berkeley, 1972.

Danner, Victor, trans. *Ibn ᶜAṭā᾽illāh's Sufi Aphorisms (Kitāb al-ḥikam)*. Leiden, 1973.

Dārā Shikōh. *Sakīnat al-auliyā*ʾ Edited by M. Jālālī Nāʾinī. Tehran, 1344 sh./1965. In Persian.

———. *Sirr-i akbar*. Edited by Tara Chand and M. Jālālī Nāʾinī. Tehran, 1961. In Persian.

Dard, Khwāja Mīr. *Chahār risāla*. Bhopal, 1310 h./1892–93. In Persian. Contains *Nāla-yi Dard, Āh-i sard, Dard-i dil*, and *Shamᶜ-i maḥfil*.

———. *Dīwān-i fārsī*. Delhi, 1310 h./1892–93.

———. *ᶜIlm ul-kitāb*. Bhopal, 1309 h./1891–92. In Persian.

———. *Urdū Dīwān*. Edited by Khalīl ur-Raḥmān Daʾūdī. Lahore, 1962. In Urdu.

Darqawi, ad-. *Letters of a Sufi Master*. Translated by Titus Burckhardt. London, 1961.

Daudpota, Umar Mūhammad. *Kalām-i Girhōṛī*. Hyderabad, Sind, 1956. In Sindhi.

Davis, F. Hadland. *The Persian Mystics: Jami*. Ca. 1908. Reprint. Lahore, n.d.

Dāyā Rāzī, Najmuddīn. *Mirṣād ul- ᶜibād*. Tehran, 1312 sh./1933. In Persian.

Daylamī, ᶜAlī ibn Aḥmad ad-. *Kitāb ᶜaṭf al-alif alʾ-maʾlūf ilāʾl-lām al-maᶜṭūf*. Edited by Jean-Claude Vadet. Cairo, 1962. In Arabic.

———. *Sīrat-i Ibn al-Ḫafīf ash-Shīrāzī*. Translated by Junayd-i Shīrāzī. Edited by Annemarie Schimmel. Ankara, 1955. In Persian.

Demeersemann, André. "Ce qu'Ibn Khaldoun pense d'al-Ghazzālī." *Institut des belles lettres arabes* 21 (1958).

Depont, O., and Coppolani, Xavier. *Les confrèries religieuses musulmanes*. Algiers, 1897.

Dermenghem, Émile. *Le culte des saints dans l'Islam Maghrebin*. Paris, 1954.

———. *Vies des saints musulmans*. Algiers, 1942.

———, trans. *L'éloge du vin (al-Khamrīya): poème mystique de Omar ibn al-Faridh, et son commentaire par Abdalghani an-Nabolosi*. Paris, 1931.

Digby, Simon. "Encounters with Jogis in Indian Sufi Hagiography." Mimeographed. London: School of Oriental and African Studies, January 1970.

Dingemans, Herman Henry. *Al-Ghazālī's boek der liefde*. Leiden, 1938.

Dubler, César E. *Über islamischen Grab- und Heiligenkult*. Zurich, 1960.

Eaton, Richard M. "Sufis of Bijapur: Some Social Roles of Medieval Muslim Saints." Paper read at the Conference of South East Asian Studies, 29 March 1972, New York.

Emre, Ismail. *Doğuşlar 2*. Adana, 1965. In Turkish.

———. *Yeni Yunus Emre ve Doğuşları*. Istanbul, 1951. In Turkish.

Engelke, Irmgard. *Sulejman Tschelebis Lobgedicht auf die Geburt des Propheten*. Halle, 1926.

Ergun, Sadettin Nüzhet. *Bektaşi Edebiyatı Antolojisi*. Istanbul, 1944. In Turkish.

Esin, Emel. "The Turkish Bakši and the Painter Muhammad Siyāh Ḳalam." *Acta Orientalia* 32 (1970).

Ess, Joseph van. *Die Gedankenwelt des Ḥāriṯ al-Muḥāsibī, anhand von Übersetzungen aus seinen Schriften dargestellt und erläutert.* Bonn, 1961.

Ethé, Hermann. "Die Rubāʿīs des Abu Saʿid ibn Abulchair." *Sitzungsberichte der bayrischen Akademie der Wissenschaften, philologisch-historische Klasse.* Munich, 1875, 1878.

———. *König und Derwisch. Romantisch-mystisches Epos vom Scheich Hilali, dem persischen Original treu nachgebildet.* Leipzig, 1870.

———. "Neupersische Literatur." In *Grundriss der Iranischen Philologie,* compiled by Wilhelm Geiger and Ernst Kuhn. Strasbourg, 1895–1901.

Ettinghausen, Richard. "The Emperor's Choice." *Festschrift. E. Panofsky.* New York, 1961.

———. "Persian Ascension Miniatures of the 14th Century." *Academia dei Lincei,* 1957.

Fakhrī Harawī. *Rauḍat as-salāṭīn.* Edited by Sayyid Hussamuddin Rashdi. Hyderabad, Sind, 1968. In Persian.

Fānī Murādābādī. *Hindū shuʿarā kā naʿtiya kalām.* Lyallpur, 1962. In Urdu.

Farhadi, Abdulghafur Rawan. "Le majlis de al-Ḥallāj, de Shams-i Tabrezi et du Molla de Roum." *Revue des études islamiques,* 1954.

Faris, Nabih A. *The Book of Knowledge.* Lahore, 1962. Translation of a chapter of Ghazzālī's *Iḥyāʾ*.

———. *The Foundations of the Articles of Faith.* Lahore, 1963. Translation of a chapter of Ghazzālī's *Iḥyāʾ*.

———. *The Mysteries of Almsgiving.* Beirut, 1966. Translation of a chapter of Ghazzālī's *Iḥyāʾ*.

Farrukh, Omar. *At-taṣawwuf fīʾl-Islām.* Beirut, 1957. In Arabic.

Faruqi, Bashir Ahmad. *The Mujaddid's Conception of God.* Lahore, 1952.

———. *The Mujaddid's Conception of Tauḥīd.* Lahore, 1940.

Feldman, Herbert. *From Crisis to Crisis: Pakistan 1962–1969.* London, 1972.

Field, Claud H. *Al-Ghazālī: The Alchemy of Happiness.* London, 1910.

———. *Mystics and Saints of Islam.* London, 1910.

Firkāwī, Maḥmud al-. *Commentaire du livre des étapes.* Edited by Serge de Laugier de Beaureceuil. Cairo, 1953. In Arabic.

Fischel, Walter J. "Jews and Judaism at the Court of the Moghul Emperors in Medieval India." *Islamic Culture,* 1951.

Fischer, August. "Vergöttlichung und Tabuisierung der Namen Muhammads." In *Beiträge zur Arabistik, Semitistik und Islamkunde,* compiled by Richard Hartmann and Helmuth Scheel. Leipzig, 1944.

Fleischer, Johann Leberecht. "Über die farbigen Lichterscheinungen der Sufis." *Zeitschrift der Deutschen Morgenländischen Gesellschaft* 16 (1862).

Fletcher, Joseph. *The Old and New Teachings in Chinese Islam*. Forthcoming.

Flügel, Gustav. *Die arabischen, persischen und türkischen Handschriften in der K. K. Hofbibliothek zu Wien*. Vienna, 1865–67.

Frick, Heinrich. *Ghazali's Selbstbiographie, ein Vergleich mit Augustins Konfessionen*. Leipzig, 1919.

Friedman, Yohanan, *Shaykh Ahmad Sirhindi: An Outline of His Thought and a Study of His Image in the Eyes of Posterity*. Montreal, 1971.

Fück, Johann. "Die sufische Dichtung in der Landessprache des Panjab." *Orientalistische Literaturzeitung* 43 (1940).

Furūzānfar, Badīʿuz-Zamān. *Aḥādīth-i Mathnawī*. Tehran, 1334 sh./1955. In Persian.

———. *Maʾākhidh-i qiṣaṣ wa tamthīlāt-ī Mathnawī*. Tehran, 1333 sh./1954. In Persian.

———. *Risāla dar taḥqīq-i aḥwāl wa zindagī-i Maulānā Jalāloddīn Muḥammad, mashhūr be-Maulawī*. Tehran, 1315 sh./1936. In Persian.

———. *Sharh-i Mathnawī-yi sharīf*. Tehran, 1348 sh./1969. In Persian.

Fuzuli. *Divan*. Edited by Abdülbâki Gölpınarlı. Istanbul, 1948. In Turkish.

Gairdner, W. H. Temple. *Al-Ghazzālī's "Mishkāt al-anwār": The Niche for Lights*. London, 1915.

Garcin de Tassy, M. Joseph Héliodore. *La poésie philosophique et religieuse chez les persans d'après le "Manṭiq uṭ-ṭair."* Paris, 1857–60.

Gardet, Louis. *Expériences mystiques en terres nonchrétiennes*. Paris, 1953.

———. "La mention du nom divin, *dhikr*, dans la mystique musulmane." *Revue Thomiste*, 1952–53.

Gawhary, Mohammad al-. "Die Gottesnamen im magischen Gebrauch in den al-Būnī zugeschriebenen Werken." Ph.D. dissertation, University of Bonn, 1968.

Geertz, Clifford. *Islam Observed: Religious Development in Morocco and Indonesia*. New Haven, 1968.

Ghanī, M. Qāsim. *Taʾrīkh-i taṣawwuf dar Islām*. Tehran, 1330 sh./1951. In Persian.

Ghazzālī, Abū Ḥāmid al-. *Iḥyāʾ ʿulūm ad-dīn*. 4 vols. Bulaq, 1289 h./1872–73. Commentary by Sayyid Murtaḍā az-Zabīdī. *Itḥāf as-sādat al-muttaqīn*. 10 vols. Cairo, 1311 h./1893–94.

———. *Al-Maqṣad al-asnāʾ fī sharḥ maʿānī asmāʾ Allāh al-Ḥusnā*. Edited by Fadlou Shehadi. Beirut, 1971.

———. *Al-munqidh min aḍ-ḍalāl*. Edited by A. Maḥmūd. Cairo, 1952.

Ghazzālī, Aḥmad. *Sawāniḥ. Aphorismen über die Liebe*. Edited by Hellmut Ritter. Istanbul, 1942. In Persian.

Gibb, Elias John Wilkinson. *A History of Ottoman Poetry*. 6 vols. 1900–1909. Reprint. London, 1958–63.
Gibb, Hamilton A. R. *Mohammedanism: An Historical Survey*. London, 1949.
Gilsenan, Michael. *Saint and Sufi in Modern Egypt: An Essay in the Sociology of Religion*. Oxford, 1973.
———. "Some Factors in the Decline of the Sufi Orders in Modern Egypt." *Moslem World* 57, no. 1 (1967).
Gīsūdarāz, Muhammad. *Dīwān anīs al-ᶜushshāq*. Lithographed in India, n.d. In Persian.
Göbel-Gross, Erhard. "Sirr-i akbar, Die Upanishad-Übersetzung Dārā Shikōhs." Ph.D. dissertation, University of Marburg, 1962.
Goldziher, Ignaz. "Arabische Synonymik der Askese." *Der Islam* 8 (1918).
———. "Aus dem muhammedanischen Heiligenkult in Aegypten." *Globus* 71 (1897).
———. *Al-Ghazzālī's Streitschrift gegen die Batiniyya*. Leiden, 1916.
———. "Die Gottesliebe in der islamischen Theologie." *Der Islam* 9 (1919).
———. "Linguistisches aus der Literatur der muhammedanischen Mystik." *Zeitschrift der Deutschen Morgenländischen Gesellschaft* 26 (1872).
———. "Materialien zur Entwicklungsgeschichte des Sufismus." *Wiener Zeitschrift für die Kunde des Morgenlandes* 13 (1899).
———. *Die Richtungen der islamischen Koranauslegung*. Leiden, 1920.
———. "Zauberelemente im islamischen Gebet." In *Orientalische Studien Theodor Nöldeke zum siebzigsten Geburtstag gewidmet*. Compiled by Carl Bezold. 2 vols. Giessen, 1906.
Goldziher, Ignaz, and de Somogyi, Joseph. "The Spanish Arabs and Islam." *Moslem World* 54, no. 1 (1964).
Gölpınarlı, Abdülbâki. *Islam ve Türk Illerinde Fütuvvet teşkilatı ve kaynakları*. Istanbul, 1952. In Turkish.
———. *Melâmilik ve Melâmiler*. Istanbul, 1931. In Turkish.
———. *Mevlâna Celâleddin, hayatı, felsefesi, eserlerinden seçmeler*. Istanbul, 1951. 3d ed. 1959. In Turkish.
———. *Mevlâna'dan sonra Mevlevilik*. Istanbul, 1953. In Turkish.
———. *Yunus Emre, Hayatı*. Istanbul, 1936. In Turkish.
Gosche, Reinhard. *Über Ghazzalis Leben und Werke*. Berlin, 1858.
Gramlich, Richard. *Die schiitischen Derwischorden Persiens, Teil I, Die Affiliationen*. Wiesbaden, 1965.
Grunebaum, Gustave E. von. *Der Islam im Mittelalter*. Zurich, 1963.
———. *Medieval Islam*. Chicago, 1953.
———. "The Place of Parapsychological Phenomena in Islam." In *Malik Ram Felicitation Volume, I*. Delhi, 1972.
Habib, Madeleine. "Some Notes on the Naqshbandi Order." *Moslem World* 59 (1969).

Ḥabibi, Abdul Ḥayy. *D Pashto adabiyāto tārīkh.* Kabul, 1342 sh./1964. In Pashto.

———. *Pata Khazāna.* Kabul, 1339 sh./1961. In Pashto.

Ḥāfiẓ, Shamsuddīn Muhammad. *Die Lieder des Hafiz, persisch mit dem Kommentar des Sudi.* Edited by Hermann Brockhaus. 1854–63. Reprint. 1965. In Persian and Turkish.

Ḥallāj, Ḥusayn ibn Manṣūr al-. "*Dîwân.* Essai de reconstitution by Louis Massignon." *Journal asiatique,* January-July 1931.

———. *Kitāb aṭ-ṭawāsīn, texte arabe . . . avec la version persane d'al-Baqlī.* Edited and translated by Louis Massignon. Paris, 1913.

Hallauer, Jakob. *Die Vita des Ibrahim ibn Edhem in der Tedhkiret al-Ewlija des Ferid ed-Din Attar.* Leipzig, 1925.

Hammer-Purgstall, Joseph von. *Geschichte der schönen Redekünste Persiens.* Vienna, 1818.

———, comp. *Das arabische Hohe Lied der Liebe, das ist Ibnol Faridh's Taije in Text und Übersetzung zum ersten Male herausgegeben.* Vienna, 1854.

———. *Zwei Abhandlungen zur Mystik und Magie des Islams.* Edited by Annemarie Schimmel. Vienna, 1974.

Haq, M. Anwarul. *The Faith-Movement of Mawlānā Muḥammad Ilyās.* London, 1972.

Haqq, Enamul. *Muslim Bengali Literature.* Karachi, 1957.

———. "Sufi Movement in Bengal." *Indo-Iranica* 3, nos. 1–2 (1948).

Hartmann, Richard. "Futuwwa and Malāma." *Zeitschrift der Deutschen Morgenländischen Gesellschaft* 72 (1918).

———. "Die Himmelsreise Muhammads und ihre Bedeutung in der Religion des Islam." In *Vorträge der Bibliothek Warburg.* Hamburg, 1928–29.

———. *Al-Kuschairis Darstellung des Sufitums.* Berlin, 1914.

———. "As-Sulamī's *Risālat al-Malāmatīya.*" *Der Islam* 8 (1918).

———. "Zur Frage nach der Herkunft und den Anfängen des Sufitums." *Der Islam* 6/7(1915).

Hashmi, Bashir Ahmad. "Sarmad." *Islamic Culture,* 1933–34.

Hasluck, Frederick William. *Christianity and Islam under the Sultans.* 2 vols. Oxford, 1929.

Hasrat, Bikrama Jit. *Dara Shikuh: Life and Works.* Calcutta, 1953.

Hastie, William. *The Festival of Spring from the "Divan" of Jeláleddin.* Glasgow, 1903.

Heer, Nicholas. "Some Biographical and Bibliographical Notes on al-Ḥakīm at-Tirmidhī." In *The World of Islam: Studies in Honour of Philip K. Hitti.* Edited by James Kritzeck and R. Bayly Winder. London, 1960.

———. "A Sufi Psychological Treatise." *Moslem World* 51 (1961).

Heiler, Friedrich. *Erscheinungsformen und Wesen der Religion.* Stuttgart, 1961.

———. *Das Gebet.* 5th ed. Munich, 1923. Translated by Samuel McComb as *Prayer.* New York, 1932.

Hickman, William. "Eshrefoghlu Rumi: Reconstitution of His *dīwān*." Ph.D. dissertation, Harvard University, 1972.

Ḥilmī, Muḥammad Muṣṭafā. *Al-ḥayāt ar-rūḥiyya fīʾl-Islām*. Cairo, 1954. In Arabic.

———. *Ibn al-Fāriḍ waʾl-ḥubb al-ilāhī*. Cairo, 1945. In Arabic.

A History of Freedom Movement. Karachi, 1957.

Horovitz, Joseph. "Muhammads Himmelfahrt." *Der Islam* 9 (1919).

Horten, Max. *Indische Strömungen in der islamischen Mystik*. Heidelberg, 1927–28.

———. *Die religiösen Vorstellungen des Volkes im heutigen Islam*. Halle, 1917.

———. "Der Sinn der islamischen Mystik." *Scientia*, July 1927.

Hoshyārpūrī, Hafeez. *Mathnawiyāt-i Hīr Ranjhā*. Karachi, 1957. In Persian.

Huart, Clemens, trans. *Les saints des derviches tourneurs*, by Shamsaddin Aḥmad Aflākī. Paris, 1918–22.

Hujwīrī, ʿAlī ibn ʿUthmān al-. *Kashf al-maḥjūb*. Edited by V. A. Žukovskij. Leningrad, 1926. Reprint. Tehran, 1336 sh./1957.

———. *The "Kashf al-Maḥjūb," the Oldest Persian Treatise on Sufism by al-Hujwiri*. Translated by Reynold A. Nicholson. Gibb Memorial Series, no. 17. 1911. Reprint. London, 1959.

Huri, Sofi. "Yunus Emre: In Memoriam." *Moslem World* 49, no. 2 (1959).

Husain, Yusuf. *Glimpses of Medieval Indian Culture*. 2d ed. London, 1959.

———. *L'Inde mystique au moyen âge*. Paris, 1929.

Husaini, A. S. "Uways al-Qarani and the Uwaysi Sufis." *Moslem World* 57, no. 2 (1967).

Husaini, Saiyid Abdul Qadir. *The Pantheistic Monism of Ibn al-Arabi*. Lahore, 1970.

Ḥusayn, ʿAlī Ṣafī. *Al-adab aṣ-ṣūfī fī Miṣr fīʾl-qarn as-sābiʿ al-hijrī*. Cairo, 1964. In Arabic.

ʿIbādī, Quṭbaddīn al-. *At-taṣfiya fī aḥwāl aṣ-ṣūfiya, or Ṣūfīnāme*. Edited by Ghulām Muḥammad Yūsufī. Tehran, 1347 sh./1968. In Persian.

Ibn ʿAbbād ar-Rondī. *"Ar-rasāʾil aṣ-ṣugrā": Lettres de direction spirituelle*. Edited by Paul Nwyia. Beirut, 1957.

Ibn ʿArabī, Muḥyīuddīn. *Dhakhāʾir al-aʿlāq*. Cairo, 1968. Commentary on the *Tarjumān al-ashwāq*. In Arabic.

———. *Fuṣūṣ al-ḥikam*. Edited by Abūʾl-ʿAlāʾ Affifi. Cairo, 1946. In Arabic.

———. *Al-futūḥāt al-makkiyya*. 4 vols. Cairo, 1329 h./1911. In Arabic.

———. *Al-kitāb at-tidhkārī*. Cairo, 1969. Memorial in honor of Ibn ʿArabī.

———. *Sufis of Andalusia: The Rūḥ al-quds and Al-Durrat al-fākhirah*. Translated by R. W. J. Austin. London, 1971.

———. *The "Tarjumān al-ashwāq": A Collection of Mystical Odes by*

Muḥyīu'ddīn ibn al-ʿArabī. Edited and translated by Reynold A. Nicholson. London, 1911.

Ibn ʿAṭāʾ Allāh al-Iskandarī, Ahmad. *Kitāb al-ḥikam.* Translated by R. Archer in "Muhammadan Mysticism in Sumatra." Malayan Branch, *Journal of the Royal Asiatic Society* 15, no. 2 (1937).

———. *Miftāḥ al-falāḥ wa miṣbāh al-arwāh.* Cairo, 1961. In Arabic.

———. *Munājāt.* Istanbul Universitesi Kütüphanesi, Arab. 1574. In Arabic.

Ibn al-Jauzī. *Talbīs Iblīs.* Cairo, 1340 h./1921–22. In Arabic. Translated by David Samuel Margoliouth as "The Devil's Delusion." *Islamic Culture* 12 (1938).

Ibn Kathīr. *Maulid rasūl Allāh.* Edited by Ṣalāḥuddin al-Munajjid. Beirut, 1961.

Ibn Khaldūn. *Shifāʾ as-sāʾil li-tahdhīb al-masāʾil.* Edited by M. ibn Tavit at-Tanci. Istanbul, 1957. In Arabic.

Ibn Qayyim al-Jauziyya. *Kitāb asrār aṣ-ṣalāt.* Istanbul Universitesi Kütüphanesi, Arab. 2347. In Arabic.

Ibn Sīnā, Abū ʿAlī. *"Risāla fiʾl-ʿishq": Traitée sur l'amour.* Edited by August Ferdinand Mehren. Leiden, 1894. In Arabic.

Ibn Taghribirdi, Abuʾl-Maḥāsin. *An-nujūm az-zāhira fi mulūk Miṣr waʾl-Qāhira.* Edited by William Popper. 8 vols. Berkeley, 1908–36.

Ibn Taymiyya. "Ar-radd ʿalā Ibn ʿArabī waʾṣ-Ṣūfiyya." In *Majmūʿa rasāʾil shaykh al-Islām Ibn Taymiyya.* Cairo, 1348 h./1929–30.

Iḥsān, Abūʾl-Fayḍ. "Rauḍat al-qayyūmiya." Ms. in Library of the Asiatic Society of Bengal.

Ikbal Ali Shah, Sirdar. *Islamic Sufism.* London, 1933.

Ikram, Sheikh Muhammed. *Muslim Rule in India and Pakistan.* Lahore, 1966.

———. *Rūd-i kauthar.* 4th ed. Lahore, 1969. In Urdu.

Iqbal, Afzal. *The Life and Thought of Rumi.* Lahore, ca. 1956.

Iqbal, Muhammad. *The Development of Metaphysics in Iran.* Cambridge, 1908.

———. *Jāwīdnāme.* Lahore, 1932. In Persian. Translated into English by Shaikh Maḥmūd Aḥmad, Lahore, 1961, and by A. J. Arberry, London, 1966; into Italian by Alessandro Bausani, 1955; into French by Eva Meyerovitch, 1962; into German verse by Annemarie Schimmel, 1957; and into Turkish prose by Annemarie Schimmel, 1958.

———. *Six Lectures on the Reconstruction of Religious Thought in Islam.* Lahore, 1930.

———. *Zabūr-i ʿajam.* Lahore, 1927. Part translated by A. J. Arberry as *Persian Psalms.* Lahore, 1948.

ʿIrāqī, Fakhruddīn. *Dīwān.* Edited by Saʿid Nafisi. Tehran, 1338 sh./1959. In Persian.

———. *The Song of the Lovers (ʿushshāqnāme).* Edited and translated by A. J. Arberry. Oxford, 1939.

Iṣfahānī, Abū Nuᶜaym al-. *Ḥilyat al-auliyāʾ*. 10 vols. Cairo, 1932. In Arabic.

Ivanow, Vladimir. "A Biography of Shaykh Aḥmad-i Jām." *Journal of the Royal Asiatic Society*, 1917.

———. "Ṭabaqāt of Anṣārī in the Old Language of Herat." *Journal of the Royal Asiatic Society*, January-July 1923.

Izutsu, Toshihiko. "The Basic Structure of Metaphysical Thinking in Islam." In *Collected Papers on Islamic Philosophy and Mysticism*, edited by Mehdi Mohaghegh and Hermann Landolt. Tehran, 1971.

———. *A Comparative Study of the Key Philosophical Concepts of Sufism and Taoism*. 2 vols. Tokyo, 1966–67.

———. "The Paradox of Light and Darkness in the Garden of Mystery of Shabastari." In *Anagogic Qualities of Literature*, edited by Joseph P. Strelka. University Park, Pa., 1971.

Jabre, Farid. "L'Extase de Plotin et le *Fanāʾ* de Ghazālī." *Studia Islamica* 6 (1956).

———. *Al-Ghazālī: Al-Munqidh min aḍ-ḍalāl (erreur et délivrance)*. Beirut, 1959.

———. *La notion de certitude selon Ghazālī*. Paris, 1958.

———. *La notion de maᶜrifa chez Ghazālī*. Beirut, 1958.

Jacob, Georg. *Beiträge zur Kenntnis des Derwisch-Ordens der Bektaschis*. Berlin, 1908.

———. *Geschichte des Schattenspiels*. Hannover, 1925.

Jaᶜfrī, Raīs Aḥmad. *Iqbāl aur ᶜashq-i rasūl*. Lahore, 1956. In Urdu.

Jagtiani, Lalchand A. *Muḥammad rasūl Allāh*. Hyderabad, Sind, 1911. In Sindhi.

Jāmī, Maulānā ᶜAbdurraḥmān. *Dīwān-i kāmil*. Edited by Hāshim Riżā. Tehran, 1341 sh./1962. In Persian.

———. *Lawāʾiḥ*. Tehran, 1342 sh./1963. In Persian. Edited and translated into English by Edward Henry Whinfield and Mirza Muḥammad Kazwini. London, 1906.

———. *Nafaḥāt al-uns*. Edited by Mahdi Tauḥīdīpur. Tehran, 1336 sh./1947. In Persian

———. *"Tuḥfat al-aḥrār": The Gift of the Noble*. Edited by E. Forbes-Falconer. London, 1848. In Persian.

Jazūlī, Abū ᶜAbdallāh. *Dalāʾil al-khayrāt*. In Arabic. Numerous editions.

Jeffery, Arthur. "Ibn al-ᶜArabī's *Shajarat al-Kawn*." *Islamic Studies* 10–11 (1959).

Jīlī, ᶜAbdul Karīm al-. *Al-Insān al-kāmil*. Cairo, 1340 h./1921–22. In Arabic.

Jotwani, Motilal. *Shāh ᶜAbdul Karīm*. New Delhi, 1970.

———. "Shah Latif: Man and Poet." *Indian Literatures* 6, no. 2 (1963).

Junayd-i Shirāzī. *Shadd al-izār fī khaṭṭ al-auzār ᶜan zuwwār al-mazār*. Edited by Muhammed Qazvīnī and ᶜAbbās Iqbāl. Tehran, 1328 sh./1949.

Jurji, Edward Jabra, ed. and trans. *Illumination in Islamic Mysticism*. Princeton, 1938.

———. "The Illuministic Sufis." *Journal of the American Oriental Society*, 1937.
Kalābādhī, Abū Bakr Muḥammad al-. *At-taᶜarruf li-madhhab ahl at-taṣawwuf*. Edited by A. J. Arberry. Cairo, 1934. In Arabic.
Kalīm, Abū Ṭālib. *Dīwān*. Edited by Partaw Baiḍāʾī. Tehran, 1336 sh./1957. In Persian.
Karaosmanoğlu, Yakup Kadri. *Erenlerin bağından*. Istanbul, 1922. In Turkish. Translated by Annemarie Schimmel as *Aus dem Garten der Weisen*. In *Das Geisterhaus*, edited by Otto Spies. Kevelaer, 1949.
———. *Nur Baba*. Istanbul, 1922. In Turkish. Translated by Annemarie Schimmel as *Flamme und Falter*. Gummersbach, 1948.
Kayğusuz Abdal, Hatayi, Kul Himmet. Istanbul, 1953. In Turkish.
Kazi, Elsa, trans. *"Risalo" of Shah Abdul Latif*. Hyderabad, Sind, 1965.
Keddie, Nikki R., ed. *Scholars, Saints, and Sufis: Muslim Religious Institutions since 1500*. Berkeley, 1972.
Keklik, Nihat. *Sadreddin Koneviʾnin Felsefesinde Allah, Kainat, ve Insan*. Istanbul, 1967.
Khaja Khan. *Studies in Tasawwuf*. Madras, 1923.
Khalifa. See ᶜAbdul Ḥakīm, Khalīfa.
Khānqāhī, A. Ṭāhir al-. *Guzīda dar akhlāq ū taṣawwuf*. Edited by Iraj Afshar. Tehran, 1347 sh./1968. In Persian.
Khāqānī. *Dīwān*. Edited by Żiāuddīn Sajjadi. Tehran, 1338 sh./1959. In Persian.
Kharrāz, Abū Bakr al-. *Kitāb aṣ-ṣidq: The Book of Truthfulness*. Edited by A. J. Arberry. Oxford, 1937. In Arabic.
Khawam, René. *Propos d'amour des mystiques musulmanes*. Paris, 1960.
Khushḥāl Khān Khattak. *Muntakhabāt*. Peshawar, 1958. In Pashto.
Kindermann, Heinz, trans. *Über die guten Sitten beim Essen und Trinken*. Leiden, 1964. Translation of a chapter of Ghazzālī's *Iḥyāʾ*.
Kissling, Hans Joachim. "Aq Šems ed-Din: Ein türkischer Heiliger aus der Endzeit von Byzans." *Byzantinische Zeitschrift* 44 (1951).
———. "Aus der Geschichte des Chalvetiyye-Ordens." *Zeitschrift der Deutschen Morgenländischen Gesellschaft* 102 (1953).
———. "Einiges über den Zeijnije-Orden im osmanischen Reiche." *Der Islam* 39 (1964).
———. "Die islamischen Derwischorden." *Zeitschrift für Religions- und Geistesgeschichte* 12 (1960).
———. "Das Menaqybname Scheich Bedr ad-Dins." *Zeitschrift der Deutschen Morgenländischen Gesellschaft* 101 (1950).
———. "The Role of the Dervish Orders in the Ottoman Empire." In *Studies in Islamic Cultural History*, edited by Gustave E. von Grunebaum. Chicago, 1954.
———. "Šaᶜbān Veli und die Šaᶜbaniyye." In *Serta Monacensia Franz Babinger zum 15. Januar 1951 als Festgruss dargebracht*. Compiled by Hans Joachim Kissling and A. Schmaus.
———. "The Sociological and Educational Role of the Dervish Orders

in the Ottoman Empire." *Memoirs of the American Anthropological Association* 76 (1954).

———. "Die Wunder der Derwische." *Zeitschrift der Deutschen Morgenländischen Gesellschaft* 107 (1956).

———. "Zum islamischen Heiligenwesen auf dem Balkan." *Zeitschrift für Balkanologie*, 1963.

———. "Zur Frage der Anfänge des Bektaschitums in Albanien." *Oriens* 15 (1962).

———. "Zur Geschichte des Derwischordens der Bajramiyya." *Südostforschungen* 15 (1956).

Klappstein, Paul. *Vier turkestanische Heilige, ein Beitrag zum Verständnis der islamischen Mystik*. Berlin, 1919.

Kocatürk, Vasfi Mahir. *Tekke Şiiri Antolojisi*. Ankara, 1955. In Turkish.

Kofler, Hans, trans. *Das Buch der Siegelringsteine der Weisheit*. Graz, 1970. Translation of Ibn ᶜArabī's *Fuṣūṣ al-ḥikam*.

Köprülü, Mehmet Fuat. *Eski şairlerimiz*. Istanbul, 1931. In Turkish.

———. *Türk edebiyatında ilk mutesavvıflar*. 2d ed. Ankara, 1966. In Turkish.

Kriss, Rudolf, and Kriss-Heinrich, Hubert. *Volksglaube im Bereich des Islams*. 2 vols. Wiesbaden, 1960–61.

Kubrā, Najmuddīn. *Die fawāʾiḥ al-ǧamāl wa fawātiḥ al-ǧalāl des Naǧmuddīn Kubrā*. Edited by Fritz Meier. Wiesbaden, 1957. In Arabic.

———. *Risāla fi faḍīlat aṣ-ṣalāt*. Istanbul Universitesi Kütüphanesi, Arab. 4530. In Arabic.

Kühnel, Ernst. *Islamische Schriftkunst*. 1942. Reprint. Graz, 1972.

Lāhījī, Muhammad. *Mafātīḥ al-iᶜjāz fī sharḥ gulshan-i rāz*. Edited by Kaiwān Samīᶜī. Tehran, 1337 sh./1958. In Persian.

Landolt, Hermann. "Simnānī on Waḥdat al-Wujūd." In *Collected Papers on Islamic Philosophy and Mysticism*, edited by Mehdi Mohaghegh and Hermann Landolt. Tehran, 1971.

———, ed. and trans. *Correspondence spirituelle, échangé entre Nuroddin Esfarayeni (ob. 717/1317) et son disciple ᶜAlāoddawleh Semnānī (ob. 736/1336)*. Tehran and Paris, 1972.

Lane, Edward William. *The Manners and Customs of the Modern Egyptians*. London, 1860.

Laugier de Beaureceuil, Serge de. *Khwadja Abdullah Ansari, mystique hanbalite*. Beirut, 1965.

Le Chatelier, A. *Confrèries musulmanes du Hejaz*. Paris, 1887.

Leeuwen, Arend Theodor van. "Essai de bibliographie d'al Ghazzālī." *Institut des belles lettres arabes* 21 (1958).

———. *Ghazālī as apologeet van den Islam*. Leiden, 1947.

Lentz, Wolfgang. "ᶜAṭṭār als Allegoriker." *Der Islam* 35 (1960).

Lewis, I. M. "Sufism in Somaliland." *Bulletin of the School of Oriental and African Studies* 17 (1955), 18 (1956).

Lings, Martin. *A Sufi Saint of the Twentieth Century*. 2d ed. London, 1971.

Littmann, Enno. *Aḥmed il-Bedawī, Ein Lied auf den ägyptischen Nationalheiligen.* Mainz, 1950.

———. *Islamisch-arabische Heiligenlieder.* Wiesbaden, 1951.

———. *Mohammad im Volksepos.* Copenhagen, 1950.

Loosen, Paul. "Die weisen Narren des Naisaburi." *Zeitschrift für Assyriologie* 27 (1912).

Macdonald, Duncan Black. "Emotional Religion in Islam as Affected by Music and Singing, Being a Translation of a Book of the *Iḥyāʾ ʿUlūm ad-Dīn* of al-Ghazzālī." *Journal of the Royal Asiatic Society,* 1901.

———. "The Life of al-Ghazzālī." *Journal of the American Oriental Society* 20 (1899).

McKane, William. *Al-Ghazālī's Book of Fear and Hope.* Leiden, 1962.

Mackeen, A. Mohamed. "The Sufi-Qawm Movement." *Moslem World* 53, no. 3 (1963).

McPherson, Joseph Williams. *The Moulid of Egypt.* Cairo, 1941.

Maḥmūd, ʿAbdul Ḥalīm. *Al-madrasa ash-shādhiliyya al-ḥadītha wa imāmuhā Abūʾl-Ḥasan ash-Shādhilī.* Cairo, ca. 1968. In Arabic.

Maḥmūd, ʿAbdul Qādir. *Al-falsafatuʾṣ-ṣūfiyya fīʾl-Islam.* Cairo, 1967. In Arabic.

Makhzan Shāh ʿAbdul Laṭīf Bhitāʾī. Hyderabad, Sind, 1954. In Sindhi.

Makkī, Abū Ṭālib al-. *Qūt al-qulūb fī muʿāmalāt al-maḥbūb.* 2 vols. Cairo, 1310 h./1892–93. In Arabic.

Malik, Hafeez, ed. *Muhammad Iqbal: Poet-Philosopher of Pakistan.* New York, 1971.

Manūfī, M. A. F. al-. *At-taṣawwuf al-Islāmī al-khāliṣ.* Cairo, 1969. In Arabic.

Mardin, Ömer Fevzi. *Varidat-i Süleyman Şerhi.* Istanbul, 1951. In Turkish.

Marshall, D. N. *Mughals in India: A Bibliography.* Bombay, 1967.

Martin, B. G. "A Short History of the Khalwati Order of Dervishes." In *Scholars, Saints, and Sufis: Muslim Religious Institutions since 1500,* edited by Nikki R. Keddie. Berkeley, 1972.

Mason, Herbert. *Two Medieval Muslim Statesmen.* The Hague, 1971.

Massignon, Louis. "L'alternative de la pensée mystique en Islam: monisme existentiel ou monisme testimonial." *Annulaire du Collège de France* 52 (1952).

———. *La cité des morts au Caire.* Cairo, 1958.

———. "Le 'coeur' (*al-qalb*) dans la prière et la méditation musulmane." *Études carmélitaines* 9 (1950).

———. *Essai sur les origines du lexique technique de la mystique musulmane.* Paris, 1928.

———. "L'homme parfait en Islam et son originalité eschatologique." *Eranos-Jahrbuch* 15 (1947).

———. "Interférences philosophiques et percées métaphysiques dans la mystique Hallajienne: notion de l'Essentiel désir." *Mélanges Maréchal* 2 (1950).

———. "La legende de Hallacé Mansur en pays turcs." *Revue des études islamiques,* 1941–46.
———. "L'oeuvre Hallagienne d'Attār." *Revue des études islamiques,* 1941–46.
———. *La passion d'al-Ḥosayn ibn Mansour Al-Hallāj, martyr mystique de l'Islam exécuté à Bagdad le 26 Mars 922.* 2 vols. Paris, 1922.
———. "Qiṣṣat Ḥusayn al-Ḥallāj." In *Donum Natalicum H. S. Nyberg.* Stockholm, 1954.
———. *Quatre textes inédits relatifs à la biographie d'al-Hallaj.* Paris, 1914.
———. *Receuil des textes inédits concernant l'histoire de la mystique en pays d'Islam.* Paris, 1929.
———. "Salmān Pāk et les prémices spirituelles de l'Islam iranien." *Société des études iraniennes* 7 (1934).
———. "La survie d'al-Ḥallāj." *Bulletin d'études arabes Damas* 11 (1945–46).
———. "La vie et les oeuvres de Rūzbehān Baqlī." In *Studia Orientalia Ioanni Pedersen dicata septuagenario.* Copenhagen, 1953.
Massignon, Louis, and Huart, Clemens. "Les entretiens de Lahore." *Journal asiatique* 209 (1926).
Massignon, Louis, and Kassim, A. M. "Un essai de bloc islamo-hindou au XVII siècle: l'humanisme mystique du Prince Dara." *Revue du monde musulman* 63 (1926).
Massignon, Louis, and Kraus, Paul. *Akhbār al-Ḥallāj, texte ancien relatif à la prédication et au supplice du mystique musulman al-Ḥosayn b. Manṣour al-Ḥallāj.* 1936. 3d ed. Paris, 1957.
Mayne, Peter. *Saints of Sind.* London, 1956.
Mehr, Ghulām Rasūl. *Sayyid Aḥmad Shahīd.* Lahore, ca. 1955. In Urdu.
Meier, Fritz. "Der Derwischtanz." *Asiatische Studien* 8 (1954).
———. "Der Geistmensch bei dem persischen Dichter ᶜAṭṭār." *Eranos-Jahrbuch* 13 (1946).
———. "Ḫurāsān und das Ende der klassischen Sufik." In *La Persia nel medioevo.* Rome, 1971.
———. "Ein Knigge für Sufis." In *Scritti in onore di Giuseppe Furlani.* Rome, 1957.
———. "Das Problem der Natur im esoterischen Monismus des Islams." *Eranos-Jahrbuch* 14 (1946).
———. "Qušayrīs Tartīb as-sulūk." *Oriens* 16 (1963).
———. "Die Schriften des ᶜAzīz-i Nasafī." *Wiener Zeitschrift für die Kunde des Morgenlandes* 52 (1953).
———. "Soufisme et déclin culturel." In *Classicisme et déclin culturel dans l'histoire de l'Islam,* edited by Gustave E. von Grunebaum. Paris, 1957.
———. "Stambuler Handschriften dreier persischen Mystiker: ᶜAin al-Quḍāt al-Hamadānī, Nağm ad-dīn al-Kubrā, Nağm ad-dīn ad-Dājā." *Der Islam* 24 (1937).
———. *Vom Wesen der islamischen Mystik.* Basel, 1943.

———. "Die Welt der Urbilder bei ᶜAlī Hamadānī." *Eranos-Jahrbuch* 18 (1950).

———. "Ein wichtiger Handschriftenfund zur Sufik." *Oriens* 20 (1967).

———. "Zur Biographie Aḥmad-i Ǧām's und zur Quellenkunde von Ǧāmī's *Nafaḥātuʾl-uns*." *Zeitschrift der Deutschen Morgenländischen Gesellschaft* 97 (1943).

———, ed. *Die "fawāʾiḥ al-ǧamāl wa fawātiḥ al-ǧalāl" des Naǧmuddīn al-Kubrā*. Wiesbaden, 1957.

———, ed. *"Firdaus al-muršidīya fī asrār aṣ-ṣamadīya": Die Vita des Scheich Abū Isḥāq al-Kāzarūnī*. Leipzig, 1948.

Merx, Adalbert. *Ideen und Grundlinien einer allgemeinen Geschichte der Mystik*. Heidelberg, 1893.

Meyerovitch, Eva. *Mystique et poésie en Islam, Djalal-ud Din Rumi et l'ordre des dervishes tourneurs*. Paris, 1972.

Mez, Adam. *Die Renaissance des Islam*. Heidelberg, 1922. Translated by S. Khuda Bakhsh and David Samuel Margoliouth. Patna, 1937.

Michon, Jean-Louis. *Le Soufi Marocain Aḥmad ibn ᶜAjība et son miᶜrāj*. Paris, 1973.

Miller, W. McE. "Shiᶜah Mysticism: The Sufis of Gunabad." *Moslem World* 13 (1923).

Mir Valiuddin. *Love of God*. Hyderabad, Deccan, 1968.

Miyēn Shāh ᶜInāt jō kalām. Edited by Dr. Nabi Bakhsh Baloch. Hyderabad, Sind, 1963. In Sindhi.

Moayyad, Heshmat. *Die Maqāmāt des Ġaznawī, eine legendäre Vita Aḥmad-i Ǧāms, genannt Žandapīl, 1049–1141*. Frankfurt, 1958.

Mohaghegh, Mehdi, and Landolt, Hermann, eds. *Collected Papers on Islamic Philosophy and Mysticism*. Tehran, 1971.

Mohan Singh (Diwāna). *An Introduction to Panjabi Literature*. Amritsar, 1951.

———. *Sikh Mysticism*. Amritsar, India, 1964. Translated into German as *Mystik und Yoga der Sikh-Meister*. Zurich, 1967.

Molé, Marijan. "Autour du Daré Mansour: l'apprentissage mystique de Bahāʾ ad-Dīn Naqshband." *Revue des études islamiques* 27 (1959).

———. "La Dance exstatique en Islam." *Sources orientales* 6 (1963).

———. "Les Kubrawiyya entre sunnisme et shiisme." *Revue des études islamiques*, 1961.

———. *Les mystiques musulmans*. Paris, 1965.

———. "Professions de foi de deux Kubrawis." *Bulletin de l'Institut Français de Damas* 17 (1961–63).

———. "Un traité de ᶜAlāʾad-dawla Simnānī sur ᶜAlī ibn Abī Ṭālib." *Bulletin de l'Institut Français de Damas* 16 (1958–60).

———, ed. *ᶜAziz an-Nasafi, Le livre de l'homme parfait*. Paris and Tehran, 1962.

Moreno, Martino Mario. *Antologia della Mistica Arabo-Persiana*. Bari, 1951.

Muḥāsibī, al-Ḥārith al-. *Kitāb ar-riᶜāya li-ḥuqūq Allāh*. Edited by Margaret Smith. Gibb Memorial Series, n.s. 15. London, 1940. In Arabic.

———. "Kitab aṣ-ṣabr wa'r-riḍā." Edited by Otto Spies. *Islamica* 6 (1932).

———. *Kitāb at-tawahhum.* Edited by A. J. Arberry. Cairo, 1937. In Arabic.

———. *Kitāb bad' man anāba ilā'llāhi ta'āla, Die Schrift des Ḥāriṯ al-Muḥāsibī über den Anfang der Umkehr zu Gott.* Edited and translated by Hellmut Ritter. Glückstadt, 1935.

Mujeeb, Mohammed. *The Indian Muslims.* Montreal and London, 1969.

Munāwī, 'Abdur Ra'ūf al-. *Al-kawākib ad-durriyya.* Cairo, 1938. In Arabic.

Nabahānī, Yusūf b. Ismā'īl an-. *Jāmi' karāmāt al-auliyā'.* Bulaq, Egypt, 1329 h./1911. In Arabic.

Nadīm, an-. *The Fihrist of al-Nadim.* Edited and translated by Bayard Dodge. 2 vols. New York, 1970.

Nadwī, Maulānā 'Abdas Salām. *Shi'r al-Hind.* Azamgarh, ca. 1936. In Urdu.

Nagel, Tilman. *Frühe Ismailiya und Fatimiden im Lichte der risālat iftitāḥ ad-da'wā.* Bonn, 1972.

Nasr, Seyyed H. *Ideals and Realities of Islam.* London, 1966.

———. *Sufi Essais.* London, 1972.

———. *Three Muslim Sages.* Cambridge, Mass., 1963.

Nicholson, Reynold A. "An Early Arabic Version of the *Mi'rāj* of Abū Yazīd al-Bisṭāmī." *Islamica* 2 (1925).

———. "The Goal of Muhammadan Mysticism." *Journal of the Royal Asiatic Society,* 1913.

———. "A Historical Enquiry concerning the Origin and Development of Sufism." *Journal of the Royal Asiatic Society,* 1906.

———. *The Idea of Personality in Sufism.* Cambridge, 1923.

———. "The Lives of 'Umar Ibnu'l-Fāriḍ and Muḥiyyu'ddīn Ibnu'l-'Arabi." *Journal of the Royal Asiatic Society,* 1906.

———. *The Mystics of Islam.* 1914. Reprint. Chester Springs, Pa., 1962.

———. *A Persian Forerunner of Dante.* Towyn-on-Sea, 1944.

———. *Rumi: Poet and Mystic.* London, 1950.

———. *Studies in Islamic Mysticism.* 1921. Reprint. Cambridge, 1967.

———. *Tales of Mystic Meaning.* London, 1931.

———, ed. and trans. *Selected Poems from the "Divan-i Shams-i Tabriz."* 1898. Reprint. Cambridge, 1961.

Nieuwenhuijze, C. A. O. van. *Samsu'l Din van Pasai, Bijdrage tot de kennis der Sumatraansche mystiek.* Leiden, 1945.

Niffarī, Muḥammad ibn 'Abdi'l-Jabbar an-. *The Mawāqif and Mukhāṭabāt of Muḥammad ibn 'Abdi'l-Jabbār al-Niffari, with other fragments.* Edited and translated by A. J. Arberry. Gibb Memorial Series, n.s. 9. London, 1935. In Arabic.

Niyāzī Miṣrī. *Dīvān.* Istanbul, 1955. In Turkish.

Nizami, Khaliq Ahmad. *The Life and Times of Shaikh Farīd Ganj-i Shakar*. Aligarh, 1955.

———. "Malfūẓāt kī tārīkhī ahammiyat." In *Arshi Presentation Volume*. Edited by Malik Ram. Delhi, 1961. In Urdu.

———. "Naqshbandi Influence on Mughal Rulers and Politics." *Islamic Culture* 39 (1965).

———. *Shāh Walīullāh kē siyāsī maktūbāt*. Aligarh, 1950. In Urdu.

———. "Some Aspects of Khānqāh Life in Medieval India." *Studia Islamica* 8 (1957).

———. *Some Aspects of Religion and Politics in India during the 13th Century*. Bombay, 1961.

———. *Taʾrīkh-e mashāʾikh-i Chisht*. Delhi, 1953. In Urdu.

Nwyia, Paul, S. J. *Exegèse coranique et langage mystique*. Beirut, 1970.

———. *Ibn ʿAbbād de Ronda*. Beirut, 1961.

———. *Ibn ʿAṭāʾ Allāh et la naissance de la confrèrie šāḏilite*. Beirut, 1972.

———. *Trois oeuvres inédites de mystiques musulmans: Šaqīq al-Balḫī, Ibn ʿAṭā, Niffarī*. Beirut, 1973.

———, ed. *Ar-rasāʾil aṣ-ṣuġrā: Lettres de direction spirituelle*, by Ibn ʿAbbād ar-Rundi. Beirut, 1957. In Arabic.

Nyberg, Hendrik Samuel. *Kleinere Schriften des Ibn ʿArabi*. Leiden, 1919.

Obermann, Julius. *Der religiöse und philosophische Subjektivismus Gazzālīs*. Leipzig, 1921.

Önder, Mehmet. *Mevlâna*. Ankara, 1971. In Turkish.

———. *Mevlâna bibliografyasi: 1. Basmalar (Kitap-makale). 2. Yazmalat*. Ankara, 1973–74. In Turkish.

———. *Mevlâna Şehri Konya*. Konya, 1962. In Turkish.

———. *Mevlâna Şiirleri Antolojisi*. 2d ed. Konya, 1958. In Turkish.

Padwick, Constance E. *Muslim Devotions*. London, 1960.

Palacios, M. Asín. *Algazel, Dogmatica, Moral y Ascetica*. Zaragoza, 1901.

———. *La Espiritualidad de Algazel y su sentido Cristiano*. 4 vols. Madrid and Granada, 1934–41.

———. *El Islam cristianizado. Estudio de "Sufismo" a trave de les obras de Abenarabi de Murcia*. Madrid, 1931.

———. "Šaḏilies y alumbrados." *Al-Andalus* 9 (1944), 16 (1951).

Palmer, E. H. *Oriental Mysticism: A Treatise on the Sufiistic and Unitarian Theosophy of the Persians*. 1867. Reprint. London, 1969.

Parsram, Jethmal. *Sufis of Sind*. Madras, 1924.

Pedersen, Johannes. *Muhammedansk mystik*. Copenhagen, 1923.

Pir Sultan Abdal. Varlık Klasikleri, no. 13. Istanbul, 1953.

Profitlich, Manfred. *Die Terminologie Ibn ʿArabis im "Kitāb wasāʾil as-sāʾil" des Ibn Saudakīn*. Freiburg, 1973.

Qāniʿ, Mīr ʿAlī Shīr. *Maklīnāme*. Edited by Sayyid Hussamuddin Rashdi. Karachi, 1967. In Persian and Sindhi.

———. *Maqālāt ash-shuʿarāʾ*. Edited by Sayyid Hussamuddin Rashdi. Karachi, 1956. In Persian.

———. *Tuḥfat al-kirām.* Hyderabad, Sind, 1957. Sindhi translation of the Persian original.
Qanungo, Kalika-Ranjan. *Dara Shukoh.* Calcutta, 1935.
Qāsim, ᶜAbduʾl-Ḥakīm. *Ayyām al-insān as-sabᶜa.* Cairo, 1971. In Arabic.
Qāsimī, Ghulam Muṣṭafā. "Hāshimīya Library." In *Mihrān jā Motī.* Karachi, 1959. In Sindhi.
Quddūsī, Iᶜjāzul Ḥaqq. *ᶜAbdul Quddūs Gangōhī.* Karachi, 1961. In Urdu.
———. *Tadhkira-yi ṣūfiya-yi Bengāl.* Lahore, 1965. In Urdu.
———. *Tadhkira-yi ṣūfiya-yi Panjāb.* Karachi, 1962. In Urdu.
———. *Tadhkira-yi ṣūfiya-yi Sarḥad.* Lahore, 1966. In Urdu.
———. *Tadhkira-yi ṣūfiya-yi Sind.* Karachi, 1959. In Urdu.
Qureshi, Ishtiaq Husain. *The Muslim Community of the Indo-Pakistan Subcontinent.* The Hague, 1962.
Qushayri, Abuʾl-Qāsim al-. *Ar-rasāʾil al-qushayriyya.* Edited and translated by F. M. Hasan. Karachi, 1964. In Urdu.
———. *Ar-risāla fī ᶜilm at-taṣawwuf.* Cairo, 1330 h./1912. In Arabic.
———. *Kitāb al-miᶜrāj.* Edited by A. H. Abdel Kader. Cairo, 1964. In Arabic.
Rahim, Abdar. "The Saints in Bengal: Shaikh Jalāl ad-Din Tabrezi and Shāh Jalāl." *Journal of the Pakistan Historical Society* 7 (1960).
Rahman, Fazlur. "Dream, Imagination, and ᶜālam al-mithāl." *Islamic Studies* 3–4 (1964–65). Also in *The Dream and Human Societies,* edited by Gustave E. von Grunebaum and Roger Caillois. Berkeley, 1966.
———. *Islam.* London, 1966.
Ramakrishna, Lajwanti. *Panjabi Sufi Poets.* London and Calcutta, 1938.
Rasheed, Ghulam Dastagir. "The Development of Naᶜtia Poetry in Persian Literature." *Islamic Culture,* 1965.
Raverty, H. G. *Selections from the Poetry of the Afghans.* London, 1862.
Redhouse, James W., trans. *The Mesnevi (usually known as the Mesnevīyi sherīf, or holy Mesnevi) of Mevlana (our lord) Jelalʾuʾd-Din Muhammad, er-Rumi. Book the First.* London, 1881.
Regnier, Yves. *Le "dīvān" de Yunus Emre.* Paris, 1963.
Reinert, Benedikt. *Die Lehre vom tawakkul in der älteren Sufik.* Berlin, 1968.
Rice, Cyprian, O. P. *The Persian Sufis.* 2d ed. London, 1969.
Richter, Gustav. *Dschelaladdin Rumi. Eine Stildeutung in drei Vorträgen.* Breslau, 1932.
Ritter, Hellmut. "Die Anfänge der Hurufisekte." *Oriens* 7 (1954).
———. "Die Aussprüche des Bāyezid Bisṭāmī." In *Westöstliche Abhandlungen, Festschrift für Rudolf Tschudi,* edited by Fritz Meier. Wiesbaden, 1954.
———. "Al-Bīrūnī's übersetzung des Yoga-Sutra des Patanjali." *Oriens* 9 (1956).
———. "Ḥasan al-Baṣrī, Studien zur Geschichte der islamischen Frömmigkeit." *Der Islam* 21 (1933).

———. *Das Meer der Seele. Gott, Welt und Mensch in den Geschichten Farīduddin ʿAṭṭārs.* Leiden, 1955.
———. "Die Mevlânafeier in Konya vom 11–17. Dezember 1960." *Oriens* 15 (1962).
———. "Muslim Mystics' Strife with God." *Oriens* 5 (1952).
———. "Neue literatur über Maulānā Calāluddīn Rūmī und seinen orden." *Oriens* 13–14 (1960–61).
———. "Philologika X." *Der Islam* 25 (1936).
———. "Philologika XIV–XVI." *Oriens* 11–14 (1961).
———. "Philologika VIII: Anṣāri Herewī.–Senāʾi Ġaznewī." *Der Islam* 22 (1934).
———. "Philologika VII: Arabische und persische Schriften über die profane und die mystische Liebe." *Der Islam* 21 (1933).
———. "Philologika XI: Maulānā Ġalāluddīn Rūmī und sein Kreis." *Der Islam* 26 (1937).
———. "Philologika IX: Die vier Suhrawardī." *Der Islam* 24–25 (1935–36).
———. "Das Proömium des Maṯnawī-i Maulawī." *Zeitschrift der Deutschen Morgenländischen Gesellschaft* 93 (1932).
———. "Der Reigen der 'Tanzenden Derwische." *Zeitschrift für Vergleichende Musikwissenschaft* 1 (1933).
———, trans. *Das Elixier der Glückseligkeit, aus den persischen und arabischen Quellen in Auswahl übertragen.* Jena, 1923. Translation of al-Ghazzālī's *Kīmīyā as-saʿāda.*
Rizvi, Syed Athar Abbas. "The Rawshaniyya Movement." *Abr Nahrain* 6 (1965–66), 7 (1967–68).
Rosen, Georg. *Mesnevi oder Doppelverse des Scheich Mevlāna Dschalal ad-Din Rumi.* Munich, 1913.
Rückert, Friedrich. *Dschelaladdin, Ghaselen.* N.p., 1819.
Rūmī, Maulāna Jalāluddīn. *Dīwān-i kabīr yā Kulliyāt-i Shams.* Edited by Badīʿuz-Zamān Furūzānfar. 10 vols. Tehran, 1336 sh./1957. In Persian.
———. *Fīhi mā fīhi.* Edited by ʿAbdul Majid Daryābādi. Azamgarh, 1928. Edited by Badīʾuz-Zamān Furūzānfar. Tehran, 1338 sh./1959. Translated into Turkish from the Persian original by Meliha Tarıkâhya. Ankara, 1954.
———. *Mathnawī-i maʿnawī.* Edited and translated by Reynold A. Nicholson. 8 vols. Gibb Memorial Series, n.s. 4. London, 1925–40.
———. *Mevlâna'nin Mektupları.* Translated by Abdulbâki Gölpınarlı. Istanbul, 1964. In Turkish.
———. *Rubāʿiyāt.* Ms. Istanbul Esat Efendi 2693. In Persian.
Rypka, Jan. *History of Iranian Literature.* Dordrecht, 1968.
Sachal Sarmast. *Dīwān-i Āshikar.* Edited by Makhdūm Amīr Aḥmad. Lahore, 1957. In Persian.
———. *Risālō Sindhī.* Edited by Othman Ali Anṣāri. Karachi, 1958. In Sindhi.

———. *Siraiki kalām.* Edited by Maulwī Ḥakīm M. Ṣādiq Rānīpūrī. Karachi, 1959. In Siraiki.

Sadarangani, H. I. *Persian Poets of Sind.* Karachi, 1956.

Sanāʾī, Abūʾl-Majd Majdūd. *Dīwān.* Edited by Mudarris Rażawī. Tehran, 1341 sh./1962. In Persian.

———. *The First Book of the Ḥadīqatuʾl-Ḥaqīqat or the Enclosed Garden of the Truth of the Ḥakīm Sana'i of Ghazna.* Edited and translated by Major J. Stephenson. 1908. Reprint. New York, 1971.

———. *Ḥadīqat al-ḥaqīqat wa sharīʿat aṭ-ṭarīqat.* Edited by Mudarris Rażawī. Tehran, 1329 sh./1950. In Persian.

———. *Mathnawīhā.* Edited by Mudarris Rażawī. Tehran, 1348 sh./1969. Includes *Sanāʾīābād.* In Persian.

Sarrāj, Abū Naṣr as-. *Kitāb al-lumaʿ fiʾt-taṣawwuf.* Edited by Reynold A. Nicholson. Gibb Memorial Series, no. 22. Leiden and London, 1914. In Arabic.

Schaeder, Hans Heinrich. *Goethes Erlebnis des Ostens.* Leipzig, 1938.

———. "Ḥasan al-Baṣrī." *Der Islam* 13 (1923).

———. "Die islamische Lehre vom Vollkommenen Menschen, ihre Herkunft und ihre dichterische Gestaltung." *Zeitschrift der Deutschen Morgenländischen Gesellschaft* 79 (1925).

———. "Die persische Vorlage von Goethes Seliger Sehnsucht." *Festschrift E. Spranger.* Berlin, 1942.

———. "Zur Deutung der islamischen Mystik." *Orientalistische Literaturzeitung* 30 (1935).

Schaya, Léon. *La doctrine soufique de l'unité.* Paris, 1962.

Schimmel, Annemarie. "The Activities of the Sindhi Adabi Board." *Die Welt des Islams,* n.s. 4, nos. 3–4 (1961).

———. *Aus dem goldenen Becher. Türkische Poesie vom 13. bis 20. Jahrhundert.* Istanbul, 1973.

———. *Die Bildersprache Dschelaladdin Rumis.* Walldorf, 1949.

———. "Drei türkische Mystiker: Yunus Emre, Kayğusuz Abdal, Pir Sultan Abdal." *Mitteilungen der Deutsch-Türkischen Gesellschaft,* no. 48 (1962).

———. *Dschelaladdin Rumi, Aus dem Diwan.* Stuttgart, 1964.

———. *Gabriel's Wing: A Study into the Religious Ideas of Sir Muhammad Iqbal.* Leiden, 1963.

———. "Die Gestalt des Satan in Muhammad Iqbal's Werk." *Kairos,* no. 2 (1963).

———. "Das Gelübde im türkischen Volksglauben." *Die Welt des Orients,* n.s. 6, nos. 1–2.

———. *Al-Halladsch, Märtyrer der Gottesliebe.* Cologne, 1969.

———. "Ibn Khafīf, an Early Representative of Sufism." *Journal of the Pakistan Historical Society,* 1959.

———. "The Idea of Prayer in the Thought of Iqbal." *Moslem World* 48, no. 3 (1958).

———. "The Influence of Sufism on Indo-Muslim Poetry." In *Anagogic*

Qualities of Literature, edited by Joseph P. Strelka. University Park, Pa., 1971.

———. *Islamic Calligraphy.* Leiden, 1970.

———. "Islamic Literatures of India." In *History of Indian Literature,* edited by Jan Gonda. Wiesbaden, 1973.

———. "The Martyr-Mystic Ḥallāj in Sindhi Folk-Poetry." *Numen* 9, no. 3 (1962).

———. "Maulānā Rūmī's Story on Prayer." In *Yādnāme Jan Rypka.* Edited by Jiří Bečka. Prague, 1967.

———. *Mevlâna Celâlettin Rumi'nin şark ve garpta tesirleri.* Ankara, 1963. In Turkish.

———. "Mir Dard's Gedanken über das Verhältnis von Mystik und Wort." In *Festgabe deutscher Iranisten zur 2500-Jahrfeier Irans,* edited by Wilhelm Eilers. Stuttgart, 1971.

———. "Neue Veröffentlichungen zur Volkskunde von Sind." *Die Welt des Islams,* n.s. 9, nos. 1–4 (1964).

———. "Nur ein störrisches Pferd." In *Ex orbe Religionum, Festschrift Geo Widengren.* Leiden, 1972.

———. "The Origin and Early Development of Sufism." *Journal of the Pakistan Historical Society,* 1958.

———."The Place of the Prophet in Iqbal's Thought." *Islamic Studies* 1, no. 4 (1962).

———. "Poetry and Calligraphy." *Pakistan Quarterly* 17, no. 1 (1969).

———. "Raymundus Lullus und seine Auseinandersetzung mit dem Islam." *Eine Heilige Kirche* 1 (1953–54).

———. "Der Regen als Symbol in der Religionsgeschichte." In *Religion und Religionen: Festschrift Gustav Mensching.* Bonn, 1966.

———. "Rose und Nachtigall." *Numen* 5, no. 2 (1958).

———. "The Ruby of the Heart." In *Zakir Husain Presentation Volume,* edited by Malik Ram. New Delhi, 1968.

———. "Rumi's Influence on Muslim Literature." In *Güldeste.* Konya, 1971.

———. "Samiha Ayverdi, eine Istanbuler Schriftstellerin." In *Festschrift Otto Spies,* edited by Wilhelm Hoenerbach. Wiesbaden, 1967.

———. "Schah Abdul Latif." *Kairos,* nos. 3–4 (1961).

———. "Schriftsymbolik im Islam." In *Festschrift Ernst Kühnel,* edited by Richard Ettinghausen. Berlin, 1959.

———. "Shah ʿAbdul Laṭīf's Beschreibung des wahren Sufi." In *Festschrift für Fritz Meier,* compiled by Richard Gramlich. Wiesbaden, 1974.

———. "Shah ʿInāyat of Jhok: A Sindhi Mystic of the Early 18th Century." In *Liber Amicorum in Honour of C. J. Bleeker.* Leiden, 1969.

———. "A Sincere Muhammadan's Way to Salvation." In *Memorial Volume S. F. G. Brandon,* edited by Eric J. Sharpe and John R. Hinnels. Manchester, 1973.

———. "Sindhi Literature." In *History of Indian Literature,* edited by Jan Gonda. Wiesbaden, 1974.

———. "Some Aspects of Mystical Prayer in Islam." *Die Welt des Islams,* n.s. 2, no. 2 (1952).
———. "Some Glimpses of the Religious Life in Egypt during the Later Mamluk Period." *Islamic Studies* 4, no. 4 (1965).
———. "Studien zum Begriff der mystischen Liebe im Islam." Dr. sc. rel. dissertation, University of Marburg, 1954.
———. "Sufismus und Heiligenverehrung im spätmittelalterlichen Ägypten." In *Festschrift für W. Caskel,* edited by Erich Gräf. Leiden, 1968.
———. "The Symbolical Language of Maulāna Jalāl al-Dīn Rūmī." *Studies in Islam* 1 (1964).
———. "Translations and Commentaries of the Qurān in the Sindhi Language." *Oriens* 15 (1963).
———. "The Veneration of the Prophet Muhammad, as Reflected in Sindhi Poetry." In *The Saviour God,* edited by Samuel G. F. Brandon. Manchester, 1963.
———. "Yunus Emre." *Numen* 8, no. 1 (1961).
———. "Zu einigen Versen Dschelāladdīn Rūmīs." *Anatolica* 1 (1967).
———. "Zur Biographie des Abū ᶜAbdallāh ibn Chafīf aš-Šīrāzī." *Die Welt des Orients,* 1955.
———."Zur Geschichte der mystischen Liebe im Islam." *Die Welt des Orients,* 1952.
Scholem, Gershom. "Die krypto-jüdische Sekte der Dönme (Sabbatianer) in der Türkei." *Numen* 7, no. 1 (1960).
Schrieke, Bernherd. "Die Himmelsreise Muhammads." *Der Islam* 6 (1961).
Schroeder, Eric. *Muhammad's People.* Portland, Maine, 1955.
Schuon, Frithjof. *Dimensions of Islam.* Translated by Peter N. Townsend. London, 1970.
———. *Understanding Islam.* Translated by D. M. Matheson. 3d ed. London, 1972.
Seale, Morris S. "The Ethics of Malāmātīya Sufism and the Sermon of the Mount." *Moslem World* 58, no. 1 (1968).
Shabistarī, Maḥmūd. *The Dialogue of the Gulshan-i Rāz.* London, 1887.
———. *Gulshan-i rāz: The Rose-Garden of Mysteries.* Edited and translated by Edward Henry Whinfield. London, 1880.
———. *The Secret Garden.* Translated by Juraj Paska. New York and London, 1969.
Shāh ᶜAbdul Laṭīf. *Risālō.* Edited by Kalyan B. Adwani. Bombay, 1958. In Sindhi.
Shaᶜrānī, ᶜAbdul Wahhāb ash-. *Bayān al-asrār.* Istanbul, Aya Sofya 248. In Arabic.
———. *Lawāqiḥ al-anwār al-qudsiyya.* Cairo, 1311 h./1893–94. In Arabic.
———. *Risāla fi talqīn adh-dhikr.* Istanbul Universitesi Kütüphanesi, Arab. 3531. In Arabic.

Sharib, Zahur U. *The Life and Teachings of Khawaja Moinud-din Hasan Chishti.* Ajmer, 1959.

Shaybī, Kāmil M. ash-. *Aṣ-ṣila bayn at-taṣawwuf waʾt-tashayyuʿ.* Cairo, ca. 1967. In Arabic.

Shehadi, Fadlou. *Ghazālī's Unique Unknowable God.* Leiden, 1964.

Shiblī, Abū Bakr. *Dīwān.* Edited by Kāmil M. ash-Shaybī. Cairo, 1967. In Arabic.

Sipahsālār, Farīdūn Aḥmad. *Risāla dar aḥwāl-i Maulānā Jalāluddīn Rūmī.* Edited by Saʿid Nafisi. Tehran, 1325 sh./1946. In Persian.

Smith, Margaret. *An Early Mystic of Baghdad.* London, 1935.

———. "Al-Ghazzālī, ar-risāla al-laduniyya." *Journal of the Royal Asiatic Society,* 1938.

———. *Rābiʿa the Mystic and Her Fellow-Saints in Islam.* Cambridge, 1928.

———. *Readings from the Mystics of Islam.* London, 1950.

———. *Studies in Early Mysticism in the Near and Middle East.* London, 1931.

———. *The Sufi Path of Love.* London, 1954.

Smith, W. Cantwell. "The Crystallization of Religious Communities in Mughal India." In *Yādnāme-ye Īrān-e Minorsky.* Tehran, 1969.

Sohbet Dergisi. Istanbul, 1952–53. In Turkish.

Sorley, Herbert Tower. *Shah Abdul Latif of Bhit: His Poetry, Life, and Times.* 1940. Reprint. Oxford, 1966.

Spies, Gertrud. *Maḥmūd von Ghazna bei Farīd ud'din ʿAṭṭār.* Basel, 1959.

Spies, Otto. "Drei biographische Werke über Sufis." *Le monde oriental,* 1930.

Storey, C. A. *Persian Literature.* Vol. 1. London, 1953.

Subhan, John A. *Sufism: Its Saints and Shrines.* 2d ed. Lucknow, 1960.

Subki, Tājuddīn as-. *Tabaqāt ash-shāfiʿiyya al-kubrā.* Cairo, 1324 h./1906–1907. In Arabic.

Suhrawardī, Shihābuddīn ʿUmar as-. *ʿAwārif al-maʿārif.* Bulaq, Egypt, 1289 h./1872–73. At the margin of Ghazzāli's *Iḥyāʾ.* In Arabic.

———. *The "ʿAwarif ul-Maʿarif" written in the thirteenth century by Shaikh Shahabud-d-Din Umar bin Muhammad-i Sahrwardi.* Translated by H. Wilberforce Clarke. 1891. Reprint. New York, 1970.

Suhrawardī Maqtūl. "Le bruissement de l'aile de Gabriel." Edited and translated by Henri Corbin and Paul Kraus. *Journal asiatique,* July 1935.

———. *Oeuvres en Persan.* Edited by Henri Corbin. Paris, 1970. In Persian.

———. *Opera metaphysica et mystica.* Edited by Henri Corbin. Vol. 1. Istanbul, 1945. Vol. 2 Tehran and Paris, 1952. In Arabic.

Sulamī, ʿAbduʾr Raḥmān as-. *Kitāb ādāb aṣ-ṣuḥba.* Edited by Meir J. Kister. Jerusalem, 1954. In Arabic.

———. *Kitāb al-arbaʿīn.* Hyderabad, Deccan, 1950. In Arabic.

———. *Kitāb ṭabaqāt aṣ-Ṣūfiyya.* Edited by Nūraddīn Sharība. Cairo,

1953. Edited by Johannes Pedersen. Leiden, 1960. In Arabic.
Süleyman Çelebi. *The Mevlidi Sherif by Suleyman Chelebi.* Translated by F. Lyman MacCallum. London, 1943.
———. *Mevlûd-i şerif.* Istanbul, n.d. In Turkish.
Sulṭān Bāhoo. *Abyāt.* Translated by Maqbool Elahi. Lahore, 1967.
Şuşut, Hasan Lutfi. *Fakir sözleri.* Istanbul, 1958. In Turkish.
———. *Islam tasavvufunda Hacegân Hanedanı.* Istanbul, 1958. In Turkish.
Swartz, Merlin S. *Ibn al-Jawzī's "kitāb al-quṣṣāṣ waʾl-mudhakkirin."* Beirut, 1971. In Arabic.
Taeschner, Franz. "Das futūwa-Rittertum des islamischen Mittelalters." In *Beiträge zur Arabistik, Semitistik und Islamkunde,* edited by Richard Hartmann and H. Scheel. Leipzig, 1944.
———. "As-Sulamīs *kitāb al-futuwwa.*" In *Festschrift J. Pedersen.* Copenhagen, 1953.
Ṭāhir, Ḥamza. "At-taṣawwuf ash-shaᶜbī fīʾl-adab at-turkī." *Majalla Kulliyyat al-adab* 12, no. 2 (1950). In Arabic.
Teufel, Johann Karl. *Eine Lebensbeschreibung des Scheichs ᶜAlī-i Hamaḏānī.* Leiden, 1962.
Tholuck, Friedrich August Deofidus. *Blüthensammlung aus der Morgenländischen Mystik.* Berlin, 1825.
———. *Ssufismus sive theosophia persarum pantheistica.* Berlin 1821.
Tikku, Girdhari L. *Persian Poetry in Kashmir, 1339–1846: An Introduction.* Berkeley, 1971.
Tilmīdh Ḥusayn. *Mirʾāt al-mathnawī.* Hyderabad, Deccan, 1352 h./1933–34. In Persian.
Trimingham, J. Spencer. *The Sufi Orders in Islam.* Oxford, 1971.
Trumpp, Ernst. "Einige Bemerkungen zum Sufismus." *Zeitschrift der Deutschen Morgenländischen Gesellschaft* 16 (1862).
———. "Sorathi. Ein Sindhi-Gedichtaus dem grossen Divan des Sayyid ᶜAbd-ul-Laṭīf." *Zeitschrift der Deutschen Morgenländischen Gesellschaft* 17 (1863).
Tunc, Cihad. "Sahl ibn ᶜAbdullah at-Tustarī und die Sālimīya." Ph.D. dissertation, University of Bonn, 1970.
Umaruddin, Muhammad. *The Ethical Philosophy of al-Ghazzālī.* Aligarh, 1951.
Underhill, Evelyn. *Mysticism: A Study in the Nature and Development of Man's Spiritual Consciousness.* 1911. Paperback. New York, 1956.
ᶜUrfī Shīrazī, Muḥammad. *Kulliyāt.* Edited by ᶜAlī Jawāhirī. Tehran, 1336 sh./1957. In Persian.
Usborne, Charles Frederick. *Hir Ranjha.* Edited by Mumtaz Hasan. Karachi, 1966.
Uzluk, Şehabettin. *Mevlevilikte Resim, Resimde Mevleviler.* Ankara, 1957. In Turkish.
Vacca, Virginia. "Aspetti politici e sociali dei 'sufi' musulmani." *Oriente moderne* 35, no. 1 (1955).

———. *Vite e detti di Santi Musulmani*. Torino, n.d.
Vahiduddin, Syed. *Indisch-Moslemische Werterlebnisse*. Leipzig, 1937.
Vaudeville, Charlotte. *Kabir Granthvali. (Doha)*. Pondicherry, 1957.
Vryonis, Speros, Jr. *The Decline of Medieval Hellenism in Asia Minor and the Process of Islamization from the Eleventh through the Fifteenth Century*. Berkeley, 1971.
Waheed Mirza. *The Life and Works of Amir Khusru*. 3d ed. Lahore, 1962.
Walad, Sultan. *Divan-i Sultan Veled*. Edited by F. Nafiz Uzluk. Istanbul, 1941. In Persian.
———. *Divan-i Turki*. Edited by Kilisli Muallim Rifᶜat. Istanbul, 1341 h./1922–23. In Turkish.
———. *Waladnāme*. Edited by Jalāl Humāʾī. Tehran, 1315 sh./1936. In Persian.
Walīullāh, Shāh. *Ḥujjat Allāh al-bāligha*. Cairo, ca. 1955. In Arabic.
———. *Lamaḥāt*. Edited by Ghulām Muṣṭafā Qāsimi. Hyderabad, Sind, ca. 1966. In Arabic.
———. *Saṭaᶜāt*. Edited by Ghulām Muṣṭafā Qāsimi. Hyderabad, Sind, 1964. In Arabic.
Walsh, John R. "Yunus Emre: A Medieval Hymnodist." *Numen* 7, nos. 2–3 (1960).
Watt, W. Montgomery. *The Faith and Practice of Al-Ghazali*. London, 1953.
———. *Muslim Intellectual: A Study of Al-Ghazali*. Edinburgh, 1963.
Wehr, Hans. *Al-Ghazālīs Buch vom Gottvertrauen*. Halle, 1940.
Wellecz, Emmy. *Akbar's Religious Thought as Reflected in Moghul Painting*. London, 1952.
Wensinck, Arend Jan. *Abuʾl-faraǧ Barhebraeus: The Book of the Dove*. Leiden, 1919.
———. *Concordance et indices de la tradition musulmane*. Leiden, 1936–71.
———. "Ghazalī's Mishkāt al-anwār." *Semietische Studien*. Leiden, 1941.
———. *La pensée de Ghazzālī*. Paris, 1940.
Whinfield, E. H., trans. *"Masnavi-i Maʾnavi": Spiritual Couplets*. London, 1887.
Widengren, Geo. *The Ascension to Heaven and the Heavenly Book*. Uppsala, 1950.
———. "Harlekin und Mönchskutte, Clownhut und Derwischmütze." *Orientalia Suecana* 2 (1953).
———. *Muhammad, the Apostle of God, and His Ascension*. Uppsala, 1955.
Wilms, Franz-Elmar, trans. *Al-Ghazālīs Schrift wider die Gottheit Jesu*. Leiden, 1966.
Wilzer, Susanna. "Untersuchungen zu Ġazzālī's kitāb at-tauba." *Der Islam* 32–33 (1955–57).

Wüstenfeld, Ferdinand. "Die Çufiten in Süd-Arabien im XI. (XVII) Jahrhundert." *Nachrichten von der Gesellschaft der Wissenschaften zu Göttingen, Philologisch-historische Klasse* 30, no. 1 (1883).

Yāfiᶜī, ᶜAbdallāh al-. *Rauḍ ar-riyāḥīn*. Cairo, 1332 h./1913–14. In Arabic.

Yaḥyā, Osman. *Histoire et classification de l'oeuvre d'Ibn ᶜArabī*. 2 vols. Damascus, 1964.

———. "Mission en Turquie: recherches sur les manuscrits du Soufisme." *Revue des études islamiques*, 1958.

———. "L'oeuvre de Tirmiḏī, essai bibliographique." In *Mélanges Louis Massignon*. 3 vols. Damascus, 1956–57.

Yūnus Emre. *Divan*. Edited by Abdülbâki Gölpınarlı. Istanbul, 1943. In Turkish.

———. *Risalat an-nushiyye ve Divan*. Edited by Abdülbâki Gölpınarlı. Istanbul, 1965. In Turkish.

Zaehner, Robert C. *Hindu and Muslim Mysticism*. London, 1960.

Zarrinkoob, A. H. "Persian Sufism in Its Historical Perspective." *Iranian Studies* 3, nos. 3–4 (1970).

Ziadah, Nicolas A. *Sanusiyah: A Study of a Revivalist Movement in Islam*. Leiden, 1958.

Zolondek, Leon, trans. *Book XX of al-Ghazālī's "Iḥyāᵓ ᶜulūm ad-Dīn."* Leiden, 1963.

INDEX OF KORANIC QUOTATIONS

INDEX OF PROPHETIC TRADITIONS

(The AM citation gives the location of the full Arabic text of the tradition in Badīʿuz-Zamān Furūzānfar's *Aḥādīth-i Mathnawī* [Tehran, 1334 sh./1955].)

ḤADĪTH

Beware of the *firāsa* of the faithful, 205 (AM no. 33)
Die before ye die, 70, 135, 320, 392 (AM no. 352)
Could the reedflute sing . . . , allusion to: The faithful is like the flute, 116 (AM no. 728)
The faithful is the mirror of the faithful, 228 (AM no. 104)
The first thing God created . . . , 215 (AM no. 342)
First tie your camel's knee, 120 (AM no. 20)
Gabriel not to answer the prayers immediately, 158 (AM no. 730)
God and His messenger should be more beloved to the faithful than anything else, 131
God created Adam in His form, 188, 225, 417 (AM no. 346)
God has not created anything he loves more than Muhammad and his family, 70
God has seventy thousand veils of light and darkness, 96 (AM no. 128)
God is beautiful and loves beauty, 291 (AM no. 106)
God kneaded Adam forty days, 16, 188 (AM no. 633)
God made dear to me perfume and women, 272, 431 (AM no. 182)
God's grace precedes His wrath, 128 (AM no. 54)
The heart of the faithful is between two fingers of the Merciful, 197, 415 (AM no. 13)
Hunger is God's food, 115 (AM no. 460)
I cannot reckon up Thy praise, 126, 162, 222 (AM no. 3)
I feel the breath of the Merciful coming from Yemen, 28, 262 (AM no. 195)
If it were permissible to prostrate oneself before anyone but God, 435
If ye knew what I know, 31 (AM no. 157)
If you had trust in God as ye ought, 118 (AM no. 535)
I have a time with God, 220 (AM no. 100)
I saw Gabriel in the form of Daḥyā al-Kalbī, 290
I saw my Lord in the most beautiful form, 290
I saw my Lord . . . with his cap awry, 290
I take refuge with Thee from knowledge that profiteth naught, 17
I was a prophet when Adam was still between water and clay, 215 (AM no. 301)
Knowledge (*ʿilm*) is the greatest veil, 140
Man is with him whom he loves, 141 (AM no. 482)
Men are asleep, and when they die they awake, 382 (AM no. 222)
Miracles are the menstruation of men, 212
The most afflicted people are the prophets, 136 (AM no. 320)
My eyes sleep, but my heart is awake, 27 (AM no. 188)
My *shayṭān* has become a Muslim, 113, 196 (AM no. 459)
O Lord, keep me one day full fed and one day hungry, 15
O Lord, Thou hast commanded me to be grateful (prayer of Moses), 164
Paradise lies at the feet of the mothers, 430 (AM no. 488)
The Pen has dried up, 197, 414 (AM no. 97)
Poverty is blackness of face, 123
Poverty is my pride, 121, 428 (AM no. 54)
The prayer of the sitting man is worth half of that of the standing person, 149

ḤADĪTH QUDSĪ

INDEX OF NAMES AND PLACES

J

N

S

INDEX OF SUBJECTS

A

A (*alif*), 153, 421, 422; as symbol of God's unity, 18, 153, 377, 385, 417–19; connected with Aḥmad, 369; as the "equator" of the face, 413. *See also* M; Sūra 2:1, *alif-lām-mīm*, 416

ᶜ*Abd* ("slave," "servant," man in general), 253. *See also* Slave of God

Abdāl (the forty, or seven, saints), 200, 202; women, 431, 434

Abdālān-i Rūm (a group of medieval dervishes), 335

ᶜ*Abduhu* ("His servant"): Muhammad the Prophet called, in Sūra 17:1, 220

ᶜ*Ābid* ("worshiper," lowest degree in the Bektashi hierarchical grouping), 340

Abrār (the seven "pious"), 200

Abstinence, 31, 37, 80; fasting and, 115. See also *Wara*ᶜ

Active intellect: corresponding to *ḥaqīqa muḥammadiyya*, 224

Adab (etiquette, correct behavior), 84, 127, 235, 237, 255; books on, 94; as "servant of religion," 230

ᶜ*Adam* ("not-being," often, the innermost abyss of the Godhead), 322

Advaita ("nonduality" in Hindu philosophy), 5, 387

Affiliation. *See* Silsila

Affliction, 16, 90, 124, 126, 131, 136, 167, 380, 395, 421, 428; as sign of divine love, 4, 36, 62, 80, 198, 394; necessary for spiritual development, 44, 137; *faqr* as, 58; leisure as, 114; patience in, 156; and pain, 198, 394. *See also* Suffering, Tribulation

Aḥad ("one," one of God's names), 224, 387, 419

Aḥadiyya ("oneness," unicity), 418

Aham brahmāsmi ("I am Brahman," unitive expression in the Vedic Upanishads), 64

Ahl al-bayt (Muhammad's family), 82

*Ahl al-ma*ᶜ*rifa* ("gnostics"), 86

Ahl aṣ-ṣuffa, aṣḥāb aṣ-ṣuffa ("the people of the Bench," the pious poor around Muhammad in Medina), 14, 28

Aḥwāl. See *Ḥāl*

Akhi (member of a religious sodality in medieval Turkey), 246

Akhyār (300 "good" in the hierarchy of saints), 200

ᶜ*Ālam al-mithāl* (the world of imagination, of spiritual values or ideas that are to be realized in this world), 193, 213, 270

Alast ("Am I not your Lord" [Sūra 7:171]), 24, 298; connected with *dhikr*, 172

Alast, Day of. *See* Covenant, primordial

Alchemy, 65; spiritual, 5, 237; expressions of, 70; of hunger, 115

Alchemist, 42

Alif-i ṣayqal (degree of polishing steel), 419

ᶜ*Ālim rabbānī* (divinely inspired master), 74

Alın yazısı ("what is written on the forehead" [Turkish], fate), 414

Allāhu Akbar ("God is most great"), 80, 150, 152. See *Takbīr*

ᶜ*Amā* (pure being), 266

ᶜ*Amal* ("work, action"), 274

Amāna ("trust") (Sūra 33:72), 188

Amīr majlis (high official in Mamluk Egypt), 234

Amr (divine command), 223

*Anā*ʾ*-l Ḥaqq* ("I am the creative Truth," "I am God," Ḥallāj's claim), 55, 64, 66, 72, 74, 75, 145, 298, 393, 396. *See also* Ḥallāj, Ḥusayn ibn Manṣūr al-

Angelology, 260, 261

Angels, 71, 116, 140, 153, 169, 189, 193, 196, 200, 256, 261, 262, 268, 318, 321, 377, 412; prostration of before Adam, 55, 188; of death, 90, 135, 148, 389; and green color, 102; fallen, 161, 193, 194; of resurrection, 200, 224; archangel, 219, 220, 262; guardian, 262; of inspiration, 265; questioning, 331; quality of, 369, 378; recording, 389. *See also* Gabriel; Isrāfīl; *Malakūt*; Sarosh

Annihilation, 17, 130, 135, 153, 178, 196, 199, 284, 307, 321, 373, 384, 391; fish of, 6, 416; as the object of *dhikr*, 58, 174; of the lover, 60, 134; in the Prophet, 378; in the sheikh, 387. See also *Fanā*

ᶜAnqā. *See* Sīmurgh

T